CODE OF FEDERAL REGULATIONS

I0058233

Title 6
Domestic Security

Revised as of January 1, 2019

Containing a codification of documents
of general applicability and future effect

As of January 1, 2019

Published by the Office of the Federal Register
National Archives and Records Administration
as a Special Edition of the Federal Register

Table of Contents

Cite this Code: **CFR**

To cite the regulations in this volume use title, part and section number. Thus, 6 CFR 3.1 refers to title 6, part 3, section 1.

Explanation

The Code of Federal Regulations is a codification of the general and permanent rules published in the Federal Register by the Executive departments and agencies of the Federal Government. The Code is divided into 50 titles which represent broad areas subject to Federal regulation. Each title is divided into chapters which usually bear the name of the issuing agency. Each chapter is further subdivided into parts covering specific regulatory areas.

Each volume of the Code is revised at least once each calendar year and issued on a quarterly basis approximately as follows:

Title 1 through Title 16..as of January 1
Title 17 through Title 27 ....as of April 1
Title 28 through Title 41 ....as of July 1
Title 42 through Title 50...as of October 1

The appropriate revision date is printed on the cover of each volume.

LEGAL STATUS

The contents of the Federal Register are required to be judicially noticed (44 U.S.C. 1507). The Code of Federal Regulations is prima facie evidence of the text of the original documents (44 U.S.C. 1510).

HOW TO USE THE CODE OF FEDERAL REGULATIONS

The Code of Federal Regulations is kept up to date by the individual issues of the Federal Register. These two publications must be used together to determine the latest version of any given rule.

To determine whether a Code volume has been amended since its revision date (in this case, January 1, 2019), consult the "List of CFR Sections Affected (LSA)," which is issued monthly, and the "Cumulative List of Parts Affected," which appears in the Reader Aids section of the daily Federal Register. These two lists will identify the Federal Register page number of the latest amendment of any given rule.

EFFECTIVE AND EXPIRATION DATES

Each volume of the Code contains amendments published in the Federal Register since the last revision of that volume of the Code. Source citations for the regulations are referred to by volume number and page number of the Federal Register and date of publication. Publication dates and effective dates are usually not the same and care must be exercised by the user in determining the actual effective date. In instances where the effective date is beyond the cut-off date for the Code a note has been inserted to reflect the future effective date. In those instances where a regulation published in the Federal Register states a date certain for expiration, an appropriate note will be inserted following the text.

OMB CONTROL NUMBERS

The Paperwork Reduction Act of 1980 (Pub. L. 96–511) requires Federal agencies to display an OMB control number with their information collection request.

Many agencies have begun publishing numerous OMB control numbers as amendments to existing regulations in the CFR. These OMB numbers are placed as close as possible to the applicable recordkeeping or reporting requirements.

PAST PROVISIONS OF THE CODE

Provisions of the Code that are no longer in force and effect as of the revision date stated on the cover of each volume are not carried. Code users may find the text of provisions in effect on any given date in the past by using the appropriate List of CFR Sections Affected (LSA). For the convenience of the reader, a "List of CFR Sections Affected" is published at the end of each CFR volume. For changes to the Code prior to the LSA listings at the end of the volume, consult previous annual editions of the LSA. For changes to the Code prior to 2001, consult the List of CFR Sections Affected compilations, published for 1949-1963, 1964-1972, 1973-1985, and 1986-2000.

"[RESERVED]" TERMINOLOGY

The term "[Reserved]" is used as a place holder within the Code of Federal Regulations. An agency may add regulatory information at a "[Reserved]" location at any time. Occasionally "[Reserved]" is used editorially to indicate that a portion of the CFR was left vacant and not accidentally dropped due to a printing or computer error.

INCORPORATION BY REFERENCE

What is incorporation by reference? Incorporation by reference was established by statute and allows Federal agencies to meet the requirement to publish regulations in the Federal Register by referring to materials already published elsewhere. For an incorporation to be valid, the Director of the Federal Register must approve it. The legal effect of incorporation by reference is that the material is treated as if it were published in full in the Federal Register (5 U.S.C. 552(a)). This material, like any other properly issued regulation, has the force of law.

What is a proper incorporation by reference? The Director of the Federal Register will approve an incorporation by reference only when the requirements of 1 CFR part 51 are met. Some of the elements on which approval is based are:

(a) The incorporation will substantially reduce the volume of material published in the Federal Register.

(b) The matter incorporated is in fact available to the extent necessary to afford fairness and uniformity in the administrative process.

(c) The incorporating document is drafted and submitted for publication in accordance with 1 CFR part 51.

What if the material incorporated by reference cannot be found? If you have any problem locating or obtaining a copy of material listed as an approved incorporation by reference, please contact the agency that issued the regulation containing that incorporation. If, after contacting the agency, you find the material is not available, please notify the Director of the Federal Register, National Archives and Records Administration, 8601 Adelphi Road, College Park, MD 20740-6001, or call 202-741-6010.

CFR INDEXES AND TABULAR GUIDES

A subject index to the Code of Federal Regulations is contained in a separate volume, revised annually as of January 1, entitled CFR INDEX AND FINDING AIDS. This volume contains the Parallel Table of Authorities and Rules. A list of CFR titles, chapters, subchapters, and parts and an alphabetical list of agencies publishing in the CFR are also included in this volume.

An index to the text of "Title 3—The President" is carried within that volume.

The Federal Register Index is issued monthly in cumulative form. This index is based on a consolidation of the "Contents" entries in the daily Federal Register.

A List of CFR Sections Affected (LSA) is published monthly, keyed to the revision dates of the 50 CFR titles.

REPUBLICATION OF MATERIAL

There are no restrictions on the republication of material appearing in the Code of Federal Regulations.

INQUIRIES

For a legal interpretation or explanation of any regulation in this volume, contact the issuing agency. The issuing agency's name appears at the top of odd-numbered pages.

For inquiries concerning CFR reference assistance, call 202–741–6000 or write to the Director, Office of the Federal Register, National Archives and Records Administration, 8601 Adelphi Road, College Park, MD 20740-6001 or e-mail *fedreg.info@nara.gov*.

SALES

The Government Publishing Office (GPO) processes all sales and distribution of the CFR. For payment by credit card, call toll-free, 866-512-1800, or DC area, 202-512-1800, M-F 8 a.m. to 4 p.m. e.s.t. or fax your order to 202-512-2104, 24 hours a day. For payment by check, write to: US Government Publishing Office – New Orders, P.O. Box 979050, St. Louis, MO 63197-9000.

ELECTRONIC SERVICES

The full text of the Code of Federal Regulations, the LSA (List of CFR Sections Affected), The United States Government Manual, the Federal Register, Public Laws, Public Papers of the Presidents of the United States, Compilation of Presidential Documents and the Privacy Act Compilation are available in electronic format via *www.govinfo.gov*. For more information, contact the GPO Customer Contact Center, U.S. Government Publishing Office. Phone 202-512-1800, or 866-512-1800 (toll-free). E-mail, *ContactCenter@gpo.gov*.

The Office of the Federal Register also offers a free service on the National Archives and Records Administration's (NARA) World Wide Web site for public law numbers, Federal Register finding aids, and related information. Connect to NARA's web site at *www.archives.gov/federal-register*.

The e-CFR is a regularly updated, unofficial editorial compilation of CFR material and Federal Register amendments, produced by the Office of the Federal Register and the Government Publishing Office. It is available at *www.ecfr.gov*.

OLIVER A. POTTS,
Director,
Office of the Federal Register
January 1, 2019

THIS TITLE

Title 6—DOMESTIC SECURITY is composed of one volume. This volume contains chapter I—Department of Homeland Security, Office of the Secretary and chapter X—Privacy and Civil Liberties Oversight Board. The contents of this volume represent all current regulations codified under this title of the CFR as of January 1, 2019.

For this volume, Gabrielle E. Burns was Chief Editor. The Code of Federal Regulations publication program is under the direction of John Hyrum Martinez, assisted by Stephen J. Frattini.

Title 6—Domestic Security

1

CHAPTER I—DEPARTMENT OF HOMELAND SECURITY, OFFICE OF THE SECRETARY

PARTS 1-2 [RESERVED]

PART 3—PETITIONS FOR RULEMAKING

Sec.
3.1 Definitions.
3.3 Applicability.
3.5 Format and mailing instructions.
3.7 Content of a rulemaking petition.
3.9 Responding to a rulemaking petition.

AUTHORITY: 5 U.S.C. 301, 553(e); 6 U.S.C. 112.

SOURCE: 81 FR 47286, July 21, 2016, unless otherwise noted.

§ 3.1 Definitions.

As used in this part:

Component means each separate organizational entity within the U.S. Department of Homeland Security (DHS) that reports directly to the Office of the Secretary.

DHS means the U.S. Department of Homeland Security, including its components.

Rulemaking petition means a petition to issue, amend, or repeal a rule, as described at 5 U.S.C. 553(e).

§ 3.3 Applicability.

(a) *General requirement.* Except as provided in paragraph (b) of this section, this part prescribes the exclusive process for interested persons to submit a rulemaking petition on a matter within DHS's jurisdiction.

(b) *Exceptions*—(1) *U.S. Coast Guard.* This part does not apply to any petition for rulemaking directed to the U.S. Coast Guard. Such petitions are governed by 33 CFR 1.05–20.

(2) *Federal Emergency Management Agency.* This part does not apply to any petition for rulemaking directed to the Federal Emergency Management Agency. Such petitions are governed by 44 CFR 1.18.

§ 3.5 Format and mailing instructions.

(a) *Format.* A rulemaking petition must include in a prominent location—

(1) The words "Petition for Rulemaking" or "Rulemaking Petition;" and

(2) The petitioner's name and a mailing address, in addition to any other contact information (such as telephone number or email) that the petitioner chooses to include.

(b) *Mailing instructions*—(1) *General mailing address.* Any interested person may submit a rulemaking petition by sending it to the following address: U.S. Department of Homeland Security, Office of the General Counsel, Mail Stop 0485, Attn: Regulatory Affairs Law Division, 245 Murray Lane SW., Washington, DC 20528–0485.

(2) *Transportation Security Administration mailing address.* Any interested person may submit a rulemaking petition regarding a Transportation Security Administration program or authority directly to the Transportation Security Administration by sending it to the following address: Transportation Security Administration, Office of the Chief Counsel, TSA–2, Attn: Regulations and Security Standards Division, 601 South 12th Street, Arlington, VA 20598–6002.

(3) DHS does not accept rulemaking petitions delivered by courier.

§ 3.7 Content of a rulemaking petition.

(a) DHS will be better positioned to understand and respond to a rulemaking petition if the petition describes with reasonable particularity the rule that the petitioner is asking DHS to issue, amend, or repeal, and the factual and legal basis for the petition. For instance, DHS would be better able to understand and respond to a petition that includes—

(1) A description of the specific problem that the requested rulemaking would address;

(2) An explanation of how the requested rulemaking would resolve this problem;

(3) Data and other information that would be relevant to DHS's consideration of the petition;

(4) A description of the substance of the requested rulemaking; and

(5) Citation to the pertinent existing regulations provisions (if any) and pertinent DHS legal authority for taking action.

(b) [Reserved]

§ 3.9 Responding to a rulemaking petition.

(a) *Public procedure.* DHS may, in its discretion, seek broader public comment on a rulemaking petition prior to its disposition under this section.

(b) *Disposition.* DHS may respond to the petition by letter or by FEDERAL REGISTER publication. DHS may grant or deny the petition, in whole or in part.

(c) *Grounds for denial.* DHS may deny the petition for any reason consistent with law, including, but not limited to, the following reasons: The petition has no merit, the petition is contrary to pertinent statutory authority, the petition is not supported by the relevant information or data, or the petition cannot be addressed because of other priorities or resource constraints.

(d) *Summary disposition.* DHS may, by written letter, deny or summarily dismiss without prejudice any petition that is moot, premature, repetitive, or frivolous, or that plainly does not warrant further consideration.

PART 4 [RESERVED]

PART 5—DISCLOSURE OF RECORDS AND INFORMATION

Subpart A—Procedures for Disclosure of Records Under the Freedom of Information Act

Subpart B—Privacy Act

Subpart C—Disclosure of Information in Litigation

AUTHORITY: 6 U.S.C. 101 *et seq.;* Pub. L. 107–296, 116 Stat. 2135; 5 U.S.C. 301.

Subpart A also issued under 5 U.S.C. 552.

Subpart B also issued under 5 U.S.C. 552a.

SOURCE: 68 FR 4056, Jan. 27, 2003, unless otherwise noted.

Subpart A—Procedures for Disclosure of Records Under the Freedom of Information Act

SOURCE: 81 FR 83632, Nov. 22, 2016, unless otherwise noted.

§5.1 General provisions.

(a)(1) This subpart contains the rules that the Department of Homeland Security follows in processing requests for records under the Freedom of Information Act (FOIA), 5 U.S.C. 552 as amended.

(2) The rules in this subpart should be read in conjunction with the text of the FOIA and the Uniform Freedom of Information Fee Schedule and Guidelines published by the Office of Management and Budget at 52 FR 10012 (March 27, 1987) (hereinafter "OMB Guidelines"). Additionally, DHS has additional policies and procedures relevant to the FOIA process. These resources are available at *http:// www.dhs.gov/freedom-information-act-foia*. Requests made by individuals for records about themselves under the Privacy Act of 1974, 5 U.S.C. 552a, are processed under subpart B of part 5 as well as under this subpart.

(b) As referenced in this subpart, component means the FOIA office of each separate organizational entity within DHS that reports directly to the Office of the Secretary.

(c) DHS has a decentralized system for processing requests, with each component handling requests for its records.

(d) *Unofficial release of DHS information.* The disclosure of exempt records, without authorization by the appropriate DHS official, is not an official release of information; accordingly, it is not a FOIA release. Such a release does not waive the authority of the Department of Homeland Security to assert FOIA exemptions to withhold the same records in response to a FOIA request. In addition, while the authority may exist to disclose records to individuals in their official capacity, the provisions of this part apply if the same individual seeks the records in a private or personal capacity.

§5.2 Proactive disclosure of DHS records.

Records that are required by the FOIA to be made available for public inspection in an electronic format are accessible on DHS's Web site, *http:// www.dhs.gov/freedom-information-act-foia-and-privacy-act*. Each component is responsible for determining which of its records are required to be made publicly available, as well as identifying additional records of interest to the public that are appropriate for public disclosure, and for posting and indexing such records. Each component shall ensure that posted records and indices are updated on an ongoing basis. Each component has a FOIA Public Liaison who can assist individuals in locating records particular to a component. A list of DHS's FOIA Public Liaisons is available at *http://www.dhs.gov/ foia-contact-information* and in appendix I to this subpart. Requesters who do not have access to the internet may contact the Public Liaison for the component from which they seek records for assistance with publicly available records.

§5.3 Requirements for making requests.

(a) *General information.* (1) DHS has a decentralized system for responding to FOIA requests, with each component designating a FOIA office to process records from that component. All components have the capability to receive requests electronically, either through email or a web portal. To make a request for DHS records, a requester should write directly to the FOIA office of the component that maintains the records being sought. A request will receive the quickest possible response if it is addressed to the FOIA office of the component that maintains the records sought. DHS's FOIA Reference Guide contains or refers the reader to descriptions of the functions of each component and provides other information that is helpful in determining where to make a request. Each component's FOIA office and any additional requirements for submitting a request to a given component are listed in appendix I of this subpart. These references can all be used by requesters to determine where to send their requests within DHS.

(2) A requester may also send his or her request to the Privacy Office, U.S. Department of Homeland Security, 245 Murray Lane SW STOP–0655, or via the internet at *http://www.dhs.gov/dhs-foia-request-submission-form,* or via fax to (202) 343–4011. The Privacy Office will forward the request to the component(s) that it determines to be most likely to maintain the records that are sought.

(3) A requester who is making a request for records about him or herself must comply with the verification of identity provision set forth in subpart B of this part.

(4) Where a request for records pertains to a third party, a requester may receive greater access by submitting either a notarized authorization signed by that individual, in compliance with the verification of identity provision set forth in subpart B of this part, or a declaration made in compliance with the requirements set forth in 28 U.S.C. 1746 by that individual, authorizing disclosure of the records to the requester, or by submitting proof that the individual is deceased (*e.g.,* a copy of a death certificate or an obituary). As an exercise of its administrative discretion, each component can require a requester to supply additional information if necessary in order to verify that a particular individual has consented to disclosure.

(b) *Description of records sought.* Requesters must describe the records sought in sufficient detail to enable DHS personnel to locate them with a reasonable amount of effort. A reasonable description contains sufficient information to permit an organized, non-random search for the record based on the component's filing arrangements and existing retrieval systems. To the extent possible, requesters should include specific information that may assist a component in identifying the requested records, such as the date, title or name, author, recipient, subject matter of the record, case number, file designation, or reference number. Requesters should refer to appendix I of this subpart for additional component-specific requirements. In general, requesters should include as much detail

as possible about the specific records or the types of records that they are seeking. Before submitting their requests, requesters may contact the component's FOIA Officer or FOIA public liaison to discuss the records they are seeking and to receive assistance in describing the records. If after receiving a request, a component determines that it does not reasonably describe the records sought, the component should inform the requester what additional information is needed or why the request is otherwise insufficient. Requesters who are attempting to reformulate or modify such a request may discuss their request with the component's designated FOIA Officer, its FOIA Public Liaison, or a representative of the DHS Privacy Office, each of whom is available to assist the requester in reasonably describing the records sought.

(c) If a request does not adequately describe the records sought, DHS may at its discretion either administratively close the request or seek additional information from the requester. Requests for clarification or more information will be made in writing (either via U.S. mail or electronic mail whenever possible). Requesters may respond by U.S. Mail or by electronic mail regardless of the method used by DHS to transmit the request for additional information. In order to be considered timely, responses to requests for additional information must be postmarked or received by electronic mail within 30 working days of the postmark date or date of the electronic mail request for additional information or received by electronic mail by 11:59:59 p.m. ET on the 30th working day. If the requester does not respond to a request for additional information within thirty (30) working days, the request may be administratively closed at DHS's discretion. This administrative closure does not prejudice the requester's ability to submit a new request for further consideration with additional information.

§5.4 Responsibility for responding to requests.

(a) *In general.* Except in the instances described in paragraphs (c) and (d) of this section, the component that first receives a request for a record and maintains that record is the component responsible for responding to the request. In determining which records are responsive to a request, a component ordinarily will include only records in its possession as of the date that it begins its search. If any other date is used, the component shall inform the requester of that date. A record that is excluded from the requirements of the FOIA pursuant to 5 U.S.C. 552(c), shall not be considered responsive to a request.

(b) *Authority to grant or deny requests.* The head of a component, or designee, is authorized to grant or to deny any requests for records that are maintained by that component.

(c) *Re-routing of misdirected requests.* Where a component's FOIA office determines that a request was misdirected within DHS, the receiving component's FOIA office shall route the request to the FOIA office of the proper component(s).

(d) *Consultations, coordination and referrals.* When a component determines that it maintains responsive records that either originated with another component or agency, or which contains information provided by, or of substantial interest to, another component or agency, then it shall proceed in accordance with either paragraph (d)(1), (2), or (3) of this section, as appropriate:

(1) The component may respond to the request, after consulting with the component or the agency that originated or has a substantial interest in the records involved.

(2) The component may respond to the request after coordinating with the other components or agencies that originated the record. This may include situations where the standard referral procedure is not appropriate where disclosure of the identity of the component or agency to which the referral would be made could harm an interest protected by an applicable exemption, such as the exemptions that protect personal privacy or national security interests. For example, if a non-law enforcement component responding to a request for records on a living third party locates records within its files originating with a law enforce-

ment agency, and if the existence of that law enforcement interest in the third party was not publicly known, then to disclose that law enforcement interest could cause an unwarranted invasion of the personal privacy of the third party. Similarly, if a component locates material within its files originating with an Intelligence Community agency, and the involvement of that agency in the matter is classified and not publicly acknowledged, then to disclose or give attribution to the involvement of that Intelligence Community agency could cause national security harms. In such instances, in order to avoid harm to an interest protected by an applicable exemption, the component that received the request should coordinate with the originating component or agency to seek its views on the disclosability of the record. The release determination for the record that is the subject of the coordination should then be conveyed to the requester by the component that originally received the request.

(3) The component may refer the responsibility for responding to the request or portion of the request to the component or agency best able to determine whether to disclose the relevant records, or to the agency that created or initially acquired the record as long as that agency is subject to the FOIA. Ordinarily, the component or agency that created or initially acquired the record will be presumed to be best able to make the disclosure determination. The referring component shall document the referral and maintain a copy of the records that it refers.

(e) *Classified information.* On receipt of any request involving classified information, the component shall determine whether information is currently and properly classified and take appropriate action to ensure compliance with 6 CFR part 7. Whenever a request involves a record containing information that has been classified or may be appropriate for classification by another component or agency under any applicable executive order concerning the classification of records, the receiving component shall refer the responsibility for responding to the request regarding that information to the component or agency that classified the information, or should consider the information for classification. Whenever a component's record contains information classified by another component or agency, the component shall coordinate with or refer the responsibility for responding to that portion of the request to the component or agency that classified the underlying information.

(f) *Notice of referral.* Whenever a component refers any part of the responsibility for responding to a request to another component or agency, it will notify the requester of the referral and inform the requester of the name of each component or agency to which the records were referred, unless disclosure of the identity of the component or agency would harm an interest protected by an applicable exemption, in which case the component should coordinate with the other component or agency, rather than refer the records.

(g) *Timing of responses to consultations and referrals.* All consultations and referrals received by DHS will be handled according to the date that the FOIA request initially was received by the first component or agency, not any later date.

(h) *Agreements regarding consultations and referrals.* Components may establish agreements with other components or agencies to eliminate the need for consultations or referrals with respect to particular types of records.

(i) *Electronic records and searches*—(1) *Significant interference.* The FOIA allows components to not conduct a search for responsive documents if the search would cause significant interference with the operation of the component's automated information system.

(2) *Business as usual approach.* A "business as usual" approach exists when the component has the capability to process a FOIA request for electronic records without a significant expenditure of monetary or personnel resources. Components are not required to conduct a search that does not meet this business as usual criterion.

(i) Creating computer programs or purchasing additional hardware to extract email that has been archived for emergency retrieval usually are not considered business as usual if extensive monetary or personnel resources are needed to complete the project.

(ii) Creating a computer program that produces specific requested fields or records contained within a well-defined database structure usually is considered business as usual. The time to create this program is considered as programmer or operator search time for fee assessment purposes and the FOIA requester may be assessed fees in accordance with § 5.11(c)(1)(iii). However, creating a computer program to merge files with disparate data formats and extract specific elements from the resultant file is not considered business as usual, but a special service, for which additional fees may be imposed as specified in § 5.11. Components are not required to perform special services and creation of a computer program for a fee is up to the discretion of the component and is dependent on component resources and expertise.

(3) *Data links.* Components are not required to expend DHS funds to establish data links that provide real time or near-real-time data to a FOIA requester.

§ 5.5 **Timing of responses to requests.**

(a) *In general.* Components ordinarily will respond to requests according to their order of receipt. Appendix I to this subpart contains the list of components that are designated to accept requests. In instances involving misdirected requests that are re-routed pursuant to § 5.4(c), the response time will commence on the date that the request is received by the proper component, but in any event not later than ten working days after the request is first received by any DHS component designated in appendix I of this subpart.

(b) *Multitrack processing.* All components must designate a specific track for requests that are granted expedited processing, in accordance with the standards set forth in paragraph (e) of this section. A component may also designate additional processing tracks that distinguish between simple and more complex requests based on the estimated amount of work or time needed to process the request. Among the factors a component may consider are the number of pages involved in processing the request or the need for consultations or referrals. Components shall advise requesters of the track into which their request falls, and when appropriate, shall offer requesters an opportunity to narrow their request so that the request can be placed in a different processing track.

(c) *Unusual circumstances.* Whenever the statutory time limits for processing a request cannot be met because of "unusual circumstances," as defined in the FOIA, and the component extends the time limits on that basis, the component shall, before expiration of the twenty-day period to respond, notify the requester in writing of the unusual circumstances involved and of the date by which processing of the request can be expected to be completed. Where the extension exceeds ten working days, the component shall, as described by the FOIA, provide the requester with an opportunity to modify the request or agree to an alternative time period for processing. The component shall make available its designated FOIA Officer and its FOIA Public Liaison for this purpose. The component shall also alert requesters to the availability of the Office of Government Information Services (OGIS) to provide dispute resolution services.

(d) *Aggregating requests.* For the purposes of satisfying unusual circumstances under the FOIA, components may aggregate requests in cases where it reasonably appears that multiple requests, submitted either by a requester or by a group of requesters acting in concert, constitute a single request that would otherwise involve unusual circumstances. Components will not aggregate multiple requests that involve unrelated matters.

(e) *Expedited processing.* (1) Requests and appeals will be processed on an expedited basis whenever the component determines that they involve:

(i) Circumstances in which the lack of expedited processing could reasonably be expected to pose an imminent threat to the life or physical safety of an individual;

(ii) An urgency to inform the public about an actual or alleged federal government activity, if made by a person who is primarily engaged in disseminating information;

(iii) The loss of substantial due process rights; or

(iv) A matter of widespread and exceptional media interest in which there exist possible questions about the government's integrity which affect public confidence.

(2) A request for expedited processing may be made at any time. Requests based on paragraphs (e)(1)(i), (ii), and (iii) of this section must be submitted to the component that maintains the records requested. When making a request for expedited processing of an administrative appeal, the request should be submitted to the DHS Office of General Counsel or the component Appeals Officer. Address information is available at the DHS Web site, *http:// www.dhs.gov/freedom-information-act-foia*, or by contacting the component FOIA officers via the information listed in appendix I. Requests for expedited processing that are based on paragraph (e)(1)(iv) of this section must be submitted to the Senior Director of FOIA Operations, the Privacy Office, U.S. Department of Homeland Security, 245 Murray Lane SW STOP–0655, Washington, DC 20598–0655. A component that receives a misdirected request for expedited processing under the standard set forth in paragraph (e)(1)(iv) of this section shall forward it immediately to the DHS Senior Director of FOIA Operations, the Privacy Office, for determination. The time period for making the determination on the request for expedited processing under paragraph (e)(1)(iv) of this section shall commence on the date that the Privacy Office receives the request, provided that it is routed within ten working days, but in no event shall the time period for making a determination on the request commence any later than the eleventh working day after the request is received by any component designated in appendix I of this subpart.

(3) A requester who seeks expedited processing must submit a statement, certified to be true and correct, explaining in detail the basis for making the request for expedited processing. For example, under paragraph (e)(1)(ii) of this section, a requester who is not a full-time member of the news media

11

must establish that he or she is a person who primarily engages in information dissemination, though it need not be his or her sole occupation. Such a requester also must establish a particular urgency to inform the public about the government activity involved in the request—one that extends beyond the public's right to know about government activity generally. The existence of numerous articles published on a given subject can be helpful to establishing the requirement that there be an "urgency to inform" the public on the topic. As a matter of administrative discretion, a component may waive the formal certification requirement.

(4) A component shall notify the requester within ten calendar days of the receipt of a request for expedited processing of its decision whether to grant or deny expedited processing. If expedited processing is granted, the request shall be given priority, placed in the processing track for expedited requests, and shall be processed as soon as practicable. If a request for expedited processing is denied, any appeal of that decision shall be acted on expeditiously.

§ 5.6   Responses to requests.

(a) *In general.* Components should, to the extent practicable, communicate with requesters having access to the Internet using electronic means, such as email or web portal.

(b) *Acknowledgments of requests.* A component shall acknowledge the request and assign it an individualized tracking number if it will take longer than ten working days to process. Components shall include in the acknowledgment a brief description of the records sought to allow requesters to more easily keep track of their requests.

(c) *Grants of requests.* Ordinarily, a component shall have twenty (20) working days from when a request is received to determine whether to grant or deny the request unless there are unusual or exceptional circumstances. Once a component makes a determination to grant a request in full or in part, it shall notify the requester in writing. The component also shall inform the requester of any fees charged

under § 5.11 and shall disclose the requested records to the requester promptly upon payment of any applicable fees. The component shall inform the requester of the availability of its FOIA Public Liaison to offer assistance.

(d) *Adverse determinations of requests.* A component making an adverse determination denying a request in any respect shall notify the requester of that determination in writing. Adverse determinations, or denials of requests, include decisions that the requested record is exempt, in whole or in part; the request does not reasonably describe the records sought; the information requested is not a record subject to the FOIA; the requested record does not exist, cannot be located, or has been destroyed; or the requested record is not readily reproducible in the form or format sought by the requester. Adverse determinations also include denials involving fees, including requester categories or fee waiver matters, or denials of requests for expedited processing.

(e) *Content of denial.* The denial shall be signed by the head of the component, or designee, and shall include:

(1) The name and title or position of the person responsible for the denial;

(2) A brief statement of the reasons for the denial, including any FOIA exemption applied by the component in denying the request;

(3) An estimate of the volume of any records or information withheld, for example, by providing the number of pages or some other reasonable form of estimation. This estimation is not required if the volume is otherwise indicated by deletions marked on records that are disclosed in part, or if providing an estimate would harm an interest protected by an applicable exemption; and

(4) A statement that the denial may be appealed under § 5.8(a), and a description of the requirements set forth therein.

(5) A statement notifying the requester of the assistance available from the agency's FOIA Public Liaison and the dispute resolution services offered by OGIS.

(f) *Markings on released documents.* Markings on released documents must be clearly visible to the requester. Records disclosed in part shall be marked to show the amount of information deleted and the exemption under which the deletion was made unless doing so would harm an interest protected by an applicable exemption. The location of the information deleted also shall be indicated on the record, if technically feasible.

(g) *Use of record exclusions.* (1) In the event that a component identifies records that may be subject to exclusion from the requirements of the FOIA pursuant to 5 U.S.C. 552(c), the head of the FOIA office of that component must confer with Department of Justice's Office of Information Policy (OIP) to obtain approval to apply the exclusion.

(2) Any component invoking an exclusion shall maintain an administrative record of the process of invocation and approval of the exclusion by OIP.

§5.7 **Confidential commercial information.**

(a) *Definitions*—(1) *Confidential commercial information* means commercial or financial information obtained by DHS from a submitter that may be protected from disclosure under Exemption 4 of the FOIA.

(2) *Submitter* means any person or entity from whom DHS obtains confidential commercial information, directly or indirectly.

(b) *Designation of confidential commercial information.* A submitter of confidential commercial information must use good faith efforts to designate by appropriate markings, either at the time of submission or within a reasonable time thereafter, any portion of its submission that it considers to be protected from disclosure under Exemption 4. These designations will expire ten years after the date of the submission unless the submitter requests and provides justification for a longer designation period.

(c) *When notice to submitters is required.* (1) A component shall promptly provide written notice to a submitter whenever records containing such information are requested under the FOIA if, after reviewing the request, the responsive records, and any appeal by the requester, the component determines that it may be required to disclose the records, provided:

(i) The requested information has been designated in good faith by the submitter as information considered protected from disclosure under Exemption 4; or

(ii) The component has a reason to believe that the requested information may be protected from disclosure under Exemption 4.

(2) The notice shall either describe the commercial information requested or include a copy of the requested records or portions of records containing the information. In cases involving a voluminous number of submitters, notice may be made by posting or publishing the notice in a place or manner reasonably likely to accomplish it.

(d) *Exceptions to submitter notice requirements.* The notice requirements of paragraphs (c) and (g) of this section shall not apply if:

(1) The component determines that the information is exempt under the FOIA;

(2) The information lawfully has been published or has been officially made available to the public;

(3) Disclosure of the information is required by a statute other than the FOIA or by a regulation issued in accordance with the requirements of Executive Order 12600 of June 23, 1987; or

(4) The designation made by the submitter under paragraph (b) of this section appears obviously frivolous, except that, in such a case, the component shall give the submitter written notice of any final decision to disclose the information and must provide that notice within a reasonable number of days prior to a specified disclosure date.

(e) *Opportunity to object to disclosure.* (1) A component will specify a reasonable time period, but no fewer than 10 working days, within which the submitter must respond to the notice referenced above. If a submitter has any objections to disclosure, it should provide the component a detailed written statement that specifies all grounds for withholding the particular information under any exemption of the FOIA. In order to rely on Exemption 4 as basis for nondisclosure, the submitter must explain why the information constitutes a trade secret, or commercial or financial information that is privileged or confidential.

(2) A submitter who fails to respond within the time period specified in the notice shall be considered to have no objection to disclosure of the information. Information received by the component after the date of any disclosure decision will not be considered by the component. Any information provided by a submitter under this subpart may itself be subject to disclosure under the FOIA.

(f) *Analysis of objections.* A component shall consider a submitter's objections and specific grounds for nondisclosure in deciding whether to disclose the requested information.

(g) *Notice of intent to disclose.* Whenever a component decides to disclose information over the objection of a submitter, the component shall provide the submitter written notice, which shall include:

(1) A statement of the reasons why each of the submitter's disclosure objections was not sustained;

(2) A description of the information to be disclosed; and

(3) A specified disclosure date, which shall be a reasonable time subsequent to the notice, but no fewer than 10 working days.

(h) *Notice of FOIA lawsuit.* Whenever a requester files a lawsuit seeking to compel the disclosure of confidential commercial information, the component shall promptly notify the submitter.

(i) *Requester notification.* The component shall notify a requester whenever it provides the submitter with notice and an opportunity to object to disclosure; whenever it notifies the submitter of its intent to disclose the requested information; and whenever a submitter files a lawsuit to prevent the disclosure of the information.

(j) *Scope.* This section shall not apply to any confidential commercial information provided to CBP by a business submitter. Section 5.12 applies to such information. Section 5.12 also defines "confidential commercial information" as used in this paragraph.

§ 5.8 Administrative appeals.

(a) *Requirements for filing an appeal.* (1) A requester may appeal adverse determinations denying his or her request or any part of the request to the appropriate Appeals Officer. A requester may also appeal if he or she questions the adequacy of the component's search for responsive records, or believes the component either misinterpreted the request or did not address all aspects of the request (*i.e.*, it issued an incomplete response), or if the requester believes there is a procedural deficiency (*e.g.*, fees were improperly calculated). For the address of the appropriate component Appeals Officer, contact the applicable component FOIA liaison using the information in appendix I to this subpart, visit *www.dhs.gov/foia*, or call 1–866–431–0486. An appeal must be in writing, and to be considered timely it must be postmarked or, in the case of electronic submissions, transmitted to the Appeals Officer within 90 working days after the date of the component's response. An electronically filed appeal will be considered timely if transmitted to the Appeals Officer by 11:59:59 p.m. ET or EDT on the 90th working day. The appeal should clearly identify the component determination (including the assigned request number if the requester knows it) that is being appealed and should contain the reasons the requester believes the determination was erroneous. To facilitate handling, the requester should mark both the letter and the envelope, or the transmittal line in the case of electronic transmissions "Freedom of Information Act Appeal."

(2) An adverse determination by the component appeals officer will be the final action of DHS.

(b) *Adjudication of appeals.* (1) The DHS Office of the General Counsel or its designee (*e.g.*, component Appeals Officers) is the authorized appeals authority for DHS;

(2) On receipt of any appeal involving classified information, the Appeals Officer shall consult with the Chief Security Officer, and take appropriate action to ensure compliance with 6 CFR part 7;

(3) If the appeal becomes the subject of a lawsuit, the Appeals Officer is not required to act further on the appeal.

(c) *Appeal decisions.* The decision on the appeal will be made in writing. A decision that upholds a component's determination will contain a statement that identifies the reasons for the affirmance, including any FOIA exemptions applied. The decision will provide the requester with notification of the statutory right to file a lawsuit and will inform the requester of the mediation services offered by the Office of Government Information Services, of the National Archives and Records Administration, as a non-exclusive alternative to litigation. Should the requester elect to mediate any dispute related to the FOIA request with the Office of Government Information Services, DHS and its components will participate in the mediation process in good faith. If the adverse decision is reversed or modified on appeal, in whole or in part, the requester will be notified in a written decision and the request will be thereafter be further processed in accordance with that appeal decision.

(d) *Time limit for issuing appeal decision.* The statutory time limit for responding to appeals is generally 20 working days after receipt. However, the Appeals Officer may extend the time limit for responding to an appeal provided the circumstances set forth in 5 U.S.C. 552(a)(6)(B)(i) are met.

(e) *Appeal necessary before seeking court review.* If a requester wishes to seek court review of a component's adverse determination on a matter appealable under paragraph (a)(1) of this section, the requester must generally first appeal it under this subpart. However, a requester is not required to first file an appeal of an adverse determination of a request for expedited processing prior to seeking court review.

§5.9 Preservation of records.

Each component shall preserve all correspondence pertaining to the requests that it receives under this subpart, as well as copies of all requested records, until disposition or destruction is authorized pursuant to title 44 of the United States Code or the General Records Schedule 4.2 and/or 14 of the National Archives and Records Administration. Records will not be disposed of or destroyed while they are the subject of a pending request, appeal, or lawsuit under the FOIA.

§5.10 FOIA requests for information contained in a Privacy Act system of records.

(a) *Information subject to Privacy Act.* (1) If a requester submits a FOIA request for information about him or herself that is contained in a Privacy Act system of records applicable to the requester (*i.e.*, the information contained in the system of records is retrieved by the component using the requester's name or other personal identifier, and the information pertains to an individual covered by the Privacy Act) the request will be processed under both the FOIA and the Privacy Act.

(2) If the information the requester is seeking is not subject to the Privacy Act (*e.g.*, the information is filed under another subject, such as an organization, activity, event, or an investigation not retrievable by the requester's name or personal identifier), the request, if otherwise properly made, will be treated only as a FOIA request. In addition, if the information is covered by the Privacy Act and the requester does not provide proper verification of the requester's identity, the request, if otherwise properly made, will be processed only under the FOIA.

(b) *When both Privacy Act and FOIA exemptions apply.* Only if both a Privacy Act exemption and a FOIA exemption apply can DHS withhold information from a requester if the information sought by the requester is about him or herself and is contained in a Privacy Act system of records applicable to the requester.

(c) *Conditions for release of Privacy Act information to third parties in response to a FOIA request.* If a requester submits a FOIA request for Privacy Act information about another individual, the information will not be disclosed without that person's prior written consent that provides the same verification information that the person would have been required to submit for information about him or herself, unless—

(1) The information is required to be released under the FOIA, as provided by 5 U.S.C. 552a (b)(2); or

(2) In most circumstances, if the individual is deceased.

(d) *Privacy Act requirements.* See DHS's Privacy Act regulations in 5 CFR part 5, subpart B for additional information regarding the requirements of the Privacy Act.

§5.11 Fees.

(a) *In general.* Components shall charge for processing requests under the FOIA in accordance with the provisions of this section and with the OMB Guidelines. Components will ordinarily use the most efficient and least expensive method for processing requested records. In order to resolve any fee issues that arise under this section, a component may contact a requester for additional information. A component ordinarily will collect all applicable fees before sending copies of records to a requester. If you make a FOIA request, it shall be considered a firm commitment to pay all applicable fees charged under §5.11, up to $25.00, unless you seek a waiver of fees. Requesters must pay fees by check or money order made payable to the Treasury of the United States.

(b) *Definitions.* Generally, "requester category" means one of the three categories in which agencies place requesters for the purpose of determining whether a requester will be charged fees for search, review and duplication; categories include commercial requesters, noncommercial scientific or educational institutions or news media requesters, and all other requesters. The term "fee waiver" means that processing fees will be waived, or reduced, if a requester can demonstrate that certain statutory standards are satisfied including that the information is in the public interest and is not requested for a primarily commercial interest. For purposes of this section:

(1) *Commercial use request* is a request that asks for information for a use or a purpose that furthers a commercial, trade, or profit interest, which can include furthering those interests through litigation. A component's decision to place a requester in the commercial use category will be made on a case-by-case basis based on the requester's intended use of the information.

(2) *Direct costs* are those expenses that an agency expends in searching for and duplicating (and, in the case of commercial use requests, reviewing) records in order to respond to a FOIA request. For example, direct costs include the salary of the employee performing the work (*i.e.,* the basic rate of pay for the employee, plus 16 percent of that rate to cover benefits) and the cost of operating computers and other electronic equipment, such as photocopiers and scanners. Direct costs do not include overhead expenses such as the costs of space, and of heating or lighting a facility.

(3) *Duplication* is reproducing a copy of a record or of the information contained in it, necessary to respond to a FOIA request. Copies can take the form of paper, audiovisual materials, or electronic records, among others.

(4) *Educational institution* is any school that operates a program of scholarly research. A requester in this fee category must show that the request is made in connection with his or her role at the educational institution. Components may seek verification from the requester that the request is in furtherance of scholarly research.

Example 1. A request from a professor of geology at a university for records relating to soil erosion, written on letterhead of the Department of Geology, would be presumed to be from an educational institution if the request adequately describes how the requested information would further a specific research goal of the educational institution.

Example 2. A request from the same professor of geology seeking immigration information from the U.S. Immigration and Customs Enforcement in furtherance of a murder mystery he is writing would not be presumed to be an institutional request, regardless of whether it was written on institutional stationery.

Example 3. A student who makes a request in furtherance of their coursework or other school-sponsored activities and provides a copy of a course syllabus or other reasonable documentation to indicate the research purpose for the request, would qualify as part of this fee category.

NOTE: These examples are provided for guidance purposes only. Each individual request will be evaluated under the particular facts, circumstances, and information provided by the requester.

(5) *Noncommercial scientific institution* is an institution that is not operated on a "commercial" basis, as defined in paragraph (b)(1) of this section, and that is operated solely for the purpose of conducting scientific research the results of which are not intended to promote any particular product or industry. A requester in this category must show that the request is authorized by and is made under the auspices of a qualifying institution and that the records are sought to further scientific research and not for a commercial use.

(6) *Representative of the news media* is any person or entity that actively gathers information of potential interest to a segment of the public, uses its editorial skills to turn the raw materials into a distinct work, and distributes that work to an audience. The term "news" means information that is about current events or that would be of current interest to the public. Examples of news media entities include television or radio stations that broadcast "news" to the public at large and publishers of periodicals that disseminate "news" and make their products available through a variety of means to the general public, including but not limited to, news organizations that disseminate solely on the Internet. A request for records that supports the news-dissemination function of the requester shall not be considered to be for a commercial use. In contrast, data brokers or others who merely compile and market government information for direct economic return shall not be presumed to be news media entities. "Freelance" journalists must demonstrate a solid basis for expecting publication through a news media entity in order to be considered as working for a news media entity. A publication contract would provide the clearest evidence that publication is expected; however, components shall also consider a requester's past publication record in making this determination.

(7) *Review* is the page-by-page, line-by-line examination of a record located in response to a request in order to determine whether any portion of it is exempt from disclosure. Review time includes processing any record for disclosure, such as doing all that is necessary to prepare the record for disclo-

sure, including the process of redacting the record and marking the appropriate exemptions. Review costs are properly charged even if a record ultimately is not disclosed. Review time also includes time spent both obtaining and considering any formal objection to disclosure made by a confidential commercial information submitter under §5.7 or §5.12, but it does not include time spent resolving general legal or policy issues regarding the application of exemptions.

(8) *Search* is the process of looking for and retrieving records or information responsive to a request. Search time includes page-by-page or line-by-line identification of information within records; and the reasonable efforts expended to locate and retrieve information from electronic records. Components shall ensure that searches are done in the most efficient and least expensive manner reasonably possible by readily available means.

(c) *Charging fees.* In responding to FOIA requests, components shall charge the following fees unless a waiver or reduction of fees has been granted under paragraph (k) of this section. Because the fee amounts provided below already account for the direct costs associated with a given fee type, unless otherwise stated in §5.11, components should not add any additional costs to those charges.

(1) *Search.* (i) Search fees shall be charged for all requests subject to the restrictions of paragraph (d) of this section. Components may properly charge for time spent searching even if they do not locate any responsive records or if they determine that the records are entirely exempt from disclosure.

(ii) For each quarter hour spent by personnel searching for requested records, including electronic searches that do not require new programming, the fees will be as follows: Managerial—$10.25; professional—$7.00; and clerical/administrative—$4.00.

(iii) Requesters will be charged the direct costs associated with conducting any search that requires the creation of a new computer program, as referenced in section 5.4, to locate the requested records. Requesters shall be notified of the costs associated with creating such a program and must agree to pay the associated costs before the costs may be incurred.

(iv) For requests that require the retrieval of records stored by an agency at a federal records center operated by the National Archives and Records Administration (NARA), additional costs shall be charged in accordance with the Transactional Billing Rate Schedule established by NARA.

(2) *Duplication.* Duplication fees will be charged to all requesters, subject to the restrictions of paragraph (d) of this section. A component shall honor a requester's preference for receiving a record in a particular form or format where it is readily reproducible by the component in the form or format requested. Where photocopies are supplied, the component will provide one copy per request at a cost of ten cents per page. For copies of records produced on tapes, disks, or other media, components will charge the direct costs of producing the copy, including operator time. Where paper documents must be scanned in order to comply with a requester's preference to receive the records in an electronic format, the requester shall pay the direct costs associated with scanning those materials. For other forms of duplication, components will charge the direct costs.

(3) *Review.* Review fees will be charged to requesters who make commercial use requests. Review fees will be assessed in connection with the initial review of the record, *i.e.,* the review conducted by a component to determine whether an exemption applies to a particular record or portion of a record. No charge will be made for review at the administrative appeal stage of exemptions applied at the initial review stage. However, when the appellate authority determines that a particular exemption no longer applies, any costs associated with a component's re-review of the records in order to consider the use of other exemptions may be assessed as review fees. Review fees will be charged at the same rates as those charged for a search under paragraph (c)(1)(ii) of this section.

(d) *Restrictions on charging fees.* (1) No search fees will be charged for requests by educational institutions, non-commercial scientific institutions, or representatives of the news media, unless the records are sought for a commercial use.

(2) If a component fails to comply with the FOIA's time limits in which to respond to a request, it may not charge search fees, or, in the instances of requests from requesters described in paragraph (d)(1) of this section, may not charge duplication fees, except as described in (d)(2)(i) through (iii).

(i) If a component has determined that unusual circumstances as defined by the FOIA apply and the component provided timely written notice to the requester in accordance with the FOIA, a failure to comply with the time limit shall be excused for an additional 10 days.

(ii) If a component has determined that unusual circumstances, as defined by the FOIA, apply and more than 5,000 pages are necessary to respond to the request, a component may charge search fees, or, in the case of requesters described in paragraph (d)(1) of this section, may charge duplication fees, if the following steps are taken. The component must have provided timely written notice of unusual circumstances to the requester in accordance with the FOIA and the component must have discussed with the requester via written mail, email, or telephone (or made not less than three good-faith attempts to do so) how the requester could effectively limit the scope of the request in accordance with 5. U.S.C. 552(a)(6)(B)(ii). If this exception is satisfied, the component may charge all applicable fees incurred in the processing of the request.

(iii) If a court has determined that exceptional circumstances exist, as defined by the FOIA, a failure to comply with the time limits shall be excused for the length of time provided by the court order.

(3) No search or review fees will be charged for a quarter-hour period unless more than half of that period is required for search or review.

(4) Except for requesters seeking records for a commercial use, components will provide without charge:

(i) The first 100 pages of duplication (or the cost equivalent for other media); and

(ii) The first two hours of search.

(5) When, after first deducting the 100 free pages (or its cost equivalent) and the first two hours of search, a total fee calculated under paragraph (c) of this section is $14.00 or less for any request, no fee will be charged.

(e) *Notice of anticipated fees in excess of $25.00.* (1) When a component determines or estimates that the fees to be assessed in accordance with this section will exceed $25.00, the component shall notify the requester of the actual or estimated amount of the fees, including a breakdown of the fees for search, review and/or duplication, unless the requester has indicated a willingness to pay fees as high as those anticipated. If only a portion of the fee can be estimated readily, the component shall advise the requester accordingly. If the requester is a noncommercial use requester, the notice will specify that the requester is entitled to his or her statutory entitlements of 100 pages of duplication at no charge and, if the requester is charged search fees, two hours of search time at no charge, and will advise the requester whether those entitlements have been provided. Two hours of search time will be provided free of charge to non-commercial requesters regardless of whether they agree to pay estimated fees.

(2) In cases in which a requester has been notified that the actual or estimated fees are in excess of $25.00, the request shall not be considered received and further work will not be completed until the requester commits in writing to pay the actual or estimated total fee, or designates some amount of fees he or she is willing to pay, or in the case of a noncommercial use requester who has not yet been provided with his or her statutory entitlements, designates that he or she seeks only that which can be provided by the statutory entitlements. The requester must provide the commitment or designation in writing, and must, when applicable, designate an exact dollar amount the requester is willing to pay. Components are not required to accept payments in installments.

(3) If the requester has indicated a willingness to pay some designated amount of fees, but the component estimates that the total fee will exceed that amount, the component will toll the processing of the request while it notifies the requester of the estimated fees in excess of the amount the requester has indicated a willingness to pay. The component shall inquire whether the requester wishes to revise the amount of fees he or she is willing to pay and/or modify the request. Once the requester responds, the time to respond will resume from where it was at the date of the notification.

(4) Components will make available their FOIA Public Liaison or other FOIA professional to assist any requester in reformulating a request to meet the requester's needs at a lower cost.

(f) *Charges for other services.* Although not required to provide special services, if a component chooses to do so as a matter of administrative discretion, the direct costs of providing the service will be charged. Examples of such services include certifying that records are true copies, providing multiple copies of the same document, or sending records by means other than first class mail.

(g) *Charging interest.* Components may charge interest on any unpaid bill starting on the 31st day following the date of billing the requester. Interest charges will be assessed at the rate provided in 31 U.S.C. 3717 and will accrue from the billing date until payment is received by the component. Components will follow the provisions of the Debt Collection Act of 1982 (Pub. L. 97–365, 96 Stat. 1749), as amended, and its administrative procedures, including the use of consumer reporting agencies, collection agencies, and offset.

(h) *Aggregating requests.* When a component reasonably believes that a requester or a group of requesters acting in concert is attempting to divide a single request into a series of requests for the purpose of avoiding fees, the component may aggregate those requests and charge accordingly. Components may presume that multiple requests of this type made within a 30-day period have been made in order to avoid fees. For requests separated by a longer period, components will aggregate them only where there is a reasonable basis for determining that aggregation is warranted in view of all the circumstances involved. Multiple requests involving unrelated matters will not be aggregated.

(i) *Advance payments.* (1) For requests other than those described in paragraphs (i)(2) and (3) of this section, a component shall not require the requester to make an advance payment before work is commenced or continued on a request. Payment owed for work already completed (*i.e.,* payment before copies are sent to a requester) is not an advance payment.

(2) When a component determines or estimates that a total fee to be charged under this section will exceed $250.00, it may require that the requester make an advance payment up to the amount of the entire anticipated fee before beginning to process the request. A component may elect to process the request prior to collecting fees when it receives a satisfactory assurance of full payment from a requester with a history of prompt payment.

(3) Where a requester has previously failed to pay a properly charged FOIA fee to any component or agency within 30 calendar days of the billing date, a component may require that the requester pay the full amount due, plus any applicable interest on that prior request and the component may require that the requester make an advance payment of the full amount of any anticipated fee, before the component begins to process a new request or continues to process a pending request or any pending appeal. Where a component has a reasonable basis to believe that a requester has misrepresented his or her identity in order to avoid paying outstanding fees, it may require that the requester provide proof of identity.

(4) In cases in which a component requires advance payment, the request shall not be considered received and further work will not be completed until the required payment is received. If the requester does not pay the advance payment within 30 calendar days after the date of the component's fee determination, the request will be closed.

(j) *Other statutes specifically providing for fees.* The fee schedule of this section does not apply to fees charged under any statute that specifically requires an agency to set and collect fees for particular types of records. In instances where records responsive to a request are subject to a statutorily-based fee schedule program, the component will inform the requester of the contact information for that source.

(k) *Requirements for waiver or reduction of fees.* (1) Records responsive to a request shall be furnished without charge or at a reduced rate below that established under paragraph (c) of this section, where a component determines, on a case-by-case basis, based on all available information, that the requester has demonstrated that:

(i) Disclosure of the requested information is in the public interest because it is likely to contribute significantly to public understanding of the operations or activities of the government; and

(ii) Disclosure of the information is not primarily in the commercial interest of the requester.

(2) In deciding whether disclosure of the requested information is in the public interest because it is likely to contribute significantly to public understanding of operations or activities of the government, components will consider the following factors:

(i) The subject of the request must concern identifiable operations or activities of the federal government, with a connection that is direct and clear, not remote or attenuated.

(ii) Disclosure of the requested records must be meaningfully informative about government operations or activities in order to be "likely to contribute" to an increased public understanding of those operations or activities. The disclosure of information that already is in the public domain, in either the same or a substantially identical form, would not contribute to such understanding where nothing new would be added to the public's understanding.

(iii) The disclosure must contribute to the understanding of a reasonably broad audience of persons interested in the subject, as opposed to the individual understanding of the requester.

A requester's expertise in the subject area as well as his or her ability and intention to effectively convey information to the public shall be considered. It shall be presumed that a representative of the news media will satisfy this consideration.

(iv) The public's understanding of the subject in question must be enhanced by the disclosure to a significant extent. However, components shall not make value judgments about whether the information at issue is "important" enough to be made public.

(3) To determine whether disclosure of the requested information is primarily in the commercial interest of the requester, components will consider the following factors:

(i) Components shall identify any commercial interest of the requester, as defined in paragraph (b)(1) of this section, that would be furthered by the requested disclosure. Requesters shall be given an opportunity to provide explanatory information regarding this consideration.

(ii) A waiver or reduction of fees is justified where the public interest is greater than any identified commercial interest in disclosure. Components ordinarily shall presume that where a news media requester has satisfied the public interest standard, the public interest will be the interest primarily served by disclosure to that requester. Disclosure to data brokers or others who merely compile and market government information for direct economic return shall not be presumed to primarily serve the public interest.

(4) Where only some of the records to be released satisfy the requirements for a waiver of fees, a waiver shall be granted for those records.

(5) Requests for a waiver or reduction of fees should be made when the request is first submitted to the component and should address the criteria referenced above. A requester may submit a fee waiver request at a later time so long as the underlying record request is pending or on administrative appeal. When a requester who has committed to pay fees subsequently asks for a waiver of those fees and that waiver is denied, the requester will be required to pay any costs incurred up to the date the fee waiver request was received.

(6) *Summary of fees.* The following table summarizes the chargeable fees (excluding direct fees identified in §5.11) for each requester category.

Category	Search fees	Review fees	Duplication fees
Commercial-use	Yes	Yes	Yes.
Educational or Non-Commercial Scientific Institution.	No	No	Yes (100 pages free).
News Media	No	No	Yes (100 pages free).
Other requesters	Yes (2 hours free)	No	Yes (100 pages free).

§5.12 Confidential commercial information; CBP procedures.

(a) *In general.* For purposes of this section, "commercial information" is defined as trade secret, commercial, or financial information obtained from a person. Commercial information provided to CBP by a business submitter and that CBP determines is privileged or confidential commercial or financial information will be treated as privileged or confidential and will not be disclosed pursuant to a Freedom of Information Act request or otherwise made known in any manner except as provided in this section.

(b) *Notice to business submitters of FOIA requests for disclosure.* Except as provided in paragraph (b)(2) of this section, CBP will provide business submitters with prompt written notice of receipt of FOIA requests or appeals that encompass their commercial information. The written notice will describe either the exact nature of the commercial information requested, or enclose copies of the records or those portions of the records that contain the commercial information. The written notice also will advise the business submitter of its right to file a disclosure objection statement as provided under paragraph (c)(1) of this section. CBP will provide notice to business submitters of FOIA requests for the business submitter's commercial information for a period of not more than 10 years after the date the business submitter provides CBP with the information, unless the business submitter requests, and provides acceptable justification for, a specific notice period of greater duration.

(1) *When notice is required.* CBP will provide business submitters with notice of receipt of a FOIA request or appeal whenever:

(i) The business submitter has in good faith designated the information as commercially- or financially-sensitive information. The business submitter's claim of confidentiality should be supported by a statement by an authorized representative of the business entity providing specific justification that the information in question is considered confidential commercial or financial information and that the information has not been disclosed to the public; or

(ii) CBP has reason to believe that disclosure of the commercial information could reasonably be expected to cause substantial competitive harm.

(2) *When notice is not required.* The notice requirements of this section will not apply if:

(i) CBP determines that the commercial information will not be disclosed;

(ii) The commercial information has been lawfully published or otherwise made available to the public; or

(iii) Disclosure of the information is required by law (other than 5 U.S.C. 552).

(c) *Procedure when notice given*—(1) *Opportunity for business submitter to object to disclosure.* A business submitter receiving written notice from CBP of receipt of a FOIA request or appeal encompassing its commercial information may object to any disclosure of the commercial information by providing CBP with a detailed statement of reasons within 10 days of the date of the notice (exclusive of Saturdays, Sundays, and legal public holidays). The statement should specify all the grounds for withholding any of the commercial information under any exemption of the FOIA and, in the case of Exemption 4, should demonstrate why

the information is considered to be a trade secret or commercial or financial information that is privileged or confidential. The disclosure objection information provided by a person pursuant to this paragraph may be subject to disclosure under the FOIA.

(2) *Notice to FOIA requester.* When notice is given to a business submitter under paragraph (b)(1) of this section, notice will also be given to the FOIA requester that the business submitter has been given an opportunity to object to any disclosure of the requested commercial information.

(d) *Notice of intent to disclose.* CBP will consider carefully a business submitter's objections and specific grounds for nondisclosure prior to determining whether to disclose commercial information. Whenever CBP decides to disclose the requested commercial information over the objection of the business submitter, CBP will provide written notice to the business submitter of CBP's intent to disclose, which will include:

(1) A statement of the reasons for which the business submitter's disclosure objections were not sustained;

(2) A description of the commercial information to be disclosed; and

(3) A specified disclosure date which will not be less than 10 days (exclusive of Saturdays, Sundays, and legal public holidays) after the notice of intent to disclose the requested information has been issued to the business submitter. Except as otherwise prohibited by law, CBP will also provide a copy of the notice of intent to disclose to the FOIA requester at the same time.

(e) *Notice of FOIA lawsuit.* Whenever a FOIA requester brings suit seeking to compel the disclosure of commercial information covered by paragraph (b)(1) of this section, CBP will promptly notify the business submitter in writing.

§ 5.13 Other rights and services.

Nothing in this subpart shall be construed to entitle any person, as of right, to any service or to the disclosure of any record to which such person is not entitled under the FOIA.

APPENDIX I TO SUBPART A TO PART 5—
FOIA CONTACT INFORMATION

Department of Homeland Security Chief FOIA Officer

Chief Privacy Officer/Chief FOIA Officer, The Privacy Office, U.S. Department of Homeland Security,245 Murray Lane SW., STOP-0655, Washington, DC. 20528-0655

Department of Homeland Security Deputy Chief FOIA Officer

Deputy Chief FOIA Officer, The Privacy Office, U.S. Department of Homeland Security, 245 Murray Lane SW., STOP-0655, Washington, DC 20528-0655

Senior Director, FOIA Operations

Sr. Director, FOIA Operations, The Privacy Office, U.S. Department of Homeland Security, 245 Murray Lane SW., STOP-0655, Washington, DC 20528-0655, Phone: 202-343-1743 or 866-431-0486,Fax: 202-343-4011, Email: *foia@hq.dhs.gov*

Director, FOIA Production and Quality Assurance

Public Liaison, FOIA Production and Quality Assurance, The Privacy Office, U.S. Department of Homeland Security,245 Murray Lane SW., STOP-0655, Washington, DC 20528-0655, Phone: 202-343-1743 or 866-431-0486, Fax: 202-343-4011, Email: *foia@hq.dhs.gov*

U.S. Customs & Border Protection (CBP)

FOIA Officer/Public Liaison, 90 K Street NE., 9th Floor, Washington, DC 20229-1181, Phone: 202-325-0150, Fax: 202-325-0230

Office of Civil Rights and Civil Liberties (CRCL)

FOIA Officer/Public Liaison, U.S. Department of Homeland Security, Washington, DC 20528, Phone: 202-357-1218, Email: *CRCL@dhs.gov*

Federal Emergency Management Agency (FEMA)

FOIA Officer/Public Liaison, 500 C Street SW., Room 7NE, Washington, DC 20472, Phone: 202-646-3323,Email: *fema-foia@dhs.gov*

Federal Law Enforcement Training Center (FLETC)

FOIA Officer/Public Liaison, Building #681, Suite 187B, Glynco, GA 31524, Phone: 912-267-3103,Fax: 912-267-3113, Email: *fletc-foia@dhs.gov*

National Protection and Programs Directorate (NPPD)

FOIA Officer/Public Liaison, U.S. Department of Homeland Security, Washington,

DC 20528, Phone: 703-235-2211, Fax: 703-235-2052, Email: *NPPD.FOIA@dhs.gov*

Office of Biometric Identity Management (OBIM) FOIA Officer, Department of Homeland Security, Washington, DC 20598-0628, Phone: 202-298-5454, Fax: 202-298-5445, E-Mail: *OBIM-FOIA@ice.dhs.gov*

Office of Intelligence & Analysis (I&A)

FOIA Officer/Public Liaison, U.S. Department of Homeland Security, Washington, DC 20528, Phone: 202-447-4883, Fax: 202-612-1936, Email: *I&AFOIA@hq.dhs.gov*

Office of Inspector General (OIG)

FOIA Public Liaison, DHS-OIG Counsel, STOP 0305, 245 Murray Lane SW., Washington, DC 20528-0305,Phone: 202-254-4001, Fax: 202-254-4398, Email: *FOIA.OIG@oig.dhs.gov*

Office of Operations Coordination and Planning (OPS)

FOIA Officer/Public Liaison,U.S. Department of Homeland Security,Washington, DC 20528,Phone: 202-447-4156,Fax: 202-282-9811,Email: *FOIAOPS@DHS.GOV*

Science & Technology Directorate (S&T)

FOIA Officer/Public Liaison,U.S. Department of Homeland Security,Washington, DC 20528,Phone: 202-254-6342,Fax: 202-254-6739,Email: *stfoia@hq.dhs.gov*

Transportation Security Administration (TSA)

FOIA Officer/Public Liaison,Freedom of Information Act Branch,601 S. 12th Street,11th Floor, East Tower, TSA-20,Arlington, VA 20598-6020,Phone: 1-866-FOIA-TSA or 571-227-2300,Fax: 571-227-1406,Email: *foia.tsa@dhs.gov*

U.S. Citizenship & Immigration Services (USCIS)

FOIA Officer/Public Liaison,National Records Center, FOIA/PA Office,P.O. Box 648010,Lee's Summit, Mo. 64064-8010,Phone: 1-800-375-5283 (USCIS National Customer Service Unit),Fax: 816-350-5785,Email: *uscis.foia@uscis.dhs.gov*

United States Coast Guard (USCG)

Commandant (CG-611),2100 2nd St., SW.,Attn: FOIA Officer/Public Liaison,Washington, DC 20593-0001,FOIA Requester Service Center Contact: Amanda Ackerson,Phone: 202-475-3522,Fax: 202-475-3927,Email: *efoia@uscg.mil*

United States Immigration & Customs Enforcement (ICE)

Freedom of Information Act Office,FOIA Officer/Public Liaison 500 12th Street, SW., Stop 5009,Washington, DC 20536-5009,

FOIA Requester Service Center Contact,Phone: 866-633-1182,Fax: 202-732-4265,Email: *ice-foia@dhs.gov*

United States Secret Service (USSS)

Freedom of Information and Privacy Acts Branch,FOIA Officer/Public Liaison,245 Murray Drive, Building 410,Washington, DC 20223,Phone: 202-406-6370,Fax: 202-406-5586,Email: *FOIA@usss.dhs.gov*

Please direct all requests for information from the Office of the Secretary, Citizenship and Immigration Services Ombudsman, Domestic Nuclear Detection Office, Office of the Executive Secretary, Office of Intergovernmental Affairs, Management Directorate, Office of Policy, Office of the General Counsel, Office of Health Affairs, Office of Legislative Affairs, Office of Public Affairs and the Privacy Office, to the DHS Privacy Office at:

The Privacy Office,U.S. Department of Homeland Security,245 Murray Lane SW.,STOP-0655,Washington, DC 20528-0655,Phone: 202-343-1743 or 866-431-0486,Fax: 202-343-4011,Email: *foia@hq.dhs.gov*

Subpart B—Privacy Act

§ 5.20 General provisions.

(a) *Purpose and scope.* (1) This subpart contains the rules that the Department of Homeland Security (Department) follows under the Privacy Act of 1974 (5 U.S.C. 552a). These rules should be read together with the Privacy Act, which provides additional information about records maintained on individuals. The rules in this subpart apply to all records in systems of records maintained by the Department that are retrieved by an individual's name or personal identifier. They describe the procedures by which individuals may request access to records about themselves, request amendment or correction of those records, and request an accounting of disclosures of those by the Department. In addition, the Department processes all Privacy Act requests for access to records under the Freedom of Information Act (FOIA) (5 U.S.C. 552), following the rules contained in subpart A of this part, which gives requests the benefit of both statutes.

(2) The provisions established by this subpart shall apply to all Department components that are transferred to the Department. Except to the extent a Department component has adopted separate guidance under the Privacy Act, the provisions of this subpart shall apply to each component of the Department. Departmental components may issue their own guidance under this subpart pursuant to approval by the Department.

(b) *Definitions.* As used in this subpart:

(1) Component means each separate bureau, office, board, division, commission, service, or administration of the Department.

(2) Request for access to a record means a request made under Privacy Act subsection (d)(1).

(3) Request for amendment or correction of a record means a request made under Privacy Act subsection (d)(2).

(4) Request for an accounting means a request made under Privacy Act subsection (c)(3).

(5) Requester means an individual who makes a request for access, a request for amendment or correction, or a request for an accounting under the Privacy Act.

(c) *Authority to request records for a law enforcement purpose.* The head of a component or designee thereof is authorized to make written requests under subsection (b)(7) of the Privacy Act for records maintained by other agencies that are necessary to carry out an authorized law enforcement activity.

(d) *Notice on Departmental use of (b)(1) exemption.* As a general matter, when applying the (b)(1) exemption for disclosures within an agency on a need to know basis, the Department will consider itself a single entity, meaning that information may be disclosed between components of the Department under the (b)(1) exemption.

(e) *Interim Retention of Authorities.* As an interim solution, all agencies and components under the Department will retain the necessary authority from their original purpose in order to conduct these necessary activities. This includes the authority to maintain Privacy Act systems of records, disseminate information pursuant to existing or new routine uses, and retention of exemption authorities under sections (j) and (k) of the Privacy Act, where applicable. This retention of an agency or component's authorities and information practices will remain in effect until this regulation is promulgated as a final rule, or the Department revises all systems of records notices. This retention of authority is necessary to allow components to fulfill their mission and purpose during the transition period of the establishment of the Department. During this transition period, the Department shall evaluate with the components the existing authorities and information practices and determine what revisions (if any) are appropriate and should be made to these existing authorities and practices. The Department anticipates that such revisions will be made either through the issuance of a revised system of records notices or through subsequent final regulations.

§5.21 Requests for access to records.

(a) *How made and addressed.* You may make a request for access to a Department of Homeland Security record about yourself by appearing in person or by writing directly to the Department component that maintains the record. Your request should be sent or delivered to the component's Privacy Act office at the address listed in appendix A to this part. In most cases, a component's central Privacy Act office is the place to send a Privacy Act request. For records held by a field office of the U.S. Customs Service, U.S. Secret Service, U.S. Coast Guard, or any other Department component with field offices, however, you must write directly to that Customs, Secret Service, Coast Guard, or other field office address, which can be found in most telephone books or by calling the component's central Privacy Act office. (The functions of each component are summarized elsewhere in this title and in the description of the Department and its components in the "United States Government Manual," which is issued annually and is available in most libraries, as well as for sale from the Government Printing Office's Superintendent of Documents. This manual also can be accessed electronically at the Government Printing Office's World Wide Web site (which can be found at *http://www.access.gpo.gov/su_docs*). Some records are maintained under a government-wide systems of records notice, for example, Official Personnel Files are maintained under the authority of the Office of Personnel Management. In order to access records maintained under a government-wide notice, please send your request to the Privacy Act office of the original department or agency from which the component was transferred to the Department. If you cannot determine where within the Department to send your request, you may send it to the Departmental Disclosure Officer, Department of Homeland Security, Washington, DC 20528, and that office will forward it to the component(s) it believes most likely to have the records that you seek. For the quickest possible handling, you should mark both your request letter and the envelope "Privacy Act Request."

(b) *Description of records sought.* You must describe the records that you want in enough detail to enable Department personnel to locate the system of records containing them with a reasonable amount of effort. Whenever possible, your request should describe the records sought, the time periods in which you believe they were compiled, and the name or identifying number of each system of records in which you believe they are kept. The Department publishes notices in the FEDERAL REGISTER that describe its components' systems of records. A description of the Department's systems of records also may be found as part of the "Privacy Act Compilation" published by the National Archives and Records Administration's Office of the Federal Register. This compilation is available in most large reference and university libraries. This compilation also can be accessed electronically at the Government Printing Office's World Wide Web site (which can be found at *http://www.access.gpo.gov/su_docs*).

(c) *Agreement to pay fees.* If you make a Privacy Act request for access to records, it shall be considered an agreement by you to pay all applicable fees charged under §5.29, up to $25.00. The component responsible for responding

25

to your request ordinarily shall confirm this agreement in an acknowledgement letter. When making a request, you may specify a willingness to pay a greater or lesser amount.

(d) *Verification of identity.* When you make a request for access to records about yourself, you must verify your identity. You must state your full name, current address, and date and place of birth. You must sign your request and your signature must either be notarized or submitted by you under 28 U.S.C. 1746, a law that permits statements to be made under penalty of perjury as a substitute for notarization. While no specific form is required, you may obtain forms for this purpose from the Departmental Disclosure Officer, Department of Homeland Security, Washington, DC 20528. In order to help the identification and location of requested records, you may also, at your option, include your social security number.

(e) *Verification of guardianship.* When making a request as the parent or guardian of a minor or as the guardian of someone determined by a court to be incompetent, for access to records about that individual, you must establish:

(1) The identity of the individual who is the subject of the record, by stating the name, current address, date and place of birth, and, at your option, the social security number of the individual;

(2) Your own identity, as required in paragraph (d) of this section;

(3) That you are the parent or guardian of that individual, which you may prove by providing a copy of the individual's birth certificate showing your parentage or by providing a court order establishing your guardianship; and

(4) That you are acting on behalf of that individual in making the request.

(f) *Verification in the case of third party information requests.* If you are making a request for records concerning an individual on behalf of that individual, you must provide a statement from the individual verifying the identity of the individual as provided in paragraph (d) of this section. You must also provide a statement from the individual certifying the individual's

agreement that records concerning the individual may be released to you.

§ 5.22 Responsibility for responding to requests for access to records.

(a) *In general.* Except as stated in paragraphs (c), (d), and (e) of this section, the component that first receives a request for access to a record, and has possession of that record, is the component responsible for responding to the request. In determining which records are responsive to a request, a component ordinarily shall include only those records in its possession as of the date the component begins its search for them. If any other date is used, the component shall inform the requester of that date.

(b) *Authority to grant or deny requests.* The head of a component, or the component head's designee, is authorized to grant or deny any request for access or amendment to a record of that component.

(c) *Consultations and referrals.* When a component receives a request for access to a record in its possession, it shall determine whether another component, or another agency of the Federal Government, is better able to determine whether the record is exempt from access under the Privacy Act. If the receiving component determines that it is best able to process the record in response to the request, then it shall do so. If the receiving component determines that it is not best able to process the record, then it shall either:

(1) Respond to the request regarding that record, after consulting with the component or agency best able to determine whether the record is exempt from access and with any other component or agency that has a substantial interest in it; or

(2) Refer the responsibility for responding to the request regarding that record to the component best able to determine whether it is exempt from access, or to another agency that originated the record (but only if that agency is subject to the Privacy Act). Ordinarily, the component or agency that originated a record will be presumed to be best able to determine whether it is exempt from access.

(d) *Law enforcement information.* Whenever a request is made for access to a record containing information that relates to an investigation of a possible violation of law and that was originated by another component or agency, the receiving component shall either refer the responsibility for responding to the request regarding that information to that other component or agency or shall consult with that other component or agency.

(e) *Classified information.* Whenever a request is made for access to a record containing information that has been classified by or may be appropriate for classification by another component or agency under Executive Order 12958 or any other executive order concerning the classification of records, the receiving component shall refer the responsibility for responding to the request regarding that information to the component or agency that classified the information, should consider the information for classification, or has the primary interest in it, as appropriate. Whenever a record contains information that has been derivatively classified by a component because it contains information classified by another component or agency, the component shall refer the responsibility for responding to the request regarding that information to the component or agency that classified the underlying information.

(f) *Release of Medical Records.* Pursuant to 5 U.S.C. 552a(f)(3), where requests are made for access to medical records, including psychological records, the decision to release directly to the individual, or to withhold direct release, shall be made by a medical practitioner. Where the medical practitioner has ruled that direct release will cause harm to the individual who is requesting access, normal release through the individual's chosen medical practitioner will be recommended. Final review and decision on appeals of disapprovals of direct release will rest with the General Counsel.

(g) *Notice of referral.* Whenever a component refers all or any part of the responsibility for responding to a request to another component or agency, it ordinarily shall notify the requester of the referral and inform the requester of the name of each component or agency to which the request has been referred and of the part of the request that has been referred.

(h) *Timing of responses to consultations and referrals.* All consultations and referrals shall be handled according to the date the Privacy Act access request was initially received by the first component or agency, not any later date.

(i) *Agreements regarding consultations and referrals.* Components may make agreements with other components or agencies to eliminate the need for consultations or referrals for particular types of records.

§ 5.23 **Responses to requests for access to records.**

(a) *Acknowledgements of requests.* On receipt of a request, a component ordinarily shall send an acknowledgement letter to the requester which shall confirm the requester's agreement to pay fees under § 5.21(c) and provide an assigned request number for further reference.

(b) *Grants of requests for access.* Once a component makes a determination to grant a request for access in whole or in part, it shall notify the requester in writing. The component shall inform the requester in the notice of any fee charged under § 5.29 and shall disclose records to the requester promptly on payment of any applicable fee. If a request is made in person, the component may disclose records to the requester directly, in a manner not unreasonably disruptive of its operations, on payment of any applicable fee and with a written record made of the grant of the request. If a requester is accompanied by another person, the requester shall be required to authorize in writing any discussion of the records in the presence of the other person.

(c) *Adverse determinations of requests for access.* A component making an adverse determination denying a request for access in any respect shall notify the requester of that determination in writing. Adverse determinations, or denials of requests, consist of: a determination to withhold any requested record in whole or in part; a determination that a requested record does not exist or cannot be located; a determination that what has been requested is not a record subject to the Privacy Act; a determination on any disputed fee matter; and a denial of a request for expedited treatment. The notification letter shall be signed by the head of the component, or the component head's designee, and shall include:

(1) The name and title or position of the person responsible for the denial;

(2) A brief statement of the reason(s) for the denial, including any Privacy Act exemption(s) applied by the component in denying the request; and

(3) A statement that the denial may be appealed under § 5.25(a) and a description of the requirements of § 5.25(a).

§ 5.24 Classified information.

In processing a request for access to a record containing information that is classified under Executive Order 12958 or any other executive order, the originating component shall review the information to determine whether it should remain classified. Information determined to no longer require classification shall not be withheld from a requester on the basis of Exemption (k)(1) of the Privacy Act. On receipt of any appeal involving classified information, the Associate General Counsel (General Law), shall take appropriate action to ensure compliance with part 7 of this title.

§ 5.25 Appeals.

(a) *Appeals.* If you are dissatisfied with a component's response to your request for access to records, you may appeal an adverse determination denying your request in any respect to the Associate General Counsel (General Law), Department of Homeland Security, Washington, DC 20528. You must make your appeal in writing and it must be received by the Associate General Counsel (General Law) within 60 days of the date of the letter denying your request. Your appeal letter may include as much or as little related information as you wish, as long as it clearly identifies the component determination (including the assigned request number, if known) that you are appealing. For the quickest possible handling, you should mark both your appeal letter and the envelope "Privacy Act Appeal."

(b) *Responses to appeals.* The decision on your appeal will be made in writing. A decision affirming an adverse determination in whole or in part will include a brief statement of the reason(s) for the affirmance, including any Privacy Act exemption applied, and will inform you of the Privacy Act provisions for court review of the decision. If the adverse determination is reversed or modified on appeal in whole or in part, you will be notified in a written decision and your request will be reprocessed in accordance with that appeal decision. An adverse determination by the Associate General Counsel (General Law) will be the final action of the Department.

(c) *When appeal is required.* If you wish to seek review by a court of any adverse determination or denial of a request, you must first appeal it under this section. An appeal will not be acted on if the request becomes a matter of litigation.

§ 5.26 Requests for amendment or correction of records.

(a) *How made and addressed.* Unless the record is not subject to amendment or correction as stated in paragraph (f) of this section, you may make a request for amendment or correction of a record of the Department about you by writing directly to the Department component that maintains the record, following the procedures in § 5.21. Your request should identify each particular record in question, state the amendment or correction that you want, and state why you believe that the record is not accurate, relevant, timely, or complete. You may submit any documentation that you think would be helpful. If you believe that the same record is in more than one system of records, you should state that and address your request to each component that maintains a system of records containing the record.

(b) *Component responses.* Within ten working days of receiving your request for amendment or correction of records, a component shall send you a written acknowledgment of its receipt of your request, and it shall promptly notify you whether your request is granted or denied. If the component grants your request in whole or in part, it shall describe the amendment or correction made and shall advise you of your right to obtain a copy of the corrected or amended record, in disclosable form. If the component denies your request in whole or in part, it shall send you a letter signed by the head of the component, or the component head's designee, that shall state:

(1) The reason(s) for the denial; and

(2) The procedure for appeal of the denial under paragraph (c) of this section, including the name and business address of the official who will act on your appeal.

(c) *Appeals.* You may appeal a denial of a request for amendment or correction to the Associate General Counsel (General Law) in the same manner as a denial of a request for access to records (see §5.25) and the same procedures shall be followed. If your appeal is denied, you shall be advised of your right to file a Statement of Disagreement as described in paragraph (d) of this section and of your right under the Privacy Act for court review of the decision.

(d) *Statements of Disagreement.* If your appeal under this section is denied in whole or in part, you have the right to file a Statement of Disagreement that states your reason(s) for disagreeing with the Department's denial of your request for amendment or correction. Statements of Disagreement must be concise, must clearly identify each part of any record that is disputed, and should be no longer than one typed page for each fact disputed. Your Statement of Disagreement must be sent to the component involved, which shall place it in the system of records in which the disputed record is maintained and shall mark the disputed record to indicate that a Statement of Disagreement has been filed and where in the system of records it may be found.

(e) *Notification of amendment/correction or disagreement.* Within 30 working days of the amendment or correction of a record, the component that maintains the record shall notify all persons, organizations, or agencies to which it previously disclosed the record, if an accounting of that disclosure was made, that the record has been amended or corrected. If an individual has

filed a Statement of Disagreement, the component shall append a copy of it to the disputed record whenever the record is disclosed and may also append a concise statement of its reason(s) for denying the request to amend or correct the record.

(f) *Records not subject to amendment or correction.* The following records are not subject to amendment or correction:

(1) Transcripts of testimony given under oath or written statements made under oath;

(2) Transcripts of grand jury proceedings, judicial proceedings, or quasi-judicial proceedings, which are the official record of those proceedings;

(3) Presentence records that originated with the courts; and

(4) Records in systems of records that have been exempted from amendment and correction under Privacy Act (5 U.S.C. 552a(j) or (k)) by notice published in the FEDERAL REGISTER.

§5.27 **Requests for an accounting of record disclosures.**

(a) *How made and addressed.* Except where accountings of disclosures are not required to be kept (as stated in paragraph (b) of this section), you may make a request for an accounting of any disclosure that has been made by the Department to another person, organization, or agency of any record about you. This accounting contains the date, nature, and purpose of each disclosure, as well as the name and address of the person, organization, or agency to which the disclosure was made. Your request for an accounting should identify each particular record in question and should be made by writing directly to the Department component that maintains the record, following the procedures in §5.21.

(b) *Where accountings are not required.* Components are not required to provide accountings to you where they relate to:

(1) Disclosures for which accountings are not required to be kept, such as disclosures that are made to employees within the agency and disclosures that are made under the FOIA;

(2) Disclosures made to law enforcement agencies for authorized law enforcement activities in response to

29

written requests from those law enforcement agencies specifying the law enforcement activities for which the disclosures are sought; or

(3) Disclosures made from law enforcement systems of records that have been exempted from accounting requirements.

(c) *Appeals.* You may appeal a denial of a request for an accounting to the Associate General Counsel (General Law) in the same manner as a denial of a request for access to records (see § 5.25) and the same procedures will be followed.

§ 5.28 Preservation of records.

Each component will preserve all correspondence pertaining to the requests that it receives under this subpart, as well as copies of all requested records, until disposition or destruction is authorized by title 44 of the United States Code or the National Archives and Records Administration's General Records Schedule 14. Records will not be disposed of while they are the subject of a pending request, appeal, or lawsuit under the Act.

§ 5.29 Fees.

(a) Components shall charge fees for duplication of records under the Privacy Act in the same way in which they charge duplication fees under § 5.11.

(b) The Department shall not process a request under the Privacy Act from persons with an unpaid fee from any previous Privacy Act request to any Federal agency until that outstanding fee has been paid in full to the agency.

§ 5.30 Notice of court-ordered and emergency disclosures.

(a) *Court-ordered disclosures.* When a record pertaining to an individual is required to be disclosed by a court order, the component shall make reasonable efforts to provide notice of this to the individual. Notice shall be given within a reasonable time after the component's receipt of the order, except that in a case in which the order is not a matter of public record, the notice shall be given only after the order becomes public. This notice shall be mailed to the individual's last known address and shall contain a copy of the

order and a description of the information disclosed. Notice shall not be given if disclosure is made from a criminal law enforcement system of records that has been exempted from the notice requirement.

(b) *Emergency disclosures.* Upon disclosing a record pertaining to an individual made under compelling circumstances affecting health or safety, the component shall notify that individual of the disclosure. This notice shall be mailed to the individual's last known address and shall state the nature of the information disclosed; the person, organization, or agency to which it was disclosed; the date of disclosure; and the compelling circumstances justifying the disclosure.

§ 5.31 Security of systems of records.

(a) *In general.* Each component shall establish administrative and physical controls to prevent unauthorized access to its systems of records, to prevent unauthorized disclosure of records, and to prevent physical damage to or destruction of records. The stringency of these controls shall correspond to the sensitivity of the records that the controls protect. At a minimum, each component's administrative and physical controls shall ensure that:

(1) Records are protected from public view;

(2) The area in which records are kept is supervised during business hours to prevent unauthorized persons from having access to them;

(3) Records are inaccessible to unauthorized persons outside of business hours; and

(4) Records are not disclosed to unauthorized persons or under unauthorized circumstances in either oral or written form.

(b) *Procedures required.* Each component shall have procedures that restrict access to records to only those individuals within the Department who must have access to those records in order to perform their duties and that prevent inadvertent disclosure of records.

§ 5.32 Contracts for the operation of record systems.

Under 5 U.S.C. 552a(m), any approved contract for the operation of a record system will contain the standard contract requirements issued by the General Services Administration to ensure compliance with the requirements of the Privacy Act for that record system. The contracting component will be responsible for ensuring that the contractor complies with these contract requirements.

§ 5.33 Use and collection of social security numbers.

Each component shall ensure that employees authorized to collect information are aware:

(a) That individuals may not be denied any right, benefit, or privilege as a result of refusing to provide their social security numbers, unless the collection is authorized either by a statute or by a regulation issued prior to 1975; and

(b) That individuals requested to provide their social security numbers must be informed of:

(1) Whether providing social security numbers is mandatory or voluntary;

(2) Any statutory or regulatory authority that authorizes the collection of social security numbers; and

(3) The uses that will be made of the numbers.

§ 5.34 Standards of conduct for administration of the Privacy Act.

Each component will inform its employees of the provisions of the Privacy Act, including the Act's civil liability and criminal penalty provisions. Unless otherwise permitted by law, the Department shall:

(a) Collect from individuals only the information that is relevant and necessary to discharge the responsibilities of the Department;

(b) Collect information about an individual directly from that individual whenever practicable and when the information may result in adverse determinations about an individual's rights, benefits, and privileges under federal programs;

(c) Inform each individual from whom information is collected of:

(1) The legal authority to collect the information and whether providing it is mandatory or voluntary;

(2) The principal purpose for which the Department intends to use the information;

(3) The routine uses the Department may make of the information; and

(4) The effects on the individual, if any, of not providing the information;

(d) Ensure that the component maintains no system of records without public notice and that it notifies appropriate Department officials of the existence or development of any system of records that is not the subject of a current or planned public notice;

(e) Maintain all records that are used by the Department in making any determination about an individual with such accuracy, relevance, timeliness, and completeness as is reasonably necessary to ensure fairness to the individual in the determination;

(f) Except as to disclosures made to an agency or made under the FOIA, make reasonable efforts, prior to disseminating any record about an individual, to ensure that the record is accurate, relevant, timely, and complete;

(g) Maintain no record describing how an individual exercises his or her First Amendment rights, unless it is expressly authorized by statute or by the individual about whom the record is maintained, or is pertinent to and within the scope of an authorized law enforcement activity;

(h) When required by the Privacy Act, maintain an accounting in the specified form of all disclosures of records by the Department to persons, organizations, or agencies;

(i) Maintain and use records with care to prevent the unauthorized or inadvertent disclosure of a record to anyone.

§ 5.35 Sanctions and penalties.

Under the provisions of the Privacy Act, 5 U.S.C. 552a, civil and criminal penalties may be assessed.

§ 5.36 Other rights and services.

Nothing in this subpart shall be construed to entitle any person, as of right, to any service or to the disclosure of any record to which such person is not entitled under the Privacy Act.

Subpart C—Disclosure of Information in Litigation

SOURCE: 68 FR 4070, Jan. 27, 2003, unless otherwise noted.

§ 5.41 Purpose and scope; definitions.

(a) This subpart C sets forth the procedures to be followed with respect to:

(1) Service of summonses and complaints or other requests or demands directed to the Department of Homeland Security (Department) or to any Department employee or former employee in connection with federal or state litigation arising out of or involving the performance of official activities of the Department; and

(2) The oral or written disclosure, in response to subpoenas, orders, or other requests or demands of federal or state judicial or quasi-judicial or administrative authority as well as state legislative authorities (collectively, "demands"), whether civil or criminal in nature, or in response to requests for depositions, affidavits, admissions, responses to interrogatories, document production, interviews, or other litigation-related matters, including pursuant to the Federal Rules of Civil Procedure, the Federal Rules of Criminal Procedure, or applicable state rules (collectively, "requests"), of any material contained in the files of the Department, any information relating to material contained in the files of the Department, or any information acquired while the subject of the demand or request is or was employed by the Department, or served as Secretary of the Department, as part of the performance of that person's duties or by virtue of that person's official status.

(b) The provisions established by this subpart shall apply to all Department components that are transferred to the Department. Except to the extent a Department component has adopted separate guidance governing the subject matter of a provision of this subpart, the provisions of this subpart shall apply to each component of the Department. Departmental components may issue their own guidance under this subpart subject to the approval of the General Counsel of the Department.

(c) For purposes of this subpart, and except as the Department may otherwise determine in a particular case, the term employee includes all former Secretaries of Homeland Security and all employees of the Department of Homeland Security or other federal agencies who are or were appointed by, or subject to the supervision, jurisdiction, or control of the Secretary of Homeland Security, whether residing or working in the United States or abroad, including United States nationals, foreign nationals, and contractors. The procedures established within this subpart also apply to former employees of the Department where specifically noted.

(d) For purposes of this subpart, the term litigation encompasses all pretrial, trial, and post-trial stages of all judicial or administrative actions, hearings, investigations, or similar proceedings before courts, commissions, boards (including the Board of Appellate Review), grand juries, or other judicial or quasi-judicial bodies or tribunals, whether criminal, civil, or administrative in nature. This subpart governs, *inter alia*, responses to discovery requests, depositions, and other pre-trial, trial, or post-trial proceedings, as well as responses to informal requests by attorneys or others in situations involving litigation. However, this subpart shall not apply to any claims against the Department by Department of Homeland Security employees (present or former), or applicants for Department employment, for which jurisdiction resides with the U.S. Equal Employment Opportunity Commission; the U.S. Merit Systems Protection Board; the Office of Special Counsel; the Federal Labor Relations Authority; the Foreign Service Labor Relations Board; the Foreign Service Grievance Board; or a labor arbitrator operating under a collective bargaining agreement between the Department and a labor organization representing Department employees; or their successor agencies or entities.

(e) For purposes of this subpart, official information means all information of any kind, however stored, that is in the custody and control of the Department, relates to information in the custody and control of the Department, or was acquired by Department employees, or former employees, as part of their official duties or because of their official status within the Department while such individuals were employed by or served on behalf of the Department.

(f) Nothing in this subpart affects disclosure of information under the Freedom of Information Act (FOIA), 5 U.S.C. 552, the Privacy Act, 5 U.S.C. 552a, Executive Order 12958 on national security information (3 CFR, 1995 Comp., p. 333), the Government in the Sunshine Act, 5 U.S.C. 552b, the Department's implementing regulations or pursuant to congressional subpoena. Nothing in this subpart permits disclosure of information by the Department, its present and former employees, or the Secretary, that is protected or prohibited by statute or other applicable law.

(g) This subpart is intended only to inform the public about Department procedures concerning the service of process and responses to demands or requests and is not intended to and does not create, and may not be relied upon to create any right or benefit, substantive or procedural, enforceable at law by a party against the Department or the United States.

(h) Nothing in this subpart affects the rules and procedures, under applicable U.S. law and international conventions, governing diplomatic and consular immunity.

(i) Nothing in this subpart affects the disclosure of official information to other federal agencies or Department of Justice attorneys in connection with litigation conducted on behalf or in defense of the United States, its agencies, officers, and employees, or litigation in which the United States has an interest; or to federal, state, local, or foreign prosecuting and law enforcement authorities in conjunction with criminal law enforcement investigations, prosecutions, or other proceedings, e.g., extradition, deportation.

§5.42 Service of summonses and complaints.

(a) Only the Office of the General Counsel is authorized to receive and accept on behalf of the Department summonses or complaints sought to be served upon the Department, the Secretary, or Department employees. All such documents should be delivered or addressed to the Office of the General Counsel, United States Department of Homeland Security, Washington, DC, 20528. The authorization for receipt shall in no way affect the requirements of service elsewhere provided in applicable rules and regulations.

(b) In the event any summons or complaint described in §5.41(a) is delivered to an employee of the Department other than in the manner specified in this part, the recipient thereof shall decline to accept the proffered service and may notify the person attempting to make service of the Departmental regulations set forth herein.

(c) Except as otherwise provided §§5.42(d) and 5.43(c), the Department is not an authorized agent for service of process with respect to civil litigation against Department employees purely in their personal, non-official capacity. Copies of summonses or complaints directed to Department employees in connection with legal proceedings arising out of the performance of official duties may, however, be served upon the Office of the General Counsel.

(d) Although the Department is not an agent for the service of process upon its employees with respect to purely personal, non-official litigation, the Department recognizes that its employees should not use their official positions to evade their personal obligations and will, therefore, counsel and encourage Department employees to accept service of process in appropriate cases.

(e) Documents for which the Office of the General Counsel accepts service in official capacity only shall be stamped "Service Accepted in Official Capacity Only". Acceptance of service shall not constitute an admission or waiver with respect to jurisdiction, propriety of service, improper venue, or any other defense in law or equity available under applicable laws or rules.

§5.43 Service of subpoenas, court orders, and other demands or requests for official information or action.

(a) Except in cases in which the Department is represented by legal counsel who have entered an appearance or otherwise given notice of their representation, only the Office of the General Counsel is authorized to receive and accept subpoenas, or other demands or requests directed to the Secretary, the Department, or any component thereof, or its employees, whether civil or criminal in nature, for:

(1) Material, including documents, contained in the files of the Department;

(2) Information, including testimony, affidavits, declarations, admissions, responses to interrogatories, or informal statements, relating to material contained in the files of the Department or which any Department employee acquired in the course and scope of the performance of his official duties;

(3) Garnishment or attachment of compensation of current or former employees; or

(4) The performance or non-performance of any official Department duty.

(b) In the event that any subpoena, demand, or request is sought to be delivered to a Department employee other than in the manner prescribed in paragraph (a) of this section, such employee shall, after consultation with the Office of the General Counsel, decline service and direct the server of process to the Departmental regulations. If the subpoena, demand, or other request is nonetheless delivered to the employee, the employee shall immediately forward a copy of that document to the Office of the General Counsel.

(c) Except as otherwise provided in this subpart, the Department is not an agent for service, or otherwise authorized to accept on behalf of its employees, any subpoenas, show-cause orders, or similar compulsory process of federal or state courts, or requests from private individuals or attorneys, which are not related to the employees' official duties except upon the express, written authorization of the individual Department employee to whom such demand or request is directed.

(d) Acceptance of such documents by the Office of the General Counsel does not constitute a waiver of any defenses that might otherwise exist with respect to service under the Federal Rules of Civil or Criminal Procedure or other applicable rules.

(e) Copies of any subpoenas, show cause orders, or similar compulsory process of federal or state courts, or requests from private individuals or attorneys, directed to former employees of the Department in connection with legal proceedings arising out of the performance of official duties shall also be served upon the Office of the General Counsel. The Department shall not, however, serve as an agent for service for the former employee, nor is the Department otherwise authorized to accept service on behalf of its former employees. If the demand involves their official duties, former employees who receive subpoenas, show cause orders, or similar compulsory process of federal or state courts should also notify in the component of the Department in which they were employed if the service involves their official duties while so employed.

(f) If the subpoena, demand, or other request is nonetheless delivered to the employee, the employee shall immediately forward a copy of that document to the Office of the General Counsel.

§ 5.44 Testimony and production of documents prohibited unless approved by appropriate Department officials.

(a) No employee, or former employee, of the Department shall, in response to a demand or request, including in connection with any litigation, provide oral or written testimony by deposition, declaration, affidavit, or otherwise concerning any information acquired while such person is or was an employee of the Department as part of the performance of that person's official duties or by virtue of that person's official status, unless authorized to do so by the Office of the General Counsel, or as authorized in § 5.44(b).

(b) No employee, or former employee, shall, in response to a demand or request, including in connection with any litigation, produce any document or any material acquired as part of the performance of that employee's duties or by virtue of that employee's official status, unless authorized to do so by the Office of the General Counsel or the delegates thereof, as appropriate.

§5.45 Procedure when testimony or production of documents is sought; general.

(a) If official information is sought, through testimony or otherwise, by a request or demand, the party seeking such release or testimony must (except as otherwise required by federal law or authorized by the Office of the General Counsel) set forth in writing, and with as much specificity as possible, the nature and relevance of the official information sought. Where documents or other materials are sought, the party should provide a description using the types of identifying information suggested in §5.3(b). Subject to §5.47, Department employees may only produce, disclose, release, comment upon, or testify concerning those matters which were specified in writing and properly approved by the appropriate Department official designated in §5.44. *See United States ex rel. Touhy* v. *Ragen,* 340 U.S. 462 (1951). The Office of the General Counsel may waive the requirement of this subsection in appropriate circumstances.

(b) To the extent it deems necessary or appropriate, the Department may also require from the party seeking such testimony or documents a plan of all reasonably foreseeable demands, including but not limited to the names of all employees and former employees from whom discovery will be sought, areas of inquiry, expected duration of proceedings requiring oral testimony, and identification of potentially relevant documents.

(c) The appropriate Department official designated in §5.42 will notify the Department employee and such other persons as circumstances may warrant of its decision regarding compliance with the request or demand.

(d) The Office of the General Counsel will consult with the Department of Justice regarding legal representation for Department employees in appropriate cases.

§5.46 Procedure when response to demand is required prior to receiving instructions.

(a) If a response to a demand is required before the appropriate Department official designated in §5.44 renders a decision, the Department, if necessary, will request that the Department of Justice or the appropriate Department attorney take appropriate steps to stay, postpone, or obtain relief from the demand pending decision. If necessary, the attorney will:

(1) Appear with the employee upon whom the demand has been made;

(2) Furnish the court or other authority with a copy of the regulations contained in this subpart;

(3) Inform the court or other authority that the demand has been, or is being, as the case may be, referred for the prompt consideration of the appropriate Department official; and

(4) Respectfully request the court or authority to stay the demand pending receipt of the requested instructions.

(b) In the event that an immediate demand for production or disclosure is made in circumstances which would preclude the proper designation or appearance of a Department of Justice or appropriate Department attorney on the employee's behalf, the employee, if necessary, shall respectfully request from the demanding court or authority for a reasonable stay of proceedings for the purpose of obtaining instructions from the Department.

§5.47 Procedure in the event of an adverse ruling.

If a stay of, or other relief from, the effect of the demand in response to a request made pursuant to §5.46 is declined or not obtained, or if the court or other judicial or quasi-judicial authority declines to stay the effect of the demand in response to a request made pursuant to §5.46, or if the court or other authority rules that the demand must be complied with irrespective of the Department's instructions not to produce the material or disclose the information sought, the employee upon whom the demand has been made shall respectfully decline to comply with the demand, citing this subpart and *United States ex rel. Touhy* v. *Ragen,* 340 U.S. 462 (1951).

§5.48 Considerations in determining whether the Department will comply with a demand or request.

(a) In deciding whether to comply with a demand or request, Department officials and attorneys shall consider, among any other pertinent considerations:

(1) Whether such compliance would be unduly burdensome or otherwise inappropriate under the applicable rules of discovery or the rules of procedure governing the case or matter in which the demand arose;

(2) Whether compliance is appropriate under the relevant substantive law concerning privilege or disclosure of information;

(3) The public interest;

(4) The need to conserve the time of Department employees for the conduct of official business;

(5) The need to avoid spending the time and money of the United States for private purposes;

(6) The need to maintain impartiality between private litigants in cases where a substantial government interest is not implicated;

(7) Whether compliance would have an adverse effect on performance by the Department of its mission and duties; and

(8) The need to avoid involving the Department in controversial issues not related to its mission.

(b) Among those demands and requests in response to which compliance will not ordinarily be authorized are those with respect to which any of the following factors, *inter alia*, exist:

(1) Compliance would violate a statute or a rule of procedure;

(2) Compliance would violate a specific regulation or Executive order;

(3) Compliance would reveal information properly classified in the interest of national security;

(4) Compliance would reveal confidential commercial or financial information or trade secrets without the owner's consent;

(5) Compliance would reveal the internal deliberative processes of the Executive Branch; or

(6) Compliance would potentially impede or prejudice an on-going law enforcement investigation.

§ 5.49 Prohibition on providing expert or opinion testimony.

(a) Except as provided in this section, and subject to 5 CFR 2635.805, Department employees shall not provide opinion or expert testimony based upon information which they acquired in the scope and performance of their official Department duties, except on behalf of the United States or a party represented by the Department of Justice.

(b) Any expert or opinion testimony by a former employee of the Department shall be excepted from 5.49(a) where the testimony involves only general expertise gained while employed at the Department.

(c) Upon a showing by the requestor of exceptional need or unique circumstances and that the anticipated testimony will not be adverse to the interests of the United States, the appropriate Department official designated in § 5.44 may, consistent with 5 CFR 2635.805, in their discretion and with the concurrence of the Office of the General Counsel, grant special, written authorization for Department employees, or former employees, to appear and testify as expert witnesses at no expense to the United States.

(d) If, despite the final determination of the appropriate Department official designated in § 5.44, a court of competent jurisdiction or other appropriate authority orders the appearance and expert or opinion testimony of a current or former Department employee, that person shall immediately inform the Office of the General Counsel of such order. If the Office of the General Counsel determines that no further legal review of or challenge to the court's order will be made, the Department employee, or former employee, shall comply with the order. If so directed by the Office of the General Counsel, however, the employee, or former employee, shall respectfully decline to testify.

APPENDIX A TO PART 5—FOIA/PRIVACY ACT OFFICES OF THE DEPARTMENT OF HOMELAND SECURITY

I. For the following Headquarters components of the Department of Homeland Security, FOIA and Privacy Act requests should be sent to the Departmental Disclosure Office, Department of Homeland Security, Washington, DC 20528. The Headquarters components are:

A

Office of the Secretary
Office of the Deputy Secretary
Office of the Under Secretary for Management

B

Office of the General Counsel
Office of the Inspector General
Office of International Affairs
Office of Legislative Affairs
Office of Public Affairs
Office of National Capital Region Coordination
Office of Professional Responsibility
Office for State and Local Government Coordination

C

Directorate of Border and Transportation Security
Directorate of Emergency Preparedness and Response
Directorate of Information Analysis and Infrastructure Protection
Directorate of Science and Technology
II. Requests made to components that have transferred or will transfer into the Department of Homeland Security, should be sent as follows:
A. Former components of the Department of Agriculture:
1. Animal and Plant Health Inspection Service, USDA, APHIS, LPA, FOIA, 4700 River Road, Unit 50, Riverdale, MD 20737–1232
2. Plum Island Animal Disease Center; Submit request to the APHIS address above or, FOIA Coordinator, USDA-REE-ARS-Information Staff, 5601 Sunnyside Avenue, Bldg. 1, Room 2248, Mail Stop 5128, Beltsville, MD 20705–5128

B. Former components of the Department of Commerce:
1. Critical Infrastructure Assurance Office (A former office of the Bureau of Industry and Security); Freedom of Information Coordinator, Bureau of Industry and Security, Room 6883, U.S. Department of Commerce, Washington, DC 20230
2. FIRESTAT (formerly the Integrated Hazard Information System of the National Oceanic and Atmospheric Administration), National Oceanic and Atmospheric Administration, Public Reference Facility (OFAx2), 1315 East-West Highway (SSMC3), Room 10703, Silver Spring, MD 20910
C. Former components of the Department of Defense:
1. National Communications Service (A former component of the Defense Information Systems Agency), Defense Information Systems Agency, ATTN: RGC/FOIA Officer, 701 S. Courthouse Rd., Arlington, VA 22204–2199

D. Former components and programs of the Department of Energy:
The address for each component and program listed below is: U.S. Department of Energy, 1000 Independence Avenue, SW., Washington, DC 20585
1. Energy Assurance Office
2. Environmental Measurements Laboratory
3. Nuclear Incident Response Team
4. The chemical and biological national security and supporting programs and activities of the non-proliferation and verification research and development program.
5. The life sciences activities related to microbial pathogens of Biological and Environmental Research Program.
6. The nuclear smuggling programs and activities within the proliferation detection program of the non-proliferation and verification research and development program.
7. The nuclear assessment program and activities of the assessment, detection, and cooperation program of the international materials protection and cooperation program, and the advanced scientific computing research program and activities at Lawrence Livermore National Laboratory.
8. National Infrastructure Simulation and Analysis Center
E. Former components of the Department of Health and Human Services:
1. The address for each component and program listed below is: Department of Health and Human Services, Freedom of Information Officer, Room 645–F, Hubert H. Humphrey Building, Independence Avenue, SW., Washington, DC 20201;
a. Metropolitan Medical Response System,
b. National Disaster Medical System, and
c. Office of Emergency Preparedness
d. Strategic National Stockpile
2. Centers for Disease Control and Agency for Toxic Substances and Disease Registry, Attn: FOI Office, MS-D54, 1600 Clifton Road, NE., Atlanta, GA 30333.
F. Former components of the Department of Justice:
1. Immigration and Naturalization Service, Director, Freedom of Information/Privacy Act Program, Department of Justice, 425 Eye Street, NW., 2nd Floor, ULLICO Building, Washington, DC 20536 (for field offices, consult your phone book).
2. The address for each component and program listed below is: Federal Bureau of Investigation, Chief, FOIPA Section, 935 Pennsylvania Avenue, NW., Department of Justice, Washington, DC 20535–0001;
a. National Infrastructure Protection Center,
b. National Domestic Preparedness Office, and
c. Domestic Emergency Support Team.

3. Office of Domestic Preparedness, U.S. Department of Justice, Office of Justice Programs, Office of the General Counsel, Attention: FOIA Staff, 810 7th Street, NW., Room 5400, Washington, DC 20531.

G. Former components of the Department of State:

Visa Office, Information and Privacy Coordinator, Office of Information Resources, Management Programs and Services, A/RPS/IPS, SA-2, Department of State, Washington, DC 20522-6001, Re: Freedom of Information Act Request.

H. Former components of the Department of Transportation:

1. Federal Aviation Administration, National Freedom of Information Act Staff, ARC-40, 800 Independence Avenue, SW., Washington, DC 20591 (for regional centers, consult your phone book).
2. Transportation Security Administration, TSA-1, FOIA Division, 400 Seventh Street, SW., Washington, DC 20590.
3. United States Coast Guard, HQ USCG Commandant, G-CIM, 2100 Second Street, SW., Washington, DC 20593-0001 (for district offices, consult your phone book).

I. Former components of the Department of Treasury:

1. Federal Law Enforcement Training Center, Freedom of Information Act Officer, Townhouse 389, Glynco, GA 31524
2. U.S. Customs Service, Freedom of Information Act Request, Mint Annex, 1300 Pennsylvania Avenue, NW., Washington, DC 20229 (for field offices, consult your phone book).
3. U.S. Secret Service, Freedom of Information Act Request, 950 H Street, NW., Suite 3000, Washington, DC 20223, e-mail *FOIA@USSS.Treas.gov*. Appeals should be addressed to the Deputy Director, United States Secret Service, Freedom of Information and Privacy Act Appeal Officer, at these same contact points.

J. Federal Emergency Management Agency: Federal Emergency Management Agency, Office of General Counsel, 500 C Street, SW., Room 840, Washington, DC 20472 (for regional offices, consult your phone book).

K. Former components of the General Services Administration:

1. For the Federal Computer Incident Response Center and the Federal Protective Service: Chief, FOIA Information Management Branch, GSA (CAIM), 1800 F Street, NW., Washington, DC 20405 (for regional offices, consult your phone book).

APPENDIX B TO PART 5 [RESERVED]

APPENDIX C TO PART 5—DHS SYSTEMS OF RECORDS EXEMPT FROM THE PRIVACY ACT

This appendix implements provisions of the Privacy Act of 1974 that permit the Department of Homeland Security (DHS) to exempt its systems of records from provisions of the Act. During the course of normal agency operations, exempt materials from other systems of records may become part of the records in these and other DHS systems. To the extent that copies of records from other exempt systems of records are entered into any DHS system, DHS hereby claims the same exemptions for those records that are claimed for the original primary systems of records from which they originated and claims any additional exemptions in accordance with this rule.

Portions of the following DHS systems of records are exempt from certain provisions of the Privacy Act pursuant to 5 U.S.C. 552(j) and (k):

1. The DHS/ALL—001 Freedom of Information Act and Privacy Act Records System of Records consists of electronic and paper records and will be used by DHS and its components. The DHS/ALL—001 Freedom of Information Act and Privacy Act Records System of Records is a repository of information held by DHS in connection with its several and varied missions and functions, including, but not limited to the enforcement of civil and criminal laws; investigations, inquiries, and proceedings there under; national security and intelligence activities; and protection of the President of the United States or other individuals pursuant to section 3056 and 3056A of Title 18. The DHS/ALL—001 Freedom of Information Act and Privacy Act Records System of Records contains information that is collected by, on behalf of, in support of, or in cooperation with DHS and its components and may contain personally identifiable information collected by other federal, state, local, tribal, foreign, or international government agencies. The Secretary of Homeland Security has exempted this system from the following provisions of the Privacy Act, subject to limitations set forth in 5 U.S.C. 552a(c)(3) and (4): (d); (e)(1), (e)(2), (e)(3), (e)(4)(G), (e)(4)(H), (e)(4)(I), (e)(5), (e)(8), (e)(12); (f); (g)(1); and (h) pursuant to 5 U.S.C. 552a(j)(2). Additionally, the Secretary of Homeland Security has exempted this system from the following provisions of the Privacy Act, subject to limitations set forth in 5 U.S.C. 552a(c)(3): (d); (e)(1), (e)(4)(G), (e)(4)(H), (e)(4)(I); and (f) pursuant to 5 U.S.C. §552a(k)(1), (k)(2), (k)(3), (k)(5), and (k)(6). Exemptions from these particular subsections are justified, on a case-by-case basis to be determined at the time a request is made, for the following reasons:

(a) From subsection (c)(3) and (4) (Accounting for Disclosures) because release of the accounting of disclosures could alert the subject of an investigation of an actual or potential criminal, civil, or regulatory violation to the existence of that investigation and reveal investigative interest on the part of DHS as well as the recipient agency. Disclosure of the accounting would therefore present a serious impediment to law enforcement efforts and/or efforts to preserve national security. Disclosure of the accounting would also permit the individual who is the subject of a record to impede the investigation, to tamper with witnesses or evidence, and to avoid detection or apprehension, which would undermine the entire investigative process.

(b) From subsection (d) (Access to Records) because access to the records contained in this system of records could inform the subject of an investigation of an actual or potential criminal, civil, or regulatory violation to the existence of that investigation and reveal investigative interest on the part of DHS or another agency. Access to the records could permit the individual who is the subject of a record to impede the investigation, to tamper with witnesses or evidence, and to avoid detection or apprehension. Amendment of the records could interfere with ongoing investigations and law enforcement activities and would impose an unreasonable administrative burden by requiring investigations to be continually re-investigated. In addition, permitting access and amendment to such information could disclose security-sensitive information that could be detrimental to homeland security.

(c) From subsection (e)(1) (Relevancy and Necessity of Information) because in the course of investigations into potential violations of federal law, the accuracy of information obtained or introduced occasionally may be unclear, or the information may not be strictly relevant or necessary to a specific investigation. In the interests of effective law enforcement, it is appropriate to retain all information that may aid in establishing patterns of unlawful activity.

(d) From subsection (e)(2) (Collection of Information from Individuals) because requiring that information be collected from the subject of an investigation would alert the subject to the nature or existence of the investigation, thereby interfering with that investigation and related law enforcement activities.

(e) From subsection (e)(3) (Notice to Subjects) because providing such detailed information could impede law enforcement by compromising the existence of a confidential investigation or reveal the identity of witnesses or confidential informants.

(f) From subsections (e)(4)(G), (e)(4)(H), and (e)(4)(I) (Agency Requirements) and (f) (Agency Rules), because portions of this sys-tem are exempt from the individual access provisions of subsection (d) for the reasons noted above, and therefore DHS is not required to establish requirements, rules, or procedures with respect to such access. Providing notice to individuals with respect to existence of records pertaining to them in the system of records or otherwise setting up procedures pursuant to which individuals may access and view records pertaining to themselves in the system would undermine investigative efforts and reveal the identities of witnesses, and potential witnesses, and confidential informants.

(g) From subsection (e)(5) (Collection of Information) because with the collection of information for law enforcement purposes, it is impossible to determine in advance what information is accurate, relevant, timely, and complete. Compliance with subsection (e)(5) would preclude DHS agents from using their investigative training and exercise of good judgment to both conduct and report on investigations.

(h) From subsection (e)(8) (Notice on Individuals) because compliance would interfere with DHS's ability to obtain, serve, and issue subpoenas, warrants, and other law enforcement mechanisms that may be filed under seal and could result in disclosure of investigative techniques, procedures, and evidence.

(i) From subsection (e)(12) (Computer Matching) if the agency is a recipient agency or a source agency in a matching program with a non-Federal agency, with respect to any establishment or revision of a matching program, at least 30 days prior to conducting such program, publish in the FEDERAL REGISTER notice of such establishment or revision.

(j) From subsection (g)(1) (Civil Remedies) to the extent that the system is exempt from other specific subsections of the Privacy Act.

(k) From subsection (h) (Legal Guardians) the parent of any minor, or the legal guardian of any individual who has been declared to be incompetent due to physical or mental incapacity or age by a court of competent jurisdiction, may act on behalf of the individual.

2. The DHS/ALL–029 Civil Rights and Civil Liberties Records System of Records consists of electronic and paper records and will be used by DHS and its components. The DHS/ALL–029 Civil Rights and Civil Liberties Records System of Records is a repository of information held by DHS in connection with its several and varied missions and functions, including, but not limited to the enforcement of civil and criminal laws; investigations, inquiries, and proceedings thereunder; national security and intelligence activities; and protection of the President of the United States or other individuals pursuant to Section 3056 and 3056A of Title 18. The DHS/ALL–029 Civil Rights and Civil Liberties

Records System of Records contains information that is collected by, on behalf of, in support of, or in cooperation with DHS and its components and may contain personally identifiable information collected by other Federal, state, local, Tribal, foreign, or international government agencies. The Secretary of Homeland Security has exempted this system from the following provisions of the Privacy Act, subject to limitations set forth in 5 U.S.C. 552a(c)(3); (d); (e)(1), (e)(4)(G), (e)(4)(H), (e)(4)(I); and (f) pursuant to 5 U.S.C. §552a(k)(1), (k)(2), (k)(3), and (k)(5). Exemptions from these particular subsections are justified, on a case-by-case basis to be determined at the time a request is made, for the following reasons:

(a) From subsection (c)(3) (Accounting for Disclosures) because release of the accounting of disclosures could alert the individual who is the subject of an investigation of an actual or potential criminal, civil, or regulatory violation to the existence of that investigation and reveal investigative interest on the part of DHS as well as the recipient agency. Disclosure of the accounting would, therefore, present a serious impediment to law enforcement efforts and/or efforts to preserve national security. Disclosure of the accounting would also permit the individual who is the subject of a record to impede the investigation, to tamper with witnesses or evidence, and to avoid detection or apprehension, which would undermine the entire investigative process.

(b) From subsection (d) (Access to Records) because access to the records contained in this system of records could inform the individual who is the subject of an investigation of an actual or potential criminal, civil, or regulatory violation to the existence of that investigation and reveal investigative interest on the part of DHS or another agency. Access to the records could permit the individual who is the subject of a record to impede the investigation, to tamper with witnesses or evidence, and to avoid detection or apprehension. Amendment of the records could interfere with ongoing investigations and law enforcement activities and would impose an unreasonable administrative burden by requiring investigations to be continually reinvestigated. In addition, permitting access and amendment to such information could disclose security-sensitive information that could be detrimental to homeland security.

(c) From subsection (e)(1) (Relevancy and Necessity of Information) because in the course of investigations into potential violations of Federal law, the accuracy of information obtained or introduced occasionally may be unclear, or the information may not be strictly relevant or necessary to a specific investigation. In the interests of effective law enforcement, it is appropriate to retain all information that may aid in establishing patterns of unlawful activity.

(d) From subsections (e)(4)(G), (e)(4)(H), and (e)(4)(I) (Agency Requirements) and (f) (Agency Rules), because portions of this system are exempt from the individual access provisions of subsection (d) for the reasons noted above, and therefore DHS is not required to establish requirements, rules, or procedures with respect to such access. Providing notice to individuals with respect to existence of records pertaining to them in the system of records or otherwise setting up procedures pursuant to which individuals may access and view records pertaining to themselves in the system would undermine investigative efforts and reveal the identities of witnesses, and potential witnesses, and confidential informants.

3. DHS–ALL–005, Redress and Response Records System. A portion of the following system of records is exempt from 5 U.S.C. 552a(c)(3) and (4); (d)(1), (2), (3), and (4); (e)(1), (2), (3), (4)(G) through (I), (5), and (8); (f), and (g); however, these exemptions apply only to the extent that information in this system records is recompiled or is created from information contained in other systems of records subject to such exemptions pursuant to 5 U.S.C. 552a(j)(2), (k)(1), (k)(2), and (k)(5). Further, no exemption shall be asserted with respect to information submitted by and collected from the individual or the individual's representative in the course of any redress process associated with this system of records. After conferring with the appropriate component or agency, DHS may waive applicable exemptions in appropriate circumstances and where it would not appear to interfere with or adversely affect the law enforcement or national security purposes of the systems from which the information is recompiled or in which it is contained. Exemptions from the above particular subsections are justified, on a case-by-case basis to be determined at the time a request is made, when information in this system records is recompiled or is created from information contained in other systems of records subject to exemptions for the following reasons:

(a) From subsection (c)(3) because making available to a record subject the accounting of disclosures from records concerning him or her would specifically reveal any investigative interest in the individual. Revealing this information could reasonably be expected to compromise ongoing efforts to investigate a known or suspected terrorist by notifying the record subject that he or she is under investigation. This information could also permit the record subject to take measures to impede the investigation, e.g., destroy evidence, intimidate potential witnesses, or flee the area to avoid or impede the investigation.

(b) From subsection (c)(4) because portions of this system are exempt from the access and amendment provisions of subsection (d).

(c) From subsections (d)(1), (2), (3), and (4) because these provisions concern individual access to and amendment of certain records contained in this system, including law enforcement counterterrorism, investigatory, and intelligence records. Compliance with these provisions could alert the subject of an investigation of the fact and nature of the investigation, and/or the investigative interest of intelligence or law enforcement agencies; compromise sensitive information related to national security; interfere with the overall law enforcement process by leading to the destruction of evidence, improper influencing of witnesses, fabrication of testimony, and/or flight of the subject; could identify a confidential source or disclose information which would constitute an unwarranted invasion of another's personal privacy; reveal a sensitive investigative or intelligence technique; or constitute a potential danger to the health or safety of law enforcement personnel, confidential informants, and witnesses. Amendment of these records would interfere with ongoing counterterrorism, law enforcement, or intelligence investigations and analysis activities and impose an impossible administrative burden by requiring investigations, analyses, and reports to be continuously reinvestigated and revised.

(d) From subsection (e)(1) because it is not always possible for DHS or other agencies to know in advance what information is relevant and necessary for it to complete an identity comparison between the individual seeking redress and a known or suspected terrorist. Also, because DHS and other agencies may not always know what information about an encounter with a known or suspected terrorist will be relevant to law enforcement for the purpose of conducting an operational response.

(e) From subsection (e)(2) because application of this provision could present a serious impediment to counterterrorism, law enforcement, or intelligence efforts in that it would put the subject of an investigation, study, or analysis on notice of that fact, thereby permitting the subject to engage in conduct designed to frustrate or impede that activity. The nature of counterterrorism, law enforcement, or intelligence investigations is such that vital information about an individual frequently can be obtained only from other persons who are familiar with such individual and his/her activities. In such investigations it is not feasible to rely upon information furnished by the individual concerning his own activities.

(f) From subsection (e)(3), to the extent that this subsection is interpreted to require DHS to provide notice to an individual if DHS or another agency receives or collects information about that individual during an investigation or from a third party. Should the subsection be so interpreted, exemption from this provision is necessary to avoid impeding counterterrorism, law enforcement, or intelligence efforts by putting the subject of an investigation, study, or analysis on notice of that fact, thereby permitting the subject to engage in conduct intended to frustrate or impede that activity.

(g) From subsections (e)(4)(G), (H) and (I) (Agency Requirements) because portions of this system are exempt from the access and amendment provisions of subsection (d).

(h) From subsection (e)(5) because many of the records in this system coming from other system of records are derived from other domestic and foreign agency record systems and therefore it is not possible for DHS to vouch for their compliance with this provision; however, the DHS has implemented internal quality assurance procedures to ensure that data used in the redress process is as thorough, accurate, and current as possible. In addition, in the collection of information for law enforcement, counterterrorism, and intelligence purposes, it is impossible to determine in advance what information is accurate, relevant, timely, and complete. With the passage of time, seemingly irrelevant or untimely information may acquire new significance as further investigation brings new details to light. The restrictions imposed by (e)(5) would limit the ability of those agencies' trained investigators and intelligence analysts to exercise their judgment in conducting investigations and impede the development of intelligence necessary for effective law enforcement and counterterrorism efforts. The DHS has, however, implemented internal quality assurance procedures to ensure that the data used in the redress process is as thorough, accurate, and current as possible.

(i) From subsection (e)(8) because to require individual notice of disclosure of information due to compulsory legal process would pose an impossible administrative burden on DHS and other agencies and could alert the subjects of counterterrorism, law enforcement, or intelligence investigations to the fact of those investigations when not previously known.

(j) From subsection (f) (Agency Rules) because portions of this system are exempt from the access and amendment provisions of subsection (d).

(k) From subsection (g) to the extent that the system is exempt from other specific subsections of the Privacy Act.

4. The Department of Homeland Security Automated Biometric Identification System (IDENT) consists of electronic and paper records and will be used by DHS and its components. IDENT is the primary repository of biometric information held by DHS in connection with its several and varied missions

41

and functions, including, but not limited to: The enforcement of civil and criminal laws (including the immigration law); investigations, inquiries, and proceedings thereunder; and national security and intelligence activities. IDENT is a centralized and dynamic DHS-wide biometric database that also contains limited biographic and encounter history information needed to place the biometric information in proper context. The information is collected by, on behalf of, in support of, or in cooperation with DHS and its components and may contain personally identifiable information collected by other Federal, State, local, tribal, foreign, or international government agencies.

Pursuant to exemptions 5 U.S.C. 552a(j)(2) of the Privacy Act, portions of this system are exempt from 5 U.S.C. 552a(c)(3) and (4); (d); (e)(1), (e)(2), (e)(3), (e)(4)(G), (e)(4)(H), (e)(5) and (e)(8); (f)(2) through (5); and (g). Pursuant to 5 U.S.C. 552a(k)(2), this system is exempt from the following provisions of the Privacy Act, subject to the limitations set forth in those subsections: 5 U.S.C. 552a (c)(3), (d), (e)(1), (e)(4)(G), and (e)(4)(H). Exemptions from these particular subsections are justified, on a case-by-case basis to be determined at the time a request is made, for the following reasons:

(a) From subsection (c)(3) and (4) (Accounting for Disclosures) because release of the accounting of disclosures could alert the subject of an investigation of an actual or potential criminal, civil, or regulatory violation to the existence of the investigation; and reveal investigative interest on the part of DHS as well as the recipient agency. Disclosure of the accounting would therefore present a serious impediment to law enforcement efforts and/or efforts to preserve national security. Disclosure of the accounting would also permit the individual who is the subject of a record to impede the investigation, to tamper with witnesses or evidence, and to avoid detection or apprehension, which would undermine the entire investigative process.

(b) From subsection (d) (Access to Records) because access to the records contained in this system of records could inform the subject of an investigation of an actual or potential criminal, civil, or regulatory violation, to the existence of the investigation, and reveal investigative interest on the part of DHS or another agency. Access to the records could permit the individual who is the subject of a record to impede the investigation, to tamper with witnesses or evidence, and to avoid detection or apprehension. Amendment of the records could interfere with ongoing investigations and law enforcement activities and would impose an impossible administrative burden by requiring investigations to be continuously reinvestigated. In addition, permitting access and amendment to such information could

disclose security-sensitive information that could be detrimental to homeland security.

(c) From subsection (e)(1) (Relevancy and Necessity of Information) because in the course of investigations into potential violations of Federal law, the accuracy of information obtained or introduced occasionally may be unclear or the information may not be strictly relevant or necessary to a specific investigation. In the interests of effective law enforcement, it is appropriate to retain all information that may aid in establishing patterns of unlawful activity.

(d) From subsection (e)(2) (Collection of Information from Individuals) because requiring that information be collected from the subject of an investigation would alert the subject to the nature or existence of an investigation, thereby interfering with the related investigation and law enforcement activities.

(e) From subsection (e)(3) (Notice to Subjects) because providing such detailed information would impede law enforcement in that it could compromise the existence of a confidential investigation or reveal the identity of witnesses or confidential informants.

(f) From subsections (e)(4)(G) and (H) (Agency Requirements), and (f)(2 through 5) (Agency Rules) because portions of this system are exempt from the individual access provisions of subsection (d) and thereby would not require DHS to establish requirements or rules for records which are exempted from access.

(g) From subsection (e)(5) (Collection of Information) because in the collection of information for law enforcement purposes it is impossible to determine in advance what information is accurate, relevant, timely, and complete. Compliance with (e)(5) would preclude DHS agents from using their investigative training and exercise of good judgment to both conduct and report on investigations.

(h) From subsection (e)(8) (Notice on Individuals) because compliance would interfere with DHS' ability to obtain, serve, and issue subpoenas, warrants, and other law enforcement mechanisms that may be filed under seal, and could result in disclosure of investigative techniques, procedures, and evidence.

(i) From subsection (g) to the extent that the system is exempt from other specific subsections of the Privacy Act.

5. The DHS/OIG–002 Investigative Records System of Records consists of electronic and paper records used by the DHS OIG. The DHS/OIG–002 Investigative Records System of Records is a repository of information held by DHS in connection with its several and varied missions and functions, including, but not limited to the enforcement of civil and criminal laws; investigations, inquiries, and proceedings there under; and national security and intelligence activities. The

DHS/OIG–002 Investigative Records System of Records contains information that is collected by, on behalf of, in support of, or in cooperation with DHS components and may contain personally identifiable information collected by other federal, state, local, tribal, foreign, or international government agencies. The Secretary of Homeland Security has exempted this system from the following provisions of the Privacy Act, subject to limitations set forth in 5 U.S.C. 552a(c)(3) and (c)(4); (d); (e)(1), (e)(2), (e)(3), (e)(4)(G), (e)(4)(H), (e)(5) and (e)(8); (f); and (g) pursuant to 5 U.S.C. 552a(j)(2). Additionally, the Secretary of Homeland Security has exempted this system from the following provisions of the Privacy Act, subject to limitations set forth in 5 U.S.C. 552a(c)(3); (d); (e)(1), (e)(4)(G), (e)(4)(H); and (f) pursuant to 5 U.S.C. 552a(k)(1), (k)(2) and (k)(5). Exemptions from these particular subsections are justified, on a case-by-case basis to be determined at the time a request is made, for the following reasons:

(a) From subsection (c)(3) and (c)(4) (Accounting for Disclosures) because release of the accounting of disclosures could alert the subject of an investigation of an actual or potential criminal, civil, or regulatory violation, to the existence of the investigation; and reveal investigative interest on the part of DHS as well as the recipient agency. Disclosure of the accounting would therefore present a serious impediment to law enforcement efforts and/or efforts to preserve national security. Disclosure of the accounting would also permit the individual who is the subject of a record to impede the investigation, tamper with witnesses or evidence, and avoid detection or apprehension, which would undermine the entire investigative process.

(b) From subsection (d) (Access to Records) because access to the records contained in this system of records could inform the subject of an investigation of an actual or potential criminal, civil, or regulatory violation, to the existence of the investigation, and reveal investigative interest on the part of DHS or another agency. Access to the records could permit the individual who is the subject of a record to impede the investigation, tamper with witnesses or evidence, and avoid detection or apprehension. Amendment of the records could interfere with ongoing investigations and law enforcement activities and would impose an impossible administrative burden by requiring investigations to be continuously reinvestigated. In addition, permitting access and amendment to such information could disclose security-sensitive information that could be detrimental to homeland security.

(c) From subsection (e)(1) (Relevancy and Necessity of Information) because in the course of investigations into potential violations of federal law, the accuracy of information obtained or introduced occasionally may be unclear or the information may not be strictly relevant or necessary to a specific investigation. In the interests of effective law enforcement, it is appropriate to retain all information that may aid in establishing patterns of unlawful activity.

(d) From subsection (e)(2) (Collection of Information from Individuals) because requiring that information be collected from the subject of an investigation would alert the subject as to the nature or existence of an investigation, thereby interfering with the related investigation and law enforcement activities.

(e) From subsection (e)(3) (Notice to Subjects) because providing such detailed information would impede law enforcement in that it could compromise investigations by: revealing the existence of an otherwise confidential investigation and thereby providing an opportunity for the subject of an investigation to conceal evidence, alter patterns of behavior, or take other actions that could thwart investigative efforts; revealing the identity of witnesses in investigations thereby providing an opportunity for the subjects of the investigations or others to harass, intimidate, or otherwise interfere with the collection of evidence or other information from such witnesses; or revealing the identity of confidential informants, which would negatively affect the informants' usefulness in any ongoing or future investigations and discourage members of the public from cooperating as confidential informants in any future investigations.

(f) From subsections (e)(4)(G) and (e)(4)(H) (Agency Requirements) and (f) (Agency Rules), because portions of this system are exempt from the individual access provisions of subsection (d) for the reasons noted above, and therefore DHS is not required to establish rules or procedures with respect to such access. Providing notice to individuals with respect to existence of records pertaining to them in this system of records or otherwise setting up procedures pursuant to which individuals may access and view records pertaining to themselves in the system would undermine investigative efforts and reveal the identities of witnesses, potential witnesses, and confidential informants.

(g) From subsection (e)(5) (Collection of Information) because in the collection of information for law enforcement purposes it is impossible to determine in advance what information is accurate, relevant, timely, and complete. Compliance with (e)(5) would preclude DHS agents from using their investigative training and exercise of good judgment to both conduct and report on investigations.

(h) From subsection (e)(8) (Notice on Individuals) because compliance would interfere with DHS' ability to obtain, serve, and issue subpoenas, warrants and other law enforcement mechanisms that may be filed under seal, and could result in disclosure of investigative techniques, procedures, and evidence.

(i) From subsection (g) (Civil Remedies) to the extent that the system is exempt from other specific subsections of the Privacy Act relating to individuals' rights to access and amend their records contained in the system. Therefore, DHS is not required to establish rules or procedures pursuant to which individuals may seek a civil remedy for the agency's refusals to amend a record; refusal to comply with a request for access to records; failure to maintain accurate, relevant, timely, and complete records; or failure to otherwise comply with an individual's right to access or amend records.

6. The Immigration and Customs Enforcement (ICE) Pattern Analysis and Information Collection (ICEPIC) System consists of electronic and paper records and will be used by DHS and its components. ICEPIC is a repository of information held by DHS in connection with its several and varied missions and functions, including, but not limited to: The enforcement of civil and criminal laws (including the immigration law); investigations, inquiries, and proceedings there under; and national security and intelligence activities. ICEPIC contains information that is collected by, on behalf of, in support of, or in cooperation with DHS and its components and may contain personally identifiable information collected by other Federal, State, local, tribal, foreign, or international government agencies.

Pursuant to exemption 5 U.S.C. 552a(j)(2) of the Privacy Act, portions of this system are exempt from 5 U.S.C. 552a(c)(3) and (4); (d); (e)(1), (e)(2), (e)(3), (e)(4)(G), (e)(4)(H), (e)(5) and (e)(8); (f), and (g). Pursuant to 5 U.S.C. 552a(k)(2), this system is exempt from the following provisions of the Privacy Act, subject to the limitations set forth in those subsections: 5 U.S.C. 552a(c)(3), (d), (e)(1), (e)(4)(G), (e)(4)(H), and (f). Exemptions from these particular subsections are justified, on a case-by-case basis to be determined at the time a request is made, for the following reasons:

(a) From subsection (c)(3) and (4) (Accounting for Disclosures) because release of the accounting of disclosures could alert the subject of an investigation of an actual or potential criminal, civil, or regulatory violation to the existence of the investigation, and reveal investigative interest on the part of DHS as well as the recipient agency. Disclosure of the accounting would therefore present a serious impediment to law enforcement efforts and/or efforts to preserve national security. Disclosure of the accounting would also permit the individual who is the subject of a record to impede the investigation, to tamper with witnesses or evidence, and to avoid detection or apprehension, which would undermine the entire investigative process.

(b) From subsection (d) (Access to Records) because access to the records contained in this system of records could inform the subject of an investigation of an actual or potential criminal, civil, or regulatory violation, to the existence of the investigation, and reveal investigative interest on the part of DHS or another agency. Access to the records could permit the individual who is the subject of a record to impede the investigation, to tamper with witnesses or evidence, and to avoid detection or apprehension. Amendment of the records could interfere with ongoing investigations and law enforcement activities and would impose an impossible administrative burden by requiring investigations to be continuously reinvestigated. In addition, permitting access and amendment to such information could disclose security-sensitive information that could be detrimental to homeland security.

(c) From subsection (e)(1) (Relevancy and Necessity of Information) because in the course of investigations into potential violations of Federal law, the accuracy of information obtained or introduced occasionally may be unclear or the information may not be strictly relevant or necessary to a specific investigation. In the interests of effective law enforcement, it is appropriate to retain all information that may aid in establishing patterns of unlawful activity.

(d) From subsection (e)(2) (Collection of Information from Individuals) because requiring that information be collected from the subject of an investigation would alert the subject to the nature or existence of an investigation, thereby interfering with the related investigation and law enforcement activities.

(e) From subsection (e)(3) (Notice to Subjects) because providing such detailed information would impede law enforcement in that it could compromise investigations by: revealing the existence of an otherwise confidential investigation and thereby provide an opportunity for the subject of an investigation to conceal evidence, alter patterns of behavior, or take other actions that could thwart investigative efforts; reveal the identity of witnesses in investigations, thereby providing an opportunity for the subjects of the investigations or others to harass, intimidate, or otherwise interfere with the collection of evidence or other information from such witnesses; or reveal the identity of confidential informants, which would negatively affect the informant's usefulness in any ongoing or future investigations and discourage members of the public from cooperating as confidential informants in any future investigations.

(f) From subsections (e)(4)(G) and (H) (Agency Requirements), and (f) (Agency

Rules) because portions of this system are exempt from the individual access provisions of subsection (d) for the reasons noted above, and therefore DHS is not required to establish requirements, rules, or procedures with respect to such access. Providing notice to individuals with respect to existence of records pertaining to them in the system of records or otherwise setting up procedures pursuant to which individuals may access and view records pertaining to themselves in the system would undermine investigative efforts and reveal the identities of witnesses, and potential witnesses, and confidential informants.

(g) From subsection (e)(5) (Collection of Information) because in the collection of information for law enforcement purposes it is impossible to determine in advance what information is accurate, relevant, timely, and complete. Compliance with (e)(5) would preclude DHS agents from using their investigative training and exercise of good judgment to both conduct and report on investigations.

(h) From subsection (e)(8) (Notice on Individuals) because compliance would interfere with DHS' ability to obtain, serve, and issue subpoenas, warrants, and other law enforcement mechanisms that may be filed under seal, and could result in disclosure of investigative techniques, procedures, and evidence.

(i) From subsection (g) to the extent that the system is exempt from other specific subsections of the Privacy Act relating to individuals' rights to access and amend their records contained in the system. Therefore DHS is not required to establish rules or procedures pursuant to which individuals may seek a civil remedy for the agency's: Refusal to amend a record; Refusal to comply with a request for access to records; failure to maintain accurate, relevant timely and complete records; or failure to otherwise comply with an individual's right to access or amend records.

7. The Office of Intelligence and Analysis (I&A) Enterprise Records System (ERS) consists of records including intelligence information and other properly acquired information received from agencies and components of the federal government, foreign governments, organizations or entities, international organizations, state and local government agencies (including law enforcement agencies), and private sector entities, as well as information provided by individuals, regardless of the medium used to submit the information or the agency to which it was submitted. This system also contains: Information regarding persons on watch lists with known or suspected links to terrorism; the results of intelligence analysis and reporting; ongoing law enforcement investigative information, information systems security analysis and reporting; active immigra-

tion, customs, border and transportation, security related records; historical law enforcement, operational, immigration, customs, border and transportation security, and other administrative records; relevant and appropriately acquired financial information; and public-source data such as that contained in media reports and commercially available databases, as appropriate. Data about the providers of information, including the means of transmission of the data, is also retained.

(a) Pursuant to 5 U.S.C. 552a(k)(1), (2), (3), and (5), this system of records is exempt from 5 U.S.C. 552a(c)(3), (d)(1), (2), (3), (4), and (5), (e)(1), (e)(4)(G), (H), and (I), and (f). These exemptions apply only to the extent that information in this system is subject to exemption. Where compliance would not appear to interfere with or adversely affect the intelligence, counterterrorism, homeland security, and related law enforcement purposes of this system, the applicable exemption may be waived by DHS.

(b) Exemptions from the particular subsections are justified for the following reasons:

(1) From subsection (c)(3) (Accounting for Disclosures) because making available to a record subject the accounting of disclosures from records concerning him/her would specifically reveal any interest in the individual of an intelligence, counterterrorism, homeland security, or related investigative nature. Revealing this information could reasonably be expected to compromise ongoing efforts of the Department to identify, understand, analyze, investigate, and counter the activities of:

(i) Known or suspected terrorists and terrorist groups;

(ii) Groups or individuals known or believed to be assisting or associated with known or suspected terrorists or terrorist groups;

(iii) Individuals known, believed to be, or suspected of being engaged in activities constituting a threat to homeland security, including (1) activities which impact or concern the security, safety, and integrity of our international borders, including any illegal activities that either cross our borders or are otherwise in violation of the immigration or customs laws and regulations of the United States; (2) activities which could reasonably be expected to assist in the development or use of a weapon of mass effect; (3) activities meant to identify, create, or exploit the vulnerabilities of, or undermine, the "key resources" (as defined in section 2(9) of the Homeland Security Act of 2002) and "critical infrastructure" (as defined in 42 U.S.C. 5195c(c)) of the United States, including the cyber and national telecommunications infrastructure and the availability of a viable national security and emergency preparedness communications infrastructure; (4) activities detrimental to the security of transportation and transportation systems; (5) activities which violate or are suspected of violating the laws relating to counterfeiting of obligations and securities of the United States and other financial crimes, including access device fraud, financial institution fraud, identity theft, computer fraud; and computer-based attacks on our nation's financial, banking, and telecommunications infrastructure; (6) activities, not wholly conducted within the United States, which violate or are suspected of violating the laws which prohibit the production, transfer, or sale of narcotics or substances controlled in accordance with Title 21 of the United States Code, or those associated activities otherwise prohibited by Titles 21 and 46 of the United States Code; (7) activities which impact, concern, or otherwise threaten the safety and security of the President and Vice President, their families, heads of state, and other designated individuals; the White House, Vice President's residence, foreign missions, and other designated buildings within the United States; (8) activities which impact, concern, or otherwise threaten domestic maritime safety and security, maritime mobility and navigation, or the integrity of the domestic maritime environment; (9) activities which impact, concern, or otherwise threaten the national operational capability of the Department to respond to natural and manmade major disasters and emergencies, including acts of terrorism; (10) activities involving the importation, possession, storage, development, or transportation of nuclear or radiological material without authorization or for use against the United States;

(iv) Foreign governments, organizations, or persons (foreign powers); and

(v) Individuals engaging in intelligence activities on behalf of a foreign power or terrorist group.

Thus, by notifying the record subject that he/she is the focus of such efforts or interest on the part of DHS, or other agencies with whom DHS is cooperating and to whom the disclosures were made, this information could permit the record subject to take measures to impede or evade such efforts, including the taking of steps to deceive DHS personnel and deny them the ability to adequately assess relevant information and activities, and could inappropriately disclose to the record subject the sensitive methods and/or confidential sources used to acquire the relevant information against him/her. Moreover, where the record subject is the actual target of a law enforcement investigation, this information could permit him/her to take measures to impede the investigation, for example, by destroying evidence, intimidating potential witnesses, or avoiding detection or apprehension.

(2) From subsections (d)(1), (2), (3), and (4) (Access to Records) because these provisions concern individual rights of access to and amendment of records (including the review of agency denials of either) contained in this system, which consists of intelligence, counterterrorism, homeland security, and related investigatory records concerning efforts of the Department, as described more fully in subsection (b)(1), above. Compliance with these provisions could inform or alert the subject of an intelligence, counterterrorism, homeland security, or investigatory effort undertaken on behalf of the Department, or by another agency with whom DHS is cooperating, of the fact and nature of such efforts, and/or the relevant intelligence, counterterrorism, homeland security, or investigatory interest of DHS and/or other intelligence, counterterrorism, or law enforcement agencies. Moreover, compliance could also compromise sensitive information either classified in the interest of national security, or which otherwise requires, as appropriate, safeguarding and protection from unauthorized disclosure; identify a confidential source or disclose information which would constitute an unwarranted invasion of another individual's personal privacy; reveal a sensitive intelligence or investigative technique or method, including interfering with intelligence or law enforcement investigative processes by permitting the destruction of evidence, improper influencing or intimidation of witnesses, fabrication of statements or testimony, and flight from detection or apprehension; or constitute a potential danger to the health or safety of intelligence, counterterrorism, homeland security, and law enforcement personnel, confidential sources and informants, and potential witnesses. Amendment of the records would interfere with ongoing intelligence, counterterrorism, homeland security, and law enforcement investigations and activities, including incident reporting and analysis activities, and impose an impossible administrative burden by requiring investigations, reports, and analyses to be continuously reinvestigated and revised.

(3) From subsection (e)(1) (Relevant and Necessary) because it is not always possible for DHS to know in advance of its receipt the relevance and necessity of each piece of information it acquires in the course of an intelligence, counterterrorism, or investigatory effort undertaken on behalf of the Department, or by another agency with whom DHS is cooperating. In the context of the authorized intelligence, counterterrorism, and investigatory activities undertaken by DHS personnel, relevance and necessity are questions of analytic judgment and timing, such that what may appear relevant and necessary when acquired ultimately may be deemed unnecessary upon further analysis

and evaluation. Similarly, in some situations, it is only after acquired information is collated, analyzed, and evaluated in light of other available evidence and information that its relevance and necessity can be established or made clear. Constraining the initial acquisition of information included within the ERS in accordance with the relevant and necessary requirement of subsection (e)(1) could discourage the appropriate receipt of and access to information which DHS and I&A are otherwise authorized to receive and possess under law, and thereby impede efforts to detect, deter, prevent, disrupt, or apprehend terrorists or terrorist groups, and/or respond to terrorist or other activities which threaten homeland security. Notwithstanding this claimed exemption, which would permit the acquisition and temporary maintenance of records whose relevance to the purpose of the ERS may be less than fully clear, DHS will only disclose such records after determining whether such disclosures are themselves consistent with the published ERS routine uses. Moreover, it should be noted that, as concerns the receipt by I&A, for intelligence purposes, of information in any record which identifies a U.S. Person, as defined in Executive Order 12333, as amended, such receipt, and any subsequent use or dissemination of that identifying information, is undertaken consistent with the procedures established and adhered to by I&A pursuant to that Executive Order. Specifically, I&A intelligence personnel may acquire information which identifies a particular U.S. Person, retain it within or disseminate it from ERS, as appropriate, only when it is determined that the personally identifying information is necessary for the conduct of I&A's functions, and otherwise falls into one of a limited number of authorized categories, each of which reflects discrete activities for which information on individuals would be utilized by the Department in the overall execution of its statutory mission.

(4) From subsections (e)(4) (G), (H) and (I) (Access), and (f) (Agency Rules), inasmuch as it is unnecessary for the publication of rules and procedures contemplated therein since the ERS, pursuant to subsections (1) and (2), above, will be exempt from the underlying duties to provide to individuals notification about, access to, and the ability to amend or correct the information pertaining to them in, this system of records. Furthermore, to the extent that subsection (e)(4)(I) is construed to require more detailed disclosure than the information accompanying the system notice for ERS, as published in today's FEDERAL REGISTER, exemption from it is also necessary to protect the confidentiality, privacy, and physical safety of sources of information, as well as the methods for acquiring it. Finally, greater specificity concerning the description of categories of sources of

properly classified records could also compromise or otherwise cause damage to the national or homeland security.

8. The information in MAGNET establishes Maritime Domain Awareness. Maritime Domain Awareness is the collection of as much information as possible about the maritime world. In other words, MAGNET establishes a full awareness of the entities (people, places, things) and their activities within the maritime industry. MAGNET collects the information and connects the information in order to fulfill this need.

Coast Guard Intelligence (through MAGNET) will provide awareness to the field as well as to strategic planners by aggregating data from existing sources internal and external to the Coast Guard or DHS. MAGNET will correlate and provide the medium to display information such as ship registry, current ship position, crew background, passenger lists, port history, cargo, known criminal vessels, and suspect lists. Coast Guard Intelligence (CG–2) will serve as MAGNET's executive agent and will share appropriate aggregated data to other law enforcement and intelligence agencies.

(a) Pursuant to 5 U.S.C. 522a(j)(2), (k)(1), and (k)(2) this system of records is exempt from 5 U.S.C. 552a(c)(3) and (4), (d)(1), (d)(2), (d)(3), (d)(4), (e)(1), (e)(2), (e)(3), (e)(4) (G), (H), and (I), e(5), e(8), e(12), (f), and (g). These exemptions apply only to the extent that information in this system is subject to exemption. Where compliance would not appear to interfere with or adversely affect the intelligence, counterterrorism, homeland security, and related law enforcement purposes of this system, the applicable exemption may be waived by DHS.

(b) Exemptions from the particular subsections are justified for the following reasons:

(1) From subsection (c)(3) (Accounting of Certain Disclosures) because making available to a record subject the accounting of disclosures from records concerning him/her would specifically reveal any interest in the individual of an intelligence, counterterrorism, homeland security, law enforcement or related investigative nature. Revealing this information could reasonably be expected to compromise ongoing efforts of the Department to identify, understand, analyze, investigate, and counter the activities of:

(i) Known or suspected terrorists and terrorist groups;

(ii) Groups or individuals known or believed to be assisting or associated with known or suspected terrorists or terrorist groups;

(iii) Individuals known, believed to be, or suspected of being engaged in activities constituting a threat to homeland security, including (1) activities which impact or concern the security, safety, and integrity of our international borders, including any illegal activities that either cross our borders or are otherwise in violation of the immigration or customs laws and regulations of the United States; (2) activities which could reasonably be expected to assist in the development or use of a weapon of mass effect; (3) activities meant to identify, create, or exploit the vulnerabilities of, or undermine, the "key resources" (as defined in section 2(9) of the Homeland Security Act of 2002) and "critical infrastructure" (as defined in 42 U.S.C. 5195c(c)) of the United States, including the cyber and national telecommunications infrastructure and the availability of a viable national security and emergency preparedness communications infrastructure; (4) activities detrimental to the security of transportation and transportation systems; (5) activities which violate or are suspected of violating the laws relating to counterfeiting of obligations and securities of the United States and other financial crimes, including access device fraud, financial institution fraud, identity theft, computer fraud; and computer-based attacks on our nation's financial, banking, and telecommunications infrastructure; (6) activities, not wholly conducted within the United States, which violate or are suspected of violating the laws which prohibit the production, transfer, or sale of narcotics or substances controlled in accordance with Title 21 of the United States Code, or those associated activities otherwise prohibited by Titles 21 and 46 of the United States Code; (7) activities which impact, concern, or otherwise threaten the safety and security of the President and Vice President, their families, heads of state, and other designated individuals; the White House, Vice President's residence, foreign missions, and other designated buildings within the United States; (8) activities which impact, concern, or otherwise threaten domestic maritime safety and security, maritime mobility and navigation, or the integrity of the domestic maritime environment; (9) activities which impact, concern, or otherwise threaten the national operational capability of the Department to respond to natural and manmade major disasters and emergencies, including acts of terrorism; (10) activities involving the importation, possession, storage, development, or transportation of nuclear or radiological material without authorization or for use against the United States;

(iv) Foreign governments, organizations, or persons (foreign powers); and

(v) Individuals engaging in intelligence activities on behalf of a foreign power or terrorist group.

Thus, by notifying the record subject that he/she is the focus of such efforts or interest on the part of DHS, or other agencies with whom DHS is cooperating and to whom the disclosures were made, this information could permit the record subject to take measures to impede or evade such efforts, including the taking of steps to deceive DHS personnel and deny them the ability to adequately assess relevant information and activities, and could inappropriately disclose to the record subject the sensitive methods and/or confidential sources used to acquire the relevant information against him/her. Moreover, where the record subject is the actual target of a law enforcement investigation, this information could permit him/her to take measures to impede the investigation, for example, by destroying evidence, intimidating potential witnesses, or avoiding detection or apprehension.

(2) From subsection (c)(4) (Accounting for Disclosure, notice of dispute) because certain records in this system are exempt from the access and amendment provisions of subsection (d), this requirement to inform any person or other agency about any correction or notation of dispute that the agency made with regard to those records, should not apply.

(3) From subsections (d)(1), (2), (3), and (4) (Access to Records) because these provisions concern individual rights of access to and amendment of records (including the review of agency denials of either) contained in this system, which consists of intelligence, counterterrorism, homeland security, and related investigatory records concerning efforts of the Department, as described more fully in subsection (b)(1), above. Compliance with these provisions could inform or alert the subject of an intelligence, counterterrorism, homeland security, or investigatory effort undertaken on behalf of the Department, or by another agency with whom DHS is cooperating, of the fact and nature of such efforts, and/or the relevant intelligence, counterterrorism, homeland security, or investigatory interest of DHS and/or other intelligence, counterterrorism, or law enforcement agencies. Moreover, compliance could also compromise sensitive information either classified in the interest of national security, or which otherwise requires, as appropriate, safeguarding and protection from unauthorized disclosure; identify a confidential source or disclose information which would constitute an unwarranted invasion of another individual's personal privacy; reveal a sensitive intelligence or investigative technique or method, including interfering with intelligence or law enforcement investigative processes by permitting the destruction of evidence, improper influencing or intimidation of witnesses, fabrication of statements or testimony, and flight from detection or apprehension; or constitute a potential danger to the health or safety of intelligence, counterterrorism, homeland security, and law enforcement personnel, confidential sources and informants, and potential witnesses. Amendment of the records

would interfere with ongoing intelligence, counterterrorism, homeland security, and law enforcement investigations and activities, including incident reporting and analysis activities, and impose an impossible administrative burden by requiring investigations, reports, and analyses to be continuously reinvestigated and revised.

(4) From subsection (e)(1) (Relevant and Necessary) because it is not always possible for DHS to know in advance of its receipt the relevance and necessity of each piece of information it acquires in the course of an intelligence, counterterrorism, or investigatory effort undertaken on behalf of the Department, or by another agency with whom DHS is cooperating. In the context of the authorized intelligence, counterterrorism, and investigatory activities undertaken by DHS personnel, relevance and necessity are questions of analytic judgment and timing, such that what may appear relevant and necessary when acquired ultimately may be deemed unnecessary upon further analysis and evaluation. Similarly, in some situations, it is only after acquired information is collated, analyzed, and evaluated in light of other available evidence and information that its relevance and necessity can be established or made clear. Constraining the initial acquisition of information included within the MAGNET in accordance with the relevant and necessary requirement of subsection (e)(1) could discourage the appropriate receipt of and access to information which DHS and MAGNET are otherwise authorized to receive and possess under law, and thereby impede efforts to detect, deter, prevent, disrupt, or apprehend terrorists or terrorist groups, and/or respond to terrorist or other activities which threaten homeland security. Notwithstanding this claimed exemption, which would permit the acquisition and temporary maintenance of records whose relevance to the purpose of the MAGNET may be less than fully clear, DHS will only disclose such records after determining whether such disclosures are themselves consistent with the published MAGNET routine uses. Moreover, it should be noted that, as concerns the receipt by USCG, for intelligence purposes, of information in any record which identifies a U.S. Person, as defined in Executive Order 12333, as amended, such receipt, and any subsequent use or dissemination of that identifying information, is undertaken consistent with the procedures established and adhered to by USCG pursuant to that Executive Order. Specifically, USCG intelligence personnel may acquire information which identifies a particular U.S. Person, retain it within or disseminate it from MAGNET, as appropriate, only when it is determined that the personally identifying information is necessary for the conduct of USCG's functions, and otherwise falls into one of a limited number of authorized cat-

egories, each of which reflects discrete activities for which information on individuals would be utilized by the Department in the overall execution of its statutory mission.

(5) From subsection (e)(2) (Collection of Information from Individuals) because application of this provision could present a serious impediment to counterterrorism or law enforcement efforts in that it would put the subject of an investigation, study or analysis on notice of that fact, thereby permitting the subject to engage in conduct designed to frustrate or impede that activity. The nature of counterterrorism and law enforcement investigations is such that vital information about an individual frequently can be obtained only from other persons who are familiar with such individual and his/her activities. In such investigations it is not feasible to rely solely upon information furnished by the individual concerning his own activities.

(6) From subsection (e)(3) (Notice to Subjects), to the extent that this subsection is interpreted to require DHS to provide notice to an individual if DHS or another agency receives or collects information about that individual during an investigation or from a third party. Should the subsection be so interpreted, exemption from this provision is necessary to avoid impeding counterterrorism or law enforcement efforts by putting the subject of an investigation, study or analysis on notice of that fact, thereby permitting the subject to engage in conduct intended to frustrate or impede that activity.

(7) From subsections (e)(4) (G), (H) and (I) (Access), and (f) (Agency Rules), inasmuch as it is unnecessary for the publication of rules and procedures contemplated therein since the MAGNET, pursuant to subsections (3), above, will be exempt from the underlying duties to provide to individuals notification about, access to, and the ability to amend or correct the information pertaining to them in, this system of records. Furthermore, to the extent that subsection (e)(4)(I) is construed to require more detailed disclosure than the information accompanying the system notice for MAGNET, as published in today's FEDERAL REGISTER, exemption from it is also necessary to protect the confidentiality, privacy, and physical safety of sources of information, as well as the methods for acquiring it. Finally, greater specificity concerning the description of categories of sources of properly classified records could also compromise or otherwise cause damage to the national or homeland security.

(8) From subsection (e)(5) (Collection of Information) because many of the records in this system coming from other system of records are derived from other domestic and foreign agency record systems and therefore it is not possible for DHS to vouch for their compliance with this provision; however, the

DHS has implemented internal quality assurance procedures to ensure that data used in its screening processes is as complete, accurate, and current as possible. In addition, in the collection of information for law enforcement and counterterrorism purposes, it is impossible to determine in advance what information is accurate, relevant, timely, and complete. With the passage of time, seemingly irrelevant or untimely information may acquire new significance as further investigation brings new details to light. The restrictions imposed by (e)(5) would limit the ability of those agencies' trained investigators and intelligence analysts to exercise their judgment in conducting investigations and impede the development of intelligence necessary for effective law enforcement and counterterrorism efforts.

(9) From subsection (e)(8) (Notice on Individuals) because to require individual notice of disclosure of information due to compulsory legal process would pose an impossible administrative burden on DHS and other agencies and could alert the subjects of counterterrorism or law enforcement investigations to the fact of those investigations then not previously known.

(10) From subsection (e)(12) (Matching Agreements) because requiring DHS to provide notice of alterations to existing matching agreements would impair DHS operations by indicating which data elements and information are valuable to DHS's analytical functions, thereby providing harmful disclosure of information to individuals who would seek to circumvent or interfere with DHS's missions.

(11) From subsection (g) (Civil Remedies) to the extent that the system is exempt from other specific subsections of the Privacy Act.

9. The Law Enforcement Information Data Base (LEIDB)/Pathfinder is a historical repository of selected Coast Guard message traffic. LEIDB/Pathfinder supports law enforcement intelligence activities. LEIDB/Pathfinder users can query archived message traffic and link relevant information across multiple data records within LEIDB/Pathfinder. Users have system tools enabling the user to identify potential relationships between information contained in otherwise unrelated documents. These tools allow the analysts to build high precision and low return queries, which minimize false hits and maximize analyst productivity while working with unstructured, unformatted, free test documents.

(a) Pursuant to 5 U.S.C. 552a(j)(2), (k)(1), and (k)(2) certain records or information in the above mentioned system of records are exempt from 5 U.S.C. 552a(c)(3) and (4); (d)(1), (2), (3), and (4); (e)(1), (2), (3), (4)(G) through (I), (e)(5), and (8); (f), and (g). These exemptions apply only to the extent that information in this system is subject to exemption. Where compliance would not appear to interfere with or adversely affect the intelligence, counterterrorism, homeland security, and related law enforcement purposes of this system, the applicable exemption may be waived by DHS.

(b) Exemptions from the particular subsections are justified for the following reasons:

(1) From subsection (c)(3) (Accounting for Disclosures) because making available to a record subject the accounting of disclosures from records concerning him/her would specifically reveal any interest in the individual of an intelligence, counterterrorism, homeland security, or related investigative nature. Revealing this information could reasonably be expected to compromise ongoing efforts of the Department to identify, understand, analyze, investigate, and counter the activities of:

(i) Known or suspected terrorists and terrorist groups;

(ii) Groups or individuals known or believed to be assisting or associated with known or suspected terrorists or terrorist groups;

(iii) Individuals known, believed to be, or suspected of being engaged in activities constituting a threat to homeland security, including (1) activities which impact or concern the security, safety, and integrity of our international borders, including any illegal activities that either cross our borders or are otherwise in violation of the immigration or customs laws and regulations of the United States; (2) activities which could reasonably be expected to assist in the development or use of a weapon of mass effect; (3) activities meant to identify, create, or exploit the vulnerabilities of, or undermine, the "key resources" (as defined in section 2(9) of the Homeland Security Act of 2002) and "critical infrastructure" (as defined in 42 U.S.C. 5195c(c)) of the United States, including the cyber and national telecommunications infrastructure and the availability of a viable national security and emergency preparedness communications infrastructure; (4) activities detrimental to the security of transportation and transportation systems; (5) activities which violate or are suspected of violating the laws relating to counterfeiting of obligations and securities of the United States and other financial crimes, including access device fraud, financial institution fraud, identity theft, computer fraud; and computer-based attacks on our nation's financial, banking, and telecommunications infrastructure; (6) activities, not wholly conducted within the United States, which violate or are suspected of violating the laws which prohibit the production, transfer, or sale of narcotics or substances controlled in accordance with Title 21 of the United States Code, or those associated activities otherwise prohibited by Titles 21 and 46 of the United States Code; (7)

activities which impact, concern, or otherwise threaten the safety and security of the President and Vice President, their families, heads of state, and other designated individuals; the White House, Vice President's residence, foreign missions, and other designated buildings within the United States; (8) activities which impact, concern, or otherwise threaten domestic maritime safety and security, maritime mobility and navigation, or the integrity of the domestic maritime environment; (9) activities which impact, concern, or otherwise threaten the national operational capability of the Department to respond to natural and manmade major disasters and emergencies, including acts of terrorism; (10) activities involving the importation, possession, storage, development, or transportation of nuclear or radiological material without authorization or for use against the United States;

(iv) Foreign governments, organizations, or persons (foreign powers); and

(v) Individuals engaging in intelligence activities on behalf of a foreign power or terrorist group.

Thus, by notifying the record subject that he/she is the focus of such efforts or interest on the part of DHS, or other agencies with whom DHS is cooperating and to whom the disclosures were made, this information could permit the record subject to take measures to impede or evade such efforts, including the taking of steps to deceive DHS personnel and deny them the ability to adequately assess relevant information and activities, and could inappropriately disclose to the record subject the sensitive methods and/or confidential sources used to acquire the relevant information against him/her. Moreover, where the record subject is the actual target of a law enforcement investigation, this information could permit him/her to take measures to impede the investigation, for example, by destroying evidence, intimidating potential witnesses, or avoiding detection or apprehension.

(2) From subsection (c)(4) (Accounting for Disclosure, notice of dispute) because certain records in this system are exempt from the access and amendment provisions of subsection (d), this requirement to inform any person or other agency about any correction or notation of dispute that the agency made with regard to those records, should not apply.

(3) From subsections (d)(1), (2), (3), and (4) (Access to Records) because these provisions concern individual rights of access to and amendment of records (including the review of agency denials of either) contained in this system, which consists of intelligence, counterterrorism, homeland security, and related investigatory records concerning efforts of the Department, as described more fully in subsection (b)(1), above. Compliance with these provisions could inform or alert the subject of an intelligence, counterterrorism, homeland security, or investigatory effort undertaken on behalf of the Department, or by another agency with whom DHS is cooperating, of the fact and nature of such efforts, and/or the relevant intelligence, counterterrorism, homeland security, or investigatory interest of DHS and/or other intelligence, counterterrorism, or law enforcement agencies. Moreover, compliance could also compromise sensitive information either classified in the interest of national security, or which otherwise requires, as appropriate, safeguarding and protection from unauthorized disclosure; identify a confidential source or disclose information which would constitute an unwarranted invasion of another individual's personal privacy; reveal a sensitive intelligence or investigative technique or method, including interfering with intelligence or law enforcement investigative processes by permitting the destruction of evidence, improper influencing or intimidation of witnesses, fabrication of statements or testimony, and flight from detection or apprehension; or constitute a potential danger to the health or safety of intelligence, counterterrorism, homeland security, and law enforcement personnel, confidential sources and informants, and potential witnesses. Amendment of the records would interfere with ongoing intelligence, counterterrorism, homeland security, and law enforcement investigations and activities, including incident reporting and analysis activities, and impose an impossible administrative burden by requiring investigations, reports, and analyses to be continuously reinvestigated and revised.

(4) From subsection (e)(1) (Relevant and Necessary) because it is not always possible for DHS to know in advance of its receipt the relevance and necessity of each piece of information it acquires in the course of an intelligence, counterterrorism, or investigatory effort undertaken on behalf of the Department, or by another agency with whom DHS is cooperating. In the context of the authorized intelligence, counterterrorism, and investigatory activities undertaken by DHS personnel, relevance and necessity are questions of analytic judgment and timing, such that what may appear relevant and necessary when acquired ultimately may be deemed unnecessary upon further analysis and evaluation. Similarly, in some situations, it is only after acquired information is collated, analyzed, and evaluated in light of other available evidence and information that its relevance and necessity can be established or made clear. Constraining the initial acquisition of information included within the LEIDB in accordance with the relevant and necessary requirement of subsection (e)(1) could discourage the appropriate receipt of and access to information

which DHS and USCG are otherwise authorized to receive and possess under law, and thereby impede efforts to detect, deter, prevent, disrupt, or apprehend terrorists or terrorist groups, and/or respond to terrorist or other activities which threaten homeland security. Notwithstanding this claimed exemption, which would permit the acquisition and temporary maintenance of records whose relevance to the purpose of the LEIDB may be less than fully clear, DHS will only disclose such records after determining whether such disclosures are themselves consistent with the published LEIDB routine uses. Moreover, it should be noted that, as concerns the receipt by USCG, for intelligence purposes, of information in any record which identifies a U.S. Person, as defined in Executive Order 12333, as amended, such receipt, and any subsequent use or dissemination of that identifying information, is undertaken consistent with the procedures established and adhered to by USCG pursuant to that Executive Order. Specifically, USCG intelligence personnel may acquire information which identifies a particular U.S. Person, retain it within or disseminate it from LEIDB, as appropriate, only when it is determined that the personally identifying information is necessary for the conduct of USCG's functions, and otherwise falls into one of a limited number of authorized categories, each of which reflects discrete activities for which information on individuals would be utilized by the Department in the overall execution of its statutory mission.

(5) From subsection (e)(2) (Collection of Information from Individuals) because application of this provision could present a serious impediment to counterterrorism or law enforcement efforts in that it would put the subject of an investigation, study or analysis on notice of that fact, thereby permitting the subject to engage in conduct designed to frustrate or impede that activity. The nature of counterterrorism, and law enforcement investigations is such that vital information about an individual frequently can be obtained only from other persons who are familiar with such individual and his/her activities. In such investigations it is not feasible to rely solely upon information furnished by the individual concerning his own activities.

(6) From subsection (e)(3) (Notice to Subjects), to the extent that this subsection is interpreted to require DHS to provide notice to an individual if DHS or another agency receives or collects information about that individual during an investigation or from a third party. Should the subsection be so interpreted, exemption from this provision is necessary to avoid impeding counterterrorism or law enforcement efforts by putting the subject of an investigation, study or analysis on notice of that fact, thereby permitting the subject to engage in conduct intended to frustrate or impede that activity.

(7) From subsections (e)(4) (G), (H) and (I) (Access), inasmuch as it is unnecessary for the publication of rules and procedures contemplated therein since the LEIDB, pursuant to subsections (2) and (3), above, will be exempt from the underlying duties to provide to individuals notification about, access to, and the ability to amend or correct the information pertaining to them in, this system of records. Furthermore, to the extent that subsection (e)(4)(I) is construed to require more detailed disclosure than the information accompanying the system notice for LEIDB, as published in today's FEDERAL REGISTER, exemption from it is also necessary to protect the confidentiality, privacy, and physical safety of sources of information, as well as the methods for acquiring it. Finally, greater specificity concerning the description of categories of sources of properly classified records could also compromise or otherwise cause damage to the national or homeland security.

(8) From subsection (e)(5) (Collection of Information) because many of the records contained in this system are derived from other domestic and foreign sources, it is not possible for DHS to vouch for those records' compliance with this provision; however, the DHS has implemented internal quality assurance procedures to ensure that data used in its screening processes is as complete, accurate, and current as possible. In addition, in the collection of information for law enforcement and counterterrorism purposes, it is impossible to determine in advance what information is accurate, relevant, timely, and complete. With the passage of time, seemingly irrelevant or untimely information may acquire new significance as further investigation brings new details to light. The restrictions imposed by (e)(5) would limit the ability of those agencies' trained investigators and intelligence analysts to exercise their judgment in conducting investigations and impede the development of intelligence necessary for effective law enforcement and counterterrorism efforts.

(9) From subsection (e)(8) (Notice on Individuals) because to require individual notice of disclosure of information due to compulsory legal process would pose an impossible administrative burden on DHS and other agencies and could alert the subjects of counterterrorism or law enforcement investigations to the fact of those investigations then not previously known.

(10) From subsection (f) (Agency Rules) because portions of this system are exempt from the access and amendment provisions of subsection (d). Access to, and amendment of, system records that are not exempt or for which exemption is waived may be obtained under procedures described in the related SORN or subpart B of this part.

(11) From subsection (g) to the extent that the system is exempt from other specific subsections of the Privacy Act relating to individuals' rights to access and amend their records contained in the system. Therefore DHS is not required to establish rules or procedures pursuant to which individuals may seek a civil remedy for the agency's: Refusal to amend a record; refusal to comply with a request for access to records; failure to maintain accurate, relevant timely and complete records; or failure to otherwise comply with an individual's right to access or amend records.

10. DHS–ICE–001, The Immigration and Customs Enforcement (ICE) Student and Exchange Visitor Information System (SEVIS) collects and maintains pertinent information on nonimmigrant students and exchange visitors and the schools and exchange visitor program sponsors that host them while in the United States. The system permits DHS to monitor compliance by these individuals with the terms of their admission into the United States. Pursuant to exemptions (j)(2), (k)(1), (k)(2) and (k)(5) of the Privacy Act, portions of this system are exempt from 5 U.S.C. 552a(c)(3); (d); (e)(1); (e)(4)(G), (H) and (I). Exemptions from the particular subsections are justified, on a case by case basis, to be determined at the time a request is made, for the following reasons:

(a) From subsection (c)(3) (Accounting for Disclosures) because release of the accounting of disclosures could alert the subject of an investigation, of an actual or potential criminal, civil, or regulatory violation to the existence of the investigation and reveal investigative interest on the part of DHS as well as the recipient agency. Disclosure of the accounting would therefore present a serious impediment to law enforcement efforts and/or efforts to preserve national security. Disclosure of the accounting would also permit the individual who is the subject of a record to impede the investigation and avoid detection or apprehension, which undermines the entire system.

(b) From subsection (d) (Access to Records) because access to the records contained in this system of records could inform the subject of an investigation, of an actual or potential criminal, civil, or regulatory violation to the existence of the investigation and reveal investigative interest on the part of DHS or another agency. Access to the records could permit the individual who is the subject of a record to impede the investigation and avoid detection or apprehension. Amendment of the records could interfere with ongoing investigations and law enforcement activities and impose an impossible administrative burden by requiring investigations to be continuously reinvestigated. In addition, permitting access and amendment to such information also could

disclose security-sensitive information that could be detrimental to homeland security.

(c) From subsection (e)(1) (Relevancy and Necessity of Information) because in the course of investigations into potential violations of federal law, the accuracy of information obtained or introduced occasionally may be unclear or the information may not be strictly relevant or necessary to a specific investigation. In the interests of effective enforcement of federal laws, it is appropriate to retain all information that may aid in establishing patterns of unlawful activity.

(d) From subsections (e)(4)(G), (H) and (I) (Agency Requirements), and (f) (Agency Rules), because portions of this system are exempt from the access provisions of subsection (d).

11. The General Counsel Electronic Management System (GEMS) consists of records and information created or collected by attorneys for U.S. Immigration and Customs Enforcement, which will be used in the preparation and presentation of cases before a court or other adjudicating body. ICE attorneys work closely with ICE law enforcement personnel throughout the process of adjudicating immigration cases. GEMS allows ICE attorneys to store all the materials pertaining to immigration adjudications, including documents related to investigations, case notes and other hearing related information, and briefs and memoranda of law related to cases. Having this information in one system should not only facilitate the work of the ICE attorneys involved in the particular case, but also will provide a legal resource for other attorneys who are adjudicating similar cases. The system will also provide management capabilities for tracking time and effort expended in the preparation and presentation of cases. Pursuant to exemptions 5 U.S.C. 552a(j)(2) of the Privacy Act, portions of this system are exempt from 5 U.S.C. 552a(c)(3) and (4); (d); (e)(1), (e)(2), (e)(3), (e)(4)(G), (e)(4)(H), (e)(5) and (e)(8); (f)(2) through (5); and (g). Pursuant to 5 U.S.C. 552a (k)(1) and (k)(2), this system is exempt from the following provisions of the Privacy Act, subject to the limitations set forth in those subsections: 5 U.S.C. 552a (c)(3), (d), (e)(1), (e)(4)(G), (e)(4)(H), and (f). Exemptions from these particular subsections are justified, on a case-by-case basis to be determined at the time a request is made, for the following reasons:

(a) From subsection (c)(3) (Accounting for Disclosures) because release of the accounting of disclosures could alert the subject of an investigation of an actual or potential criminal, civil, or regulatory violation, to the existence of the investigation, which in some cases may be classified, and reveal investigative interest on the part of DHS or ICE. Disclosure of the accounting would therefore present a serious impediment to law enforcement efforts and/or efforts to preserve national security. Disclosure of the accounting would also permit the individual who is the subject of a record to impede the investigation, tamper with witnesses or evidence, and avoid detection or apprehension, which would undermine the entire investigative process.

(b) From subsection (d) (Access to Records) because access to the records contained in this system of records could inform the subject of an investigation pertaining to an immigration matter, which in some cases may be classified, and prematurely reveal investigative interest on the part of DHS or another agency. Access to the records could permit the individual who is the subject of a record to impede the investigation, tamper with witnesses or evidence, and avoid detection or apprehension. Amendment of the records could interfere with ongoing investigations and law enforcement activities and would impose an impossible administrative burden by requiring investigations to be continuously reinvestigated. In addition, permitting access and amendment to such information could disclose security-sensitive information that could be detrimental to homeland security.

(c) From subsection (e)(1) (Relevancy and Necessity of Information) because in the course of investigations into potential violations of federal immigration law, the accuracy of information obtained or introduced occasionally may be unclear or the information may not be strictly relevant or necessary to a specific investigation. In the interests of effective law enforcement and for the protection of national security, it is appropriate to retain all information that may aid in establishing patterns of unlawful activity.

(d) From subsection (e)(2) (Collection of Information from Individuals) because requiring that information be collected from the subject of an investigation would alert the subject of the nature or existence of an investigation, which could cause interference with the investigation, a related inquiry or other law enforcement activities, some of which may be classified.

(e) From subsection (e)(3) (Notice to Subjects) because providing such detailed information would impede law enforcement in that it could compromise the existence of a confidential investigation or reveal the identity of witnesses or confidential informants.

(f) From subsections (e)(4)(G) and (H) (Agency Requirements), (f) (Agency Rules), and (g) (Civil Remedies) because portions of this system are exempt from the individual access provisions of subsection (d).

(g) From subsection (e)(5) (Collection of Information) because in the collection of information for law enforcement purposes it is impossible to determine in advance what in-

formation is accurate, relevant, timely, and complete.

(h) From subsection (e)(8) (Notice on Individuals) because compliance would interfere with ICE's ability to obtain, serve, and issue subpoenas, warrants and other law enforcement mechanisms that may be filed under seal, and could result in disclosure of investigative techniques, procedures, and evidence.

(i) From subsection (g) to the extent that the system is exempt from other specific subsections of the Privacy Act.

12. DHS/CBP–005, Advanced Passenger Information System. A portion of the following system of records is exempt from 5 U.S.C. 552a(c)(3) and (4); (d)(1), (2), (3), and (4); (e)(1), (2), (3), (4)(G) through (I), (5), and (8); (f), and (g); however, these exemptions apply only to the extent that information in this system records is recompiled or is created from information contained in other systems of records subject to such exemptions pursuant to 5 U.S.C. 552a(j)(2), and (k)(2). Further, no exemption shall be asserted with respect to information submitted by and collected from the individual or the individual's representative in the course of any redress process associated with this system of records. After conferring with the appropriate component or agency, DHS may waive applicable exemptions in appropriate circumstances and where it would not appear to interfere with or adversely affect the law enforcement or national security purposes of the systems from which the information is recompiled or in which it is contained. Exemptions from the above particular subsections are justified, on a case-by-case basis to be determined at the time a request is made, when information in this system records is recompiled or is created from information contained in other systems of records subject to exemptions for the following reasons:

(a) From subsection (c)(3) (Accounting for Disclosure) because making available to a record subject the accounting of disclosures from records concerning him or her would specifically reveal any investigative interest in the individual. Revealing this information could reasonably be expected to compromise ongoing efforts to investigate a known or suspected terrorist by notifying the record subject that he or she is under investigation. This information could also permit the record subject to take measures to impede the investigation, e.g., destroy evidence, intimidate potential witnesses, or flee the area to avoid or impede the investigation.

(b) From subsection (c)(4) (Accounting for Disclosure, notice of dispute) because portions of this system are exempt from the access and amendment provisions of subsection (d).

(c) From subsections (d)(1), (2), (3), and (4) (Access to Records) because these provisions concern individual access to and amendment of certain records contained in this system, including law enforcement counterterrorism, investigatory, and intelligence records. Compliance with these provisions could alert the subject of an investigation of the fact and nature of the investigation, and/or the investigative interest of intelligence or law enforcement agencies; compromise sensitive information related to national security; interfere with the overall law enforcement process by leading to the destruction of evidence, improper influencing of witnesses, fabrication of testimony, and/or flight of the subject; could identify a confidential source or disclose information which would constitute an unwarranted invasion of another's personal privacy; reveal a sensitive investigative or intelligence technique; or constitute a potential danger to the health or safety of law enforcement personnel, confidential informants, and witnesses. Amendment of these records would interfere with ongoing counterterrorism, law enforcement, or intelligence investigations and analysis activities and impose an impossible administrative burden by requiring investigations, analyses, and reports to be continuously re-investigated and revised.

(d) From subsection (e)(1) (Relevancy and Necessity of Information) because it is not always possible for DHS or other agencies to know in advance what information is relevant and necessary for it to complete an identity comparison between the individual seeking redress and a known or suspected terrorist. Also, because DHS and other agencies may not always know what information about an encounter with a known or suspected terrorist will be relevant to law enforcement for the purpose of conducting an operational response.

(e) From subsection (e)(2) (Collection of Information from Individuals) because application of this provision could present a serious impediment to counterterrorism, law enforcement, or intelligence efforts in that it would put the subject of an investigation, study, or analysis on notice of that fact, thereby permitting the subject to engage in conduct designed to frustrate or impede that activity. The nature of counterterrorism, law enforcement, or intelligence investigations is such that vital information about an individual frequently can be obtained only from other persons who are familiar with such individual and his/her activities. In such investigations it is not feasible to rely upon information furnished by the individual concerning his own activities.

(f) From subsection (e)(3) (Notice to Subjects), to the extent that this subsection is interpreted to require DHS to provide notice to an individual if DHS or another agency receives or collects information about that individual during an investigation or from a third party. Should the subsection be so interpreted, exemption from this provision is

necessary to avoid impeding counterterrorism, law enforcement, or intelligence efforts by putting the subject of an investigation, study, or analysis on notice of that fact, thereby permitting the subject to engage in conduct intended to frustrate or impede that activity.

(g) From subsections (e)(4)(G), (H) and (I) (Agency Requirements) because portions of this system are exempt from the access and amendment provisions of subsection (d).

(h) From subsection (e)(5) (Collection of Information) because many of the records in this system coming from other system of records are derived from other domestic and foreign agency record systems and therefore it is not possible for DHS to vouch for their compliance with this provision; however, the DHS has implemented internal quality assurance procedures to ensure that data used in the redress process is as thorough, accurate, and current as possible. In addition, in the collection of information for law enforcement, counterterrorism, and intelligence purposes, it is impossible to determine in advance what information is accurate, relevant, timely, and complete. With the passage of time, seemingly irrelevant or untimely information may acquire new significance as further investigation brings new details to light. The restrictions imposed by (e)(5) would limit the ability of those agencies' trained investigators and intelligence analysts to exercise their judgment in conducting investigations and impede the development of intelligence necessary for effective law enforcement and counterterrorism efforts. The DHS has, however, implemented internal quality assurance procedures to ensure that the data used in the redress process is as thorough, accurate, and current as possible.

(i) From subsection (e)(8) (Notice on Individuals) because to require individual notice of disclosure of information due to compulsory legal process would pose an impossible administrative burden on DHS and other agencies and could alert the subjects of counterterrorism, law enforcement, or intelligence investigations to the fact of those investigations when not previously known.

(j) From subsection (f) (Agency Rules) because portions of this system are exempt from the access and amendment provisions of subsection (d).

(k) From subsection (g) (Civil Remedies) to the extent that the system is exempt from other specific subsections of the Privacy Act.

13. The Department of Homeland Security General Training Records system of records consists of electronic and paper records and will be used by DHS and its components. The Department of Homeland Security General Training Records system of records consists of electronic and paper records and will be used by DHS and its components and offices

to maintain records about individual training, including enrollment and participation information, information pertaining to class schedules, programs, and instructors, training trends and needs, testing and examination materials, and assessments of training efficacy. The data will be collected by employee name or other unique identifier. The collection and maintenance of this information will assist DHS in meeting its obligation to train its personnel and contractors in order to ensure that the agency mission can be successfully accomplished. Pursuant to exemptions 5 U.S.C. 552a(k)(6) of the Privacy Act, portions of this system are exempt from 5 U.S.C. 552a(d) to the extent that records in this system relate to testing or examination materials used solely to determine individual qualifications for appointment in the Federal service. Access to or amendment of this information by the data subject would compromise the objectivity and fairness of the testing and examination process.

14. The U.S. ICE–005 Trade Transparency Analysis and Research (TTAR) System consists of electronic and paper records and will be used by the Department of Homeland Security (DHS). TTAR is a repository of information held by DHS in connection with its several and varied missions and functions, including, but not limited to: The enforcement of civil and criminal laws; investigations, inquiries, and proceedings there under; and national security and intelligence activities. TTAR contains information that is collected by other federal and foreign government agencies and may contain personally identifiable information. Pursuant to exemption 5 U.S.C. 552a(j)(2) of the Privacy Act, portions of this system are exempt from 5 U.S.C. 552a(c)(3) and (4); (d); (e)(1), (e)(2), (e)(3), (e)(4)(G), (e)(4)(H), (e)(5) and (e)(8); (f), and (g). Pursuant to 5 U.S.C. 552a(k)(2), this system is exempt from the following provisions of the Privacy Act, subject to the limitations set forth in those subsections: 5 U.S.C. 552a(c)(3), (d), (e)(1), (e)(4)(G), (e)(4)(H), and (f). Exemptions from these particular subsections are justified, on a case-by-case basis to be determined at the time a request is made, for the following reasons:

(a) From subsection (c)(3) and (4) (Accounting for Disclosures) because release of the accounting of disclosures could alert the subject of an investigation of an actual or potential criminal, civil, or regulatory violation to the existence of the investigation, and reveal investigative interest on the part of DHS as well as the recipient agency. Disclosure of the accounting would therefore present a serious impediment to law enforcement efforts and/or efforts to preserve national security. Disclosure of the accounting would also permit the individual who is the subject of a record to impede the investigation, to tamper with witnesses or evidence, and to avoid detection or apprehension,

which would undermine the entire investigative process.

(b) From subsection (d) (Access to Records) because access to the records contained in this system of records could inform the subject of an investigation of an actual or potential criminal, civil, or regulatory violation, to the existence of the investigation, and reveal investigative interest on the part of DHS or another agency. Access to the records could permit the individual who is the subject of a record to impede the investigation, to tamper with witnesses or evidence, and to avoid detection or apprehension. Amendment of the records could interfere with ongoing investigations and law enforcement activities and would impose an impossible administrative burden by requiring investigations to be continuously reinvestigated. In addition, permitting access and amendment to such information could disclose security-sensitive information that could be detrimental to homeland security.

(c) From subsection (e)(1) (Relevancy and Necessity of Information) because in the course of investigations into potential violations of Federal law, the accuracy of information obtained or introduced occasionally may be unclear or the information may not be strictly relevant or necessary to a specific investigation. In the interests of effective law enforcement, it is appropriate to retain all information that may aid in establishing patterns of unlawful activity.

(d) From subsection (e)(2) (Collection of Information from Individuals) because requiring that information be collected from the subject of an investigation would alert the subject to the nature or existence of an investigation, thereby interfering with the related investigation and law enforcement activities.

(e) From subsection (e)(3) (Notice to Subjects) because providing such detailed information would impede law enforcement in that it could compromise investigations by: Revealing the existence of an otherwise confidential investigation and thereby provide an opportunity for the subject of an investigation to conceal evidence, alter patterns of behavior, or take other actions that could thwart investigative efforts; reveal the identity of witnesses in investigations, thereby providing an opportunity for the subjects of the investigations or others to harass, intimidate, or otherwise interfere with the collection of evidence or other information from such witnesses; or reveal the identity of confidential informants, which would negatively affect the informant's usefulness in any ongoing or future investigations and discourage members of the public from cooperating as confidential informants in any future investigations.

(f) From subsections (e)(4)(G) and (H) (Agency Requirements), and (f) (Agency Rules) because portions of this system are exempt from the individual access provisions of subsection (d) for the reasons noted above, and therefore DHS is not required to establish requirements, rules, or procedures with respect to such access. Providing notice to individuals with respect to existence of records pertaining to them in the system of records or otherwise setting up procedures pursuant to which individuals may access and view records pertaining to themselves in the system would undermine investigative efforts and reveal the identities of witnesses, potential witnesses, and confidential informants.

(g) From subsection (e)(5) (Collection of Information) because in the collection of information for law enforcement purposes it is impossible to determine in advance what information is accurate, relevant, timely, and complete. Compliance with (e)(5) would preclude DHS agents from using their investigative training and exercise of good judgment to both conduct and report on investigations.

(h) From subsection (e)(8) (Notice on Individuals) because compliance would interfere with DHS's ability to obtain, serve, and issue subpoenas, warrants, and other law enforcement mechanisms that may be filed under seal, and could result in disclosure of investigative techniques, procedures, and evidence.

(i) From subsection (g) to the extent that the system is exempt from other specific subsections of the Privacy Act relating to individuals' rights to access and amend their records contained in the system. Therefore DHS is not required to establish rules or procedures pursuant to which individuals may seek a civil remedy for the agency's: Refusal to amend a record; refusal to comply with a request for access to records; failure to maintain accurate, relevant, timely and complete records; or failure to otherwise comply with an individual's right to access or amend records.

15. The DHS/ALL—013 Claims Records system of records consists of electronic and paper records and will be used by DHS and its components. The DHS/ALL—013 Claims Records system is a repository of information held by DHS in connection with its several and varied missions and functions, including, but not limited to: the enforcement of civil and criminal laws; investigations, inquiries, and proceedings there under; and national security, intelligence activities; and protection of the President of the United States or other individuals pursuant to section 3056 and 3056A of Title 18. The DHS/ALL—013 Claims Records system contains information that is collected by, on behalf of, in support of, or in cooperation with DHS and its components and may contain personally identifiable information collected by other Federal, State, local, Tribal, foreign, or international government agencies. The

Secretary of Homeland Security has exempted this system from the following provisions of the Privacy Act, subject to limitations set forth in 5 U.S.C. 552a(c)(3) and (4); (d); (e)(1), (e)(2), (e)(3), (e)(4)(G), (e)(4)(H), (e)(4)(I), (e)(5) and (e)(8); (f), and (g) pursuant to 5 U.S.C. 552a(j)(2). Additionally, the Secretary of Homeland Security has exempted this system from the following provisions of the Privacy Act, subject to limitations set forth in 5 U.S.C. 552a(c)(3), (d), (e)(1), (e)(4)(G), (e)(4)(H), (I), and (f) pursuant to 5 U.S.C. 552a(k)(1), (k)(2), and (k)(3). Exemptions from these particular subsections are justified, on a case-by-case basis to be determined at the time a request is made, for the following reasons:

(a) From subsection (c)(3) and (4) (Accounting for Disclosures) because release of the accounting of disclosures could alert the subject of an investigation of an actual or potential criminal, civil, or regulatory violation to the existence of the investigation, and reveal investigative interest on the part of DHS as well as the recipient agency. Disclosure of the accounting would therefore present a serious impediment to law enforcement efforts and/or efforts to preserve national security. Disclosure of the accounting would also permit the individual who is the subject of a record to impede the investigation, to tamper with witnesses or evidence, and to avoid detection or apprehension, which would undermine the entire investigative process.

(b) From subsection (d) (Access to Records) because access to the records contained in this system of records could inform the subject of an investigation of an actual or potential criminal, civil, or regulatory violation, to the existence of the investigation, and reveal investigative interest on the part of DHS or another agency. Access to the records could permit the individual who is the subject of a record to impede the investigation, to tamper with witnesses or evidence, and to avoid detection or apprehension. Amendment of the records could interfere with ongoing investigations and law enforcement activities and would impose an impossible administrative burden by requiring investigations to be continuously reinvestigated. In addition, permitting access and amendment to such information could disclose security-sensitive information that could be detrimental to homeland security.

(c) From subsection (e)(1) (Relevancy and Necessity of Information) because in the course of investigations into potential violations of Federal law, the accuracy of information obtained or introduced occasionally may be unclear or the information may not be strictly relevant or necessary to a specific investigation. In the interests of effective law enforcement, it is appropriate to retain all information that may aid in establishing patterns of unlawful activity.

(d) From subsection (e)(2) (Collection of Information from Individuals) because requiring that information be collected from the subject of an investigation would alert the subject to the nature or existence of an investigation, thereby interfering with the related investigation and law enforcement activities.

(e) From subsection (e)(3) (Notice to Subjects) because providing such detailed information would impede law enforcement in that it could compromise investigations by: revealing the existence of an otherwise confidential investigation and thereby provide an opportunity for the subject of an investigation to conceal evidence, alter patterns of behavior, or take other actions that could thwart investigative efforts; reveal the identity of witnesses in investigations, thereby providing an opportunity for the subjects of the investigations or others to harass, intimidate, or otherwise interfere with the collection of evidence or other information from such witnesses; or reveal the identity of confidential informants, which would negatively affect the informant's usefulness in any ongoing or future investigations and discourage members of the public from cooperating as confidential informants in any future investigations.

(f) From subsections (e)(4)(G), (H), and (I) (Agency Requirements), and (f) (Agency Rules) because portions of this system are exempt from the individual access provisions of subsection (d) for the reasons noted above, and therefore DHS is not required to establish requirements, rules, or procedures with respect to such access. Providing notice to individuals with respect to existence of records pertaining to them in the system of records or otherwise setting up procedures pursuant to which individuals may access and view records pertaining to themselves in the system would undermine investigative efforts and reveal the identities of witnesses, and potential witnesses, and confidential informants.

(g) From subsection (e)(5) (Collection of Information) because in the collection of information for law enforcement purposes it is impossible to determine in advance what information is accurate, relevant, timely, and complete. Compliance with (e)(5) would preclude DHS agents from using their investigative training and exercise of good judgment to both conduct and report on investigations.

(h) From subsection (e)(8) (Notice on Individuals) because compliance would interfere with DHS' ability to obtain, serve, and issue subpoenas, warrants, and other law enforcement mechanisms that may be filed under seal, and could result in disclosure of investigative techniques, procedures, and evidence.

(i) From subsection (g) to the extent that the system is exempt from other specific subsections of the Privacy Act relating to individuals' rights to access and amend their records contained in the system. Therefore DHS is not required to establish rules or procedures pursuant to which individuals may seek a civil remedy for the agency's: refusal to amend a record; refusal to comply with a request for access to records; failure to maintain accurate, relevant timely and complete records; or failure to otherwise comply with an individual's right to access or amend records.

16. The DHS/ALL—018 Grievances, Appeals and Disciplinary Action Records system of records consists of electronic and paper records and will be used by DHS and its components. The DHS/ALL—018 Grievances, Appeals and Disciplinary Action Records system is a repository of information held by DHS in connection with its several and varied missions and functions, including, but not limited to: the enforcement of civil and criminal laws; investigations, inquiries, and proceedings there under; national security and intelligence activities; and protection of the President of the United States or other individuals pursuant to section 3056 and 3056A of Title 18. The DHS/ALL—018 Grievances, Appeals and Disciplinary Action Records system contains information that is collected by, on behalf of, in support of, or in cooperation with DHS and its components and may contain personally identifiable information collected by other Federal, State, local, tribal, foreign, or international government agencies. The Secretary of Homeland Security has exempted this system from the following provisions of the Privacy Act, subject to the limitations set forth in 5 U.S.C. 552a(c)(3) and (4); (d); (e)(1), (e)(2), (e)(3), (e)(4)(G), (e)(4)(H), (e)(4)(I), (e)(5) and (e)(8); (f), and (g) pursuant to 5 U.S.C. 552a(j)(2). Additionally, the Secretary of Homeland Security has exempted this system from the following provisions of the Privacy Act, subject to the limitations set forth in 5 U.S.C. 552a(c)(3), (d), (e)(1), (e)(4)(G), (e)(4)(H), (e)(4)(I), and (f) pursuant to 5 U.S.C. 552a(k)(1), (k)(2), (k)(3), and (k)(5). Exemptions from these particular subsections are justified, on a case-by-case basis to be determined at the time a request is made, for the following reasons:

(a) From subsection (c)(3) and (4) (Accounting for Disclosures) because release of the accounting of disclosures could alert the subject of an investigation of an actual or potential criminal, civil, or regulatory violation to the existence of the investigation, and reveal investigative interest on the part of DHS as well as the recipient agency. Disclosure of the accounting would therefore present a serious impediment to law enforcement efforts and/or efforts to preserve national security. Disclosure of the accounting would also permit the individual who is the subject of a record to impede the investigation, to tamper with witnesses or evidence, and to avoid detection or apprehension, which would undermine the entire investigative process.

(b) From subsection (d) (Access to Records) because access to the records contained in this system of records could inform the subject of an investigation of an actual or potential criminal, civil, or regulatory violation, to the existence of the investigation, and reveal investigative interest on the part of DHS or another agency. Access to the records could permit the individual who is the subject of a record to impede the investigation, to tamper with witnesses or evidence, and to avoid detection or apprehension. Amendment of the records could interfere with ongoing investigations and law enforcement activities and would impose an impossible administrative burden by requiring investigations to be continuously reinvestigated. In addition, permitting access and amendment to such information could disclose security-sensitive information that could be detrimental to homeland security.

(c) From subsection (e)(1) (Relevancy and Necessity of Information) because in the course of investigations into potential violations of Federal law, the accuracy of information obtained or introduced occasionally may be unclear or the information may not be strictly relevant or necessary to a specific investigation. In the interests of effective law enforcement, it is appropriate to retain all information that may aid in establishing patterns of unlawful activity.

(d) From subsection (e)(2) (Collection of Information from Individuals) because requiring that information be collected from the subject of an investigation would alert the subject to the nature or existence of an investigation, thereby interfering with the related investigation and law enforcement activities.

(e) From subsection (e)(3) (Notice to Subjects) because providing such detailed information would impede law enforcement in that it could compromise investigations by: revealing the existence of an otherwise confidential investigation and thereby provide an opportunity for the subject of an investigation to conceal evidence, alter patterns of behavior, or take other actions that could thwart investigative efforts; reveal the identity of witnesses in investigations, thereby providing an opportunity for the subjects of the investigations or others to harass, intimidate, or otherwise interfere with the collection of evidence or other information from such witnesses; or reveal the identity of confidential informants, which would negatively affect the informant's usefulness in any ongoing or future investigations and discourage members of the public from cooperating as confidential informants in any future investigations.

(f) From subsections (e)(4)(G), (H), and (I) (Agency Requirements), and (f) (Agency Rules) because portions of this system are exempt from the individual access provisions of subsection (d) for the reasons noted above, and therefore DHS is not required to establish requirements, rules, or procedures with respect to such access. Providing notice to individuals with respect to existence of records pertaining to them in the system of records or otherwise setting up procedures pursuant to which individuals may access and view records pertaining to themselves in the system would undermine investigative efforts and reveal the identities of witnesses, and potential witnesses, and confidential informants.

(g) From subsection (e)(5) (Collection of Information) because in the collection of information for law enforcement purposes it is impossible to determine in advance what information is accurate, relevant, timely, and complete. Compliance with (e)(5) would preclude DHS agents from using their investigative training and exercise of good judgment to both conduct and report on investigations.

(h) From subsection (e)(8) (Notice on Individuals) because compliance would interfere with DHS' ability to obtain, serve, and issue subpoenas, warrants, and other law enforcement mechanisms that may be filed under seal, and could result in disclosure of investigative techniques, procedures, and evidence.

(i) From subsection (g) to the extent that the system is exempt from other specific subsections of the Privacy Act relating to individuals' rights to access and amend their records contained in the system. Therefore DHS is not required to establish rules or procedures pursuant to which individuals may seek a civil remedy for the agency's: Refusal to amend a record; refusal to comply with a request for access to records; failure to maintain accurate, relevant timely and complete records; or failure to otherwise comply with an individual's right to access or amend records.

17. The DHS/ALL—006 Accident Records system of records consists of electronic and paper records and will be used by DHS and its components. The DHS/ALL—006 Accident Records system is a repository of information held by DHS in connection with its several and varied missions and functions, including, but not limited to: the enforcement of civil and criminal laws; investigations, inquiries, and proceedings thereunder; national security and intelligence activities; and protection of the President of the United States or other individuals pursuant to section 3056 and 3056A of Title 18. The DHS/ALL—006 Accident Records system contains information that is collected by, on behalf of, in support

of, or in cooperation with DHS and its components and may contain personally identifiable information collected by other Federal, State, local, tribal, foreign, or international government agencies. The Secretary of Homeland Security has exempted this system from the following provisions of the Privacy Act, subject to the limitations set forth in 5 U.S.C. 552a(d) pursuant to 5 U.S.C. 552a(k)(3). Exemptions from these particular subsections are justified, on a case-by-case basis to be determined at the time a request is made, for the following reasons: From subsection (d) (Access to Records) because access to the records contained in this system of records could inform the subject of information related to the protection of a President of the United States or other individuals pursuant to section 3056 and 3056A of Title 18. Permitting access and amendment to such information could disclose security-sensitive information that could be detrimental to homeland security.

18. The DHS/ALL—020 Internal Affairs Records system of records consists of electronic and paper records and will be used by DHS and its components. The DHS/ALL—020 Internal Affairs Records system is a repository of information held by DHS in connection with its several and varied missions and functions, including, but not limited to: The enforcement of civil and criminal laws; investigations, inquiries, and proceedings thereunder; national security and intelligence activities; and protection of the President of the United States or other individuals pursuant to section 3056 and 3056A of Title 18. The DHS/ALL—020 Internal Affairs Records system contains information that is collected by, on behalf of, in support of, or in cooperation with DHS and its components and may contain personally identifiable information collected by other Federal, State, local, tribal, foreign, or international government agencies. The Secretary of Homeland Security has exempted this system from the following provisions of the Privacy Act, subject to the limitations set forth in 5 U.S.C. 552a(c)(3) and (4); (d); (e)(1), (e)(2), (e)(3), (e)(4)(G), (e)(4)(H), (e)(4)(I), (e)(5) and (e)(8); (f), and (g) pursuant to 5 U.S.C. 552a(j)(2). Additionally, the Secretary of Homeland Security has exempted this system from the following provisions of the Privacy Act, subject to the limitations set forth in 5 U.S.C. 552a (c)(3), (d), (e)(1), (e)(4)(G), (e)(4)(H), (e)(4)(I), and (f) pursuant to 5 U.S.C. 552a(k)(1), (k)(2), (k)(3), and (k)(5). Exemptions from these particular subsections are justified, on a case-by-case basis to be determined at the time a request is made, for the following reasons:

(a) From subsection (c)(3) and (4) (Accounting for Disclosures) because release of the accounting of disclosures could alert the subject of an investigation of an actual or potential criminal, civil, or regulatory violation to the existence of the investigation, and reveal investigative interest on the part of DHS as well as the recipient agency. Disclosure of the accounting would therefore present a serious impediment to law enforcement efforts and/or efforts to preserve national security. Disclosure of the accounting would also permit the individual who is the subject of a record to impede the investigation, to tamper with witnesses or evidence, and to avoid detection or apprehension, which would undermine the entire investigative process.

(b) From subsection (d) (Access to Records) because access to the records contained in this system of records could inform the subject of an investigation of an actual or potential criminal, civil, or regulatory violation, to the existence of the investigation, and reveal investigative interest on the part of DHS or another agency. Access to the records could permit the individual who is the subject of a record to impede the investigation, to tamper with witnesses or evidence, and to avoid detection or apprehension. Amendment of the records could interfere with ongoing investigations and law enforcement activities and would impose an impossible administrative burden by requiring investigations to be continuously reinvestigated. In addition, permitting access and amendment to such information could disclose security-sensitive information that could be detrimental to homeland security.

(c) From subsection (e)(1) (Relevancy and Necessity of Information) because in the course of investigations into potential violations of Federal law, the accuracy of information obtained or introduced occasionally may be unclear or the information may not be strictly relevant or necessary to a specific investigation. In the interests of effective law enforcement, it is appropriate to retain all information that may aid in establishing patterns of unlawful activity.

(d) From subsection (e)(2) (Collection of Information from Individuals) because requiring that information be collected from the subject of an investigation would alert the subject to the nature or existence of an investigation, thereby interfering with the related investigation and law enforcement activities.

(e) From subsection (e)(3) (Notice to Subjects) because providing such detailed information would impede law enforcement in that it could compromise investigations by: revealing the existence of an otherwise confidential investigation and thereby provide an opportunity for the subject of an investigation to conceal evidence, alter patterns of behavior, or take other actions that could thwart investigative efforts; reveal the identity of witnesses in investigations, thereby providing an opportunity for the subjects of the investigations or others to harass, intimidate, or otherwise interfere with the collection of evidence or other information from such witnesses; or reveal the identity of confidential informants, which would negatively affect the informant's usefulness in any ongoing or future investigations and discourage members of the public from cooperating as confidential informants in any future investigations.

(f) From subsections (e)(4)(G), (H), and (I) (Agency Requirements), and (f) (Agency Rules) because portions of this system are exempt from the individual access provisions of subsection (d) for the reasons noted above, and therefore DHS is not required to establish requirements, rules, or procedures with respect to such access. Providing notice to individuals with respect to existence of records pertaining to them in the system of records or otherwise setting up procedures pursuant to which individuals may access and view records pertaining to themselves in the system would undermine investigative efforts and reveal the identities of witnesses, and potential witnesses, and confidential informants.

(g) From subsection (e)(5) (Collection of Information) because in the collection of information for law enforcement purposes it is impossible to determine in advance what information is accurate, relevant, timely, and complete. Compliance with (e)(5) would preclude DHS agents from using their investigative training, and exercise of good judgment to both conduct and report on investigations.

(h) From subsection (e)(8) (Notice on Individuals) because compliance would interfere with DHS' ability to obtain, serve, and issue subpoenas, warrants, and other law enforcement mechanisms that may be filed under seal, and could result in disclosure of investigative techniques, procedures, and evidence.

(i) From subsection (g) to the extent that the system is exempt from other specific subsections of the Privacy Act relating to individuals' rights to access and amend their records contained in the system. Therefore DHS is not required to establish rules or procedures pursuant to which individuals may seek a civil remedy for the agency's: refusal to amend a record; refusal to comply with a request for access to records; failure to maintain accurate, relevant timely and complete records; or failure to otherwise comply with an individual's right to access or amend records.

19. The DHS/ALL—024 Facility and Perimeter Access Control and Visitor Management system of records consists of electronic and paper records and will be used by DHS and its components. The DHS/ALL—024 Facility and Perimeter Access Control and Visitor Management system is a repository of information held by DHS in connection with its several and varied missions and functions, including, but not limited to: the enforcement of civil and criminal laws; investigations, inquiries, and proceedings there under; and national security and intelligence activities. The DHS/ALL—024 Facility and Perimeter Access Control and Visitor Management system contains information that is collected by, on behalf of, in support of, or in cooperation with DHS and its components and may contain personally identifiable information collected by other Federal, State, local, tribal, foreign, or international government agencies. The Secretary of Homeland Security has exempted this system from the following provisions of the Privacy Act, subject to the limitations set forth in 5 U.S.C. 552a (c)(3), (d), (e)(1), (e)(4)(G), (e)(4)(H), (e)(4)(I), and (f) pursuant to 5 U.S.C. 552a(k)(1), (k)(2), and (k)(5). Exemptions from these particular subsections are justified, on a case-by-case basis to be determined at the time a request is made, for the following reasons:

(a) From subsection (c)(3) (Accounting for Disclosures) because release of the accounting of disclosures could alert the subject of an investigation of an actual or potential criminal, civil, or regulatory violation to the existence of the investigation, and reveal investigative interest on the part of DHS as well as the recipient agency. Disclosure of the accounting would therefore present a serious impediment to law enforcement efforts and/or efforts to preserve national security. Disclosure of the accounting would also permit the individual who is the subject of a record to impede the investigation, to tamper with witnesses or evidence, and to avoid detection or apprehension, which would undermine the entire investigative process.

(b) From subsection (d) (Access to Records) because access to the records contained in this system of records could inform the subject of an investigation of an actual or potential criminal, civil, or regulatory violation, to the existence of the investigation, and reveal investigative interest on the part of DHS or another agency. Access to the records could permit the individual who is the subject of a record to impede the investigation, to tamper with witnesses or evidence, and to avoid detection or apprehension. Amendment of the records could interfere with ongoing investigations and law enforcement activities and would impose an impossible administrative burden by requiring investigations to be continuously reinvestigated. In addition, permitting access and amendment to such information could disclose security-sensitive information that could be detrimental to homeland security.

(c) From subsection (e)(1) (Relevancy and Necessity of Information) because in the course of investigations into potential violations of Federal law, the accuracy of information obtained or introduced occasionally

61

may be unclear or the information may not be strictly relevant or necessary to a specific investigation. In the interests of effective law enforcement, it is appropriate to retain all information that may aid in establishing patterns of unlawful activity.

(d) From subsections (e)(4)(G), (e)(4)(H), and (e)(4)(I) (Agency Requirements), and (f) (Agency Rules) because portions of this system are exempt from the individual access provisions of subsection (d) for the reasons noted above, and therefore DHS is not required to establish requirements, rules, or procedures with respect to such access. Providing notice to individuals with respect to existence of records pertaining to them in the system of records or otherwise setting up procedures pursuant to which individuals may access and view records pertaining to themselves in the system would undermine investigative efforts and reveal the identities of witnesses, and potential witnesses, and confidential informants.

20. The DHS/CBP—009 Electronic System for Travel Authorization system of records consists of electronic and paper records and will be used by DHS and it's Components. The DHS/CBP—009 Electronic System for Travel Authorization system is a repository of information held by DHS in connection with its several and varied missions and functions, including, but not limited to: The enforcement of civil and criminal laws; investigations, inquiries, and proceedings thereunder; and national security and intelligence activities. The DHS/CBP—009 Electronic System for Travel Authorization system contains information that is collected by, on behalf of, in support of, or in cooperation with DHS and its components and may contain personally identifiable information collected by other Federal, State, local, tribal, foreign, or international government agencies. The Secretary of Homeland Security has exempted this system from the following provisions of the Privacy Act, subject to the limitations set forth in 5 U.S.C. 552a(c)(3), (e)(8), and (g) pursuant to 5 U.S.C. 552a(j)(2), and (k)(2). Further, no exemption shall be asserted with respect to information maintained in the system as it relates to data submitted by or on behalf of a person who travels to visit the United States and crosses the border, nor shall an exemption be asserted with respect to the resulting determination (approval or denial). After conferring with the appropriate component or agency, DHS may waive applicable exemptions in appropriate circumstances and where it would not appear to interfere with or adversely affect the law enforcement purposes of the systems from which the information is recompiled or in which it is contained. Exemptions from the above particular subsections are justified, on a case-by-case basis to be determined at the time a request is made, when information in this system of records may impede a law enforcement or national security investigation:

(a) From subsection (c)(3) (Accounting for Disclosure) because making available to a record subject the accounting of disclosures from records concerning him or her would specifically reveal any investigative interest in the individual. Revealing this information could reasonably be expected to compromise ongoing efforts to investigate a violation of U.S. law, including investigations of a known or suspected terrorist, by notifying the record subject that he or she is under investigation. This information could also permit the record subject to take measures to impede the investigation, e.g., destroy evidence, intimidate potential witnesses, or flee the area to avoid or impede the investigation.

(b) From subsection (e)(8) (Notice on Individuals) because to require individual notice of disclosure of information due to compulsory legal process would pose an impossible administrative burden on DHS and other agencies and could alert the subjects of counterterrorism or law enforcement investigations to the fact of those investigations when not previously known.

(c) From subsection (g) (Civil Remedies) to the extent that the system is exempt from other specific subsections of the Privacy Act.

21. The DHS/CBP—010 Persons Engaged in International Trade in CBP Licensed/Regulated Activities system of records consists of electronic and paper records and will be used by DHS and its components. The DHS/CBP—010 Persons Engaged in International Trade in CBP Licensed/Regulated Activities is a repository of information held by DHS in connection with its several and varied missions and functions, including, but not limited to: The enforcement of civil and criminal laws; investigations, inquiries, and proceedings thereunder; and national security and intelligence activities. The DHS/CBP—010 Persons Engaged in International Trade in CBP Licensed/Regulated Activities contains information that is collected by, on behalf of, in support of, or in cooperation with DHS and its components and may contain personally identifiable information collected by other Federal, State, local, tribal, foreign, or international government agencies. The Secretary of Homeland Security has exempted this system from the following provisions of the Privacy Act, subject to the limitations set forth in 5 U.S.C. 552a(c)(3) and (4); (d); (e)(1), (e)(2), (e)(3), (e)(4)(G), (e)(4)(H), (e)(4)(I), (e)(5) and (e)(8); (f), and (g) pursuant to 5 U.S.C. 552a(j)(2). Additionally, the Secretary of Homeland Security has exempted this system from the following provisions of the Privacy Act, subject to the limitations set forth in 5 U.S.C. 552a (c)(3), (d), (e)(1), (e)(4)(G), (e)(4)(H), (e)(4)(I), and (f) pursuant to 5 U.S.C. 552a(k)(2). Exemptions from these particular subsections are justified, on a

case-by-case basis to be determined at the time a request is made, for the following reasons:

(a) From subsection (c)(3) and (4) (Accounting for Disclosures) because release of the accounting of disclosures could alert the subject of an investigation of an actual or potential criminal, civil, or regulatory violation to the existence of the investigation, and reveal investigative interest on the part of DHS as well as the recipient agency. Disclosure of the accounting would therefore present a serious impediment to law enforcement efforts and/or efforts to preserve national security. Disclosure of the accounting would also permit the individual who is the subject of a record to impede the investigation, to tamper with witnesses or evidence, and to avoid detection or apprehension, which would undermine the entire investigative process.

(b) From subsection (d) (Access to Records) because access to the records contained in this system of records could inform the subject of an investigation of an actual or potential criminal, civil, or regulatory violation, to the existence of the investigation, and reveal investigative interest on the part of DHS or another agency. Access to the records could permit the individual who is the subject of a record to impede the investigation, to tamper with witnesses or evidence, and to avoid detection or apprehension. Amendment of the records could interfere with ongoing investigations and law enforcement activities and would impose an impossible administrative burden by requiring investigations to be continuously reinvestigated. In addition, permitting access and amendment to such information could disclose security-sensitive information that could be detrimental to national security.

(c) From subsection (e)(1) (Relevancy and Necessity of Information) because in the course of investigations into potential violations of Federal law, the accuracy of information obtained or introduced occasionally may be unclear or the information may not be strictly relevant or necessary to a specific investigation. In the interests of effective law enforcement, it is appropriate to retain all information that may aid in establishing patterns of unlawful activity.

(d) From subsection (e)(2) (Collection of Information from Individuals) because requiring that information be collected from the subject of an investigation would alert the subject to the nature or existence of an investigation, thereby interfering with the related investigation and law enforcement activities.

(e) From subsection (e)(3) (Notice to Subjects) because providing such detailed information would impede law enforcement in that it could compromise investigations by: Revealing the existence of an otherwise confidential investigation and thereby provide an opportunity for the subject of an investigation to conceal evidence, alter patterns of behavior, or take other actions that could thwart investigative efforts; reveal the identity of witnesses in investigations, thereby providing an opportunity for the subjects of the investigations or others to harass, intimidate, or otherwise interfere with the collection of evidence or other information from such witnesses; or reveal the identity of confidential informants, which would negatively affect the informant's usefulness in any ongoing or future investigations and discourage members of the public from cooperating as confidential informants in any future investigations.

(f) From subsections (e)(4)(G), (H), and (I) (Agency Requirements), and (f) (Agency Rules) because portions of this system are exempt from the individual access provisions of subsection (d) for the reasons noted above, and therefore DHS is not required to establish requirements, rules, or procedures with respect to such access. Providing notice to individuals with respect to existence of records pertaining to them in the system of records or otherwise setting up procedures pursuant to which individuals may access and view records pertaining to themselves in the system would undermine investigative efforts and reveal the identities of witnesses, and potential witnesses, and confidential informants.

(g) From subsection (e)(5) (Collection of Information) because in the collection of information for law enforcement purposes it is impossible to determine in advance what information is accurate, relevant, timely, and complete. Compliance with (e)(5) would preclude DHS agents from using their investigative training and exercise of good judgment to both conduct and report on investigations.

(h) From subsection (e)(8) (Notice on Individuals) because compliance would interfere with DHS' ability to obtain, serve, and issue subpoenas, warrants, and other law enforcement mechanisms that may be filed under seal, and could result in disclosure of investigative techniques, procedures, and evidence.

(i) From subsection (g) to the extent that the system is exempt from other specific subsections of the Privacy Act relating to individuals' rights to access and amend their records contained in the system. Therefore DHS is not required to establish rules or procedures pursuant to which individuals may seek a civil remedy for the agency's: Refusal to amend a record; refusal to comply with a request for access to records; failure to maintain accurate, relevant, timely and complete records; or failure to otherwise comply with an individual's right to access or amend records.

22. The DHS/CBP—011 TECS system of records consists of electronic and paper

records and will be used by DHS, its Components, and other Federal agencies. The DHS/CBP–011 TECS is a repository of information held by DHS in connection with its several and varied missions and functions, including, but not limited to: The enforcement of civil and criminal laws; investigations, inquiries, and proceedings thereunder; and national security and intelligence activities. The DHS/CBP–011 TECS contains information that is collected by, on behalf of, in support of, or in cooperation with DHS and its components and may contain personally identifiable information collected by other Federal, State, local, Tribal, foreign, or international government agencies. The Secretary of Homeland Security has exempted this system from the following provisions of the Privacy Act, subject to the limitations set forth in 5 U.S.C. 552a(c)(3) and (4); (d); (e)(1), (e)(2), (e)(3), (e)(4)(G), (e)(4)(H), (e)(4)(I), (e)(5) and (e)(8); (f), and (g) pursuant to 5 U.S.C. 552a(j)(2). Additionally, the Secretary of Homeland Security has exempted this system from the following provisions of the Privacy Act, subject to the limitations set forth in 5 U.S.C. 552a (c)(3), (d), (e)(1), (e)(4)(G), (e)(4)(H), (e)(4)(I), and (f) pursuant to 5 U.S.C. 552a(k)(2). Exemptions from these particular subsections are justified, on a case-by-case basis to be determined at the time a request is made, for the following reasons:

(a) From subsection (c)(3) and (4) (Accounting for Disclosures) because release of the accounting of disclosures could alert the subject of an investigation of an actual or potential criminal, civil, or regulatory violation to the existence of the investigation, and reveal investigative interest on the part of DHS as well as the recipient agency. Disclosure of the accounting would therefore present a serious impediment to law enforcement efforts and/or efforts to preserve national security. Disclosure of the accounting would also permit the individual who is the subject of a record to impede the investigation, to tamper with witnesses or evidence, and to avoid detection or apprehension, which would undermine the entire investigative process.

(b) From subsection (d) (Access to Records) because access to the records contained in this system of records could inform the subject of an investigation of an actual or potential criminal, civil, or regulatory violation, to the existence of the investigation, and reveal investigative interest on the part of DHS or another agency. Access to the records could permit the individual who is the subject of a record to impede the investigation, to tamper with witnesses or evidence, and to avoid detection or apprehension. Amendment of the records could interfere with ongoing investigations and law enforcement activities and would impose an impossible administrative burden by requiring investigations to be continuously re-investigated. In addition, permitting access and amendment to such information could disclose security-sensitive information that could be detrimental to national security.

(c) From subsection (e)(1) (Relevancy and Necessity of Information) because in the course of investigations into potential violations of Federal law, the accuracy of information obtained or introduced occasionally may be unclear or the information may not be strictly relevant or necessary to a specific investigation. In the interests of effective law enforcement, it is appropriate to retain all information that may aid in establishing patterns of unlawful activity.

(d) From subsection (e)(2) (Collection of Information from Individuals) because requiring that information be collected from the subject of an investigation or subject of interest would alert the subject to the nature or existence of an investigation, thereby interfering with the related investigation and law enforcement activities or national security matter.

(e) From subsection (e)(3) (Notice to Subjects) because providing such detailed information would impede law enforcement in that it could compromise investigations by: Revealing the existence of an otherwise confidential investigation and thereby provide an opportunity for the subject of an investigation to conceal evidence, alter patterns of behavior, or take other actions that could thwart investigative efforts; reveal the identity of witnesses in investigations, thereby providing an opportunity for the subjects of the investigations or others to harass, intimidate, or otherwise interfere with the collection of evidence or other information from such witnesses; or reveal the identity of confidential informants, which would negatively affect the informant's usefulness in any ongoing or future investigations and discourage members of the public from cooperating as confidential informants in any future investigations.

(f) From subsections (e)(4)(G), (H), and (I) (Agency Requirements), and (f) (Agency Rules) because portions of this system are exempt from the individual access provisions of subsection (d) for the reasons noted above, and therefore DHS is not required to establish requirements, rules, or procedures with respect to such access. Providing notice to individuals with respect to existence of records pertaining to them in the system of records or otherwise setting up procedures pursuant to which individuals may access and view records pertaining to themselves in the system would undermine investigative efforts and reveal the identities of witnesses, and potential witnesses, and confidential informants.

(g) From subsection (e)(5) (Collection of Information) because in the collection of information for law enforcement purposes it is impossible to determine in advance what information is accurate, relevant, timely, and complete. Compliance with (e)(5) would preclude DHS agents from using their investigative training and exercise of good judgment to both conduct and report on investigations.

(h) From subsection (e)(8) (Notice on Individuals) because compliance would interfere with DHS' ability to obtain, serve, and issue subpoenas, warrants, and other law enforcement mechanisms that may be filed under seal, and could result in disclosure of investigative techniques, procedures, and evidence.

(i) From subsection (g) to the extent that the system is exempt from other specific subsections of the Privacy Act relating to individuals' rights to access and amend their records contained in the system. Therefore DHS is not required to establish rules or procedures pursuant to which individuals may seek a civil remedy for the agency's: Refusal to amend a record; refusal to comply with a request for access to records; failure to maintain accurate, relevant, timely and complete records; or failure to otherwise comply with an individual's right to access or amend records.

23. The DHS/CBP—012 Closed Circuit Television system of records consists of electronic and paper records and will be used by DHS and its components. The DHS/CBP—012 Closed Circuit Television system is a repository of information held by DHS in connection with its several and varied missions and functions, including, but not limited to: The enforcement of civil and criminal laws; investigations, inquiries, and proceedings thereunder; and national security and intelligence activities. The DHS/CBP—012 Closed Circuit Television system contains information that is collected by, on behalf of, in support of, or in cooperation with DHS and its components and may contain personally identifiable information collected by other Federal, State, local, tribal, foreign, or international government agencies. The Secretary of Homeland Security has exempted this system from the following provisions of the Privacy Act, subject to the limitations set forth in 5 U.S.C. 552a(c)(3) and (4); (d); (e)(1), (e)(2), (e)(3), (e)(4)(G), (e)(4)(H), (e)(4)(I), (e)(5) and (e)(8); (f), and (g) pursuant to 5 U.S.C. 552a(j)(2). Additionally, the Secretary of Homeland Security has exempted this system from the following provisions of the Privacy Act, subject to the limitations set forth in 5 U.S.C. 552a(c)(3), (d), (e)(1), (e)(4)(G), (e)(4)(H), (e)(4)(I), and (f) pursuant to 5 U.S.C. 552a(k)(2). Exemptions from these particular subsections are justified, on a case-by-case basis to be determined at the time a request is made, for the following reasons:

(a) From subsection (c)(3) and (4) (Accounting for Disclosures) because release of the accounting of disclosures could alert the subject of an investigation of an actual or potential criminal, civil, or regulatory violation to the existence of the investigation, and reveal investigative interest on the part of DHS as well as the recipient agency. Disclosure of the accounting would therefore present a serious impediment to law enforcement efforts and/or efforts to preserve national security. Disclosure of the accounting would also permit the individual who is the subject of a record to impede the investigation, to tamper with witnesses or evidence, and to avoid detection or apprehension, which would undermine the entire investigative process.

(b) From subsection (d) (Access to Records) because access to the records contained in this system of records could inform the subject of an investigation of an actual or potential criminal, civil, or regulatory violation, to the existence of the investigation, and reveal investigative interest on the part of DHS or another agency. Access to the records could permit the individual who is the subject of a record to impede the investigation, to tamper with witnesses or evidence, and to avoid detection or apprehension. Amendment of the records could interfere with ongoing investigations and law enforcement activities and would impose an impossible administrative burden by requiring investigations to be continuously reinvestigated. In addition, permitting access and amendment to such information could disclose security-sensitive information that could be detrimental to homeland security.

(c) From subsection (e)(1) (Relevancy and Necessity of Information) because in the course of investigations into potential violations of Federal law, the accuracy of information obtained or introduced occasionally may be unclear or the information may not be strictly relevant or necessary to a specific investigation. In the interests of effective law enforcement, it is appropriate to retain all information that may aid in establishing patterns of unlawful activity.

(d) From subsection (e)(2) (Collection of Information from Individuals) because requiring that information be collected from the subject of an investigation would alert the subject to the nature or existence of an investigation, thereby interfering with the related investigation and law enforcement activities.

(e) From subsection (e)(3) (Notice to Subjects) because providing such detailed information would impede law enforcement in that it could compromise investigations by: Revealing the existence of an otherwise confidential investigation and thereby provide an opportunity for the subject of an investigation to conceal evidence, alter patterns of behavior, or take other actions that could thwart investigative efforts; reveal the identity of witnesses in investigations, thereby providing an opportunity for the subjects of the investigations or others to harass, intimidate, or otherwise interfere with the collection of evidence or other information from such witnesses; or reveal the identity of confidential informants, which would negatively affect the informant's usefulness in any ongoing or future investigations and discourage members of the public from cooperating as confidential informants in any future investigations.

(f) From subsections (e)(4)(G), (H), and (I) (Agency Requirements), and (f) (Agency Rules) because portions of this system are exempt from the individual access provisions of subsection (d) for the reasons noted above, and therefore DHS is not required to establish requirements, rules, or procedures with respect to such access. Providing notice to individuals with respect to existence of records pertaining to them in the system of records or otherwise setting up procedures pursuant to which individuals may access and view records pertaining to themselves in the system would undermine investigative efforts and reveal the identities of witnesses, and potential witnesses, and confidential informants.

(g) From subsection (e)(5) (Collection of Information) because in the collection of information for law enforcement purposes it is impossible to determine in advance what information is accurate, relevant, timely, and complete. Compliance with (e)(5) would preclude DHS agents from using their investigative training and exercise of good judgment to both conduct and report on investigations.

(h) From subsection (e)(8) (Notice on Individuals) because compliance would interfere with DHS' ability to obtain, serve, and issue subpoenas, warrants, and other law enforcement mechanisms that may be filed under seal, and could result in disclosure of investigative techniques, procedures, and evidence.

(i) From subsection (g) to the extent that the system is exempt from other specific subsections of the Privacy Act relating to individuals' rights to access and amend their records contained in the system. Therefore DHS is not required to establish rules or procedures pursuant to which individuals may seek a civil remedy for the agency's: Refusal to amend a record; refusal to comply with a request for access to records; failure to maintain accurate, relevant, timely and complete records; or failure to otherwise comply with an individual's right to access or amend records.

24. The DHS/CBP—013 Seized Assets and Case Tracking System (SEACATS) consists of electronic and paper records and will be used by DHS and its components. The DHS/CBP—013 Seized Assets and Case Tracking System is a repository of information held by DHS in connection with its several and

varied missions and functions, including, but not limited to: The enforcement of civil and criminal laws; investigations, inquiries, and proceedings thereunder; and national security and intelligence activities. The DHS/CBP—013 Seized Assets and Case Tracking System contains information that is collected by, on behalf of, in support of, or in cooperation with DHS and its components and may contain personally identifiable information collected by other Federal, State, local, tribal, foreign, or international government agencies. The Secretary of Homeland Security has exempted this system from the following provisions of the Privacy Act, subject to the limitations set forth in 5 U.S.C. 552a(c)(3) and (4); (d); (e)(1), (e)(2), (e)(3), (e)(4)(G), (e)(4)(H), (e)(4)(I), (e)(5) and (e)(8); (f), and (g) pursuant to 5 U.S.C. 552a(j)(2). Additionally, the Secretary of Homeland Security has exempted this system from the following provisions of the Privacy Act, subject to the limitations set forth in 5 U.S.C. 552a (c)(3), (d), (e)(1), (e)(4)(G), (e)(4)(H), (I), and (f) pursuant to 5 U.S.C. 552a(k)(2). Exemptions from these particular subsections are justified, on a case-by-case basis to be determined at the time a request is made, for the following reasons:

(a) From subsection (c)(3) and (4) (Accounting for Disclosures) because release of the accounting of disclosures could alert the subject of an investigation of an actual or potential criminal, civil, or regulatory violation to the existence of the investigation, and reveal investigative interest on the part of DHS as well as the recipient agency. Disclosure of the accounting would therefore present a serious impediment to law enforcement efforts and/or efforts to preserve national security. Disclosure of the accounting would also permit the individual who is the subject of a record to impede the investigation, to tamper with witnesses or evidence, and to avoid detection or apprehension, which would undermine the entire investigative process.

(b) From subsection (d) (Access to Records) because access to the records contained in this system of records could inform the subject of an investigation of an actual or potential criminal, civil, or regulatory violation, to the existence of the investigation, and reveal investigative interest on the part of DHS or another agency. Access to the records could permit the individual who is the subject of a record to impede the investigation, to tamper with witnesses or evidence, and to avoid detection or apprehension. Amendment of the records could interfere with ongoing investigations and law enforcement activities and would impose an impossible administrative burden by requiring investigations to be continuously reinvestigated. In addition, permitting access and amendment to such information could disclose security-sensitive information that could be detrimental to national security.

(c) From subsection (e)(1) (Relevancy and Necessity of Information) because in the course of investigations into potential violations of Federal law, the accuracy of information obtained or introduced occasionally may be unclear or the information may not be strictly relevant or necessary to a specific investigation. In the interests of effective law enforcement, it is appropriate to retain all information that may aid in establishing patterns of unlawful activity.

(d) From subsection (e)(2) (Collection of Information from Individuals) because requiring that information be collected from the subject of an investigation would alert the subject to the nature or existence of an investigation, thereby interfering with the related investigation and law enforcement activities.

(e) From subsection (e)(3) (Notice to Subjects) because providing such detailed information would impede law enforcement in that it could compromise investigations by: Revealing the existence of an otherwise confidential investigation and thereby provide an opportunity for the subject of an investigation to conceal evidence, alter patterns of behavior, or take other actions that could thwart investigative efforts; reveal the identity of witnesses in investigations, thereby providing an opportunity for the subjects of the investigations or others to harass, intimidate, or otherwise interfere with the collection of evidence or other information from such witnesses; or reveal the identity of confidential informants, which would negatively affect the informant's usefulness in any ongoing or future investigations and discourage members of the public from cooperating as confidential informants in any future investigations.

(f) From subsections (e)(4)(G), (H), and (I) (Agency Requirements), and (f) (Agency Rules) because portions of this system are exempt from the individual access provisions of subsection (d) for the reasons noted above, and therefore DHS is not required to establish requirements, rules, or procedures with respect to such access. Providing notice to individuals with respect to existence of records pertaining to them in the system of records or otherwise setting up procedures pursuant to which individuals may access and view records pertaining to themselves in the system would undermine investigative efforts and reveal the identities of witnesses, and potential witnesses, and confidential informants.

(g) From subsection (e)(5) (Collection of Information) because in the collection of information for law enforcement purposes it is impossible to determine in advance what information is accurate, relevant, timely, and complete. Compliance with (e)(5) would preclude the officers and agents of DHS compo-

nents' from using their investigative training and exercise of good judgment to both conduct and report on investigations.

(h) From subsection (e)(8) (Notice on Individuals) because compliance would interfere with DHS' ability to obtain, serve, and issue subpoenas, warrants, and other law enforcement mechanisms that may be filed under seal, and could result in disclosure of investigative techniques, procedures, and evidence.

(i) From subsection (g) to the extent that the system is exempt from other specific subsections of the Privacy Act relating to individuals' rights to access and amend their records contained in the system. Therefore DHS is not required to establish rules or procedures pursuant to which individuals may seek a civil remedy for the agency's: Refusal to amend a record; refusal to comply with a request for access to records; failure to maintain accurate, relevant timely and complete records; or failure to otherwise comply with an individual's right to access or amend records.

25. The Department of Homeland Security (DHS)/U.S. Customs and Border Protection-014 Regulatory Audit Archive System (RAAS) System of Records consists of electronic and paper records and will be used by DHS and its Components. The DHS/CBP-014 RAAS System of Records is a repository of information held by DHS in connection with its several and varied missions and functions, including, but not limited to: the enforcement of civil and criminal laws; investigations; inquiries; and proceedings there under. The DHS/CBP-014 RAAS System of Records contains information that is collected by, on behalf of, in support of, or in cooperation with DHS and its Components and may contain personally identifiable information collected by other Federal, State, local, tribal, foreign, or international government agencies. The Secretary of Homeland Security, pursuant to 5 U.S.C. 552a(k)(2), has exempted this system from the following provisions of the Privacy Act: 5 U.S.C. 552a(c)(3). Exemptions from these particular subsections are justified, on a case-by-case basis to be determined at the time a request is made, for the following reasons:

(a) From subsection (c)(3) (Accounting for Disclosures) because release of the accounting of disclosures could alert the subject of an investigation of an actual or potential criminal, civil, or regulatory violation to the existence of that investigation and reveal investigative interest on the part of DHS as well as the recipient agency. Disclosure of the accounting would therefore present a serious impediment to law enforcement efforts and/or efforts to preserve national security. Disclosure of the accounting would also permit the individual who is the subject of a record to impede the investigation, to tamper with witnesses or evidence, and to avoid detection or apprehension, which would undermine the entire investigative process.

(b) From subsection (d) (Access to Records) because access to the records contained in this system of records could inform the subject of an investigation of an actual or potential criminal, civil, or regulatory violation, to the existence of the investigation, and reveal investigative interest on the part of DHS or another agency. Access to the records could permit the individual who is the subject of a record to impede the investigation, to tamper with witnesses or evidence, and to avoid detection or apprehension. Amendment of the records could interfere with ongoing investigations and law enforcement activities and would impose an impossible administrative burden by requiring investigations to be continuously reinvestigated. In addition, permitting access and amendment to such information could disclose security-sensitive information that could be detrimental to homeland security.

(c) From subsection (e)(1) (Relevancy and Necessity of Information) because in the course of investigations into potential violations of Federal law, the accuracy of information obtained or introduced occasionally may be unclear or the information may not be strictly relevant or necessary to a specific investigation. In the interests of effective law enforcement, it is appropriate to retain all information that may aid in establishing patterns of unlawful activity.

(d) From subsections (e)(4)(G), (H), and (I) (Agency Requirements), and (f) (Agency Rules) because portions of this system are exempt from the individual access provisions of subsection (d) for the reasons noted above, and therefore DHS is not required to establish requirements, rules, or procedures with respect to such access. Providing notice to individuals with respect to existence of records pertaining to them in the system of records or otherwise setting up procedures pursuant to which individuals may access and view records pertaining to themselves in the system would undermine investigative efforts and reveal the identities of witnesses, and potential witnesses, and confidential informants.

26. DHS/CBP-001, Import Information System (IIS). A portion of the following system of records is exempt from 5 U.S.C. 552a(c)(3), (e)(8), and (g)(1) pursuant to 5 U.S.C. 552a(j)(2), and from 5 U.S.C. 552a(c)(3) pursuant to 5 U.S.C. 552a(k)(2). Further, no exemption shall be asserted with respect to information maintained in the system as it relates to data submitted by or on behalf of a person who travels to visit the United States and crosses the border, nor shall an exemption be asserted with respect to the resulting determination (approval or denial). After conferring with the appropriate component

or agency, DHS may waive applicable exemptions in appropriate circumstances and where it would not appear to interfere with or adversely affect the law enforcement purposes of the systems from which the information is recompiled or in which it is contained. Exemptions from the above particular subsections are justified, on a case-by-case basis to be determined at the time a request is made, when information in this system of records is may impede a law enforcement, intelligence activities and national security investigation:

(a) From subsection (c)(3) (Accounting for Disclosure) because making available to a record subject the accounting of disclosures from records concerning him or her would specifically reveal any investigative interest in the individual. Revealing this information could reasonably be expected to compromise ongoing efforts to investigate a violation of U.S. law, including investigations of a known or suspected terrorist, by notifying the record subject that he or she is under investigation. This information could also permit the record subject to take measures to impede the investigation, e.g., destroy evidence, intimidate potential witnesses, or flee the area to avoid or impede the investigation.

(b) From subsection (e)(8) (Notice on Individuals) because to require individual notice of disclosure of information due to compulsory legal process would pose an impossible administrative burden on DHS and other agencies and could alert the subjects of counterterrorism or law enforcement investigations to the fact of those investigations when not previously known.

(c) From subsection (g)(1) (Civil Remedies) to the extent that the system is exempt from other specific subsections of the Privacy Act.

27. The DHS/CBP-009 Nonimmigrant Information system of records consists of electronic and paper records and will be used by DHS and it's Components. The DHS/CBP-009 Nonimmigrant Information System is a repository of information held by DHS in connection with its several and varied missions and functions, including, but not limited to: The enforcement of civil and criminal laws; Investigations, inquiries, and proceedings thereunder; and national security and intelligence activities. The DHS/CBP-009 Nonimmigrant Information System contains information that is collected by, on behalf of, in support of, or in cooperation with DHS and its components and may contain personally identifiable information collected by other Federal, State, local, Tribal, foreign, or international government agencies. This system may contain records or information pertaining to the accounting of disclosures made from the Nonimmigrant Information System to other law enforcement and counterterrorism agencies (Federal, State, Local, Foreign, International or Tribal) in

accordance with the published routine uses. The Secretary of Homeland Security has exempted this system from the following provisions of the Privacy Act, subject to the limitations set forth in 5 U.S.C. 522(c)(3), (e) (8), and (g) of the Privacy Act of 1974, as amended, as necessary and appropriate to protect accounting of these disclosures only, pursuant to 5 U.S.C. 552a (j)(2), and (k)(2). Further, no exemption shall be asserted with respect to biographical or travel information submitted by, and collected from, a person's travel documents or submitted from a government computer system to support or to validate those travel documents. After conferring with the appropriate component or agency, DHS may waive applicable exemptions in appropriate circumstances and where it would not appear to interfere with or adversely affect the law enforcement purposes of the systems from which the information is recompiled or in which it is contained. Exemptions from the above particular subsections are justified, on a case-by-case basis to be determined at the time a request is made, when information in this system of records is recompiled or is created from information contained in other systems of records subject to exemptions for the following reasons:

(a) From subsection (c)(3) (Accounting for Disclosure) because making available to a record subject the accounting of disclosures from records concerning him or her would specifically reveal any investigative interest in the individual. Revealing this information could reasonably be expected to compromise ongoing efforts to investigate a violation of U.S. law, including investigations of a known or suspected terrorist, by notifying the record subject that he or she is under investigation. This information could also permit the record subject to take measures to impede the investigation, e.g., destroy evidence, intimidate potential witnesses, or flee the area to avoid or impede the investigation.

(b) From subsection (e)(8) (Notice on Individuals) because to require individual notice of disclosure of information due to compulsory legal process would pose an impossible administrative burden on DHS and other agencies and could alert the subjects of counterterrorism or law enforcement investigations to the fact of those investigations when not previously known.

(c) From subsection (g) (Civil Remedies) to the extent that the system is exempt from other specific subsections of the Privacy Act.

28. The DHS/ICE—007 Law Enforcement Support Center (LESC) Alien Criminal Response Information Management (ACRIMe) system of records consists of electronic and paper records and will be used by DHS and its components. The DHS/ICE—007 Law Enforcement Support Center Alien Criminal Response Information Management system

is a repository of information held by DHS in connection with its several and varied missions and functions, including, but not limited to: The enforcement of civil and criminal laws; investigations, inquiries, and proceedings thereunder; and national security and intelligence activities. The DHS/ICE—007 Law Enforcement Support Center Alien Criminal Response Information Management system contains information that is collected by, on behalf of, in support of, or in cooperation with DHS and its components and may contain personally identifiable information collected by other Federal, State, local, tribal, foreign, or international government agencies. The Secretary of Homeland Security has exempted this system of records from the following provisions of the Privacy Act, subject to the limitations set forth in 5 U.S.C. 552a(c)(3) and (4); (d); (e)(1), (e)(2), (e)(3), (e)(4)(G), (e)(4)(H), and (e)(5) and (e)(8); (f), and (g) pursuant to 5 U.S.C. 552a(j)(2). Additionally, the Secretary of Homeland Security has exempted this system from the following provisions of the Privacy Act, subject to the limitations set forth in 5 U.S.C. 552a (c)(3), (d), (e)(1), (e)(4)(G), (e)(4)(H), and (f) pursuant to 5 U.S.C. 552a(k)(2). Exemptions from these particular subsections are justified, on a case-by-case basis to be determined at the time a request is made, for the following reasons:

(a) From subsection (c)(3) and (4) (Accounting for Disclosures) because release of the accounting of disclosures could alert the subject of an investigation of an actual or potential criminal, civil, or regulatory violation to the existence of the investigation, and reveal investigative interest on the part of DHS as well as the recipient agency. Disclosure of the accounting would therefore present a serious impediment to law enforcement efforts and/or efforts to preserve national security. Disclosure of the accounting would also permit the individual who is the subject of a record to impede the investigation, to tamper with witnesses or evidence, and to avoid detection or apprehension, which would undermine the entire investigative process.

(b) From subsection (d) (Access to Records) because access to the records contained in this system of records could inform the subject of an investigation of an actual or potential criminal, civil, or regulatory violation, to the existence of the investigation, and reveal investigative interest on the part of DHS or another agency. Access to the records could permit the individual who is the subject of a record to impede the investigation, to tamper with witnesses or evidence, and to avoid detection or apprehension. Amendment of the records could interfere with ongoing investigations and law enforcement activities and would impose an impossible administrative burden by requiring investigations to be continuously reinvestigated. In addition, permitting access and amendment to such information could disclose security-sensitive information that could be detrimental to homeland security.

(c) From subsection (e)(1) (Relevancy and Necessity of Information) because in the course of investigations into potential violations of Federal law, the accuracy of information obtained or introduced occasionally may be unclear or the information may not be strictly relevant or necessary to a specific investigation. In the interests of effective law enforcement, it is appropriate to retain all information that may aid in identifying or establishing patterns of unlawful activity.

(d) From subsection (e)(2) (Collection of Information from Individuals) because requiring that information be collected from the subject of an investigation would alert the subject to the nature or existence of an investigation, thereby interfering with the related investigation and law enforcement activities.

(e) From subsection (e)(3) (Notice to Subjects) because providing such detailed information would impede law enforcement in that it could compromise investigations by: Revealing the existence of an otherwise confidential investigation and thereby provide an opportunity for the subject of an investigation to conceal evidence, alter patterns of behavior, or take other actions that could thwart investigative efforts; reveal the identity of witnesses in investigations, thereby providing an opportunity for the subjects of the investigations or others to harass, intimidate, or otherwise interfere with the collection of evidence or other information from such witnesses; or reveal the identity of confidential informants, which would negatively affect the informant's usefulness in any ongoing or future investigations and discourage members of the public from cooperating as confidential informants in any future investigations.

(f) From subsections (e)(4)(G), (H) (Agency Requirements), and (f) (Agency Rules) because portions of this system are exempt from the individual access provisions of subsection (d) for the reasons noted above, and therefore DHS is not required to establish requirements, rules, or procedures with respect to such access. Providing notice to individuals with respect to existence of records pertaining to them in the system of records or otherwise setting up procedures pursuant to which individuals may access and view records pertaining to themselves in the system would undermine investigative efforts and reveal the identities of witnesses, and potential witnesses, and confidential informants.

(g) From subsection (e)(5) (Collection of Information) because in the collection of information for law enforcement purposes it is

impossible to determine in advance what information is accurate, relevant, timely, and complete. Compliance with (e)(5) would preclude DHS agents from using their investigative training and exercise of good judgment to both conduct and report on investigations.

(h) From subsection (e)(8) (Notice on Individuals) because compliance would interfere with DHS' ability to obtain, serve, and issue subpoenas, warrants, and other law enforcement mechanisms that may be filed under seal, and could result in disclosure of investigative techniques, procedures, and evidence.

(i) From subsection (g) to the extent that the system is exempt from other specific subsections of the Privacy Act relating to individuals' rights to access and amend their records contained in the system. Therefore DHS is not required to establish rules or procedures pursuant to which individuals may seek a civil remedy for the agency's: Refusal to amend a record; refusal to comply with a request for access to records; failure to maintain accurate, relevant, timely and complete records; or failure to otherwise comply with an individual's right to access or amend records.

29. The DHS/ICE—008 Search, Arrest, and Seizure system of records consists of electronic and paper records and will be used by DHS and its components. The DHS/ICE—008 Search, Arrest, and Seizure system is a repository of information held by DHS in connection with its several and varied missions and functions, including, but not limited to: The enforcement of civil and criminal laws; investigations, inquiries, and proceedings thereunder; and national security and intelligence activities. The DHS/ICE—008 Search, Arrest, and Seizure system contains information that is collected by, on behalf of, in support of, or in cooperation with DHS and its components and may contain personally identifiable information collected by other Federal, State, local, tribal, foreign, or international government agencies. The Secretary of Homeland Security has exempted this system from the following provisions of the Privacy Act, subject to the limitations set forth in 5 U.S.C. 552a(c)(3) and (4); (d); (e)(1), (e)(2), (e)(3), (e)(4)(G), (e)(4)(H), (e)(5) and (e)(8); (f), and (g) pursuant to 5 U.S.C. 552a(j)(2). Additionally, the Secretary of Homeland Security has exempted this system from the following provisions of the Privacy Act, subject to the limitations set forth in 5 U.S.C. 552a(c)(3), (d), (e)(1), (e)(4)(G), (e)(4)(H), and (f) pursuant to 5 U.S.C. 552a(k)(2). Exemptions from these particular subsections are justified, on a case-by-case basis to be determined at the time a request is made, for the following reasons:

(a) From subsection (c)(3) and (4) (Accounting for Disclosures) because release of the accounting of disclosures could alert the subject of an investigation of an actual or potential criminal, civil, or regulatory violation to the existence of the investigation, and reveal investigative interest on the part of DHS as well as the recipient agency. Disclosure of the accounting would therefore present a serious impediment to law enforcement efforts and/or efforts to preserve national security. Disclosure of the accounting would also permit the individual who is the subject of a record to impede the investigation, to tamper with witnesses or evidence, and to avoid detection or apprehension, which would undermine the entire investigative process.

(b) From subsection (d) (Access to Records) because access to the records contained in this system of records could inform the subject of an investigation of an actual or potential criminal, civil, or regulatory violation, to the existence of the investigation, and reveal investigative interest on the part of DHS or another agency. Access to the records could permit the individual who is the subject of a record to impede the investigation, to tamper with witnesses or evidence, and to avoid detection or apprehension. Amendment of the records could interfere with ongoing investigations and law enforcement activities and would impose an impossible administrative burden by requiring investigations to be continuously reinvestigated. In addition, permitting access and amendment to such information could disclose security-sensitive information that could be detrimental to homeland security.

(c) From subsection (e)(1) (Relevancy and Necessity of Information) because in the course of investigations into potential violations of Federal law, the accuracy of information obtained or introduced occasionally may be unclear or the information may not be strictly relevant or necessary to a specific investigation. In the interests of effective law enforcement, it is appropriate to retain all information that may aid in establishing patterns of unlawful activity.

(d) From subsection (e)(2) (Collection of Information from Individuals) because requiring that information be collected from the subject of an investigation would alert the subject to the nature or existence of an investigation, thereby interfering with the related investigation and law enforcement activities.

(e) From subsection (e)(3) (Notice to Subjects) because providing such detailed information would impede law enforcement in that it could compromise investigations by: Revealing the existence of an otherwise confidential investigation and thereby provide an opportunity for the subject of an investigation to conceal evidence, alter patterns of behavior, or take other actions that could thwart investigative efforts; reveal the identity of witnesses in investigations, thereby

providing an opportunity for the subjects of the investigations or others to harass, intimidate, or otherwise interfere with the collection of evidence or other information from such witnesses; or reveal the identity of confidential informants, which would negatively affect the informant's usefulness in any ongoing or future investigations and discourage members of the public from cooperating as confidential informants in any future investigations.

(f) From subsections (e)(4)(G) and (H) (Agency Requirements), and (f) (Agency Rules) because portions of this system are exempt from the individual access provisions of subsection (d) for the reasons noted above, and therefore DHS is not required to establish requirements, rules, or procedures with respect to such access. Providing notice to individuals with respect to existence of records pertaining to them in the system of records or otherwise setting up procedures pursuant to which individuals may access and view records pertaining to themselves in the system would undermine investigative efforts and reveal the identities of witnesses, and potential witnesses, and confidential informants.

(g) From subsection (e)(5) (Collection of Information) because in the collection of information for law enforcement purposes it is impossible to determine in advance what information is accurate, relevant, timely, and complete. Compliance with (e)(5) would preclude DHS agents from using their investigative training and exercise of good judgment to both conduct and report on investigations.

(h) From subsection (e)(8) (Notice on Individuals) because compliance would interfere with DHS' ability to obtain, serve, and issue subpoenas, warrants, and other law enforcement mechanisms that may be filed under seal, and could result in disclosure of investigative techniques, procedures, and evidence.

(i) From subsection (g) to the extent that the system is exempt from other specific subsections of the Privacy Act relating to individuals' rights to access and amend their records contained in the system. Therefore DHS is not required to establish rules or procedures pursuant to which individuals may seek a civil remedy for the agency's: Refusal to amend a record; refusal to comply with a request for access to records; failure to maintain accurate, relevant, timely and complete records; or failure to otherwise comply with an individual's right to access or amend records.

30. The DHS/ICE—009 External Investigations system of records consists of electronic and paper records and will be used by DHS and its components. The DHS/ICE—009 External Investigations system is a repository of information held by DHS in connection with its several and varied missions and

functions, including, but not limited to: The enforcement of civil and criminal laws; investigations, inquiries, and proceedings there under; and national security and intelligence activities. The DHS/ICE—009 External Investigations system contains information that is collected by, on behalf of, in support of, or in cooperation with DHS and its components and may contain personally identifiable information collected by other Federal, State, local, tribal, foreign, or international government agencies. The Secretary of Homeland Security has exempted this system from the following provisions of the Privacy Act, subject to the limitations set forth in 5 U.S.C. 552a(c)(3) and (4); (d); (e)(1), (e)(2), (e)(3), (e)(4)(G), (e)(4)(H), and (e)(5) and (e)(8); (f), and (g) pursuant to 5 U.S.C. 552a(j)(2). Additionally, the Secretary of Homeland Security has exempted this system from the following provisions of the Privacy Act, subject to the limitations set forth in 5 U.S.C. 552a(c)(3), (d), (e)(1), (e)(4)(G), (e)(4)(H), and (f) pursuant to 5 U.S.C. 552a(k)(2). Exemptions from these particular subsections are justified, on a case-by-case basis to be determined at the time a request is made, for the following reasons:

(a) From subsections (c)(3) and (4) (Accounting for Disclosures) because release of the accounting of disclosures could alert the subject of an investigation of an actual or potential criminal, civil, or regulatory violation to the existence of the investigation, and reveal investigative interest on the part of DHS as well as the recipient agency. Disclosure of the accounting would therefore present a serious impediment to law enforcement efforts and/or efforts to preserve national security. Disclosure of the accounting would also permit the individual who is the subject of a record to impede the investigation, to tamper with witnesses or evidence, and to avoid detection or apprehension, which would undermine the entire investigative process.

(b) From subsection (d) (Access to Records) because access to the records contained in this system of records could inform the subject of an investigation of an actual or potential criminal, civil, or regulatory violation, to the existence of the investigation, and reveal investigative interest on the part of DHS or another agency. Access to the records could permit the individual who is the subject of a record to impede the investigation, to tamper with witnesses or evidence, and to avoid detection or apprehension. Amendment of the records could interfere with ongoing investigations and law enforcement activities and would impose an impossible administrative burden by requiring investigations to be continuously reinvestigated. In addition, permitting access and amendment to such information could disclose security-sensitive information that could be detrimental to homeland security.

(c) From subsection (e)(1) (Relevancy and Necessity of Information) because in the course of investigations into potential violations of Federal law, the accuracy of information obtained or introduced occasionally may be unclear or the information may not be strictly relevant or necessary to a specific investigation. In the interests of effective law enforcement, it is appropriate to retain all information that may aid in establishing patterns of unlawful activity.

(d) From subsection (e)(2) (Collection of Information from Individuals) because requiring that information be collected from the subject of an investigation would alert the subject to the nature or existence of an investigation, thereby interfering with the related investigation and law enforcement activities.

(e) From subsection (e)(3) (Notice to Subjects) because providing such detailed information would impede law enforcement in that it could compromise investigations by: Revealing the existence of an otherwise confidential investigation and thereby provide an opportunity for the subject of an investigation to conceal evidence, alter patterns of behavior, or take other actions that could thwart investigative efforts; reveal the identity of witnesses in investigations, thereby providing an opportunity for the subjects of the investigations or others to harass, intimidate, or otherwise interfere with the collection of evidence or other information from such witnesses; or reveal the identity of confidential informants, which would negatively affect the informant's usefulness in any ongoing or future investigations and discourage members of the public from cooperating as confidential informants in any future investigations.

(f) From subsections (e)(4)(G) and (H) (Agency Requirements), and (f) (Agency Rules) because portions of this system are exempt from the individual access provisions of subsection (d) for the reasons noted above, and therefore DHS is not required to establish requirements, rules, or procedures with respect to such access. Providing notice to individuals with respect to existence of records pertaining to them in the system of records or otherwise setting up procedures pursuant to which individuals may access and view records pertaining to themselves in the system would undermine investigative efforts and reveal the identities of witnesses, and potential witnesses, and confidential informants.

(g) From subsection (e)(5) (Collection of Information) because in the collection of information for law enforcement purposes it is impossible to determine in advance what information is accurate, relevant, timely, and complete. Compliance with (e)(5) would preclude DHS agents from using their investigative training and exercise of good judgment to both conduct and report on investigations.

(h) From subsection (e)(8) (Notice on Individuals) because compliance would interfere with DHS' ability to obtain, serve, and issue subpoenas, warrants, and other law enforcement mechanisms that may be filed under seal, and could result in disclosure of investigative techniques, procedures, and evidence.

(i) From subsection (g) to the extent that the system is exempt from other specific subsections of the Privacy Act relating to individuals' rights to access and amend their records contained in the system. Therefore DHS is not required to establish rules or procedures pursuant to which individuals may seek a civil remedy for the agency's: Refusal to amend a record; refusal to comply with a request for access to records; failure to maintain accurate, relevant, timely and complete records; or failure to otherwise comply with an individual's right to access or amend records.

31. The DHS/ICE—010 Confidential and Other Sources of Information (COSI) system of records consists of electronic and paper records and will be used by DHS and its components. The DHS/ICE—010 Confidential and Other Sources of Information system is a repository of information held by DHS in connection with its several and varied missions and functions, including, but not limited to: the enforcement of civil and criminal laws; and investigations, inquiries, and proceedings there under; and national security and intelligence activities. The DHS/ICE—010 Confidential and Other Sources of Information system contains information that is collected by, on behalf of, in support of, or in cooperation with DHS and its components and may contain personally identifiable information collected by other Federal, State, local, tribal, foreign, or international government agencies. The Secretary of Homeland Security has exempted this system from the following provisions of the Privacy Act, subject to the limitations set forth in 5 U.S.C. 552a(c)(3) and (4); (d); (e)(1), (e)(2), (e)(3), (e)(4)(G), (e)(4)(H), (e)(5) and (e)(8); (f), and (g) pursuant to 5 U.S.C. 552a(j)(2). Additionally, the Secretary of Homeland Security has exempted this system from the following provisions of the Privacy Act, subject to the limitations set forth in 5 U.S.C. 552a (c)(3), (d), (e)(1), (e)(4)(G), (e)(4)(H), and (f) pursuant to 5 U.S.C. 552a(k)(2). Exemptions from these particular subsections are justified, on a case-by-case basis to be determined at the time a request is made, for the following reasons:

(a) From subsection (c)(3) and (4) (Accounting for Disclosures) because release of the accounting of disclosures could alert the subject of an investigation of an actual or potential criminal, civil, or regulatory violation to the existence of the investigation, and reveal investigative interest on the part of DHS as well as the recipient agency. Disclosure of the accounting would therefore present a serious impediment to law enforcement efforts and/or efforts to preserve national security. Disclosure of the accounting would also permit the individual who is the subject of a record to impede the investigation, to tamper with witnesses or evidence, and to avoid detection or apprehension, which would undermine the entire investigative process.

(b) From subsection (d) (Access to Records) because access to the records contained in this system of records could inform the subject of an investigation of an actual or potential criminal, civil, or regulatory violation, to the existence of the investigation, and reveal investigative interest on the part of DHS or another agency. Access to the records could permit the individual who is the subject of a record to impede the investigation, to tamper with witnesses or evidence, and to avoid detection or apprehension. Amendment of the records could interfere with ongoing investigations and law enforcement activities and would impose an impossible administrative burden by requiring investigations to be continuously reinvestigated. In addition, permitting access and amendment to such information could disclose security-sensitive information that could be detrimental to homeland security.

(c) From subsection (e)(1) (Relevancy and Necessity of Information) because in the course of investigations into potential violations of Federal law, the accuracy of information obtained or introduced occasionally may be unclear or the information may not be strictly relevant or necessary to a specific investigation. In the interests of effective law enforcement, it is appropriate to retain all information that may aid in establishing patterns of unlawful activity.

(d) From subsection (e)(2) (Collection of Information from Individuals) because requiring that information be collected from the subject of an investigation would alert the subject to the nature or existence of an investigation, thereby interfering with the related investigation and law enforcement activities.

(e) From subsection (e)(3) (Notice to Subjects) because providing such detailed information would impede law enforcement in that it could compromise investigations by: Revealing the existence of an otherwise confidential investigation and thereby provide an opportunity for the subject of an investigation to conceal evidence, alter patterns of behavior, or take other actions that could thwart investigative efforts; reveal the identity of witnesses in investigations, thereby providing an opportunity for the subjects of the investigations or others to harass, intimidate, or otherwise interfere with the collection of evidence or other information from such witnesses; or reveal the identity of confidential informants, which would negatively affect the informant's usefulness in any ongoing or future investigations and discourage members of the public from cooperating as confidential informants in any future investigations.

(f) From subsections (e)(4)(G) and (H) (Agency Requirements), and (f) (Agency Rules) because portions of this system are exempt from the individual access provisions of subsection (d) for the reasons noted above, and therefore DHS is not required to establish requirements, rules, or procedures with respect to such access. Providing notice to individuals with respect to existence of records pertaining to them in the system of records or otherwise setting up procedures pursuant to which individuals may access and view records pertaining to themselves in the system would undermine investigative efforts and reveal the identities of witnesses, and potential witnesses, and confidential informants.

(g) From subsection (e)(5) (Collection of Information) because in the collection of information for law enforcement purposes it is impossible to determine in advance what information is accurate, relevant, timely, and complete. Compliance with (e)(5) would preclude DHS agents from using their investigative training and exercise of good judgment to both conduct and report on investigations.

(h) From subsection (e)(8) (Notice on Individuals) because compliance would interfere with DHS' ability to obtain, serve, and issue subpoenas, warrants, and other law enforcement mechanisms that may be filed under seal, and could result in disclosure of investigative techniques, procedures, and evidence.

(i) From subsection (g) to the extent that the system is exempt from other specific subsections of the Privacy Act relating to individuals' rights to access and amend their records contained in the system. Therefore DHS is not required to establish rules or procedures pursuant to which individuals may seek a civil remedy for the agency's: Refusal to amend a record; refusal to comply with a request for access to records; failure to maintain accurate, relevant, timely, and complete records; or failure to otherwise comply with an individual's right to access or amend records.

32. The DHS/USCIS—006 Fraud Detection and National Security Data System (FDNS–DS) system of records consists of a stand alone database and paper files that will be used by DHS and its components. The DHS/USCIS—006 Fraud Detection and National Security Data System is a case management system used to record, track, and manage immigration inquiries, investigative referrals, law enforcement requests, and case determinations involving benefit fraud, crimi-

nal activity, public safety and national security concerns. The Secretary of Homeland Security has exempted this system from the following provisions of the Privacy Act, subject to the limitations set forth in 5 U.S.C. 552a(c)(3); (d); (e)(1), (e)(4)(G), (e)(4)(H), (e)(4)(I), and (f) pursuant to 5 U.S.C. 552a (k)(2). These exemptions apply only to the extent that records in the system are subject to exemption pursuant to 5 U.S.C. 552a (k)(2). Exemptions from these particular subsections are justified, on a case-by-case basis to be determined at the time a request is made, for the following reasons:

(a) From subsection (c)(3) (Accounting for Disclosures) because release of the accounting of disclosures could alert the subject of an investigation of an actual or potential criminal, civil, or regulatory violation to the existence of the investigation; and reveal investigative interest on the part of DHS as well as the recipient agency. Disclosure of the accounting would therefore present a serious impediment to law enforcement efforts and/or efforts to preserve national security. Disclosure of the accounting would also permit the individual who is the subject of a record to impede the investigation, to tamper with witnesses or evidence, and to avoid detection or apprehension, which would undermine the entire investigative process.

(b) From subsection (d) (Access to Records) because access to the records contained in this system of records could inform the subject of an investigation of an actual or potential criminal, civil, or regulatory violation, to the existence of the investigation, and reveal investigative interest on the part of DHS or another agency. Access to the records could permit the individual who is the subject of a record to impede the investigation, to tamper with witnesses or evidence, and to avoid detection or apprehension. Amendment of the records could interfere with ongoing investigations and law enforcement activities and would impose an impossible administrative burden by requiring investigations to be continuously reinvestigated. In addition, permitting access and amendment to such information could disclose security-sensitive information that could be detrimental to homeland security.

(c) From subsection (e)(1) (Relevancy and Necessity of Information) because in the course of investigations into potential violations of Federal law, the accuracy of information obtained or introduced occasionally may be unclear or the information may not be strictly relevant or necessary to a specific investigation. In the interests of effective law enforcement, it is appropriate to retain all information that may aid in establishing patterns of unlawful activity.

(d) From subsections (e)(4)(G) and (e)(4)(H) (Agency Requirements) because portions of this system are exempt from the individual access provisions of subsection (d) which exempts providing access because it could alert a subject to the nature or existence of an investigation, and thus there could be no procedures for that particular data. Procedures do exist for access for those portions of the system that are not exempted.

(e) From subsection (e)(4)(I) (Agency Requirements) because providing such source information would impede law enforcement or intelligence by compromising the nature or existence of a confidential investigation.

(f) From subsection (f) (Agency Rules) because portions of this system are exempt from the access and amendment provisions of subsection (d).

33. The DHS/USCG—028 Family Advocacy Case Records system of records consists of electronic and paper records and will be used by DHS and its components. The DHS/USCG—028 Family Advocacy Case Records is a repository of information held by DHS in connection with its several and varied missions and functions, including, but not limited to: the enforcement of civil and criminal laws; investigations, inquiries, and proceedings there under. The DHS/USCG—028 Family Advocacy Case Records contains information that is collected by, on behalf of, in support of, or in cooperation with DHS and its components and may contain personally identifiable information collected by other Federal, State, local, tribal, foreign, or international government agencies. The Secretary of Homeland Security has exempted this system from the following provisions of the Privacy Act, subject to the limitations set forth in 5 U.S.C. 552a (c)(3), (d), (e)(1), (e)(4)(G), (e)(4)(H), (e)(4)(I), and (f) pursuant to 5 U.S.C. 552a(k)(2). Exemptions from these particular subsections are justified, on a case-by-case basis to be determined at the time a request is made, for the following reasons:

(a) From subsection (c)(3) (Accounting for Disclosures) because release of the accounting of disclosures could alert the subject of an investigation of an actual or potential criminal, civil, or regulatory violation to the existence of the investigation, and reveal investigative interest on the part of DHS as well as the recipient agency. Disclosure of the accounting would therefore present a serious impediment to law enforcement efforts and/or efforts to preserve national security. Disclosure of the accounting would also permit the individual who is the subject of a record to impede the investigation, to tamper with witnesses or evidence, and to avoid detection or apprehension, which would undermine the entire investigative process.

(b) From subsection (d) (Access to Records) because access to the records contained in this system of records could inform the subject of an investigation of an actual or potential criminal, civil, or regulatory violation, to the existence of the investigation, and reveal investigative interest on the part of DHS or another agency. Access to the records could permit the individual who is the subject of a record to impede the investigation, to tamper with witnesses or evidence, and to avoid detection or apprehension. Amendment of the records could interfere with ongoing investigations and law enforcement activities and would impose an impossible administrative burden by requiring investigations to be continuously reinvestigated. In addition, permitting access and amendment to such information could disclose security-sensitive information that could be detrimental to homeland security.

(c) From subsection (e)(1) (Relevancy and Necessity of Information) because in the course of investigations into potential violations of Federal law, the accuracy of information obtained or introduced occasionally may be unclear or the information may not be strictly relevant or necessary to a specific investigation. In the interests of effective law enforcement, it is appropriate to retain all information that may aid in establishing patterns of unlawful activity.

(d) From subsections (e)(4)(G), (H), and (I) (Agency Requirements), and (f) (Agency Rules) because portions of this system are exempt from the individual access provisions of subsection (d) for the reasons noted above, and therefore DHS is not required to establish requirements, rules, or procedures with respect to such access. Providing notice to individuals with respect to existence of records pertaining to them in the system of records or otherwise setting up procedures pursuant to which individuals may access and view records pertaining to themselves in the system would undermine investigative efforts and reveal the identities of witnesses, and potential witnesses, and confidential informants.

34. The DHS/USCG–029 Notice of Arrival and Departure System of Records consists of electronic and paper records and will be used by DHS and its components. The DHS/USCG–029 Notice of Arrival and Departure System of Records is a repository of information held by DHS in connection with its several and varied missions and functions, including, but not limited to the enforcement of civil and criminal laws; investigations, inquiries, and proceedings there under. The DHS/USCG–029 Notice of Arrival and Departure System of Records contains information that is collected by, on behalf of, in support of, or in cooperation with DHS and its components and may contain personally identifiable information collected by other federal, state, local, tribal, foreign, or international government agencies.

The Secretary of Homeland Security, pursuant to 5 U.S.C. 552a(j)(2), exempted this system from the following provisions of the Privacy Act: Sections (c)(3), (e)(8), and (g) of the Privacy Act of 1974, as amended, as is necessary and appropriate to protect this information. Further, DHS has exempted section (c)(3) of the Privacy Act of 1974, as amended, pursuant to 5 U.S.C. 552a(k)(2), as is necessary and appropriate to protect this information.

Exemptions from these particular subsections are justified, on a case-by-case basis to be determined at the time a request is made, for the following reasons:

(a) From subsection (c)(3) (Accounting for Disclosures) because release of the accounting of disclosures could alert the subject of an investigation of an actual or potential criminal, civil, or regulatory violation to the existence of that investigation and reveal investigative interest on the part of DHS as well as the recipient agency. Disclosure of the accounting would therefore present a serious impediment to law enforcement efforts and/or efforts to preserve national security. Disclosure of the accounting would also permit the individual who is the subject of a record to impede the investigation, to tamper with witnesses or evidence, and to avoid detection or apprehension, which would undermine the entire investigative process. When an investigation has been completed, information on disclosures made may continue to be exempted if the fact that an investigation occurred remains sensitive after completion.

(b) From subsection (e)(8) (Notice on Individuals) because compliance would interfere with DHS's ability to obtain, serve, and issue subpoenas, warrants, and other law enforcement mechanisms that may be filed under seal and could result in disclosure of investigative techniques, procedures, and evidence.

(c) From subsection (g)(1) (Civil Remedies) to the extent that the system is exempt from other specific subsections of the Privacy Act.

35. The DHS/Secret Service—001 Criminal Investigation Information system of records consists of electronic and paper records and will be used by DHS and its components. The DHS/Secret Service—001 Criminal Investigation Information system is a repository of information held by DHS in connection with its several and varied missions and functions, including, but not limited to: The enforcement of civil and criminal laws; investigations, inquiries, and proceedings there under; the protection of the President of the United States or other individuals and locations pursuant to section 3056 and 3056A of Title 18. The DHS/Secret Service—001 Criminal Investigation Information system contains information that is collected by, on behalf of, in support of, or in cooperation with DHS and its components and may contain personally identifiable information collected by other Federal, State, local, tribal, foreign, international government agencies, as well as private corporate, education and other entities. The Secretary of Homeland

Security has exempted this system from the following provisions of the Privacy Act, subject to the limitations set forth in 5 U.S.C. 552a(c)(3) and (4); (d); (e)(1), (e)(2), (e)(3), (e)(4)(G), (e)(4)(H), (e)(4)(I), (e)(5) and (e)(8); (f), and (g) pursuant to 5 U.S.C. 552a(j)(2). Additionally, the Secretary of Homeland Security has exempted this system from the following provisions of the Privacy Act, subject to the limitations set forth in 5 U.S.C. 552a(c)(3), (d), (e)(1), (e)(4)(G), (e)(4)(H), (I), and (f) pursuant to 5 U.S.C. 552a(k)(1), (k)(2), and (k)(3). Exemptions from these particular subsections are justified, on a case-by-case basis to be determined at the time a request is made, for the following reasons:

(a) From subsection (c)(3) and (4) (Accounting for Disclosures) because release of the accounting of disclosures could alert the subject of an investigation of an actual or potential criminal, civil, or regulatory violation to the existence of the investigation, or protective inquiry, and reveal investigative interest on the part of DHS as well as the recipient agency. Disclosure of the accounting would therefore present a serious impediment to law enforcement efforts and/or the Secret Service's protective mission. Disclosure of the accounting would also permit the individual who is the subject of a record to impede the investigation, or inquiry, to tamper with witnesses or evidence, and to avoid detection or apprehension, which would undermine the entire investigative or inquiry process.

(b) From subsection (d) (Access to Records) because access to the records contained in this system of records could inform the subject of an investigation of an actual or potential criminal, civil, or regulatory violation, or protective inquiry to the existence of the investigation or inquiry, and reveal investigative interest on the part of DHS or another agency. Access to the records could permit the individual who is the subject of a record to impede the investigation or inquiry, to tamper with witnesses or evidence, and to avoid detection or apprehension. Amendment of the records could interfere with ongoing investigations and law enforcement or protective activities and/or could disclose security-sensitive information that could be detrimental to homeland security or the protective mission of the Secret Service.

(c) From subsection (e)(1) (Relevancy and Necessity of Information) because in the course of investigations into potential violations of Federal law or protective inquiries, the accuracy of information obtained or introduced occasionally may be unclear or the information may not be strictly relevant or necessary to a specific investigation or protective inquiry. In the interests of effective law enforcement, and/or the protective mission of the Secret Service, it is appropriate to retain all information that may aid in establishing patterns of unlawful activity, or a threat to an individual, location or event protected or secured by the Secret Service.

(d) From subsection (e)(2) (Collection of Information from Individuals) because requiring that information be collected from the subject of an investigation or protective inquiry would alert the subject to the nature or existence of an investigation or inquiry, thereby interfering with the related investigation or inquiry and law enforcement or protective activities.

(e) From subsection (e)(3) (Notice to Individuals Providing Information) because providing such detailed information would impede law enforcement or protective activities in that it could compromise investigations or inquires by: Revealing the existence of an otherwise confidential investigation or inquiry and thereby provide an opportunity for the subject of an investigation or inquiry to conceal evidence, alter patterns of behavior, or take other actions that could thwart investigative or protective efforts; reveal the identity of witnesses in investigations or inquiries, thereby providing an opportunity for the subjects of the investigations or inquiries or others to harass, intimidate, or otherwise interfere with the collection of evidence or other information from such witnesses; or reveal the identity of confidential informants, which would negatively affect the informant's usefulness in any ongoing or future investigations or protective activities and discourage members of the public from cooperating as confidential informants in any future investigations or protective activities.

(f) From subsections (e)(4)(G), (H), and (I) (Agency Requirements), and (f) (Agency Rules) because portions of this system are exempt from the individual access provisions of subsection (d) for the reasons noted above, and therefore DHS is not required to establish requirements, rules, or procedures with respect to such access. Providing notice to individuals with respect to the existence of records pertaining to them in the system of records or otherwise setting up procedures pursuant to which individuals may access and view records pertaining to themselves in the system would undermine investigative or protective efforts and reveal the identities of witnesses, and potential witnesses, and confidential informants.

(g) From subsection (e)(5) (Maintenance of Information Used in Making any Determination) because in the collection of information for law enforcement and protective purposes it is impossible to determine in advance what information is accurate, relevant, timely, and complete. Compliance with (e)(5) would preclude Secret Service DHS agents from using their investigative and protective training and exercising good judgment to both conduct and report on investigations or other protective activities.

(h) From subsection (e)(8) (Notice on Individuals) because compliance would interfere with DHS' ability to obtain, serve, and issue subpoenas, warrants, and other law enforcement mechanisms that may be filed under seal, or/and could result in disclosure of investigative or protective techniques, procedures, and evidence.

(i) From subsection (g) (Civil Remedies) to the extent that the system is exempt from other specific subsections of the Privacy Act relating to individuals' rights to access and amend their records contained in the system. Therefore DHS is not required to establish rules or procedures pursuant to which individuals may seek a civil remedy for the agency's: Refusal to amend a record; refusal to comply with a request for access to records; failure to maintain accurate, relevant, timely and complete records; or failure to otherwise comply with an individual's right to access or amend records.

36. The DHS/Secret Service—003 Non-Criminal Investigation Information system of records consists of electronic and paper records and will be used by DHS and its components. The DHS/Secret Service—003 Non-Criminal Investigation Information system is a repository of information held by DHS in connection with its several and varied missions and functions, including, but not limited to: The enforcement of civil and criminal laws; criminal, civil, protective and background investigations and inquiries, and proceedings thereunder; the protection of the President of the United States or other individuals and locations pursuant to section 3056 and 3056A of Title 18; and the hiring of employees through an application process which includes the use of polygraph examinations. The DHS/Secret Service—003 Non-Criminal Investigation Information system contains information that is collected by, on behalf of, in support of, or in cooperation with DHS and its components and may contain personally identifiable information collected by other Federal, State, local, tribal, foreign, or international government agencies, as well as private corporate, educational and other entities. The Secretary of Homeland Security has exempted this system from the following provisions of the Privacy Act, subject to the limitations set forth in 5 U.S.C. 552a(c)(3) and (4); (d); (e)(1), (e)(2), (e)(3), (e)(4)(G), (e)(4)(H), (e)(4)(I), (e)(5) and (e)(8); (f), and (g) pursuant to 5 U.S.C. 552a(j)(2). Additionally, the Secretary of Homeland Security has exempted this system from the following provisions of the Privacy Act, subject to the limitations set forth in 5 U.S.C. 552a(c)(3), (d), (e)(1), (e)(4)(G), (e)(4)(H), (e)(4)(I), and (f) pursuant to 5 U.S.C. 552a(k)(1), (k)(2), (k)(3), (k)(5), and (k)(6). Exemptions from these particular subsections are justified, on a case-by-case basis to be

determined at the time a request is made, for the following reasons:

(a) From subsection (c)(3) and (4) (Accounting for Disclosures) because release of the accounting of disclosures could alert the subject of an investigation of an actual or potential criminal, civil, or regulatory violation to the existence of the investigation, or protective inquiry, and reveal investigative interest on the part of DHS as well as the recipient agency. Disclosure of the accounting would therefore present a serious impediment to law enforcement efforts and/or the Secret Service's protective mission. Disclosure of the accounting would also permit the individual who is the subject of a record to impede the investigation or inquiry, to tamper with witnesses or evidence, and to avoid detection or apprehension, which would undermine the entire investigative or inquiry process.

(b) From subsection (d) (Access to Records) because access to the records contained in this system of records could inform the subject of an investigation of an actual or potential criminal, civil, or regulatory violation, or protective inquiry to the existence of the investigation or inquiry, and reveal investigative interest on the part of DHS or another agency. Access to the records could permit the individual who is the subject of a record to impede the investigation or inquiry, to tamper with witnesses or evidence, and to avoid detection or apprehension. Amendment of the records could interfere with ongoing investigations and law enforcement or protective activities and/or could disclose security-sensitive information that could be detrimental to homeland security or the protective mission of the Secret Service.

(c) From subsection (e)(1) (Relevancy and Necessity of Information) because in the course of investigations into potential violations of Federal law or protective inquiries, the accuracy of information obtained or introduced occasionally may be unclear or the information may not be strictly relevant or necessary to a specific investigation or protective inquiry. In the interests of effective law enforcement and/or the protective mission of the Secret Service, it is appropriate to retain all information that may aid in establishing patterns of unlawful activity, or a threat to an individual, location or event protected or secured by the Secret Service.

(d) From subsection (e)(2) (Collection of Information from Individuals) because requiring that information be collected from the subject of an investigation or protective inquiry would alert the subject to the nature or existence of an investigation or inquiry, thereby interfering with the related investigation or inquiry and law enforcement or protective activities.

(e) From subsection (e)(3) (Notice to Individuals Providing Information) because providing such detailed information would impede law enforcement or protective activities in that it could compromise investigations or inquiries by: Revealing the existence of an otherwise confidential investigation or inquiry and thereby provide an opportunity for the subject of an investigation or inquiry to conceal evidence, alter patterns of behavior, or take other actions that could thwart investigative or protective efforts; reveal the identity of witnesses in investigations or inquiries, thereby providing an opportunity for the subjects of the investigations or inquiries or others to harass, intimidate, or otherwise interfere with the collection of evidence or other information from such witnesses; or reveal the identity of confidential informants, which would negatively affect the informant's usefulness in any ongoing or future investigations or protective activities and discourage members of the public from cooperating as confidential informants in any future investigations or protective activities.

(f) From subsections (e)(4)(G), (H), and (I) (Agency Requirements), and (f) (Agency Rules) because portions of this system are exempt from the individual access provisions of subsection (d) for the reasons noted above, and therefore DHS is not required to establish requirements, rules, or procedures with respect to such access. Providing notice to individuals with respect to the existence of records pertaining to them in the system of records or otherwise setting up procedures pursuant to which individuals may access and view records pertaining to themselves in the system would undermine investigative or protective efforts and reveal the identities of witnesses, and potential witnesses, and confidential informants.

(g) From subsection (e)(5) (Maintenance of Information Used in Making any Determination) because in the collection of information for law enforcement and protective purposes it is impossible to determine in advance what information is accurate, relevant, timely, and complete. Compliance with (e)(5) would preclude Secret Service agents from using their investigative and protective training, and exercising good judgment to both conduct and report on investigations or other protective activities.

(h) From subsection (e)(8) (Notice on Individuals) because compliance would interfere with DHS' ability to obtain, serve, and issue subpoenas, warrants, and other law enforcement mechanisms that may be filed under seal, or could result in disclosure of investigative or protective techniques, procedures, and evidence.

(i) From subsection (g) (Civil Remedies) to the extent that the system is exempt from other specific subsections of the Privacy Act relating to individuals' rights to access and amend their records contained in the system. Therefore DHS is not required to establish rules or procedures pursuant to which individuals may seek a civil remedy for the agency's: Refusal to amend a record; refusal to comply with a request for access to records; failure to maintain accurate, relevant, timely and complete records; or failure to otherwise comply with an individual's right to access or amend records.

37. The DHS/Secret Service—004 Protection Information system of records consists of electronic and paper records and will be used by DHS and its components. The DHS/Secret Service—004 Protection Information system is a repository of information held by DHS in connection with its several and varied missions and functions, including, but not limited to: the enforcement of civil and criminal laws; investigations, inquiries, and proceedings thereunder; and the protection of the President of the United States or other individuals and locations pursuant to Sections 3056 and 3056A of Title 18. The DHS/Secret Service—004 Protection Information system contains information that is collected by, on behalf of, in support of, or in cooperation with DHS and its components and may contain personally identifiable information collected by other Federal, State, local, Tribal, foreign, or international government agencies, as well as private corporate or other entities. The Secretary of Homeland Security has exempted this system from the following provisions of the Privacy Act, subject to the limitations set forth in 5 U.S.C. 552a(c)(3) and (4); (d); (e)(1), (e)(2), (e)(3), (e)(4)(G), (e)(4)(H), (e)(4)(I), (e)(5) and (e)(8); (f), and (g) pursuant to 5 U.S.C. 552a(j)(2). Additionally, the Secretary of Homeland Security has exempted this system from the following provisions of the Privacy Act, subject to the limitations set forth in 5 U.S.C. 552a (c)(3), (d), (e)(1), (e)(4)(G), (e)(4)(H), (e)(4)(I), and (f) pursuant to 5 U.S.C. 552a(k)(1), (k)(2), and (k)(3). Exemptions from these particular subsections are justified, on a case-by-case basis to be determined at the time a request is made, for the following reasons:

(a) From subsection (c)(3) and (4) (Accounting for Disclosures) because release of the accounting of disclosures could alert the subject of an investigation of an actual or potential criminal, civil, or regulatory violation or a protective inquiry to the existence of the investigation or inquiry, and reveal investigative interest on the part of DHS as well as the recipient agency. Disclosure of the accounting would therefore present a serious impediment to law enforcement efforts and/or the Secret Service's protective mission. Disclosure of the accounting would also permit the individual who is the subject of a record to impede the investigation or inquiry, to tamper with witnesses or evidence, and to avoid detection or apprehension, which would undermine the entire investigative or inquiry process.

(b) From subsection (d) (Access to Records) because access to the records contained in this system of records could inform the subject of an investigation of an actual or potential criminal, civil, or regulatory violation, or protective inquiry to the existence of the investigation or inquiry, and reveal investigative interest on the part of DHS or another agency. Access to the records could permit the individual who is the subject of a record to impede the investigation, or inquiry to tamper with witnesses or evidence, and to avoid detection or apprehension. Amendment of the records could interfere with ongoing investigations, law enforcement or protective activities and/or could disclose security-sensitive information that could be detrimental to homeland security or the protective mission of the Secret Service.

(c) From subsection (e)(1) (Relevancy and Necessity of Information) because in the course of investigations into potential violations of Federal law or protective inquiries, the accuracy of information obtained or introduced occasionally may be unclear or the information may not be strictly relevant or necessary to a specific investigation or protective inquiry. In the interests of effective law enforcement and/or the protective mission of the Secret Service, it is appropriate to retain all information that may aid in establishing patterns of unlawful activity, or a possible threat to an individual, location or event protected or secured by the Secret Service.

(d) From subsection (e)(2) (Collection of Information from Individuals) because requiring that information be collected from the subject of an investigation or protective inquiry would alert the subject to the nature or existence of an investigation or inquiry, thereby interfering with the related investigation or inquiry and law enforcement or protective activities.

(e) From subsection (e)(3) (Notice to Individuals Providing Information) because providing such detailed information would impede law enforcement or protective activities in that it could compromise investigations or inquiries by: Revealing the existence of an otherwise confidential investigation or inquiry and thereby provide an opportunity for the subject of an investigation or inquiry to conceal evidence, alter patterns of behavior, or take other actions that could thwart investigative or protective efforts; reveal the identity of witnesses, thereby providing an opportunity for the subjects of the investigations or inquiries or others to harass, intimidate, or otherwise interfere with the collection of evidence or other information from such witnesses; or reveal the identity of confidential informants, which would negatively affect the informant's usefulness in any ongoing or future investigations or protective activities and discourage members of the public from cooperating as confidential informants in any future investigations or protective activities.

(f) From subsections (e)(4)(G), (H), and (I) (Agency Requirements), and (f) (Agency Rules) because portions of this system are exempt from the individual access provisions of subsection (d) for the reasons noted above, and therefore DHS is not required to establish requirements, rules, or procedures with respect to such access. Providing notice to individuals with respect to the existence of records pertaining to them in the system of records or otherwise setting up procedures pursuant to which individuals may access and view records pertaining to themselves in the system would undermine investigative and protective efforts and reveal the identities of witnesses, and potential witnesses, and confidential informants.

(g) From subsection (e)(5) (Maintenance of Information Used in Making any Determination) because in the collection of information for law enforcement and protective purposes it is impossible to determine in advance what information is accurate, relevant, timely, and complete. Compliance with (e)(5) would preclude Secret Service agents from using their investigative and protective training and exercising good judgment to both conduct and report on investigations or other protective activities.

(h) From subsection (e)(8) (Notice on Individuals) because compliance would interfere with DHS' ability to obtain, serve, and issue subpoenas, warrants, and other law enforcement mechanisms that may be filed under seal, and could result in disclosure of investigative or protective techniques, procedures, and evidence.

(i) From subsection (g) (Civil Remedies) to the extent that the system is exempt from other specific subsections of the Privacy Act relating to individuals' rights to access and amend their records contained in the system. Therefore DHS is not required to establish rules or procedures pursuant to which individuals may seek a civil remedy for the agency's: refusal to amend a record; refusal to comply with a request for access to records; failure to maintain accurate, relevant, timely and complete records; or failure to otherwise comply with an individual's right to access or amend records.

38. The DHS/ALL—025 Law Enforcement Authority in Support of the Protection of Property Owned or Occupied by the Department of Homeland Security system of records consists of electronic and paper records and will be used by DHS and its components. The DHS/ALL—025 Law Enforcement Authority in Support of the Protection of Property Owned or Occupied by the Department of Homeland Security system is a repository of information held by DHS in connection with its several and varied missions and functions, including, but not limited to: The enforcement of civil and criminal laws; investigations, inquiries, and proceedings there under; and national security and intelligence activities. The DHS/ALL—025 Law Enforcement Authority in Support of the Protection of Property Owned or Occupied by the Department of Homeland Security system contains information that is collected by, on behalf of, in support of, or in cooperation with DHS and its components and may contain personally identifiable information collected by other Federal, State, local, tribal, foreign, or international government agencies. The Secretary of Homeland Security has exempted this system from the following provisions of the Privacy Act, subject to the limitations set forth in 5 U.S.C. 552a (c)(3), (d), (e)(1), (e)(4)(G), (e)(4)(H), (e)(4)(I), and (f) pursuant to 5 U.S.C. 552a(k)(1), (k)(2), and (k)(5). Exemptions from these particular subsections are justified, on a case-by-case basis to be determined at the time a request is made, for the following reasons:

(a) From subsection (c)(3) (Accounting for Disclosures) because release of the accounting of disclosures could alert the subject of an investigation of an actual or potential criminal, civil, or regulatory violation to the existence of the investigation, and reveal investigative interest on the part of DHS as well as the recipient agency. Disclosure of the accounting would therefore present a serious impediment to law enforcement efforts and/or efforts to preserve national security. Disclosure of the accounting would also permit the individual who is the subject of a record to impede the investigation, to tamper with witnesses or evidence, and to avoid detection or apprehension, which would undermine the entire investigative process.

(b) From subsection (d) (Access to Records) because access to the records contained in this system of records could inform the subject of an investigation of an actual or potential criminal, civil, or regulatory violation, to the existence of the investigation, and reveal investigative interest on the part of DHS or another agency. Access to the records could permit the individual who is the subject of a record to impede the investigation, to tamper with witnesses or evidence, and to avoid detection or apprehension. Amendment of the records could interfere with ongoing investigations and law enforcement activities and would impose an impossible administrative burden by requiring investigations to be continuously reinvestigated. In addition, permitting access and amendment to such information could disclose security-sensitive information that could be detrimental to homeland security.

(c) From subsection (e)(1) (Relevancy and Necessity of Information) because in the course of investigations into potential violations of Federal law, the accuracy of information obtained or introduced occasionally

may be unclear or the information may not be strictly relevant or necessary to a specific investigation. In the interests of effective law enforcement, it is appropriate to retain all information that may aid in establishing patterns of unlawful activity.

(d) From subsections (e)(4)(G), (e)(4)(H), and (e)(4)(I) (Agency Requirements), and (f) (Agency Rules) because portions of this system are exempt from the individual access provisions of subsection (d) for the reasons noted above, and therefore DHS is not required to establish requirements, rules, or procedures with respect to such access. Providing notice to individuals with respect to existence of records pertaining to them in the system of records or otherwise setting up procedures pursuant to which individuals may access and view records pertaining to themselves in the system would undermine investigative efforts and reveal the identities of witnesses, and potential witnesses, and confidential informants.

39. The DHS/ALL—017 General Legal Records system of records consists of electronic and paper records and will be used by DHS and its components. The DHS/ALL—017 General Legal Records system of records is a repository of information held by DHS in connection with its several and varied missions and functions, including, but not limited to: The enforcement of civil and criminal laws; investigations, inquiries, and proceedings thereunder; national security and intelligence activities; and protection of the President of the United States or other individuals pursuant to section 3056 and 3056A of Title 18. The DHS/ALL—017 General Legal Records system of records contains information that is collected by, on behalf of, in support of, or in cooperation with DHS and its components and may contain personally identifiable information collected by other Federal, State, local, tribal, foreign, or international government agencies. The Secretary of Homeland Security has exempted this system from the following provisions of the Privacy Act, subject to the limitations set forth in 5 U.S.C. 552a(c)(3) and (4); (d); (e)(1), (e)(2), (e)(3), (e)(4)(G), (e)(4)(H), (e)(4)(I), (e)(5) and (e)(8); (f), and (g), pursuant to exemption 5 U.S.C. 552a(j)(2). Additionally, the Secretary of Homeland Security has exempted this system from the following provisions of the Privacy Act, subject to the limitations set forth in 5 U.S.C. 552a (c)(3), (d), (e)(1), (e)(4)(G), (e)(4)(H), (I), and (f), pursuant to 5 U.S.C. 552a(k)(1), (k)(2), (k)(3) and (k)(5). Exemptions from these particular subsections are justified, on a case-by-case basis to be determined at the time a request is made, for the following reasons:

(a) From subsection (c)(3) and (4) (Accounting for Disclosures) because release of the accounting of disclosures could alert the subject of an investigation of an actual or potential criminal, civil, or regulatory viola-

tion to the existence of the investigation, and reveal investigative interest on the part of DHS as well as the recipient agency. Disclosure of the accounting would therefore present a serious impediment to law enforcement efforts and/or efforts to preserve national security. Disclosure of the accounting would also permit the individual who is the subject of a record to impede the investigation, to tamper with witnesses or evidence, and to avoid detection or apprehension, which would undermine the entire investigative process.

(b) From subsection (d) (Access to Records) because access to the records contained in this system of records could inform the subject of an investigation of an actual or potential criminal, civil, or regulatory violation, to the existence of the investigation, and reveal investigative interest on the part of DHS or another agency. Access to the records could permit the individual who is the subject of a record to impede the investigation, to tamper with witnesses or evidence, and to avoid detection or apprehension. Amendment of the records could interfere with ongoing investigations and law enforcement activities and would impose an impossible administrative burden by requiring investigations to be continuously reinvestigated. In addition, permitting access and amendment to such information could disclose security-sensitive information that could be detrimental to homeland security.

(c) From subsection (e)(1) (Relevancy and Necessity of Information) because in the course of investigations into potential violations of Federal law, the accuracy of information obtained or introduced occasionally may be unclear or the information may not be strictly relevant or necessary to a specific investigation. In the interests of effective law enforcement, it is appropriate to retain all information that may aid in establishing patterns of unlawful activity.

(d) From subsection (e)(2) (Collection of Information from Individuals) because requiring that information be collected from the subject of an investigation would alert the subject to the nature or existence of an investigation, thereby interfering with the related investigation and law enforcement activities.

(e) From subsection (e)(3) (Notice to Subjects) because providing such detailed information would impede law enforcement in that it could compromise investigations by: Revealing the existence of an otherwise confidential investigation and thereby provide an opportunity for the subject of an investigation to conceal evidence, alter patterns of behavior, or take other actions that could thwart investigative efforts; reveal the identity of witnesses in investigations, thereby providing an opportunity for the subjects of

81

the investigations or others to harass, intimidate, or otherwise interfere with the collection of evidence or other information from such witnesses; or reveal the identity of confidential informants, which would negatively affect the informant's usefulness in any ongoing or future investigations and discourage members of the public from cooperating as confidential informants in any future investigations.

(f) From subsections (e)(4)(G), (H), and (I) (Agency Requirements), and (f) (Agency Rules) because portions of this system are exempt from the individual access provisions of subsection (d) for the reasons noted above, and therefore DHS is not required to establish requirements, rules, or procedures with respect to such access. Providing notice to individuals with respect to existence of records pertaining to them in the system of records or otherwise setting up procedures pursuant to which individuals may access and view records pertaining to themselves in the system would undermine investigative efforts and reveal the identities of witnesses, and potential witnesses, and confidential informants.

(g) From subsection (e)(5) (Collection of Information) because in the collection of information for law enforcement purposes it is impossible to determine in advance what information is accurate, relevant, timely, and complete. Compliance with (e)(5) would preclude DHS agents from using their investigative training and exercise of good judgment to both conduct and report on investigations.

(h) From subsection (e)(8) (Notice on Individuals) because compliance would interfere with DHS' ability to obtain, serve, and issue subpoenas, warrants, and other law enforcement mechanisms that may be filed under seal, and could result in disclosure of investigative techniques, procedures, and evidence.

(i) From subsection (g) to the extent that the system is exempt from other specific subsections of the Privacy Act relating to individuals' rights to access and amend their records contained in the system. Therefore DHS is not required to establish rules or procedures pursuant to which individuals may seek a civil remedy for the agency's: Refusal to amend a record; refusal to comply with a request for access to records; failure to maintain accurate, relevant, timely and complete records; or failure to otherwise comply with an individual's right to access or amend records.

40. The DHS/ALL—023 Personnel Security Management system of records consists of electronic and paper records and will be used by DHS and its components. The DHS/ALL—023 Personnel Security Management system is a repository of information held by DHS in connection with its several and varied missions and functions, including, but not limited to: The enforcement of civil and criminal laws; investigations, inquiries, and proceedings thereunder; national security and intelligence activities; and protection of the President of the United States or other individuals pursuant to section 3056 and 3056A of Title 18. The DHS/ALL—023 Personnel Security Management system contains information that is collected by, on behalf of, in support of, or in cooperation with DHS and its components and may contain personally identifiable information collected by other Federal, State, local, tribal, foreign, or international government agencies. The Secretary of Homeland Security has exempted this system from the following provisions of the Privacy Act, subject to the limitations set forth in 5 U.S.C. 552a (c)(3), (d), (e)(1), (e)(4)(G), (e)(4)(H), (e)(4)(I), and (f) pursuant to 5 U.S.C. 552a(k)(1), (k)(2), (k)(3), and (k)(5). Exemptions from these particular subsections are justified, on a case-by-case basis to be determined at the time a request is made, for the following reasons:

(a) From subsection (c)(3) (Accounting for Disclosures) because release of the accounting of disclosures could alert the subject of an investigation of an actual or potential criminal, civil, or regulatory violation to the existence of the investigation, and reveal investigative interest on the part of DHS as well as the recipient agency. Disclosure of the accounting would therefore present a serious impediment to law enforcement efforts and/or efforts to preserve national security. Disclosure of the accounting would also permit the individual who is the subject of a record to impede the investigation, to tamper with witnesses or evidence, and to avoid detection or apprehension, which would undermine the entire investigative process.

(b) From subsection (d) (Access to Records) because access to the records contained in this system of records could inform the subject of an investigation of an actual or potential criminal, civil, or regulatory violation, to the existence of the investigation, and reveal investigative interest on the part of DHS or another agency. Access to the records could permit the individual who is the subject of a record to impede the investigation, to tamper with witnesses or evidence, and to avoid detection or apprehension. Amendment of the records could interfere with ongoing investigations and law enforcement activities and would impose an impossible administrative burden by requiring investigations to be continuously reinvestigated. In addition, permitting access and amendment to such information could disclose security-sensitive information that could be detrimental to homeland security.

(c) From subsection (e)(1) (Relevancy and Necessity of Information) because in the course of investigations into potential violations of Federal law, the accuracy of information obtained or introduced occasionally

may be unclear or the information may not be strictly relevant or necessary to a specific investigation. In the interests of effective law enforcement, it is appropriate to retain all information that may aid in establishing patterns of unlawful activity.

(d) From subsections (e)(4)(G), (H), and (I) (Agency Requirements), and (f) (Agency Rules) because portions of this system are exempt from the individual access provisions of subsection (d) for the reasons noted above, and therefore DHS is not required to establish requirements, rules, or procedures with respect to such access. Providing notice to individuals with respect to existence of records pertaining to them in the system of records or otherwise setting up procedures pursuant to which individuals may access and view records pertaining to themselves in the system would undermine investigative efforts and reveal the identities of witnesses, and potential witnesses, and confidential informants.

41. The DHS/NPPD/US–VISIT—001 Arrival and Departure Information system of records notice is a system for the storage and use of biographic, biometric indicator, and encounter data consolidated from various systems regarding aliens who have applied for entry, entered, or departed the United States. Information in the DHS/NPPD/US–VISIT—001 Arrival and Departure Information system of records notice is used primarily to facilitate the investigation of subjects of interest who may have violated their immigration status by remaining in the United States beyond their authorized stay; thereby supporting the several and varied missions and functions of DHS, including but not limited to: the enforcement of civil and criminal laws (including the immigration law); investigations, inquiries; national security and intelligence activities in support of the DHS mission to identify and prevent acts of terrorism against the United States. The information is collected by, on behalf of, in support of, or in cooperation with DHS and its components and may contain personally identifiable information collected by other Federal, State, local, tribal, foreign, or international government agencies. The Secretary of Homeland Security has exempted this system from the following provisions of the Privacy Act, subject to the limitations set forth in 5 U.S.C. 552a(c)(3) and (4); (d); (e)(1), (e)(2), (e)(3), (e)(4)(G), (e)(4)(H), (e)(5) and (e)(8); (f); and (g) pursuant to 5 U.S.C. 552a(j)(2). Additionally, the Secretary of Homeland Security has exempted this system from the following provisions of the Privacy Act, subject to the limitations set forth in 5 U.S.C. 552a(c)(3); (d); (e)(1), (e)(4)(G), (e)(4)(H); and (f) pursuant to 5 U.S.C. 552a(k)(1), (k)(2), (k)(3) and (k)(5). Exemptions from these particular subsections are justified, on a case-by-case basis to be determined at the time a request is made, for the following reasons:

(a) From subsection (c)(3) and (4) (Accounting for Disclosures) because release of the accounting of disclosures could alert the subject of an investigation of an actual or potential criminal, civil, or regulatory violation to the existence of the investigation; and reveal investigative interest on the part of DHS as well as the recipient agency. Disclosure of the accounting would therefore present a serious impediment to law enforcement efforts and/or efforts to preserve national security. Disclosure of the accounting would also permit the individual who is the subject of a record to impede the investigation, to tamper with witnesses or evidence, and to avoid detection or apprehension, which would undermine the entire investigative process.

(b) From subsection (d) (Access to Records) because access to the records contained in this system of records could inform the subject of an investigation of an actual or potential criminal, civil, or regulatory violation, to the existence of the investigation, and reveal investigative interest on the part of DHS or another agency. Access to the records could permit the individual who is the subject of a record to impede the investigation, to tamper with witnesses or evidence, and to avoid detection or apprehension. Amendment of the records could interfere with ongoing investigations and law enforcement activities and would impose an impossible administrative burden by requiring investigations to be continuously re-investigated. In addition, permitting access and amendment to such information could disclose security-sensitive information that could be detrimental to homeland security.

(c) From subsection (e)(1) (Relevancy and Necessity of Information) because in the course of investigations into potential violations of Federal law, the accuracy of information obtained or introduced occasionally may be unclear or the information may not be strictly relevant or necessary to a specific investigation. In the interests of effective law enforcement, it is appropriate to retain all information that may aid in establishing patterns of unlawful activity.

(d) From subsection (e)(2) (Collection of Information from Individuals) because requiring that information be collected from the subject of an investigation would alert the subject to the nature or existence of an investigation, thereby interfering with the related investigation and law enforcement activities.

(e) From subsection (e)(3) (Notice to Subjects) because providing such detailed information would impede law enforcement in that it could compromise investigations by: revealing the existence of an otherwise confidential investigation and thereby provide an opportunity for the subject of an investigation to conceal evidence, alter patterns of behavior, or take other actions that could thwart investigative efforts; reveal the identities of witnesses in investigations, thereby providing an opportunity for the subjects of the investigations or others to harass, intimidate, or otherwise interfere with the collection of evidence or other information from such witnesses; or reveal the identity of confidential informants, which would negatively affect the informant's usefulness in any ongoing or future investigations and discourage members of the public from cooperating as confidential informants in any future investigations.

(f) From subsections (e)(4)(G) and (H) (Agency Requirements), and (f) (Agency Requirements) because portions of this system are exempt from the individual access provisions of subsection (d) for the reasons noted above, and therefore DHS is not required to establish requirements, rules, or procedures with respect to such access. Providing notice to individuals with respect to existence of records pertaining to them in the system of records or otherwise setting up procedures pursuant to which individuals may access and view records pertaining to themselves in the system would undermine investigative efforts and reveal the identities of witnesses, and potential witnesses, and confidential informants.

(g) From subsection (e)(5) (Collection of Information) because in the collection of information for law enforcement purposes it is impossible to determine in advance what information is accurate, relevant, timely, and complete. Compliance with (e)(5) would preclude DHS agents from using their investigative training and exercise of good judgment to both conduct and report on investigations.

(h) From subsection (e)(8) (Notice on Individuals) because compliance would interfere with DHS' ability to obtain, serve, and issue subpoenas, warrants, and other law enforcement mechanisms that may be filed under seal, and could result in disclosure of investigative techniques, procedures, and evidence.

(i) From subsection (g) (Civil Remedies) to the extent that the system is exempt from other specific subsections of the Privacy Act relating to individuals' rights to access and amend their records contained in the system. Therefore DHS is not required to establish rules or procedures pursuant to which individuals may seek a civil remedy for the agency's: refusal to amend a record; refusal to comply with a request for access to records; failure to maintain accurate, relevant, timely and complete records; or failure to otherwise comply with an individual's right to access or amend records.

42. The DHS/NPPD/US–VISIT—003 Technical Reconciliation Analysis Classification system of records (TRACS) consists of stand alone database and paper files that will be used by DHS and its components. This sys-

tem of records will be used to perform a range of information management and analytic functions involving collecting, verifying, and resolving tracking of data primarily on individuals who are not United States citizens or legal permanent residents (LPRs). However, it will contain data on: (1.) U.S. citizens or LPRs who have a connection to the DHS mission (e.g., individuals who have submitted a visa application to the UK, or have made requests for a license or credential as part of a background check or security screening in connection with their hiring or retention, performance of a job function or the issuance of a license or credential for employment at DHS); (2.) U.S. citizens and LPRs who have an incidental connection to the DHS mission (e.g., individuals living at the same address as individuals who have remained in this country beyond their authorized stays); and (3.) individuals who have, over time, changed their status and became U.S. citizens or LPRs. The DHS/NPPD/US–VISIT—003 Technical Reconciliation Analysis Classification system of records is managed and maintained by the US–VISIT Program. The data contained in the DHS/NPPD/US–VISIT—003 Technical Reconciliation Analysis Classification system of records is primarily derived from DHS/NPPD/U.S–VISIT—001 Arrival and Departure Information System (ADIS); DHS/CBP—011 TECS; DHS/ICE—001 Student and Exchange Visitor Information System (SEVIS); DHS/ICE/CBP/USCIS—001–03 Enforcement Operational Immigration Records (ENFORCE/IDENT); DHS/ICE—011 Removable Alien Records System (RARS); DHS/USCIS—001 Alien File (A–File) and Central Index System (CIS); DHS/USCIS—007 Benefits Information System covering Computer Linked Application Information Management System 3 (Claims 3) and Computer Linked Application Information Management System 4 (Claims 4); DHS/USCIS Refugees, Asylum & Parole System (RAPS); and from the Department of State's Consolidated Consular Database (CCD). The DHS/NPPD/US–VISIT—003 Technical Reconciliation Analysis Classification system of records also contains data from web searches for addresses and phone numbers. This data is collected by, on behalf of, in support of, or in cooperation with DHS and its components. The Secretary of Homeland Security has exempted this system from the following provisions of the Privacy Act, subject to the limitations set forth in 5 U.S.C. 552a(c)(3) and (4); (d); (e)(1), (e)(2), (e)(3), (e)(4)(G), (e)(4)(H), (e)(4)(I), (e)(5) and (e)(8); (f); and (g) pursuant to 5 U.S.C. 552a(j)(2). Additionally, the Secretary of Homeland Security has exempted this system from the following provisions of the Privacy Act, subject to the limitations set forth in 5 U.S.C. 552a(c)(3); (d); (e)(1), (e)(4)(G), (e)(4)(H), (e)(4)(I); and (f) pursuant to 5 U.S.C. 552a(k)(1), (k)(2), and (k)(5). Exemptions from these particular subsections are justified, on a case-by-case basis to be determined at the time a request is made, for the following reasons:

(a) From subsection (c)(3) and (4) (Accounting for Disclosures) because release of the accounting of disclosures could alert the subject of an investigation of an actual or potential criminal, civil, or regulatory violation to the existence of the investigation, and reveal investigative interest on the part of DHS as well as the recipient agency. Disclosure of the accounting would therefore present a serious impediment to law enforcement efforts and/or efforts to preserve national security. Disclosure of the accounting would also permit the individual who is the subject of a record to impede the investigation, to tamper with witnesses or evidence, and to avoid detection or apprehension, which would undermine the entire investigative process.

(b) From subsection (d) (Access to Records) because access to the records contained in this system of records could inform the subject of an investigation of an actual or potential criminal, civil, or regulatory violation, to the existence of the investigation, and reveal investigative interest on the part of DHS or another agency. Access to the records could permit the individual who is the subject of a record to impede the investigation, to tamper with witnesses or evidence, and to avoid detection or apprehension. Amendment of the records could interfere with ongoing investigations and law enforcement activities and would impose an impossible administrative burden by requiring investigations to be continuously re-investigated. In addition, permitting access and amendment to such information could disclose security-sensitive information that could be detrimental to homeland security.

(c) From subsection (e)(1) (Relevancy and Necessity of Information) because in the course of investigations into potential violations of Federal law, the accuracy of information obtained or introduced occasionally may be unclear or the information may not be strictly relevant or necessary to a specific investigation. In the interests of effective law enforcement, it is appropriate to retain all information that may aid in establishing patterns of unlawful activity.

(d) From subsection (e)(2) (Collection of Information from Individuals) because requiring that information be collected from the subject of an investigation would alert the subject to the nature or existence of an investigation, thereby interfering with the related investigation and law enforcement activities.

(e) From subsection (e)(3) (Notice to Subjects) because providing such detailed information would impede law enforcement in that it could compromise investigations by:

revealing the existence of an otherwise confidential investigation and thereby provide an opportunity for the subject of an investigation to conceal evidence, alter patterns of behavior, or take other actions that could thwart investigative efforts; reveal the identity of witnesses in investigations, thereby providing an opportunity for the subjects of the investigations or others to harass, intimidate, or otherwise interfere with the collection of evidence or other information from such witnesses; or reveal the identity of confidential informants, which would negatively affect the informant's usefulness in any ongoing or future investigations and discourage members of the public from cooperating as confidential informants in any future investigations.

(f) From subsections (e)(4)(G), and (e)(4)(H) (Agency Requirements) because portions of this system are exempt from the individual access provisions of subsection (d) which exempts providing access because it could alert a subject to the nature or existence of an investigation, and thus there could be no procedures for that particular data. Procedures do exist for access for those portions of the system that are not exempted.

(g) From subsection (e)(4)(I) (Agency Requirements) because providing such source information would impede enforcement or intelligence by compromising the nature or existence of a confidential investigation.

(h) From subsection (e)(5) (Collection of Information) because in the collection of information for law enforcement purposes it is impossible to determine in advance what information is accurate, relevant, timely, and complete. Compliance with (e)(5) would preclude DHS agents from using their investigative training and exercise of good judgment to both conduct and report on investigations.

(i) From subsection (e)(8) (Notice on Individuals) because compliance would interfere with DHS' ability to obtain, serve, and issue subpoenas, warrants, and other law enforcement mechanisms that may be filed under seal, and could result in disclosure of investigative techniques, procedures, and evidence.

(j) From subsection (f) (Agency Rules) because portions of this system are exempt from the access and amendment provisions of subsection (d).

(k) From subsection (g) to the extent that the system is exempt from other specific subsections of the Privacy Act.

43. The DHS/USCG—013 Marine Information for Safety and Law Enforcement system of records consists of electronic and paper records and will be used by DHS and its components. The DHS/USCG—013 Marine Information for Safety and Law Enforcement system of records is a repository of information held by DHS in connection with its several and varied missions and functions, including,

but not limited to: the enforcement of civil and criminal laws; investigations, inquiries, and proceedings there under; national security and intelligence activities. The DHS/USCG—013 Marine Information for Safety and Law Enforcement system of records contains information that is collected by, on behalf of, in support of, or in cooperation with DHS and its components and may contain personally identifiable information collected by other Federal, State, local, tribal, foreign, or international government agencies. The Secretary of Homeland Security has exempted this system from the following provisions of the Privacy Act, subject to the limitations set forth in 5 U.S.C. 552a(c)(3) and (4); (d); (e)(1), (e)(2), (e)(3), (e)(4)(G), (e)(4)(H), (e)(4)(I), (e)(5) and (e)(8); (f); and (g) pursuant to 5 U.S.C. 552a(j)(2). Additionally, the Secretary of Homeland Security has exempted this system from the following provisions of the Privacy Act, subject to the limitations set forth in 5 U.S.C. 552a(c)(3); (d); (e)(1), (e)(4)(G), (e)(4)(H); (I); and (f) pursuant to 5 U.S.C. 552a(k)(2). Exemptions from these particular subsections are justified, on a case-by-case basis to be determined at the time a request is made, for the following reasons:

(a) From subsections (c)(3) and (4) (Accounting for Disclosures) because release of the accounting of disclosures could alert the subject of an investigation of an actual or potential criminal, civil, or regulatory violation to the existence of the investigation, and reveal investigative interest on the part of DHS as well as the recipient agency. Disclosure of the accounting would therefore present a serious impediment to law enforcement efforts and/or efforts to preserve national security. Disclosure of the accounting would also permit the individual who is the subject of a record to impede the investigation, to tamper with witnesses or evidence, and to avoid detection or apprehension, which would undermine the entire investigative process.

(b) From subsection (d) (Access to Records) because access to the records contained in this system of records could inform the subject of an investigation of an actual or potential criminal, civil, or regulatory violation, to the existence of the investigation, and reveal investigative interest on the part of DHS or another agency. Access to the records could permit the individual who is the subject of a record to impede the investigation, to tamper with witnesses or evidence, and to avoid detection or apprehension. Amendment of the records could interfere with ongoing investigations and law enforcement activities and would impose an impossible administrative burden by requiring investigations to be continuously re-investigated. In addition, permitting access and amendment to such information could disclose security-sensitive information that could be detrimental to homeland security.

(c) From subsection (e)(1) (Relevancy and Necessity of Information) because in the course of investigations into potential violations of Federal law, the accuracy of information obtained or introduced occasionally may be unclear or the information may not be strictly relevant or necessary to a specific investigation. In the interests of effective law enforcement, it is appropriate to retain all information that may aid in establishing patterns of unlawful activity.

(d) From subsection (e)(2) (Collection of Information from Individuals) because requiring that information be collected from the subject of an investigation would alert the subject to the nature or existence of an investigation, thereby interfering with the related investigation and law enforcement activities.

(e) From subsection (e)(3) (Notice to Subjects) because providing such detailed information would impede law enforcement in that it could compromise investigations by: revealing the existence of an otherwise confidential investigation and thereby provide an opportunity for the subject of an investigation to conceal evidence, alter patterns of behavior, or take other actions that could thwart investigative efforts; reveal the identity of witnesses in investigations, thereby providing an opportunity for the subjects of the investigations or others to harass, intimidate, or otherwise interfere with the collection of evidence or other information from such witnesses; or reveal the identity of confidential informants, which would negatively affect the informant's usefulness in any ongoing or future investigations and discourage members of the public from cooperating as confidential informants in any future investigations.

(f) From subsections (e)(4)(G), (H), and (I) (Agency Requirements), and (f) (Agency Rules) because portions of this system are exempt from the individual access provisions of subsection (d) for the reasons noted above, and therefore DHS is not required to establish requirements, rules, or procedures with respect to such access. Providing notice to individuals with respect to existence of records pertaining to them in the system of records or otherwise setting up procedures pursuant to which individuals may access and view records pertaining to themselves in the system would undermine investigative efforts and reveal the identities of witnesses, and potential witnesses, and confidential informants.

(g) From subsection (e)(5) (Collection of Information) because in the collection of information for law enforcement purposes it is impossible to determine in advance what information is accurate, relevant, timely, and complete. Compliance with (e)(5) would preclude DHS agents from using their investigative training and exercise of good judgment to both conduct and report on investigations.

(h) From subsection (e)(8) (Notice on Individuals) because compliance would interfere with DHS' ability to obtain, serve, and issue subpoenas, warrants, and other law enforcement mechanisms that may be filed under seal, and could result in disclosure of investigative techniques, procedures, and evidence.

(i) From subsection (g) to the extent that the system is exempt from other specific subsections of the Privacy Act relating to individuals' rights to access and amend their records contained in the system. Therefore DHS is not required to establish rules or procedures pursuant to which individuals may seek a civil remedy for the agency's: refusal to amend a record; refusal to comply with a request for access to records; failure to maintain accurate, relevant timely and complete records; or failure to otherwise comply with an individual's right to access or amend records.

44. The DHS/USCG—030 Merchant Seaman's Records system of records consists of electronic and paper records and will be used by DHS and its components. The DHS/USCG—030 Merchant Seaman's Records system of records is a repository of information held by DHS in connection with its several and varied missions and functions, including, but not limited to: the enforcement of civil and criminal laws; investigations, inquiries, and proceedings there under. The DHS/USCG—030 Merchant Seaman's Records system of records contains information that is collected by, on behalf of, in support of, or in cooperation with DHS and its components and may contain personally identifiable information collected by other Federal, State, local, tribal, foreign, or international government agencies. The Secretary of Homeland Security has exempted this system from the following provisions of the Privacy Act, subject to the limitations set forth in 5 U.S.C. 552a(c)(3); (d); (e)(1), (e)(4)(G), (e)(4)(H), (e)(4)(I); and (f) pursuant to 5 U.S.C. 552a(k)(2). Exemptions from these particular subsections are justified, on a case-by-case basis to be determined at the time a request is made, for the following reasons:

(a) From subsection (c)(3) (Accounting for Disclosures) because release of the accounting of disclosures could alert the subject of an investigation of an actual or potential criminal, civil, or regulatory violation to the existence of the investigation, and reveal investigative interest on the part of DHS as well as the recipient agency. Disclosure of the accounting would therefore present a serious impediment to law enforcement efforts and/or efforts to preserve national security. Disclosure of the accounting would also permit the individual who is the subject of a record to impede the investigation, to tamper with witnesses or evidence, and to avoid detection or apprehension, which would undermine the entire investigative process.

(b) From subsection (d) (Access to Records) because access to the records contained in this system of records could inform the subject of an investigation of an actual or potential criminal, civil, or regulatory violation, to the existence of the investigation, and reveal investigative interest on the part of DHS or another agency. Access to the records could permit the individual who is the subject of a record to impede the investigation, to tamper with witnesses or evidence, and to avoid detection or apprehension. Amendment of the records could interfere with ongoing investigations and law enforcement activities and would impose an impossible administrative burden by requiring investigations to be continuously reinvestigated. In addition, permitting access and amendment to such information could disclose security-sensitive information that could be detrimental to homeland security.

(c) From subsection (e)(1) (Relevancy and Necessity of Information) because in the course of investigations into potential violations of Federal law, the accuracy of information obtained or introduced occasionally may be unclear or the information may not be strictly relevant or necessary to a specific investigation. In the interests of effective law enforcement, it is appropriate to retain all information that may aid in establishing patterns of unlawful activity.

(d) From subsections (e)(4)(G), (e)(4)(H), and (e)(4)(I) (Agency Requirements), and (f) (Agency Rules) because portions of this system are exempt from the individual access provisions of subsection (d) for the reasons noted above, and therefore DHS is not required to establish requirements, rules, or procedures with respect to such access. Providing notice to individuals with respect to existence of records pertaining to them in the system of records or otherwise setting up procedures pursuant to which individuals may access and view records pertaining to themselves in the system would undermine investigative efforts and reveal the identities of witnesses, and potential witnesses, and confidential informants.

45. The DHS/CBP—006 Automated Targeting system of records performs screening of both inbound and outbound cargo, travelers, and conveyances. As part of this screening function and to facilitate DHS's border enforcement mission, the DHS/CBP—006 Automated Targeting system of records compares information received with CBP's law enforcement databases, the Federal Bureau of Investigation Terrorist Screening Center's Terrorist Screening Database (TSDB), information on outstanding wants or warrants, information from other government agencies regarding high-risk parties, and risk-based rules developed by analysts using law enforcement data, intelligence,

and past case experience. The modules also facilitate analysis of the screening results of these comparisons. This supports the several and varied missions and functions of DHS, including but not limited to: The enforcement of civil and criminal laws (including the immigration law); investigations, inquiries; national security and intelligence activities in support of the DHS mission to identify and prevent acts of terrorism against the United States. The information is collected by, on behalf of, in support of, or in cooperation with DHS and its components and may contain personally identifiable information collected by other Federal, State, local, tribal, foreign, or international government agencies. Certain records or information in DHS/CBP—006 Automated Targeting system of records are exempt from the Privacy Act. With respect to the ATS–P module, exempt records are the targeting rule sets, risk assessment analyses, and business confidential information contained in the PNR that relates to the air and vessel carriers. No exemption shall be asserted regarding PNR data about the requester, provided by either the requester or a booking agent, brokers, or another person on the requester's behalf. This information, upon request, may be provided to the requester in the form in which it was collected from the respective carrier, but may not include certain business confidential information of the air carrier that is also contained in the record, such as use and application of frequent flier miles, internal annotations to the air fare, etc. For other DHS/CBP—006 Automated Targeting system of records modules the only information maintained in the system is the targeting rule sets, risk assessment analyses, and a pointer to the data from the source system of records. The Secretary of Homeland Security has exempted this system from the following provisions of the Privacy Act, subject to the limitations set forth in 5 U.S.C. 552a(c)(3) and (4); (d)(1), (2), (3), and (4); (e)(1), (2), (3), (4)(G) through (I), (e)(5), and (8); (f); and (g) pursuant to 5 U.S.C. 552a(j)(2). Additionally, the Secretary of Homeland Security has exempted this system from the following provisions of the Privacy Act, subject to the limitations set forth in 5 U.S.C. 552a(c)(3) and (4); (d)(1), (2), (3), and (4); (e)(1), (2), (3), (4)(G) through (I), (e)(5), and (8); (f); and (g) pursuant to 5 U.S.C. 552a(k)(2). These exemptions also apply to the extent that information in this system of records is recompiled or is created from information contained in other systems of records. After conferring with the appropriate component or agency, DHS may waive applicable exemptions in appropriate circumstances and where it would not appear to interfere with or adversely affect the law enforcement purposes of the systems from which the information is recompiled or in which it is contained. Exemptions from these

particular subsections are justified, on a case-by-case basis to be determined at the time a request is made, for the following reasons:

(a) From subsection (c)(3) and (4) (Accounting for Disclosure) because making available to a record subject the accounting of disclosures from records concerning him or her would specifically reveal any investigative interest in the individual. Revealing this information could reasonably be expected to compromise ongoing efforts to investigate a known or suspected criminal or terrorist, or other person of interest, by notifying the record subject that he or she is under investigation. This information could also permit the record subject to take measures to impede the investigation, e.g., destroy evidence, intimidate potential witnesses, or flee the area to avoid or impede the investigation. Exemptions from these particular subsections are justified, on a case-by-case basis to be determined at the time a request is made, for the following reasons: (a) From subsection (c)(3) (Accounting for Disclosure) because making available to a record subject the accounting of disclosures from records concerning him or her would specifically reveal any investigative interest in the individual. Revealing this information could reasonably be expected to compromise ongoing efforts to investigate a known or suspected terrorist by notifying the record subject that he or she is under investigation. This information could also permit the record subject to take measures to impede the investigation, e.g., destroy evidence, intimidate potential witnesses, or flee the area to avoid or impede the investigation.

(b) From subsection (c)(4) (Accounting for Disclosure, notice of dispute) because certain records in this system are exempt from the access and amendment provisions of subsection (d), this requirement to inform any person or other agency about any correction or notation of dispute that the agency made with regard to those records, should not apply.

(c) From subsections (d)(1), (2), (3), and (4) (Access to Records) because these provisions concern individual access to and amendment of certain records contained in this system, including law enforcement, counterterrorism, and investigatory records. Compliance with these provisions could alert the subject of an investigation to the fact and nature of the investigation, and/or the investigative interest of intelligence or law enforcement agencies; compromise sensitive information related to law enforcement, including matters bearing on national security; interfere with the overall law enforcement process by leading to the destruction of evidence, improper influencing of witnesses, fabrication of testimony, and/or flight of the subject; could identify a confidential source;

reveal a sensitive investigative or intelligence technique; or constitute a potential danger to the health or safety of law enforcement personnel, confidential informants, and witnesses. Amendment of these records would interfere with ongoing counterterrorism or law enforcement investigations and analysis activities and impose an impossible administrative burden by requiring investigations, analyses, and reports to be continuously reinvestigated and revised.

(d) From subsection (e)(1) (Relevancy and Necessity of Information) because it is not always possible for DHS or other agencies to know in advance what information is relevant and necessary for it to complete screening of cargo, conveyances, and passengers. Information relating to known or suspected criminals or terrorists or other persons of interest, is not always collected in a manner that permits immediate verification or determination of relevancy to a DHS purpose. For example, during the early stages of an investigation, it may not be possible to determine the immediate relevancy of information that is collected—only upon later evaluation or association with further information, obtained subsequently, may it be possible to establish particular relevance to a law enforcement program. Lastly, this exemption is required because DHS and other agencies may not always know what information about an encounter with a known or suspected criminal or terrorist or other person of interest will be relevant to law enforcement for the purpose of conducting an operational response.

(e) From subsection (e)(2) (Collection of Information from Individuals) because application of this provision could present a serious impediment to counterterrorism or other law enforcement efforts in that it would put the subject of an investigation, study or analysis on notice of that fact, thereby permitting the subject to engage in conduct designed to frustrate or impede that activity. The nature of counterterrorism, and law enforcement investigations is such that vital information about an individual frequently can be obtained only from other persons who are familiar with such individual and his/her activities. In such investigations it is not feasible to rely solely upon information furnished by the individual concerning his own activities.

(f) From subsection (e)(3) (Notice to Subjects), to the extent that this subsection is interpreted to require DHS to provide notice to an individual if DHS or another agency receives or collects information about that individual during an investigation or from a third party. Should the subsection be so interpreted, exemption from this provision is necessary to avoid impeding counterterrorism or other law enforcement efforts by putting the subject of an investigation, study or analysis on notice of that fact,

thereby permitting the subject to engage in conduct intended to frustrate or impede that activity.

(g) From subsections (e)(4)(G), (H) and (I) (Agency Requirements) because portions of this system are exempt from the access and amendment provisions of subsection (d).

(h) From subsection (e)(5) (Collection of Information) because many of the records in this system coming from other systems of records are derived from other domestic and foreign agency record systems and therefore it is not possible for DHS to vouch for their compliance with this provision; however, the DHS has implemented internal quality assurance procedures to ensure that data used in its screening processes is as complete, accurate, and current as possible. In addition, in the collection of information for law enforcement and counterterrorism purposes, it is impossible to determine in advance what information is accurate, relevant, timely, and complete. With the passage of time, seemingly irrelevant or untimely information may acquire new significance as further investigation brings new details to light. The restrictions imposed by (e)(5) would limit the ability of those agencies' trained investigators and intelligence analysts to exercise their judgment in conducting investigations and impede the development of intelligence necessary for effective law enforcement and counterterrorism efforts.

(i) From subsection (e)(8) (Notice on Individuals) because to require individual notice of disclosure of information due to compulsory legal process would pose an impossible administrative burden on DHS and other agencies and could alert the subjects of counterterrorism or law enforcement investigations to the fact of those investigations when not previously known.

(j) From subsection (f) (Agency Rules) because portions of this system are exempt from the access and amendment provisions of subsection (d). Access to, and amendment of, system records that are not exempt or for which exemption is waived may be obtained under procedures described in the related SORN or subpart B of this part.

(k) From subsection (g) (Civil Remedies) to the extent that the system is exempt from other specific subsections of the Privacy Act.

46. The DHS/CBP–007 Border Crossing Information System of Records consists of electronic and paper records and will be used by DHS and its Components. The DHS/CBP–007 Border Crossing Information System of Records is a repository of information held by DHS in connection with its several and varied missions and functions including, but not limited to the enforcement of civil and criminal laws; investigations, inquiries, and proceedings thereunder; and law enforcement, border security, and intelligence activities. The DHS/CBP–007 Border Crossing

Information System of Records contains information that is collected by, on behalf of, in support of, or in cooperation with DHS and its Components and may contain personally identifiable information collected by other Federal, State, local, tribal, foreign, or international government agencies. At the time of border crossing and during the process of determining admissibility, CBP collects two types of data for which it claims different exemptions.

(a) CBP will not assert any exemption to limit an individual from accessing or amending his or her record with respect to information maintained in the system that is collected from a person at the time of crossing and submitted by that person's air, sea, bus, or rail carriers. The Privacy Act requires DHS to maintain an accounting of the disclosures made pursuant to all routine uses. Pursuant to 5 U.S.C. 552a(j)(2), CBP will not disclose the fact that a law enforcement or intelligence agency has sought particular records because it may affect ongoing law enforcement activities. The Secretary of Homeland Security has exempted this system from subsections (c)(3), (e)(8), and (g) of the Privacy Act of 1974, as amended, as is necessary and appropriate to protect this information. Further, DHS will claim exemption from subsection (c)(3) of the Privacy Act of 1974, as amended, pursuant to 5 U.S.C. 552a(k)(2) as is necessary and appropriate to protect this information. Exemptions from these particular subsections are justified, on a case-by-case basis to be determined at the time a request is made, for the following reasons:

(i) From subsection (c)(3) (Accounting for Disclosures) because release of the accounting of disclosures could alert the subject of an investigation of an actual or potential criminal, civil, or regulatory violation to the existence of that investigation and reveal investigative interest on the part of DHS as well as the recipient agency. Disclosure of the accounting would therefore present a serious impediment to law enforcement efforts and/or efforts to preserve national security. Disclosure of the accounting would also permit the individual who is the subject of a record to impede the investigation, to tamper with witnesses or evidence, and to avoid detection or apprehension, which would undermine the entire investigative process.

(ii) From subsection (e)(8) (Notice on Individuals) because compliance would interfere with DHS's ability to obtain, serve, and issue subpoenas, warrants, and other law enforcement mechanisms that may be filed under seal and could result in disclosure of investigative techniques, procedures, and evidence.

(iii) From subsection (g) (Civil Remedies) to the extent that the system is exempt from other specific subsections of the Privacy Act.

(b) Additionally, this system contains records or information recompiled from or created from information contained in other systems of records that are exempt from certain provisions of the Privacy Act. For these records or information only, the Secretary of Homeland Security, pursuant to 5 U.S.C. 552a(j)(2), has exempted this system from the following provisions of the Privacy Act: 5 U.S.C. 552a(c)(3), (c)(4); (d)(1)–(4); (e)(1), (e)(2), (e)(3), (e)(4)(G), (e)(4)(H), (e)(4)(I), (e)(5) and (e)(8); (f); and (g). Additionally, the Secretary of Homeland Security, pursuant to 5 U.S.C. 552a(k)(2), has exempted this system from the following provisions of the Privacy Act, 5 U.S.C. 552a(c)(3); (d)(1)–(4); (e)(1), (e)(4)(G), (e)(4)(H), (e)(4)(I); and (f). Exemptions from these particular subsections are justified, on a case-by-case basis to be determined at the time a request is made, for the following reasons:

(i) From subsection (c)(3) and (c)(4) (Accounting for Disclosures) because release of the accounting of disclosures could alert the subject of an investigation of an actual or potential criminal, civil, or regulatory violation to the existence of that investigation and reveal investigative interest on the part of DHS as well as the recipient agency. Disclosure of the accounting would therefore present a serious impediment to law enforcement efforts and/or efforts to preserve national security. Disclosure of the accounting would also permit the individual who is the subject of a record to impede the investigation, to tamper with witnesses or evidence, and to avoid detection or apprehension, which would undermine the entire investigative process.

(ii) From subsection (d) (Access to Records) because access to the 6records contained in this system of records could inform the subject of an investigation of an actual or potential criminal, civil, or regulatory violation to the existence of that investigation and reveal investigative interest on the part of DHS or another agency. Access to the records could permit the individual who is the subject of a record to impede the investigation, and to avoid detection or apprehension. Amendment of the records could interfere with ongoing investigations and law enforcement activities and would impose an unreasonable administrative burden by requiring investigations to be continually reinvestigated. In addition, permitting access and amendment to such information could disclose security-sensitive information that could be detrimental to homeland security.

(iii) From subsection (e)(1) (Relevancy and Necessity of Information) because in the course of investigations into potential violations of federal law, the accuracy of information obtained or introduced occasionally may be unclear, or the information may not be strictly relevant or necessary to a specific investigation. In the interests of effective law enforcement, it is appropriate to retain all information that may aid in establishing patterns of unlawful activity.

(iv) From subsection (e)(2) (Collection of Information from Individuals) because requiring that information be collected from the subject of an investigation would alert the subject to the nature or existence of the investigation, thereby interfering with that investigation and related law enforcement activities.

(v) From subsection (e)(3) (Notice to Subjects) because providing such detailed information could impede law enforcement by compromising the existence of a confidential investigation or reveal the identity of witnesses or confidential informants.

(vi) From subsections (e)(4)(G), (e)(4)(H), and (e)(4)(I) (Agency Requirements) and (f) (Agency Rules), because portions of this system are exempt from the individual access provisions of subsection (d) for the reasons noted above, and therefore DHS is not required to establish requirements, rules, or procedures with respect to such access. Providing notice to individuals with respect to existence of records pertaining to them in the system of records or otherwise setting up procedures pursuant to which individuals may access and view records pertaining to themselves in the system would undermine investigative efforts and reveal the identities of witnesses, potential witnesses, and confidential informants.

(vii) From subsection (e)(5) (Collection of Information) because with the collection of information for law enforcement purposes, it is impossible to determine in advance what information is accurate, relevant, timely, and complete. Compliance with subsection (e)(5) would preclude DHS agents from using their investigative training and exercise of good judgment to both conduct and report on investigations.

(viii) From subsection (e)(8) (Notice on Individuals) because compliance would interfere with DHS's ability to obtain, serve, and issue subpoenas, warrants, and other law enforcement mechanisms that may be filed under seal and could result in disclosure of investigative techniques, procedures, and evidence.

(ix) From subsection (g) (Civil Remedies) to the extent that the system is exempt from other specific subsections of the Privacy Act.

47. The Visa Security Program Records (VSPR) system of records consists of electronic and paper records and will be used by the Department of Homeland Security (DHS) U.S. Immigration and Customs Enforcement (ICE). VSPR consists of information created in support of the Visa Security Program, the purpose of which is to identify persons who may be ineligible for a U.S. visa because of criminal history, terrorism association, or other factors and convey that information to the State Department, which decides wheth-

er to issue the visa. VSPR contains records on visa applicants for whom a visa security review is conducted. VSPR contains information that is collected by, on behalf of, in support of, or in cooperation with DHS and its components and may contain personally identifiable information collected by other Federal, State, local, Tribal, foreign, or international government agencies. Pursuant to exemption 5 U.S.C. 552a(j)(2) of the Privacy Act, portions of this system are exempt from 5 U.S.C. 552a(c)(3) and (4); (d); (e)(1), (e)(2), (e)(3), (e)(4)(G), and (e)(4)(H), (e)(5) and (e)(8); (f); and (g). Pursuant to 5 U.S.C. 552a(k)(1) and (k)(2), this system is exempt from the following provisions of the Privacy Act, subject to the limitations set forth in those subsections: 5 U.S.C. 552a(c)(3), (d), (e)(1), (e)(4)(G), (e)(4)(H), and (f). Exemptions from these particular subsections are justified, on a case-by-case basis to be determined at the time a request is made, for the following reasons:

(a) From subsection (c)(3) and (4) (Accounting for Disclosures) because release of the accounting of disclosures could alert the individual to the existence of an investigation in the form of a visa security review predicated on classified, national security, law enforcement, foreign government, or other sensitive information. Disclosure of the accounting would therefore present a serious impediment to ICE's Visa Security Program, immigration enforcement efforts and/or efforts to preserve national security. Disclosure of the accounting would also permit the individual who is the subject of a record to impede the investigation, thereby undermining the entire investigative process.

(b) From subsection (d) (Access to Records) because access to the records contained in this system of records could alert the individual to the existence of an investigation in the form of a visa security review predicated on classified, national security, law enforcement, foreign government, or other sensitive information. Revealing the existence of an otherwise confidential investigation could also provide the visa applicant an opportunity to conceal adverse information or take other actions that could thwart investigative efforts; and reveal the identity of other individuals with information pertinent to the visa security review, thereby providing an opportunity for the applicant to interfere with the collection of adverse or other relevant information from such individuals. Access to the records would therefore present a serious impediment to the enforcement of Federal immigration laws, law enforcement efforts and/or efforts to preserve national security. Amendment of the records could interfere with ICE's ongoing investigations and law enforcement activities and would impose an impossible administrative burden by requiring investigations

91

to be continuously reinvestigated. In addition, permitting access and amendment to such information could disclose classified and other security-sensitive information that could be detrimental to national or homeland security.

(c) From subsection (e)(1) (Relevancy and Necessity of Information) because in the course of investigations of visa applications, the accuracy of information obtained or introduced occasionally may be unclear or the information may not be strictly relevant or necessary to a specific investigation. In the interest of effective enforcement of Federal immigration laws, it is appropriate to retain all information that may be relevant to the determination whether an individual is eligible for a U.S. visa.

(d) From subsection (e)(2) (Collection of Information From Individuals) because requiring that information be collected from the visa applicant would alert the subject to the fact of an investigation in the form of a visa security review, and to the existence of adverse information about the individual, thereby interfering with the related investigation and law enforcement activities.

(e) From subsection (e)(3) (Notice to Subjects) because providing such detailed information would impede immigration enforcement activities in that it could compromise investigations by: Revealing the existence of an otherwise confidential investigation and thereby provide an opportunity for the visa applicant to conceal adverse information, or take other actions that could thwart investigative efforts; Reveal the identity of other individuals with information pertinent to the visa security review, thereby providing an opportunity for the applicant to interfere with the collection of adverse or other relevant information from such individuals; reveal the identity of confidential informants, which would negatively affect the informant's usefulness in any ongoing or future investigations and discourage members of the public from cooperating as confidential informants in any future investigations.

(f) From subsections (e)(4)(G) and (H) (Agency Requirements), and (f) (Agency Rules) because portions of this system are exempt from the individual access provisions of subsection (d) for the reasons noted above, and therefore DHS is not required to establish requirements, rules, or procedures with respect to such access. Providing notice to individuals with respect to existence of records pertaining to them in the system of records or otherwise setting up procedures pursuant to which individuals may access and view records pertaining to themselves in the system would undermine investigative and immigration enforcement efforts as described above.

(g) From subsection (e)(5) (Collection of Information) because in the collection of information for law enforcement purposes it is impossible to determine in advance what information is accurate, relevant, timely, and complete. Compliance with (e)(5) would preclude DHS agents from using their investigative training and exercise of good judgment to both conduct and report on investigations.

(h) From subsection (e)(8) because to require individual notice of disclosure of information due to compulsory legal process would pose an impossible administrative burden on DHS and other agencies and could alert the subjects of counterterrorism, law enforcement, or intelligence investigations to the fact of those investigations when not previously known.

(i) From subsection (g) to the extent that the system is exempt from other specific subsections of the Privacy Act relating to individuals' rights to access and amend their records contained in the system. Therefore DHS is not required to establish rules or procedures pursuant to which individuals may seek a civil remedy for the agency's: Refusal to amend a record; refusal to comply with a request for access to records; failure to maintain accurate, relevant, timely and complete records; or failure to otherwise comply with an individual's right to access or amend records.

48. The DHS/ICE–011 Immigration and Enforcement Operational Records system of records consists of electronic and paper records and will be used by DHS and its components. The DHS/ICE–011 Immigration and Enforcement Operational Records system of records is a repository of information held by DHS in connection with its several and varied missions and functions, including, but not limited to: The enforcement of civil and criminal laws; investigations, inquiries, and proceedings there under; and national security and intelligence activities. The DHS/ICE–011 Immigration and Enforcement Operational Records system of records contains information that is collected by, on behalf of, in support of, or in cooperation with DHS and its components and may contain personally identifiable information collected by other federal, state, local, tribal, foreign, or international government agencies. The Secretary of Homeland Security has exempted this system from the following provisions of the Privacy Act, subject to the limitations set forth in 5 U.S.C. 552a(c)(3) and (4); (d); (e)(1), (e)(2), (e)(3), (e)(4)(G), (e)(4)(H), (e)(5), and (e)(8); (f); and (g) pursuant to 5 U.S.C. 552a(j)(2). Additionally, the Secretary of Homeland Security has exempted this system from the following provisions of the Privacy Act, subject to the limitations set forth in 5 U.S.C. 552a(c)(3); (d); (e)(1), (e)(4)(G), (e)(4)(H); and (f) pursuant to 5 U.S.C. 552a(k)(2). Exemptions from these particular subsections are justified, on a case-by-case basis to be determined at the time a request is made, for the following reasons:

(a) From subsection (c)(3) and (4) (Accounting for Disclosures) because release of the accounting of disclosures could alert the subject of an investigation of an actual or potential criminal, civil, or regulatory violation to the existence of the investigation, and reveal investigative interest on the part of DHS as well as the recipient agency. Disclosure of the accounting would therefore present a serious impediment to law enforcement efforts and/or efforts to preserve national security. Disclosure of the accounting would also permit the individual who is the subject of a record to impede the investigation, to tamper with witnesses or evidence, and to avoid detection or apprehension, which would undermine the entire investigative process.

(b) From subsection (d) (Access to Records) because access to the records contained in this system of records could inform the subject of an investigation of an actual or potential criminal, civil, or regulatory violation, to the existence of the investigation, and reveal investigative interest on the part of DHS or another agency. Access to the records could permit the individual who is the subject of a record to impede the investigation, to tamper with witnesses or evidence, and to avoid detection or apprehension. Amendment of the records could interfere with ongoing investigations and law enforcement activities and would impose an impossible administrative burden by requiring investigations to be continuously re-investigated. In addition, permitting access and amendment to such information could disclose security-sensitive information that could be detrimental to homeland security.

(c) From subsection (e)(1) (Relevancy and Necessity of Information) because in the course of investigations into potential violations of Federal law, the accuracy of information obtained or introduced occasionally may be unclear or the information may not be strictly relevant or necessary to a specific investigation. In the interests of effective law enforcement, it is appropriate to retain all information that may aid in establishing patterns of unlawful activity.

(d) From subsection (e)(2) (Collection of Information from Individuals) because requiring that information be collected from the subject of an investigation would alert the subject to the nature or existence of an investigation, thereby interfering with the related investigation and law enforcement activities.

(e) From subsection (e)(3) (Notice to Subjects) because providing such detailed information would impede law enforcement in that it could compromise investigations by: Revealing the existence of an otherwise confidential investigation and thereby provide an opportunity for the subject of an investigation to conceal evidence, alter patterns of behavior, or take other actions that could thwart investigative efforts; reveal the identity of witnesses in investigations, thereby providing an opportunity for the subjects of the investigations or others to harass, intimidate, or otherwise interfere with the collection of evidence or other information from such witnesses; or reveal the identity of confidential informants, which would negatively affect the informant's usefulness in any ongoing or future investigations and discourage members of the public from cooperating as confidential informants in any future investigations.

(f) From subsections (e)(4)(G) and (H) (Agency Requirements), and (f) (Agency Rules) because portions of this system are exempt from the individual access provisions of subsection (d) for the reasons noted above, and therefore DHS is not required to establish requirements, rules, or procedures with respect to such access. Providing notice to individuals with respect to existence of records pertaining to them in the system of records or otherwise setting up procedures pursuant to which individuals may access and view records pertaining to themselves in the system would undermine investigative efforts and reveal the identities of witnesses, and potential witnesses, and confidential informants.

(g) From subsection (e)(5) (Collection of Information) because in the collection of information for law enforcement purposes it is impossible to determine in advance what information is accurate, relevant, timely, and complete. Compliance with (e)(5) would preclude DHS agents from using their investigative training and exercise of good judgment to both conduct and report on investigations.

(h) From subsection (e)(8) (Notice on Individuals) because compliance would interfere with DHS' ability to obtain, serve, and issue subpoenas, warrants, and other law enforcement mechanisms that may be filed under seal, and could result in disclosure of investigative techniques, procedures, and evidence.

(i) From subsection (g) to the extent that the system is exempt from other specific subsections of the Privacy Act relating to individuals' rights to access and amend their records contained in the system. Therefore DHS is not required to establish rules or procedures pursuant to which individuals may seek a civil remedy for the agency's: Refusal to amend a record; refusal to comply with a request for access to records; failure to maintain accurate, relevant timely and complete records; or failure to otherwise comply with an individual's right to access or amend records.

49. The DHS/USCIS—009 Compliance Tracking and Management System of Records consists of electronic and paper files that will be used by DHS and its components. This system of records will be used to

perform a range of information management and analytic functions involving minimizing misuse, abuse, discrimination, breach of privacy, and fraudulent use of SAVE and E-Verify. The Secretary of Homeland Security has exempted this system from the following provisions of the Privacy Act, subject to the limitation set forth in 5 U.S.C. 552a(c)(3), (d), (e)(1), (e)(4)(G), (e)(4)(H), (e)(4)(I), and (f) pursuant to 5 U.S.C. 552a(k)(2). Exemptions from these particular subsections are justified, on a case-by-case basis to be determined at the time a request is made, for the following reasons:

(a) From subsection (c)(3) (Accounting for Disclosures) because release of the accounting of disclosures could alert the subject of an investigation of an actual or potential criminal, civil, or regulatory violation to the existence of the investigation, and reveal investigative interest on the part of DHS as well as the recipient agency. Disclosure of the accounting would therefore present a serious impediment to law enforcement efforts and/or efforts to preserve national security. Disclosure of the accounting would also permit the individual who is the subject of a record to impede the investigation, to tamper with witnesses or evidence, and to avoid detection or apprehension, which would undermine the entire investigative process.

(b) From subsection (d) (Access to Records) because access to the records contained in this system of records could inform the subject of an investigation of an actual or potential criminal, civil, or regulatory violation, to the existence of the investigation, and reveal investigative interest on the part of DHS or another agency. Access to the records could permit the individual who is the subject of a record to impede the investigation, to tamper with witnesses or evidence, and to avoid detection or apprehension. Amendment of the records could interfere with ongoing investigations and law enforcement activities and would impose an impossible administrative burden by requiring investigations to be continuously reinvestigated. In addition, permitting access and amendment to such information could disclose security-sensitive information that could be detrimental to homeland security.

(c) From subsection (e)(1) (Relevancy and Necessity of Information) because in the course of investigations into potential violations of Federal law, the accuracy of information obtained or introduced occasionally may be unclear or the information may not be strictly relevant or necessary to a specific investigation. In the interest of effective law enforcement, it is appropriate to retain all information that may aid in establishing patterns of unlawful activity.

(d) From subsections (e)(4)(G), (H), and (I) (Agency Requirements), and (f) (Agency Rules) because portions of this system are exempt from the individual access provisions of subsection (d) for the reasons noted above, and therefore DHS is not required to establish requirements, rules, or procedures with respect to such access. Providing notice to individuals with respect to existence of records pertaining to them in the system of records or otherwise setting up procedures pursuant to which individuals may access and view records pertaining to themselves in the system would undermine investigative efforts and reveal the identities of witnesses, and potential witnesses, and confidential informants.

50. The Immigration and Customs Enforcement (ICE)—006 Intelligence Records System (IIRS) consists of electronic and paper records and will be used by the Department of Homeland Security (DHS). IIRS is a repository of information held by DHS in connection with its several and varied missions and functions, including, but not limited to: the enforcement of civil and criminal laws; investigations, inquiries, and proceedings thereunder; and national security and intelligence activities. IIRS contains information that is collected by other federal and foreign government agencies and may contain personally identifiable information. Pursuant to exemption 5 U.S.C. 552a(j)(2) of the Privacy Act, portions of this system are exempt from 5 U.S.C. 552a(c)(3) and (4); (d); (e)(1), (e)(2), (e)(3), (e)(4)(G), (e)(4)(H), (e)(5) and (e)(8); (f), and (g). Pursuant to 5 U.S.C. 552a(k)(2), this system is exempt from the following provisions of the Privacy Act, subject to the limitations set forth in those subsections: 5 U.S.C. 552a(c)(3), (d), (e)(1), (e)(4)(G), (e)(4)(H), and (f). Exemptions from these particular subsections are justified, on a case-by-case basis to be determined at the time a request is made, for the following reasons:

(a) From subsection (c)(3) and (4) (Accounting for Disclosures) because release of the accounting of disclosures could alert the subject of an investigation of an actual or potential criminal, civil, or regulatory violation to the existence of the investigation, and reveal investigative interest on the part of DHS as well as the recipient agency. Disclosure of the accounting would therefore present a serious impediment to law enforcement efforts and/or efforts to preserve national security. Disclosure of the accounting would also permit the individual who is the subject of a record to impede the investigation, to tamper with witnesses or evidence, and to avoid detection or apprehension, which would undermine the entire investigative process.

(b) From subsection (d) (Access to Records) because access to the records contained in this system of records could inform the subject of an investigation of an actual or potential criminal, civil, or regulatory violation, to the existence of the investigation, and reveal investigative interest on the part of DHS or another agency. Access to the records could permit the individual who is the subject of a record to impede the investigation, to tamper with witnesses or evidence, and to avoid detection or apprehension. Amendment of the records could interfere with ongoing investigations and law enforcement activities and would impose an impossible administrative burden by requiring investigations to be continuously re-investigated. In addition, permitting access and amendment to such information could disclose security-sensitive information that could be detrimental to homeland security.

(c) From subsection (e)(1) (Relevancy and Necessity of Information) because in the course of investigations into potential violations of Federal law, the accuracy of information obtained or introduced occasionally may be unclear or the information may not be strictly relevant or necessary to a specific investigation. In the interests of effective law enforcement, it is appropriate to retain all information that may aid in establishing patterns of unlawful activity.

(d) From subsection (e)(2) (Collection of Information from Individuals) because requiring that information be collected from the subject of an investigation would alert the subject to the nature or existence of an investigation, thereby interfering with the related investigation and law enforcement activities.

(e) From subsection (e)(3) (Notice to Subjects) because providing such detailed information would impede law enforcement in that it could compromise investigations by: revealing the existence of an otherwise confidential investigation and thereby provide an opportunity for the subject of an investigation to conceal evidence, alter patterns of behavior, or take other actions that could thwart investigative efforts; reveal the identity of witnesses in investigations, thereby providing an opportunity for the subjects of the investigations or others to harass, intimidate, or otherwise interfere with the collection of evidence or other information from such witnesses; or reveal the identity of confidential informants, which would negatively affect the informant's usefulness in any ongoing or future investigations and discourage members of the public from cooperating as confidential informants in any future investigations.

(f) From subsections (e)(4)(G) and (H) (Agency Requirements), and (f) (Agency Rules) because portions of this system are exempt from the individual access provisions of subsection (d) for the reasons noted above, and therefore DHS is not required to establish requirements, rules, or procedures with respect to such access. Providing notice to individuals with respect to existence of records pertaining to them in the system of records or otherwise setting up procedures pursuant to which individuals may access

and view records pertaining to themselves in the system would undermine investigative efforts and reveal the identities of witnesses, and potential witnesses, and confidential informants.

(g) From subsection (e)(5) (Collection of Information) because in the collection of information for law enforcement purposes it is impossible to determine in advance what information is accurate, relevant, timely, and complete. Compliance with (e)(5) would preclude DHS agents from using their investigative training and exercise of good judgment to both conduct and report on investigations.

(h) From subsection (e)(8) (Notice on Individuals) because compliance would interfere with DHS' ability to obtain, serve, and issue subpoenas, warrants, and other law enforcement mechanisms that may be filed under seal, and could result in disclosure of investigative techniques, procedures, and evidence.

(i) From subsection (g) to the extent that the system is exempt from other specific subsections of the Privacy Act relating to individuals' rights to access and amend their records contained in the system. Therefore DHS is not required to establish rules or procedures pursuant to which individuals may seek a civil remedy for the agency's: refusal to amend a record; refusal to comply with a request for access to records; failure to maintain accurate, relevant timely and complete records; or failure to otherwise comply with an individual's right to access or amend records.

51. The DHS/ALL—027 The History of the Department of Homeland Security System of Records consists of electronic and paper records and will be used by DHS and its components. The DHS/ALL—027 The History of the Department of Homeland Security System of Records is a repository of information held by DHS in connection with its several and varied missions and functions, including, but not limited to the enforcement of civil and criminal laws; investigations, inquiries, and proceedings thereunder; national security and intelligence activities; and protection of the President of the United States or other individuals pursuant to section 3056 and 3056A of Title 18. The DHS/ALL—027 The History of the Department of Homeland Security System of Records contain information that is collected by, on behalf of, in support of, or in cooperation with DHS and its components and may contain personally identifiable information collected by other federal, state, local, tribal, foreign, or international government agencies. The Secretary of Homeland Security has exempted this system from the following provisions of the Privacy Act, subject to limitations set forth in 5 U.S.C. 552a(c)(3) and (4); (d); (e)(1), (e)(2), (e)(3), (e)(4)(G), (e)(4)(H), (e)(4)(I),

(e)(5), (e)(8), (e)(12); (f); (g)(1); and (h) pursuant to 5 U.S.C. 552a(j)(2). Additionally, the Secretary of Homeland Security has exempted this system from the following provisions of the Privacy Act, subject to limitations set forth in 5 U.S.C. 552a(c)(3); (d); (e)(1), (e)(4)(G), (e)(4)(H), (e)(4)(I); and (f) pursuant to 5 U.S.C. 552a(k)(1), (k)(2), (k)(3), and (k)(5). Exemptions from these particular subsections are justified, on a case-by-case basis to be determined at the time a request is made, for the following reasons:

(a) From subsection (c)(3) and (4) (Accounting for Disclosures) because release of the accounting of disclosures could alert the subject of an investigation of an actual or potential criminal, civil, or regulatory violation to the existence of that investigation and reveal investigative interest on the part of DHS as well as the recipient agency. Disclosure of the accounting would therefore present a serious impediment to law enforcement efforts and/or efforts to preserve national security. Disclosure of the accounting would also permit the individual who is the subject of a record to impede the investigation, to tamper with witnesses or evidence, and to avoid detection or apprehension, which would undermine the entire investigative process.

(b) From subsection (d) (Access to Records) because access to the records contained in this system of records could inform the subject of an investigation of an actual or potential criminal, civil, or regulatory violation to the existence of that investigation and reveal investigative interest on the part of DHS or another agency. Access to the records could permit the individual who is the subject of a record to impede the investigation, to tamper with witnesses or evidence, and to avoid detection or apprehension. Amendment of the records could interfere with ongoing investigations and law enforcement activities and would impose an unreasonable administrative burden by requiring investigations to be continually reinvestigated. In addition, permitting access and amendment to such information could disclose security-sensitive information that could be detrimental to homeland security.

(c) From subsection (e)(1) (Relevancy and Necessity of Information) because in the course of investigations into potential violations of federal law, the accuracy of information obtained or introduced occasionally may be unclear, or the information may not be strictly relevant or necessary to a specific investigation. In the interests of effective law enforcement, it is appropriate to retain all information that may aid in establishing patterns of unlawful activity.

(d) From subsection (e)(2) (Collection of Information from Individuals) because requiring that information be collected from the subject of an investigation would alert the subject to the nature or existence of the investigation, thereby interfering with that investigation and related law enforcement activities.

(e) From subsection (e)(3) (Notice to Subjects) because providing such detailed information could impede law enforcement by compromising the existence of a confidential investigation or reveal the identity of witnesses or confidential informants.

(f) From subsections (e)(4)(G), (e)(4)(H), and (e)(4)(I) (Agency Requirements) and (f) (Agency Rules), because portions of this system are exempt from the individual access provisions of subsection (d) for the reasons noted above, and therefore DHS is not required to establish requirements, rules, or procedures with respect to such access. Providing notice to individuals with respect to existence of records pertaining to them in the system of records or otherwise setting up procedures pursuant to which individuals may access and view records pertaining to themselves in the system would undermine investigative efforts and reveal the identities of witnesses, and potential witnesses, and confidential informants.

(g) From subsection (e)(5) (Collection of Information) because with the collection of information for law enforcement purposes, it is impossible to determine in advance what information is accurate, relevant, timely, and complete. Compliance with subsection (e)(5) would preclude DHS agents from using their investigative training and exercise of good judgment to both conduct and report on investigations.

(h) From subsection (e)(8) (Notice on Individuals) because compliance would interfere with DHS's ability to obtain, serve, and issue subpoenas, warrants, and other law enforcement mechanisms that may be filed under seal and could result in disclosure of investigative techniques, procedures, and evidence.

(i) From subsection (e)(12) (Computer Matching) if the agency is a recipient agency or a source agency in a matching program with a non-Federal agency, with respect to any establishment or revision of a matching program, at least 30 days prior to conducting such program, publish in the FEDERAL REGISTER notice of such establishment or revision.

(j) From subsection (g)(1) (Civil Remedies) to the extent that the system is exempt from other specific subsections of the Privacy Act.

(k) From subsection (h) (Legal Guardians) the parent of any minor, or the legal guardian of any individual who has been declared to be incompetent due to physical or mental incapacity or age by a court of competent jurisdiction, may act on behalf of the individual.

52. The DHS/ALL—031 ISE SAR Initiative System of Records consists of electronic

records and will be used by DHS and its components. The DHS/ALL—031 ISE SAR Initiative System of Records is a repository of information held by DHS in connection with its several and varied missions and functions, including, but not limited to the enforcement of civil and criminal laws; investigations, inquiries, and proceedings there under; national security and intelligence activities; and protection of the President of the U.S. or other individuals pursuant to Section 3056 and 3056A of Title 18. The DHS/ALL—031 ISE SAR Initiative System of Records contains information that is collected by, on behalf of, in support of, or in cooperation with DHS, its components, as well as other federal, state, local, tribal, or foreign agencies or private sector organization and may contain personally identifiable information collected by other federal, state, local, tribal, foreign, or international government agencies. The Secretary of Homeland Security has exempted this system from the following provisions of the Privacy Act, subject to the limitations set forth in 5 U.S.C. 552a(c)(3) and (4); (d); (e)(1), (e)(2), (e)(3), (e)(4)(G), (e)(4)(H), (e)(4)(I), (e)(5), (e)(8), and (e)(12); (f); (g)(1); and (h) of the Privacy Act pursuant to 5 U.S.C. 552a(j)(2). Additionally, the Secretary of Homeland Security has exempted this system from the following provisions of the Privacy Act, subject to the limitation set forth in 5 U.S.C. 552a(c)(3); (d); (e)(1), (e)(4)(G), (e)(4)(H), (e)(4)(I); and (f) of the Privacy Act pursuant to 5 U.S.C. 552a(k)(2) and (k)(3). Exemptions from these particular subsections are justified, on a case-by-case basis to be determined at the time a request is made, for the following reasons:

(a) From subsection (c)(3) and (c)(4) (Accounting for Disclosures) because release of the accounting of disclosures could alert the subject of an investigation of an actual or potential criminal, civil, or regulatory violation to the existence of that investigation and reveal investigative interest on the part of DHS as well as the recipient agency. Disclosure of the accounting would therefore present a serious impediment to law enforcement efforts and/or efforts to preserve national security. Disclosure of the accounting would also permit the individual who is the subject of a record to impede the investigation, to tamper with witnesses or evidence, and to avoid detection or apprehension, which would undermine the entire investigative process.

(b) From subsection (d) (Access to Records) because access to the records contained in this system of records could inform the subject of an investigation of an actual or potential criminal, civil, or regulatory violation to the existence of that investigation and reveal investigative interest on the part of DHS or another agency. Access to the records could permit the individual who is the subject of a record to impede the investigation, to tamper with witnesses or evidence, and to avoid detection or apprehension. Amendment of the records could interfere with ongoing investigations and law enforcement activities and would impose an unreasonable administrative burden by requiring investigations to be continually reinvestigated. In addition, permitting access and amendment to such information could disclose security-sensitive information that could be detrimental to homeland security.

(c) From subsection (e)(1) (Relevancy and Necessity of Information) because in the course of investigations into potential violations of federal law, the accuracy of information obtained or introduced occasionally may be unclear, or the information may not be strictly relevant or necessary to a specific investigation. In the interests of effective law enforcement, it is appropriate to retain all information that may aid in establishing patterns of unlawful activity.

(d) From subsection (e)(2) (Collection of Information from Individuals) because requiring that information be collected from the subject of an investigation would alert the subject to the nature or existence of the investigation, thereby interfering with that investigation and related law enforcement activities.

(e) From subsection (e)(3) (Notice to Subjects) because providing such detailed information could impede law enforcement by compromising the existence of a confidential investigation or reveal the identity of witnesses or confidential informants.

(f) From subsections (e)(4)(G), (e)(4)(H), and (e)(4)(I) (Agency Requirements) and (f) (Agency Rules), because portions of this system are exempt from the individual access provisions of subsection (d) for the reasons noted above, and therefore DHS is not required to establish requirements, rules, or procedures with respect to such access. Providing notice to individuals with respect to existence of records pertaining to them in the system of records or otherwise setting up procedures pursuant to which individuals may access and view records pertaining to themselves in the system would undermine investigative efforts and reveal the identities of witnesses, and potential witnesses, and confidential informants.

(g) From subsection (e)(5) (Collection of Information) because with the collection of information for law enforcement purposes, it is impossible to determine in advance what information is accurate, relevant, timely, and complete. Compliance with subsection (e)(5) would preclude DHS agents from using their investigative training and exercise of good judgment to both conduct and report on investigations.

(h) From subsection (e)(8) (Notice on Individuals) because compliance would interfere with DHS's ability to obtain, serve, and issue subpoenas, warrants, and other law enforcement mechanisms that may be filed under seal and could result in disclosure of investigative techniques, procedures, and evidence.

(i) From subsection (e)(12) (Computer Matching) if the agency is a recipient agency or a source agency in a matching program with a non-Federal agency, with respect to any establishment or revision of a matching program, at least 30 days prior to conducting such program, publish in the FEDERAL REGISTER notice of such establishment or revision.

(j) From subsection (g)(1) (Civil Remedies) to the extent that the system is exempt from other specific subsections of the Privacy Act.

(k) From subsection (h) (Legal Guardians) the parent of any minor, or the legal guardian of any individual who has been declared to be incompetent due to physical or mental incapacity or age by a court of competent jurisdiction, may act on behalf of the individual.

53. The DHS/USCIS–012 CIDR System of Records consists of electronic and paper records and will be used by DHS and its components. The DHS/USCIS–012 CIDR System of Records is a repository of information held by DHS in connection with its several and varied missions and functions, including, but not limited to the enforcement of civil and criminal laws; investigations, inquiries, and proceedings thereunder; national security and intelligence activities; and protection of the President of the U.S. or other individuals pursuant to Section 3056 and 3056A of Title 18. The DHS/USCIS–012 CIDR System of Records contains information that is collected by, on behalf of, in support of, or in cooperation with DHS and its components and may contain PII collected by other federal, state, local, tribal, foreign, or international government agencies. The Secretary of Homeland Security has exempted this system from the following provisions of the Privacy Act, subject to limitations set forth in 5 U.S.C. 552a(c)(3); (d); (e)(1), (e)(4)(G), (e)(4)(H), (e)(4)(I); and (f) pursuant to 5 U.S.C. 552a (k)(1) and (k)(2). Exemptions from these particular subsections are justified, on a case-by-case basis to be determined at the time a request is made, for the following reasons:

(a) From subsection (c)(3) (Accounting for Disclosures) because release of the accounting of disclosures could alert the subject of an investigation of an actual or potential criminal, civil, or regulatory violation to the existence of the investigation, and reveal investigative interest on the part of DHS as well as the recipient agency. Disclosure of the accounting would therefore present a serious impediment to law enforcement efforts and/or efforts to preserve national security. Disclosure of the accounting could also permit the individual who is the subject of a record to impede the investigation, to tamper with witnesses or evidence, and to avoid detection or apprehension, which would undermine the entire investigative process.

(b) From subsection (d) (Access to Records) because access to the records contained in this system of records could inform the subject of an investigation of an actual or potential criminal, civil, or regulatory violation, to the existence of the investigation, and reveal investigative interest on the part of DHS or another agency. Access to the records could permit the individual who is the subject of a record to impede the investigation, to tamper with witnesses or evidence, and to avoid detection or apprehension. Amendment of the records could interfere with ongoing investigations and law enforcement activities and would impose an impossible administrative burden by requiring investigations to be continuously reinvestigated. In addition, permitting access and amendment to such information could disclose security-sensitive information that could be detrimental to homeland security.

(c) From subsection (e)(1) (Relevancy and Necessity of Information) because in the course of investigations into potential violations of federal law, the accuracy of information obtained or introduced occasionally may be unclear or the information may not be strictly relevant or necessary to a specific investigation. In the interests of effective law enforcement, it is appropriate to retain all information that may aid in establishing patterns of unlawful activity.

(d) From subsections (e)(4)(G), (e)(4)(H), and (e)(4)(I) (Agency Requirements), and (f) (Agency Rules) because portions of this system are exempt from the individual access provisions of subsection (d) for the reasons noted above, and therefore DHS is not required to establish requirements, rules, or procedures with respect to such access. Providing notice to individuals with respect to existence of records pertaining to them in the system of records or otherwise setting up procedures pursuant to which individuals may access and view records pertaining to themselves in the system would undermine investigative efforts and reveal the identities of witnesses, and potential witnesses, and confidential informants.

54. The DHS/USCG—008 Courts Martial Case Files System of Records consists of electronic and paper records and will be used by DHS/USCG. The DHS/USCG—008 Courts Martial Case Files System of Records is a repository of information held by DHS/USCG in connection with its several and varied missions and functions, including, but not limited to: the enforcement of civil and criminal laws; investigations, inquiries, and proceedings thereunder; and national security and intelligence activities. The DHS/USCG—008 Courts Martial Case Files System

of Records contains information that is collected by, on behalf of, in support of, or in cooperation with DHS/USCG and may contain personally identifiable information collected by other federal, state, local, tribal, foreign, or international government agencies. The Secretary of Homeland Security has exempted this system from the following provisions of the Privacy Act, subject to the limitations set forth in 5 U.S.C. 552a(c)(3) and (c)(4); (d); (e)(1), (e)(2), (e)(3), (e)(4)(G), (e)(4)(H), (e)(4)(I), (e)(5) and (e)(8); (f); and (g) pursuant to 5 U.S.C. 552a(j)(2). Additionally, the Secretary of Homeland Security has exempted this system from the following provisions of the Privacy Act, subject to the limitations set forth in 5 U.S.C. 552a(c)(3); (d); (e)(1), (e)(4)(G), (e)(4)(H), (e)(4)(I); and (f) pursuant to 5 U.S.C. 552a(k)(1) and (k)(2). Exemptions from these particular subsections are justified, on a case-by-case basis to be determined at the time a request is made, for the following reasons:

(a) From subsection (c)(3) and (c)(4) (Accounting for Disclosures) because release of the accounting of disclosures could alert the subject of an investigation of an actual or potential criminal, civil, or regulatory violation to the existence of the investigation, and reveal investigative interest on the part of DHS as well as the recipient agency. Disclosure of the accounting would therefore present a serious impediment to law enforcement efforts and/or efforts to preserve national security. Disclosure of the accounting would also permit the individual who is the subject of a record to impede the investigation, to tamper with witnesses or evidence, and to avoid detection or apprehension, which would undermine the entire investigative process.

(b) From subsection (d) (Access to Records) because access to the records contained in this system of records could inform the subject of an investigation of an actual or potential criminal, civil, or regulatory violation, to the existence of the investigation, and reveal investigative interest on the part of DHS or another agency. Access to the records could permit the individual who is the subject of a record to impede the investigation, to tamper with witnesses or evidence, and to avoid detection or apprehension. Amendment of the records could interfere with ongoing investigations and law enforcement activities and would impose an impossible administrative burden by requiring investigations to be continuously reinvestigated. In addition, permitting access and amendment to such information could disclose security-sensitive information that could be detrimental to homeland security.

(c) From subsection (e)(1) (Relevancy and Necessity of Information) because in the course of investigations into potential violations of federal law, the accuracy of information obtained or introduced occasionally may be unclear or the information may not be strictly relevant or necessary to a specific investigation. In the interests of effective law enforcement, it is appropriate to retain all information that may aid in establishing patterns of unlawful activity.

(d) From subsection (e)(2) (Collection of Information from Individuals) because requiring that information be collected from the subject of an investigation would alert the subject to the nature or existence of an investigation, thereby interfering with the related investigation and law enforcement activities.

(e) From subsection (e)(3) (Notice to Subjects) because providing such detailed information would impede law enforcement in that it could compromise investigations by revealing the existence of an otherwise confidential investigation and thereby provide an opportunity for the subject of an investigation to conceal evidence, alter patterns of behavior, or take other actions that could thwart investigative efforts; reveal the identity of witnesses in investigations, thereby providing an opportunity for the subjects of the investigations or others to harass, intimidate, or otherwise interfere with the collection of evidence or other information from such witnesses; or reveal the identity of confidential informants, which would negatively affect the informant's usefulness in any ongoing or future investigations and discourage members of the public from cooperating as confidential informants in any future investigations.

(f) From subsections (e)(4)(G), (e)(4)(H), and (e)(4)(I) (Agency Requirements), and (f) (Agency Rules) because portions of this system are exempt from the individual access provisions of subsection (d) for the reasons noted above, and therefore DHS is not required to establish requirements, rules, or procedures with respect to such access. Providing notice to individuals with respect to existence of records pertaining to them in the system of records or otherwise setting up procedures pursuant to which individuals may access and view records pertaining to themselves in the system would undermine investigative efforts and reveal the identities of witnesses, and potential witnesses, and confidential informants.

(g) From subsection (e)(5) (Collection of Information) because in the collection of information for law enforcement purposes it is impossible to determine in advance what information is accurate, relevant, timely, and complete. Compliance with (e)(5) would preclude DHS agents from using their investigative training and exercise of good judgment to both conduct and report on investigations.

(h) From subsection (e)(8) (Notice on Individuals) because compliance would interfere with DHS' ability to obtain, serve, and issue subpoenas, warrants, and other law enforcement mechanisms that may be filed under seal, and could result in disclosure of investigative techniques, procedures, and evidence.

(i) From subsection (g) to the extent that the system is exempt from other specific subsections of the Privacy Act relating to individuals' rights to access and amend their records contained in the system. Therefore DHS is not required to establish rules or procedures pursuant to which individuals may seek a civil remedy for the agency's: refusal to amend a record; refusal to comply with a request for access to records; failure to maintain accurate, relevant, timely and complete records; or failure to otherwise comply with an individual's right to access or amend records.

55. The DHS/FEMA–011 Training and Exercise Program Records System of Records consists of electronic and paper records and will be used by FEMA. The DHS/FEMA–011 Training and Exercise Program Records System of Records consists of electronic and paper records and will be used by DHS and its components and offices to maintain records about individual training, including enrollment and participation information, information pertaining to class schedules, programs, and instructors, training trends and needs, testing and examination materials, and assessments of training efficacy. The data will be collected by employee name or other unique identifier. The collection and maintenance of this information will assist DHS in meeting its obligation to train its personnel and contractors in order to ensure that the agency mission can be successfully accomplished. The DHS/FEMA–011 General Training and Exercise Program Records System of Records contains information that is collected by, on behalf of, in support of, or in cooperation with DHS and its components and may contain personally identifiable information collected by other Federal, State, local, tribal, foreign, or international government agencies. The Secretary of Homeland Security has exempted this system from the following provisions of the Privacy Act, subject to limitations set forth in 5 U.S.C. 552a(c)(3); (d); (e)(1), (e)(4)(G), (e)(4)(H), (e)(4)(I); and (f) pursuant to 5 U.S.C. 552a (k)(6) where it states: "For testing or examination material used solely to determine individual qualifications for appointment or promotion in the Federal service the disclosure of which would compromise the objectivity or fairness of the testing or examination process."

Exemptions from these particular subsections are justified, on a case-by-case basis to be determined at the time a request is made, for the following reasons:

(a) From subsection (c)(3) (Accounting for Disclosures) because release of the accounting of disclosures could alert the subject of an investigation of an actual or potential criminal, civil, or regulatory violation to the existence of that investigation and reveal investigative interest on the part of DHS as well as the recipient agency. Disclosure of the accounting would therefore present a serious impediment to law enforcement efforts and/or efforts to preserve national security. Disclosure of the accounting would also permit the individual who is the subject of a record to impede the investigation, to tamper with witnesses or evidence, and to avoid detection or apprehension, which would undermine the entire investigative process.

(b) From subsection (d) (Access to Records) because access to the records contained in this system of records could inform the subject of an investigation of an actual or potential criminal, civil, or regulatory violation to the existence of that investigation and reveal investigative interest on the part of DHS or another agency. Access to the records could permit the individual who is the subject of a record to impede the investigation, to tamper with witnesses or evidence, and to avoid detection or apprehension. Amendment of the records could interfere with ongoing investigations and law enforcement activities and would impose an unreasonable administrative burden by requiring investigations to be continually reinvestigated. In addition, permitting access and amendment to such information could disclose security-sensitive information that could be detrimental to homeland security.

(c) From subsection (e)(1) (Relevancy and Necessity of Information) because in the course of investigations into potential violations of federal law, the accuracy of information obtained or introduced occasionally may be unclear, or the information may not be strictly relevant or necessary to a specific investigation. In the interests of effective law enforcement, it is appropriate to retain all information that may aid in establishing patterns of unlawful activity.

(d) From subsections (e)(4)(G), (e)(4)(H), and (e)(4)(I) (Agency Requirements) and (f) (Agency Rules), because portions of this system are exempt from the individual access provisions of subsection (d) for the reasons noted above, and therefore DHS is not required to establish requirements, rules, or procedures with respect to such access. Providing notice to individuals with respect to existence of records pertaining to them in the system of records or otherwise setting up procedures pursuant to which individuals may access and view records pertaining to themselves in the system would undermine investigative efforts and reveal the identities of witnesses, and potential witnesses, and confidential informants.

56. The DHS/TSA–023 Workplace Violence Prevention Program System of Records consists of electronic and paper records and is used by the TSA in the administration of its

Workplace Violence Prevention Program, an internal TSA program designed to prevent and respond to workplace violence. The DHS/TSA–023 Workplace Violence Prevention Program System of Records is a repository of information held by TSA in connection with its several and varied missions and functions, including, but not limited to: The enforcement of civil and criminal laws; investigations, inquiries, and proceedings there under. The DHS/TSA–023 Workplace Violence Prevention Program System of Records contains information collected by TSA, and may contain personally identifiable information collected by other federal, state, local, tribal, foreign, or international government agencies. The Secretary of Homeland Security has exempted portions of this system from the following provisions of the Privacy Act, subject to the limitations set forth in (c)(3); (d); (e)(1), (e)(4)(G); (e)(4)(H); (e)(4)(I); and (f) of the Privacy Act pursuant to 5 U.S.C. 552a(k)(2). Exemptions from these particular subsections are justified, on a case-by-case basis to be determined at the time a request is made, for the following reasons:

(a) From subsection (c)(3) (Accounting for Disclosures) because release of the accounting of disclosures could alert the subject of an investigation of an actual or potential criminal, civil, or regulatory violation to the existence of that investigation and reveal investigative interest on the part of DHS as well as the recipient agency. Disclosure of the accounting would therefore present a serious impediment to law enforcement efforts and/or efforts to preserve national security. Disclosure of the accounting would also permit the individual who is the subject of a record to impede the investigation, to tamper with witnesses or evidence, and to avoid detection or apprehension, which would undermine the entire investigative process.

(b) From subsection (d) (Access to Records) because access to the records contained in this system of records could inform the subject of an investigation of an actual or potential criminal, civil, or regulatory violation to the existence of that investigation and reveal investigative interest on the part of DHS or another agency. Access to the records could permit the individual who is the subject of a record to impede the investigation, to tamper with witnesses or evidence, and to avoid detection or apprehension. Amendment of the records could interfere with ongoing investigations and law enforcement activities and would impose an unreasonable administrative burden by requiring investigations to be continually reinvestigated. In addition, permitting access and amendment to such information could disclose security-sensitive information that could be detrimental to homeland security.

(c) From subsection (e)(1) (Relevancy and Necessity of Information) because in the course of investigations into potential violations of federal law, the accuracy of information obtained or introduced occasionally may be unclear, or the information may not be strictly relevant or necessary to a specific investigation. In the interests of effective law enforcement, it is appropriate to retain all information that may aid in establishing patterns of unlawful activity.

(d) From subsections (e)(4)(G), (e)(4)(H), and (e)(4)(I) (Agency Requirements) and (f) (Agency Rules), because portions of this system are exempt from the individual access provisions of subsection (d) for the reasons noted above, and therefore DHS is not required to establish requirements, rules, or procedures with respect to such access. Providing notice to individuals with respect to existence of records pertaining to them in the system of records or otherwise setting up procedures pursuant to which individuals may access and view records pertaining to themselves in the system would undermine investigative efforts and reveal the identities of witnesses, and potential witnesses, and confidential informants.

57. The DHS/OPS–002 National Operations Center Tracker and Senior Watch Officer Logs Records System of Records consists of electronic and paper records and will be used by DHS and its components. The DHS/OPS–002 National Operations Center Tracker and Senior Watch Officer Logs Records System of Records is a repository of information held by DHS in connection with its several and varied missions and functions, including, but not limited to the enforcement of civil and criminal laws; investigations, inquiries, and proceedings there under; national security and intelligence activities; and protection of the President of the U.S. or other individuals pursuant to Section 3056 and 3056A of Title 18. The DHS/OPS–002 National Operations Center Tracker and Senior Watch Officer Logs Records System of Records contains information that is collected by, on behalf of, in support of, or in cooperation with DHS and its components and may contain personally identifiable information collected by other federal, state, local, tribal, foreign, or international government agencies. The Secretary of Homeland Security is exempting this system from the following provisions of the Privacy Act, subject to limitations set forth in 5 U.S.C. 552a(c)(3); (d); (e)(1), (e)(4)(G), (e)(4)(H), (e)(4)(I); and (f) pursuant to 5 U.S.C. 552a(k)(1), (k)(2), and (k)(3). Exemptions from these particular subsections are justified, on a case-by-case basis to be determined at the time a request is made, for the following reasons:

(a) From subsection (c)(3) (Accounting for Disclosures) because release of the accounting of disclosures could alert the subject of an investigation of an actual or potential criminal, civil, or regulatory violation to the existence of that investigation and reveal investigative interest on the part of DHS as well as the recipient agency. Disclosure of the accounting would therefore present a serious impediment to law enforcement efforts and/or efforts to preserve national security. Disclosure of the accounting would also permit the individual who is the subject of a record to impede the investigation, to tamper with witnesses or evidence, and to avoid detection or apprehension, which would undermine the entire investigative process.

(b) From subsection (d) (Access to Records) because access to the records contained in this system of records could inform the subject of an investigation of an actual or potential criminal, civil, or regulatory violation to the existence of that investigation and reveal investigative interest on the part of DHS or another agency. Access to the records could permit the individual who is the subject of a record to impede the investigation, to tamper with witnesses or evidence, and to avoid detection or apprehension. Amendment of the records could interfere with ongoing investigations and law enforcement activities and would impose an unreasonable administrative burden by requiring investigations to be continually reinvestigated. In addition, permitting access and amendment to such information could disclose security-sensitive information that could be detrimental to homeland security.

(c) From subsection (e)(1) (Relevancy and Necessity of Information) because in the course of investigations into potential violations of federal law, the accuracy of information obtained or introduced occasionally may be unclear, or the information may not be strictly relevant or necessary to a specific investigation. In the interests of effective law enforcement, it is appropriate to retain all information that may aid in establishing patterns of unlawful activity.

(d) From subsections (e)(4)(G), (e)(4)(H), and (e)(4)(I) (Agency Requirements) and (f) (Agency Rules), because portions of this system are exempt from the individual access provisions of subsection (d) for the reasons noted above, and therefore DHS is not required to establish requirements, rules, or procedures with respect to such access. Providing notice to individuals with respect to existence of records pertaining to them in the system of records or otherwise setting up procedures pursuant to which individuals may access and view records pertaining to themselves in the system would undermine investigative efforts and reveal the identities of witnesses, and potential witnesses, and confidential informants.

59. The DHS/NPPD–001 NICC Records System of Records consists of electronic and paper records and will be used by DHS and its components. The DHS/NPPD–001 NICC Records System of Records is a repository of information held by DHS in connection with

its several and varied missions and functions, including, but not limited to the enforcement of civil and criminal laws; investigations, inquiries, and proceedings there under; national security and intelligence activities The DHS/NPPD–001 NICC Records System of Records contains information that is collected by, on behalf of, in support of, or in cooperation with DHS and its components and may contain personally identifiable information collected by other Federal, state, local, Tribal, foreign, or international government agencies. The Secretary of Homeland Security has exempted this system from the following provisions of the Privacy Act, subject to limitations set forth in 5 U.S.C. 552a(c)(3); (d); (e)(1), (e)(4)(G), (e)(4)(H), (e)(4)(I), and (f) pursuant to 5 U.S.C. 552a(k)(1) and (k)(2). Exemptions from these particular subsections are justified, on a case-by-case basis to be determined at the time a request is made, for the following reasons:

(a) From subsection (c)(3) (Accounting for Disclosures) because release of the accounting of disclosures could alert the subject of an investigation of an actual or potential criminal, civil, or regulatory violation to the existence of that investigation and reveal investigative interest on the part of DHS as well as the recipient agency. Disclosure of the accounting would therefore present a serious impediment to law enforcement efforts and/or efforts to preserve national security. Disclosure of the accounting would also permit the individual who is the subject of a record to impede the investigation, to tamper with witnesses or evidence, and to avoid detection or apprehension, which would undermine the entire investigative process.

(b) From subsection (d) (Access to Records) because access to the records contained in this system of records could inform the subject of an investigation of an actual or potential criminal, civil, or regulatory violation to the existence of that investigation and reveal investigative interest on the part of DHS or another agency. Access to the records could permit the individual who is the subject of a record to impede the investigation, to tamper with witnesses or evidence, and to avoid detection or apprehension. Amendment of the records could interfere with ongoing investigations and law enforcement activities and would impose an unreasonable administrative burden by requiring investigations to be continually reinvestigated. In addition, permitting access and amendment to such information could disclose security-sensitive information that could be detrimental to homeland security.

(c) From subsection (e)(1) (Relevancy and Necessity of Information) because in the course of investigations into potential violations of Federal law, the accuracy of information obtained or introduced occasionally may be unclear, or the information may not be strictly relevant or necessary to a specific investigation. In the interests of effective law enforcement, it is appropriate to retain all information that may aid in establishing patterns of unlawful activity.

(d) From subsections (e)(4)(G), (e)(4)(H), and (e)(4)(I) (Agency Requirements) and (f) (Agency Rules), because portions of this system are exempt from the individual access provisions of subsection (d) for the reasons noted above, and therefore DHS is not required to establish requirements, rules, or procedures with respect to such access. Providing notice to individuals with respect to existence of records pertaining to them in the system of records or otherwise setting up procedures pursuant to which individuals may access and view records pertaining to themselves in the system would undermine investigative efforts and reveal the identities of witnesses, and potential witnesses, and confidential informants.

64. The DHS/USCIS–015 Electronic Immigration System-2 Account and Case Management System of Records consists of electronic and paper records and will be used by DHS and its components. The DHS/USCIS–015 Electronic Immigration System-2 Account and Case Management is a repository of information held by USCIS to serve its mission of processing immigration benefits. This system also supports certain other DHS programs whose functions include, but are not limited to, the enforcement of civil and criminal laws; investigations, inquiries, and proceedings there under; and national security and intelligence activities. The DHS/USCIS–015 Electronic Immigration System-2 Account and Case Management System of Records contains information that is collected by, on behalf of, in support of, or in cooperation with DHS and its components and may contain personally identifiable information collected by other federal, state, local, Tribal, foreign, or international government agencies. This system is exempted from the following provisions of the Privacy Act pursuant to 5 U.S.C. 552a(k)(2): 5 U.S.C. 552a(c)(3); (d); (e)(1), (e)(4)(G), (e)(4)(H), (e)(4)(I); and (f). Additionally, many of the functions in this system require retrieving records from law enforcement systems. Where a record received from another system has been exempted in that source system under 5 U.S.C. 552a(j)(2), DHS will claim the same exemptions for those records that are claimed for the original primary systems of records from which they originated and claims any additional exemptions in accordance with this rule. Exemptions from these particular subsections are justified, on a case-by-case basis determined at the time a request is made, for the following reasons:

(a) From subsection (c)(3) (Accounting for Disclosures) because release of the accounting of disclosures could alert the subject of an investigation of an actual or potential criminal, civil, or regulatory violation to the existence of that investigation and reveal investigative interest on the part of DHS as well as the recipient agency. Disclosure of the accounting would therefore present a serious impediment to law enforcement efforts and/or efforts to preserve national security. Disclosure of the accounting would also permit the individual who is the subject of a record to impede the investigation, to tamper with witnesses or evidence, and to avoid detection or apprehension, which would undermine the entire investigative process.

(b) From subsection (d) (Access to Records) because access to the records contained in this system of records could inform the subject of an investigation of an actual or potential criminal, civil, or regulatory violation to the existence of that investigation and/or reveal investigative interest on the part of DHS or another agency. Access to the records could permit the individual who is the subject of a record to impede the investigation, to tamper with witnesses or evidence, and to avoid detection or apprehension. Amendment of the records could interfere with ongoing investigations and law enforcement activities and would impose an unreasonable administrative burden by requiring investigations to be continually reinvestigated. In addition, permitting access and amendment to such information could disclose security-sensitive information that could be detrimental to homeland security.

(c) From subsection (e)(1) (Relevancy and Necessity of Information) because in the course of investigations into potential violations of federal law, the accuracy of information obtained or introduced occasionally may be unclear, or the information may not be strictly relevant or necessary to a specific investigation. In the interests of effective law enforcement, it is appropriate to retain all information that may aid in establishing patterns of unlawful activity.

(d) From subsections (e)(4)(G), (e)(4)(H), and (e)(4)(I) (Agency Requirements) and (f) (Agency Rules) because portions of this system are exempt from the individual access provisions of subsection (d) for the reasons noted above, and therefore DHS is not required to establish requirements, rules, or procedures with respect to such access. Providing notice to individuals with respect to existence of records pertaining to them in the system of records, or otherwise setting up procedures pursuant to which individuals may access and view records pertaining to themselves in the system, would undermine investigative efforts and reveal the identities of witnesses, and potential witnesses, and confidential informants.

65. The DHS/USCIS–016 Electronic Immigration System-3 Automated Background Functions System of Records consists of electronic and paper records and will be used by DHS and its components. The DHS/

USCIS–016 Electronic Immigration System-3 Automated Background Functions System of Records is a repository of information held by USCIS to serve its mission of processing immigration benefits. This system also supports certain other DHS programs whose functions include, but are not limited to, the enforcement of civil and criminal laws; investigations, inquiries, and proceedings there under; and national security and intelligence activities. The DHS/USCIS–016 Electronic Immigration System-3 Automated Background Functions System of Records contains information that is collected by, on behalf of, in support of, or in cooperation with DHS and its components and may contain personally identifiable information collected by other federal, state, local, Tribal, foreign, or international government agencies. This system is exempted from the following provisions of the Privacy Act pursuant to 5 U.S.C. 552a(k)(2): 5 U.S.C. 552a(c)(3); (d); (e)(1), (e)(4)(G), (e)(4)(H), (e)(4)(I); and (f). Additionally, many of the functions in this system require retrieving records from law enforcement systems. Where a record received from another system has been exempted in that source system under 5 U.S.C. 552a(j)(2), DHS will claim the same exemptions for those records that are claimed for the original primary systems of records from which they originated and claims any additional exemptions in accordance with this rule. Exemptions from these particular subsections are justified, on a case-by-case basis determined at the time a request is made, for the following reasons:

(a) From subsection (c)(3) (Accounting for Disclosures) because release of the accounting of disclosures could alert the subject of an investigation of an actual or potential criminal, civil, or regulatory violation to the existence of that investigation and reveal investigative interest on the part of DHS as well as the recipient agency. Disclosure of the accounting would therefore present a serious impediment to law enforcement efforts and/or efforts to preserve national security. Disclosure of the accounting would also permit the individual who is the subject of a record to impede the investigation, to tamper with witnesses or evidence, and to avoid detection or apprehension, which would undermine the entire investigative process.

(b) From subsection (d) (Access to Records) because access to the records contained in this system of records could inform the subject of an investigation of an actual or potential criminal, civil, or regulatory violation to the existence of that investigation and/or reveal investigative interest on the part of DHS or another agency. Access to the records could permit the individual who is the subject of a record to impede the investigation, to tamper with witnesses or evidence, and to avoid detection or apprehension. Amendment of the records could inter-fere with ongoing investigations and law enforcement activities and would impose an unreasonable administrative burden by requiring investigations to be continually reinvestigated. In addition, permitting access and amendment to such information could disclose security-sensitive information that could be detrimental to homeland security.

(c) From subsection (e)(1) (Relevancy and Necessity of Information) because in the course of investigations into potential violations of federal law, the accuracy of information obtained or introduced occasionally may be unclear, or the information may not be strictly relevant or necessary to a specific investigation. In the interests of effective law enforcement, it is appropriate to retain all information that may aid in establishing patterns of unlawful activity.

(d) From subsections (e)(4)(G), (e)(4)(H), and (e)(4)(I) (Agency Requirements) and (f) (Agency Rules), because portions of this system are exempt from the individual access provisions of subsection (d) for the reasons noted above, and therefore DHS is not required to establish requirements, rules, or procedures with respect to such access. Providing notice to individuals with respect to existence of records pertaining to them in the system of records, or otherwise setting up procedures pursuant to which individuals may access and view records pertaining to themselves in the system, would undermine investigative efforts and reveal the identities of witnesses, and potential witnesses, and confidential informants.

66. The DHS/ALL–030 Use of the Terrorist Screening Database System of Records consists of electronic and paper records and will be used by DHS and its Components. The DHS/ALL–030 Use of the Terrorist Screening Database System of Records is a repository of information held by DHS in connection with its several and varied missions and functions, including, the enforcement of civil and criminal laws; investigations, inquiries, and proceedings thereunder; and national security and intelligence activities. The Terrorist Screening Database belongs to the Department of Justice (DOJ)/Federal Bureau of Investigation (FBI). DHS does not change or alter these records. All records within the DHS/ALL–030 Use of the Terrorist Screening Database System of Records are collected and disseminated by the DOJ/FBI and are covered by the DOJ/FBI–019, "Terrorist Screening Records Center System," 72 FR 77846 (Dec. 14, 2011). Because DHS does not make any changes to the records obtained from DOJ/FBI, the same exemptions outlined in the DOJ/FBI SORN, and reasons provided in its implementing regulations for use of such exemptions at 28 CFR 16.96, transfer and apply. The Secretary of Homeland Security, pursuant to 5 U.S.C. 552a(j)(2), has exempted this system from the following provisions of the Privacy Act: 5 U.S.C. 552a(c)(3), (c)(4), (d),

(e)(1), (e)(2), (e)(3), (e)(5), (e)(8), and (g). When a record has been received from DOJ/FBI–019 Terrorist Screening Records System of Records and has been exempted in that source system, DHS will claim the same exemptions for those records that are claimed for that original primary system of records from which they originated and claims any additional exemptions set forth here. Exemptions from these particular subsections are justified, on a case-by-case basis to be determined at the time a request is made, for the following reasons:

(a) From subsection (c)(3) and (4) (Accounting for Disclosures) because release of the accounting of disclosures could alert the subject of an investigation of an actual or potential criminal, civil, or regulatory violation to the existence of that investigation and reveal investigative interest on the part of DHS as well as the recipient agency. Disclosure of the accounting would therefore present a serious impediment to law enforcement efforts and/or efforts to preserve national security. Disclosure of the accounting would also permit the individual who is the subject of a record to impede the investigation, to tamper with witnesses or evidence, and to avoid detection or apprehension, which would undermine the entire investigative process.

(b) From subsection (d) (Access to Records) because access to the records contained in this system of records could inform the subject of an investigation of an actual or potential criminal, civil, or regulatory violation to the existence of that investigation and reveal investigative interest on the part of DHS or another agency. Access to the records could permit the individual who is the subject of a record to impede the investigation, to tamper with witnesses or evidence, and to avoid detection or apprehension. Amendment of the records could interfere with ongoing investigations and law enforcement activities and would impose an unreasonable administrative burden by requiring investigations to be continually reinvestigated. In addition, permitting access and amendment to such information could disclose security-sensitive information that could be detrimental to homeland security.

(c) From subsection (e)(1) (Relevancy and Necessity of Information) because in the course of investigations into potential violations of Federal law, the accuracy of information obtained or introduced occasionally may be unclear, or the information may not be strictly relevant or necessary to a specific investigation. In the interests of effective law enforcement, it is appropriate to retain all information that may aid in establishing patterns of unlawful activity.

(d) From subsection (e)(2) (Collection of Information from Individuals) because requiring that information be collected from the subject of an investigation would alert the subject to the nature or existence of the investigation, thereby interfering with that investigation and related law enforcement activities.

(e) From subsection (e)(3) (Notice to Subjects) because providing such detailed information could impede law enforcement by compromising the existence of a confidential investigation or reveal the identity of witnesses or confidential informants.

(f) From subsection (e)(5) (Collection of Information) because with the collection of information for law enforcement purposes, it is impossible to determine in advance what information is accurate, relevant, timely, and complete. Compliance with subsection (e)(5) would preclude DHS agents from using their investigative training and exercise of good judgment to both conduct and report on investigations.

(g) From subsection (e)(8) (Notice on Individuals) because compliance would interfere with DHS's ability to obtain, serve, and issue subpoenas, warrants, and other law enforcement mechanisms that may be filed under seal and could result in disclosure of investigative techniques, procedures, and evidence.

(h) From subsection (g) (Civil Remedies) to the extent that the system is exempt from other specific subsections of the Privacy Act.

67. The DHS/FEMA–012 Suspicious Activity Reporting System of Records consists of electronic and paper records and will be used by DHS/FEMA and its components. The DHS/FEMA—012 Suspicious Activity Reporting System of Records is a repository of information held by DHS/FEMA to serve its mission to support our citizens and first responders to ensure that as a nation we work together to build, sustain, and improve our capability to prepare for, protect against, respond to, recover from, and mitigate all hazards. This system also supports certain other DHS/FEMA programs whose functions include, but are not limited to, the enforcement of civil and criminal laws; investigations, inquiries, and proceedings there under; and national security and intelligence activities. The DHS/FEMA–012 Suspicious Activity Reporting System of Records contains information that is collected by, on behalf of, in support of, or in cooperation with DHS/FEMA and its components and may contain personally identifiable information collected by other federal, state, local, tribal, foreign, or international government agencies. The Secretary of Homeland Security has exempted this system from the following provisions of the Privacy Act pursuant to 5 U.S.C. 552a(k)(2); (c)(3); (d); (e)(1), (e)(4)(G), (e)(4)(H), (e)(4)(I); and (f). Exemptions from these particular subsections are justified, on a case-by-case basis determined at the time a request is made, for the following reasons:

(a) From subsection (c)(3) (Accounting for Disclosures) because release of the accounting of disclosures could alert the subject of an investigation of an actual or potential criminal, civil, or regulatory violation to the existence of that investigation and reveal investigative interest on the part of DHS/FEMA as well as the recipient agency. Disclosure of the accounting would therefore present a serious impediment to law enforcement efforts and/or efforts to preserve national security. Disclosure of the accounting would also permit the individual who is the subject of a record to impede the investigation, to tamper with witnesses or evidence, and to avoid detection or apprehension, which would undermine the entire investigative process.

(b) From subsection (d) (Access to Records) because access to the records contained in this system of records could inform the subject of an investigation of an actual or potential criminal, civil, or regulatory violation to the existence of that investigation and reveal investigative interest on the part of DHS/FEMA or another agency. Access to the records could permit the individual who is the subject of a record to impede the investigation, to tamper with witnesses or evidence, and to avoid detection or apprehension. Amendment of the records could interfere with ongoing investigations and law enforcement activities and would impose an unreasonable administrative burden by requiring investigations to be continually reinvestigated. In addition, permitting access and amendment to such information could disclose security-sensitive information that could be detrimental to homeland security.

(c) From subsection (e)(1) (Relevancy and Necessity of Information) because in the course of investigations into potential violations of federal law, the accuracy of information obtained or introduced occasionally may be unclear, or the information may not be strictly relevant or necessary to a specific investigation. In the interests of effective law enforcement, it is appropriate to retain all information that may aid in establishing patterns of unlawful activity.

(d) From subsections (e)(4)(G), (e)(4)(H), and (e)(4)(I) (Agency Requirements) and (f) (Agency Rules), because portions of this system are exempt from the individual access provisions of subsection (d) for the reasons noted above, and therefore DHS/FEMA is not required to establish requirements, rules, or procedures with respect to such access. Providing notice to individuals with respect to existence of records pertaining to them in the system of records or otherwise setting up procedures pursuant to which individuals may access and view records pertaining to themselves in the system would undermine investigative efforts and reveal the identities of witnesses, and potential witnesses, and confidential informants.

68. The DHS OPS–003 Operations Collection, Planning, Coordination, Reporting, Analysis, and Fusion System of Records consists of electronic and paper records and will be used by DHS and its components. The DHS OPS–003 Operations Collection, Planning, Coordination, Reporting, Analysis, and Fusion System of Records is a repository of information held by DHS to serve its several and varied missions and functions. This system also supports certain other DHS programs whose functions include, but are not limited to, the enforcement of civil and criminal laws; investigations, inquiries, and proceedings there under; national security and intelligence activities; and protection of the President of the U.S. or other individuals pursuant to Section 3056 and 3056A of Title 18. The DHS OPS–003 Operations Collection, Planning, Coordination, Reporting, Analysis, and Fusion System of Records contains information that is collected by, on behalf of, in support of, or in cooperation with DHS and its components and may contain personally identifiable information collected by other federal, state, local, tribal, foreign, or international government agencies. This system is exempt from the following provisions of the Privacy Act pursuant to 5 U.S.C. 552a(k)(1), (k)(2), (k)(3): 5 U.S.C. 552a(c)(3); (d); (e)(1), (e)(4)(G), (e)(4)(H), (e)(4)(I); and (f). Exemptions from these particular subsections are justified, on a case-by-case basis to be determined at the time a request is made, for the following reasons:

(a) From subsection (c)(3) (Accounting for Disclosures) because release of the accounting of disclosures could alert the subject of an investigation of an actual or potential criminal, civil, or regulatory violation to the existence of that investigation and reveal investigative interest on the part of DHS as well as the recipient agency. Disclosure of the accounting would therefore present a serious impediment to law enforcement efforts and/or efforts to preserve national security. Disclosure of the accounting would also permit the individual who is the subject of a record to impede the investigation, to tamper with witnesses or evidence, and to avoid detection or apprehension, which would undermine the entire investigative process.

(b) From subsection (d) (Access and Amendment) because access to the records contained in this system of records could inform the subject of an investigation of an actual or potential criminal, civil, or regulatory violation to the existence of that investigation and reveal investigative interest on the part of DHS or another agency. Access to the records could permit the individual who is the subject of a record to impede the investigation, to tamper with witnesses or evidence, and to avoid detection or apprehension. Amendment of the records could interfere with ongoing investigations and law enforcement activities and would impose an unreasonable administrative burden by requiring investigations to be continually reinvestigated. In addition, permitting access and amendment to such information could disclose security-sensitive information that could be detrimental to homeland security.

(c) From subsection (e)(1) (Relevancy and Necessity of Information) because in the course of investigations into potential violations of federal law, the accuracy of information obtained or introduced occasionally may be unclear, or the information may not be strictly relevant or necessary to a specific investigation. In the interests of effective law enforcement, it is appropriate to retain all information that may aid in establishing patterns of unlawful activity.

(d) From subsections (e)(4)(G), (e)(4)(H), and (e)(4)(I) (Agency Requirements) and (f) (Agency Rules), because portions of this system are exempt from the individual access provisions of subsection (d) for the reasons noted above, and therefore DHS is not required to establish requirements, rules, or procedures with respect to such access. Providing notice to individuals with respect to existence of records pertaining to them in the system of records or otherwise setting up procedures pursuant to which individuals may access and view records pertaining to themselves in the system would undermine investigative efforts and reveal the identities of witnesses, and potential witnesses, and confidential informants.

69. The DHS/CBP—017 Analytical Framework for Intelligence (AFI) System of Records consists of electronic and paper records and will be used by DHS and its components. The DHS/CBP—017 Analytical Framework for Intelligence (AFI) System of Records is a repository of information held by DHS to enhance DHS's ability to: Identify, apprehend, and/or prosecute individuals who pose a potential law enforcement or security risk; aid in the enforcement of the customs and immigration laws, and other laws enforced by DHS at the border; and enhance United States security. This system also supports certain other DHS programs whose functions include, but are not limited to, the enforcement of civil and criminal laws; investigations, inquiries, and proceedings there under; and national security and intelligence activities. The DHS/CBP—017 Analytical Framework for Intelligence (AFI) System of Records contains information that is collected by, on behalf of, in support of, or in cooperation with DHS and its components and may contain personally identifiable information collected by other federal, state, local, tribal, foreign, or international government agencies.

(a) The Secretary of Homeland Security has exempted this system from certain provisions of the Privacy Act as follows:

(1) Pursuant to 5 U.S.C. 552a(j)(2), the system is exempt from 5 U.S.C. 552a(c)(3) and (c)(4), (e)(1), (e)(2), (e)(3), (e)(4)(G), (e)(4)(H), (e)(4)(I), (e)(5), (e)(8), (f), and (g).

(2) Pursuant to 5 U.S.C. 552a(j)(2), the system (except for any records that were ingested by AFI where the source system of records already provides access and/or amendment under the Privacy Act) is exempt from 5 U.S.C. 552a(d)(1), (d)(2), (d)(3), and (d)(4).

(3) Pursuant to 5 U.S.C. 552a(k)(1), the system is exempt from 5 U.S.C. 552a(c)(3); (e)(1), (e)(4)(G), (e)(4)(H), (e)(4)(I); and (f).

(4) Pursuant to 5 U.S.C. 552a(k)(1), the system is exempt from (d)(1), (d)(2), (d)(3), and (d)(4).

(5) Pursuant to 5 U.S.C. 552a(k)(2), the system is exempt from 5 U.S.C. 552a(c)(3); (e)(1), (e)(4)(G), (e)(4)(H), (e)(4)(I); and (f).

(6) Pursuant to 5 U.S.C. 552a(k)(2),the system (except for any records that were ingested by AFI where the source system of records already provides access and/or amendment under the Privacy Act) is exempt from (d)(1), (d)(2), (d)(3), and (d)(4).

(b) Exemptions from these particular subsections are justified, on a case-by-case basis to be determined at the time a request is made, for the following reasons:

(1) From subsection (c)(3) and (4) (Accounting for Disclosures) because release of the accounting of disclosures could alert the subject of an investigation of an actual or potential criminal, civil, or regulatory violation to the existence of that investigation and reveal investigative interest on the part of DHS as well as the recipient agency. Disclosure of the accounting would therefore present a serious impediment to law enforcement efforts and/or efforts to preserve national security. Disclosure of the accounting would also permit the individual who is the subject of a record to impede the investigation, to tamper with witnesses or evidence, and to avoid detection or apprehension, which would undermine the entire investigative process.

(2) From subsection (d) (Access to Records) because access to the records contained in this system of records could inform the subject of an investigation of an actual or potential criminal, civil, or regulatory violation to the existence of that investigation and reveal investigative interest on the part of DHS or another agency. Access to the records could permit the individual who is the subject of a record to impede the investigation, to tamper with witnesses or evidence, and to avoid detection or apprehension. Amendment of the records could interfere with ongoing investigations and law enforcement activities and would impose an unreasonable administrative burden by requiring investigations to be continually reinvestigated. In addition, permitting access and amendment to such information could

disclose security-sensitive information that could be detrimental to homeland security.

(3) From subsection (e)(1) (Relevancy and Necessity of Information) because in the course of investigations into potential violations of federal law, the accuracy of information obtained or introduced occasionally may be unclear, or the information may not be strictly relevant or necessary to a specific investigation. In the interests of effective law enforcement and national security, it is appropriate to retain all information that may aid in establishing patterns of unlawful activity.

(4) From subsection (e)(2) (Collection of Information from Individuals) because requiring that information be collected from the subject of an investigation would alert the subject to the nature or existence of the investigation, thereby interfering with that investigation and related law enforcement and national security activities.

(5) From subsection (e)(3) (Notice to Individuals) because providing such detailed information could impede law enforcement and national security by compromising the existence of a confidential investigation or reveal the identity of witnesses or confidential informants.

(6) From subsections (e)(4)(G), (e)(4)(H), and (e)(4)(I) (Agency Requirements) and (f) (Agency Rules), because portions of this system are exempt from the individual access provisions of subsection (d) for the reasons noted above, and therefore DHS is not required to establish requirements, rules, or procedures with respect to such access. Providing notice to individuals with respect to existence of records pertaining to them in the system of records or otherwise setting up procedures pursuant to which individuals may access and view records pertaining to themselves in the system would undermine investigative efforts and reveal the identities of witnesses, and potential witnesses, and confidential informants.

(7) From subsection (e)(5) (Collection of Information) because with the collection of information for law enforcement purposes, it is impossible to determine in advance what information is accurate, relevant, timely, and complete. Compliance with subsection (e)(5) would preclude DHS agents from using their investigative training and exercise of good judgment to both conduct and report on investigations.

(8) From subsection (e)(8) (Notice on Individuals) because compliance would interfere with DHS's ability to obtain, serve, and issue subpoenas, warrants, and other law enforcement mechanisms that may be filed under seal and could result in disclosure of investigative techniques, procedures, and evidence.

(9) From subsection (g)(1) (Civil Remedies) to the extent that the system is exempt from other specific subsections of the Privacy Act.

70. DHS/USCIS–ICE–CBP–001 Alien File, Index, and National File Tracking System of Records consists of electronic and paper records and will be used by USCIS, ICE, and CBP. DHS/USCIS–ICE–CBP–001 Alien File, Index, and National File Tracking System of Records is a repository of information held by DHS in connection with its several and varied missions and functions, including, but not limited to: The enforcement of civil and criminal laws; investigations, inquiries, and proceedings thereunder; and national security and intelligence activities. DHS/USCIS–ICE–CBP–001 Alien File, Index, and National File Tracking System of Records contains information that is collected by, on behalf of, in support of, or in cooperation with DHS and its components and may contain personally identifiable information collected by other federal, state, local, tribal, territorial, foreign, or international government agencies. The Secretary of Homeland Security has exempted this system from the following provisions of the Privacy Act pursuant to 5 U.S.C. 552a(j)(2): 5 U.S.C. 552a(c)(3) and (c)(4), (d), (e)(1), (e)(2), (e)(3), (e)(4)(G), (e)(4)(H), (e)(4)(I), (e)(5), (e)(8), (e)(12), (f), (g)(1), and (h). Additionally, the Secretary of Homeland Security has exempted this system from the following provisions of the Privacy Act pursuant to 5 U.S.C. 552a(k)(1) and (k)(2): 5 U.S.C. 552a(c)(3), (d), (e)(1), (e)(4)(G), (e)(4)(H), (e)(4)(I), and (f). Exemptions from these particular subsections may be justified, on a case-by-case basis to be determined at the time a request is made, for the following reasons:

(a) From subsection (c)(3) and (4) (Accounting for Disclosures) because release of the accounting of disclosures could alert the subject of an investigation of an actual or potential criminal, civil, or regulatory violation to the existence of that investigation and reveal investigative interest on the part of DHS as well as the recipient agency. Disclosure of the accounting would therefore present a serious impediment to law enforcement efforts and/or efforts to preserve national security. Disclosure of the accounting would also permit the individual who is the subject of a record to impede the investigation, to tamper with witnesses or evidence, and to avoid detection or apprehension, which would undermine the entire investigative process.

(b) From subsection (d) (Access to Records) because access to the records contained in this system of records could inform the subject of an investigation of an actual or potential criminal, civil, or regulatory violation to the existence of that investigation and reveal investigative interest on the part of DHS or another agency. Access to the records could permit the individual who is the subject of a record to impede the investigation, to tamper with witnesses or evidence, and to avoid detection or apprehension. Amendment of the records could interfere with ongoing investigations and law enforcement activities and would impose an unreasonable administrative burden by requiring investigations to be continually reinvestigated. In addition, permitting access and amendment to such information could disclose security-sensitive information that could be detrimental to homeland security.

(c) From subsection (e)(1) (Relevancy and Necessity of Information) because in the course of investigations into potential violations of federal law, the accuracy of information obtained or introduced occasionally may be unclear, or the information may not be strictly relevant or necessary to a specific investigation. In the interests of effective law enforcement, it is appropriate to retain all information that may aid in establishing patterns of unlawful activity.

(d) From subsection (e)(2) (Collection of Information from Individuals) because requiring that information be collected from the subject of an investigation would alert the subject to the nature or existence of the investigation, thereby interfering with that investigation and related law enforcement activities.

(e) From subsection (e)(3) (Notice to Individuals) because providing such detailed information could impede law enforcement by compromising the existence of a confidential investigation or reveal the identity of witnesses, DHS employees, or confidential informants.

(f) From subsections (e)(4)(G), (e)(4)(H), and (e)(4)(I) (Agency Requirements) and (f) (Agency Rules), because portions of this system are exempt from the individual access provisions of subsection (d) for the reasons noted above, and therefore DHS is not required to establish requirements, rules, or procedures with respect to such access. Providing notice to individuals with respect to existence of records pertaining to them in the system of records or otherwise setting up procedures pursuant to which individuals may access and view records pertaining to themselves in the system would undermine investigative efforts and reveal the identities of witnesses, potential witnesses, and confidential informants.

(g) From subsection (e)(5) (Collection of Information) because with the collection of information for law enforcement purposes, it is impossible to determine in advance what information is accurate, relevant, timely, and complete. Compliance with subsection (e)(5) would impede DHS officials' ability to effectively use their investigative training and exercise good judgment to both conduct and report on investigations.

(h) From subsection (e)(8) (Notice on Individuals) because compliance would interfere with DHS's ability to obtain, serve, and issue subpoenas, warrants, and other law enforcement mechanisms that may be filed under seal and could result in disclosure of investigative techniques, procedures, and evidence.

(i) From subsection (e)(12) (Computer Matching) if the agency is a recipient agency or a source agency in a matching program with a non-Federal agency, with respect to any establishment or revision of a matching program, at least 30 days prior to conducting such program, publish in the FEDERAL REGISTER notice of such establishment or revision.

(j) From subsection (g)(1) (Civil Remedies) to the extent that the system is exempt from other specific subsections of the Privacy Act.

(k) From subsection (h) (Legal Guardians) if the parent of any minor, or the legal guardian of any individual who has been declared to be incompetent due to physical or mental incapacity or age by a court of competent jurisdiction, is acting on behalf of the individual.

71. The Department of Homeland Security (DHS)/Transportation Security Administration (TSA)-021 TSA Pre✓™ Application Program System of Records consists of electronic and paper records and will be used by DHS/TSA. The DHS/TSA–021 TSA Pre✓™ Application Program System of Records is a repository of information held by DHS/TSA on individuals who voluntarily provide personally identifiable information (PII) to TSA in return for enrollment in a program that will make them eligible for expedited security screening at designated airports. This System of Records contains PII in biographic application data, biometric information, pointer information to law enforcement databases, payment tracking, and U.S. application membership decisions that support the TSA Pre✓™ Application Program membership decisions. The DHS/TSA–021 TSA Pre✓™ Application Program System of Records contains information that is collected by, on behalf of, in support of, or in cooperation with DHS and its components and may contain PII collected by other federal, state, local, tribal, territorial, or foreign government agencies. The Secretary of Homeland Security, pursuant to 5 U.S.C. 552a(k)(1) and (k)(2), has exempted this system from the following provisions of the Privacy Act: 5 U.S.C. 552a(c)(3); (d); (e)(1); (e)(4)(G), (H), and (I); and (f). Where a record received from another system has been exempted in that source system under 5 U.S.C. 552a(k)(1) and (k)(2), DHS will claim the same exemptions for those records that are claimed for the original primary systems of records from which they originated and claims any additional exemptions set forth here. Exemptions from these particular subsections are justified, on a case-by-case basis

to be determined at the time a request is made, for the following reasons:

(a) From subsection (c)(3) (Accounting for Disclosures) because release of the accounting of disclosures could alert the subject of an investigation of an actual or potential criminal, civil, or regulatory violation to the existence of that investigation and reveal investigative interest on the part of DHS as well as the recipient agency. Disclosure of the accounting would therefore present a serious impediment to law enforcement efforts and/or efforts to preserve national security. Disclosure of the accounting also would permit the individual who is the subject of a record to impede the investigation, to tamper with witnesses or evidence, and to avoid detection or apprehension, which would undermine the entire investigative process.

(b) From subsection (d) (Access to Records) because access to the records contained in this system of records could inform the subject of an investigation of an actual or potential criminal, civil, or regulatory violation to the existence of that investigation and reveal investigative interest on the part of DHS or another agency. Access to the records could permit the individual who is the subject of a record to impede the investigation, to tamper with witnesses or evidence, and to avoid detection or apprehension. Amendment of the records could interfere with ongoing investigations and law enforcement activities and would impose an unreasonable administrative burden by requiring investigations to be continually reinvestigated. In addition, permitting access and amendment to such information could disclose security-sensitive information that could be detrimental to homeland security.

(c) From subsection (e)(1) (Relevancy and Necessity of Information) because in the course of investigations into potential violations of federal law, the accuracy of information obtained or introduced occasionally may be unclear, or the information may not be strictly relevant or necessary to a specific investigation. In the interests of effective law enforcement, it is appropriate to retain all information that may aid in establishing patterns of unlawful activity.

(d) From subsections (e)(4)(G), (H), and (I) (Agency Requirements) and (f) (Agency Rules), because portions of this system are exempt from the individual access provisions of subsection (d) for the reasons noted above, and therefore DHS is not required to establish requirements, rules, or procedures with respect to such access. Providing notice to individuals with respect to the existence of records pertaining to them in the system of records or otherwise setting up procedures pursuant to which individuals may access and view records pertaining to themselves in the system would undermine investigative efforts and reveal the identities of witnesses, potential witnesses, and confidential informants.

72. The DHS/ICE–014 Homeland Security Investigations Forensic Laboratory System of Records consists of electronic and paper records that will be used by DHS and its components. The DHS/ICE–014 Homeland Security Investigations Forensic Laboratory System of Records contains records of evidence and cases submitted to the HSI-FL. This information will include information on the individual submitting the request, identify the evidence submitted, track the evidence as it moves throughout the HSI-FL, capture case notes and results of examinations, store electronic images of evidence, and produce reports of findings. Other case-related records are maintained, including descriptions of expert witness testimony provided by HSI–FL employees. Records in the DHS/ICE–014 Homeland Security Investigations Forensic Laboratory System of Records also include the library of genuine, altered, and counterfeit travel and identity documents provided to the HSI-FL by international organizations, government agencies, and law enforcement organizations from across the United States and around the world to research methods of document production and authenticate documents through comparative forensic examinations. The DHS/ICE–014 Homeland Security Investigations Forensic Laboratory System of Records contains information that is collected by, on behalf of, in support of, or in cooperation with DHS and its components, and may contain personally identifiable information (PII) collected by other federal, state, local, tribal, foreign, or international government agencies. The Secretary of the Department of Homeland Security, pursuant to 5 U.S.C. 552a(j)(2), has exempted this system from the following provisions of the Privacy Act, subject to limitations set forth in 5 U.S.C. 552a(c)(3), (c)(4); (d); (e)(1), (e)(2), (e)(3), (e)(4)(G), (e)(4)(H), (e)(4)(I), (e)(5), (e)(8); (f); and (g). Additionally, the Secretary of Homeland Security, pursuant to 5 U.S.C. 552a(k)(2), has exempted this system from the following provisions of the Privacy Act, subject to limitations set forth in 5 U.S.C. 552a(c)(3); (d); (e)(1), (e)(4)(G), (e)(4)(H), (e)(4)(I); and (f). Where a record received from another system has been exempted in that source system under 5 U.S.C. 552a(j)(2), DHS will claim the same exemptions for those records that are claimed for the original primary systems of records from which they originated and claims any additional exemptions set forth here. Exemptions from these particular subsections are justified, on a case-by-case basis to be determined at the time a request is made, for the following reasons:

(a) From subsection (c)(3) and (4) (Accounting for Disclosures) because release of the accounting of disclosures could alert the subject of an investigation of an actual or potential criminal, civil, or regulatory violation to the existence of that investigation and reveal investigative interest on the part of DHS as well as the recipient agency. Disclosure of the accounting would therefore present a serious impediment to law enforcement efforts and/or efforts to preserve national security. Disclosure of the accounting would also permit the individual who is the subject of a record to impede the investigation, to tamper with witnesses or evidence, and to avoid detection or apprehension, which would undermine the entire investigative process.

(b) From subsection (d) (Access to Records) because access to the records contained in this system of records could inform the subject of an investigation of an actual or potential criminal, civil, or regulatory violation to the existence of that investigation and reveal investigative interest on the part of DHS or another agency. Access to the records could permit the individual who is the subject of a record to impede the investigation, to tamper with witnesses or evidence, and to avoid detection or apprehension. Amendment of the records could interfere with ongoing investigations and law enforcement activities and would impose an unreasonable administrative burden by requiring investigations to be continually re-investigated. In addition, permitting access and amendment to such information could disclose security-sensitive information that could be detrimental to homeland security.

(c) From subsection (e)(1) (Relevancy and Necessity of Information) because in the course of investigations into potential violations of federal law, the accuracy of information obtained or introduced occasionally may be unclear, or the information may not be strictly relevant or necessary to a specific investigation. In the interests of effective law enforcement, it is appropriate to retain all information that may aid in establishing patterns of unlawful activity.

(d) From subsection (e)(2) (Collection of Information from Individuals) because requiring that information be collected from the subject of an investigation would alert the subject to the nature or existence of the investigation, thereby interfering with that investigation and related law enforcement activities.

(e) From subsection (e)(3) (Notice to Subjects) because providing such detailed information could impede law enforcement by compromising the existence of a confidential investigation or reveal the identity of witnesses or confidential informants.

(f) From subsections (e)(4)(G), (e)(4)(H), and (e)(4)(I) (Agency Requirements) and (f) (Agency Rules), because portions of this system are exempt from the individual access provisions of subsection (d) for the reasons noted above, and therefore DHS is not required to establish requirements, rules, or procedures with respect to such access. Providing notice to individuals with respect to existence of records pertaining to them in the system of records or otherwise setting up procedures pursuant to which individuals may access and view records pertaining to themselves in the system would undermine investigative efforts and reveal the identities of witnesses, and potential witnesses, and confidential informants.

(g) From subsection (e)(5) (Collection of Information) because with the collection of information for law enforcement purposes, it is impossible to determine in advance what information is accurate, relevant, timely, and complete. Compliance with subsection (e)(5) would preclude DHS agents from using their investigative training and exercise of good judgment to both conduct and report on investigations.

(h) From subsection (e)(8) (Notice on Individuals) because compliance would interfere with DHS's ability to obtain, serve, and issue subpoenas, warrants, and other law enforcement mechanisms that may be filed under seal and could result in disclosure of investigative techniques, procedures, and evidence.

(i) From subsection (g)(1) (Civil Remedies) to the extent that the system is exempt from other specific subsections of the Privacy Act.

73. The DHS/NPPD—002 Chemical Facility Anti-Terrorism Standards Personnel Surety Program System of Records consists of electronic and paper records and will be used by DHS and its components. The DHS/NPPD—002 Chemical Facility Anti-Terrorism Standards Personnel Surety Program System of Records is a repository of information held by DHS in connection with its several and varied missions and functions, including, but not limited to the enforcement of civil and criminal laws; investigations, inquiries, and proceedings thereunder; and national security and intelligence activities. The DHS/NPPD—002 Chemical Facility Anti-Terrorism Standards Personnel Surety Program System of Records contains information that is collected by, on behalf of, in support of, or in cooperation with DHS and its components and may contain personally identifiable information collected by other federal, state, local, tribal, foreign, or international government agencies. The Secretary of Homeland Security has exempted this system from the following provisions of the Privacy Act, subject to limitations set forth therein: 5 U.S.C. 552a(c)(3); (d); (e)(1), (e)(4)(G), (e)(4)(H), (e)(4)(I); and (f). These exemptions are made pursuant to 5 U.S.C. 552a(k)(1) and (k)(2).

In addition to records under the control of DHS, the DHS/NPPD—002 Chemical Facility Anti-Terrorism Standards Personnel Surety Program System of Records may include records originating from systems of records of other law enforcement and intelligence agencies, which may be exempt from certain provisions of the Privacy Act. DHS does not, however, assert exemption from any provisions of the Privacy Act with respect to information submitted by high-risk chemical facilities.

To the extent the DHS/NPPD—002 Chemical Facility Anti-Terrorism Standards Personnel Surety Program System of Records contains records originating from other systems of records, DHS will rely on the exemptions claimed for those records in the originating systems of records. Exemptions from these particular subsections are justified, on a case-by-case basis to be determined at the time a request is made, for the following reasons:

(a) From subsection (c)(3) (Accounting for Disclosures) because release of the accounting of disclosures could alert the subject of an investigation of an actual or potential criminal, civil, or regulatory violation to the existence of that investigation and reveal investigative interest, on the part of DHS as well as the recipient agency. Disclosure of the accounting would therefore present a serious impediment to law enforcement efforts and/or efforts to preserve national security. Disclosure of the accounting would also permit the individual who is the subject of a record to impede the investigation, to tamper with witnesses or evidence, and to avoid detection or apprehension, which would undermine the entire investigative process.

(b) From subsection (d) (Access to Records) because access to the records contained in this system of records could inform the subject of an investigation of an actual or potential criminal, civil, or regulatory violation to the existence of that investigation and reveal investigative interest on the part of DHS or another agency. Access to the records could permit the individual who is the subject of a record to impede the investigation, to tamper with witnesses or evidence, and to avoid detection or apprehension. Amendment of the records could interfere with ongoing investigations and law enforcement activities and would impose an unreasonable administrative burden by requiring investigations to be continually reinvestigated. In addition, permitting access and amendment to such information could disclose security-sensitive information that could be detrimental to homeland security.

(c) From subsection (e)(1) (Relevancy and Necessity of Information) because in the course of investigations into potential violations of federal law, the accuracy of information obtained or introduced occasionally may be unclear, or the information may not be strictly relevant or necessary to a specific investigation. In the interests of effective law enforcement, it is appropriate to retain all information that may aid in establishing patterns of unlawful activity.

(d) From subsections (e)(4)(G), (e)(4)(H), and (e)(4)(I) (Agency Requirements) and (f) (Agency Rules), because portions of this system are exempt from the individual access provisions of subsection (d) for the reasons noted above, and therefore DHS is not required to establish requirements, rules, or procedures with respect to such access. Providing notice to individuals with respect to existence of records pertaining to them in the system of records or otherwise setting up procedures pursuant to which individuals may access and view records pertaining to themselves in the system would undermine investigative efforts and reveal the identities of witnesses, potential witnesses, and confidential informants.

74. The DHS/CBP–022 Electronic Visa Update System (EVUS) System of Records consists of electronic and paper records and will be used by DHS and its components. EVUS is a repository of information held by DHS/CBP in connection with its several and varied missions and functions, including, but not limited to the enforcement of civil and criminal laws; investigations, inquiries, and proceedings there under; and national security and intelligence activities. EVUS contains information that is collected by, on behalf of, in support of, or in cooperation with DHS and its components and may contain personally identifiable information collected by other federal, state, local, tribal, foreign, or international government agencies. The Secretary of Homeland Security, pursuant to 5 U.S.C. 552a(j)(2), has exempted this system from the following provisions of the Privacy Act: 5 U.S.C. 552a(c)(3), (e)(8), and (g). Additionally, the Secretary of Homeland Security, pursuant to 5 U.S.C. 552a(k)(2) has exempted this system from the following provisions of the Privacy Act: 5 U.S.C. 552a(c)(3). Exemptions from these particular subsections are justified, on a case-by-case basis to be determined at the time a request is made, for the following reasons:

(a) From subsection (c)(3) (Accounting for Disclosures) because release of the accounting of disclosures could alert the subject of an investigation of an actual or potential criminal, civil, or regulatory violation to the existence of that investigation and reveal investigative interest on the part of DHS as well as the recipient agency. Disclosure of the accounting would therefore present a serious impediment to law enforcement efforts and/or efforts to preserve national security. Disclosure of the accounting would also permit the individual who is the subject of a record to impede the investigation, to tamper with witnesses or evidence, and to avoid detection or apprehension, which would undermine the entire investigative process.

(b) From subsection (e)(8) (Notice on Individuals) because compliance would interfere with DHS's ability to obtain, serve, and issue subpoenas, warrants, and other law enforcement mechanisms that may be filed under seal and could result in disclosure of investigative techniques, procedures, and evidence.

(c) From subsection (g) (Civil Remedies) to the extent that the system is exempt from other specific subsections of the Privacy Act.

75. The DHS/ICE–015 LeadTrac System of Records consists of electronic and paper records and will be used by ICE investigative and homeland security personnel. The DHS/ICE–015 LeadTrac System of Records is a repository of information held by ICE for analytical and investigative purposes. The system is used to conduct research supporting the production of law enforcement activities; provide lead information for investigative inquiry and follow-up; assist in the conduct of ICE criminal and administrative investigations; assist in the disruption of terrorist or other criminal activity; and discover previously unknown connections among existing ICE investigations. The DHS/ICE–015 LeadTrac System of Records contains aggregated data from ICE and DHS law enforcement and homeland security IT systems, as well as data uploaded by ICE personnel for analysis from various public, private, and commercial sources during the course of an investigation or analytical project. The Secretary of Homeland Security, pursuant to 5 U.S.C. 552a(j)(2), has exempted this system from the following provisions of the Privacy Act: 5 U.S.C. 552a(c)(3), (c)(4); (d); (e)(1), (e)(2), (e)(3), (e)(4)(G), (e)(4)(H), (e)(4)(I), (e)(5), (e)(8); (f); and (g). Additionally, the Secretary of Homeland Security, pursuant to 5 U.S.C. 552a(k)(2), has exempted this system from the following provisions of the Privacy Act: 5 U.S.C. 552a(c)(3), (c)(4); (d); (e)(1), (e)(4)(G), (e)(4)(H), (e)(4)(I); and (f). When a record received from another system has been exempted in that source system under 5 U.S.C. 552a(j)(2) or (k)(2), DHS will claim the same exemptions for those records that are claimed for the original primary systems of records from which they originated and claims any additional exemptions set forth here.

Exemptions from these particular subsections are justified, on a case-by-case basis to be determined at the time a request is made, for the following reasons:

(a) From subsection (c)(3) and (4) (Accounting for Disclosures) because release of the accounting of disclosures could alert the subject of an investigation of an actual or potential criminal, civil, or regulatory violation to the existence of that investigation and reveal investigative interest on the part of DHS as well as the recipient agency. Disclosure of the accounting would therefore present a serious impediment to law enforcement efforts and/or efforts to preserve national security. Disclosure of the accounting would also permit the individual who is the

subject of a record to impede the investigation, to tamper with witnesses or evidence, and to avoid detection or apprehension, which would undermine the entire investigative process. Disclosure of corrections or notations of dispute may impede investigations by requiring DHS to inform each witness or individual contacted during the investigation of each correction or notation pertaining to information provided them during the investigation.

(b) From subsection (d) (Access to Records) because access to the records contained in this system of records could inform the subject of an investigation of an actual or potential criminal, civil, or regulatory violation to the existence of that investigation and reveal investigative interest on the part of DHS or another agency. Access to the records could permit the individual who is the subject of a record to impede the investigation, to tamper with witnesses or evidence, and to avoid detection or apprehension. Amendment of the records could interfere with ongoing investigations and law enforcement activities and would impose an unreasonable administrative burden by requiring investigations to be continually reinvestigated. In addition, permitting access and amendment to such information could disclose classified and other security-sensitive information that could be detrimental to homeland security.

(c) From subsection (e)(1) (Relevancy and Necessity of Information) because in the course of investigations into potential violations of federal law, the accuracy of information obtained or introduced occasionally may be unclear, or the information may not be strictly relevant or necessary to a specific investigation. In the interests of effective law enforcement, it is appropriate to retain all information that may aid in establishing patterns of unlawful activity.

(d) From subsection (e)(2) (Collection of Information from Individuals) because requiring that information be collected from the subject of an investigation would alert the subject to the nature or existence of the investigation, thereby interfering with that investigation and related law enforcement activities.

(e) From subsection (e)(3) (Notice to Subjects) because providing such detailed information could impede law enforcement by compromising the existence of a confidential investigation or reveal the identity of witnesses or confidential informants.

(f) From subsections (e)(4)(G), (e)(4)(H), and (e)(4)(I) (Agency Requirements) and (f) (Agency Rules), because portions of this system are exempt from the individual access provisions of subsection (d) for the reasons noted above, and therefore DHS is not required to establish requirements, rules, or procedures with respect to such access. Providing notice to individuals with respect to existence of records pertaining to them in the system of records or otherwise establishing procedures pursuant to which individuals may access and view records pertaining to themselves in the system would undermine investigative efforts and reveal the identities of witnesses, potential witnesses, and confidential informants.

(g) From subsection (e)(5) (Collection of Information) because with the collection of information for law enforcement purposes, it is impossible to determine in advance what information is accurate, relevant, timely, and complete. Compliance with subsection (e)(5) would preclude DHS agents from using their investigative training and exercise of good judgment to both conduct and report on investigations.

(h) From subsection (e)(8) (Notice on Individuals) because compliance would interfere with DHS's ability to obtain, serve, and issue subpoenas, warrants, and other law enforcement mechanisms that may be filed under seal and could result in disclosure of investigative techniques, procedures, and evidence.

(i) From subsection (g)(1) (Civil Remedies) to the extent that the system is exempt from other specific subsections of the Privacy Act.

76. The DHS/CBP–023 Border Patrol Enforcement Records (BPER) System of Records consists of electronic and paper records and will be used by DHS and its components. The DHS/CBP–023 BPER System of Records is a repository of information held by DHS/CBP in connection with its several and varied missions and functions, including, but not limited to the enforcement of civil and criminal laws; investigations, inquiries, and proceedings there under; and national security and intelligence activities. The DHS/CBP–023 BPER System of Records contains information that is collected by, on behalf of, in support of, or in cooperation with DHS and its components and may contain personally identifiable information collected by other federal, state, local, tribal, foreign, or international government agencies. The Secretary of Homeland Security, pursuant to 5 U.S.C. 552a(j)(2), has exempted this system from the following provisions of the Privacy Act: 5 U.S.C. 552a (c)(3), (c)(4); (d); (e)(1), (e)(2), (e)(3), (e)(4)(G), (e)(4)(H), (e)(5), (e)(8); and (g). Additionally, the Secretary of Homeland Security, pursuant to 5 U.S.C. 552a(k)(2), has exempted this system from the following provisions of the Privacy Act: 5 U.S.C. 552a (c)(3); (d); (e)(1), (e)(4)(G), and (e)(4)(H). Exemptions from these particular subsections are justified, on a case-by-case basis to be determined at the time a request is made, for the following reasons:

(a) From subsection (c)(3) and (4) (Accounting for Disclosures) because release of the accounting of disclosures could alert the subject of an investigation of an actual or potential criminal, civil, or regulatory violation to the existence of that investigation and reveal investigative interest on the part of DHS as well as the recipient agency. Disclosure of the accounting would therefore present a serious impediment to law enforcement efforts and/or efforts to preserve national security. Disclosure of the accounting would also permit the individual who is the subject of a record to impede the investigation, to tamper with witnesses or evidence, and to avoid detection or apprehension, which would undermine the entire investigative process.

(b) From subsection (d) (Access to Records) because access to the records contained in this system of records could inform the subject of an investigation of an actual or potential criminal, civil, or regulatory violation to the existence of that investigation and reveal investigative interest on the part of DHS or another agency. Access to the records could permit the individual who is the subject of a record to impede the investigation, to tamper with witnesses or evidence, and to avoid detection or apprehension. Amendment of the records could interfere with ongoing investigations and law enforcement activities and would impose an unreasonable administrative burden by requiring investigations to be continually reinvestigated. In addition, permitting access and amendment to such information could disclose security-sensitive information that could be detrimental to homeland security.

(c) From subsection (e)(1) (Relevancy and Necessity of Information) because in the course of investigations into potential violations of federal law, the accuracy of information obtained or introduced occasionally may be unclear, or the information may not be strictly relevant or necessary to a specific investigation. In the interests of effective law enforcement, it is appropriate to retain all information that may aid in establishing patterns of unlawful activity.

(d) From subsection (e)(2) (Collection of Information from Individuals) because requiring that information be collected from the subject of an investigation would alert the subject to the nature or existence of the investigation, thereby interfering with that investigation and related law enforcement activities.

(e) From subsection (e)(3) (Notice to Subjects) because providing such detailed information could impede law enforcement by compromising the existence of a confidential investigation or reveal the identity of witnesses or confidential informants.

(f) From subsections (e)(4)(G) and (e)(4)(H) (Agency Requirements) because portions of this system are exempt from the individual access provisions of subsection (d) for the reasons noted above, and therefore DHS is not required to establish requirements, rules, or procedures with respect to such access. Providing notice to individuals with respect to existence of records pertaining to them in the system of records or otherwise setting up procedures pursuant to which individuals may access and view records pertaining to themselves in the system would undermine investigative efforts and reveal the identities of witnesses, and potential witnesses, and confidential informants.

(g) From subsection (e)(5) (Collection of Information) because with the collection of information for law enforcement purposes, it is impossible to determine in advance what information is accurate, relevant, timely, and complete. Compliance with subsection (e)(5) would preclude DHS agents from using their investigative training and exercise of good judgment to both conduct and report on investigations.

(h) From subsection (e)(8) (Notice on Individuals) because compliance would interfere with DHS's ability to obtain, serve, and issue subpoenas, warrants, and other law enforcement mechanisms that may be filed under seal and could result in disclosure of investigative techniques, procedures, and evidence.

(i) From subsection (g)(1) (Civil Remedies) to the extent that the system is exempt from other specific subsections of the Privacy Act.

77. The DHS/USCG–031 USCG Law Enforcement (ULE) System of Records consists of electronic and paper records and will be used by DHS and its components. The DHS/USCG–031 USCG Law Enforcement (ULE) System of Records is a repository of information held by DHS in connection with its several and varied missions and functions, including, but not limited to the enforcement of civil and criminal laws; investigations, inquiries, and proceedings there under; and national security and intelligence activities. The DHS/USCG–031 USCG Law Enforcement (ULE) System of Records contains information that is collected by, on behalf of, in support of, or in cooperation with DHS and its components and may contain personally identifiable information collected by other federal, state, local, tribal, foreign, or international government agencies. The Secretary of Homeland Security, pursuant to 5 U.S.C. 552a(j)(2), has exempted this system from the following provisions of the Privacy Act: 5 U.S.C. 552a (c)(3–4); (d); (e)(1–3), (e)(5), (e)(8); and (g). Additionally, the Secretary of Homeland Security, pursuant to 5 U.S.C. 552a(k)(2) has exempted this system from the following provisions of the Privacy Act: 5 U.S.C. 552a (c)(3); (d); (e)(1), (e)(4)(G), (e)(4)(H), (e)(4)(I); and (f). When a record received from another system has been exempted in that source system under 5 U.S.C. 552a(j)(2), DHS will claim the same exemptions for those records that are claimed for the original primary systems of records from which they originated and

claims any additional exemptions set forth here.

Exemptions from these particular subsections are justified, on a case-by-case basis to be determined at the time a request is made, for the following reasons:

(a) From subsection (c)(3) and (4) (Accounting for Disclosures) because release of the accounting of disclosures could alert the subject of an investigation of an actual or potential criminal, civil, or regulatory violation to the existence of that investigation and reveal investigative interest on the part of DHS as well as the recipient agency. Disclosure of the accounting would therefore present a serious impediment to law enforcement efforts and/or efforts to preserve national security. Disclosure of the accounting would also permit the individual who is the subject of a record to impede the investigation, to tamper with witnesses or evidence, and to avoid detection or apprehension, which would undermine the entire investigative process.

(b) From subsection (d) (Access to Records) because access to the records contained in this system of records could inform the subject of an investigation of an actual or potential criminal, civil, or regulatory violation to the existence of that investigation and reveal investigative interest on the part of DHS or another agency. Access to the records could permit the individual who is the subject of a record to impede the investigation, to tamper with witnesses or evidence, and to avoid detection or apprehension. Amendment of the records could interfere with ongoing investigations and law enforcement activities and would impose an unreasonable administrative burden by requiring investigations to be continually reinvestigated. In addition, permitting access and amendment to such information could disclose security-sensitive information that could be detrimental to homeland security.

(c) From subsection (e)(1) (Relevancy and Necessity of Information) because in the course of investigations into potential violations of federal law, the accuracy of information obtained or introduced occasionally may be unclear, or the information may not be strictly relevant or necessary to a specific investigation. In the interests of effective law enforcement, it is appropriate to retain all information that may aid in establishing patterns of unlawful activity.

(d) From subsection (e)(2) (Collection of Information from Individuals) because requiring that information be collected from the subject of an investigation would alert the subject to the nature or existence of the investigation, thereby interfering with that investigation and related law enforcement activities.

(e) From subsection (e)(3) (Notice to Subjects) because providing such detailed information could impede law enforcement by compromising the existence of a confidential investigation or reveal the identity of witnesses or confidential informants.

(f) From subsection (e)(5) (Collection of Information) because with the collection of information for law enforcement purposes, it is impossible to determine in advance what information is accurate, relevant, timely, and complete. Compliance with subsection (e)(5) would preclude DHS agents from using their investigative training and exercise of good judgment to both conduct and report on investigations.

(g) From subsection (e)(8) (Notice on Individuals) because compliance would interfere with DHS's ability to obtain, serve, and issue subpoenas, warrants, and other law enforcement mechanisms that may be filed under seal and could result in disclosure of investigative techniques, procedures, and evidence.

(h) From subsection (g) (Civil Remedies) to the extent that the system is exempt from other specific subsections of the Privacy Act.

78. The DHS/ALL–039 Foreign Access Management System of Records consists of electronic and paper records and will be used by DHS and its components. The DHS/ALL–039 Foreign Access Management System of Records is a repository of information held by DHS in connection with its several and varied missions and functions, including, but not limited to the enforcement of civil and criminal laws; investigations, inquiries, and proceedings there under; and national security and intelligence activities. The DHS/ALL–039 Foreign Access Management System of Records contains information that is collected by, on behalf of, in support of, or in cooperation with DHS and its components and may contain personally identifiable information collected by other federal, state, local, tribal, foreign, or international government agencies. The Secretary of Homeland Security, pursuant to 5 U.S.C. 552a(k)(1), (k)(2), and (k)(5), has exempted this system from the following provisions of the Privacy Act: 5 U.S.C. 552a(c)(3); (d); (e)(1), (e)(4)(G), (e)(4)(H), (e)(4)(I); and (f). When a record received from another system has been exempted in that source system under 5 U.S.C. 552a(j)(2), DHS will claim the same exemptions for those records that are claimed for the original primary systems of records from which they originated and claims any additional exemptions set forth here. Exemptions from these particular subsections are justified, on a case-by-case basis to be determined at the time a request is made, for the following reasons:

(a) From subsection (c)(3) (Accounting for Disclosures) because release of the accounting of disclosures could alert the subject of an investigation of an actual or potential criminal, civil, or regulatory violation to the existence of that investigation and reveal investigative interest on the part of DHS as well as the recipient agency. Disclosure of the accounting would therefore present a serious impediment to law enforcement efforts and efforts to preserve national security. Disclosure of the accounting would also permit the individual who is the subject of a record to impede the investigation, to tamper with witnesses or evidence, and to avoid detection or apprehension, which would undermine the entire investigative process. When an investigation has been completed, information on disclosures made may continue to be exempted if the fact that an investigation occurred remains sensitive after completion.

(b) From subsection (d) (Access and Amendment to Records) because access to the records contained in this system of records could inform the subject of an investigation of an actual or potential criminal, civil, or regulatory violation to the existence of that investigation and reveal investigative interest on the part of DHS or another agency. Access to the records could permit the individual who is the subject of a record to impede the investigation, to tamper with witnesses or evidence, and to avoid detection or apprehension. Amendment of the records could interfere with ongoing investigations and law enforcement activities and would impose an unreasonable administrative burden by requiring investigations to be continually reinvestigated. In addition, permitting access and amendment to such information could disclose security-sensitive information that could be detrimental to homeland security.

(c) From subsection (e)(1) (Relevancy and Necessity of Information) because in the course of investigations into potential violations of federal law, the accuracy of information obtained or introduced occasionally may be unclear, or the information may not be strictly relevant or necessary to a specific investigation. In the interests of effective law enforcement, it is appropriate to retain all information that may aid in establishing patterns of unlawful activity.

(d) From subsections (e)(4)(G), (e)(4)(H), and (e)(4)(I) (Agency Requirements) and (f) (Agency Rules), because portions of this system are exempt from the individual access provisions of subsection (d) for the reasons noted above, and therefore DHS is not required to establish requirements, rules, or procedures with respect to such access. Providing notice to individuals with respect to existence of records pertaining to them in the system of records or otherwise setting up procedures pursuant to which individuals may access and view records pertaining to themselves in the system would undermine investigative efforts and reveal the identities of witnesses, and potential witnesses, and confidential informants.

79. The DHS/CBP–024 CBP Intelligence Records System (CIRS) System of Records

consists of electronic and paper records and will be used by DHS and its components. The CIRS is a repository of information held by DHS in connection with its several and varied missions and functions, including, but not limited to the enforcement of civil and criminal laws; investigations, inquiries, and proceedings there under; and national security and intelligence activities. The CIRS contains information that is collected by, on behalf of, in support of, or in cooperation with DHS and its components and may contain personally identifiable information collected by other Federal, state, local, tribal, foreign, or international government agencies. The Secretary of Homeland Security, pursuant to 5 U.S.C. 552a(j)(2), has exempted this system from the following provisions of the Privacy Act: 5 U.S.C. 552a(c)(3) and (4); (d); (e)(1), (e)(2), (e)(3), (e)(4)(G), (e)(4)(H), (e)(4)(I); (e)(5), and (e)(8); (f); and (g). Additionally, the Secretary of Homeland Security, pursuant to 5 U.S.C. 552a(k)(1) and (k)(2), has exempted this system from the following provisions of the Privacy Act, 5 U.S.C. 552a(c)(3); (d); (e)(1), (e)(4)(G), (e)(4)(H), (e)(4)(I), and (f). When this system receives a record from another system exempted in that source system under 5 U.S.C. 552a(k)(1), (k)(2), or (j)(2), DHS will claim the same exemptions for those records that are claimed for the original primary systems of records from which they originated and claims any additional exemptions set forth here. Exemptions from these particular subsections are justified, on a case by case basis to be determined at the time a request is made, for the following reasons:

(a) From subsection (c)(3) and (4) (Accounting for Disclosures) because release of the accounting of disclosures could alert the subject of an investigation of an actual or potential criminal, civil, or regulatory violation to the existence of that investigation and reveal investigative interest on the part of DHS as well as the recipient agency. Disclosure of the accounting would therefore present a serious impediment to law enforcement efforts and/or efforts to preserve national security. Disclosure of the accounting would also permit the individual who is the subject of a record to impede the investigation, to tamper with witnesses or evidence, and to avoid detection or apprehension, which would undermine the entire investigative process. Information on a completed investigation may be withheld and exempt from disclosure if the fact that an investigation occurred remains sensitive after completion.

(b) From subsection (d) (Access and Amendment to Records) because access to the records contained in this system of records could inform the subject of an investigation of an actual or potential criminal, civil, or regulatory violation to the existence of that investigation and reveal inves-

tigative interest on the part of DHS or another agency. Access to the records could permit the individual who is the subject of a record to impede the investigation, to tamper with witnesses or evidence, and to avoid detection or apprehension. Amendment of the records could interfere with ongoing investigations and law enforcement activities and would impose an unreasonable administrative burden by requiring investigations to be continually reinvestigated. In addition, permitting access and amendment to such information could disclose security-sensitive information that could be detrimental to homeland security.

(c) From subsection (e)(1) (Relevancy and Necessity of Information) because in the course of investigations into potential violations of Federal law, the accuracy of information obtained or introduced occasionally may be unclear, or the information may not be strictly relevant or necessary to a specific investigation. In the interests of effective law enforcement, it is appropriate to retain all information that may aid in establishing patterns of unlawful activity.

(d) From subsection (e)(2) (Collection of Information from Individuals) because requiring that information be collected from the subject of an investigation would alert the subject to the nature or existence of the investigation, thereby interfering with that investigation and related law enforcement activities.

(e) From subsection (e)(3) (Notice to Subjects) because providing such detailed information could impede law enforcement by compromising the existence of a confidential investigation or reveal the identity of witnesses or confidential informants.

(f) From subsections (e)(4)(G), (e)(4)(H), and (e)(4)(I) (Agency Requirements) and (f) (Agency Rules) because portions of this system are exempt from the individual access and amendment provisions of subsection (d) for the reasons noted above, and therefore DHS is not required to establish requirements, rules, or procedures with respect to such access. Providing notice to individuals with respect to existence of records pertaining to them in the system of records or otherwise setting up procedures pursuant to which individuals may access, amend, and view records pertaining to themselves in the system would undermine investigative efforts and reveal the identities of witnesses, and potential witnesses, and confidential informants.

(g) From subsection (e)(5) (Collection of Information) because with the collection of information for law enforcement purposes, it is impossible to determine in advance what information is accurate, relevant, timely, and complete. Compliance with subsection (e)(5) would preclude DHS agents from using their investigative training and exercise of good judgment to both conduct and report on investigations.

(h) From subsection (e)(8) (Notice on Individuals) because compliance would interfere with DHS's ability to obtain, serve, and issue subpoenas, warrants, and other law enforcement mechanisms that may be filed under seal and could result in disclosure of investigative techniques, procedures, and evidence.

(i) From subsection (g) to the extent that the system is exempt from other specific subsections of the Privacy Act relating to individuals' rights to access and amend their records contained in the system. Therefore, DHS is not required to establish rules or procedures pursuant to which individuals may seek a civil remedy for the agency's refusal to amend a record, refusal to comply with a request for access to records, failure to maintain accurate, relevant timely and complete records, or its failure to otherwise comply with an individual's right to access or amend records.

[71 FR 20523, Apr. 21, 2006]

EDITORIAL NOTE: For FEDERAL REGISTER citations affecting appendix C to part 5, see the List of CFR Sections Affected, which appears in the Finding Aids section of the printed volume and at *www.govinfo.gov.*

PART 7—CLASSIFIED NATIONAL SECURITY INFORMATION

AUTHORITY: 5 U.S.C. 301; Pub. L. 107–296; E.O. 13526; 3 CFR, 1995 Comp., p. 333; E.O. 13142, 64 FR 66089, 3 CFR, 1999 Comp., p. 236; 32 CFR part 2001.

SOURCE: 79 FR 44095, July 30, 2014, unless otherwise noted.

§ 7.1   Purpose.

The purpose of this part is to ensure that information within the Department of Homeland Security (DHS) relating to the national security is classified, safeguarded, and declassified pursuant to the provisions of Executive Order 13526, and implementing directives from the Information Security Oversight Office (ISOO) of the National Archives and Records Administration (NARA).

§ 7.2   Scope.

(a) This part applies to all employees, detailees, and non-contractor personnel inside and outside the Executive Branch who are granted access to classified information by the DHS, in accordance with the standards in Executive Order 13526, and its implementing directives, and Executive Order 13549, "Classified National Security Information Program for State, Local, Tribal, and Private Sector Entities," and its implementing directives.

(b) This part does not apply to contractors, grantees and other categories of personnel falling under the purview of Executive Order 12829, National Industrial Security Program, as amended, and its implementing directives.

(c) This part is independent of and does not affect any classification procedures or requirements of the Atomic Energy Act of 1954, as amended (42 U.S.C. 2011 *et seq.*).

(d) This part does not, and is not intended to, create any right to judicial review, or any other right or benefit or trust responsibility, substantive or procedural, enforceable by a party against the United States, its agencies or instrumentalities, its officers or employees, or any other person. This part creates limited rights to administrative review of decisions. This part does not, and is not intended to, create any right to judicial review of administrative action.

§7.3 Definitions.

The terms defined or used in Executive Order 13526, and the implementing directives in 32 CFR part 2001 and 2004 are applicable to this part.

Subpart A—Administration

§7.10 Authority of the DHS Chief Security Officer.

(a) The DHS Chief Security Officer (hereafter "Chief Security Officer") is designated as the Senior Agency Official as required by section 5.4(d) of Executive Order 13526, and, except as specifically provided elsewhere in this part, is authorized to administer the DHS Classified National Security Information program pursuant to Executive Order 13526.

(b) To the extent that 32 CFR part 2001 refers to the agency head or "designee," the Chief Security Officer is such designee unless determined otherwise by the Secretary. The Chief Security Officer may further delegate the associated authorities.

(c) The Chief Security Officer shall, among other actions:

(1) Oversee and administer the DHS's program established under Executive Order 13526;

(2) Promulgate implementing regulations;

(3) Establish and maintain DHS-wide security education and training programs, to include implementation and management of mandatory training for DHS officials who have been delegated original classification authority and those who perform derivative classification actions and suspension of such authority for failure to attend such training;

(4) Establish and maintain an ongoing self-inspection program that shall include regularly reviewing representative samples of DHS's original and derivative classification actions, correcting instances of misclassification, and reporting annually to the Director of ISOO on the DHS self-inspection program;

(5) Establish procedures to prevent unnecessary access to classified information, including procedures that:

(i) Require that a need for access to classified information is established before initiating administrative procedures to grant access; and

(ii) Ensure that the number of persons granted access to classified information is limited to the minimum necessary for operational and security requirements and needs;

(6) Develop special contingency plans for the safeguarding of classified information used in or near hostile or potentially hostile areas;

(7) Coordinate with the DHS Chief Human Capital Officer, as appropriate, to ensure that the performance contract or other system used to rate personnel performance includes the management of classified information as a critical element or item to be evaluated in the rating of:

(i) Original classification authorities;

(ii) Security managers or security specialists; and

(iii) All other personnel whose duties significantly involve the creation or handling of classified information, including persons who apply derivative classification markings;

(8) Account for the costs associated with implementing this part and report the cost to the Director of ISOO;

(9) Assign in a prompt manner personnel to respond to any request, appeal, challenge, complaint, or suggestion concerning Executive Order 13526, that pertains to classified information that originated in a DHS component that no longer exists and for which there is no clear successor in function;

(10) Establish a secure capability to receive information, allegations, or complaints regarding over-classification or incorrect classification and to provide a ready source for guidance on proper classification;

(11) Report violations, take corrective measures and assess appropriate sanctions as warranted, in accordance with Executive Order 13526;

(12) Oversee DHS creation and participation in special access programs authorized under Executive Order 13526;

(13) Direct and administer DHS's personnel security program in accordance with Executive Order 12968 and other applicable law;

(14) Direct and administer DHS implementation and compliance with the National Industrial Security Program

in accordance with Executive Order 12829 and other applicable guidance; and

(15) Perform any other duties as the Secretary may designate.

(d) The Chief Security Officer shall maintain a current list of all officials authorized pursuant to this part to originally classify or declassify documents.

(e) The Chief Security Officer shall establish and maintain a means for appointing, tracking, and training DHS officials who do or will perform original and derivative classification actions.

(f) The Chief Security Officer shall administer a program for the implementation, management, and oversight of access to and safeguarding of classified information provided to state, local, tribal, and private sector personnel pursuant to Executive Order 13549, "Classified National Security Information Program for State, Local, Tribal, and Private Sector Entities," and its implementing directives.

(g) Nothing in this part will be interpreted to abrogate or affect the responsibilities of the Director of National Intelligence under the National Security Act of 1947, Public Law 235 (1947), as amended, and E.O. 12333, United States Intelligence Activities (1981), as amended, or any responsibilities of the Under Secretary for Intelligence and Analysis conferred by presidential or intelligence community directive implicating those authorities, insofar as those authorities concern classified sources, methods, and activities, classified national intelligence, or sensitive compartmented information and are executed consistent with delegations or designations of authority issued pursuant to the statutory authority of the Secretary.

§ 7.11 Components' responsibilities.

Each DHS component shall appoint a security officer or security liaison to implement this part. The security officer/security liaison shall:

(a) Implement, observe, and enforce security regulations or procedures within their component with respect to the classification, declassification, safeguarding, handling, and storage of classified national security information;

(b) Report violations of the provisions of this part to the Chief Security Officer committed by employees of their component, as required by implementing directives;

(c) Ensure that employees of their component attend mandatory security education and training, as required by the DHS classified information security procedures, to include those component officials delegated the authority to classify information originally and those who perform derivative classification actions;

(d) Continuously review the requirements for personnel access to classified information as a part of the continuous need-to-know evaluation, and initiate action to administratively withdraw or reduce the level of access authorized, as appropriate; and

(e) Cooperate fully with any request from the Chief Security Officer for assistance in the implementation of this part.

§ 7.12 Violations of classified information requirements.

(a) Any person who suspects or has knowledge of a violation of this part, including the known or suspected loss or compromise of classified information, shall promptly report such violations or possible violations, pursuant to requirements set forth in DHS directives.

(b) DHS employees and detailees may be reprimanded, suspended without pay, terminated from classification authority, suspended from or denied access to classified information, or subject to other sanctions in accordance with applicable law and DHS regulations or directives if they:

(1) Knowingly, willfully, or negligently disclose to unauthorized persons information properly classified under Executive Order 13526, or its predecessor orders;

(2) Knowingly, willfully, or negligently classify or continue the classification of information in violation of Executive Order 13526, or its implementing directives; or

(3) Knowingly, willfully, or negligently create or continue a special

access program contrary to the requirements of Executive Order 13526; or,

(4) Knowingly, willfully, or negligently violate any other provision of Executive Order 13526, or DHS implementing directives, or;

(5) Knowingly, willfully, or negligently grant eligibility for, or allow access to, classified information in violation of Executive Order 13526, or its implementing directives, this part, or DHS implementing directives promulgated by the Chief Security Officer.

§ 7.13 **Judicial proceedings.**

(a) Any DHS official or organization, except for the Office of Inspector General in matters involving the Office of Inspector General only, receiving an order or subpoena from a federal or state court, or an administrative subpoena from a federal agency, to produce classified information (see 6 CFR 5.41 through 5.49), required to submit classified information for official DHS litigation purposes, or receiving classified information from another organization for production of such in litigation, shall notify the Office of the General Counsel, unless the demand for production is made by the Office of the General Counsel, and immediately determine from the agency originating the classified information whether the information can be declassified. If declassification is not possible, DHS representatives will take appropriate action to protect such information, pursuant to the provisions of this section.

(b) If a determination is made under paragraph (a) of this section to produce classified information in a judicial proceeding in any manner, the DHS General Counsel attorney, or the Office of Inspector General attorney, if the matter involves the Office of Inspector General only, in conjunction with the Department of Justice, shall take appropriate steps to protect classified information in judicial proceedings and retrieve the information when the information is no longer required in such judicial proceedings, in accordance with the Department of Justice procedures, and in Federal criminal cases, pursuant to the requirements of Classified Information Procedures Act (CIPA), Public Law 96–456, 94 Stat. 2025,

(18 U.S.C. App.), and the "Security Procedures Established Pursuant to Public Law 96–456, 94 Stat. 2025, by the Chief Justice of the United States for the Protection of Classified Information," and other applicable authorities.

Subpart B—Classified Information

§ 7.20 **Classification and declassification authority.**

(a) Top Secret original classification authority may only be exercised by the Secretary and by officials with a demonstrable and continuing need to exercise such authority and to whom such authority is delegated in writing by the Secretary. The Chief Security Officer, as the Senior Agency Official, is delegated authority to originally classify information up to and including Top Secret. No official who is delegated Top Secret original classification authority by the Secretary may further delegate such authority.

(b) The Chief Security Officer may delegate Secret and Confidential original classification authority to other officials with a demonstrable and continuing need to exercise such authority. No official who is delegated original classification authority by the Secretary or the Chief Security Officer may further delegate such authority.

(c) Persons who are delegated original classification authority shall attend mandatory classification training within 60 days of the delegation, and annually thereafter. Persons who fail to attend mandatory training shall have such authority suspended until such time as the training occurs.

(1) Except for suspensions of the Inspector General's classification authority, the Chief Security Officer may waive a suspension of authority for no longer than 60 days following the due date of the training when unavoidable circumstances exist that prevent the person from attending the training.

(2) For cases involving suspension of the Inspector General's classification authority under paragraph (c) of this section, only the Secretary or Deputy Secretary may waive such a suspension.

(d) Officials authorized to classify information at a specified level are also authorized to classify information at a lower level. In the absence of an official authorized to exercise classification authority, the person designated to act in lieu of such official may exercise the official's classification authority.

(e) Declassification authority may be exercised by the official who authorized the original classification, if that official is still serving in the same position and has original classification authority; the originator's current successor in function, if that individual has original classification authority; a supervisory official of either the originator or his or her successor in function, if the supervisory official has original classification authority; or officials delegated declassification authority by the Secretary or the Chief Security Officer.

§ 7.21   Classification of information, limitations.

(a) Information may be originally classified only if all of the following standards are met:

(1) An original classification authority is classifying the information;

(2) The information is owned by, produced by or for, or is under the control of the United States Government;

(3) The information falls within one or more of the categories of information specified in section 1.4 of Executive Order 13526; and

(4) The original classification authority determines that the unauthorized disclosure of the information reasonably could be expected to cause identifiable and describable damage to the national security.

(b) Information shall be classified as Top Secret, Secret, or Confidential in accordance with and in compliance with the standards and criteria in Executive Order 13526. No other terms shall be used to identify United States classified information except as otherwise provided by statute.

(c) If there is significant doubt about the need to classify information it shall not be classified. If classification is warranted but there is significant doubt about the appropriate level of classification it shall be classified at the lower level.

(d) Original classification decisions made by a DHS original classification authority shall be incorporated into a security classification guide in a timely manner but no later than one year from the date of the original decision. Such decisions shall be reported to the Office of the Chief Security Officer, Administrative Security Division, within thirty days following the original classification decision.

(e) All DHS security classification guides shall be coordinated through and receive the concurrence of the Office of the Chief Security Officer, Administrative Security Division, prior to approval and publication by an original classification authority.

(f) Information shall not be classified in order to:

(1) Conceal inefficiency, violations of law, or administrative error;

(2) Prevent embarrassment to a person, organization, or agency;

(3) Restrain competition;

(4) Prevent or delay release of information that does not require protection in the interest of national security.

(g) Information may not be reclassified after it has been declassified and released to the public under proper authority unless:

(1) The reclassification is approved in writing by the Secretary based on a document-by-document determination that the reclassification of the information is required to prevent significant and demonstrable damage to the national security;

(2) The reclassification of the information meets the standards and criteria for classification pursuant to Executive Order 13526;

(3) The information may be reasonably recovered without bringing undue attention to the information; and

(4) The reclassification action is reported promptly to the Assistant to the President for National Security Affairs (National Security Advisor) and the Director of ISOO.

(5) For documents in the physical and legal custody of the National Archives and Records Administration that have previously been made available for public use and determined to warrant reclassification per paragraphs (g)(1) through (4) of this section, the Secretary shall notify the Archivist of the

United States, who shall suspend public access pending approval by the Director of ISOO. Any such decision made by the Director of ISOO may be appealed by the Secretary to the President through the National Security Advisor.

(h) Information that has not previously been disclosed to the public under proper authority may be classified or reclassified after DHS has received a request for it under the Freedom of Information Act (5 U.S.C. 552), the Presidential Records Act, 44 U.S.C. 2204(c)(1), the Privacy Act of 1974 (5 U.S.C. 552a), or the mandatory review provisions of Executive Order 13526, section 3.5. When it is necessary to classify or reclassify such information, it shall be done so on a document-by-document basis with the personal participation of and under the direction of the Secretary or Deputy Secretary.

§7.22 Classification pending review.

(a) Whenever persons who do not have original classification authority originate or develop information that they believe requires immediate classification and safeguarding, and no authorized original classifier is available, that person shall:

(1) Safeguard the information in a manner appropriate for the classification level they believe it to be;

(2) Apply the appropriate overall classification markings; and

(3) Within five working days, securely transmit the information to the organization that has appropriate subject matter interest and original classification authority.

(b) When it is not clear which component would be the appropriate original classifier, the information shall be sent to the Office of the Chief Security Officer, Administrative Security Division, to determine the appropriate organization.

(c) The applicable original classification authority shall decide within 30 days of receipt whether the information warrants classification pursuant to Executive Order 13526 and shall render such decision in writing.

§7.23 Emergency release of classified information.

(a) The DHS Undersecretary for Management has delegated to certain DHS employees the authority to disclose classified information to an individual or individuals not otherwise eligible for access in emergency situations when there is an imminent threat to life or in defense of the homeland.

(b) In exercising this authority, the delegees shall adhere to the following conditions:

(1) Limit the amount of classified information disclosed to a minimum to achieve the intended purpose;

(2) Limit the number of individuals who receive it to only those persons with a specific need-to-know;

(3) Transmit the classified information through approved communication channels by the most secure and expeditious method possible, or by other means deemed necessary in exigent circumstances;

(4) Provide instructions about what specific information is classified and how it should be safeguarded. Physical custody of classified information must remain with an authorized Federal Government entity, in all but the most extraordinary circumstances as determined by the delegated official;

(5) Provide appropriate briefings to the recipients on their responsibilities not to disclose the information and obtain from the recipients a signed DHS Emergency Release of Classified Information Non-disclosure Form. In emergency situations requiring immediate verbal release of information, the signed nondisclosure agreement memorializing the briefing may be received after the emergency abates;

(6) Within 72 hours of the disclosure of classified information, or the earliest opportunity that the emergency permits, but no later than 7 days after the release, the disclosing authority must notify the DHS Office of the Chief Security Officer, Administrative Security Division, and the originating agency of the information disclosed. A copy of the signed nondisclosure agreements should be forwarded with the notification, or as soon thereafter as practical.

(7) Release of information pursuant to this authority does not constitute declassification of the information.

(8) Authority to disclose classified information under the above conditions may not be further delegated.

§ 7.24   Duration of classification.

(a) At the time of original classification, original classification authorities shall apply a date or event in which the information will be automatically declassified.

(b) The original classification authority shall attempt to establish a specific date or event that is not more than 10 years from the date of origination in which the information will be automatically declassified. If the original classification authority cannot determine an earlier specific date or event it shall be marked for automatic declassification 10 years from the date of origination.

(c) If the original classification authority determines that the sensitivity of the information requires classification beyond 10 years, it may be marked for automatic declassification for up to 25 years from the date of the original classification decision.

(d) Original classification authorities do not have the authority to classify or retain the classification of information beyond 25 years from the date of origination. The only exceptions to this rule are information that would clearly and demonstrably be expected to reveal the identity of a confidential human source or human intelligence source, or, key design concepts of weapons of mass destruction. In these instances, the information shall be marked for declassification based on implementing directives issued pursuant to Executive Order 13526. In all other instances, classification beyond 25 years shall only be authorized in accordance with § 7.28 and Executive Order 13526.

§ 7.25   Identification and markings.

(a) Classified information, in all forms, must be marked in a manner that is immediately apparent pursuant to the standards set forth in section 1.6 of Executive Order 13526; 32 CFR part 2001, subpart B; and internal DHS guidance approved and distributed by the Office of the Chief Security Officer.

(b) Foreign government information shall retain its original classification markings or be assigned a U.S. classification that provides a degree of protection at least equivalent to that required by the entity that furnished the information.

(c) Information assigned a level of classification under predecessor Executive Orders shall remain classified at that level of classification, except as otherwise provided herein, i.e., the information is reclassified or declassified.

§ 7.26   Derivative classification.

(a) Derivative classification is defined as the incorporating, paraphrasing, restating, or generating in a new form information that is already classified, and marking the newly developed material consistent with the classification markings that apply to the source information. Information is also derivatively classified when classification is based on instructions provided in a security classification guide.

(b) Persons need not possess original classification authority to derivatively classify information based on source documents or classification guides.

(c) Persons who perform derivative classification actions shall be designated as authorized derivative classifiers as specified in directives published by the Office of the Chief Security Officer.

(d) Persons who are designated as authorized derivative classifiers shall attend mandatory classification training before performing derivative classification actions, and once every two years thereafter. Persons who fail to attend mandatory training shall have such authority suspended until such time as the training occurs.

(1) Except for suspensions of the Office of Inspector General's classification authority, the Chief Security Officer may waive the suspension of authority for no longer than 60 days following the due date of the training when unavoidable circumstances exist that prevent the person from attending the training.

(2) For cases involving suspension of the Office of Inspector General's classification authority under paragraph (d) of this section, only the Secretary or Deputy Secretary may waive such a suspension.

(e) Persons who apply derivative classification markings shall observe original classification decisions and carry forward to any newly created documents the pertinent classification markings.

(f) Information classified derivatively from other classified information shall be classified and marked in accordance with the standards set forth in sections 2.1 and 2.2 of Executive Order 13526, 32 CFR part 2001, and internal DHS guidance provided by the Office of the Chief Security Officer.

§ 7.27 Declassification and downgrading.

(a) Classified information shall be declassified as soon as it no longer meets the standards for classification. Declassification and downgrading is governed by part 3 of Executive Order 13526, implementing ISOO directives at 32 CFR part 2001, subpart C, and applicable internal DHS direction provided by the Office of the Chief Security Officer.

(b) Information shall be declassified or downgraded by the official who authorized the original classification if that official is still serving in the same position and has original classification authority, the originator's successor if that position has original classification authority, or a supervisory official of either if that position has original classification authority, or, by officials delegated such authority in writing by the Secretary or the Chief Security Officer, or, pursuant to section 3.1.(e) of Executive Order 13526, the Director of the Information Security Oversight Office.

(c) It is presumed that information that continues to meet the classification requirements under Executive Order 13526 requires continued protection. In some exceptional cases during declassification reviews, the need to protect classified information may be outweighed by the public interest in disclosure of the information, and in these cases the information should be declassified. If it appears that the public interest in disclosure of the information may outweigh the need to protect the information, the declassification reviewing official shall refer the information with a recommendation for decision to the Chief Security Offi-

cer. The Chief Security Officer shall review the information and after consulting with the applicable original classification authority and other components and agencies with equities, make a recommendation to the Secretary on whether the public interest in disclosure outweighs the damage to national security that might reasonably be expected from disclosure. The Secretary shall decide whether to declassify the information. The decision of the Secretary shall be final. This provision does not amplify or modify the substantive criteria or procedures for classification or create any substantive or procedural rights subject to judicial review.

(d) Each component shall develop schedules for declassification of records in the National Archives.

§ 7.28 Automatic declassification.

(a) Subject to paragraph (b) of this section and paragraphs 3.3(b)–(d) and (g)–(j) of Executive Order 13526, all classified information contained in records that are more than 25 years old that have been determined to have permanent historical value shall be declassified automatically on December 31st of the year that is 25 years from the date of origin.

(b) At least one year before information is declassified automatically under this section, the Chief Security Officer shall notify the ISOO of any specific information that DHS proposes to exempt from automatic declassification. The notification shall include:

(1) A description of the information;

(2) An explanation of why the information is exempt from automatic declassification and must remain classified for a longer period of time; and

(3) A specific date or event for declassification of the information whenever the information exempted does not identify a confidential human source or human intelligence source, or, key design concepts of weapons of mass destruction.

(c) Proposed exemptions under this section shall be forwarded to the Chief Security Officer. When the Chief Security Officer determines the exemption request is consistent with this section, he or she will submit the exemption request to the Executive Secretary of the

Interagency Security Classification Appeals Panel (ISCAP) for approval.

(d) Declassification guides that narrowly and precisely define exempted information may be used to exempt information from automatic declassification. Declassification guides must include the exemption notification information detailed in paragraph (b) of this section, and be approved pursuant to paragraph (c) of this section. The creation of declassification guides to cite proposed or ISCAP-approved DHS exemptions shall be coordinated through and processed by the Office of the Chief Security Officer, Administrative Security Division.

§ 7.29 National Declassification Center.

(a) The Chief Security Officer and applicable components will support the NARA, National Declassification Center (NDC), which was established to streamline declassification processes, facilitate quality-assurance measures, and implement standardized training regarding the declassification of records determined to have permanent historical value. The Chief Security Officer will assign DHS personnel on an as-needed basis to address declassification matters and priorities containing DHS equities.

(b) The Office of the Chief Security Officer shall provide the NDC with all DHS classification and declassification guides that include ISCAP-approved exemptions from automatic declassification.

(c) The Chief Security Officer, or his designee, shall oversee DHS-wide support to the NDC, including representing DHS in consultations with the NDC Director.

§ 7.30 Documents of permanent historical value.

The original classification authority, to the greatest extent possible, shall declassify classified information contained in records determined to have permanent historical value under 44 U.S.C. 2107 before they are accessioned into the National Archives.

§ 7.31 Classification challenges.

(a) Authorized holders of information classified by DHS or any other agency who, in good faith, believe that specific information is improperly or unnecessarily classified are encouraged and expected to challenge the classification status of that information pursuant to section 1.8 of Executive Order 13526. Authorized holders may submit classification challenges in writing to the original classification authority with jurisdiction over the information in question. If an original classification authority cannot be determined, the challenge shall be submitted to the Office of the Chief Security Officer, Administrative Security Division. The challenge need not be more specific than a question as to why the information is or is not classified, or is classified at a certain level.

(b) If anonymity of the challenger is requested, the challenger may submit the challenge to the Office of the Chief Security Officer, Administrative Security Division. The Administrative Security Division will act as an agent for the challenger and the identity of the challenger will be redacted.

(c) The original classification authority shall no later than 60 days from receipt of the challenge, provide a written response to the submitter. The original classification authority may classify or declassify the information subject to the challenge and, if applicable, state specific reasons why the original classification determination was proper. If the original classification authority is not able to respond within 60 days, he or she shall inform the individual who filed the challenge in writing of that fact, and the anticipated determination date.

(d) The individual challenging the classification will be notified of the determination made by the original classification authority and that the individual may appeal this determination to the Chief Security Officer, or in cases involving appeals by Office of Inspector General employees, the Secretary or Deputy Secretary. Upon receipt of such appeals, the Chief Security Officer, or in cases involving appeals by Office of Inspector General employees, the Secretary or Deputy Secretary, shall convene a DHS Classification Appeals Panel (DHS/CAP). The DHS/CAP shall, at a minimum, consist of representatives from the Office of the Chief Security Officer, the Office of

General Counsel, and a representative from the component having jurisdiction over the information. Additional members may be added as determined by the Chief Security Officer. The DHS/CAP shall be chaired by the Chief Security Officer.

(e) If the requester files an appeal through the DHS/CAP, and the appeal is denied, the requester shall be notified of the right to appeal the denial to the Interagency Security Classification Appeals Panel (ISCAP) pursuant to section 5.3 of Executive Order 13526, and the rules issued by the ISCAP pursuant to section 5.3 of Executive Order 13526.

(f) Any individual who challenges a classification and believes that any action has been taken against him or her in retaliation or retribution because of that challenge may report the facts to the Office of Inspector General via its Hotline or Web site, or other appropriate office.

(g) Nothing in this section shall prohibit a person from informally challenging the classified status of information directly to the original classification authority.

(h) Classification challenge provisions are not applicable to documents required to be submitted for prepublication review or other administrative process pursuant to an approved non-disclosure agreement.

(i) Requests for review of classified material for declassification by persons other than authorized holders are governed by §7.32.

§7.32 Mandatory declassification review.

(a) Any individual, as "individual" is defined by 5 U.S.C. 552a(a)(2) (with the exception of a foreign government entity or any representative thereof), may request that classified information be reviewed for declassification pursuant to the mandatory declassification review provisions of section 3.5 of Executive Order 13526. Such requests must be sent to the Departmental Disclosure Officer, Privacy Office, 245 Murray Lane SW., Building 410, Washington, DC 20528.

(b) The request must describe the document or material with enough specificity to allow it to be located by the component with a reasonable amount of effort. Components will generally consider deficient any requests for declassification review of, for instance, broad categories of information, entire file series of records, or similar non-specific requests.

(1) When the description of the information in the request is deficient, the component shall solicit as much additional identifying information as possible from the requester.

(2) If the information or material requested cannot be obtained with a reasonable amount of effort, the component shall provide the requester, through the DHS Disclosure Officer, with written notification of the reasons why no action will be taken and of the requester's right to appeal.

(c) Requests for review of information that has been subjected to a declassification review request within the preceding two years shall not be processed. The DHS Disclosure Officer will notify the requester of such denial.

(d) Mandatory Declassification Review provisions are not applicable to documents required to be submitted for prepublication review or other administrative process pursuant to an approved non-disclosure agreement.

(e) Requests for information exempted from search or review under sections 701, 702, or 703 of the National Security Act of 1947, as added and amended (50 U.S.C. 431–433), or other provisions of law, shall not be processed. The DHS Disclosure Officer will notify the requester of such denial.

(f) If documents or material being reviewed for declassification under this section contain information that has been originally classified by another government agency, the reviewing authority shall notify the DHS Disclosure Officer. Unless the association of that organization with the requested information is itself classified, the DHS Disclosure Officer will then notify the requester of the referral.

(g) A DHS component may refuse to confirm or deny the existence, or non-existence, of requested information when its existence or non-existence, is properly classified.

(h) DHS components shall make a final determination on the request as soon as practicable but within one year from receipt. When information cannot be declassified in its entirety, components shall make reasonable efforts to redact those portions that still meet the standards for classification and release those declassified portions of the requested information that constitute a coherent segment.

(i) DHS components shall notify the DHS Disclosure Officer of the determination made in the processing of a mandatory review request. Such notification shall include the number of pages declassified in full; the number of pages declassified in part; and the number of pages where declassification was denied.

(j) The DHS Disclosure Officer shall maintain a record of all mandatory review actions for reporting in accordance with applicable Federal requirements.

(k) The mandatory declassification review system shall provide for administrative appeal in cases where the review results in the information remaining classified. The requester shall be notified of the results of the review and of the right to appeal the denial of declassification. To address such appeals, the DHS Disclosure Office shall convene a DHS Classification Appeals Panel (DHS/CAP). The DHS/CAP shall, at a minimum, consist of representatives from the Disclosure Office, the Office of the Chief Security Officer, the Office of General Counsel, and a representative from the component having jurisdiction over the information. Additional members may be added as determined by the DHS Disclosure Officer. The DHS/CAP shall be chaired by the DHS Disclosure Officer.

(l) If the requester files an appeal through the DHS/CAP, and the appeal is denied, the requester shall be notified of the right to appeal the denial to the ISCAP pursuant to section 5.3 of Executive Order 13526, and the rules issued by the ISCAP pursuant to section 5.3 of Executive Order 13526.

PART 9—RESTRICTIONS UPON LOBBYING

Subpart A—General

Sec.
9.1 Conditions on use of funds.
9.2 Definitions.
9.3 Certification and disclosure.

Subpart B—Activities by Own Employees

9.11 Agency and legislative liaison.
9.15 Professional and technical services.
9.20 Reporting.

Subpart C—Activities by Other than Own Employees

9.23 Professional and technical services.

Subpart D—Penalties and Enforcement

9.31 Penalties.
9.32 Penalty procedures.
9.33 Enforcement.

Subpart E—Exemptions

9.41 Secretary of Defense.

Subpart F—Agency Reports

9.51 Semi-annual compilation.
9.52 Inspector General report.
APPENDIX A TO PART 9—CERTIFICATION REGARDING LOBBYING
APPENDIX B TO PART 9—DISCLOSURE FORM TO REPORT LOBBYING

AUTHORITY: Sec. 319, Pub. L. 101–121, 103 Stat. 750 (31 U.S.C. 1352); Pub. L. 107–296, 116 Stat. 2135 (6 U.S.C. 1 et seq.); 5 U.S.C. 301.

SOURCE: 68 FR 10912, Mar. 6, 2003, unless otherwise noted.

Subpart A—General

§ 9.1 Conditions on use of funds.

(a) No appropriated funds may be expended by the recipient of a Federal contract, grant, loan, or cooperative agreement to pay any person for influencing or attempting to influence an officer or employee of any agency, a Member of Congress, an officer or employee of Congress, or an employee of a Member of Congress in connection with any of the following covered Federal actions: the awarding of any Federal contract, the making of any Federal grant, the making of any Federal loan, the entering into of any cooperative agreement, and the extension, continuation, renewal, amendment, or modification of any Federal contract, grant, loan, or cooperative agreement.

(b) Each person who requests or receives from an agency a Federal contract, grant, loan, or cooperative agreement shall file with that agency a certification, set forth in appendix A to this part, that the person has not made, and will not make, any payment prohibited by paragraph (a) of this section.

(c) Each person who requests or receives from an agency a Federal contract, grant, loan, or a cooperative agreement shall file with that agency a disclosure form, set forth in appendix B to this part, if such person has made or has agreed to make any payment using non appropriated funds (to include profits from any covered Federal action), which would be prohibited under paragraph (a) of this section if paid for with appropriated funds.

(d) Each person who requests or receives from an agency a commitment providing for the United States to insure or guarantee a loan shall file with that agency a statement, set forth in appendix A to this part, whether that person has made or has agreed to make any payment to influence or attempt to influence an officer or employee of any agency, a Member of Congress, an officer or employee of Congress, or an employee of a Member of Congress in connection with that loan insurance or guarantee.

(e) Each person who requests or receives from an agency a commitment providing for the United States to insure or guarantee a loan shall file with that agency a disclosure form, set forth in appendix B to this part, if that person has made or has agreed to make any payment to influence or attempt to influence an officer or employee of any agency, a Member of Congress, an officer or employee of Congress, or an employee of a Member of Congress in connection with that loan insurance or guarantee.

§9.2 Definitions.

For purposes of this part:

(a) *Agency* has the same meaning as provided in 5 U.S.C. 552(f), and includes Federal executive departments and agencies as well as independent regulatory commissions and Government corporations, as defined in 31 U.S.C. 9101(1).

(b) The term *covered Federal action*:

(1) Means any of the following Federal actions:

(i) The awarding of any Federal contract;

(ii) The making of any Federal grant;

(iii) The making of any Federal loan;

(iv) The entering into of any cooperative agreement; and

(v) The extension, continuation, renewal, amendment, or modification of any Federal contract, grant, loan, or cooperative agreement.

(2) Does not include receiving from an agency a commitment providing for the United States to insure or guarantee a loan. Loan guarantees and loan insurance are addressed independently within this part.

(c) *Federal contract* means an acquisition contract awarded by an agency, including those subject to the Federal Acquisition Regulation (FAR) (48 CFR Chapter 1) and any other acquisition contract for real or personal property or services not subject to the FAR.

(d) *Federal cooperative agreement* means a cooperative agreement entered into by an agency.

(e) *Federal grant* means an award of financial assistance in the form of money, or property in lieu of money, by the Federal Government or a direct appropriation made by law to any person. The term does not include technical assistance that provides services instead of money, or other assistance in the form of revenue sharing, loans, loan guarantees, loan insurance, interest subsidies, insurance, or direct United States cash assistance to an individual.

(f) *Federal loan* means a loan made by an agency. The term does not include loan guarantee or loan insurance.

(g) *Indian tribe* and *tribal organization* have the meaning provided in section 4 of the Indian Self-Determination and Education Assistance Act (25 U.S.C. 450B). Alaskan Natives are included under the definition of Indian tribe in that Act.

(h) *Influencing or attempting to influence* means making, with the intent to influence, any communication to or appearance before an officer or employee or any agency, a Member of Congress, an officer or employee of Congress, or an employee of a Member of Congress in connection with any covered Federal action.

(i) *Loan guarantee* or loan insurance means an agency's guarantee or insurance of a loan made by a person.

129

(j) *Local government* means a unit of government in a State and, if chartered, established, or otherwise recognized by a State for the performance of a governmental duty, including a local public authority, a special district, an intrastate district, a council of governments, a sponsor group representative organization, and any other instrumentality of a local government.

(k) *Officer or employee of an agency* includes the following individuals who are employed by an agency:

(1) An individual appointed to a position in the Government pursuant to title 5 of the United States Code, including any position by temporary appointment or any appointment as an acting official as outlined in section 1511(c) of the Homeland Security Act;

(2) A member of the uniformed services as defined in 37 U.S.C. 101(3);

(3) A special Government employee as defined in section 18 U.S.C. 202; and

(4) An individual who is a member of a Federal advisory committee, as defined by the Federal Advisory Committee Act at 5 U.S.C. App. 2.

(l) *Person* means an individual, corporation, company, association, authority, firm, partnership, society, State, and local government, regardless of whether such entity is operated for profit or not for profit. This term excludes an Indian tribe, tribal organization, or any other Indian organization with respect to expenditures specifically permitted by other Federal law.

(m) *Reasonable compensation* means, with respect to a regularly employed officer or employee of any person, compensation that is consistent with the normal compensation for such officer or employee for work that is not furnished to, not funded by, or not furnished in cooperation with the Federal Government.

(n) *Reasonable payment* means, with respect to professional and other technical services, a payment in an amount that is consistent with the amount normally paid for such services in the private sector.

(o) *Recipient* includes all contractors, subcontractors at any tier, and sub grantees at any tier of the recipient of funds received in connection with a Federal contract, grant, loan, or coop-

erative agreement. The term excludes an Indian tribe, tribal organization, or any other Indian organization with respect to expenditures specifically permitted by other Federal law.

(p) *Regularly employed* means, with respect to an officer or employee of a person requesting or receiving a Federal contract, grant, loan, or cooperative agreement or a commitment providing for the United States to insure or guarantee a loan, an officer or employee who is employed by such person for at least 130 working days within one year immediately preceding the date of the submission that initiates agency consideration of such person for receipt of such contract, grant, loan, cooperative agreement, loan insurance commitment, or loan guarantee commitment. An officer or employee who is employed by such person for less than 130 working days within one year immediately preceding the date of the submission that initiates agency consideration of such person shall be considered to be regularly employed as soon as he or she is employed by such person for 130 working days.

(q) *State* means a State of the United States, the District of Columbia, the Commonwealth of Puerto Rico, a territory or possession of the United States, an agency or instrumentality of a State, and a multi-State, regional, or interstate entity having governmental duties and powers.

§ 9.3   Certification and disclosure.

(a) Each person shall file a certification, and a disclosure form, if required, with each submission that initiates agency consideration of such person for:

(1) Award of a Federal contract, grant, or cooperative agreement exceeding $100,000; or

(2) An award of a Federal loan or a commitment providing for the United States to insure or guarantee a loan exceeding $150,000.

(b)(1) Each person shall file a certification, and a disclosure form, if required, upon receipt by such person of:

(i) A Federal contract, grant, or cooperative agreement exceeding $100,000; or

(ii) A Federal loan or a commitment providing for the United States to insure or guarantee a loan exceeding $150,000.

(2) A filing described in paragraph (b)(1) of this section shall not be required if such person previously filed a certification, and a disclosure form required under paragraph (a) of this section.

(c) Each person shall file a disclosure form at the end of each calendar quarter in which there occurs any event that requires disclosure or that materially affects the accuracy of the information contained in any disclosure form previously filed by such person under paragraph (a) or (b) of this section. An event that materially affects the accuracy of the information reported includes:

(1) A cumulative increase of $25,000 or more in the amount paid or expected to be paid for influencing or attempting to influence a covered Federal action;

(2) A change in the person(s) or individual(s) influencing or attempting to influence a covered Federal action; or

(3) A change in the officer(s), employee(s), or Member(s) contacted to influence or attempt to influence a covered Federal action.

(d)(1) The requirements of paragraph (d)(2) of this section apply to any person who requests or receives from a person referred to in paragraph (a) or (b) of this section:

(i) A subcontract exceeding $100,000 at any tier under a Federal contract;

(ii) A subgrant, contract, or subcontract exceeding $100,000 at any tier under a Federal grant;

(iii) A contract or subcontract exceeding $100,000 at any tier under a Federal loan exceeding $150,000; or

(iv) A contract or subcontract exceeding $100,000 at any tier under a Federal cooperative agreement.

(2) A person described in paragraph (d)(1) of this section shall file a certification, and a disclosure form, if required, to the next tier.

(e) All disclosure forms, but not certifications, shall be forwarded from tier to tier until received by the person referred to in paragraph (a) or (b) of this section. That person shall forward all disclosure forms to the agency.

(f) Any certification or disclosure form filed under paragraph (e) of this section shall be treated as a material representation of fact upon which all receiving tiers shall rely. All liability arising from an erroneous representation shall be borne solely by the tier filing that representation and shall not be shared by any tier to which the erroneous representation is forwarded. Submitting an erroneous certification or disclosure constitutes a failure to file the required certification or disclosure, respectively. If a person fails to file a required certification or disclosure, the United States may pursue all available remedies, including those authorized by section 31 U.S.C. 1352.

(g) No reporting is required for an activity paid for with appropriated funds if that activity is allowable under either subpart B or C of this part.

Subpart B—Activities by Own Employees

§ 9.11 Agency and legislative liaison.

(a) The prohibition on the use of appropriated funds, in §9.1(a), does not apply in the case of a payment of reasonable compensation made to an officer or employee of a person requesting or receiving a Federal contract, grant, loan, or cooperative agreement if the payment is for agency and legislative liaison activities not directly related to a covered Federal action.

(b) For purposes of paragraph (a) of this section, providing any information specifically requested by an agency or Congress is allowable at any time.

(c) For purposes of paragraph (a) of this section, the following agency and legislative liaison activities are allowable at any time only where they are not related to a specific solicitation for any covered Federal action:

(1) Discussing with an agency (including individual demonstrations) the qualities and characteristics of the person's products or services, conditions or terms of sale, and service capabilities; and

(2) Technical discussions and other activities regarding the application or adaptation of the person's products or services for an agency's use.

(d) For purposes of paragraph (a) of this section, the following agencies and

legislative liaison activities are allowable only where they are prior to formal solicitation of any covered Federal action:

(1) Providing any information not specifically requested but necessary for an agency to make an informed decision about initiation of a covered Federal action;

(2) Technical discussions regarding the preparation of an unsolicited proposal prior to its official submission; and

(3) Capability presentations by persons seeking awards from an agency pursuant to the provisions of the Small Business Act, as amended.

(e) Only those activities expressly authorized by this section are allowable under this section.

§ 9.15 Professional and technical services.

(a) The prohibition on the use of appropriated funds, in § 9.1(a), does not apply in the case of a payment of reasonable compensation made to an officer or employee of a person requesting or receiving a Federal contract, grant, loan, or cooperative agreement or an extension, continuation, renewal, amendment, or modification of a Federal contract, grant, loan, or cooperative agreement if payment is for professional or technical services rendered directly in the preparation, submission, or negotiation of any bid, proposal, or application for that Federal contract, grant, loan, or cooperative agreement or for meeting requirements imposed by or pursuant to law as a condition for receiving that Federal contract, grant, loan, or cooperative agreement.

(b) For purposes of paragraph (a) of this section, *professional and technical services* shall be limited to advice and analysis directly applying any professional or technical discipline. For example, drafting of a legal document accompanying a bid or proposal by a lawyer is allowable. Similarly, technical advice provided by an engineer on the performance or operational capability of a piece of equipment rendered directly in the negotiation of a contract is allowable. However, communications with the intent to influence made by a professional (such as a licensed lawyer) or a technical person (such as a licensed accountant) are not allowable under this section unless they provide advice and analysis directly applying their professional or technical expertise and unless the advice or analysis is rendered directly and solely in the preparation, submission or negotiation of a covered Federal action. Thus, for example, communications with the intent to influence made by a lawyer that do not provide legal advice or analysis directly and solely related to the legal aspects of his or her client's proposal, but generally advocate one proposal over another are not allowable under this section because the lawyer is not providing professional legal services. Similarly, communications with the intent to influence made by an engineer providing an engineering analysis prior to the preparation or submission of a bid or proposal are not allowable under this section since the engineer is providing technical services but not directly in the preparation, submission or negotiation of a covered Federal action.

(c) Requirements imposed by or pursuant to law as a condition for receiving a covered Federal award include those required by law or regulation, or reasonably expected to be required by law or regulation, and any other requirements in the actual award documents.

(d) Only those services expressly authorized by this section are allowable under this section.

§ 9.20 Reporting.

No reporting is required with respect to payments of reasonable compensation made to regularly employed officers or employees of a person.

Subpart C—Activities by Other than Own Employees

§ 9.23 Professional and technical services.

(a) The prohibition on the use of appropriated funds, in § 9.1(a), does not apply in the case of any reasonable payment to a person, other than an officer or employee of a person requesting or receiving a covered Federal action, if the payment is for professional or technical services rendered directly in the preparation, submission, or negotiation of any bid, proposal, or application for that Federal contract, grant, loan, or cooperative agreement or for meeting requirements imposed by or pursuant to law as a condition for receiving that Federal contract, grant, loan, or cooperative agreement.

(b) The reporting requirements in §9.3(a) and (b) regarding filing a disclosure form by each person, if required, shall not apply with respect to professional or technical services rendered directly in the preparation, submission, or negotiation of any commitment providing for the United States to insure or guarantee a loan.

(c) For purposes of paragraph (a) of this section, *professional and technical services* shall be limited to advice and analysis directly applying any professional or technical discipline. For example, drafting of a legal document accompanying a bid or proposal by a lawyer is allowable. Similarly, technical advice provided by an engineer on the performance or operational capability of a piece of equipment rendered directly in the negotiation of a contract is allowable. However, communications with the intent to influence made by a professional (such as a licensed lawyer) or a technical person (such as a licensed accountant) are not allowable under this section unless they provide advice and analysis directly applying their professional or technical expertise and unless the advice or analysis is rendered directly and solely in the preparation, submission or negotiation of a covered Federal action. Thus, for example, communications with the intent to influence made by a lawyer that do not provide legal advice or analysis directly and solely related to the legal aspects of his or her client's proposal, but generally advocate one proposal over another are not allowable under this section because the lawyer is not providing professional legal services. Similarly, communications with the intent to influence made by an engineer providing an engineering analysis prior to the preparation or submission of a bid or proposal are not allowable under this section since the engineer is providing technical services but not directly in the preparation,

submission or negotiation of a covered Federal action.

(d) Requirements imposed by or pursuant to law as a condition for receiving a covered Federal action include those required by law or regulation, or reasonably expected to be required by law or regulation, and any other requirements in the actual award documents.

(e) Persons other than officers or employees of a person requesting or receiving a covered Federal action include consultants and trade associations.

(f) Only those services expressly authorized by this section are allowable under this section.

Subpart D—Penalties and Enforcement

§ 9.31 Penalties.

(a) Any person who makes an expenditure prohibited herein shall be subject to a civil penalty of not less than $10,000 and not more than $100,000 for each such expenditure.

(b) Any person who fails to file or amend the disclosure form (see appendix B to this part) to be filed or amended if required herein, shall be subject to a civil penalty of not less than $10,000 and not more than $100,000 for each such failure.

(c) A filing or amended filing on or after the date on which an administrative action for the imposition of a civil penalty is commenced does not prevent the imposition of such civil penalty for a failure occurring before that date. An administrative action is commenced with respect to a failure when an investigating official determines in writing to commence an investigation of an allegation of such failure.

(d) In determining whether to impose a civil penalty, and the amount of any such penalty, by reason of a violation by any person, the agency shall consider the nature, circumstances, extent, and gravity of the violation, the effect on the ability of such person to continue in business, any prior violations by such person, the degree of culpability of such person, the ability of the person to pay the penalty, and such other matters as may be appropriate.

(e) First offenders under paragraphs (a) or (b) of this section shall be subject to a civil penalty of $10,000, absent aggravating circumstances. Second and subsequent offenses by persons shall be subject to an appropriate civil penalty between $10,000 and $100,000, as determined by the agency head or his or her designee.

(f) An imposition of a civil penalty under this section does not prevent the United States from seeking any other remedy that may apply to the same conduct that is the basis for the imposition of such civil penalty.

§ 9.32 Penalty procedures.

Agencies shall impose and collect civil penalties pursuant to the provisions of the Program Fraud and Civil Remedies Act, 31 U.S.C. 3803 (except subsection (c)), 3804, 3805, 3806, 3807, 3808, and 3812, insofar as these provisions are not inconsistent with the requirements in this part.

§ 9.33 Enforcement.

The head of each agency shall take such actions as are necessary to ensure that the provisions herein are vigorously implemented and enforced in that agency.

Subpart E—Exemptions

§ 9.41 Secretary of Defense.

(a) The Secretary of Defense may exempt, on a case-by-case basis, a covered Federal action from the prohibition whenever the Secretary determines, in writing, that such an exemption is in the national interest. The Secretary shall transmit a copy of each such written exemption to Congress immediately after making such a determination.

(b) The Department of Defense may issue supplemental regulations to implement paragraph (a) of this section.

Subpart F—Agency Reports

§ 9.51 Semi-annual compilation.

(a) The head of each agency shall collect and compile the disclosure reports (see appendix B to this part) and, on May 31 and November 30 of each year, submit to the Secretary of the Senate and the Clerk of the House of Representatives a report containing a compilation of the information contained in the disclosure reports received during the six-month period ending on March 31 or September 30, respectively, of that year.

(b) The report, including the compilation, shall be available for public inspection 30 days after receipt of the report by the Secretary and the Clerk.

(c) Information that involves intelligence matters shall be reported only to the Select Committee on Intelligence of the Senate, the Permanent Select Committee on Intelligence of the House of Representatives, and the Committees on Appropriations of the Senate and the House of Representatives in accordance with procedures agreed to by such committees. Such information shall not be available for public inspection.

(d) Information that is classified under Executive Order 12356 or any successor order shall be reported only to the Committee on Foreign Relations of the Senate and the Committee on Foreign Affairs of the House of Representatives or the Committees on Armed Services of the Senate and the House of Representatives (whichever such committees have jurisdiction of matters involving such information) and to the Committees on Appropriations of the Senate and the House of Representatives in accordance with procedures agreed to by such committees. Such information shall not be available for public inspection.

(e) Agencies shall keep the originals of all disclosure reports in the official files of the agency.

§ 9.52 Inspector General report.

(a) The Inspector General, or other official as specified in paragraph (b) of this section, of each agency shall prepare and submit to Congress each year an evaluation of the compliance of that agency with, and the effectiveness of, the requirements in this part. The evaluation may include any recommended changes that may be necessary to strengthen or improve the requirements.

(b) In the case of an agency that does not have an Inspector General, the agency official comparable to an Inspector General shall prepare and submit the annual report, or, if there is no such comparable official, the head of the agency shall prepare and submit the annual report.

(c) The annual report shall be submitted at the same time the agency submits its annual budget justifications to Congress.

(d) The annual report shall include the following: All alleged violations relating to the agency's covered Federal actions during the year covered by the report, the actions taken by the head of the agency in the year covered by the report with respect to those alleged violations and alleged violations in previous years, and the amounts of civil penalties imposed by the agency in the year covered by the report.

APPENDIX A TO PART 9—CERTIFICATION REGARDING LOBBYING

Certification for Contracts, Grants, Loans, and Cooperative Agreements

I. The undersigned certifies, to the best of his or her knowledge and belief, that:

(1) No Federal appropriated funds have been paid or will be paid, by or on behalf of the undersigned, to any person for influencing or attempting to influence an officer or employee of an agency, a Member of Congress, an officer or employee of Congress, or an employee of a Member of Congress in connection with the awarding of any Federal contract, the making of any Federal grant, the making of any Federal loan, the entering into of any cooperative agreement, and the extension, continuation, renewal, amendment, or modification of any Federal contract, grant, loan, or cooperative agreement.

(2) If any funds other than Federal appropriated funds have been paid or will be paid

to any person for influencing or attempting to influence an officer or employee of any agency, a Member of Congress, an officer or employee of Congress, or an employee of a Member of Congress in connection with this Federal contract, grant, loan, or cooperative agreement, the undersigned shall complete and submit Standard Form—LLL, "Disclosure Form to Report Lobbying," in accordance with its instructions.

(3) The undersigned shall require that the language of this certification be included in the award documents for all sub awards at all tiers (including subcontracts, subgrants, and contracts under grants, loans, and cooperative agreements) and that all subrecipients shall certify and disclose accordingly.

This certification is a material representation of fact upon which reliance was placed when this transaction was made or entered into.

Submission of this certification is a prerequisite for making or entering into this transaction imposed by section 31 U.S.C. 1352. Any person who fails to file the required certification shall be subject to a civil penalty of not less than $10,000 and not more than $100,000 for each such failure.

II. Statement for Loan Guarantees and Loan Insurance:

The undersigned states, to the best of his or her knowledge and belief, that:

If any funds have been paid or will be paid to any person for influencing or attempting to influence an officer or employee of any agency, a Member of Congress, an officer or employee of Congress, or an employee of a Member of Congress in connection with this commitment providing for the United States to insure or guarantee a loan, the undersigned shall complete and submit Standard Form-LLL, "Disclosure Form to Report Lobbying," in accordance with its instructions.

Submission of this statement is a prerequisite for making or entering into this transaction imposed by 31 U.S.C. 1352. Any person who fails to file the required statement shall be subject to a civil penalty of not less than $10,000 and not more than $100,000 for each such failure.

APPENDIX B TO PART 9—DISCLOSURE FORM TO REPORT LOBBYING

DISCLOSURE OF LOBBYING ACTIVITIES   Approved by OMB
                                                                      0348-0046

Complete this form to disclose lobbying activities pursuant to 31 U.S.C. 1352
(See reverse for public burden disclosure.)

| 1. Type of Federal Action:
   a. contract
   b. grant
   c. cooperative
     agreement
  d. loan
      e. loan guarantee
      f. loan insurance | 2. Status of Federal Action:
   a. bid/offer/application
   b. Initial award
   c. post-award | 3. Report Type:
   a. initial filing
   b. material change
   For Material Change
   Only:
year _____ quarter
_____
date of last
report_____ |

| 4. Name and Address of Reporting Entity:

☐ Prime   ☐ Subawardee
                Tier_____, if known:

Congressional District, if known: | 5. If Reporting Entity in No. 4 is Subawardee,
Enter Name   and Address of Prime

Congressional District, if known: |

| 6. Federal Department/Agency: | 7. Federal Program Name/Description

CFDA Number, if applicable: _____ |

| 8. Federal Action Number, if known: | 9. Award Amount, if known:
$ |

| 10. a. Name and Address of Lobbying Entity
     (if individual, last name, first name,
MI):

                   (attach
Continuation Sheet(s) | b. Individual Performing Services (including
address if   different from No. 10a)
   (last name, first name, MI)

SF-LLL-A, if necessary) |

| 11. Amount of Payment (check all that apply):

$_____ ☐ actual ☐ planned

12. Form of Payment (check all that apply):

☐ a. cash
☐ b. in-kind; specify: nature _____
                   value | 13. Type of Payment (check all that apply):

☐ a. retainer
☐ b. one-time fee
☐ c. commission
☐ d. contingent fee
☐ e. deferred
☐ f. other; specify: |

| 14. Brief Description of Services Performed or to be Performed and Date(s) of Service,
including officer(s),   employee(s), or Member(s) contacted, for payment
indicated in Item 11:

(attach Continuation Sheet(s) SF-LLL-A, if necessary) |

| 15. Continuation Sheet(s) SF-LLL-A   Yes   No
attached: |

| 16.
   Information requested through this form is
authorized by title 31 U.S.C. section 1352. This
disclosure of lobbying activities is a material
representation of fact upon which reliance was
placed by the tier above when this transaction was
made or entered into. This disclosure is required
pursuant to 31 U.S.C. 1352. This information will
be reported to the Congress semi-annually and will
be available for public inspection. Any person who
fails to file the required disclosure shall be
subject to a civil penalty of not less than $10,000
and not more than $100,000 for each failure. | Signature:_____

Print
Name:_____

Title:_____

Telephone
No.:_____Date:_____ |

| Federal Use Only | Authorized for Local Reproduction
Standard Form--LLL |

DISCLOSURE OF LOBBYING ACTIVITIES
CONTINUATION SHEET

Approved by OMB
0348-0046

Reporting Entity:_____ Page _____ of _____

Authorized for Local Reproduction
Standard Form--LLL-A

INSTRUCTIONS FOR COMPLETION OF SF-LLL, DISCLOSURE OF LOBBYING ACTIVITIES

This disclosure form shall be completed by the reporting entity, whether subawardee of prime Federal recipient, at the initiation or receipt of a covered Federal action, or a material change to a previous filing, pursuant to title 31 U.S.C. section 1352. The filing of a form is required for each payment or agreement to make payment to any lobbying entity for influencing or attempting to influence an officer or employee of any agency, a Member of Congress, an officer or employee of Congress, or an employee of a Member of Congress in connection with a covered Federal action. Use the SF-LLL-A Continuation Sheet for additional information if the space on the form is inadequate. Complete all items that apply for both the initial filing and material change report. Refer to the implementing guidance published by the Office of Management and Budget for additional information.

1. Identify the type of covered Federal action for which lobbying activity is and/or has been secured to influence the outcome of a covered Federal action.

2. Identify the status of the covered Federal action.

3. Identify the appropriate classification of this report. If this is a follow-up report caused by a material change to the information previously reported, enter the year and quarter in which the change occurred. Enter the date of the last previously submitted report by this reporting entity for this covered Federal action.

4. Enter the full name, address, city, state and zip code of the reporting entity. Include Congressional District, if known. Check the appropriate classification of the reporting entity that designates if it is, or expects to be, a prime or subaward recipient. Identify the tier of the subawardee, e.g., the first subawardee of the prime is the 1st tier. Subawards include but are not limited to subcontracts, subgrants and contract awards under grants.

5. If the organization filing the report in item 4 checks "Subawardee," then enter the full name, address, city, state and zip code of the prime Federal recipient. Include Congressional District, if known.

6. Enter the name of the Federal agency making the award or loan commitment. Include at least one organizational level below agency name, if known. For example, Department of Transportation, United States Coast Guard.

7. Enter the Federal program name or description for the covered Federal action (item 1). If known, enter the full Catalog of Federal Domestic Assistance (CFDA) number for grants, cooperative agreements, loans, and loan commitments.

8. Enter the most appropriate Federal identifying number available for the Federal action identified in item 1 (e.g., Request for Proposal (RFP) number, Invitation for Bid (IFB) number, grant announcement number, the contract, grant, or loan award number, the application/proposal control number assigned by the Federal agency). Include prefixes, e.g., "RFP-DE-90-001."

9. For a covered Federal action where there has been an award or loan commitment by the Federal agency, enter the Federal amount of the award/loan commitment for the prime entity identified in item 4 or 5.

10. (a) Enter the full name, address, city, state and zip code of the lobbying entity engaged by the reporting entity identified in item 4 to influence the covered Federal action.

    (b) Enter the full names of the individual(s) performing services, and include full address if different from 10(a); Enter Last Name, First Name, and Middle Name (MI).

11. Enter the amount of compensation paid or reasonably expected to be paid by the reporting entity (item 4) to the lobbying entity (item 10). Indicate whether the payment has been made (actual) or will be made (planned). Check all boxes that apply. If this is a material change report, enter the cumulative amount of payment made or planned to be made.

12. Check the appropriate box(es). Check all boxes that apply. If payment is made through an in-kind contribution, specify the nature and value of the in-kind payment.

13. Check the appropriate box(es). Check all boxes that apply. If other, specify nature.

14. Provide a specific and detailed description of the services that the lobbyist has performed, or will be expected to perform, and the date(s) of any services rendered. Include all preparatory and related activity, not just time spent in actual contact with Federal officials. Identify the Federal official(s) or employee(s) contacted or the officer(s), employee(s), or Member(s) of Congress that were contacted.

15. Check whether or not a SF-LLL-A Continuation Sheet(s) is attached.

16. The certifying official shall sign and date the form, print his/her name, title and telephone number.

Public reporting burden for this collection of information is estimated to average 30 minutes per response, including time for reviewing instructions, searching existing data sources, gathering and maintaining the data needed, and completing and reviewing the collection of information. Send comments regarding the burden estimate or any other aspect of this collection of information, including suggestions for reducing this burden, to the Office of Management and Budget, Paperwork Reduction Project (0348-0046), Washington, D.C. 20503.

PART 11—CLAIMS

Subpart A—Debt Collection

Sec.
11.1 General application.
11.2 Definitions.
11.3 Demand for payment.
11.4 Collection by administrative offset.
11.5 Administrative wage garnishment.
11.6 Reporting debts.
11.7 Private collection agencies.
11.8 Suspension or revocation of eligibility for loans and loan guarantees, licenses, permits, or privileges.
11.9 Collection in installments.
11.10 Interest, penalty charges, and administrative costs.
11.11 Compromise.
11.12 Suspending or terminating collection activity.
11.13 Referrals to the Department of Justice.
11.14 Receipt of offset requests by other Federal agencies.
11.15 Applying the debt against DHS payments.

Subpart B [Reserved]

AUTHORITY: 5 U.S.C. 301, 5514; 26 U.S.C. 6402, 31 U.S.C. 3701, 3711, 3716, 3717, 3718, 3720A,

3720B, 3720D; Pub. L. 107–296, 116 Stat. 2135 (6 U.S.C. 1 *et seq.*).

Source: 72 FR 4190, Jan. 30, 2007, unless otherwise noted.

Subpart A—Debt Collection

§11.1 General application.

(a) *Application of Debt Collection Standards.* The provisions of 31 CFR parts 285, 900–904, as amended by the Secretary of the Treasury and the Attorney General, are applicable to debts and debt procedures within the jurisdiction of the Department of Homeland Security.

(b) *Authority.* The Chief Financial Officer of the Department of Homeland Security is delegated authority to administer this subpart and to redelegate authority under this subpart.

(c) *Application to DHS.* This subpart provides procedures for the collection of DHS debts, and for collection of other debts owed to the United States when a request for offset of a DHS payment is received by the DHS from another federal agency. This subpart applies to all of DHS, including all of its components. It applies to the DHS when collecting a DHS debt, to persons who owe DHS debts, and to Federal agencies requesting offset of a payment issued by the DHS as a payment agency (including salary payments to DHS employees).

(d) *Exclusions.* This subpart does not apply to debt arising from taxation under the Internal Revenue Act of 1986, as amended, or to any debt excepted from the FCCS, 31 CFR parts 900 through 904.

(e) *Non-exclusive procedure or remedy.* Nothing in this subpart precludes collection or disposition of any debt under statutes and regulations other than those described in this subpart. To the extent that the provisions of laws or other regulations apply, including the remission or mitigation of fines, penalties, forfeitures and debts arising under the tariff laws of the United States, DHS components are authorized to collect debts under those laws and regulations. DHS components and other Federal agencies may simultaneously use multiple collection remedies to collect a debt, except as prohibited by law.

(f) *Additional policies and procedures.* DHS components may, but are not required to, promulgate additional policies and procedures consistent with this subpart and other applicable Federal law, policies, and procedures.

(g) *Duplication not required.* Nothing in this subpart requires DHS to duplicate notices or administrative proceedings required by contract, this subpart, or other laws or regulations.

(h) *No private rights created.* This subpart does not create any right or benefit, substantive or procedural, enforceable at law or in equity by a party against the United States, its agencies, its officers, or any other person, nor shall the failure of any DHS component to comply with any of the provisions of this subpart or 31 CFR parts 285, 900–904 be a defense to the collection of any debt or enforcement of any other law.

§11.2 Definitions.

In addition to the definitions provided in 31 CFR parts 285, 900–904, as used in this subpart:

(a) *Department of Homeland Security* or *DHS* means the United States Department of Homeland Security and includes the Secretary and any DHS entity which reports directly or indirectly to the Secretary.

(b) *DHS debt* means a debt owed to DHS by a person.

(c) *Secretary* means the Secretary of Homeland Security.

§11.3 Demand for payment.

(a) *Notice requirements.* Generally, before DHS starts the collection actions described in this subpart, DHS sends a written notice to the debtor under 31 CFR 901.2. The notice provided under this section includes notice of any and all actions DHS may take to offset the debt, including any notices required under 31 CFR parts 285, 900–904.

(b) *Exceptions to notice requirements.* DHS may omit from any notice to a debtor any provision that is not legally required given the collection remedies to be applied to a particular debt.

§11.4 Collection by administrative offset.

(a) *General Provisions for Offset.* DHS will collect debts by administrative offset pursuant to 31 CFR parts 900–904.

(b) *Centralized Offset through the Treasury Offset Program.* DHS adopts the provisions of 31 CFR 901.3.

(c) *Non-centralized Offset for DHS Debts.* When centralized offset is not available or appropriate, DHS may collect delinquent DHS debts through non-centralized offset. In these cases, DHS may offset a payment internally or make a request directly to a Federal payment agency to offset a payment owed to the debtor. Before requesting a payment authorizing agency to conduct a non-centralized administrative offset, DHS will provide the debtor with the due process set forth in 31 CFR 901.3(b)(4) and the notice requirements of 31 CFR 901.2 (unless the due process and notice requirements are not required under that part). DHS will provide the payment authorizing agency written certification that the debtor owes the past due, legally enforceable delinquent debt in the amount stated, and that DHS has fully complied with its regulations concerning administrative offset.

(d) *Hearing Procedures for Federal Employees*—(1) *Request for a hearing.* A Federal employee who has received a notice that his or her DHS debt will be collected by means of salary offset may request a hearing concerning the existence or amount of the debt. The Federal employee also may request a hearing concerning the amount proposed to be deducted from the employee's pay each pay period. The employee must send any request for hearing, in writing, to the office designated in the notice described in section 11.4(c). The request must be received by the designated office on or before the 15th calendar day following the employee's receipt of the notice. The employee must sign the request and specify whether an oral or paper hearing is requested. If an oral hearing is requested, the employee must explain why the matter cannot be resolved by review of the documentary evidence alone. All travel expenses incurred by the Federal employee in connection with an in-person hearing will be borne by the employee.

(2) *Failure to submit timely request for hearing.* If the employee fails to submit a request for hearing within the time period described in paragraph (d)(1) of this section, the employee will have waived the right to a hearing, and salary offset may be initiated. However, DHS should accept a late request for hearing if the employee can show that the late request was the result of circumstances beyond the employee's control or because of a failure to receive actual notice of the filing deadline.

(3) *Hearing official.* DHS must obtain the services of a hearing official who is not under the supervision or control of the Secretary. The DHS Chief Financial Officer will coordinate DHS efforts to obtain the services of a hearing official.

(4) *Notice of hearing.* After the employee requests a hearing, the designated hearing official informs the employee of the form of the hearing to be provided. For oral hearings, the notice sets forth the date, time and location of the hearing. For paper hearings, the notice provides the employee the date by which he or she should submit written arguments to the designated hearing official. The hearing official gives the employee reasonable time to submit documentation in support of the employee's position. The hearing official schedules a new hearing date if requested by both parties. The hearing official gives both parties reasonable notice of the time and place of a rescheduled hearing.

(5) *Oral hearing.* The hearing official conducts an oral hearing if he or she determines the matter cannot be resolved by review of documentary evidence alone (for example, when an issue of credibility or veracity is involved). The hearing need not take the form of an evidentiary hearing, but may be conducted in a manner determined by the hearing official, including but not limited to:

(i) Informal conferences with the hearing official, in which the employee and agency representative will be given full opportunity to present evidence, witnesses and argument;

(ii) Informal meetings with an interview of the employee by the hearing official; or

(iii) Formal written submissions, with an opportunity for oral presentation.

(6) *Paper hearing.* If the hearing official determines an oral hearing is not

necessary, he or she makes the determination based upon a review of the available written record, including any documentation submitted by the employee in support of his or her position.

(7) *Failure to appear or submit documentary evidence.* In the absence of good cause shown (for example, excused illness), if the employee fails to appear at an oral hearing or fails to submit documentary evidence as required for a paper hearing, the employee waives the right to a hearing, and salary offset may be initiated. Further, the employee is deemed to admit the existence and amount of the debt as described in the notice of intent to offset. If a DHS representative does not appear at an oral hearing, the hearing official shall proceed with the hearing as scheduled, and make his or her determination based upon the oral testimony presented and the documentary evidence submitted by both parties.

(8) *Burden of proof.* DHS has the initial burden to prove the existence and amount of the debt. Thereafter, if the employee disputes the existence or amount of the debt, the employee must prove by a preponderance of the evidence that no debt exists or that the amount of the debt is incorrect. In addition, the employee may present evidence that the proposed terms of the repayment schedule are unlawful, would cause a financial hardship to the employee, or that collection of the debt may not be pursued due to operation of law.

(9) *Record.* The hearing official maintains a summary record of any hearing provided by this subpart. Witnesses testify under oath or affirmation in oral hearings.

(10) *Date of decision.* The hearing official issues a written opinion stating his or her decision, based upon documentary evidence and information developed at the hearing, as soon as practicable after the hearing but not later than 60 days after the date on which the request for hearing was received by DHS. If the employee requests a delay in the proceedings, the deadline for the decision may be postponed by the number of days by which the hearing was postponed. When a decision is not timely rendered, DHS waives penalties applied to the debt for the period beginning with the date the decision is due and ending on the date the decision is issued.

(11) *Content of decision.* The written decision includes:

(i) A statement of the facts presented to support the origin, nature, and amount of the debt;

(ii) The hearing official's findings, analysis, and conclusions; and

(iii) The terms of any repayment schedules, if applicable.

(12) *Final agency action.* The hearing official's decision is final.

(f) *Waiver not precluded.* Nothing in this subpart precludes an employee from requesting waiver of an overpayment under 5 U.S.C. 5584 or 8346(b), 10 U.S.C. 2774, 32 U.S.C. 716, or other statutory authority.

(g) *Salary offset process*—(1) *Determination of disposable pay.* The Chief Financial Officer consults with the appropriate DHS payroll office to determine the amount of a DHS employee's disposable pay and will implement salary offset when requested to do so by a DHS component or another federal agency. If the debtor is not employed by DHS, the agency employing the debtor will determine the amount of the employee's disposable pay and implement salary offset upon request.

(2) *Amount of salary offset.* The amount to be offset from each salary payment will be up to 15 percent of a debtor's disposable pay, as follows:

(i) If the amount of the debt is equal to or less than 15 percent of the disposable pay, such debt generally is collected in one lump sum payment; or

(ii) Installment deductions are made over a period of no greater than the anticipated period of employment. An installment deduction will not exceed 15 percent of the disposable pay from which the deduction is made unless the employee has agreed in writing to the deduction of a greater amount or the creditor agency has determined that smaller deductions are appropriate based on the employee's ability to pay.

(3) *Final salary payment.* After the employee has separated either voluntarily or involuntarily from the payment agency, the payment agency may make a lump sum deduction exceeding 15 percent of disposable pay from any

final salary or other payments pursuant to 31 U.S.C. 3716 in order to satisfy a debt.

(h) *Payment agency's responsibilities.* (1) As required by 5 CFR 550.1109, if the employee separates from the payment agency from which DHS requested salary offset, the payment agency must certify the total amount of its collection and notify DHS and the employee of the amounts collected. If the payment agency is aware that the employee is entitled to payments from the Civil Service Retirement Fund and Disability Fund, the Federal Employee Retirement System, or other similar payments, it must provide written notification to the agency responsible for making such retirement payments that the debtor owes a debt, the amount of the debt, and that DHS has complied with the provisions of this section. DHS must submit a properly certified claim to the new payment agency before the collection can be made.

(2) If the employee is already separated from employment and all payments due from his or her former payment agency have been made, DHS may request that money due and payable to the employee from the Civil Service Retirement Fund and Disability Fund, the Federal Employee Retirement System, or other similar funds, is administratively offset to collect the debt. Generally, DHS will collect such monies through the Treasury Offset Program as described in this section.

(3) When an employee transfers to another agency, DHS should resume collection with the employee's new payment agency in order to continue salary offset.

§ 11.5 **Administrative wage garnishment.**

DHS may collect debts from a debtor's wages by means of administrative wage garnishment in accordance with the requirements of 31 U.S.C. 3720D under the procedures established in 31 CFR 285.11.

§ 11.6 **Reporting debts.**

DHS will report delinquent debts to credit bureaus and other automated databases in accordance with 31 U.S.C. 3711(e), 31 CFR 901.4, and the Office of

Management and Budget Circular A-129, "Policies for Federal Credit Programs and Non-tax Receivables," which may be found at *http:// www.fms.treas.gov/debt.* At least sixty (60) days prior to reporting a delinquent debt to a consumer reporting agency, DHS sends a notice to the debtor in accordance with 6 CFR 11.3. DHS may authorize the Treasury Department's Financial Management Service to report to credit bureaus those delinquent debts that have been transferred to the Financial Management Service for administrative offset.

§ 11.7 **Private collection agencies.**

DHS will transfer delinquent DHS debts to the Treasury Department's Financial Management Service to obtain debt collection services provided by private collection agencies.

§ 11.8 **Suspension or revocation of eligibility for loans and loan guarantees, licenses, permits, or privileges.**

The authority to extend financial assistance in the form of a loan, loan guarantee, or loan insurance to any person delinquent on a nontax debt owed to DHS is delegated to the Chief Financial Officer.

§ 11.9 **Collection in installments.**

DHS may accept payment of a DHS debt in regular installments, in accordance with the provisions of 31 CFR 901.8 and policies and procedures adopted by the Chief Financial Officer (CFO). The CFO will consult the Office of General Counsel regarding a legally enforceable written agreement from the debtor.

§ 11.10 **Interest, penalty charges, and administrative costs.**

(a) *Assessment and notice.* DHS shall assess interest, penalties and administrative costs on DHS debts in accordance with 31 U.S.C. 3717 and 31 CFR 901.9. Administrative costs of processing and handling a delinquent debt shall be determined by DHS.

(b) *Waiver of interest, penalties, and administrative costs.* DHS may waive interest, penalties, and administrative costs, or any portion thereof, under the criteria in the FCCS, or when it determines the collection of these charges would be against equity and good conscience or not in the best interests of the United States. The authority to waive interest, penalties and administrative costs is delegated to the Chief Financial Officer. The DHS Chief Financial Officer shall issue written guidance on maintaining records of waivers.

(c) *Accrual during suspension of debt collection.* Interest and related charges will not accrue during the period a hearing official does not render a timely decision.

§11.11 Compromise.

DHS may compromise a debt in accordance with the provisions of 31 CFR part 902. The Chief Financial Officer is authorized to compromise debts owed to DHS. No debt over $10,000 may be compromised without the concurrence of the Office of the General Counsel.

§11.12 Suspending or terminating collection activity.

DHS will suspend or terminate collection activity, or discharge indebtedness, in accordance with 31 CFR part 903. The Chief Financial Officer is delegated authority to suspend or terminate collection activity, or to discharge indebtedness regarding debts owed to DHS, but for any such action involving a debt over $10,000, the Chief Financial Officer must obtain the concurrence of the Office of the General Counsel. The Chief Financial Officer is authorized to act on behalf of the Secretary in selling a debt, and in determining whether or not it is in the best interests of the United States to do so.

§11.13 Referrals to the Department of Justice.

Referrals of debts to the Department of Justice for collection will be by the General Counsel.

§11.14 Receipt of offset requests by other Federal agencies.

Other Federal agencies send non-centralized offset requests to DHS at: U.S. Department of Homeland Security, Attn: Chief Financial Officer, Mail Stop 0200, Washington, DC 20528–0200. Those agencies must comply with 31 CFR 901.3 when forwarding the requests to DHS. DHS does not review the merits of the creditor agency's determination with regard to the existence or the amount of the debt. When two or more agencies are seeking offsets from payments made to the same person, or when two or more debts are owed to a single creditor agency, DHS may determine the order in which the debts will be collected or whether one or more debts should be collected by offset simultaneously. For the purposes of this section, debts owed to DHS generally take precedence over debts owed to other agencies, but DHS may pay a debt to another agency prior to collecting for DHS. DHS determines the order of debt collection based upon the best interests of the United States.

§11.15 Applying the debt against DHS payments.

(a) *Notice to the Debtor.* DHS sends a written notice to the debtor indicating a certified debt claim was received from the creditor agency, the amount of the debt claimed to be owed by the creditor agency, the estimated date the offset will begin (if more than one payment), and the amount of the deduction(s). For employees, DHS generally begins deductions from pay at the next officially established pay interval. Deductions continue until DHS knows the debt is paid in full or until otherwise instructed by the creditor agency. Alternatively, the amount offset may be an amount agreed upon, in writing, by the debtor and the creditor agency. If a DHS employee retires or resigns, or if his or her employment ends before collection of the debt is complete, DHS continues to offset, under 31 U.S.C. 3716, up to 100% of an employee's subsequent payments until the debt is paid or otherwise resolved. Such payments include a debtor's final salary payment, lump-sum leave payment, and other payments payable to the debtor by DHS. See 31 U.S.C. 3716 and 5 CFR 550.1104(l) and 550.1104(m). If the employee is separated from DHS before the debt is paid in full, DHS will certify to the creditor agency the total amount of its collection. If DHS is aware the employee is entitled to payments from the Civil Service Retirement and Disability Fund, Federal Employee Retirement System, or other similar payments, DHS provides written notice to the agency making such retirement payments that the debtor owes a debt (including the amount) and that the provisions of 5 CFR 550.1109 have been fully complied with. The creditor agency is responsible for submitting a certified claim to the agency responsible for making such payments before collection may begin. Generally, creditor agencies will collect such monies through the Treasury Offset Program as described in section 11.4.

(b) *Notice to the debtor.* DHS provides to the debtor a copy of any notices sent to the creditor agency under this subpart.

(c) *Transfer of employee debtor to another Federal agency.* If an employee debtor transfers to another Federal agency before the debt is paid in full, DHS notifies the creditor agency and provides it a certification of the total amount of its collection on the debt. The creditor agency is responsible for submitting a certified claim to the debtor's new employing agency before collection may begin.

Subpart B [Reserved]

PART 13—PROGRAM FRAUD CIVIL REMEDIES

AUTHORITY: Pub. L. 107–296, 116 Stat. 2135 (6 U.S.C., Ch. 1, sections 101 *et seq.*); 5 U.S.C. 301; 31 U.S.C. 3801–3812.

SOURCE: 70 FR 59211, Oct. 12, 2005, unless otherwise noted.

§ 13.1 Basis, purpose, scope and effect.

(a) *Basis.* This part implements the Program Fraud Civil Remedies Act of 1986, 31 U.S.C. 3801–3812. section 3809 of title 31, United States Code, requires each authority to promulgate regulations necessary to implement the provisions of the statute.

(b) *Purpose.* This part:

(1) Establishes administrative procedures for imposing civil penalties and assessments against Persons who Make, submit, or present, or cause to be Made, submitted, or presented, false, fictitious, or fraudulent Claims or written Statements to the Authority or to certain others; and

(2) Specifies the hearing and appeal rights of Persons subject to allegations of liability for such penalties and assessments.

(c) *Scope.* This part applies to all components of the Department of Homeland Security.

(d) *Effect.* (1) This part applies to program fraud cases initiated by any component of the Department of Homeland Security on or after October 12, 2005.

(2) Program fraud cases initiated by any component of the Department of Homeland Security before October 12, 2005, but not completed before October 12, 2005, will continue to completion under the rules and procedures in effect before this part.

§13.2 Definitions.

The following definitions have general applicability throughout this part:

(a) *ALJ* means an Administrative Law Judge in the Authority appointed pursuant to 5 U.S.C. 3105 or detailed to the Authority pursuant to 5 U.S.C. 3344. An ALJ will preside at any hearing convened under the regulations in this part.

(b) *Authority* means the Department of Homeland Security.

(c) *Authority Head* means the Deputy Secretary, Department of Homeland Security, or another officer designated by the Deputy Secretary.

(d) *Benefit* means, in the context of a Statement, anything of value, including but not limited to any advantage, preference, privilege, license, permit, favorable decision, ruling, status, or loan guarantee.

(e) *Claim* means any request, demand, or submission:

(1) Made to the Authority for property, services, or money (including money representing grants, loans, insurance, or Benefits);

(2) Made to a recipient of property, services, or money from the Authority or to a party to a contract with the Authority:

(i) For property or services if the United States:

(A) Provided such property or services;

(B) Provided any portion of the funds for the purchase of such property or services; or

(C) Will reimburse such recipient or party for the purchase of such property or services; or

(ii) For the payment of money (including money representing grants, loans, insurance, or Benefits) if the United States:

(A) Provided any portion of the money requested or demanded; or

(B) Will reimburse such recipient or party for any portion of the money paid on such request or demand; or

(3) Made to the Authority which has the effect of decreasing an obligation to pay or account for property, services, or money.

(f) *Complaint* means the administrative Complaint served by the Reviewing Official on the Defendant under §13.7.

(g) *Defendant* means any Person alleged in a Complaint under §13.7 to be liable for a civil penalty or assessment under §13.3.

(h) *Government* means the Government of the United States.

(i) *Individual* means a natural Person.

(j) *Initial Decision* means the written decision of the ALJ required by §13.10 or §13.37, and includes a revised Initial Decision issued following a remand or a motion for reconsideration.

(k) *Investigating Official* means the Inspector General of the Department of Homeland Security or an officer or employee of the Office of the Inspector General designated by the Inspector General and eligible under 31 U.S.C. 3801(a)(4)(B).

(l) *Knows or Has Reason to Know*, means that a Person, with respect to a Claim or Statement:

(1) Has actual knowledge that the Claim or Statement is false, fictitious, or fraudulent;

(2) Acts in deliberate ignorance of the truth or falsity of the Claim or Statement; or

(3) Acts in reckless disregard of the truth or falsity of the Claim or Statement.

(m) *Makes* includes presents, submits, and causes to be made, presented, or submitted. As the context requires, Making or Made will likewise include the corresponding forms of such terms.

(n) *Person* means any Individual, partnership, corporation, association, or private organization, and includes the plural of that term.

(o) *Representative* means an attorney who is a member in good standing of the bar of any State, Territory, or possession of the United States, the District of Columbia, or the Commonwealth of Puerto Rico. This definition is not intended to foreclose *pro se* appearances. That is, an Individual may appear for himself or herself, and a corporation or other entity may appear by an owner, officer, or employee of the corporation or entity.

(p) *Reviewing Official* means the General Counsel of the Department of Homeland Security, or other officer or employee of the Department who is designated by the General Counsel and eligible under 31 U.S.C. 3801(a)(8).

(q) *Statement* means any representation, certification, affirmation, Document, record, or accounting or bookkeeping entry Made:

(1) With respect to a Claim or to obtain the approval or payment of a Claim (including relating to eligibility to Make a Claim); or

(2) With respect to (including relating to eligibility for):

(i) A contract with, or bid or proposal for a contract with the Authority, or any State, political subdivision of a State, or other party, if the United States Government provides any portion of the money or property under such contract or for such grant, loan, or Benefit, or if the Government will reimburse such State, political subdivision, or party for any portion of the money or property under such contract or for such grant, loan, or Benefit; or

(ii) A grant, loan, or Benefit from, the Authority, or any State, political subdivision of a State, or other party, if the United States Government provides any portion of the money or property under such contract or for such grant, loan, or Benefit, or if the Government will reimburse such State, political subdivision, or party for any portion of the money or property under such contract or for such grant, loan, or Benefit.

§ 13.3 Basis for civil penalties and assessments.

(a) *Claims.* (1) Except as provided in paragraph (c) of this section, a Person will be subject, in addition to any other remedy that may be prescribed by law, to a civil penalty of not more than $5,500 for each Claim (as adjusted in accordance with the Federal Civil Penalties Inflation Adjustment Act of 1990 (Public Law 101–140), as amended by the Debt Collection Improvement Act of 1996 (Public Law 104–134)) if such Person Makes a Claim that such Person Knows or Has Reason to Know:

(i) Is false, fictitious, or fraudulent;

(ii) Includes or is supported by any written Statement that asserts a material fact that is false, fictitious, or fraudulent;

(iii) Includes or is supported by any written Statement that:

(A) Omits a material fact;

(B) Is false, fictitious, or fraudulent as a result of such omission; and

(C) Is a Statement in which the Person Making such Statement has a duty to include such material fact; or

(iv) Is for payment for the provision of property or services that the Person has not provided as claimed.

(2) Each voucher, invoice, Claim form, or other Individual request or demand for property, services, or money constitutes a separate Claim.

(3) A Claim will be considered Made to the Authority, recipient, or party when such Claim is actually Made to an agent, fiscal intermediary, or other entity, including any State or political subdivision thereof, acting for or on behalf of the Authority, recipient, or party.

(4) Each Claim for property, services, or money is subject to a civil penalty regardless of whether such property, services, or money is actually delivered or paid.

(5) If the Government has Made any payment (including transferred property or provided services) on a Claim, a Person subject to a civil penalty under paragraph (a)(1) of this section will also be subject to an assessment of not more than twice the amount of such Claim or that portion thereof that is determined to be in violation of paragraph (a)(1) of this section. Such assessment will be in lieu of damages sustained by the Government because of such Claim.

(b) *Statements.* (1) Except as provided in paragraph (c) of this section, a Person will be subject, in addition to any other remedy that may be prescribed by law, to a civil penalty of not more than $5,500 (as adjusted in accordance with the Federal Civil Penalties Inflation Adjustment Act of 1990 (Public Law 101–140), as amended by the Debt Collection Improvement Act of 1996 (Public Law 104–134)) if such Person Makes a written Statement that:

(i) The Person Knows or Has Reason to Know:

(A) Asserts a material fact that is false, fictitious, or fraudulent; or

(B) Is false, fictitious, or fraudulent because it omits a material fact that the Person Making the Statement has a duty to include in such Statement; and

(ii) Contains, or is accompanied by, an express certification or affirmation of the truthfulness and accuracy of the contents of the Statement.

(2) Each written representation, certification, or affirmation constitutes a separate Statement.

(3) A Statement will be considered Made to the Authority when such Statement is actually Made to an agent, fiscal intermediary, or other entity, including any State or political subdivision thereof, acting for or on behalf of the Authority.

(c) *Specific intent not required.* No proof of specific intent to defraud is required to establish liability under this section.

(d) *More than one Person liable.* (1) In any case in which it is determined that more than one Person is liable for Making a Claim or Statement under this section, each such Person may be held liable for a civil penalty under this section.

(2) In any case in which it is determined that more than one Person is liable for Making a Claim under this section on which the Government has Made payment (including transferred property or provided services), an assessment may be imposed against any such Person or jointly and severally against any combination of such Persons.

§ 13.4 **Investigation.**

(a) If an Investigating Official concludes that a subpoena pursuant to the Authority conferred by 31 U.S.C. 3804(a) is warranted:

(1) The subpoena so issued will notify the Person to whom it is addressed of the Authority under which the subpoena is issued and will identify the records or Documents sought;

(2) The Investigating Official may designate a Person to act on his or her behalf to receive the Documents sought; and

(3) The Person receiving such subpoena will be required to tender to the Investigating Official or the Person designated to receive the Documents a certification that the Documents sought have been produced, or that such Documents are not available and the reasons therefore, or that such Documents, suitably identified, have been withheld based upon the assertion of an identified privilege.

(b) If the Investigating Official concludes that an action under the Act may be warranted, the Investigating Official will submit a report containing the findings and conclusions of such investigation to the Reviewing Official.

(c) Nothing in this section will preclude or limit an Investigating Official's discretion to refer allegations directly to the Department of Justice for suit under the False Claims Act or other civil relief, or to defer or postpone a report or referral to the Reviewing Official to avoid interference with a criminal investigation or prosecution.

(d) Nothing in this section modifies any responsibility of an Investigating Official to report violations of criminal law to the Attorney General.

§ 13.5 **Review by the Reviewing Official.**

(a) If, based on the report of the Investigating Official under § 13.4(b), the Reviewing Official determines that there is adequate evidence to believe that a Person is liable under § 13.3, the Reviewing Official will transmit to the Attorney General a written notice of the Reviewing Official's intention to issue a Complaint under § 13.7.

(b) Such notice will include:

(1) A Statement of the Reviewing Official's reasons for issuing a Complaint;

(2) A Statement specifying the evidence that supports the allegations of liability;

(3) A description of the Claims or Statements upon which the allegations of liability are based;

(4) An estimate of the amount of money or the value of property, services, or other Benefits requested or demanded in violation of § 13.3;

(5) A Statement of any exculpatory or mitigating circumstances that may relate to the Claims or Statements known by the Reviewing Official or the Investigating Official; and

(6) A Statement that there is a reasonable prospect of collecting an appropriate amount of penalties and assessments.

§ 13.6 **Prerequisites for issuing a Complaint.**

(a) The Reviewing Official may issue a Complaint under § 13.7 only if:

(1) The Department of Justice approves the issuance of a Complaint in a written Statement described in 31 U.S.C. 3803(b)(1); and

(2) In the case of allegations of liability under § 13.3(a) with respect to a Claim, the Reviewing Official determines that, with respect to such Claim or a group of related Claims submitted at the same time such Claim is submitted (as defined in paragraph (b) of this section), the amount of money or the value of property or services demanded or requested in violation of § 13.3(a) does not exceed $150,000.

(b) For the purposes of this section, a related group of Claims submitted at the same time will include only those Claims arising from the same transaction (e.g., grant, loan, application, or contract) that are submitted simultaneously as part of a single request, demand, or submission.

(c) Nothing in this section will be construed to limit the Reviewing Official's authority to join in a single Complaint against a Person's Claims that are unrelated or were not submitted simultaneously, regardless of the amount of money, or the value of property or services, demanded or requested.

§ 13.7 **Complaint.**

(a) On or after the date the Department of Justice approves the issuance of a Complaint in accordance with 31 U.S.C. 3803(b)(1), the Reviewing Official may serve a Complaint on the Defendant, as provided in § 13.8.

(b) The Complaint will state:

(1) The allegations of liability against the Defendant, including the statutory basis for liability, an identification of the Claims or Statements that are the basis for the alleged liability, and the reasons why liability allegedly arises from such Claims or Statements;

(2) The maximum amount of penalties and assessments for which the Defendant may be held liable;

(3) Instructions for filing an answer to request a hearing, including a specific Statement of the Defendant's right to request a hearing by filing an answer and to be represented by a Representative; and

(4) That failure to file an answer within 30 days of service of the Complaint will result in the imposition of the maximum amount of penalties and assessments without right to appeal, as provided in § 13.10.

(5) That the Defendant may obtain copies of relevant material and exculpatory information pursuant to the process outlined in § 13.20.

(c) At the same time the Reviewing Official serves the Complaint, he or she will serve the Defendant with a copy of the regulations in this part.

§ 13.8 **Service of Complaint.**

(a) Service of a Complaint must be Made by certified or registered mail or by delivery in any manner authorized by Rule 4(d) of the Federal Rules of Civil Procedure. Service of a Complaint is complete upon receipt.

(b) Proof of service, stating the name and address of the Person on whom the Complaint was served, and the manner and date of service, may be Made by:

(1) Affidavit of the Individual serving the Complaint by delivery;

(2) A United States Postal Service return receipt card acknowledging receipt; or

(3) Written acknowledgment of receipt by the Defendant or his or her Representative; or

(4) In case of service abroad, authentication in accordance with the Convention on Service Abroad of Judicial and Extrajudicial Documents in Commercial and Civil Matters.

§ 13.9 **Answer.**

(a) The Defendant may request a hearing by serving an answer on the Reviewing Official within 30 days of service of the Complaint. Service of an answer will be Made by delivering a copy to the Reviewing Official or by placing a copy in the United States mail, postage prepaid and addressed to the Reviewing Official. Service of an answer is complete upon such delivery or mailing. An answer will be deemed to be a request for hearing.

(b) In the answer, the Defendant:

(1) Will admit or deny each of the allegations of liability Made in the Complaint;

(2) Will state any defense on which the Defendant intends to rely;

(3) May state any reasons why the Defendant contends that the penalties and assessments should be less than the statutory maximum; and

(4) Will state the name, address, and telephone number of the Person authorized by the Defendant to act as Defendant's Representative, if any.

(c) If the Defendant is unable to file an answer meeting the requirements of paragraph (b) of this section within the time provided, the Defendant may, before the expiration of 30 days from service of the Complaint, serve on the Reviewing Official a general answer denying liability and requesting a hearing, and a request for an extension of time within which to serve an answer meeting the requirements of paragraph (b) of this section. The Reviewing Official will file promptly the Complaint, the general answer denying liability, and the request for an extension of time as provided in §13.11. For good cause shown, the ALJ may grant the Defendant up to 30 additional days from the original due date within which to serve an answer meeting the requirements of paragraph (b) of this section.

§13.10 Default upon failure to answer.

(a) If the Defendant does not answer within the time prescribed in §13.9(a), the Reviewing Official may refer the Complaint to an ALJ by filing the Complaint and a Statement that Defendant has failed to answer on time.

(b) Upon the referral of the Complaint, the ALJ will promptly serve on Defendant in the manner prescribed in §13.8, a notice that an Initial Decision will be issued under this section.

(c) In addition, the ALJ will assume the facts alleged in the Complaint to be true, and, if such facts establish liability under §13.3, the ALJ will issue an Initial Decision imposing the maximum amount of penalties and assessments allowed under the statute.

(d) Except as otherwise provided in this section, by failing to answer on time, the Defendant waives any right to further review of the penalties and assessments imposed under paragraph (c) of this section, and the Initial Decision will become final and binding upon the parties 30 days after it is issued.

(e) If, before such an Initial Decision becomes final, the Defendant files a motion seeking to reopen on the grounds that extraordinary circumstances prevented the Defendant from answering, the Initial Decision will be stayed pending the ALJ's decision on the motion.

(f) If, on such motion, the Defendant can demonstrate extraordinary circumstances excusing the failure to answer on time, the ALJ will withdraw the Initial Decision in paragraph (c) of this section, if such a decision has been issued, and will grant the Defendant an opportunity to answer the Complaint.

(g) A decision of the ALJ denying a Defendant's motion under paragraph (e) of this section is not subject to reconsideration under §13.38.

(h) The Defendant may appeal to the Authority Head the decision denying a motion to reopen by filing a notice of appeal in accordance with §13.26 within 15 days after the ALJ denies the motion. The timely filing of a notice of appeal will stay the Initial Decision until the Authority Head decides the issue.

(i) If the Defendant files a timely notice of appeal with the Authority Head, the ALJ will forward the record of the proceeding to the Authority Head.

(j) The Authority Head will decide expeditiously whether extraordinary circumstances excuse the Defendant's failure to answer on time based solely on the record before the ALJ.

(k) If the Authority Head decides that extraordinary circumstances excused the Defendant's failure to answer on time, the Authority Head will remand the case to the ALJ with instructions to grant the Defendant an opportunity to answer.

(l) If the Authority Head decides that the Defendant's failure to answer on time is not excused, the Authority Head will reinstate the Initial Decision of the ALJ, which will become final and binding upon the parties 30 days after the Authority Head issues such decision.

§ 13.11 Referral of Complaint and answer to the ALJ.

Upon receipt of an answer, the Reviewing Official will refer the matter to an ALJ by filing the Complaint and answer in accordance with § 13.26.

§ 13.12 Notice of hearing.

(a) When the ALJ receives the Complaint and answer, the ALJ will promptly serve a notice of hearing upon the Defendant in the manner prescribed by § 13.8.

(b) Such notice will include:

(1) The tentative time and place, and the nature of the hearing;

(2) The legal authority and jurisdiction under which the hearing is to be held;

(3) The matters of fact and law to be asserted;

(4) A description of the procedures for the conduct of the hearing;

(5) The name, address, and telephone number of the Representative of the Government and of the Defendant, if any; and

(6) Such other matters as the ALJ deems appropriate.

§ 13.13 Parties to the hearing.

(a) The parties to the hearing will be the Defendant and the Authority.

(b) Pursuant to 31 U.S.C. 3730(c)(5), a private plaintiff under the False Claims Act may participate in these proceedings to the extent authorized by the provisions of that Act.

§ 13.14 Separation of functions.

(a) The Investigating Official, the Reviewing Official, and any employee or agent of the Authority who takes part in investigating, preparing, or presenting a particular case may not, in such case or a factually related case:

(1) Participate in the hearing as the ALJ;

(2) Participate or advise in the Initial Decision or the review of the Initial Decision by the Authority Head, except as a witness or a Representative in public proceedings; or

(3) Make the collection of penalties and assessments under 31 U.S.C. 3806.

(b) The ALJ will not be responsible to, or subject to the supervision or direction of, the Investigating Official or the Reviewing Official.

(c) Except as provided in paragraph (a) of this section, the Representative for the Government may be employed anywhere in the Authority, including in the offices of either the Investigating Official or the Reviewing Official.

§ 13.15 *Ex parte* contacts.

No party or Person (except employees of the ALJ's office) will communicate in any way with the ALJ on any matter at issue in a case, unless on notice and opportunity for all parties to participate. This provision does not prohibit a Person or party from inquiring about the status of a case or asking routine questions concerning administrative functions or procedures.

§ 13.16 Disqualification of Reviewing Official or ALJ.

(a) A Reviewing Official or ALJ in a particular case may disqualify himself or herself at any time.

(b) A party may file a motion for disqualification of a Reviewing Official or an ALJ. Such motion will be accompanied by an affidavit alleging personal bias or other reason for disqualification.

(c) Such motion and affidavit will be filed promptly upon the party's discovery of reasons requiring disqualification, or such objections will be deemed waived.

(d) Such affidavit will state specific facts that support the party's belief that personal bias or other reason for disqualification exists and the time and circumstances of the party's discovery of such facts. It will be accompanied by a certificate of the Representative of record that it is Made in good faith.

(e)(1) If the ALJ determines that a Reviewing Official is disqualified, the ALJ will dismiss the Complaint without prejudice.

(2) If the ALJ disqualifies himself or herself, the case will be reassigned promptly to another ALJ.

(3) If the ALJ denies a motion to disqualify, the Authority Head may determine the matter only as part of his or

her review of the Initial Decision upon appeal, if any.

§13.17 Rights of parties.

Except as otherwise limited by this part, all parties may:

(a) Be accompanied, represented, and advised by a Representative;

(b) Participate in any conference held by the ALJ;

(c) Conduct discovery;

(d) Agree to stipulations of fact or law, which will be Made part of the record;

(e) Present evidence relevant to the issues at the hearing;

(f) Present and cross-examine witnesses;

(g) Present oral arguments at the hearing as permitted by the ALJ; and

(h) Submit written briefs and proposed findings of fact and conclusions of law after the hearing.

§13.18 Authority of the ALJ.

(a) The ALJ will conduct a fair and impartial hearing, avoid delay, maintain order, and assure that a record of the proceeding is Made.

(b) The ALJ has the authority to:

(1) Set and change the date, time, and place of the hearing upon reasonable notice to the parties;

(2) Continue or recess the hearing in whole or in part for a reasonable period of time;

(3) Hold conferences to identify or simplify the issues, or to consider other matters that may aid in the expeditious disposition of the proceeding;

(4) Administer oaths and affirmations;

(5) Issue subpoenas requiring the attendance of witnesses and the production of Documents at depositions or at hearings;

(6) Rule on motions and other procedural matters;

(7) Regulate the scope and timing of discovery;

(8) Regulate the course of the hearing and the conduct of Representatives and parties;

(9) Examine witnesses;

(10) Receive, rule on, exclude, or limit evidence;

(11) Upon motion of a party, take official notice of facts;

(12) Upon motion of a party, decide cases, in whole or in part, by summary judgment where there is no disputed issue of material fact;

(13) Conduct any conference, argument, or hearing on motions in Person or by telephone; and

(14) Exercise such other authority as is necessary to carry out the responsibilities of the ALJ under this part.

(c) The ALJ does not have the authority to Make any determinations regarding the validity of treaties or other international agreements, Federal statutes or regulations, or Departmental Orders or Directives.

§13.19 Prehearing conferences.

(a) The ALJ may schedule prehearing conferences as appropriate.

(b) Upon the motion of any party, the ALJ will schedule at least one prehearing conference at a reasonable time in advance of the hearing.

(c) The ALJ may use prehearing conferences to discuss the following:

(1) Simplification of the issues;

(2) The necessity or desirability of amendments to the pleadings, including the need for a more definite Statement;

(3) Stipulations and admissions of fact or as to the contents and authenticity of Documents;

(4) Whether the parties can agree to submission of the case on a stipulated record;

(5) Whether a party chooses to waive appearance at an oral hearing and to submit only documentary evidence (subject to the objection of other parties) and written argument;

(6) Limitation of the number of witnesses;

(7) Scheduling dates for the exchange of witness lists and of proposed exhibits;

(8) Discovery;

(9) The time and place for the hearing; and

(10) Such other matters as may tend to expedite the fair and just disposition of the proceedings.

(d) The ALJ may issue an order containing all matters agreed upon by the parties or ordered by the ALJ at a prehearing conference.

§ 13.20 Disclosure of Documents.

(a) Upon written request to the Reviewing Official, the Defendant may review, at a time and place convenient to the Authority, any relevant and material Documents, transcripts, records, and other materials that relate to the allegations set out in the Complaint and upon which the findings and conclusions of the Investigating Official under § 13.4(b) are based, unless such Documents are subject to a privilege under Federal law. Special arrangements as to confidentiality may be required by the Reviewing Official, who may also assert privilege or other related doctrines. Upon payment of fees for duplication, the Defendant may obtain copies of such Documents.

(b) Upon written request to the Reviewing Official, the Defendant also may obtain a copy of all exculpatory information in the possession of the Reviewing Official or Investigating Official relating to the allegations in the Complaint, even if it is contained in a Document that would otherwise be privileged. If the Document would otherwise be privileged, only that portion containing exculpatory information must be disclosed.

(c) The notice sent to the Attorney General from the Reviewing Official as described in § 13.5 is not discoverable under any circumstances.

(d) The Defendant may file a motion to compel disclosure of the Documents subject to the provisions of this section. Such a motion may only be filed following the serving of an answer pursuant to § 13.9.

§ 13.21 Discovery.

(a) *In general.* (1) The following types of discovery are authorized:

(i) Requests for production of Documents for inspection and copying;

(ii) Requests for admissions of the authenticity of any relevant Document or of the truth of any relevant fact;

(iii) Written interrogatories; and

(iv) Depositions.

(2) Unless mutually agreed to by the parties, discovery is available only as ordered by the ALJ. The ALJ will regulate the timing of discovery.

(b) *Documents defined.* (1) For the purpose of this section and §§ 13.22 and 13.23, the term *Documents* includes information, documents, reports, answers, records, accounts, papers, and other data and documentary evidence.

(2) Nothing in this part will be interpreted to require the creation of a Document.

(c) *Motions for discovery.* (1) A party seeking discovery may file a motion. Such a motion will be accompanied by a copy of the request for production of Documents, request for admissions, or interrogatories or, in the case of depositions, a summary of the scope of the proposed deposition.

(2) Within ten days of service, a party may file an opposition to the motion or a motion for protective order as provided in § 13.24.

(3) The ALJ may grant a motion for discovery only if he or she finds that the discovery sought:

(i) Is necessary for the expeditious, fair, and reasonable consideration of the issues;

(ii) Is not unduly costly or burdensome;

(iii) Will not unduly delay the proceeding; and

(iv) Does not seek privileged information.

(4) The burden of showing that discovery should be allowed is on the party seeking discovery.

(5) The ALJ may grant discovery subject to a protective order under § 13.24.

(d) *Depositions.* (1) If a motion for deposition is granted, the ALJ will issue a subpoena for the deponent, which may require the deponent to produce Documents. The subpoena will specify the time and place at which the deposition will be held. Deposition requests for senior level DHS officials (including career and non-career senior executive level employees) shall not be approved absent showing of compelling need that cannot be met by any other means.

(2) The party seeking to depose will serve the subpoena in the manner prescribed in § 13.8.

(3) The deponent may file a motion to quash the subpoena or a motion for a protective order within ten days of service. If the ALJ has not acted on such a motion by the return date, such date will be suspended pending the ALJ's final action on the motion.

(4) The party seeking to depose will provide for the taking of a verbatim

transcript of the deposition, which it will Make available to all other parties for inspection and copying.

(e) Each party will bear its own costs of discovery.

§ 13.22 Exchange of witness lists, Statements, and exhibits.

(a) At least 15 days before the hearing or at such other time as may be ordered by the ALJ, the parties will exchange witness lists, copies of prior Statements of proposed witnesses, and copies of proposed hearing exhibits, including copies of any written Statements that the party intends to offer in lieu of live testimony in accordance with § 13.33(b). At the time the above Documents are exchanged, any party that intends to rely on the transcript of deposition testimony in lieu of live testimony at the hearing, if permitted by the ALJ, will provide each party with a copy of the specific pages of the transcript it intends to introduce into evidence.

(b) If a party objects, the ALJ will not admit into evidence the testimony of any witness whose name does not appear on the witness list or any exhibit not provided to the opposing party as provided above unless the ALJ finds good cause for the failure or that there is no prejudice to the objecting party.

(c) Unless another party objects within the time set by the ALJ, Documents exchanged in accordance with paragraph (a) of this section will be deemed to be authentic for the purpose of admissibility at the hearing.

§ 13.23 Subpoenas for attendance at hearing.

(a) A party wishing to procure the appearance and testimony of any Individual at the hearing may request that the ALJ issue a subpoena. Requests for witness testimony of senior level DHS officials (including career and non-career senior executive level employees) shall not be approved absent a showing of compelling need that cannot be met by any other means.

(b) A subpoena requiring the attendance and testimony of an Individual may also require the Individual to produce Documents at the hearing.

(c) A party seeking a subpoena will file a written request therefore not less than 15 days before the date fixed for the hearing unless otherwise allowed by the ALJ for good cause shown. Such request will be accompanied by a proposed subpoena, which will specify and Documents to be produced and will designate the witnesses and describe the address and location thereof with sufficient particularity to permit such witnesses to be found.

(d) The subpoena will specify the time and place at which the witness is to appear and any Documents the witness is to produce.

(e) The party seeking the subpoena will serve it in the manner prescribed in § 13.8. A subpoena on a party or upon an Individual under the control of party may be served by first class mail.

(f) A party or the Individual to whom the subpoena is directed may file a motion to quash the subpoena within ten days after service or on or before the time specified in the subpoena for compliance if it is less than ten days after service. If the ALJ has not acted on such a motion by the return date, such date will be suspended pending the ALJ's final action on the motion.

§ 13.24 Protective order.

(a) A party or a prospective witness or deponent may file a motion for a protective order with respect to discovery sought by an opposing party or with respect to the hearing, seeking to limit the availability or disclosure of evidence.

(b) In issuing a protective order, the ALJ may Make any order that justice requires to protect a party or Person from annoyance, embarrassment, oppression, or undue burden or expense, including one or more of the following:

(1) That the discovery not be had;

(2) That the discovery may be had only on specified terms and conditions, including a designation of the time or place;

(3) That the discovery may be had only through a method of discovery other than that requested;

(4) That certain matters not be inquired into, or that the scope of discovery be limited to certain matters;

(5) That discovery be conducted with no one present except Persons designated by the ALJ;

(6) That the contents of discovery or evidence be sealed;

(7) That a deposition after being sealed be opened only by order of the ALJ;

(8) That a trade secret or other confidential research, development, commercial information, or facts pertaining to any criminal investigation, proceeding, or other administrative investigation not be disclosed or be disclosed only in a designated way; and

(9) That the parties simultaneously submit to the ALJ specified Documents or information enclosed in sealed envelopes to be opened as directed by the ALJ.

§ 13.25 Fees.

The party requesting a subpoena will pay the cost of the fees and mileage of any witness subpoenaed in the amounts that would be payable to a witness in a proceeding in United States District Court. A check for witness fees and mileage will accompany the subpoena when served, except that when a subpoena is issued on behalf of the Authority, a check for witness fees and mileage need not accompany the subpoena.

§ 13.26 Filing, form and service of papers.

(a) *Filing and form.* (1) Documents filed with the ALJ will include an original and two copies.

(2) Every pleading and paper filed in the proceeding will contain a caption setting forth the title of the action, the case number assigned by the ALJ, and a designation of the paper (e.g., Motion to Quash Subpoena).

(3) Every pleading and paper will be signed by, and will contain the address and telephone number of, the party or the Person on whose behalf the paper was filed, or his or her Representative.

(4) Papers are considered filed when they are mailed. Date of mailing may be established by a certificate from the party or its Representative or by proof that the Document was sent by certified or registered mail.

(b) *Service.* A party filing a Document will, at the time of filing, serve a copy of such Document on every other party. Service upon any party of any Document other than those required to be served as prescribed in § 13.8 will be

Made by delivering a copy, or by placing a copy of the Document in the United States mail, postage prepaid and addressed, to the party's last known address. When a party is represented by a Representative, service will be Made upon such Representative in lieu of the actual party.

(c) *Proof of service.* A certificate of the Individual serving the Document by Personal delivery or by mail, setting forth the manner of service, will be proof of service.

§ 13.27 Computation of time.

(a) In computing any period of time under this part or in an order issued thereunder, the time begins with the day following the act, event, or default, and includes the last day of the period, unless it is a Saturday, Sunday, or legal holiday observed by the Federal Government, in which event it includes the next business day.

(b) When the period of time allowed is less than seven days, intermediate Saturdays, Sundays, and legal holidays observed by the Federal Government will be excluded from the computation.

(c) Where a Document has been served or issued by placing it in the United States mail, an additional five days will be added to the time permitted for any responses.

§ 13.28 Motions.

(a) Any application to the ALJ for an order or ruling will be by motion. Motions will state the relief sought, the authority relied upon, and the facts alleged, and will be filed and served on all other parties.

(b) Except for motions Made during a prehearing conference or at the hearing, all motions will be in writing. The ALJ may require that oral motions be reduced to writing.

(c) Within 15 days after a written motion is served, or such other time as may be fixed by the ALJ, any party may file a response to such motion.

(d) The ALJ may not grant a written motion before the time for filing response thereto has expired, except upon consent of the parties or following a hearing on the motion, but may overrule or deny such motion without awaiting a response.

(e) The ALJ will Make a reasonable effort to dispose of all outstanding motions before the hearing begins.

(f) Except as provided by §§ 13.21(e)(3) and 13.23(f), which concern subpoenas, the filing or pendency of a motion will not automatically alter or extend a deadline or return date.

§13.29 Sanctions.

(a) The ALJ may sanction a Person, including any party or Representative, for:

(1) Failing to comply with an order, rule, or procedure governing the proceeding;

(2) Failing to prosecute or defend an action; or

(3) Engaging in other misconduct that interferes with the speedy, orderly, or fair conduct of the hearing.

(b) Sanctions include but are not limited to those specifically set forth in paragraphs (c), (d), and (e) of this section. Any such sanction will reasonably relate to the severity and nature of the failure or misconduct.

(c) When a party fails to comply with an order, including an order for taking a deposition, the production of evidence within the party's control, or a request for admission, the ALJ may:

(1) Draw an inference in favor of the requesting party with regard to the information sought;

(2) In the case of requests for admission, deem each matter of which an admission is requested to be admitted;

(3) Prohibit the party failing to comply with such order from introducing evidence concerning, or otherwise relying upon, testimony relating to the information sought; and

(4) Strike any part of the pleadings or other submissions of the party failing to comply with such request.

(d) If a party fails to prosecute or defend an action under this part begun by service of a notice of hearing, the ALJ may dismiss the action or may issue an Initial Decision imposition penalties and assessments.

(e) The ALJ may refuse to consider any motion, request, response, brief or other Document that is not filed in a timely fashion.

§13.30 The hearing and burden of proof.

(a) The ALJ will conduct a hearing on the record in order to determine whether the Defendant is liable for a civil penalty or assessment under § 13.3 and, if so, the appropriate amount of any such civil penalty or assessment considering any aggravating or mitigating factors.

(b) The Authority will prove Defendant's liability and any aggravating factors by a preponderance of the evidence.

(c) The Defendant will prove any affirmative defenses and any mitigating factors by a preponderance of the evidence.

(d) The hearing will be open to the public unless otherwise ordered by the ALJ for good cause shown.

§13.31 Determining the amount of penalties and assessments.

(a) In determining an appropriate amount of civil penalties and assessments, the ALJ and the Authority Head, upon appeal, should evaluate any circumstances that mitigate or aggravate the violation and should articulate in their opinions the reasons that support the penalties and assessments they impose. Because of the intangible costs of fraud, the expense of investigating such conduct, and the need to deter others who might be similarly tempted, ordinarily double damages and a significant civil penalty should be imposed.

(b) Although not exhaustive, the following factors are among those that may influence the ALJ and the Authority Head in determining the amount of penalties and assessments to impose with respect to the misconduct (i.e., the false fictitious, of fraudulent Claims or Statements) charged in the Complaint:

(1) The number of false, fictitious, or fraudulent Claims or Statements;

(2) The time period over which such Claims or Statements were Made;

(3) The degree of the Defendant's culpability with respect to the misconduct;

(4) The amount of money or the value of the property, services, or Benefit falsely claimed;

(5) The value of the Government's actual loss as a result of the misconduct, including foreseeable consequential damages and the costs of investigation;

(6) The relationship of the amount imposed as civil penalties to the amount of the Government's loss;

(7) The potential or actual impact of the misconduct upon national defense, public health or safety, or public confidence in the management of Government programs and operations, including particularly the impact on the intended beneficiaries of such programs;

(8) Whether the Defendant has engaged in a pattern of the same or similar misconduct;

(9) Whether the Defendant attempted to conceal the misconduct;

(10) The degree to which the Defendant has involved others in the misconduct or in concealing it;

(11) Where the misconduct of employees or agents is imputed to the Defendant, the extent to which the Defendant's practices fostered or attempted to preclude such misconduct;

(12) Whether the Defendant cooperated in or obstructed an investigation of the misconduct;

(13) Whether the Defendant assisted in identifying and prosecuting other wrongdoers;

(14) The complexity of the program or transaction, and the degree of the Defendant's sophistication with respect to it, including the extent of the Defendant's prior participation in the program or in similar transactions;

(15) Whether the Defendant has been found, in any criminal, civil, or administrative proceeding to have engaged in similar misconduct or to have dealt dishonestly with the Government of the United States or of a State, directly or indirectly; and

(16) The need to deter the Defendant and others from engaging in the same or similar misconduct.

(c) Nothing in this section will be construed to limit the ALJ or the Authority Head from considering any other factors that in any given case may mitigate or aggravate the offense for which penalties and assessments are imposed.

§ 13.32   Location of hearing.

(a) The hearing may be held:

(1) In any judicial district of the United States in which the Defendant resides or transacts business;

(2) In any judicial district of the United States in which the Claim or Statement in issue was Made; or

(3) In such other place as may be agreed upon by the Defendant and the ALJ.

(b) Each party will have the opportunity to present written and oral argument with respect to the location of the hearing.

(c) The hearing will be held at the place and at the time ordered by the ALJ.

§ 13.33   Witnesses.

(a) Except as provided in paragraph (b) of this section, testimony at the hearing will be given orally by witnesses under oath or affirmation.

(b) At the discretion of the ALJ, testimony may be admitted in the form of a written Statement or deposition. Any such written Statement must be provided to all other parties along with the last known address of such witness, in a manner that allows sufficient time for other parties to subpoena such witness for cross-examination at the hearing. Prior written Statements of witnesses proposed to testify at the hearing and deposition transcripts will be exchanged as provided in § 13.22(a).

(c) The ALJ will exercise reasonable control over the mode and order of interrogating witnesses and presenting evidence so as to:

(1) Make the interrogation and presentation effective for the ascertainment of the truth;

(2) Avoid needless consumption of time; and

(3) Protect witnesses from harassment or undue embarrassment.

(d) The ALJ will permit the parties to conduct such cross-examination as may be required for a full and true disclosure of the facts.

(e) At the discretion of the ALJ, a witness may be cross-examined on matters relevant to the proceeding without regard to the scope of his or her direct examination. To the extent permitted by the ALJ, cross-examination on matters outside the scope of direct examination will be conducted in the manner of direct examination and may proceed by leading questions only if the witness is a hostile witness, an adverse party, or a witness identified with an adverse party.

(f) Upon motion of any party, the ALJ will order witnesses excluded so that they cannot hear the testimony of other witnesses. This rule does not authorize exclusion of:

(1) A party who is an Individual;

(2) In the case of a party that is not an Individual, an officer or employee of the party;

(i) Appearing for the entity pro se; or

(ii) Designated by the party's Representative; or

(3) An Individual whose presence is shown by a party to be essential to the presentation of its case, including an Individual employed by the Government engaged in assisting the Representative for the Government.

§ 13.34 Evidence.

(a) The ALJ will determine the admissibility of evidence.

(b) Except as provided in this part, the ALJ will not be bound by the Federal Rules of Evidence. However, the ALJ may apply the Federal Rules of Evidence where appropriate, e.g., to exclude unreliable evidence.

(c) The ALJ will exclude irrelevant and immaterial evidence.

(d) Although relevant, evidence may be excluded if its probative value is substantially outweighed by the danger of unfair prejudice, confusion of the issues, or by considerations of undue delay or needless presentation of cumulative evidence.

(e) Although relevant, evidence may be excluded if it is privileged under Federal law.

(f) Evidence concerning offers of compromise or settlement will be inadmissible to the extent provided in Rule 408 of the Federal Rules of Evidence.

(g) The ALJ will permit the parties to introduce rebuttal witnesses and evidence.

(h) All Documents and other evidence offered or taken for the record will be open to examination by all parties, un-

less otherwise ordered by the ALJ pursuant to § 13.24.

§ 13.35 The record.

(a) The hearing will be recorded and transcribed. Transcripts may be obtained following the hearing from the ALJ at a cost not to exceed the actual cost of duplication.

(b) The transcript of testimony, exhibits and other evidence admitted at the hearing, and all papers and requests filed in the proceeding constitute the record for the decision by the ALJ and the Authority Head.

(c) The record may be inspected and copied (upon payment of a reasonable fee) by anyone, unless otherwise ordered by the ALJ pursuant to § 13.24.

§ 13.36 Post-hearing briefs.

The ALJ may require the parties to file post-hearing briefs. In any event, any party may file a post-hearing brief. The ALJ will fix the time for filing such briefs. Such briefs may be accompanied by proposed findings of fact and conclusions of law. The ALJ may permit the parties to file reply briefs.

§ 13.37 Initial Decision.

(a) The ALJ will issue an Initial Decision based only on the record, which will contain findings of fact, conclusions of law, and the amount of any penalties and assessments imposed.

(b) The findings of fact will include a finding on each of the following issues:

(1) Whether the Claims or Statements identified in the Complaint, or any portions thereof, violate § 13.3;

(2) If the Person is liable for penalties or assessments, the appropriate amount of any such penalties or assessments considering any mitigating or aggravating factors that he or she finds in the case, such as those described in § 13.31.

(c) The ALJ will promptly serve the Initial Decision on all parties within 90 days after the time for submission of post-hearing briefs and reply briefs (if permitted) has expired. The ALJ will at the same time serve all parties with a Statement describing the right of any Defendant determined to be liable for a civil penalty or assessment to file a motion for reconsideration with the

ALJ or a notice of appeal with the Authority Head. If the ALJ fails to meet the deadline contained in this paragraph, he or she will notify the parties of the reason for the delay and will set a new deadline.

(d) Unless the Initial Decision of the ALJ is timely appealed to the Authority Head, or a motion for reconsideration of the Initial Decision is timely filed, the Initial Decision will constitute the final decision of the Authority Head and will be final and binding on the parties 30 days after it is issued by the ALJ.

§ 13.38 Reconsideration of Initial Decision.

(a) Except as provided in paragraph (d) of this section, any party may file a motion for reconsideration of the Initial Decision within 20 days of receipt of the Initial Decision. If service was Made by mail, receipt will be presumed to be five days from the date of mailing in the absence of contrary proof.

(b) Every such motion must set forth the matters claimed to have been erroneously decided and the nature of the alleged errors. Such motion will be accompanied by a supporting brief.

(c) Responses to such motions will be allowed only upon request of the ALJ.

(d) No party may file a motion for reconsideration of an Initial Decision that has been revised in response to a previous motion for reconsideration.

(e) The ALJ may dispose of a motion for reconsideration by denying it or by issuing a revised Initial Decision.

(f) If the ALJ denies a motion for reconsideration, the Initial Decision will constitute the final decision of the Authority Head and will be final and binding on the parties 30 days after the ALJ denies the motion, unless the Initial Decision is timely appealed to the Authority Head in accordance with § 13.39.

(g) If the ALJ issues a revised Initial Decision, that decision will constitute the final decision of the Authority Head and will be final and binding on the parties 30 days after it is issued, unless it is timely appealed to the Authority Head in accordance with § 13.39.

§ 13.39 Appeal to Authority Head.

(a) Any Defendant who has served a timely answer and who is determined in an Initial Decision to be liable for a civil penalty or assessment may appeal such decision to the Authority Head by filing a notice of appeal in accordance with this section and § 13.26.

(b)(1) A notice of appeal may be filed at any time within 30 days after the ALJ issues an Initial Decision. However, if another party files a motion for reconsideration under § 13.38, consideration of the appeal will be stayed automatically pending resolution of the motion for reconsideration.

(2) If a Defendant files a timely motion for reconsideration, a notice of appeal may be filed within 30 days after the ALJ denies the motion or issues a revised Initial Decision, whichever applies.

(3) The Authority Head may extend the initial 30-day period for an additional 30 days if the Defendant files with the Authority Head a request for an extension within the initial 30-day period and shows good cause.

(c) If the Defendant files a timely notice of appeal and the time for filing motions for reconsideration under § 13.38 has expired, the ALJ will forward two copies of the notice of appeal to the Authority Head, and will forward or Make available the record of the proceeding to the Authority Head.

(d) A notice of appeal will be accompanied by a written brief specifying exceptions to the Initial Decision and reasons supporting the exceptions.

(e) The Representative for the Government may file a brief in opposition to exceptions within 30 days of receiving the notice of appeal and accompanying brief.

(f) There is no right to appear personally before the Authority Head.

(g) There is no right to appeal any interlocutory ruling by the ALJ.

(h) In reviewing the Initial Decision, the Authority Head will not consider any objection that was not raised before the ALJ unless a demonstration is Made of extraordinary circumstances causing the failure to raise the objection.

(i) If any party demonstrates to the satisfaction of the Authority Head that additional evidence not presented at such hearing is material and that there were reasonable grounds for the failure to present such evidence at such hearing, the Authority Head will remand the matter to the ALJ for consideration of such additional evidence.

(j) The Authority Head may affirm, reduce, reverse, compromise, remand, or settle any penalty or assessment determined by the ALJ in any Initial Decision.

(k) The Authority Head will promptly serve each party to the appeal with a copy of the decision of the Authority Head and with a Statement describing the right of any Person determined to be liable for a penalty or assessment to seek judicial review.

(l) Unless a petition for review is filed as provided in 31 U.S.C. 3805 after a Defendant has exhausted all administrative remedies under this part and within 60 days after the date on which the Authority Head serves the Defendant with a copy of the Authority Head's decision, a determination that a Defendant is liable under §13.3 is final and is not subject to judicial review.

§13.40 Stays ordered by the Department of Justice.

If at any time the Attorney General or an Assistant Attorney General designated by the Attorney General transmits to the Authority Head a written finding that continuation of the administrative process described in this part with respect to a Claim or Statement may adversely affect any pending or potential criminal or civil action related to such Claim or Statement, the Authority Head will stay the process immediately. The Authority Head may order the process resumed only upon receipt of the written authorization of the Attorney General.

§13.41 Stay pending appeal.

(a) An Initial Decision is stayed automatically pending disposition of a motion for reconsideration or of an appeal to the Authority Head.

(b) No administrative stay is available following a final decision of the Authority Head.

§13.42 Judicial review.

Section 3805 of title 31, United States Code, authorizes judicial review by an appropriate United States District Court of a final decision of the Author-

ity Head imposing penalties or assessments under this part and specifies the procedures for such review.

§13.43 Collection of civil penalties and assessments.

Sections 3806 and 3808(b) of title 31, United States Code, authorize actions for collection of civil penalties and assessments imposed under this part and specify the procedures for such actions.

§13.44 Right to administrative offset.

The amount of any penalty or assessment that has become final, or for which a judgment has been entered under §13.42 or §13.43, or any amount agreed upon in a compromise or settlement under §13.46, may be collected by administrative offset under 31 U.S.C. 3716, except that an administrative offset may not be Made under that subsection against a refund of an overpayment of Federal taxes, then or later owing by the United States to the Defendant.

§13.45 Deposit in Treasury of United States.

All amounts collected pursuant to this part will be deposited as miscellaneous receipts in the Treasury of the United States, except as provided in 31 U.S.C. 3806(g).

§13.46 Compromise or settlement.

(a) Parties may Make offers of compromise or settlement at any time.

(b) The Reviewing Official has the exclusive authority to compromise or settle a case under this part at any time after the date on which the Reviewing Official is permitted to issue a Complaint and before the date on which the ALJ issues an Initial Decision.

(c) The Authority Head has exclusive authority to compromise or settle a case under this part at any time after the date on which the ALJ issues an Initial Decision, except during the pendency of any review under §13.42 or during the pendency of any action to collect penalties and assessments under §13.43.

(d) The Attorney General has exclusive authority to compromise or settle a case under this part during the pendency of any review under §13.42 or of any action to recover penalties and assessments under 31 U.S.C. 3806.

(e) The Investigating Official may recommend settlement terms to the Reviewing Official, the Authority Head, or the Attorney General, as appropriate. The Reviewing Official may recommend settlement terms to the Authority Head, or the Attorney General, as appropriate.

(f) Any compromise or settlement must be in writing and signed by all parties and their Representatives.

§ 13.47   Limitations.

(a) The notice of hearing with respect to a Claim or Statement must be served in the manner specified in § 13.8 within 6 years after the date on which such Claim or Statement is Made.

(b) If the Defendant fails to serve a timely answer, service of a notice under § 13.10(b) will be deemed a notice of hearing for purposes of this section.

(c) The statute of limitations may be extended by agreement of the parties.

PART 15—ENFORCEMENT OF NON-DISCRIMINATION ON THE BASIS OF DISABILITY IN PROGRAMS OR ACTIVITIES CONDUCTED BY THE DEPARTMENT OF HOMELAND SECURITY

AUTHORITY: Pub. L. 107-296, 116 Stat. 2135 (6 U.S.C. 1 et seq.); 5 U.S.C. 301; 29 U.S.C. 794.

SOURCE: 68 FR 10886, Mar. 6, 2003, unless otherwise noted.

§ 15.1   Purpose.

The purpose of this part is to effectuate section 504 of the Rehabilitation Act of 1973 ("Section 504"), as amended by section 119 of the Rehabilitation, Comprehensive Services, and Developmental Disabilities Amendments of 1978, which prohibits discrimination on the basis of disability in programs or activities conducted by Executive agencies. The provisions established by this part shall be effective for all components of the Department, including all Department components that are transferred to the Department, except to the extent that a Department component already has existing section 504 regulations.

§ 15.2   Application.

This part applies to all programs or activities conducted by the Department of Homeland Security (Department), except for programs or activities conducted outside the United States that do not involve individuals with a disability in the United States.

§ 15.3   Definitions.

For purposes of this part:

(a) *Auxiliary aids* means services or devices that enable persons with impaired sensory, manual, or speaking skills to have an equal opportunity to participate in, and enjoy the benefits of, programs or activities conducted by the Department. For example, auxiliary aids useful for persons with impaired vision include readers, materials in Braille, audio recordings and other similar services and devices. Auxiliary aids useful for persons with impaired hearing include telephone handset amplifiers, telephones compatible with hearing aids, telecommunications devices for deaf persons (TTYs), interpreters, notetakers, written materials and other similar services and devices.

(b) *Complete complaint* means a written statement that contains the complainant's name and address, and describes the Department's alleged discriminatory action in sufficient detail to inform the Department of the nature and date of the alleged violation of section 504. It shall be signed by the complainant or by someone authorized to do so on his or her behalf. Complaints filed on behalf of classes of individuals with disabilities shall also identify (where possible) the alleged victims of discrimination.

(c) *Facility* means all or any portion of a building, structure, equipment, road, walk, parking lot, rolling stock, or other conveyance, or other real or personal property.

(d) *Individual with a disability* means any person who has a physical or mental impairment that substantially limits one or more of the individual's major life activities, has a record of such an impairment, or is regarded as having such an impairment. For purposes of this definition:

(1) *Physical or mental impairment includes:*

(i) Any physiological disorder or condition, cosmetic disfigurement, or anatomical loss affecting one or more of the following body systems: Neurological; musculoskeletal; special sense organs; respiratory, including speech organs, cardiovascular; reproductive, digestive; genitourinary; hemic and lymphatic; skin; and endocrine; or

(ii) Any mental or psychological disorder such as mental retardation, organic brain syndrome, emotional or mental illness, and specific learning disabilities. The term *physical or mental impairment* includes, but is not limited to, such diseases and conditions as orthopedic, visual, speech and hearing impairments, cerebral palsy, epilepsy, muscular dystrophy, multiple sclerosis, cancer, heart disease, diabetes, mental retardation, emotional illness, drug addiction and alcoholism.

(2) *Major life activities* includes functions such as caring for one's self, performing manual tasks, walking, seeing, hearing, speaking, breathing, learning, and working.

(3) *Has a record of such an impairment* means has a history of, or has been misclassified as having, a mental or physical impairment that substantially limits one or more of the individual's major life activities.

(4) *Is regarded as having an impairment* means:

(i) Has a physical or mental impairment that does not substantially limit major life activities but is treated by the Department as constituting such a limitation;

(ii) Has a physical or mental impairment that substantially limits major life activities only as a result of the attitudes of others toward such impairment; or

(iii) Has none of the impairments defined in paragraph (e)(1) of this section but is treated by the Department as having such an impairment.

(e) *Qualified individual with a disability* means:

(1) With respect to a Department program or activity under which a person is required to perform services or to achieve a level of accomplishment, an individual with a disability who meets the essential eligibility requirements and who can achieve the purpose of the program or activity without modifications in the program or activity that the Department can demonstrate would result in a fundamental alteration in the nature of the program; and

(2) With respect to any other program or activity, an individual with a disability who meets the essential eligibility requirements for participation in, or receipt of benefits from, that program or activity.

(3) With respect to employment, an individual with a disability who satisfies the requisite skill, experience, education and other job-related requirements of the employment position such individual holds or desires, and who, with or without reasonable accommodation, can perform the essential functions of such position.

(f) *Section 504* means section 504 of the Rehabilitation Act of 1973 (29 U.S.C. 794), as amended. As used in this part, section 504 applies only to programs or activities conducted by Executive agencies and not to federally assisted programs.

§15.10 Self-evaluation.

(a) Except as provided in paragraph (d) of this section, the Department shall, not later than March 7, 2005, evaluate its current policies and practices, and the effects thereof, to determine if they meet the requirements of this part. To the extent modification of any such policy and practice is required, the Department shall proceed to make the necessary modifications.

(b) The Department shall provide an opportunity to interested persons, including individuals with a disability or organizations representing individuals with disabilities, to participate in the self-evaluation process.

(c) The Department shall, until three years following the completion of the self-evaluation, maintain on file and make available for public inspection:

(1) A description of areas examined and any problems identified;

(2) A description of any modifications made; and

(3) A list of participants in the self-evaluation process.

(d) If a component within the Department has already complied with the self-evaluation requirement of a regulation implementing section 504, then the requirements of this section shall apply to only those programs and activities conducted by that component that were not included in the previous self-evaluation.

§ 15.11 Notice.

The Department shall make available to all Department employees and interested persons information regarding the provisions of this part and its applicability to the programs or activities conducted by the Department, and make such information available to them in such a manner as is necessary to apprise them of the protections against discrimination assured them by section 504 and this part.

§ 15.30 General prohibitions against discrimination.

(a) No qualified individual with a disability in the United States, shall, by reason of his or her disability, be excluded from the participation in, be denied benefits of, or otherwise be subjected to discrimination under any program or activity conducted by the Department.

(b)(1) The Department, in providing any aid, benefit, or service, may not directly or through contractual, licensing, or other arrangements, on the basis of disability:

(i) Deny a qualified individual with a disability the opportunity to participate in or benefit from the aid, benefit, or service;

(ii) Afford a qualified individual with a disability an opportunity to participate in or benefit from the aid, benefit, or service that is not equal to that afforded others;

(iii) Provide a qualified individual with a disability with an aid, benefit, or service that is not as effective in affording equal opportunity to obtain the same result, to gain the same benefit, or to reach the same level of achievement as that provided to others;

(iv) Provide different or separate aid, benefits or services to individuals with a disability or to any class of individuals with a disability than is provided to others unless such action is necessary to provide qualified individuals with a disability with aid, benefits or services that are as effective as those provided to others;

(v) Deny a qualified individual with a disability the opportunity to participate as a member of planning or advisory boards; or

(vi) Otherwise limit a qualified individual with a disability in the enjoyment of any right, privilege, advantage, or opportunity enjoyed by others receiving the aid, benefit, or service.

(2) For purposes of this part, aids, benefits, and services, to be equally effective, are not required to produce the identical result or level of achievement for individuals with a disability and for nondisabled persons, but must afford individuals with a disability equal opportunity to obtain the same result, to gain the same benefit, or to reach the same level of achievement in the most integrated setting appropriate to the individual's needs.

(3) Even if the Department is permitted, under paragraph (b)(1)(iv) of this section, to operate a separate or different program for individuals with a disability or for any class of individuals with a disability, the Department must permit any qualified individual with a disability who wishes to participate in the program that is not separate or different to do so.

(4) The Department may not, directly or through contractual or other arrangements, utilize criteria or methods of administration the purpose or effect of which would:

(i) Subject qualified individuals with a disability to discrimination on the basis of disability; or

(ii) Defeat or substantially impair accomplishment of the objectives of a program or activity with respect to individuals with a disability.

(5) The Department may not, in determining the site or location of a facility, make selections the purpose or effect of which would:

(i) Exclude individuals with a disability from, deny them the benefits of, or otherwise subject them to discrimination under any program or activity conducted by the Department; or

(ii) Defeat or substantially impair the accomplishment of the objectives of a program or activity with respect to individuals with a disability.

(6) The Department, in the selection of procurement contractors, may not use criteria that subject qualified individuals with a disability to discrimination on the basis of disability.

(7) The Department may not administer a licensing or certification program in a manner that subjects qualified individuals with a disability to discrimination on the basis of disability, nor may the Department establish requirements for the programs or activities of licensees or certified entities that subject qualified individuals with a disability to discrimination on the basis of disability. However, the programs or activities of entities that are licensed or certified by the Department are not, themselves, covered by this part.

(c) The exclusion of nondisabled persons from the benefits of a program limited by Federal statute or Executive order to individuals with a disability or the exclusion of a specific class of individuals with a disability from a program limited by Federal statute or Executive order to a different class of individuals with a disability is not prohibited by this part.

(d) The Department shall administer programs and activities in the most integrated setting appropriate to the needs of qualified individuals with a disability.

§ 15.40 Employment.

No qualified individual with a disability shall, on the basis of that disability, be subjected to discrimination in employment under any program or activity conducted by the Department. The definitions, requirements and procedures of section 501 of the Rehabilitation Act of 1973 (29 U.S.C. 791), as established by the Equal Employment Op-

portunity Commission in 29 CFR part 1614, shall apply to employment of Federally conducted programs or activities.

§ 15.49 Program accessibility; discrimination prohibited.

Except as otherwise provided in § 15.50, no qualified individual with a disability shall, because the Department's facilities are inaccessible to or unusable by individuals with a disability, be denied the benefits of, be excluded from participation in, or otherwise be subjected to discrimination under any program or activity conducted by the Department.

§ 15.50 Program accessibility; existing facilities.

(a) General. The Department shall operate each program or activity so that the program or activity, when viewed in its entirety, is readily accessible to and usable by individuals with a disability. This paragraph (a) does not require the Department:

(1) To make structural alterations in each of its existing facilities in order to make them accessible to and usable by individuals with a disability where other methods are effective in achieving compliance with this section; or

(2) To take any action that it can demonstrate would result in a fundamental alteration in the nature of a program or activity or in undue financial and administrative burdens. In those circumstances where Department personnel believe that the proposed action would fundamentally alter the program or activity or would result in undue financial and administrative burdens, the Department has the burden of proving that compliance with this paragraph (a) of this section would result in such alteration or burdens. The decision that compliance would result in such alteration or burdens must be made by the Secretary of Homeland Security (or his or her designee) after considering all agency resources available for use in the funding and operation of the conducted program or activity and must be accompanied by a written statement of the reasons for reaching that conclusion. If an action would result in such an alteration or such burdens, the Department shall

take any other action that would not result in such an alteration or such burdens but would nevertheless ensure that individuals with a disability receive the benefits and services of the program or activity.

(b) *Methods.* The Department may comply with the requirements of this section through such means as redesign of equipment, reassignment of services to accessible buildings, assignment of aides to beneficiaries, home visits, delivery of services at alternate accessible sites, alteration of existing facilities and construction of new facilities, use of accessible rolling stock, or any other methods that result in making its programs or activities readily accessible to and usable by individuals with a disability. The Department, in making alterations to existing buildings, shall meet accessibility requirements to the extent required by the Architectural Barriers Act of 1968, as amended (42 U.S.C. 4151–4157), and any regulations implementing it. In choosing among available methods for meeting the requirements of this section, the Department shall give priority to those methods that offer programs and activities to qualified individuals with a disability in the most integrated setting appropriate.

(c) *Time period for compliance.* The Department shall comply with the obligations established under this section not later than May 5, 2003, except that where structural changes in facilities are undertaken, such changes shall be made not later than March 6, 2006, but in any event as expeditiously as possible. If a component within the Department has already complied with the accessibility requirements of a regulation implementing section 504, then the provisions of this paragraph shall apply only to facilities for that agency's programs and activities that were not previously made readily accessible to and usable by individuals with disabilities in compliance with that regulation.

(d) *Transition plan.* In the event that structural changes to facilities will be undertaken to achieve program accessibility, the Department shall develop not later than September 8, 2003, a transition plan setting forth the steps necessary to complete such changes.

The Department shall provide an opportunity to interested persons, including individuals with disabilities or organizations representing individuals with disabilities, to participate in the development of the transition plan by submitting comments (both telephonic and written). A copy of the transition plan shall be made available for public inspection. If a component of the Department has already complied with the transition plan requirement of a regulation implementing section 504, then the requirements of this paragraph shall apply only to the agency's facilities for programs and activities that were not included in the previous transition plan. The plan shall at a minimum:

(1) Identify physical obstacles in the Department's facilities that limit the physical accessibility of its programs or activities to individuals with disabilities;

(2) Describe in detail the methods that will be used to make the facilities accessible;

(3) Specify the schedule for taking the steps necessary to achieve compliance with this section and, if the time period of the transition plan is longer than one year, identify steps that will be taken during each year of the transition period; and

(4) Indicate the official responsible for implementation of the plan.

§ 15.51   Program accessibility; new construction and alterations.

Each building or part of a building that is constructed or altered by, on behalf of, or for the use of the Department shall be designed, constructed, or altered so as to be readily accessible to and usable by individuals with a disability. The definitions, requirements, and standards of the Architectural Barriers Act (42 U.S.C. 4151–4157), as established in 41 CFR 101–19.600 through 101–19.607 apply to buildings covered by this section.

§ 15.60   Communications.

(a) The Department shall take appropriate steps to effectively communicate with applicants, participants, personnel of other Federal entities, and members of the public.

(1) The Department shall furnish appropriate auxiliary aids where necessary to afford an individual with a disability an equal opportunity to participate in, and enjoy the benefits of, a program or activity conducted by the Department.

(i) In determining what type of auxiliary aid is necessary, the Department shall give primary consideration to the requests of the individual with a disability.

(ii) The Department need not provide individually prescribed devices, readers for personal use or study, or other devices of a personal nature to applicants or participants in programs.

(2) Where the Department communicates with applicants and beneficiaries by telephone, the Department shall use telecommunication devices for deaf persons (TTYs) or equally effective telecommunication systems to communicate with persons with impaired hearing.

(b) The Department shall make available to interested persons, including persons with impaired vision or hearing, information as to the existence and location of accessible services, activities, and facilities.

(c) The Department shall post notices at a primary entrance to each of its inaccessible facilities, directing users to an accessible facility, or to a location at which they can obtain information about accessible facilities. The international symbol for accessibility shall be used at each primary entrance of an accessible facility.

(d) This section does not require the Department to take any action that it can demonstrate would result in a fundamental alteration in the nature of a program or activity or in undue financial and administrative burdens.

(e) In those circumstances where Department personnel believe that the proposed action would fundamentally alter the program or activity or would result in undue financial and administrative burdens, the Department has the burden of proving that compliance with this section would result in such alteration or burdens. The decision that compliance would result in such alteration or burdens must be made by the Secretary of Homeland Security (or his or her designee) after considering all resources available for use in the funding and operation of the conducted program or activity and must be accompanied by a written statement of the reasons for reaching that conclusion. If an action required to comply with this section would result in such an alteration or such burdens, the Department shall take any other action that would not result in such an alteration or such burdens but would nevertheless ensure that, to the maximum extent possible, individuals with a disability receive the benefits and services of the program or activity.

§15.70 Compliance procedures.

(a) Except as provided in paragraph (b) of this section, this section applies to all allegations of discrimination on the basis of disability in programs and activities conducted by the Department.

(b) The Department shall process complaints alleging violations of section 504 with respect to employment according to the procedures established by the Equal Employment Opportunity Commission in 29 CFR part 1614.

(c) All other complaints alleging violations of section 504 may be sent to the Officer for Civil Rights and Civil Liberties, Department of Homeland Security, Washington, DC 20528. The Officer for Civil Rights and Civil Liberties shall be responsible for coordinating implementation of this section.

(d)(1) Any person who believes that he or she has been subjected to discrimination prohibited by this part may by him or herself, or by his or her authorized representative, file a complaint. Any person who believes that any specific class of persons has been subjected to discrimination prohibited by this part and who is a member of that class or the authorized representative of a member of that class may file a complaint.

(2) The Department shall accept and investigate all complete complaints over which it has jurisdiction.

(3) All complete complaints must be filed within 180 days of the alleged act of discrimination. The Department may extend this time period for good cause.

(e) If the Department receives a complaint over which it does not have jurisdiction, it shall promptly notify the complainant and shall make reasonable efforts to refer the complaint to the appropriate entity of the Federal government.

(f) The Department shall notify the Architectural and Transportation Barriers Compliance Board upon receipt of any complaint alleging that a building or facility that is subject to the Architectural Barriers Act of 1968, as amended (42 U.S.C. 4151–4157), is not readily accessible to and usable by individuals with disabilities.

(g)(1) Not later than 180 days from the receipt of a complete complaint over which it has jurisdiction, the Department shall notify the complainant of the results of the investigation in a letter containing:

(i) Findings of fact and conclusions of law;

(ii) A description of a remedy for each violation found; and

(iii) A notice of the right to appeal.

(2) Department employees are required to cooperate in the investigation and attempted resolution of complaints. Employees who are required to participate in any investigation under this section shall do so as part of their official duties and during the course of regular duty hours.

(3) If a complaint is resolved informally, the terms of the agreement shall be reduced to writing and made part of the complaint file, with a copy of the agreement provided to the complainant. The written agreement shall describe the subject matter of the complaint and any corrective action to which the parties have agreed.

(h) Appeals of the findings of fact and conclusions of law or remedies must be filed by the complainant not later than 60 days after receipt from the Department of the letter required by paragraph (g)(1) of this section. The Department may extend this time for good cause.

(i) Timely appeals shall be accepted and processed by the Officer for Civil Rights and Civil Liberties, or designee thereof, who will issue the final agency decision which may include appropriate corrective action to be taken by the Department.

(j) The Department shall notify the complainant of the results of the appeal within 30 days of the receipt of the appeal. If the Department determines that it needs additional information from the complainant, it shall have 30 days from the date it received the additional information to make its determination on the appeal.

(k) The time limits cited in paragraphs (g) and (j) of this section may be extended for an individual case when the Officer for Civil Rights and Civil Liberties determines that there is good cause, based on the particular circumstances of that case, for the extension.

(l) The Department may delegate its authority for conducting complaint investigations to other Federal agencies and may contract with nongovernment investigators to perform the investigation, but the authority for making the final determination may not be delegated to another agency.

PART 17—NONDISCRIMINATION ON THE BASIS OF SEX IN EDUCATION PROGRAMS OR ACTIVITIES RECEIVING FEDERAL FINANCIAL ASSISTANCE

Subpart A—Introduction

Subpart B—Coverage

AUTHORITY: Pub. L. 107–296, 116 Stat. 2135 (6 U.S.C. 1 *et seq.*); 5 U.S.C. 301; 20 U.S.C. 1681, 1682, 1683, 1685, 1686, 1687, 1688.

SOURCE: 68 FR 10892, Mar. 6, 2003, unless otherwise noted.

Subpart A—Introduction

§ 17.100 Purpose and effective date.

(a) The purpose of these Title IX regulations is to effectuate Title IX of the Education Amendments of 1972, as amended (except sections 904 and 906 of those Amendments) (20 U.S.C. 1681, 1682, 1683, 1685, 1686, 1687, 1688), which is designed to eliminate (with certain exceptions) discrimination on the basis of sex in any education program or activity receiving Federal financial assistance, whether or not such program or activity is offered or sponsored by an educational institution as defined in these Title IX regulations. The effective date of these Title IX regulations shall be March 6, 2003.

(b) The provisions established by this part shall be effective for all components of the Department, including all Department components that are transferred to the Department, except to the extent that a Department component already has existing Title IX regulations.

§ 17.105 Definitions.

As used in these Title IX regulations, the term:

(a) *Administratively separate unit* means a school, department, or college of an educational institution (other than a local educational agency) admission to which is independent of admission to any other component of such institution.

(b) *Admission* means selection for part-time, full-time, special, associate, transfer, exchange, or any other enrollment, membership, or matriculation in or at an education program or activity operated by a recipient.

(c) *Applicant* means one who submits an application, request, or plan required to be approved by an official of the Federal agency that awards Federal financial assistance, or by a recipient, as a condition to becoming a recipient.

(d) *Department* means Department of Homeland Security.

(e) *Designated agency official* means the Officer for Civil Rights and Civil Liberties, or the designee thereof.

(f) *Educational institution* means a local educational agency (LEA) as defined by 20 U.S.C. 8801(18), a preschool, a private elementary or secondary school, or an applicant or recipient

167

that is an institution of graduate higher education, an institution of undergraduate higher education, an institution of professional education, or an institution of vocational education, as defined in this section.

(g) *Federal financial assistance* means any of the following, when authorized or extended under a law administered by the Federal agency that awards such assistance:

(1) A grant or loan of Federal financial assistance, including funds made available for:

(i) The acquisition, construction, renovation, restoration, or repair of a building or facility or any portion thereof; and

(ii) Scholarships, loans, grants, wages, or other funds extended to any entity for payment to or on behalf of students admitted to that entity, or extended directly to such students for payment to that entity.

(2) A grant of Federal real or personal property or any interest therein, including surplus property, and the proceeds of the sale or transfer of such property, if the Federal share of the fair market value of the property is not, upon such sale or transfer, properly accounted for to the Federal Government.

(3) Provision of the services of Federal personnel.

(4) Sale or lease of Federal property or any interest therein at nominal consideration, or at consideration reduced for the purpose of assisting the recipient or in recognition of public interest to be served thereby, or permission to use Federal property or any interest therein without consideration.

(5) Any other contract, agreement, or arrangement that has as one of its purposes the provision of assistance to any education program or activity, except a contract of insurance or guaranty.

(h) *Institution of graduate higher education* means an institution that:

(1) Offers academic study beyond the bachelor of arts or bachelor of science degree, whether or not leading to a certificate of any higher degree in the liberal arts and sciences;

(2) Awards any degree in a professional field beyond the first professional degree (regardless of whether the first professional degree in such

field is awarded by an institution of undergraduate higher education or professional education); or

(3) Awards no degree and offers no further academic study, but operates ordinarily for the purpose of facilitating research by persons who have received the highest graduate degree in any field of study.

(i) *Institution of professional education* means an institution (except any institution of undergraduate higher education) that offers a program of academic study that leads to a first professional degree in a field for which there is a national specialized accrediting agency recognized by the Secretary of Education.

(j) *Institution of undergraduate higher education* means:

(1) An institution offering at least two but less than four years of college-level study beyond the high school level, leading to a diploma or an associate degree, or wholly or principally creditable toward a baccalaureate degree;

(2) An institution offering academic study leading to a baccalaureate degree; or

(3) An agency or body that certifies credentials or offers degrees, but that may or may not offer academic study.

(k) *Institution of vocational education* means a school or institution (except an institution of professional or graduate or undergraduate higher education) that has as its primary purpose preparation of students to pursue a technical, skilled, or semi-skilled occupation or trade, or to pursue study in a technical field, whether or not the school or institution offers certificates, diplomas, or degrees and whether or not it offers full-time study.

(l) *Recipient* means any State or political subdivision thereof or any instrumentality of a State or political subdivision thereof, any public or private agency, institution, or organization, or other entity, or any person, to whom Federal financial assistance is extended directly or through another recipient and that operates an education program or activity that receives such assistance, including any subunit, successor, assignee, or transferee thereof.

(m) *Reviewing authority* means that component of the Department delegated authority to review the decisions of hearing officers in cases arising under these Title IX regulations.

(n) *Secretary* means Secretary of the Department of Homeland Security.

(o) *Student* means a person who has gained admission.

(p) *Title IX* means Title IX of the Education Amendments of 1972, Public Law 92–318, 86 Stat. 235, 373 (codified as amended at 20 U.S.C. 1681–1688) (except sections 904 and 906 thereof), as amended by section 3 of Public Law 93–568, 88 Stat. 1855, by section 412 of the Education Amendments of 1976, Public Law 94–482, 90 Stat. 2234, and by section 3 of Public Law 100–259, 102 Stat. 28, 28–29 (20 U.S.C. 1681, 1682, 1683, 1685, 1686, 1687, 1688).

(q) *Title IX regulations* means the provisions of this part.

(r) *Transition plan* means a plan subject to the approval of the Secretary of Education pursuant to section 901(a)(2) of the Education Amendments of 1972 (20 U.S.C. 1681(a)(2)), under which an educational institution operates in making the transition from being an educational institution that admits only students of one sex to being one that admits students of both sexes without discrimination.

§17.110 **Remedial and affirmative action and self-evaluation.**

(a) *Remedial action.* If the designated agency official finds that a recipient has discriminated against persons on the basis of sex in an education program or activity, such recipient shall take such remedial action as the designated agency official deems necessary to overcome the effects of such discrimination.

(b) *Affirmative action.* In the absence of a finding of discrimination on the basis of sex in an education program or activity, a recipient may take affirmative action consistent with law to overcome the effects of conditions that resulted in limited participation therein by persons of a particular sex. Nothing in these Title IX regulations shall be interpreted to alter any affirmative action obligations that a recipient may have under Executive Order 11246, 3 CFR, 1964–1965 Comp., p. 339; as amended by Executive Order 11375, 3 CFR, 1966–1970 Comp., p. 684; as amended by Executive Order 11478, 3 CFR, 1966–1970 Comp., p. 803; as amended by Executive Order 12086, 3 CFR, 1978 Comp., p. 230; as amended by Executive Order 12107, 3 CFR, 1978 Comp., p. 264.

(c) *Self-evaluation.* Each recipient education institution shall, within one year of March 6, 2003:

(1) Evaluate, in terms of the requirements of these Title IX regulations, its current policies and practices and the effects thereof concerning admission of students, treatment of students, and employment of both academic and nonacademic personnel working in connection with the recipient's education program or activity;

(2) Modify any of these policies and practices that do not or may not meet the requirements of these Title IX regulations; and

(3) Take appropriate remedial steps to eliminate the effects of any discrimination that resulted or may have resulted from adherence to these policies and practices.

(d) *Availability of self-evaluation and related materials.* Recipients shall maintain on file for at least three years following completion of the evaluation required under paragraph (c) of this section, and shall provide to the designated agency official upon request, a description of any modifications made pursuant to paragraph (c)(2) of this section and of any remedial steps taken pursuant to paragraph (c)(3) of this section.

§17.115 **Assurance required.**

(a) *General.* Either at the application stage or the award stage, Federal agencies must ensure that applications for Federal financial assistance or awards of Federal financial assistance contain, be accompanied by, or be covered by a specifically identified assurance from the applicant or recipient, satisfactory to the designated agency official, that each education program or activity operated by the applicant or recipient and to which these Title IX regulations apply will be operated in compliance with these Title IX regulations. An assurance of compliance with these Title IX regulations shall not be satisfactory to the designated agency official if the applicant or recipient to whom such assurance applies fails to commit itself to take whatever remedial action is necessary in accordance with § 17.110(a) to eliminate existing discrimination on the basis of sex or to eliminate the effects of past discrimination whether occurring prior to or subsequent to the submission to the designated agency official of such assurance.

(b) *Duration of obligation.* (1) In the case of Federal financial assistance extended to provide real property or structures thereon, such assurance shall obligate the recipient or, in the case of a subsequent transfer, the transferee, for the period during which the real property or structures are used to provide an education program or activity.

(2) In the case of Federal financial assistance extended to provide personal property, such assurance shall obligate the recipient for the period during which it retains ownership or possession of the property.

(3) In all other cases such assurance shall obligate the recipient for the period during which Federal financial assistance is extended.

(c) *Form.* (1) The assurances required by paragraph (a) of this section, which may be included as part of a document that addresses other assurances or obligations, shall include that the applicant or recipient will comply with all applicable Federal statutes relating to nondiscrimination. These include but are not limited to: Title IX of the Education Amendments of 1972, as amended (20 U.S.C. 1681-1683, 1685-1688).

(2) The designated agency official will specify the extent to which such assurances will be required of the applicant's or recipient's subgrantees, contractors, subcontractors, transferees, or successors in interest.

§ 17.120   Transfers of property.

If a recipient sells or otherwise transfers property financed in whole or in part with Federal financial assistance to a transferee that operates any education program or activity, and the Federal share of the fair market value of the property is not upon such sale or transfer properly accounted for to the Federal Government, both the transferor and the transferee shall be deemed to be recipients, subject to the provisions of §§ 17.205 through 17.235(a).

§ 17.125   Effect of other requirements.

(a) *Effect of other Federal provisions.* The obligations imposed by these Title IX regulations are independent of, and do not alter, obligations not to discriminate on the basis of sex imposed by Executive Order 11246, 3 CFR, 1964-1965 Comp., p. 339; as amended by Executive Order 11375, 3 CFR, 1966-1970 Comp., p. 684; as amended by Executive Order 11478, 3 CFR, 1966-1970 Comp., p. 803; as amended by Executive Order 12087, 3 CFR, 1978 Comp., p. 230; as amended by Executive Order 12107, 3 CFR, 1978 Comp., p. 264; sections 704 and 855 of the Public Health Service Act (42 U.S.C. 295m, 298b-2); Title VII of the Civil Rights Act of 1964 (42 U.S.C. 2000e *et seq.*); the Equal Pay Act of 1963 (29 U.S.C. 206); and any other Act of Congress or Federal regulation.

(b) *Effect of State or local law or other requirements.* The obligation to comply with these Title IX regulations is not obviated or alleviated by any State or local law or other requirement that would render any applicant or student ineligible, or limit the eligibility of any applicant or student, on the basis of sex, to practice any occupation or profession.

(c) *Effect of rules or regulations of private organizations.* The obligation to comply with these Title IX regulations is not obviated or alleviated by any rule or regulation of any organization, club, athletic or other league, or association that would render any applicant or student ineligible to participate or limit the eligibility or participation of any applicant or student, on the basis of sex, in any education program or activity operated by a recipient and that receives Federal financial assistance.

§ 17.130   Effect of employment opportunities.

The obligation to comply with these Title IX regulations is not obviated or alleviated because employment opportunities in any occupation or profession are or may be more limited for members of one sex than for members of the other sex.

§ 17.135 Designation of responsible employee and adoption of grievance procedures.

(a) *Designation of responsible employee.* Each recipient shall designate at least one employee to coordinate its efforts to comply with and carry out its responsibilities under these Title IX regulations, including any investigation of any complaint communicated to such recipient alleging its noncompliance with these Title IX regulations or alleging any actions that would be prohibited by these Title IX regulations. The recipient shall notify all its students and employees of the name, office address, and telephone number of the employee or employees appointed pursuant to this paragraph.

(b) *Complaint procedure of recipient.* A recipient shall adopt and publish grievance procedures providing for prompt and equitable resolution of student and employee complaints alleging any action that would be prohibited by these Title IX regulations.

§ 17.140 Dissemination of policy.

(a) *Notification of policy.* (1) Each recipient shall implement specific and continuing steps to notify applicants for admission and employment, students and parents of elementary and secondary school students, employees, sources of referral of applicants for admission and employment, and all unions or professional organizations holding collective bargaining or professional agreements with the recipient, that it does not discriminate on the basis of sex in the educational programs or activities that it operates, and that it is required by Title IX and these Title IX regulations not to discriminate in such a manner. Such notification shall contain such information, and be made in such manner, as the designated agency official finds necessary to apprise such persons of the protections against discrimination assured them by Title IX and these Title IX regulations, but shall state at least that the requirement not to discriminate in education programs or activities extends to employment therein, and to admission thereto unless §§ 17.300 through 17.310 do not apply to the recipient, and that inquiries concerning the application of Title IX and

these Title IX regulations to such recipient may be referred to the employee designated pursuant to § 17.135, or to the designated agency official.

(2) Each recipient shall make the initial notification required by paragraph (a)(1) of this section within 90 days of March 6, 2003 or of the date these Title IX regulations first apply to such recipient, whichever comes later, which notification shall include publication in:

(i) Newspapers and magazines operated by such recipient or by student, alumnae, or alumni groups for or in connection with such recipient; and

(ii) Memoranda or other written communications distributed to every student and employee of such recipient.

(b) *Publications.* (1) Each recipient shall prominently include a statement of the policy described in paragraph (a) of this section in each announcement, bulletin, catalog, or application form that it makes available to any person of a type, described in paragraph (a) of this section, or which is otherwise used in connection with the recruitment of students or employees.

(2) A recipient shall not use or distribute a publication of the type described in paragraph (b)(1) of this section that suggests, by text or illustration, that such recipient treats applicants, students, or employees differently on the basis of sex except as such treatment is permitted by these Title IX regulations.

(c) *Distribution.* Each recipient shall distribute without discrimination on the basis of sex each publication described in paragraph (b)(1) of this section, and shall apprise each of its admission and employment recruitment representatives of the policy of nondiscrimination described in paragraph (a) of this section, and shall require such representatives to adhere to such policy.

Subpart B—Coverage

§ 17.200 Application.

Except as provided in §§ 17.205 through 17.235(a), these Title IX regulations apply to every recipient and to each education program or activity operated by such recipient that receives Federal financial assistance.

§ 17.205 **Educational institutions and other entities controlled by religious organizations.**

(a) *Exemption.* These Title IX regulations do not apply to any operation of an educational institution or other entity that is controlled by a religious organization to the extent that application of these Title IX regulations would not be consistent with the religious tenets of such organization.

(b) *Exemption claims.* An educational institution or other entity that wishes to claim the exemption set forth in paragraph (a) of this section shall do so by submitting in writing to the designated agency official a statement by the highest-ranking official of the institution, identifying the provisions of these Title IX regulations that conflict with a specific tenet of the religious organization.

§ 17.210 **Military and merchant marine educational institutions.**

These Title IX regulations do not apply to an educational institution whose primary purpose is the training of individuals for a military service of the United States or for the merchant marine.

§ 17.215 **Membership practices of certain organizations.**

(a) *Social fraternities and sororities.* These Title IX regulations do not apply to the membership practices of social fraternities and sororities that are exempt from taxation under section 501(a) of the Internal Revenue Code of 1954, 26 U.S.C. 501(a), the active membership of which consists primarily of students in attendance at institutions of higher education.

(b) *YMCA, YWCA, Girl Scouts, Boy Scouts, and Camp Fire Girls.* These Title IX regulations do not apply to the membership practices of the Young Men's Christian Association (YMCA), the Young Women's Christian Association (YWCA), the Girl Scouts, the Boy Scouts, and Camp Fire Girls.

(c) *Voluntary youth service organizations.* These Title IX regulations do not apply to the membership practices of a voluntary youth service organization that is exempt from taxation under section 501(a) of the Internal Revenue Code of 1986 (26 U.S.C. 501(a)), and the membership of which has been traditionally limited to members of one sex and principally to persons of less than nineteen years of age.

§ 17.220 **Admissions.**

(a) *General.* Admissions to educational institutions prior to June 24, 1973, are not covered by these Title IX regulations.

(b) *Administratively separate units.* For the purposes only of this section, §§ 17.225, 17.230, and 17.300 through 17.310, each administratively separate unit shall be deemed to be an educational institution.

(c) *Application of §§ 17.300 through 17.310.* Except as provided in paragraphs (d) and (e) of this section, §§ 17.300 through 17.310 apply to each recipient. A recipient to which §§ 17.300 through 17.310 apply shall not discriminate on the basis of sex in admission or recruitment in violation of §§ 17.300 through 17.310.

(d) *Educational institutions.* Except as provided in paragraph (e) of this section as to recipients that are educational institutions, §§ 17.300 through 17.310 apply only to institutions of vocational education, professional education, graduate higher education, and public institutions of undergraduate higher education.

(e) *Public institutions of undergraduate higher education.* Sections 17.300 through 17.310 do not apply to any public institution of undergraduate higher education that traditionally and continually from its establishment has had a policy of admitting students of only one sex.

§ 17.225 **Educational institutions eligible to submit transition plans.**

(a) *Application.* This section applies to each educational institution to which §§ 17.300 through 17.310 apply that:

(1) Admitted students of only one sex as regular students as of June 23, 1972; or

(2) Admitted students of only one sex as regular students as of June 23, 1965, but thereafter admitted, as regular students, students of the sex not admitted prior to June 23, 1965.

(b) Provision for transition plans. An educational institution to which this section applies shall not discriminate on the basis of sex in admission or recruitment in violation of §§17.300 through 17.310.

§17.230 Transition plans.

(a) *Submission of plans.* An institution to which §17.225 applies and that is composed of more than one administratively separate unit may submit either a single transition plan applicable to all such units, or a separate transition plan applicable to each such unit.

(b) *Content of plans.* In order to be approved by the Secretary of Education, a transition plan shall:

(1) State the name, address, and Federal Interagency Committee on Education Code of the educational institution submitting such plan, the administratively separate units to which the plan is applicable, and the name, address, and telephone number of the person to whom questions concerning the plan may be addressed. The person who submits the plan shall be the chief administrator or president of the institution, or another individual legally authorized to bind the institution to all actions set forth in the plan.

(2) State whether the educational institution or administratively separate unit admits students of both sexes as regular students and, if so, when it began to do so.

(3) Identify and describe with respect to the educational institution or administratively separate unit any obstacles to admitting students without discrimination on the basis of sex.

(4) Describe in detail the steps necessary to eliminate as soon as practicable each obstacle so identified and indicate the schedule for taking these steps and the individual directly responsible for their implementation.

(5) Include estimates of the number of students, by sex, expected to apply for, be admitted to, and enter each class during the period covered by the plan.

(c) *Nondiscrimination.* No policy or practice of a recipient to which §17.225 applies shall result in treatment of applicants to or students of such recipient in violation of §§17.300 through 17.310 unless such treatment is necessitated by an obstacle identified in paragraph (b)(3) of this section and a

schedule for eliminating that obstacle has been provided as required by paragraph (b)(4) of this section.

(d) *Effects of past exclusion.* To overcome the effects of past exclusion of students on the basis of sex, each educational institution to which §17.225 applies shall include in its transition plan, and shall implement, specific steps designed to encourage individuals of the previously excluded sex to apply for admission to such institution. Such steps shall include instituting recruitment programs that emphasize the institution's commitment to enrolling students of the sex previously excluded.

§17.235 Statutory amendments.

(a) This section, which applies to all provisions of these Title IX regulations, addresses statutory amendments to Title IX.

(b) These Title IX regulations shall not apply to or preclude:

(1) Any program or activity of the American Legion undertaken in connection with the organization or operation of any Boys State conference, Boys Nation conference, Girls State conference, or Girls Nation conference;

(2) Any program or activity of a secondary school or educational institution specifically for:

(i) The promotion of any Boys State conference, Boys Nation conference, Girls State conference, or Girls Nation conference; or

(ii) The selection of students to attend any such conference;

(3) Father-son or mother-daughter activities at an educational institution or in an education program or activity, but if such activities are provided for students of one sex, opportunities for reasonably comparable activities shall be provided to students of the other sex;

(4) Any scholarship or other financial assistance awarded by an institution of higher education to an individual because such individual has received such award in a single-sex pageant based upon a combination of factors related to the individual's personal appearance, poise, and talent. The pageant, however, must comply with other nondiscrimination provisions of Federal law.

173

(c) For purposes of these Title IX regulations, program or activity or program means:

(1) All of the operations of any entity described in paragraphs (c)(1)(i) through (iv) of this section, any part of which is extended Federal financial assistance:

(i)(A) A department, agency, special purpose district, or other instrumentality of a State or of a local government; or

(B) The entity of such State or local government that distributes such assistance and each such department or agency (and each other State or local government entity) to which the assistance is extended, in the case of assistance to a State or local government;

(ii)(A) A college, university, or other postsecondary institution, or a public system of higher education; or

(B) A local educational agency (as defined in 20 U.S.C. 8801), system of vocational education, or other school system;

(iii)(A) An entire corporation, partnership, or other private organization, or an entire sole proprietorship:

(1) If assistance is extended to such corporation, partnership, private organization, or sole proprietorship as a whole; or

(2) Which is principally engaged in the business of providing education, health care, housing, social services, or parks and recreation; or

(B) The entire plant or other comparable, geographically separate facility to which Federal financial assistance is extended, in the case of any other corporation, partnership, private organization, or sole proprietorship; or

(iv) Any other entity that is established by two or more of the entities described in paragraphs (c)(1)(i), (ii), or (iii) of this section.

(2)(i) Program or activity does not include any operation of an entity that is controlled by a religious organization if the application of 20 U.S.C. 1681 to such operation would not be consistent with the religious tenets of such organization.

(ii) For example, all of the operations of a college, university, or other postsecondary institution, including but not limited to traditional educational operations, faculty and student housing, campus shuttle bus service, campus restaurants, the bookstore, and other commercial activities are part of a program or activity subject to these Title IX regulations if the college, university, or other institution receives Federal financial assistance.

(d)(1) Nothing in these Title IX regulations shall be construed to require or prohibit any person, or public or private entity, to provide or pay for any benefit or service, including the use of facilities, related to an abortion. Medical procedures, benefits, services, and the use of facilities, necessary to save the life of a pregnant woman or to address complications related to an abortion are not subject to this section.

(2) Nothing in this section shall be construed to permit a penalty to be imposed on any person or individual because such person or individual is seeking or has received any benefit or service related to a legal abortion. Accordingly, subject to paragraph (d)(1) of this section, no person shall be excluded from participation in, be denied the benefits of, or be subjected to discrimination under any academic, extracurricular, research, occupational training, employment, or other educational program or activity operated by a recipient that receives Federal financial assistance because such individual has sought or received, or is seeking, a legal abortion, or any benefit or service related to a legal abortion.

Subpart C—Discrimination on the Basis of Sex in Admission and Recruitment Prohibited

§ 17.300 Admission.

(a) *General.* No person shall, on the basis of sex, be denied admission, or be subjected to discrimination in admission, by any recipient to which §§ 17.300 through 17.310 apply, except as provided in §§ 17.225 and 17.230.

(b) *Specific prohibitions.* (1) In determining whether a person satisfies any policy or criterion for admission, or in making any offer of admission, a recipient to which §§ 17.300 through 17.310 apply shall not:

(i) Give preference to one person over another on the basis of sex, by ranking applicants separately on such basis, or otherwise;

(ii) Apply numerical limitations upon the number or proportion of persons of either sex who may be admitted; or

(iii) Otherwise treat one individual differently from another on the basis of sex.

(2) A recipient shall not administer or operate any test or other criterion for admission that has a disproportionately adverse effect on persons on the basis of sex unless the use of such test or criterion is shown to predict validly success in the education program or activity in question and alternative tests or criteria that do not have such a disproportionately adverse effect are shown to be unavailable.

(c) *Prohibitions relating to marital or parental status.* In determining whether a person satisfies any policy or criterion for admission, or in making any offer of admission, a recipient to which §§ 17.300 through 17.310 apply:

(1) Shall not apply any rule concerning the actual or potential parental, family, or marital status of a student or applicant that treats persons differently on the basis of sex;

(2) Shall not discriminate against or exclude any person on the basis of pregnancy, childbirth, termination of pregnancy, or recovery therefrom, or establish or follow any rule or practice that so discriminates or excludes;

(3) Subject to § 17.235(d), shall treat disabilities related to pregnancy, childbirth, termination of pregnancy, or recovery therefrom in the same manner and under the same policies as any other temporary disability or physical condition; and

(4) Shall not make pre-admission inquiry as to the marital status of an applicant for admission, including whether such applicant is "Miss" or "Mrs." A recipient may make pre-admission inquiry as to the sex of an applicant for admission, but only if such inquiry is made equally of such applicants of both sexes and if the results of such inquiry are not used in connection with discrimination prohibited by these Title IX regulations.

§ 17.305 Preference in admission.

A recipient to which §§ 17.300 through 17.310 apply shall not give preference to applicants for admission, on the basis of attendance at any educational institution or other school or entity that admits as students only or predominantly members of one sex, if the giving of such preference has the effect of discriminating on the basis of sex in violation of §§ 17.300 through 17.310.

§ 17.310 Recruitment.

(a) *Nondiscriminatory recruitment.* A recipient to which §§ 17.300 through 17.310 apply shall not discriminate on the basis of sex in the recruitment and admission of students. A recipient may be required to undertake additional recruitment efforts for one sex as remedial action pursuant to § 17.110(a), and may choose to undertake such efforts as affirmative action pursuant to § 17.110(b).

(b) *Recruitment at certain institutions.* A recipient to which §§ 17.300 through 17.310 apply shall not recruit primarily or exclusively at educational institutions, schools, or entities that admit as students only or predominantly members of one sex, if such actions have the effect of discriminating on the basis of sex in violation of §§ 17.300 through 17.310.

Subpart D—Discrimination on the Basis of Sex in Education Programs or Activities Prohibited

§ 17.400 Education programs or activities.

(a) *General.* Except as provided elsewhere in these Title IX regulations, no person shall, on the basis of sex, be excluded from participation in, be denied the benefits of, or be subjected to discrimination under any academic, extracurricular, research, occupational training, or other education program or activity operated by a recipient that receives Federal financial assistance. Sections 17.400 through 17.455 do not apply to actions of a recipient in connection with admission of its students to an education program or activity of a recipient to which §§ 17.300 through 17.310 do not apply, or an entity, not a recipient, to which §§ 17.300 through 17.310 would not apply if the entity were a recipient.

(b) *Specific prohibitions.* Except as provided in §§ 17.400 through 17.455, in providing any aid, benefit, or service to a student, a recipient shall not, on the basis of sex:

(1) Treat one person differently from another in determining whether such person satisfies any requirement or condition for the provision of such aid, benefit, or service;

(2) Provide different aid, benefits, or services or provide aid, benefits, or services in a different manner;

(3) Deny any person any such aid, benefit, or service;

(4) Subject any person to separate or different rules of behavior, sanctions, or other treatment;

(5) Apply any rule concerning the domicile or residence of a student or applicant, including eligibility for in-state fees and tuition;

(6) Aid or perpetuate discrimination against any person by providing significant assistance to any agency, organization, or person that discriminates on the basis of sex in providing any aid, benefit, or service to students or employees; or

(7) Otherwise limit any person in the enjoyment of any right, privilege, advantage, or opportunity.

(c) *Assistance administered by a recipient educational institution to study at a foreign institution.* A recipient educational institution may administer or assist in the administration of scholarships, fellowships, or other awards established by foreign or domestic wills, trusts, or similar legal instruments, or by acts of foreign governments and restricted to members of one sex, that are designed to provide opportunities to study abroad, and that are awarded to students who are already matriculating at or who are graduates of the recipient institution; Provided, that a recipient educational institution that administers or assists in the administration of such scholarships, fellowships, or other awards that are restricted to members of one sex provides, or otherwise makes available, reasonable opportunities for similar studies for members of the other sex. Such opportunities may be derived from either domestic or foreign sources.

(d) *Aids, benefits or services not provided by recipient.* (1) This paragraph (d) applies to any recipient that requires participation by any applicant, student, or employee in any education program or activity not operated wholly by such recipient, or that facilitates, permits, or considers such participation as part of or equivalent to an education program or activity operated by such recipient, including participation in educational consortia and cooperative employment and student-teaching assignments.

(2) Such recipient:

(i) Shall develop and implement a procedure designed to assure itself that the operator or sponsor of such other education program or activity takes no action affecting any applicant, student, or employee of such recipient that these Title IX regulations would prohibit such recipient from taking; and

(ii) Shall not facilitate, require, permit, or consider such participation if such action occurs.

§ 17.405 Housing.

(a) *General.* A recipient shall not, on the basis of sex, apply different rules or regulations, impose different fees or requirements, or offer different services or benefits related to housing, except as provided in this section (including housing provided only to married students).

(b) *Housing provided by recipient.* (1) A recipient may provide separate housing on the basis of sex.

(2) Housing provided by a recipient to students of one sex, when compared to that provided to students of the other sex, shall be as a whole:

(i) Proportionate in quantity to the number of students of that sex applying for such housing; and

(ii) Comparable in quality and cost to the student.

(c) *Other housing.* (1) A recipient shall not, on the basis of sex, administer different policies or practices concerning occupancy by its students of housing other than that provided by such recipient.

(2)(i) A recipient which, through solicitation, listing, approval of housing, or otherwise, assists any agency, organization, or person in making housing available to any of its students, shall

176

take such reasonable action as may be necessary to assure itself that such housing as is provided to students of one sex, when compared to that provided to students of the other sex, is as a whole:

(A) Proportionate in quantity; and

(B) Comparable in quality and cost to the student.

(ii) A recipient may render such assistance to any agency, organization, or person that provides all or part of such housing to students of only one sex.

§ 17.410 Comparable facilities.

A recipient may provide separate toilet, locker room, and shower facilities on the basis of sex, but such facilities provided for students of one sex shall be comparable to such facilities provided for students of the other sex.

§ 17.415 Access to course offerings.

(a) A recipient shall not provide any course or otherwise carry out any of its education program or activity separately on the basis of sex, or require or refuse participation therein by any of its students on such basis, including health, physical education, industrial, business, vocational, technical, home economics, music, and adult education courses.

(b)(1) With respect to physical education classes and activities at the elementary school level, the recipient shall comply fully with this section as expeditiously as possible, but in no event later than one year from March 6, 2003. With respect to physical education classes and activities at the secondary and post-secondary levels, the recipient shall comply fully with this section as expeditiously as possible but in no event later than three years from March 6, 2003.

(2) This section does not prohibit grouping of students in physical education classes and activities by ability as assessed by objective standards of individual performance developed and applied without regard to sex.

(3) This section does not prohibit separation of students by sex within physical education classes or activities during participation in wrestling, boxing, rugby, ice hockey, football, basketball, and other sports the purpose or major activity of which involves bodily contact.

(4) Where use of a single standard of measuring skill or progress in a physical education class has an adverse effect on members of one sex, the recipient shall use appropriate standards that do not have such effect.

(5) Portions of classes in elementary and secondary schools, or portions of education programs or activities, that deal exclusively with human sexuality may be conducted in separate sessions for boys and girls.

(6) Recipients may make requirements based on vocal range or quality that may result in a chorus or choruses of one or predominantly one sex.

§ 17.420 Access to schools operated by LEAs.

A recipient that is a local educational agency shall not, on the basis of sex, exclude any person from admission to:

(a) Any institution of vocational education operated by such recipient; or

(b) Any other school or educational unit operated by such recipient, unless such recipient otherwise makes available to such person, pursuant to the same policies and criteria of admission, courses, services, and facilities comparable to each course, service, and facility offered in or through such schools.

§ 17.425 Counseling and use of appraisal and counseling materials.

(a) *Counseling.* A recipient shall not discriminate against any person on the basis of sex in the counseling or guidance of students or applicants for admission.

(b) *Use of appraisal and counseling materials.* A recipient that uses testing or other materials for appraising or counseling students shall not use different materials for students on the basis of their sex or use materials that permit or require different treatment of students on such basis unless such different materials cover the same occupations and interest areas and the use of such different materials is shown to be essential to eliminate sex bias. Recipients shall develop and use internal procedures for ensuring that such materials do not discriminate on the basis of sex. Where the use of a counseling test or other instrument results in a substantially disproportionate number of members of one sex in any particular course of study or classification, the recipient shall take such action as is necessary to assure itself that such disproportion is not the result of discrimination in the instrument or its application.

(c) *Disproportion in classes.* Where a recipient finds that a particular class contains a substantially disproportionate number of individuals of one sex, the recipient shall take such action as is necessary to assure itself that such disproportion is not the result of discrimination on the basis of sex in counseling or appraisal materials or by counselors.

§ 17.430   Financial assistance.

(a) *General.* Except as provided in paragraphs (b) and (c) of this section, in providing financial assistance to any of its students, a recipient shall not:

(1) On the basis of sex, provide different amounts or types of such assistance, limit eligibility for such assistance that is of any particular type or source, apply different criteria, or otherwise discriminate;

(2) Through solicitation, listing, approval, provision of facilities, or other services, assist any foundation, trust, agency, organization, or person that provides assistance to any of such recipient's students in a manner that discriminates on the basis of sex; or

(3) Apply any rule or assist in application of any rule concerning eligibility for such assistance that treats persons of one sex differently from persons of the other sex with regard to marital or parental status.

(b) *Financial aid established by certain legal instruments.* (1) A recipient may administer or assist in the administration of scholarships, fellowships, or other forms of financial assistance established pursuant to domestic or foreign wills, trusts, bequests, or similar legal instruments or by acts of a foreign government that require that awards be made to members of a particular sex specified therein; Provided, that the overall effect of the award of such sex-restricted scholarships, fellowships, and other forms of financial

assistance does not discriminate on the basis of sex.

(2) To ensure nondiscriminatory awards of assistance as required in paragraph (b)(1) of this section, recipients shall develop and use procedures under which:

(i) Students are selected for award of financial assistance on the basis of nondiscriminatory criteria and not on the basis of availability of funds restricted to members of a particular sex.

(ii) An appropriate sex-restricted scholarship, fellowship, or other form of financial assistance is allocated to each student selected under paragraph (b)(2)(i) of this section; and

(iii) No student is denied the award for which he or she was selected under paragraph (b)(2)(i) of this section because of the absence of a scholarship, fellowship, or other form of financial assistance designated for a member of that student's sex.

(c) *Athletic scholarships.* (1) To the extent that a recipient awards athletic scholarships or grants-in-aid, it must provide reasonable opportunities for such awards for members of each sex in proportion to the number of students of each sex participating in interscholastic or intercollegiate athletics.

(2) A recipient may provide separate athletic scholarships or grants-in-aid for members of each sex as part of separate athletic teams for members of each sex to the extent consistent with this paragraph (c) and § 17.450.

§ 17.435   Employment assistance to students.

(a) *Assistance by recipient in making available outside employment.* A recipient that assists any agency, organization, or person in making employment available to any of its students:

(1) Shall assure itself that such employment is made available without discrimination on the basis of sex; and

(2) Shall not render such services to any agency, organization, or person that discriminates on the basis of sex in its employment practices.

(b) *Employment of students by recipients.* A recipient that employs any of its students shall not do so in a manner that violates §§ 17.500 through 17.550.

§17.440 Health and insurance benefits and services.

Subject to §17.235(d), in providing a medical, hospital, accident, or life insurance benefit, service, policy, or plan to any of its students, a recipient shall not discriminate on the basis of sex, or provide such benefit, service, policy, or plan in a manner that would violate §§17.500 through 17.550 if it were provided to employees of the recipient. This section shall not prohibit a recipient from providing any benefit or service that may be used by a different proportion of students of one sex than of the other, including family planning services. However, any recipient that provides full coverage health service shall provide gynecological care.

§17.445 Marital or parental status.

(a) *Status generally.* A recipient shall not apply any rule concerning a student's actual or potential parental, family, or marital status that treats students differently on the basis of sex.

(b) *Pregnancy and related conditions.* (1) A recipient shall not discriminate against any student, or exclude any student from its education program or activity, including any class or extracurricular activity, on the basis of such student's pregnancy, childbirth, false pregnancy, termination of pregnancy, or recovery therefrom, unless the student requests voluntarily to participate in a separate portion of the program or activity of the recipient.

(2) A recipient may require such a student to obtain the certification of a physician that the student is physically and emotionally able to continue participation as long as such a certification is required of all students for other physical or emotional conditions requiring the attention of a physician.

(3) A recipient that operates a portion of its education program or activity separately for pregnant students, admittance to which is completely voluntary on the part of the student as provided in paragraph (b)(1) of this section, shall ensure that the separate portion is comparable to that offered to non-pregnant students.

(4) Subject to §17.235(d), a recipient shall treat pregnancy, childbirth, false pregnancy, termination of pregnancy and recovery therefrom in the same

manner and under the same policies as any other temporary disability with respect to any medical or hospital benefit, service, plan, or policy that such recipient administers, operates, offers, or participates in with respect to students admitted to the recipient's educational program or activity.

(5) In the case of a recipient that does not maintain a leave policy for its students, or in the case of a student who does not otherwise qualify for leave under such a policy, a recipient shall treat pregnancy, childbirth, false pregnancy, termination of pregnancy, and recovery therefrom as a justification for a leave of absence for as long a period of time as is deemed medically necessary by the student's physician, at the conclusion of which the student shall be reinstated to the status that she held when the leave began.

§17.450 Athletics.

(a) *General.* No person shall, on the basis of sex, be excluded from participation in, be denied the benefits of, be treated differently from another person, or otherwise be discriminated against in any interscholastic, intercollegiate, club, or intramural athletics offered by a recipient, and no recipient shall provide any such athletics separately on such basis.

(b) *Separate teams.* Notwithstanding the requirements of paragraph (a) of this section, a recipient may operate or sponsor separate teams for members of each sex where selection for such teams is based upon competitive skill or the activity involved is a contact sport. However, where a recipient operates or sponsors a team in a particular sport for members of one sex but operates or sponsors no such team for members of the other sex, and athletic opportunities for members of that sex have previously been limited, members of the excluded sex must be allowed to try out for the team offered unless the sport involved is a contact sport. For the purposes of these Title IX regulations, contact sports include boxing, wrestling, rugby, ice hockey, football, basketball, and other sports the purpose or major activity of which involves bodily contact.

(c) *Equal opportunity.* (1) A recipient that operates or sponsors interscholastic, intercollegiate, club, or intramural athletics shall provide equal athletic opportunity for members of both sexes. In determining whether equal opportunities are available, the designated agency official will consider, among other factors:

(i) Whether the selection of sports and levels of competition effectively accommodate the interests and abilities of members of both sexes;

(ii) The provision of equipment and supplies;

(iii) Scheduling of games and practice time;

(iv) Travel and per diem allowance;

(v) Opportunity to receive coaching and academic tutoring;

(vi) Assignment and compensation of coaches and tutors;

(vii) Provision of locker rooms, practice, and competitive facilities;

(viii) Provision of medical and training facilities and services;

(ix) Provision of housing and dining facilities and services; and

(x) Publicity.

(2) For purposes of paragraph (c)(1) of this section, unequal aggregate expenditures for members of each sex or unequal expenditures for male and female teams if a recipient operates or sponsors separate teams will not constitute noncompliance with this section, but the designated agency official may consider the failure to provide necessary funds for teams for one sex in assessing equality of opportunity for members of each sex.

(d) *Adjustment period.* A recipient that operates or sponsors interscholastic, intercollegiate, club, or intramural athletics at the elementary school level shall comply fully with this section as expeditiously as possible but in no event later than one year from March 6, 2003. A recipient that operates or sponsors interscholastic, intercollegiate, club, or intramural athletics at the secondary or postsecondary school level shall comply fully with this section as expeditiously as possible but in no event later than three years from March 6, 2003.

§ 17.455 Textbooks and curricular material.

Nothing in these Title IX regulations shall be interpreted as requiring or prohibiting or abridging in any way the use of particular textbooks or curricular materials.

Subpart E—Discrimination on the Basis of Sex in Employment in Education Programs or Activities Prohibited

§ 17.500 Employment.

(a) *General.* (1) No person shall, on the basis of sex, be excluded from participation in, be denied the benefits of, or be subjected to discrimination in employment, or recruitment, consideration, or selection therefore, whether full-time or part-time, under any education program or activity operated by a recipient that receives Federal financial assistance.

(2) A recipient shall make all employment decisions in any education program or activity operated by such recipient in a nondiscriminatory manner and shall not limit, segregate, or classify applicants or employees in any way that could adversely affect any applicant's or employee's employment opportunities or status because of sex.

(3) A recipient shall not enter into any contractual or other relationship which directly or indirectly has the effect of subjecting employees or students to discrimination prohibited by §§ 17.500 through 17.550, including relationships with employment and referral agencies, with labor unions, and with organizations providing or administering fringe benefits to employees of the recipient.

(4) A recipient shall not grant preferences to applicants for employment on the basis of attendance at any educational institution or entity that admits as students only or predominantly members of one sex, if the giving of such preferences has the effect of discriminating on the basis of sex in violation of these Title IX regulations.

(b) *Application.* Sections 17.500 through 17.550 apply to:

(1) Recruitment, advertising, and the process of application for employment;

(2) Hiring, upgrading, promotion, consideration for and award of tenure, demotion, transfer, layoff, termination, application of nepotism policies, right of return from layoff, and rehiring;

(3) Rates of pay or any other form of compensation, and changes in compensation;

(4) Job assignments, classifications, and structure, including position descriptions, lines of progression, and seniority lists;

(5) The terms of any collective bargaining agreement;

(6) Granting and return from leaves of absence, leave for pregnancy, childbirth, false pregnancy, termination of pregnancy, leave for persons of either sex to care for children or dependents, or any other leave;

(7) Fringe benefits available by virtue of employment, whether or not administered by the recipient;

(8) Selection and financial support for training, including apprenticeship, professional meetings, conferences, and other related activities, selection for tuition assistance, selection for sabbaticals and leaves of absence to pursue training;

(9) Employer-sponsored activities, including social or recreational programs; and

(10) Any other term, condition, or privilege of employment.

§17.505 Employment criteria.

A recipient shall not administer or operate any test or other criterion for any employment opportunity that has a disproportionately adverse effect on persons on the basis of sex unless:

(a) Use of such test or other criterion is shown to predict validly successful performance in the position in question; and

(b) Alternative tests or criteria for such purpose, which do not have such disproportionately adverse effect, are shown to be unavailable.

§17.510 Recruitment.

(a) *Nondiscriminatory recruitment and hiring.* A recipient shall not discriminate on the basis of sex in the recruitment and hiring of employees. Where a recipient has been found to be presently discriminating on the basis of sex in the recruitment or hiring of employees, or has been found to have so discriminated in the past, the recipient shall recruit members of the sex so discriminated against so as to overcome the effects of such past or present discrimination.

(b) *Recruitment patterns.* A recipient shall not recruit primarily or exclusively at entities that furnish as applicants only or predominantly members of one sex if such actions have the effect of discriminating on the basis of sex in violation of §§17.500 through 17.550.

§17.515 Compensation.

A recipient shall not make or enforce any policy or practice that, on the basis of sex:

(a) Makes distinctions in rates of pay or other compensation;

(b) Results in the payment of wages to employees of one sex at a rate less than that paid to employees of the opposite sex for equal work on jobs the performance of which requires equal skill, effort, and responsibility, and that are performed under similar working conditions.

§17.520 Job classification and structure.

A recipient shall not:

(a) Classify a job as being for males or for females;

(b) Maintain or establish separate lines of progression, seniority lists, career ladders, or tenure systems based on sex; or

(c) Maintain or establish separate lines of progression, seniority systems, career ladders, or tenure systems for similar jobs, position descriptions, or job requirements that classify persons on the basis of sex, unless sex is a bona fide occupational qualification for the positions in question as set forth in §17.550.

§17.525 Fringe benefits.

(a) *"Fringe benefits" defined.* For purposes of these Title IX regulations, the term fringe benefits means any medical, hospital, accident, life insurance, or retirement benefit, service, policy or plan, any profit-sharing or bonus plan, leave, and any other benefit or service

181

of employment not subject to the provisions of § 17.515.

(b) *Prohibitions.* A recipient shall not:

(1) Discriminate on the basis of sex with regard to making fringe benefits available to employees or make fringe benefits available to spouses, families, or dependents of employees differently upon the basis of the employee's sex;

(2) Administer, operate, offer, or participate in a fringe benefit plan that does not provide for equal periodic benefits for members of each sex and for equal contributions to the plan by such recipient for members of each sex; or

(3) Administer, operate, offer, or participate in a pension or retirement plan that establishes different optional or compulsory retirement ages based on sex or that otherwise discriminates in benefits on the basis of sex.

§ 17.530 Marital or parental status.

(a) *General.* A recipient shall not apply any policy or take any employment action:

(1) Concerning the potential marital, parental, or family status of an employee or applicant for employment that treats persons differently on the basis of sex; or

(2) Which is based upon whether an employee or applicant for employment is the head of household or principal wage earner in such employee's or applicant's family unit.

(b) *Pregnancy.* A recipient shall not discriminate against or exclude from employment any employee or applicant for employment on the basis of pregnancy, childbirth, false pregnancy, termination of pregnancy, or recovery therefrom.

(c) *Pregnancy as a temporary disability.* Subject to § 17.235(d), a recipient shall treat pregnancy, childbirth, false pregnancy, termination of pregnancy, recovery therefrom, and any temporary disability resulting therefrom as any other temporary disability for all job-related purposes, including commencement, duration, and extensions of leave, payment of disability income, accrual of seniority and any other benefit or service, and reinstatement, and under any fringe benefit offered to employees by virtue of employment.

(d) *Pregnancy leave.* In the case of a recipient that does not maintain a leave policy for its employees, or in the case of an employee with insufficient leave or accrued employment time to qualify for leave under such a policy, a recipient shall treat pregnancy, childbirth, false pregnancy, termination of pregnancy, and recovery therefrom as a justification for a leave of absence without pay for a reasonable period of time, at the conclusion of which the employee shall be reinstated to the status that she held when the leave began or to a comparable position, without decrease in rate of compensation or loss of promotional opportunities, or any other right or privilege of employment.

§ 17.535 Effect of state or local law or other requirements.

(a) *Prohibitory requirements.* The obligation to comply with §§ 17.500 through 17.550 is not obviated or alleviated by the existence of any State or local law or other requirement that imposes prohibitions or limits upon employment of members of one sex that are not imposed upon members of the other sex.

(b) *Benefits.* A recipient that provides any compensation, service, or benefit to members of one sex pursuant to a State or local law or other requirement shall provide the same compensation, service, or benefit to members of the other sex.

§ 17.540 Advertising.

A recipient shall not in any advertising related to employment indicate preference, limitation, specification, or discrimination based on sex unless sex is a bona fide occupational qualification for the particular job in question.

§ 17.545 Pre-employment inquiries.

(a) *Marital status.* A recipient shall not make pre-employment inquiry as to the marital status of an applicant for employment, including whether such applicant is "Miss" or "Mrs."

(b) *Sex.* A recipient may make pre-employment inquiry as to the sex of an applicant for employment, but only if such inquiry is made equally of such applicants of both sexes and if the results of such inquiry are not used in connection with discrimination prohibited by these Title IX regulations.

§ 17.550 Sex as a bona fide occupational qualification.

A recipient may take action otherwise prohibited by §§ 17.500 through 17.550 provided it is shown that sex is a bona fide occupational qualification for that action, such that consideration of sex with regard to such action is essential to successful operation of the employment function concerned. A recipient shall not take action pursuant to this section that is based upon alleged comparative employment characteristics or stereotyped characterizations of one or the other sex, or upon preference based on sex of the recipient, employees, students, or other persons, but nothing contained in this section shall prevent a recipient from considering an employee's sex in relation to employment in a locker room or toilet facility used only by members of one sex.

Subpart F—Procedures

§ 17.600 Notice of covered programs.

Within 60 days of March 6, 2003, each component of the Department that awards Federal financial assistance shall publish in the FEDERAL REGISTER a notice of the programs covered by these Title IX regulations. Each such component shall periodically republish the notice of covered programs to reflect changes in covered programs. Copies of this notice also shall be made available upon request to the Department's office that enforces Title IX.

§ 17.605 Enforcement procedures.

The investigative, compliance, and enforcement procedural provisions of Title VI of the Civil Rights Act of 1964 (42 U.S.C. 2000d) ("Title VI") are hereby adopted and applied to these Title IX regulations. These procedures may be found at 6 CFR part 21.

§ 17.635 Forms and instructions; coordination.

(a) *Forms and instructions.* The designated agency official shall issue and promptly make available to interested persons forms and detailed instructions and procedures for effectuating these Title IX regulations.

(b) *Supervision and coordination.* The designated agency official may from time to time assign to officials of the Department, or to officials of other departments or agencies of the Government with the consent of such departments or agencies, responsibilities in connection with the effectuation of the purposes of Title IX and these Title IX regulations (other than responsibility for review as provided in § 17.625(e)), including the achievements of effective coordination and maximum uniformity within the Department and within the Executive Branch of the Government in the application of Title IX and these Title IX regulations to similar programs and in similar situations. Any action taken, determination made, or requirement imposed by an official of another department or agency acting pursuant to an assignment of responsibility under this section shall have the same effect as though such action had been taken by the designated official of this Department.

PART 19—NONDISCRIMINATION IN MATTERS PERTAINING TO FAITH-BASED ORGANIZATIONS

AUTHORITY: 5 U.S.C. 301; Pub. L. 107–296; E.O. 13279, 67 FR 77141; E.O. 13403, 71 FR 28543; E.O. 13498, 74 FR 6533; and E.O. 13559, 75 FR 71319.

SOURCE: 81 FR 19410, Apr. 4, 2016, unless otherwise noted.

§ 19.1 Purpose.

It is the policy of the Department of Homeland Security (DHS) to ensure the equal treatment of faith-based organizations in social service programs administered or supported by DHS or its component agencies, enabling those organizations to participate in providing important social services to beneficiaries. The equal treatment policies and requirements contained in this part are generally applicable to faith-based organizations participating or seeking to participate in any such programs. More specific policies and requirements regarding the participation of faith-based organizations in individual programs may be provided in the statutes, regulations, or guidance governing those programs, such as regulations in title 44 of the Code of Federal Regulations. DHS or its components may issue policy guidance and reference materials at a future time with respect to the applicability of this policy and this part to particular programs.

§ 19.2 Definitions.

For purposes of this part:

Beneficiary means an individual recipient of goods or services provided as part of a social service program specifically supported by Federal financial assistance. "Beneficiary" does not mean an individual who may incidentally benefit from Federal financial assistance provided to a State, local, or Tribal government, or a private non-profit organization. Except where expressly noted or where inapplicable, "beneficiary" includes a prospective beneficiary.

Direct Federal financial assistance or *Federal financial assistance provided directly* means that the government or an intermediary (*e.g.,* State, local, or Tribal government, or nongovernmental organization) selects the provider and either purchases services from that provider (*e.g.,* via a contract) or awards funds to that provider to carry out a service (*e.g.,* through a grant or cooperative agreement). In general, Federal financial assistance shall be treated as direct, unless it meets the definition of "indirect Federal financial assistance" or "Federal

financial assistance provided indirectly".

Explicitly religious activities include activities that involve overt religious content such as worship, religious instruction, or proselytization. An activity is not explicitly religious merely because it is motivated by religious faith.

Financial assistance means assistance that non-Federal entities receive or administer in the form of grants, sub-grants, contracts, subcontracts, prime awards, loans, loan guarantees, property, cooperative agreements, food, direct appropriations, or other assistance, including materiel for emergency response and incident management. Financial assistance includes assistance provided by DHS, its component organizations, regional offices, and DHS financial assistance administered by intermediaries such as State, local, and Tribal governments, such as formula or block grants.

Indirect Federal financial assistance or *Federal financial assistance provided indirectly* means that the choice of the service provider is placed in the hands of the beneficiary, and the cost of that service is paid through a voucher, certificate, or other similar means of government-funded payment. For purposes of this part, sub-grant recipients that receive Federal financial assistance through State-administered programs are not considered recipients of "indirect Federal financial assistance." Federal financial assistance provided to an organization is considered "indirect" within the meaning of the Establishment Clause of the First Amendment to the U.S. Constitution when:

(1) The government program through which the beneficiary receives the voucher, certificate, or other similar means of government-funded payment is neutral toward religion;

(2) The organization receives the assistance as a result of a decision of the beneficiary, not a decision of the government; and

(3) The beneficiary has at least one adequate secular option for the use of the voucher, certificate, or other similar means of government-funded payment.

Intermediary means an entity, including a non-governmental organization, acting under a contract, grant, or other agreement with the Federal government or with a State or local government, that accepts Federal financial assistance and distributes that assistance to other organizations that, in turn, provide government-funded social services. If an intermediary, acting under a contract, grant, or other agreement with the Federal government or with a State or local government that is administering a program supported by Federal financial assistance, is given the authority under the contract, grant, or agreement to select non-governmental organizations to provide services supported by the Federal government, the intermediary must ensure compliance with the provisions of Executive Order 13559 and any implementing rules or guidance by the recipient of a contract, grant or agreement. If the intermediary is a non-governmental organization, it retains all other rights of a non-governmental organization under the program's statutory and regulatory provisions.

Social service program means a program that is administered by the Federal government, or by a State or local government using Federal financial assistance, and that provides services directed at reducing poverty, improving opportunities for low-income children, revitalizing low-income communities, empowering low-income families and low-income individuals to become self-sufficient, or otherwise helping people in need. Such programs include, but are not limited to, the following:

(1) Child care services, protective services for children and adults, services for children and adults in foster care, adoption services, services related to the management and maintenance of the home, day care services for adults, and services to meet the special needs of children, older individuals, and individuals with disabilities (including physical, mental, or emotional disabilities);

(2) Transportation services;

(3) Job training and related services, and employment services;

(4) Information, referral, and counseling services;

(5) The preparation and delivery of meals and services related to soup kitchens or food banks;

(6) Health support services;

(7) Literacy and mentoring programs;

(8) Services for the prevention and treatment of juvenile delinquency and substance abuse, services for the prevention of crime and the provision of assistance to the victims and the families of criminal offenders, and services related to intervention in, and prevention of, domestic violence; and

(9) Services related to the provision of assistance for housing under Federal law.

§ 19.3 Equal ability for faith-based organizations to seek and receive financial assistance through DHS social service programs.

(a) Faith-based organizations are eligible, on the same basis as any other organization, to seek and receive direct financial assistance from DHS for social service programs or to participate in social service programs administered or financed by DHS.

(b) Neither DHS, nor a State or local government, nor any other entity that administers any social service program supported by direct financial assistance from DHS, shall discriminate for or against an organization on the basis of the organization's religious motivation, character, or affiliation.

(c) Decisions about awards of Federal financial assistance must be free from political interference or even the appearance of such interference and must be made on the basis of merit, not on the basis of religion or religious belief or lack thereof, or on the basis of religious or political affiliation.

(d) Nothing in this part shall be construed to preclude DHS or any of its components from accommodating religious organizations and persons to the fullest extent consistent with the Constitution and laws of the United States.

(e) All organizations that participate in DHS social service programs, including religious organizations, must carry out eligible activities in accordance with all program requirements and other applicable requirements governing the conduct of DHS-supported activities, including those prohibiting the use of direct financial assistance from DHS to engage in explicitly religious activities. No grant document, agreement, covenant, memorandum of understanding, or policy issued by DHS or an intermediary in administering financial assistance from DHS shall disqualify a religious organization from participating in DHS's social service programs because such organization is motivated or influenced by religious faith to provide social services or because of its religious character or affiliation.

§ 19.4 Explicitly religious activities.

(a) Organizations that receive direct financial assistance from DHS to participate in or administer any social service program may not use direct Federal financial assistance that it receives (including through a prime or sub-award) to support or engage in any explicitly religious activities (including activities that involve overt religious content such as worship, religious instruction, or proselytization) or in any other manner prohibited by law.

(b) Organizations receiving direct financial assistance from DHS for social service programs are free to engage in explicitly religious activities, but such activities must be

(1) Clearly distinct from programs specifically supported by direct federal assistance;

(2) Offered separately, in time or location, from the programs, activities, or services specifically supported by direct DHS financial assistance pursuant to DHS social service programs; and

(3) Voluntary for the beneficiaries of the programs, activities, or services specifically supported by direct DHS financial assistance pursuant to DHS social service programs.

(c) All organizations that participate in DHS social service programs, including religious organizations, must carry out eligible activities in accordance with all program requirements and other applicable requirements governing the conduct of DHS-supported activities, including those prohibiting the use of direct financial assistance from DHS to engage in explicitly religious activities. No grant document, agreement, covenant, memorandum of understanding, or policy issued by DHS or a State or local government in administering financial assistance from DHS shall disqualify a religious organization from participating in DHS's social service programs because such organization is motivated or influenced by religious faith to provide social services or because of its religious character or affiliation.

(d) The use of indirect Federal financial assistance is not subject to the restriction in paragraphs (a), (b), and (c) of this section.

(e) Nothing in this part restricts DHS's authority under applicable federal law to fund activities, such as the provision of chaplaincy services, that can be directly funded by the Government consistent with the Establishment Clause.

§ 19.5 Nondiscrimination requirements.

An organization that receives financial assistance from DHS for a social service program shall not, in providing services or in outreach activities related to such services, favor or discriminate against a beneficiary of said program or activity on the basis of religion or religious belief, a refusal to hold a religious belief, or a refusal to attend or participate in a religious practice. Organizations that favor or discriminate against a beneficiary will be subject to applicable sanctions and penalties, as established by the requirements of the particular DHS social service program or activity. However, an organization that participates in a program funded by indirect financial assistance need not modify its program activities to accommodate a beneficiary who chooses to expend the indirect aid on the organization's program.

§ 19.6 Beneficiary protections: Written notice.

(a) Faith-based or religious organizations providing social services to beneficiaries under a DHS program supported by direct Federal financial assistance must give written notice to beneficiaries of certain protections. Such notice may be given in the form set forth in appendix A of this part. This notice must state that:

(1) The organization may not discriminate against beneficiaries on the basis of religion or religious belief, a

refusal to hold a religious belief, or a refusal to attend or participate in a religious practice;

(2) The organization may not require beneficiaries to attend or participate in any explicitly religious activities that are offered by the organization, and any participation by beneficiaries in such activities must be purely voluntary;

(3) The organization must separate in time or location any privately funded explicitly religious activities from activities supported by direct Federal financial assistance;

(4) If a beneficiary objects to the religious character of the organization, the organization will undertake reasonable efforts to identify and refer the beneficiary to an alternative provider to which the beneficiary has no objection; and

(5) Beneficiaries may report an organization's violations of these protections, including any denials of services or benefits by an organization, by contacting or filing a complaint with the DHS Office for Civil Rights and Civil Liberties, or to any intermediary awarding entity.

(b) This written notice must be given to beneficiaries prior to the time they enroll in the program or receive services from such programs. When the nature of the service provided or exigent circumstances make it impracticable to provide such written notice in advance of the actual service, service providers must advise beneficiaries of their protections at the earliest available opportunity.

§19.7 Beneficiary protections: Referral requirements.

(a) If a beneficiary of a social service program covered under §19.6 objects to the religious character of an organization that provides services under the program, that organization must promptly undertake reasonable efforts to identify and refer the beneficiary to an alternative provider to which the beneficiary has no objection.

(b) A referral may be made to another religiously affiliated provider, if the beneficiary has no objection to that provider. But if the beneficiary requests a secular provider, and a secular provider is available, then a referral must be made to that provider.

(c) Except for services provided by telephone, internet, or similar means, the referral must be to an alternative provider that is in reasonable geographic proximity to the organization making the referral and that offers services that are similar in substance and quality to those offered by the organization. The alternative provider also must have the capacity to accept additional clients.

(d) When the organization makes a referral to an alternative provider, it shall keep a record of that referral. If the organization determines that it is unable to identify an alternative provider, the organization shall both keep a record and promptly notify either DHS or an intermediary awarding entity. If the organization is unable to identify an alternative provider, DHS or the intermediary shall determine whether there is any other suitable alternative provider to which the beneficiary may be referred. An intermediary that receives a request for assistance in identifying an alternative provider shall notify, and may request assistance from, DHS.

§19.8 Independence of faith-based organizations.

(a) A faith-based organization that applies for, or participates in, a social service program supported with Federal financial assistance may retain its independence and may continue to carry out its mission, including the definition, development, practice, and expression of its religious beliefs, provided that it does not use direct Federal financial assistance contrary to §19.4.

(b) Faith-based organizations may use space in their facilities to provide social services using financial assistance from DHS without removing or concealing religious articles, texts, art, or symbols.

(c) A faith-based organization using financial assistance from DHS for social service programs retains its authority over internal governance, and may also retain religious terms in its organization's name, select its board

187

members on a religious basis, and include religious references in its organization's mission statements and other governing documents.

§ 19.9 Exemption from Title VII employment discrimination requirements.

(a) A faith-based organization's exemption, set forth in section 702(a) of the Civil Rights Act of 1964 (42 U.S.C. 2000e-1), from the Federal prohibition on employment discrimination on the basis of religion is not forfeited when the organization seeks or receives financial assistance from DHS for a social service program or otherwise participates in a DHS program.

(b) Where a DHS program contains independent statutory or regulatory provisions that impose nondiscrimination requirements on all grantees, those provisions are not waived or mitigated by this part. Accordingly, grantees should consult with the appropriate DHS program office to determine the scope of any applicable requirements.

§ 19.10 Commingling of Federal assistance.

(a) If a State, local, or Tribal government voluntarily contributes its own funds to supplement Federally supported activities, the State, local, or Tribal government has the option to segregate the Federal assistance or commingle it.

(b) If the State, local, or Tribal government chooses to commingle its own and Federal funds, the requirements of this part apply to all of the commingled funds.

(c) If a State, local, or Tribal government is required to contribute matching funds to supplement a Federally supported activity, the matching funds are considered commingled with the Federal assistance and therefore subject to the requirements of this part.

APPENDIX A TO PART 19—MODEL
WRITTEN NOTICE TO BENEFICIARIES

NOTICE OF BENEFICIARY RIGHTS

Name of Organization:
Name of Program:
Contact Information for Program Staff (name, phone number, and email address, if appropriate):

Because this program is supported in whole or in part by direct financial assistance from the Federal Government, we are required to let you know that—

• We may not discriminate against you on the basis of religion or religious belief, your refusal to hold a religious belief, or your refusal to attend or participate in a religious practice;

• We may not require you to attend or participate in any explicitly religious activities that are offered by us, and any participation by you in these activities must be purely voluntary;

• We must separate in time or location any privately funded explicitly religious activities from activities supported with direct Federal financial assistance under this program;

• If you object to the religious character of our organization, we must make reasonable efforts to identify and refer you to an alternative provider to which you have no objection; however, we cannot guarantee that in every instance, an alternative provider will be available; and

• You may report violations of these protections, including any denials of services or benefits, by contacting or filing a written complaint with the Department of Homeland Security, Office for Civil Rights and Civil Liberties:

E-mail: *CRCLCompliance@hq.dhs.gov.*
Fax: 202-401-4708.
U.S. Mail: U.S. Department of Homeland Security Office for Civil Rights and Civil Liberties, Compliance Branch, 245 Murray Lane SW., Building 410, Mail Stop #0190, Washington, DC 20528.

{Where the program involves an intermediary, the recipient or intermediary should add where feasible:

You may also report violations of these protections, including any denials of services or benefits, to:

[Name and contact information for the intermediary]}

We must give you this written notice before you enroll in our program or receive services from the program.

BENEFICIARY REFERRAL REQUEST

If you object to receiving services from us based on the religious character of our organization, please complete this form and return it to the program contact identified above. If you object, we will make reasonable efforts to refer you to another service provider. With your consent, we will follow up with you or the organization to which you were referred to determine whether you contacted that organization.

Please check if applicable:
( ) I want to be referred to another service provider.

If you checked above that you wish to be referred to another service provider, please check one of the following:
( ) Please follow up with me.
Name:
Best way to reach me (phone/address/email):
( ) Please follow up with the service provider to which I was referred.
( ) Please do not follow up.
—End of Form—

PART 21—NONDISCRIMINATION ON THE BASIS OF RACE, COLOR, OR NATIONAL ORIGIN IN PROGRAMS OR ACTIVITIES RECEIVING FEDERAL FINANCIAL ASSISTANCE FROM THE DEPARTMENT OF HOMELAND SECURITY

AUTHORITY: 5 U.S.C. 310, 42 U.S.C. 2000d–2000d–7.

SOURCE: 68 FR 10904, Mar. 6, 2003, unless otherwise noted.

§21.1 Purpose.

The purpose of this part is to effectuate the provisions of title VI of the Civil Rights Act of 1964 (the Act) to the end that no person in the United States shall, on the grounds of race, color, or national origin, be excluded from participation in, be denied the benefits of, or be otherwise subjected to discrimination under any program or activity receiving Federal financial assistance from the Department of Homeland Security. The provisions established by this part shall be effective for all components of the Department, including all Department components that are transferred to the Department, except to the extent that a Department component already has existing title VI regulations.

§21.3 Application.

(a) This part applies to any program for which Federal financial assistance is authorized under a law administered by the Department, including the types of Federal financial assistance listed in appendix A to this part. It also applies to money paid, property transferred, or other Federal financial assistance extended after the effective date of this part pursuant to an application approved before that effective date. This part does not apply to:

(1) Any Federal financial assistance by way of insurance or guaranty contracts;

(2) Money paid, property transferred, or other assistance extended before the effective date of this part, except where such assistance was subject to the title VI regulations of any agency whose responsibilities are now exercised by this Department;

(3) Any assistance to any individual who is the ultimate beneficiary; or

(4) Any employment practice, under any such program, of any employer, employment agency, or labor organization, except to the extent described in §21.5(c). The fact that a type of Federal financial assistance is not listed in appendix A to this part shall not mean, if title VI of the Act is otherwise applicable, that a program is not covered. Other types of Federal financial assistance under statutes now in force or hereinafter enacted may be added to appendix A to this part.

(b) In any program receiving Federal financial assistance in the form, or for the acquisition, of real property or an interest in real property, to the extent that rights to space on, over, or under any such property are included as part of the program receiving that assistance, the nondiscrimination requirement of this part shall extend to any facility located wholly or in part in that space.

§21.4 Definitions.

Unless the context requires otherwise, as used in this part:

(a) *Applicant* means a person who submits an application, request, or plan required to be approved by the Secretary, or designee thereof, or by a primary recipient, as a condition to eligibility for Federal financial assistance, and application means such an application, request, or plan.

(b) *Facility* includes all or any part of structures, equipment, or other real or personal property or interests therein, and the provision of facilities includes the construction, expansion, renovation, remodeling, alteration or acquisition of facilities.

(c) *Federal financial assistance* includes:

(1) Grants and loans of Federal funds;

(2) The grant or donation of Federal property and interests in property;

(3) The detail of Federal personnel;

(4) The sale and lease of, and the permission to use (on other than a casual or transient basis), Federal property or any interest in such property without consideration or at a nominal consideration, or at a consideration which is reduced for the purpose of assisting the recipient, or in recognition of the public interest to be served by such sale or lease to the recipient; and

(5) Any Federal agreement, arrangement, or other contract which has as one of its purposes the provision of assistance.

(d) *Primary recipient* means any recipient that is authorized or required to extend Federal financial assistance to another recipient.

(e) *Program or activity* and *program* mean all of the operations of any entity described in paragraphs (e)(1) through (4) of this section, any part of which is extended Federal financial assistance:

(1)(i) A department, agency, special purpose district, or other instrumentality of a State or of a local government; or

(ii) The entity of such State or local government that distributes such assistance and each such department or agency (and each other State or local government entity) to which the assistance is extended, in the case of assistance to a State or local government;

(2)(i) A college, university, or other postsecondary institution, or a public system of higher education; or

(ii) A local educational agency (as defined in 20 U.S.C. 8801), system of vocational education, or other school system;

(3)(i) An entire corporation, partnership, or other private organization, or an entire sole proprietorship—

(A) If assistance is extended to such corporation, partnership, private organization, or sole proprietorship as a whole; or

(B) Which is principally engaged in the business of providing education, health care, housing, social services, or parks and recreation; or

(ii) The entire plant or other comparable, geographically separate facility to which Federal financial assistance is extended, in the case of any other corporation, partnership, private organization or sole proprietorship; or

(4) Any other entity which is established by two or more of the entities described in paragraph (e)(1), (2), or (3) of this section.

(f) *Recipient* may mean any State, territory, possession, the District of Columbia, or the Commonwealth of Puerto Rico, or any political subdivision thereof, or instrumentality thereof, any public or private agency, institution, or organization, or other entity, or any individual, in any State, territory, possession, the District of Columbia, or the Commonwealth of Puerto Rico, to whom Federal financial assistance is extended, directly or through another recipient, including any successor, assignee, or transferee thereof, but such term does not include any ultimate beneficiary.

(g) *Secretary* means the Secretary of the Department of Homeland Security or, except in § 21.17(e), any delegatee of the Secretary.

§ 21.5 **Discrimination prohibited.**

(a) *General.* No person in the United States shall, on the grounds of race, color, or national origin be excluded from participation in, be denied the benefits of, or be otherwise subjected to discrimination under, any program to which this part applies.

(b) *Specific discriminatory actions prohibited.* (1) A recipient to which this part applies may not, directly or through contractual or other arrangements, on the grounds of race, color, or national origin:

(i) Deny a person any service, financial aid, or other benefit provided under the program;

(ii) Provide any service, financial aid, or other benefit to a person which is different, or is provided in a different manner, from that provided to others under the program;

(iii) Subject a person to segregation or separate treatment in any matter related to his receipt of any service, financial aid, or other benefit under the program;

(iv) Restrict a person in any way in the enjoyment of any advantage or privilege enjoyed by others receiving any service, financial aid, or other benefit under the program;

(v) Treat a person differently from others in determining whether he satisfies any admission, enrollment, quota, eligibility, membership, or other requirement or condition which persons must meet in order to be provided any service, financial aid, or other benefit provided under the program;

(vi) Deny a person an opportunity to participate in the program through the provision of services or otherwise or afford him an opportunity to do so which is different from that afforded others under the program; or

(vii) Deny a person the opportunity to participate as a member of a planning, advisory, or similar body which is an integral part of the program.

(2) A recipient, in determining the types of services, financial aid, or other benefits, or facilities which will be provided under any such program, or the class of person to whom, or the situations in which, such services, financial aid, other benefits, or facilities will be provided under any such program, or the class of persons to be afforded an opportunity to participate in any such program; may not, directly or through contractual or other arrangements, utilize criteria or methods of administration which have the effect of subjecting persons to discrimination because of their race, color, or national origin or have the effect of defeating or substantially impairing accomplishment of the objectives of the program

with respect to individuals of a particular race, color, or national origin.

(3) In determining the site or location of facilities, a recipient or applicant may not make selections with the purpose or effect of excluding persons from, denying them the benefits of, or subjecting them to discrimination under any program to which this regulation applies, on the grounds of race, color, or national origin; or with the purpose or effect of defeating or substantially impairing the accomplishment of the objectives of the Act or this part.

(4) As used in this section the services, financial aid, or other benefits provided under a program receiving Federal financial assistance include any service, financial aid, or other benefit provided in or through a facility provided with the aid of Federal financial assistance.

(5) The enumeration of specific forms of prohibited discrimination in this paragraph does not limit the generality of the prohibition in paragraph (a) of this section.

(6) This part does not prohibit the consideration of race, color, or national origin if the purpose and effect are to remove or overcome the consequences of practices or impediments which have restricted the availability of, or participation in, the program or activity receiving Federal financial assistance, on the grounds of race, color, or national origin. Where prior discriminatory practice or usage tends, on the grounds of race, color, or national origin to exclude individuals from participation in, to deny them the benefits of, or to subject them to discrimination under any program or activity to which this part applies, the applicant or recipient must take affirmative action to remove or overcome the effects of the prior discriminatory practice or usage. Even in the absence of prior discriminatory practice or usage, a recipient in administering a program or activity to which this part applies, may take affirmative action to assure that no person is excluded from participation in or denied the benefits of the program or activity on the grounds of race, color, or national origin.

(c) *Employment practices.* (1) Where a primary objective of the Federal financial assistance to a program to which this part applies is to provide employment, a recipient subject to this part shall not, directly or through contractual or other arrangements, subject a person to discrimination on the ground of race, color, or national origin in its employment practices under such program (including recruitment or recruitment advertising, hiring, firing, upgrading, promotion, demotion, transfer, layoff, termination, rates of pay or other forms of compensation or benefits, selection for training or apprenticeship, and use of facilities). Such recipient shall take affirmative action to insure that applicants are employed, and employees are treated during employment, without regard to their race, color, or national origin. The requirements applicable to construction employment under any such program shall be those specified in or pursuant to Part III of Executive Order 11246 or any Executive order which supersedes it.

(2) Federal financial assistance to programs under laws funded or administered by the Department which have as a primary objective the providing of employment include those set forth in appendix B to this part.

(3) Where a primary objective of the Federal financial assistance is not to provide employment, but discrimination on the grounds of race, color, or national origin in the employment practices of the recipient or other persons subject to the regulation tends, on the grounds of race, color, or national origin, to exclude individuals from participation in, deny them the benefits of, or subject them to discrimination under any program to which this regulation applies, the provisions of paragraph (c)(1) of this section shall apply to the employment practices of the recipient or other persons subject to the regulation, to the extent necessary to assure equality of opportunity to, and nondiscriminatory treatment of, beneficiaries.

(d) *Facility location or site.* A recipient may not make a selection of a site or location of a facility if the purpose of that selection, or its effect when made, is to exclude individuals from participation in, to deny them the benefits of, or to subject them to discrimination under any program or activity to which this rule applies, on the grounds of race, color, or national origin; or if the purpose is to, or its effect when made will substantially impair the accomplishment of the objectives of this part.

§ 21.7 **Assurances required.**

(a) *General.* (1) Every application for Federal financial assistance to which this part applies, except an application to which paragraph (b) of this section applies, and every application for Federal financial assistance to provide a facility shall, as a condition to its approval and the extension of any Federal financial assistance pursuant to the application, contain or be accompanied by, an assurance that the program will be conducted or the facility operated in compliance with all requirements imposed by or pursuant to this part. Every award of Federal financial assistance shall require the submission of such an assurance. In the case where the Federal financial assistance is to provide or is in the form of personal property, or real property or interest therein or structures thereon, the assurance shall obligate the recipient, or, in the case of a subsequent transfer, the transferee, for the period during which the property is used for a purpose for which the Federal financial assistance is extended or for another purpose involving the provision of similar services or benefits, or for as long as the recipient retains ownership or possession of the property, whichever is longer. In all other cases the assurance shall obligate the recipient for the period during which Federal financial assistance is extended to the program. The Secretary shall specify the form of the foregoing assurances, and the extent to which like assurances will be required of subgrantees, contractors and subcontractors, transferees, successors in interest, and other participants. Any such assurance shall include provisions which give the United States a right to seek its judicial enforcement.

(2) In the case where Federal financial assistance is provided in the form

192

of a transfer of real property, structures, or improvements thereon, or interest therein, from the Federal Government, the instrument effecting or recording the transfer shall contain a covenant running with the land assuring nondiscrimination for the period during which the real property is used for a purpose for which the Federal financial assistance is extended or for another purpose involving the provision of similar services or benefits. Where no transfer of property or interest therein from the Federal Government is involved, but property is acquired or improved with Federal financial assistance, the recipient shall agree to include such covenant in any subsequent transfer of such property. When the property is obtained from the Federal Government, such covenant may also include a condition coupled with a right to be reserved by the Department to revert title to the property in the event of a breach of the covenant where, in the discretion of the Secretary, such a condition and right of reverter is appropriate to the statute under which the real property is obtained and to the nature of the grant and the grantee. In such event if a transferee of real property proposes to mortgage or otherwise encumber the real property as security for financing construction of new, or improvement of existing, facilities on such property for the purposes for which the property was transferred, the Secretary may agree, upon request of the transferee and if necessary to accomplish such financing, and upon such conditions as he deems appropriate, to subordinate such right of reversion to the lien of such mortgage or other encumbrance.

(b) *Continuing Federal financial assistance.* Every application by a State or a State agency for continuing Federal financial assistance to which this part applies (including the types of Federal financial assistance listed in appendix A to this part) shall as a condition to its approval and the extension of any Federal financial assistance pursuant to the application:

(1) Contain or be accompanied by a statement that the program is (or, in the case of a new program, will be) conducted in compliance with all requirements imposed by or pursuant to this part; and

(2) Provide or be accompanied by provision for such methods of administration for the program as are found by the Secretary to give reasonable guarantee that the applicant and all recipients of Federal financial assistance under such program will comply with all requirements imposed by or pursuant to this part.

(c) *Assurance from institutions.* (1) In the case of any application for Federal financial assistance to an institution of higher education (including assistance for construction, for research, for special training projects, for student loans or for any other purpose), the assurance required by this section shall extend to admission practices and to all other practices relating to the treatment of students.

(2) The assurance required with respect to an institution of higher education, hospital, or any other institution, insofar as the assurance relates to the institution's practices with respect to admission or other treatment of individuals as students, patients, or clients of the institution or to the opportunity to participate in the provision of services or other benefits to such individuals, shall be applicable to the entire institution.

§21.9 Compliance information.

(a) *Cooperation and assistance.* The Secretary shall to the fullest extent practicable seek the cooperation of recipients in obtaining compliance with this part and shall provide assistance and guidance to recipients to help them comply voluntarily with this part.

(b) *Compliance reports.* Each recipient shall keep such records and submit to the Secretary timely, complete, and accurate compliance reports at such times, and in such form and containing such information, as the Secretary may determine to be necessary to enable him to ascertain whether the recipient has complied or is complying with this part. In the case in which a primary recipient extends Federal financial assistance to any other recipient, such other recipient shall also submit such compliance reports to the primary recipient as may be necessary to enable the primary recipient to carry out its obligations under this part. In general, recipients should have available for the Secretary racial and ethnic data showing the extent to which members of minority groups are beneficiaries of programs receiving Federal financial assistance.

(c) *Access to sources of information.* Each recipient shall permit access by the Secretary during normal business hours to such of its books, records, accounts, and other sources of information, and its facilities as may be pertinent to ascertain compliance with this part. Where any information required of a recipient is in the exclusive possession of any other agency, institution, or person and this agency, institution, or person fails or refuses to furnish this information, the recipient shall so certify in its report and shall set forth what efforts it has made to obtain the information.

(d) *Information to beneficiaries and participants.* Each recipient shall make available to participants, beneficiaries, and other interested persons such information regarding the provisions of this part and its applicability to the program for which the recipient receives Federal financial assistance, and make such information available to them in such manner, as the Secretary finds necessary to apprise such persons of the protections against discrimination assured them by the Act and this part.

§ 21.11 Conduct of investigations.

(a) *Periodic compliance reviews.* The Secretary shall from time to time review the practices of recipients to determine whether they are complying with this part.

(b) *Complaints.* Any person who believes that he or she, or any specific class of persons, has been subjected to discrimination prohibited by this part may by himself or herself, or by a representative, file with the Secretary a written complaint. A complaint must be filed not later than 180 days after the date of the alleged discrimination, unless the time for filing is extended by the Secretary.

(c) *Investigations.* The Secretary will make a prompt investigation whenever a compliance review, report, complaint, or any other information indicates a possible failure to comply with this part. The investigation will include, where appropriate, a review of the pertinent practices and policies of the recipient, the circumstances under which the possible noncompliance with this part occurred, and other factors relevant to a determination as to whether the recipient has failed to comply with this part.

(d) *Resolution of matters.* (1) If an investigation pursuant to paragraph (c) of this section indicates a failure to comply with this part, the Secretary will so inform the recipient and the matter will be resolved by informal means whenever possible. If it has been determined that the matter cannot be resolved by informal means, action will be taken as provided for in § 21.13.

(2) If an investigation does not warrant action pursuant to paragraph (d)(1) of this section the Secretary will so inform the recipient and the complainant, if any, in writing.

(e) *Intimidatory or retaliatory acts prohibited.* No recipient or other person shall intimidate, threaten, coerce, or discriminate against any individual for the purpose of interfering with any right or privilege secured by section 601 of the Act or this part, or because he has made a complaint, testified, assisted, or participated in any manner in an investigation, proceeding, or hearing under this part. The identity of complainants shall be kept confidential except to the extent necessary to carry out the purposes of this part, including the conduct of any investigation, hearing, or judicial proceeding arising thereunder.

§ 21.13 Procedure for effecting compliance.

(a) *General.* If there appears to be a failure or threatened failure to comply with this part, and if the noncompliance or threatened noncompliance cannot be corrected by informal means, compliance with this part may be effected by the suspension or termination of or refusal to grant or to continue Federal financial assistance or by any other means authorized by law. Such other means may include, but are not limited to:

(1) A referral to the Department of Justice with a recommendation that appropriate proceedings be brought to enforce any rights of the United States under any law of the United States (including other titles of the Act), or any assurance or other contractual undertaking; and

(2) Any applicable proceeding under State or local law.

(b) *Noncompliance with §21.7.* If an applicant fails or refuses to furnish an assurance required under §21.7 or otherwise fails or refuses to comply with a requirement imposed by or pursuant to that section, Federal financial assistance may be refused in accordance with the procedures of paragraph (c) of this section. The Department shall not be required to provide assistance in such a case during the pendency of the administrative proceedings under such paragraph. However, subject to §21.21, the Department shall continue assistance during the pendency of such proceedings where such assistance is due and payable pursuant to an application approved prior to the effective date of this part.

(c) *Termination of or refusal to grant or to continue Federal financial assistance.* (1) No order suspending, terminating, or refusing to grant or continue Federal financial assistance shall become effective until:

(i) The Secretary has advised the applicant or recipient of his failure to comply and has determined that compliance cannot be secured by voluntary means;

(ii) There has been an express finding on the record, after opportunity for hearing, of a failure by the applicant or recipient to comply with a requirement imposed by or pursuant to this part;

(iii) The action has been approved by the Secretary pursuant to §21.17(e); and

(iv) The expiration of 30 days after the Secretary has filed with the committee of the House and the committee of the Senate having legislative jurisdiction over the program involved, a full written report of the circumstances and the grounds for such action.

(2) Any action to suspend or terminate or to refuse to grant or to continue Federal financial assistance shall be limited to the particular political entity, or part thereof, or other applicant or recipient as to whom such a finding has been made and shall be limited in its effect to the particular program, or part thereof, in which such noncompliance has been so found.

(d) *Other means authorized by law.* No action to effect compliance with title VI of the Act by any other means authorized by law shall be taken by this Department until:

(1) The Secretary has determined that compliance cannot be secured by voluntary means;

(2) The recipient or other person has been notified of its failure to comply and of the action to be taken to effect compliance; and

(3) The expiration of at least 10 days from the mailing of such notice to the recipient or other person. During this period of at least 10 days, additional efforts shall be made to persuade the recipient or other person to comply with the regulation and to take such corrective action as may be appropriate.

§21.15 Hearings.

(a) *Opportunity for hearing.* Whenever an opportunity for a hearing is required by §21.13(c), reasonable notice shall be given by registered or certified mail, return receipt requested, to the affected applicant or recipient. This notice shall advise the applicant or recipient of the action proposed to be taken, the specific provision under which the proposed action against it is to be taken, and the matters of fact or law asserted as the basis for this action, and either:

(1) Fix a date not less than 20 days after the date of such notice within which the applicant or recipient may request of the Secretary that the matter be scheduled for hearing; or

(2) Advise the applicant or recipient that the matter in question has been set down for hearing at a stated place and time. The time and place so fixed shall be reasonable and shall be subject to change for cause. The complainant, if any, shall be advised of the time and place of the hearing. An applicant or recipient may waive a hearing and submit written information and argument for the record. The failure of an applicant or recipient to request a hearing under this paragraph or to appear at a

hearing for which a date has been set shall be deemed to be a waiver of the right to a hearing under section 602 of the Act and § 21.13(c) and consent to the making of a decision on the basis of such information as is available.

(b) *Time and place of hearing.* Hearings shall be held at the offices of the Department in Washington, DC, at a time fixed by the Secretary unless he determines that the convenience of the applicant or recipient or of the Department requires that another place be selected. Hearings shall be held before the Secretary, or at his discretion, before a hearing examiner appointed in accordance with section 3105 of title 5, United States Code, or detailed under section 3344 of title 5, United States Code.

(c) *Right to counsel.* In all proceedings under this section, the applicant or recipient and the Department shall have the right to be represented by counsel.

(d) *Procedures, evidence, and record.* (1) The hearing, decision, and any administrative review thereof shall be conducted in conformity with sections 554 through 557 of title 5, United States Code, and in accordance with such rules of procedure as are proper (and not inconsistent with this section) relating to the conduct of the hearing, giving of notices subsequent to those provided for in paragraph (a) of this section, taking of testimony, exhibits, arguments and briefs, requests for findings, and other related matters. Both the Department and the applicant or recipient shall be entitled to introduce all relevant evidence on the issues as stated in the notice for hearing or as determined by the officer conducting the hearing at the outset of or during the hearing.

(2) Technical rules of evidence do not apply to hearings conducted pursuant to this part, but rules or principles designed to assure production of the most credible evidence available and to subject testimony to test by cross-examination shall be applied where reasonably necessary by the officer conducting the hearing. The hearing officer may exclude irrelevant, immaterial, or unduly repetitious evidence. All documents and other evidence offered or taken for the record shall be open to examination by the parties and oppor-

tunity shall be given to refute facts and arguments advanced on either side of the issues. A transcript shall be made of the oral evidence except to the extent the substance thereof is stipulated for the record. All decisions shall be based upon the hearing record and written findings shall be made.

(e) *Consolidated or joint hearings.* In cases in which the same or related facts are asserted to constitute noncompliance with this part with respect to two or more Federal statutes, authorities, or other means by which Federal financial assistance is extended and to which this part applies, or noncompliance with this part and the regulations of one or more other Federal departments or agencies issued under title VI of the Act, the Secretary may, by agreement with such other departments or agencies, where applicable, provide for the conduct of consolidated or joint hearings, and for the application to such hearings of rules or procedures not inconsistent with this part. Final decisions in such cases, insofar as this regulation is concerned, shall be made in accordance with § 21.17.

§ 21.17 Decisions and notices.

(a) *Procedure on decisions by hearing examiner.* If the hearing is held by a hearing examiner, the hearing examiner shall either make an initial decision, if so authorized, or certify the entire record including his recommended findings and proposed decision to the Secretary for a final decision, and a copy of such initial decision or certification shall be mailed to the applicant or recipient. Where the initial decision is made by the hearing examiner the applicant or recipient may, within 30 days after the mailing of such notice of initial decision, file with the Secretary his exceptions to the initial decision, with his reasons therefor. In the absence of exceptions, the Secretary may, on his own motion, within 45 days after the initial decision, serve on the applicant or recipient a notice that he will review the decision. Upon the filing of such exceptions or of notice of review, the Secretary shall review the initial decision and issue his own decision thereon including the reasons therefor. In the absence of either exceptions or a notice of review the initial decision shall, subject to paragraph (e) of this section, constitute the final decision of the Secretary.

(b) *Decisions on record or review by the Secretary.* Whenever a record is certified to the Secretary for decision or he reviews the decision of a hearing examiner pursuant to paragraph (a) of this section, or whenever the Secretary conducts the hearing, the applicant or recipient shall be given reasonable opportunity to file with him briefs or other written statements of its contentions, and a written copy of the final decision of the Secretary shall be sent to the applicant or recipient and to the complainant, if any.

(c) *Decisions on record where a hearing is waived.* Whenever a hearing is waived pursuant to §21.15, a decision shall be made by the Secretary on the record and a written copy of such decision shall be sent to the applicant or recipient, and to the complainant, if any.

(d) *Rulings required.* Each decision of a hearing examiner or the Secretary shall set forth his ruling on each finding, conclusion, or exception presented, and shall identify the requirement or requirements imposed by or pursuant to this part with which it is found that the applicant or recipient has failed to comply.

(e) *Approval by Secretary.* Any final decision by an official of the Department, other than the Secretary personally, which provides for the suspension or termination of, or the refusal to grant or continue Federal financial assistance, or the imposition of any other sanction available under this part or the Act, shall promptly be transmitted to the Secretary personally, who may approve such decision, may vacate it, or remit or mitigate any sanction imposed.

(f) *Content of orders.* The final decision may provide for suspension or termination of, or refusal to grant or continue Federal financial assistance, in whole or in part, to which this regulation applies, and may contain such terms, conditions, and other provisions as are consistent with and will effectuate the purposes of the Act and this part, including provisions designed to assure that no Federal financial assistance to which this regulation applies will thereafter be extended to the applicant or recipient determined by such decision to be in default in its performance of an assurance given by it pursuant to this part, or to have otherwise failed to comply with this part, unless and until it corrects its noncompliance and satisfies the Secretary that it will fully comply with this part.

(g) *Post termination proceedings.* (1) An applicant or recipient adversely affected by an order issued under paragraph (f) of this section shall be restored to full eligibility to receive Federal financial assistance if it satisfies the terms and conditions of that order for such eligibility or if it brings itself into compliance with this part and provides reasonable assurance that it will fully comply with this part.

(2) Any applicant or recipient adversely affected by an order entered pursuant to paragraph (f) of this section may at any time request the Secretary to restore fully its eligibility to receive Federal financial assistance. Any such request shall be supported by information showing that the applicant or recipient has met the requirements of paragraph (g)(1) of this section. If the Secretary determines that those requirements have been satisfied, he shall restore such eligibility.

(3) If the Secretary denies any such request, the applicant or recipient may submit a request for a hearing in writing, specifying why it believes such official to have been in error. It shall thereupon be given an expeditious hearing, with a decision on the record in accordance with rules or procedures issued by the Secretary. The applicant or recipient will be restored to such eligibility if it proves at such a hearing that it satisfied the requirements of paragraph (g)(1) of this section. While proceedings under this paragraph are pending, the sanctions imposed by the order issued under paragraph (f) of this section shall remain in effect.

§21.19 Judicial review.

Action taken pursuant to section 602 of the Act is subject to judicial review as provided in section 603 of the Act.

§ 21.21 Effect on other regulations, forms, and instructions.

(a) *Effect on other regulations.* All regulations, orders, or like directions issued before the effective date of this part by any officer of the Department which impose requirements designed to prohibit any discrimination against individuals on the grounds of race, color, or national origin under any program to which this part applies, and which authorize the suspension or termination of or refusal to grant or to continue Federal financial assistance to any applicant for a recipient of such assistance for failure to comply with such requirements, are hereby superseded to the extent that such discrimination is prohibited by this part, except that nothing in this part may be considered to relieve any person of any obligation assumed or imposed under any such superseded regulation, order, instruction, or like direction before the effective date of this part. Nothing in this part, however, supersedes any of the following (including future amendments thereof):

(1) Executive Order 11246 (3 CFR, 1965 Supp., p. 167) and regulations issued thereunder; or

(2) Any other orders, regulations, or instructions, insofar as such orders, regulations, or instructions prohibit discrimination on the ground of race, color, or national origin in any program or situation to which this part is inapplicable, or prohibit discrimination on any other ground.

(b) *Forms and instructions.* The Secretary shall issue and promptly make available to all interested persons forms and detailed instructions and procedures for effectuating this part as applied to programs to which this part applies and for which he is responsible.

(c) *Supervision and coordination.* The Secretary may from time to time assign to officials of the Department, or to officials of other departments or agencies of the Government with the consent of such departments or agencies, responsibilities in connection with the effectuation of the purposes of title VI of the Act and this part (other than responsibility for final decision as provided in § 21.17), including the achievement of effective coordination and maximum uniformity within the Department and within the Executive Branch of the Government in the application of title VI and this part to similar programs and in similar situations. Any action taken, determination made or requirement imposed by an official of another department or agency acting pursuant to an assignment of responsibility under this paragraph shall have the same effect as though such action had been taken by the Secretary of this Department.

APPENDIX A TO PART 21—ACTIVITIES TO WHICH THIS PART APPLIES

NOTE: Failure to list a type of Federal assistance in appendix A shall not mean, if title VI is otherwise applicable, that a program is not covered.

1. Lease of real property and the grant of permits, licenses, easements and rights-of-way covering real property under control of the U.S. Coast Guard (14 U.S.C. 93 (n) and (o)).

2. Utilization of U.S. Coast Guard personnel and facilities by any State, territory, possession, or political subdivision thereof (14 U.S.C. 141(a)).

3. Use of U.S. Coast Guard personnel for duty in connection with maritime instruction and training by the States, territories, and the Commonwealth of Puerto Rico (14 U.S.C. 148).

4. Use of obsolete and other U.S. Coast Guard material by sea scout service of Boy Scouts of America, any incorporated unit of the U.S. Coast Guard auxiliary, and public body or private organization not organized for profit (14 U.S.C. 641(a)).

5. U.S. Coast Guard Auxiliary Program (14 U.S.C. 821–832).

6. U.S. Coast Guard Boating Safety Financial Assistance program.

7. U.S. Coast Guard State Access to Oil Spill Liability Trust Fund.

8. U.S. Coast Guard Bridge Alteration.

9. Use of Customs personnel and facilities by any State, territory, possession, or political subdivision thereof.

10. Use of Customs personnel for duty in connection with instruction and training by the States, territories and the Commonwealth of Puerto Rico.

11. Grants to educational institutions, associations, States, or other entities for research, analysis, or programs or strategies relating to trade issues.

APPENDIX B TO PART 21—ACTIVITIES TO WHICH THIS PART APPLIES WHEN A PRIMARY OBJECTIVE OF THE FEDERAL FINANCIAL ASSISTANCE IS TO PROVIDE EMPLOYMENT

NOTE: Failure to list a type of Federal assistance in appendix B shall not mean, if title VI is otherwise applicable, that a program is not covered.

[Reserved]

PART 25—REGULATIONS TO SUPPORT ANTI-TERRORISM BY FOSTERING EFFECTIVE TECHNOLOGIES

Sec.
25.1 Purpose.
25.2 Definitions.
25.3 Delegation.
25.4 Designation of qualified anti-terrorism technologies.
25.5 Obligations of seller.
25.6 Procedures for designation of qualified anti-terrorism technologies.
25.7 Litigation management.
25.8 Government contractor Defense.
25.9 Procedures for certification of approved products for Homeland Security.
25.10 Confidentiality and protection of intellectual property.

AUTHORITY: Subtitle G, of Title VIII, Public Law 107–296, 116 Stat. 2238 (6 U.S.C. 441–444).

SOURCE: 71 FR 33159, June 8, 2006, unless otherwise noted.

§25.1 Purpose.

This part implements the Support Anti-terrorism by Fostering Effective Technologies Act of 2002, sections 441–444 of title 6, United States Code (the "SAFETY Act" or "the Act").

§25.2 Definitions.

Act of Terrorism—The term "Act of Terrorism" means any act determined to have met the following requirements or such other requirements as defined and specified by the Secretary:

(1) Is unlawful;

(2) Causes harm, including financial harm, to a person, property, or entity, in the United States, or in the case of a domestic United States air carrier or a United States-flag vessel (or a vessel based principally in the United States on which United States income tax is paid and whose insurance coverage is subject to regulation in the United States), in or outside the United States; and

(3) Uses or attempts to use instrumentalities, weapons or other methods designed or intended to cause mass destruction, injury or other loss to citizens or institutions of the United States.

Certification—The term "Certification" means (unless the context requires otherwise) the certification issued pursuant to section 25.9 that a Qualified Anti-Terrorism Technology for which a Designation has been issued will perform as intended, conforms to the Seller's specifications, and is safe for use as intended.

Contractor—The term "contractor" means any person, firm, or other entity with whom or with which a Seller has a contract or contractual arrangement relating to the manufacture, sale, use, or operation of anti-terrorism Technology for which a Designation is issued (regardless of whether such contract is entered into before or after the issuance of such Designation), including, without limitation, an independent laboratory or other entity engaged in testing or verifying the safety, utility, performance, or effectiveness of such Technology, or the conformity of such Technology to the Seller's specifications.

Designation—The term "Designation" means the designation of a Qualified Anti-Terrorism Technology under the SAFETY Act issued by the Under Secretary under authority delegated to the Under Secretary by the Secretary of Homeland Security.

Loss—The term "loss" means death, bodily injury, or loss of or damage to property, including business interruption loss (which is a component of loss of or damage to property).

Noneconomic damages—The term "noneconomic damages" means damages for losses for physical and emotional pain, suffering, inconvenience, physical impairment, mental anguish, disfigurement, loss of enjoyment of life, loss of society and companionship, loss of consortium, hedonic damages, injury to reputation, and any other nonpecuniary losses.

Office of SAFETY Act Implementation—The term "Office of SAFETY Act Implementation" or "OSAI" means the office within the Department of Homeland Security's Directorate of Science and Technology that assists with the implementation of the SAFETY Act. The responsibilities of the Office of SAFETY Act Implementation may include, without limitation, preparing the SAFETY Act Application Kit, receiving and facilitating the evaluation of applications, managing the SAFETY Act Web site and otherwise providing the public with information regarding the SAFETY Act and the application process.

Physical harm—The term "physical harm" as used in the Act and this part means any physical injury to the body, including an injury that caused, either temporarily or permanently, partial or total physical disability, incapacity or disfigurement. In no event shall physical harm include mental pain, anguish, or suffering, or fear of injury.

Qualified Anti-Terrorism Technology or QATT—The term "'Qualified Anti-Terrorism Technology" or "QATT" means any Technology (including information technology) designed, developed, modified, procured, or sold for the purpose of preventing, detecting, identifying, or deterring acts of terrorism or limiting the harm such acts might otherwise cause, for which a Designation has been issued pursuant to this part.

SAFETY Act or Act—The term "SAFETY Act" or "Act" means the Support Anti-terrorism by Fostering Effective Technologies Act of 2002, sections 441–444 of title 6, United States Code.

SAFETY Act Application Kit—The term "SAFETY Act Application Kit" means the Application Kit containing the instructions and forms necessary to apply for Designation or Certification. The SAFETY Act Application Kit shall be published at *http://www.safetyact.gov* or made available in hard copy upon written request to: Directorate of Science and Technology, SAFETY Act/room 4320, Department of Homeland Security, Washington, DC 20528.

SAFETY Act Confidential Information—Any and all information and data voluntarily submitted to the Department under this part (including Applications, Pre-Applications, other forms, supporting documents and other materials relating to any of the foregoing, and responses to requests for additional information), including, but not limited to, inventions, devices, Technology, know-how, designs, copyrighted information, trade secrets, confidential business information, analyses, test and evaluation results, manuals, videotapes, contracts, letters, facsimile transmissions, electronic mail and other correspondence, financial information and projections, actuarial calculations, liability estimates, insurance quotations, and business and marketing plans. Notwithstanding the foregoing, "SAFETY Act Confidential Information" shall not include any information or data that is in the public domain or becomes part of the public domain by any means other than the violation of this section.

Secretary—The term "Secretary" means the Secretary of Homeland Security as established by section 102 of the Homeland Security Act of 2002.

Seller—The term "Seller" means any person, firm, or other entity that sells or otherwise provides Qualified Anti-Terrorism Technology to any customer(s) and to whom or to which (as appropriate) a Designation and/or Certification has been issued under this part (unless the context requires otherwise).

Technology—The term "Technology" means any product, equipment, service (including support services), device, or technology (including information technology) or any combination of the foregoing. Design services, consulting services, engineering services, software development services, software integration services, threat assessments, vulnerability studies, and other analyses relevant to homeland security may be deemed a Technology under this part.

Under Secretary—The term "Under Secretary" means the Under Secretary for Science and Technology of the Department of Homeland Security.

§ 25.3 Delegation.

All of the Secretary's responsibilities, powers, and functions under the SAFETY Act, except the authority to declare that an act is an Act of Terrorism for purposes of section 865(2) of the SAFETY Act, may be exercised by the Under Secretary for Science and Technology of the Department of Homeland Security or the Under Secretary's designees.

§25.4 Designation of qualified anti-terrorism technologies.

(a) *General.* The Under Secretary may Designate as a Qualified Anti-Terrorism Technology for purposes of the protections under the system of litigation and risk management set forth in sections 441–444 of Title 6, United States Code, any qualifying Technology designed, developed, modified, provided or procured for the specific purpose of preventing, detecting, identifying, or deterring acts of terrorism or limiting the harm such acts might otherwise cause.

(b) *Criteria to be Considered.* (1) In determining whether to issue the Designation under paragraph (a) of this section, the Under Secretary may exercise discretion and judgment in considering the following criteria and evaluating the Technology:

(i) Prior United States Government use or demonstrated substantial utility and effectiveness.

(ii) Availability of the Technology for immediate deployment in public and private settings.

(iii) Existence of extraordinarily large or extraordinarily unquantifiable potential third party liability risk exposure to the Seller or other provider of such anti-terrorism Technology.

(iv) Substantial likelihood that such anti-terrorism Technology will not be deployed unless protections under the system of risk management provided under sections 441–444 of title 6, United States Code, are extended.

(v) Magnitude of risk exposure to the public if such anti-terrorism Technology is not deployed.

(vi) Evaluation of all scientific studies that can be feasibly conducted in order to assess the capability of the Technology to substantially reduce risks of harm.

(vii) Anti-terrorism Technology that would be effective in facilitating the defense against acts of terrorism, including Technologies that prevent, defeat or respond to such acts.

(viii) A determination made by Federal, State, or local officials, that the Technology is appropriate for the purpose of preventing, detecting, identifying or deterring acts of terrorism or limiting the harm such acts might otherwise cause.

(ix) Any other factor that the Under Secretary may consider to be relevant to the determination or to the homeland security of the United States.

(2) The Under Secretary has discretion to give greater weight to some factors over others, and the relative weighting of the various criteria may vary depending upon the particular Technology at issue and the threats that the Technology is designed to address. The Under Secretary may, in his discretion, determine that failure to meet a particular criterion justifies denial of an application under the SAFETY Act. However, the Under Secretary is not required to reject an application that fails to meet one or more of the criteria. The Under Secretary may conclude, after considering all of the relevant criteria and any other relevant factors, that a particular Technology merits Designation as a Qualified Anti-Terrorism Technology even if one or more particular criteria are not satisfied. The Under Secretary's considerations will take into account evolving threats and conditions that give rise to the need for the anti-terrorism Technologies.

(c) *Use of Standards.* From time to time, the Under Secretary may develop, issue, revise, adopt, and recommend technical standards for various categories or components of anti-terrorism Technologies ("Adopted Standards"). In the case of Adopted Standards that are developed by the Department or that the Department has the right or license to reproduce, the Department will make such standards available to the public consistent with necessary protection of sensitive homeland security information. In the case of Adopted Standards that the Department does not have the right or license to reproduce, the Directorate of Science and Technology will publish a list and summaries of such standards and may publish information regarding the sources for obtaining copies of such standards. Compliance with any Adopted Standard or other technical standards that are applicable to a particular anti-terrorism Technology may be considered in determining whether a Technology will be Designated pursuant to paragraph (a) of this section. Depending on whether an Adopted Standard otherwise meets the criteria set forth in section 862 of the Homeland Security Act; 6 U.S.C. 441, the Adopted Standard itself may be deemed a Technology that may be Designated as a Qualified Anti-Terrorism Technology.

(d) *Consideration of Substantial Equivalence.* In considering the criteria in paragraph (b) of this section, or evaluating whether a particular anti-terrorism Technology complies with any Adopted Standard referenced in paragraph (c) of this section, the Under Secretary may consider evidence that the Technology is substantially equivalent to other Technologies ("Predicate Technologies") that previously have been Designated as Qualified Anti-Terrorism Technologies under the SAFETY Act. A Technology may be deemed to be substantially equivalent to a Predicate Technology if:

(1) It has the same intended use as the Predicate Technology; and

(2) It has the same or substantially similar performance or technological characteristics as the Predicate Technology.

(e) *Pre-Application Consultations.* To the extent that he deems it to be appropriate, the Under Secretary may consult with prospective and current SAFETY Act applicants regarding their particular anti-terrorism Technologies. Prospective applicants may request such consultations through the Office of SAFETY Act Implementation. The confidentiality provisions in § 25.10 shall be applicable to such consultations.

(f) *Developmental Testing & Evaluation (DT&E) Designations.* With respect to any Technology that is being developed, tested, evaluated, modified or is otherwise being prepared for deployment for the purpose of preventing, detecting, identifying, or deterring acts of terrorism or limiting the harm such acts might otherwise cause, the Under Secretary may Designate such Technology as a Qualified Anti-Terrorism Technology and make such Technology eligible for the protections under the system of litigation and risk manage-

ment set forth in sections 441–444 of title 6, United States Code. A Designation made pursuant to this paragraph shall be referred to as a "DT&E Designation," and shall confer all of the rights, privileges and obligations that accompany Designations made pursuant to paragraph (a) of this section except as modified by the terms of this paragraph or the terms of the particular DT&E Designation. The intent of this paragraph is to make eligible for SAFETY Act protections qualifying Technologies that are undergoing testing and evaluation and that may need to be deployed in the field either for developmental testing and evaluation purposes or on an emergency basis, including during a period of heightened risk. DT&E Designations shall describe the subject Technology (in such detail as the Under Secretary deems to be appropriate); identify the Seller of the subject Technology; be limited to the period of time set forth in the applicable DT&E Designation, which in no instance shall exceed a reasonable period for testing or evaluating the Technology (presumptively not longer than 36 months); be terminable by the Under Secretary at any time upon notice to the Seller; be subject to the limitations on the use or deployment of the QATT set forth in the DT&E Designation; and be subject to such other limitations as established by the Under Secretary. The protections associated with a DT&E Designation shall apply only during the period specified in the applicable DT&E Designation. Consent of the Seller of a QATT Designated pursuant to this paragraph will be a condition precedent to the establishment of any deployment or use condition and any other obligation established by the Under Secretary pursuant to this paragraph. Those seeking a DT&E Designation for a QATT pursuant to this paragraph (f) shall follow the procedures for DT&E Designations set forth in the SAFETY Act Application Kit.

§ 25.5 Obligations of seller.

(a) *Liability Insurance Required.* The Seller shall obtain liability insurance of such types and in such amounts as shall be required in the applicable Designation, which shall be the amounts and types certified by the Under Secretary to satisfy otherwise compensable third-party claims arising out of, relating to, or resulting from an Act of Terrorism when Qualified Anti-Terrorism Technologies have been deployed in defense against, response to, or recovery from, such act. The Under Secretary may request at any time that the Seller of a Qualified Anti-Terrorism Technology submit any information that would:

(1) Assist in determining the amount of liability insurance required; or

(2) Show that the Seller or any other provider of Qualified Anti-Terrorism Technology otherwise has met all of the requirements of this section.

(b) *Amount of Liability Insurance.* (1) The Under Secretary may determine the appropriate amounts and types of liability insurance that the Seller will be required to obtain and maintain based on criteria he may establish to satisfy compensable third-party claims arising from, relating to or resulting from an Act of Terrorism. In determining the amount of liability insurance required, the Under Secretary may consider any factor, including, but not limited to, the following:

(i) The particular Technology at issue;

(ii) The amount of liability insurance the Seller maintained prior to application;

(iii) The amount of liability insurance maintained by the Seller for other Technologies or for the Seller's business as a whole;

(iv) The amount of liability insurance typically maintained by Sellers of comparable Technologies;

(v) Information regarding the amount of liability insurance offered on the world market;

(vi) Data and history regarding mass casualty losses;

(vii) The intended use of the Technology; and

(viii) The possible effects of the cost of insurance on the price of the product, and the possible consequences thereof for development, production, or deployment of the Technology.

(2) In determining the appropriate amounts and types of insurance that a particular Seller is obligated to carry, the Under Secretary may not require any type of insurance or any amount of insurance that is not available on the world market, and may not require any type or amount of insurance that would unreasonably distort the sales price of the Seller's anti-terrorism Technology

(c) *Scope of Coverage.* (1) Liability insurance required to be obtained pursuant to this section shall, in addition to the Seller, protect the following, to the extent of their potential liability for involvement in the manufacture, qualification, sale, use, or operation of Qualified Anti-Terrorism Technologies deployed in defense against, response to, or recovery from, an Act of Terrorism:

(i) Contractors, subcontractors, suppliers, vendors and customers of the Seller.

(ii) Contractors, subcontractors, suppliers, and vendors of the customer.

(2) Notwithstanding the foregoing, in appropriate instances the Under Secretary will specify in a particular Designation that, consistent with the Department's interpretation of the SAFETY Act, an action for the recovery of damages proximately caused by a Qualified Anti-Terrorism Technology that arises out of, relates to, or results from an Act of Terrorism may properly be brought only against the Seller and, accordingly, the liability insurance required to be obtained pursuant to this section shall be required to protect only the Seller.

(d) *Third Party Claims.* To the extent available pursuant to the SAFETY Act, liability insurance required to be obtained pursuant to this section shall provide coverage against third party claims arising out of, relating to, or resulting from an Act of Terrorism when the applicable Qualified Anti-Terrorism Technologies have been deployed in defense against, response to, or recovery from such act.

(e) *Reciprocal Waiver of Claims.* The Seller shall enter into a reciprocal waiver of claims with its contractors, subcontractors, suppliers, vendors, and customers, and contractors and subcontractors of the customers, involved in the manufacture, sale, use, or operation of Qualified Anti-Terrorism Technologies, under which each party to the waiver agrees to be responsible for losses, including business interruption losses, that it sustains, or for losses sustained by its own employees resulting from an activity resulting from an Act of Terrorism when Qualified Anti-Terrorism Technologies have been deployed in defense against, response to, or recovery from such act. Notwithstanding the foregoing, provided that the Seller has used diligent efforts in good faith to obtain all required reciprocal waivers, obtaining such waivers shall not be a condition precedent or subsequent for, nor shall the failure to obtain one or more of such waivers adversely affect, the issuance, validity, effectiveness, duration, or applicability of a Designation or a Certification. Nothing in this paragraph (e) shall be interpreted to render the failure to obtain one or more of such waivers a condition precedent or subsequent for the issuance, validity, effectiveness, duration, or applicability of a Designation or a Certification.

(f) *Information to be Submitted by the Seller.* As part of any application for a Designation, the Seller shall provide all information that may be requested by the Under Secretary or his designee, regarding a Seller's liability insurance coverage applicable to third-party claims arising out of, relating to, or resulting from an Act of Terrorism when the Seller's Qualified Anti-Terrorism Technology has been deployed in defense against, response to, or recovery from such act, including:

(1) Names of insurance companies, policy numbers, and expiration dates;

(2) A description of the types and nature of such insurance (including the extent to which the Seller is self-insured or intends to self-insure);

(3) Dollar limits per occurrence and annually of such insurance, including any applicable sublimits;

(4) Deductibles or self-insured retentions, if any, that are applicable;

(5) Any relevant exclusions from coverage under such policies or other factors that would affect the amount of insurance proceeds that would be available to satisfy third party claims arising out of, relating to, or resulting from an Act of Terrorism;

(6) The price for such insurance, if available, and the per-unit amount or percentage of such price directly related to liability coverage for the Seller's Qualified Anti-Terrorism Technology deployed in defense against, or response to, or recovery from an Act of Terrorism;

(7) Where applicable, whether the liability insurance, in addition to the Seller, protects contractors, subcontractors, suppliers, vendors and customers of the Seller and contractors, subcontractors, suppliers, vendors and customers of the customer to the extent of their potential liability for involvement in the manufacture, qualification, sale, use or operation of Qualified Anti-terrorism Technologies deployed in defense against, response to, or recovery from an Act of Terrorism; and

(8) Any limitations on such liability insurance.

(g) *Under Secretary's Certification.* For each Qualified Anti-Terrorism Technology, the Under Secretary shall certify the amount of liability insurance the Seller is required to carry pursuant to section 443(a) of title 6, United States Code, and paragraphs (a), (b), and (c) of this section. The Under Secretary shall include the insurance certification under this section as a part of the applicable Designation. The insurance certification may specify a period of time for which such insurance certification will apply. The Seller of a Qualified Anti-Terrorism Technology may at any time petition the Under Secretary for a revision of the insurance certification under this section, and the Under Secretary may revise such insurance certification in response to such a petition. The Under Secretary may at any time request information from the Seller regarding the insurance carried by the Seller or the amount of insurance available to the Seller.

(h) *Seller's Continuing Obligations.* Within 30 days after the Under Secretary's insurance certification required by paragraph (g) of this section, the Seller shall certify to the Under Secretary in writing that the Seller has obtained the required insurance. Within 30 days of each anniversary of the issuance of a Designation or at any other time as he may determine, the

Under Secretary may require, by written notice to the Seller, that the Seller certify to the Under Secretary in writing that the Seller has maintained the required insurance. The Under Secretary may terminate a Designation if the Seller fails to provide any of the insurance certifications required by this paragraph (h) or provides a false certification.

§25.6 Procedures for designation of qualified anti-terrorism technologies.

(a) *Application Procedure.* Any person, firm or other entity seeking a Designation shall submit an application to the Under Secretary or such other official as may be named from time to time by the Under Secretary. Such applications shall be submitted according to the procedures set forth in and using the appropriate forms contained in the SAFETY Act Application Kit prescribed by the Under Secretary, which shall be made available at *http://www.safetyact.gov* and by mail upon written request to: Directorate of Science and Technology, SAFETY Act/room 4320, Department of Homeland Security, Washington, DC 20528. The burden is on the applicant to make timely submission of all relevant data requested in the SAFETY Act Application Kit to substantiate an application for Designation. An applicant may withdraw a submitted application at any time and for any reason by making a written request for withdrawal with the Department. Withdrawal of a SAFETY Act application shall have no prejudicial effect on any other application.

(b) *Initial Notification.* Within 30 days after receipt of an application for a Designation, the Under Secretary his designee shall notify the applicant in writing that:

(1) The application is complete and will be reviewed and evaluated, or

(2) That the application is incomplete, in which case the missing or incomplete parts will be specified.

(c) *Review Process.* (1) The Under Secretary or his designee will review each complete application and any included supporting materials. In performing this function, the Under Secretary or his designee may but is not required to:

(i) Request additional information from the Seller;

(ii) Meet with representatives of the Seller;

(iii) Consult with, and rely upon the expertise of, any other Federal or non-Federal entity;

(iv) Perform studies or analyses of the subject Technology or the insurance market for such Technology; and

(v) Seek information from insurers regarding the availability of insurance for such Technology.

(2) For Technologies with which a Federal, State, or local government agency already has substantial experience or data (through the procurement process or through prior use or review), the review may rely in part upon such prior experience and, thus, may be expedited. The Under Secretary may consider any scientific studies, testing, field studies, or other experience with the Technology that he deems appropriate and that are available or can be feasibly conducted or obtained, including test results produced by an independent laboratory or other entity engaged to test or verify the safety, utility, performance, in order to assess the effectiveness of the Technology or the capability of the Technology to substantially reduce risks of harm. Such studies may, in the Under Secretary's discretion, include, without limitation:

(i) Public source studies;

(ii) Classified and otherwise confidential studies;

(iii) Studies, tests, or other performance records or data provided by or available to the producer of the specific Technology; and

(iv) Proprietary studies that are available to the Under Secretary.

(3) In considering whether or the extent to which it is feasible to defer a decision on a Designation until additional scientific studies can be conducted on a particular Technology, the Under Secretary will bring to bear his expertise concerning the protection of the security of the United States and will consider the urgency of the need for the Technology.

(d) *Action by the Under Secretary.* Within 90 days of notification to the Seller that an application for a Designation is complete in accordance with paragraph (b)(1) of this section, the Under Secretary shall take one of the following actions:

(1) Approve the application and issue an appropriate Designation to the applicant for the Technology, which shall include the insurance certification required by § 25.5(h) of this part;

(2) Notify the applicant in writing that the Technology is potentially eligible for a Designation, but that additional specified information is needed before a decision may be reached; or

(3) Deny the application, and notify the applicant in writing of such decision. The Under Secretary may extend the 90-day time period for up to 45 days upon notice to the Seller. The Under Secretary is not required to provide a reason or cause for such extension. The Under Secretary's decision shall be final and not subject to review, except at the discretion of the Under Secretary.

(e) *Content of Designation.* (1) A Designation shall:

(i) Describe the Qualified Anti-Terrorism Technology (in such detail as the Under Secretary deems to be appropriate);

(ii) Identify the Seller(s) of the Qualified Anti-Terrorism Technology;

(iii) Specify the earliest date of sale of the Qualified Anti-Terrorism Technology to which the Designation shall apply (which shall be determined by the Under Secretary in his discretion, and may be prior to, but shall not be later than, the effective date of the Designation);

(iv) Set forth the insurance certification required by § 25.5(g); and

(v) To the extent practicable, include such standards, specifications, requirements, performance criteria, limitations, or other information as the Department in its sole and unreviewable discretion may deem appropriate.

(2) The Designation may, but need not, specify other entities that are required to be covered by the liability insurance required to be purchased by the Seller. The failure to specify a covered person, firm, or other entity in a Designation will not preclude the application or applicability of the Act's protections to that person, firm, or other entity.

(f) *Term of Designation; Renewal.* A Designation shall be valid and effective for a term of five to eight years (as determined by the Under Secretary) commencing on the date of issuance, and the protections conferred by the Designation shall continue in full force and effect indefinitely to all sales of Qualified Anti-Terrorism Technologies covered by the Designation. At any time within two years prior to the expiration of the term of the Designation, the Seller may apply for renewal of the Designation. The Under Secretary shall make the application form for renewal available at *http://www.safetyact.gov* and by mail upon request sent to: Directorate of Science and Technology, SAFETY Act/room 4320, Department of Homeland Security, Washington, DC 20528.

(g) *Government Procurements*—(1) *Overview.* The Under Secretary may coordinate the review of a Technology for SAFETY Act purposes in connection with a Federal, State, or local government agency procurement of an anti-terrorism Technology in any manner he deems appropriate consistent with the Act and other applicable law. A determination by the Under Secretary to issue a Designation, or not to issue a Designation for a particular Technology as a QATT is not a determination that the Technology meets, or fails to meet, the requirements of any solicitation issued by any Federal government customer or non-Federal government customer. Determinations by the Under Secretary with respect to whether to issue a Designation for Technologies submitted for his review shall be based on the factors identified in § 25.4(b).

(2) *Procedure.* Any Federal, State, or local government agency that engages in or is planning to engage in the procurement of a Technology that potentially qualifies as a Qualified Anti-terrorism Technology, through the use of a solicitation of proposals or otherwise, may request that the Under Secretary issue a notice stating that the Technology to be procured either affirmatively or presumptively satisfies the technical criteria necessary to be deemed a Qualified Anti-Terrorism Technology (a "Pre-Qualification Designation Notice"). The Pre-Qualification Designation Notice will provide that the vendor(s) chosen to provide

the Technology (the "Selected Vendor(s)"), upon submitting an application for SAFETY Act Designation will: Receive expedited review of their application for Designation; either affirmatively or presumptively (as the case may be) be deemed to have satisfied the technical criteria for SAFETY Act Designation with respect to the Technology identified in the Pre-Qualification Designation Notice; and be authorized to submit a streamlined application as set forth in the Pre-Qualification Designation Notice. In instances in which the subject procurement involves Technology with respect to which a Block Designation or Block Certification has been issued, the Department may determine that the vendor providing such Technology will affirmatively receive Designation or Certification with respect to such Technology, provided the vendor satisfy each other applicable requirement for Designation or Certification. Government agencies seeking a Pre-Qualification Designation Notice shall submit a written request using the "Procurement Pre-Qualification Request" form prescribed by the Under Secretary and made available at *http://www.safetyact.gov* and by mail upon request sent to: Directorate of Science and Technology, SAFETY Act/room 4320, Department of Homeland Security, Washington, DC 20528.

(3) *Actions.* Within 60 days after the receipt of a complete Procurement Pre-Qualification Request, the Under Secretary shall take one of the following actions:

(i) Approve the Procurement Pre-Qualification Request and issue an appropriate Pre-Qualification Designation Notice to the requesting agency that it may include in the government contract or in the solicitation materials, as appropriate; or

(ii) Notify the requesting agency in writing that the relevant procurement is potentially eligible for a Pre-Qualification Designation Notice, but that additional information is needed before a decision may be reached; or

(iii) Deny the Procurement Pre-Qualification Request and notify the requesting agency in writing of such decision, including the reasons for such denial.

(4) *Contents of Notice.* A Pre-Qualification Designation Notice shall contain, at a minimum, the following:

(i) A detailed description of and detailed specifications for the Technology to which the Pre-Qualification Designation Notice applies, which may incorporate by reference all or part of the procurement solicitation documents issued or to be issued by the requesting agency;

(ii) A statement that the Technology to which the Pre-Qualification Designation Notice applies satisfies the technical criteria to be deemed a Qualified Anti-Terrorism Technology and that the Selected Vendor(s) may presumptively or will qualify for the issuance of a Designation for such Technology upon compliance with the terms and conditions set forth in such Pre-Qualification Designation Notice and the approval of the streamlined application;

(iii) A list of the portions of the application referenced in §25.6(a) that the Selected Vendor(s) must complete and submit to the Department in order to obtain Designation and the appropriate period of time for such submission;

(iv) The period of time within which the Under Secretary will take action upon such submission;

(v) The date of expiration of such Pre-Qualification Designation Notice; and

(vi) Any other terms or conditions that the Under Secretary deems to be appropriate in his discretion.

(5) *Review of Completed Applications.* The application for Designation from the Selected Vendor(s) shall be considered, processed, and acted upon in accordance with the procedures set forth in §25.6 (which shall be deemed to be modified by the terms and conditions set forth in the applicable Pre-Qualification Designation Notice). However, the review and evaluation of the Technology to be procured from the Selected Vendor(s), in relation to the criteria set forth in §25.4(b), shall ordinarily consist of a validation that that the Technology complies with the detailed description of and detailed specifications for the Technology set forth in the applicable Pre-Qualification Designation Notice.

(h) *Block Designations.* (1) From time to time, the Under Secretary, in response to an application submitted pursuant to § 25.6(a) or upon his own initiative, may issue a Designation that is applicable to any person, firm, or other entity that is a qualified Seller of the QATT described in such Designation (a "Block Designation"). A Block Designation will be issued only for Technology that relies on established performance standards or defined technical characteristics. All Block Designations shall be published by the Department within ten days after the issuance thereof at *http://www.safetyact.gov*, and copies may also be obtained by mail by sending a request to: Directorate of Science and Technology, SAFETY Act/room 4320, Department of Homeland Security, Washington, DC 20528. Any person, firm, or other entity that desires to qualify as a Seller of a QATT that has received a Block Designation shall complete only such portions of the application referenced in § 25.6(a) as are specified in such Block Designation and shall submit an application to the Department in accordance with § 25.6(a) and the terms of the Block Designation. Applicants seeking to be qualified Sellers of a QATT pursuant to a Block Designation will receive expedited review of their applications and shall not be required to provide information with respect to the technical merits of the QATT that has received Block Designation. Within 60 days (or such other period of time as may be specified in the applicable Block Designation) after the receipt by the Department of a complete application, the Under Secretary shall take one of the following actions:

(i) Approve the application and notify the applicant in writing of such approval, which notification shall include the certification required by § 25.5(g); or

(ii) Deny the application, and notify the applicant in writing of such decision, including the reasons for such denial.

(2) If the application is approved, commencing on the date of such approval the applicant shall be deemed to be a Seller under the applicable Block Designation for all purposes under the SAFETY Act, this part, and such Block Designation. A Block Designation shall be valid and effective for a term of five to eight years (as determined by the Under Secretary in his discretion) commencing on the date of issuance, and may be renewed or extended by the Under Secretary at his own initiative or in response to an application for renewal submitted by a qualified Seller under such Block Designation in accordance with § 25.6(h). Except as otherwise specifically provided in this paragraph, a Block Designation shall be deemed to be a Designation for all purposes under the SAFETY Act and this part.

(i) *Other Bases for Expedited Review of Applications.* The Under Secretary may identify other categories or types of Technologies for which expedited processing may be granted. For example, the Under Secretary may conduct expedited processing for applications addressing a particular threat or for particular types of anti-terrorism Technologies. The Under Secretary shall notify the public of any such opportunities for expedited processing by publishing such notice in the FEDERAL REGISTER.

(j) *Transfer of Designation.* Except as may be restricted by the terms and conditions of a Designation, any Designation may be transferred and assigned to any other person, firm, or other entity to which the Seller transfers and assigns all right, title, and interest in and to the Technology covered by the Designation, including the intellectual property rights therein (or, if the Seller is a licensee of the Technology, to any person, firm, or other entity to which such Seller transfers all of its right, title, and interest in and to the applicable license agreement). Such transfer and assignment of a Designation will not be effective unless and until the Under Secretary is notified in writing of the transfer using the "Application for Transfer of Designation" form issued by the Under Secretary (the Under Secretary shall make this application form available at *http://www.safetyact.gov* and by mail by written request sent to: Directorate of Science and Technology, SAFETY Act/room 4320, Department of Homeland Security, Washington, DC 20528).

Upon the effectiveness of such transfer and assignment, the transferee will be deemed to be a Seller in the place and stead of the transferor with respect to the applicable Technology for all purposes under the SAFETY Act, this part, and the transferred Designation. The transferred Designation will continue to apply to the transferor with respect to all transactions and occurrences that occurred through the time at which the transfer and assignment of the Designation became effective, as specified in the applicable Application for Transfer of Designation.

(k) *Application of Designation to Licensees.* Except as may be restricted by the terms and conditions of a Designation, any Designation shall apply to any other person, firm, or other entity to which the Seller licenses (exclusively or nonexclusively) the right to manufacture, use, or sell the Technology, in the same manner and to the same extent that such Designation applies to the Seller, effective as of the date of commencement of the license, provided that the Seller notifies the Under Secretary of such license by submitting, within 30 days after such date of commencement, a "Notice of License of Qualified Anti-terrorism Technology" form issued by the Under Secretary. The Under Secretary shall make this form available at *http://www.safetyact.gov* and by mail upon request sent to: Directorate of Science and Technology, SAFETY Act/room 4320, Department of Homeland Security, Washington, DC 20528. Such notification shall not be required for any licensee listed as a Seller on the applicable Designation.

(1) *Significant Modification of Qualified Anti-terrorism Technologies.* (1) The Department recognizes that Qualified Anti-Terrorism Technologies may routinely undergo changes or modifications in their manufacturing, materials, installation, implementation, operating processes, component assembly, or in other respects from time to time. When a Seller makes routine changes or modifications to a Qualified Anti-Terrorism Technology, such that the QATT remains within the scope of the description set forth in the applicable Designation or Certification, the Seller shall not be required to provide notice under this subsection, and the changes or modifications shall not adversely affect the force or effect of the Seller's QATT Designation or Certification.

(2) A Seller shall promptly notify the Department and provide details of any change or modification to a QATT that causes the QATT no longer to be within the scope of the Designation or Certification by submitting to the Department a completed "Notice of Modification to Qualified Anti-Terrorism Technology" form issued by the Under Secretary (a "Modification Notice"). A Seller is not required to notify the Department of any change or modification of a particular Qualified Anti-Terrorism Technology that is made post-sale by a purchaser unless the Seller has consented expressly to the modification. The Under Secretary shall make an appropriate form available at *http://www.safetyact.gov* and by mail upon request sent to: Directorate of Science and Technology, SAFETY Act/ room 4320, Department of Homeland Security, Washington, DC 20528. The Department will promptly acknowledge receipt of a Modification Notice by providing the relevant Seller with written notice to that effect. Within 60 days of the receipt of a Modification Notice, the Under Secretary may, in his sole and unreviewable discretion:

(i) Inform the submitting Seller that the QATT as changed or modified is consistent with, and is not outside the scope of, the Seller's Designation or Certification;

(ii) Issue to the Seller a modified Designation or Certification incorporating some or all of the notified changes or modifications;

(iii) Seek further information regarding the changes or modifications and temporarily suspend the 60-day period of review;

(iv) Inform the submitting Seller that the changes or modifications might cause the QATT as changed or modified to be outside the scope of the Seller's Designation or Certification, and require further review and consideration by the Department;

(v) Inform the submitting Seller that the QATT as changed or modified is outside the scope of the subject Seller's

Designation or Certification, and require that the QATT be brought back into conformance with the Seller's Designation or Certification; or

(vi) If the Seller fails to bring the subject QATT into conformance in accordance with the Under Secretary's direction pursuant to paragraph (1)(2)(v) of this section, issue a public notice stating that the QATT as changed or modified is outside the scope of the submitting Seller's Designation or Certification and, consequentially, that such Designation or Certification is not applicable to the QATT as changed or modified. If the Under Secretary does not take one or more of such actions within the 60-day period following the Department's receipt of a Seller's Modification Notice, the changes or modifications identified in the Modification Notice will be deemed to be approved by the Under Secretary and the QATT, as changed or modified, will be conclusively established to be within the scope of the description of the QATT in the Seller's Designation or Certification.

(3) Notwithstanding anything to the contrary herein, a Seller's original QATT Designation or Certification will continue in full force and effect in accordance with its terms unless modified, suspended, or terminated by the Under Secretary in his discretion, including during the pendency of the review of the Seller's Modification Notice. In no event will any SAFETY Act Designation or Certification terminate automatically or retroactively under this section. A Seller is not required to notify the Under Secretary of any change or modification that is made post-sale by a purchaser or end-user of the QATT without the Seller's consent, but the Under Secretary may, in appropriate circumstances, require an end-user to provide periodic reports on modifications or permit inspections or audits.

§ 25.7 Litigation management.

(a) Liability for all claims against a Seller arising out of, relating to, or resulting from an Act of Terrorism when such Seller's Qualified Anti-Terrorism Technology has been deployed in defense against, response to, or recovery from such act and such claims result or

may result in loss to the Seller shall not be in an amount greater than the limits of liability insurance coverage required to be maintained by the Seller under this section or as specified in the applicable Designation.

(b) In addition, in any action for damages brought under section 442 of Title 6, United States Code:

(1) No punitive damages intended to punish or deter, exemplary damages, or other damages not intended to compensate a plaintiff for actual losses may be awarded, nor shall any party be liable for interest prior to the judgment;

(2) Noneconomic damages may be awarded against a defendant only in an amount directly proportional to the percentage of responsibility of such defendant for the harm to the plaintiff, and no plaintiff may recover noneconomic damages unless the plaintiff suffered physical harm; and

(3) Any recovery by a plaintiff shall be reduced by the amount of collateral source compensation, if any, that the plaintiff has received or is entitled to receive as a result of such Acts of Terrorism that result or may result in loss to the Seller.

(c) Without prejudice to the authority of the Under Secretary to terminate a Designation pursuant to paragraph (h) of § 25.6, the liability limitations and reductions set forth in this section shall apply in perpetuity to all sales or deployments of a Qualified Anti-Terrorism Technology in defense against, response to, or recovery from any Act of Terrorism that occurs on or after the effective date of the Designation applicable to such Qualified Anti-Terrorism Technology, regardless of whether any liability insurance coverage required to be obtained by the Seller is actually obtained or maintained or not, provided that the sale of such Qualified Anti-Terrorism Technology was consummated by the Seller on or after the earliest date of sale of such Qualified Anti-Terrorism Technology specified in such Designation and prior to the earlier of the expiration or termination of such Designation.

(d) There shall exist only one cause of action for loss of property, personal injury, or death for performance or non-performance of the Seller's Qualified Anti-Terrorism Technology in relation to an Act of Terrorism. Such cause of action may be brought only against the Seller of the Qualified Anti-Terrorism Technology and may not be brought against the buyers, the buyers' contractors, or downstream users of the Technology, the Seller's suppliers or contractors, or any other person or entity. In addition, such cause of action must be brought in the appropriate district court of the United States.

§25.8 **Government contractor Defense.**

(a) *Criteria for Certification.* The Under Secretary may issue a Certification for a Qualified Anti-Terrorism Technology as an Approved Product for Homeland Security for purposes of establishing a rebuttable presumption of the applicability of the government contractor defense. In determining whether to issue such Certification, the Under Secretary or his designee shall conduct a comprehensive review of the design of such Technology and determine whether it will perform as intended, conforms to the Seller's specifications, and is safe for use as intended. The Seller shall provide safety and hazard analyses and other relevant data and information regarding such Qualified Anti-Terrorism Technology to the Department in connection with an application. The Under Secretary or his designee may require that the Seller submit any information that the Under Secretary or his designee considers relevant to the application for approval. The Under Secretary or his designee may consult with, and rely upon the expertise of, any other governmental or non-governmental person, firm, or entity, and may consider test results produced by an independent laboratory or other person, firm, or other entity engaged by the Seller.

(b) *Extent of liability.* Should a product liability or other lawsuit be filed for claims arising out of, relating to, or resulting from an Act of Terrorism when Qualified Anti-Terrorism Technologies Certified by the Under Secretary as provided in §§25.8 and 25.9 of this part have been deployed in defense against or response or recovery from such act and such claims result or may

result in loss to the Seller, there shall be a rebuttable presumption that the government contractor defense applies in such lawsuit. This presumption shall only be overcome by clear and convincing evidence showing that the Seller acted fraudulently or with willful misconduct in submitting information to the Department during the course of the consideration of such Technology under this section and §25.9 of this part. A claimant's burden to show fraud or willful misconduct in connection with a Seller's SAFETY Act application cannot be satisfied unless the claimant establishes there was a knowing and deliberate intent to deceive the Department. This presumption of the government contractor defense shall apply regardless of whether the claim against the Seller arises from a sale of the product to Federal Government or non-Federal Government customers. Such presumption shall apply in perpetuity to all deployments of a Qualified Anti-Terrorism Technology (for which a Certification has been issued by the Under Secretary as provided in this section and §25.9 of this part) in defense against, response to, or recovery from any Act of Terrorism that occurs on or after the effective date of the Certification applicable to such Technology, provided that the sale of such Technology was consummated by the Seller on or after the earliest date of sale of such Technology specified in such Certification (which shall be determined by the Under Secretary in his discretion, and may be prior to, but shall not be later than, such effective date) and prior to the expiration or termination of such Certification.

(c) *Establishing applicability of the government contractor defense.* The Under Secretary will be exclusively responsible for the review and approval of anti-terrorism Technology for purposes of establishing the government contractor defense in any product liability lawsuit for claims arising out of, relating to, or resulting from an Act of Terrorism when Qualified Anti-Terrorism Technologies approved by the Under Secretary, as provided in this final rule, have been deployed in defense against or response or recovery from such act and such claims result or may result in loss to the Seller. The Certification of a Technology as an Approved Product for Homeland Security shall be the only evidence necessary to establish that the Seller of the Qualified Anti-Terrorism Technology that has been issue a Certification is entitled to a presumption of dismissal from a cause of action brought against a Seller arising out of, relating to, or resulting from an Act of Terrorism when the Qualified Anti-Terrorism Technology was deployed in defense against or response to or recovery from such Act of Terrorism. This presumption of dismissal is based upon the statutory government contractor defense conferred by the SAFETY Act.

§ 25.9 Procedures for certification of approved products for Homeland Security.

(a) *Application procedure.* An applicant seeking a Certification of anti-terrorism Technology as an Approved Product for Homeland Security under § 25.8 shall submit information supporting such request to the Under Secretary. The Under Secretary shall make application forms available at *http://www.safetyact.gov*, and copies may also be obtained by mail by sending a request to: Directorate of Science and Technology, SAFETY Act/room 4320, Department of Homeland Security, Washington, DC 20528. An application for a Certification may not be filed unless the applicant has also filed an application for a Designation for the same Technology in accordance with § 25.6(a). Such applications may be filed simultaneously and may be reviewed simultaneously by the Department.

(b) *Initial notification.* Within 30 days after receipt of an application for a Certification, the Under Secretary or his designee shall notify the applicant in writing that:

(1) The application is complete and will be reviewed, or

(2) That the application is incomplete, in which case the missing or incomplete parts will be specified.

(c) *Review process.* The Under Secretary or his designee will review each complete application for a Certification and any included supporting materials. In performing this function,

the Under Secretary or his designee may, but is not required to:

(1) Request additional information from the Seller;

(2) Meet with representatives of the Seller;

(3) Consult with, and rely upon the expertise of, any other Federal or non-Federal entity; and

(4) Perform or seek studies or analyses of the Technology.

(d) *Action by the Under Secretary.* (1) Within 90 days after receipt of a complete application for a Certification, the Under Secretary shall take one of the following actions:

(i) Approve the application and issue an appropriate Certification to the Seller;

(ii) Notify the Seller in writing that the Technology is potentially eligible for a Certification, but that additional specified information is needed before a decision may be reached; or

(iii) Deny the application, and notify the Seller in writing of such decision.

(2) The Under Secretary may extend the time period one time for 45 days upon notice to the Seller, and the Under Secretary is not required to provide a reason or cause for such extension. The Under Secretary's decision shall be final and not subject to review, except at the discretion of the Under Secretary.

(e) *Designation is a pre-condition.* The Under Secretary may approve an application for a Certification only if the Under Secretary has also approved an application for a Designation for the same Technology in accordance with § 25.4.

(f) *Content and term of certification; renewal.* (1) A Certification shall:

(i) Describe the Qualified Anti-Terrorism Technology (in such detail as the Under Secretary deems to be appropriate);

(ii) Identify the Seller(s) of the Qualified Anti-Terrorism Technology;

(iii) Specify the earliest date of sale of the Qualified Anti-Terrorism Technology to which the Certification shall apply (which shall be determined by the Under Secretary in his discretion, and may be prior to, but shall not be later than, the effective date of the Certification); and

(iv) To the extent practicable, include such standards, specifications, requirements, performance criteria, limitations, or other information as the Department in its sole and unreviewable discretion may deem appropriate.

(2) A Certification shall be valid and effective for the same period of time for which the related Designation is issued, and shall terminate upon the termination of such related Designation. The Seller may apply for renewal of the Certification in connection with an application for renewal of the related Designation. An application for renewal must be made using the "Application for Certification of an Approved Product for Homeland Security" form issued by the Under Secretary.

(g) *Application of Certification to licensees.* A Certification shall apply to any other person, firm, or other entity to which the applicable Seller licenses (exclusively or nonexclusively) the right to manufacture, use, or and sell the Technology, in the same manner and to the same extent that such Certification applies to the Seller, effective as of the date of commencement of the license, provided that the Seller notifies the Under Secretary of such license by submitting, within 30 days after such date of commencement, a "Notice of License of Approved Anti-terrorism Technology" form issued by the Under Secretary. The Under Secretary shall make this form available at *http://www.safetyact.gov* and by mail upon request sent to: Directorate of Science and Technology, SAFETY Act/room 4320, Department of Homeland Security, Washington, DC 20528. Such notification shall not be required for any licensee listed as a Seller on the applicable Certification.

(h) *Transfer of Certification.* In the event of any permitted transfer and assignment of a Designation, any related Certification for the same anti-terrorism Technology shall automatically be deemed to be transferred and assigned to the same transferee to which such Designation is transferred and assigned. The transferred Certification will continue to apply to the transferor with respect to all transactions and occurrences that occurred through the time at which such transfer and assignment of the Certification became effective.

(i) *Issuance of Certificate; Approved Product List.* For anti-terrorism Technology reviewed and approved by the Under Secretary and for which a Certification is issued, the Under Secretary shall issue a certificate of conformance to the Seller and place the anti-terrorism Technology on an Approved Product List for Homeland Security, which shall be published by the Department.

(j) *Block Certifications.* (1) From time to time, the Under Secretary, in response to an application submitted pursuant to §25.9(a) or at his own initiative, may issue a Certification that is applicable to any person, firm or other entity that is a qualified Seller of the Approved Product for Homeland Security described in such Certification (a "Block Certification"). All Block Certifications shall be published by the Department within ten days after the issuance thereof at *http://www.safetyact.gov*, and copies may also be obtained by mail by sending a request to: Directorate of Science and Technology, SAFETY Act/room 4320, Department of Homeland Security, Washington, DC 20528. Any person, firm, or other entity that desires to qualify as a Seller of an Approved Product for Homeland Security under a Block Certification shall complete only such portions of the application referenced in §25.9(a) as are specified in such Block Certification and shall submit such application to the Department in accordance with §9(a). Applicants seeking to be qualified Sellers of an Approved Product for Homeland Security pursuant to a Block Certification will receive expedited review of their applications and shall not be required to provide information with respect to the technical merits of the Approved Product for Homeland Security that has received Block Certification. Within 60 days (or such other period of time as may be specified in the applicable Block Certification) after the receipt by the Department of a complete application, the Under Secretary shall take one of the following actions:

(i) Approve the application and notify the applicant in writing of such approval; or

(ii) Deny the application, and notify the applicant in writing of such decision, including the reasons for such denial.

(2) If the application is approved, commencing on the date of such approval, the applicant shall be deemed to be a Seller under the applicable Block Certification for all purposes under the SAFETY Act, this part, and such Block Certification. A Block Certification shall be valid and effective for the same period of time for which the related Block Designation is issued. A Block Certification may be renewed by the Under Secretary at his own initiative or in response to an application for renewal submitted by a qualified Seller under such Block Certification in accordance with § 25.9(g). Except as otherwise specifically provided in this paragraph, a Block Certification shall be deemed to be a Certification for all purposes under the SAFETY Act and this part.

§ 25.10 **Confidentiality and protection of Intellectual Property.**

(a) *General.* The Secretary, in consultation with the Office of Management and Budget and appropriate Federal law enforcement and intelligence officials, and in a manner consistent with existing protections for sensitive or classified information, shall establish confidentiality procedures for safeguarding, maintenance and use of information submitted to the Department under this part. Such protocols shall, among other things, ensure that the Department will utilize all appropriate exemptions from the Freedom of Information Act.

(b) *Non-disclosure.* Except as otherwise required by applicable law or regulation or a final order of a court of competent jurisdiction, or as expressly authorized in writing by the Under Secretary, no person, firm, or other entity may:

(1) Disclose SAFETY Act Confidential Information (as defined above) to any person, firm, or other entity, or

(2) Use any SAFETY Act Confidential Information for his, her, or its own benefit or for the benefit of any other person, firm, or other entity, unless the applicant has consented to the release of such SAFETY Act Confidential Information.

(c) *Legends.* Any person, firm, or other entity that submits data or information to the Department under this part may place a legend on such data or information indicating that the submission constitutes SAFETY Act Confidential Information. The absence of such a legend shall not prevent any data or information submitted to the Department under this part from constituting or being considered by the Department to constitute SAFETY Act Confidential Information.

PART 27—CHEMICAL FACILITY ANTI-TERRORISM STANDARDS

Subpart A—General

Subpart B—Chemical Facility Security Program

Subpart C—Orders and Adjudications

AUTHORITY: 6 U.S.C. 624; Pub. L. 101–410, 104 Stat. 890, as amended by Pub. L. 114–74, 129 Stat. 599.

SOURCE: 72 FR 17729, Apr. 9, 2007, unless otherwise noted.

Subpart A—General

§27.100 Purpose.

The purpose of this part is to enhance the security of our Nation by furthering the mission of the Department as provided in 6 U.S.C. §111(b)(1) and by lowering the risk posed by certain chemical facilities.

§27.105 Definitions.

As used in this part:

A Commercial Grade (ACG) shall refer to any quality or concentration of a chemical of interest offered for commercial sale that a facility uses, stores, manufactures, or ships.

A Placarded Amount (APA) shall refer to the STQ for a sabotage and contamination chemical of interest, as calculated in accordance with §27.203(d).

Alternative Security Program or ASP shall mean a third-party or industry organization program, a local authority, state or Federal government program or any element or aspect thereof, that the Assistant Secretary has determined meets the requirements of this part and provides for an equivalent level of security to that established by this part.

Assistant Secretary shall mean the Assistant Secretary for Infrastructure Protection, Department of Homeland Security or his designee.

Chemical Facility or facility shall mean any establishment that possesses or plans to possess, at any relevant point in time, a quantity of a chemical substance determined by the Secretary to be potentially dangerous or that meets other risk-related criteria identified by the Department. As used herein, the term chemical facility or facility shall also refer to the owner or operator of the chemical facility. Where multiple owners and/or operators function within a common infrastructure or within a single fenced area, the Assistant Secretary may determine that such owners and/or operators constitute a single chemical facility or multiple chemical facilities depending on the circumstances.

Chemical of Interest shall refer to a chemical listed in appendix A to part 27.

Chemical Security Assessment Tool or CSAT shall mean a suite of four applications, including User Registration, Top-Screen, Security Vulnerability Assessment, and Site Security Plan, through which the Department will collect and analyze key data from chemical facilities.

Chemical-terrorism Vulnerability Information or CVI shall mean the information listed in §27.400(b).

Coordinating Official shall mean the person (or his designee(s)) selected by the Assistant Secretary to ensure that the regulations are implemented in a uniform, impartial, and fair manner.

Covered Facility or Covered Chemical Facility shall mean a chemical facility determined by the Assistant Secretary to present high levels of security risk, or a facility that the Assistant Secretary has determined is presumptively high risk under §27.200.

CUM 100g shall refer to the cumulative STQ of 100 grams for designated theft/diversion-CW/CWP chemicals and which is located in appendix A to part 27 as the entry for the STQ and Minimum Concentration of certain theft/diversion-CW/CWP chemicals.

Department shall mean the Department of Homeland Security.

Deputy Secretary shall mean the Deputy Secretary of the Department of Homeland Security or his designee.

Director of the Chemical Security Division or Director shall mean the Director of the Chemical Security Division, Office of Infrastructure Protection, Department of Homeland Security or any successors to that position within the Department or his designee.

General Counsel shall mean the General Counsel of the Department of Homeland Security or his designee.

Operator shall mean a person who has responsibility for the daily operations of a facility or facilities subject to this part.

Owner shall mean the person or entity that owns any facility subject to this part.

Present high levels of security risk and high risk shall refer to a chemical facility that, in the discretion of the Secretary of Homeland Security, presents a high risk of significant adverse consequences for human life or health, national security and/or critical economic assets if subjected to terrorist attack, compromise, infiltration, or exploitation.

Risk profiles shall mean criteria identified by the Assistant Secretary for determining which chemical facilities will complete the Top-Screen or provide other risk assessment information.

Screening Threshold Quantity or STQ shall mean the quantity of a chemical of interest, upon which the facility's obligation to complete and submit the CSAT Top-Screen is based.

Secretary or Secretary of Homeland Security shall mean the Secretary of the Department of Homeland Security or any person, officer or entity within the Department to whom the Secretary's authority under section 550 is delegated.

Security Issue shall refer to the type of risks associated with a given chemical. For purposes of this part, there are four main security issues:

(1) Release (including toxic, flammable, and explosive);

(2) Theft and diversion (including chemical weapons and chemical weapons precursors, weapons of mass effect, and explosives and improvised explosive device precursors),

(3) Sabotage and contamination, and

(4) Critical to government mission and national economy.

Terrorist attack or terrorist incident shall mean any incident or attempt that constitutes terrorism or terrorist activity under 6 U.S.C. 101(15) or 18 U.S.C. 2331(5) or 8 U.S.C. 1182(a)(3)(B)(iii), including any incident or attempt that involves or would involve sabotage of chemical facilities or theft, misappropriation or misuse of a dangerous quantity of chemicals.

Tier shall mean the risk level associated with a covered chemical facility and which is assigned to a facility by the Department. For purposes of this part, there are four risk-based tiers, ranging from highest risk at Tier 1 to lowest risk at Tier 4.

Top-Screen shall mean an initial screening process designed by the Assistant Secretary through which chemical facilities provide information to the Department for use pursuant to § 27.200 of these regulations.

Under Secretary shall mean the Under Secretary for National Protection and Programs, Department of Homeland Security or any successors to that position within the Department or his designee.

[72 FR 17729, Apr. 9, 2007, as amended at 72 FR 65418, Nov. 20, 2007]

§ 27.110 Applicability.

(a) This part applies to chemical facilities and to covered facilities as set out herein.

(b) This part does not apply to facilities regulated pursuant to the Maritime Transportation Security Act of 2002, Pub. L. 107–295, as amended; Public Water Systems, as defined by section 1401 of the Safe Drinking Water Act, Pub. L. 93–523, as amended; Treatment Works as defined in section 212 of the Federal Water Pollution Control Act, Pub. L. 92–500, as amended; any facility owned or operated by the Department of Defense or the Department of Energy, or any facility subject to regulation by the Nuclear Regulatory Commission.

§ 27.115 Implementation.

The Assistant Secretary may implement the section 550 program in a phased manner, selecting certain chemical facilities for expedited initial processes under these regulations and identifying other chemical facilities or types or classes of chemical facilities for other phases of program implementation. The Assistant Secretary has flexibility to designate particular chemical facilities for specific phases of program implementation based on potential risk or any other factor consistent with this part.

§27.120 Designation of a coordinating official; Consultations and technical assistance.

(a) The Assistant Secretary will designate a Coordinating Official who will be responsible for ensuring that these regulations are implemented in a uniform, impartial, and fair manner.

(b) The Coordinating Official and his staff shall provide guidance to covered facilities regarding compliance with this part and shall, as necessary and to the extent that resources permit, be available to consult and to provide technical assistance to an owner or operator who seeks such consultation or assistance.

(c) In order to initiate consultations or seek technical assistance, a covered facility shall submit a written request for consultation or technical assistance to the Coordinating Official or contact the Department in any other manner specified in any subsequent guidance. Requests for consultation or technical guidance do not serve to toll any of the applicable timelines set forth in this part.

(d) If a covered facility modifies its facility, processes, or the types or quantities of materials that it possesses, and believes that such changes may impact the covered facility's obligations under this part, the covered facility may request a consultation with the Coordinating Official as specified in paragraph (c).

§27.125 Severability.

If a court finds any portion of this part to have been promulgated without proper authority, the remainder of this part will remain in full effect.

Subpart B—Chemical Facility Security Program

§27.200 Information regarding security risk for a chemical facility.

(a) *Information to determine security risk.* In order to determine the security risk posed by chemical facilities, the Secretary may, at any time, request information from chemical facilities that may reflect potential consequences of or vulnerabilities to a terrorist attack or incident, including questions specifically related to the nature of the business and activities conducted at the facility; information concerning the names, nature, conditions of storage, quantities, volumes, properties, customers, major uses, and other pertinent information about specific chemicals or chemicals meeting a specific criterion; information concerning facilities' security, safety, and emergency response practices, operations, and procedures; information regarding incidents, history, funding, and other matters bearing on the effectiveness of the security, safety and emergency response programs, and other information as necessary.

(b) *Obtaining information from facilities.* (1) The Assistant Secretary may seek the information provided in paragraph (a) of this section by contacting chemical facilities individually or by publishing a notice in the FEDERAL REGISTER seeking information from chemical facilities that meet certain criteria, which the Department will use to determine risk profiles. Through any such individual or FEDERAL REGISTER notification, the Assistant Secretary may instruct such facilities to complete and submit a Top-Screen process, which may be completed through a secure Department Web site or through other means approved by the Assistant Secretary.

(2) A facility must complete and submit a Top-Screen in accordance with the schedule provided in §27.210, the calculation provisions in §27.203, and the minimum concentration provisions in §27.204 if it possesses any of the chemicals listed in appendix A to this part at or above the STQ for any applicable Security Issue.

(3) Where the Department requests that a facility complete and submit a Top-Screen, the facility must designate a person who is responsible for the submission of information through the CSAT system and who attests to the accuracy of the information contained in any CSAT submissions. Such

217

submitter must be an officer of the corporation or other person designated by an officer of the corporation and must be domiciled in the United States.

(c) *Presumptively High Risk Facilities.* (1) If a chemical facility subject to paragraph (a) or (b) of this section fails to provide information requested or complete the Top-Screen within the timeframe provided in § 27.210, the Assistant Secretary may, after attempting to consult with the facility, reach a preliminary determination, based on the information then available, that the facility presumptively presents a high level of security risk. The Assistant Secretary shall then issue a notice to the entity of this determination and, if necessary, order the facility to provide information or complete the Top-Screen pursuant to these rules. If the facility then fails to do so, it may be subject to civil penalties pursuant to § 27.300, audit and inspection under § 27.250 or, if appropriate, an order to cease operations under § 27.300.

(2) If the facility deemed "presumptively high risk" pursuant to paragraph (c)(1) of this section completes the Top-Screen, and the Department determines that it does not present a high level of security risk under § 27.205, its status as "presumptively high risk" will terminate, and the Department will issue a notice to the facility to that effect.

[72 FR 17729, Apr. 9, 2007, as amended at 72 FR 65418, Nov. 20, 2007]

§ 27.203 Calculating the screening threshold quantity by security issue.

(a) *General.* In calculating whether a facility possesses a chemical of interest that meets the STQ for any security issue, a facility need not include chemicals of interest:

(1) Used as a structural component;

(2) Used as products for routine janitorial maintenance;

(3) Contained in food, drugs, cosmetics, or other personal items used by employees;

(4) In process water or non-contact cooling water as drawn from environment or municipal sources;

(5) In air either as compressed air or as part of combustion;

(6) Contained in articles, as defined in 40 CFR 68.3;

(7) In solid waste (including hazardous waste) regulated under the Resource Conservation and Recovery Act, 42 U.S.C. 6901 *et. seq.*, except for the waste described in 40 CFR 261.33;

(8) in naturally occurring hydrocarbon mixtures prior to entry of the mixture into a natural gas processing plant or a petroleum refining process unit. Naturally occurring hydrocarbon mixtures include condensate, crude oil, field gas, and produced water as defined in 40 CFR 68.3.

(b) *Release chemicals*—(1) *Release-toxic, release-flammable, and release-explosive chemicals.* Except as provided in paragraphs (b)(2) and (b)(3), in calculating whether a facility possesses an amount that meets the STQ for release chemicals of interest, the facility shall only include release chemicals of interest:

(i) In a vessel as defined in 40 CFR 68.3, in a underground storage facility, or stored in a magazine as defined in 27 CFR 555.11;

(ii) In transportation containers used for storage not incident to transportation, including transportation containers connected to equipment at a facility for loading or unloading and transportation containers detached from the motive power that delivered the container to the facility;

(iii) Present as process intermediates, by-products, or materials produced incidental to the production of a product if they exist at any given time;

(iv) In natural gas or liquefied natural gas stored in peak shaving facilities; and

(v) In gasoline, diesel, kerosene or jet fuel (including fuels that have flammability hazard ratings of 1, 2, 3, or 4, as determined by using National Fire Protection Association (NFPA) 704: Standard System for the Identification of the Hazards of Materials for Emergency Response [2007 ed.], which is incorporated by reference at 27.204(a)(2)) stored in aboveground tank farms, including tank farms that are part of pipeline systems;

(2) *Release-toxic, release-flammable, and release-explosive chemicals.* Except as provided in paragraph (c)(2)(i), in calculating whether a facility possesses an amount that meets the STQ

for release-toxic, release-flammable, and release-explosive chemicals, a facility need not include release-toxic, release-flammable, or release-explosive chemicals of interest that a facility manufactures, processes or uses in a laboratory at the facility under the supervision of a technically qualified individual as defined in 40 CFR 720.3.

(i) This exemption does not apply to specialty chemical production; manufacture, processing, or use of substances in pilot plant scale operations; or activities, including research and development, involving chemicals of interest conducted outside the laboratory.

(ii) [Reserved]

(3) *Propane.* In calculating whether a facility possesses an amount that meets the STQ for propane, a facility need not include propane in tanks of 10,000 pounds or less.

(c) *Theft and diversion chemicals.* In calculating whether a facility possesses an amount of a theft/diversion chemical of interest that meets the STQ, the facility shall only include theft/diversion chemicals of interest in a transportation packaging, as defined in 49 CFR 171.8. Where a theft/diversion-Chemical Weapons (CW) chemical is designated by "CUM 100g," a facility shall total the quantity of all such designated chemicals in its possession to determine whether the facility possesses theft/diversion-CW chemicals that meet or exceed the STQ of 100 grams.

(d) *Sabotage and contamination chemicals.* A facility meets the STQ for a sabotage/contamination chemical of interest if it ships the chemical and is required to placard the shipment of that chemical pursuant to the provisions of subpart F of 49 CFR part 172.

[72 FR 65419, Nov. 20, 2007]

§27.204 Minimum concentration by security issue.

(a) *Release chemicals*—(1) *Release-toxic chemicals.* If a release-toxic chemical of interest is present in a mixture, and the concentration of the chemical is equal to or greater than one percent (1%) by weight, the facility shall count the amount of the chemical of interest in the mixture toward the STQ. If a release-toxic chemical of interest is present in a mixture, and the concentration of the chemical is less than one percent (1%) by weight of the mixture, the facility need not count the amount of that chemical in the mixture in determining whether the facility possesses the STQ. Except for oleum, if the concentration of the chemical of interest in the mixture is one percent (1%) or greater by weight, but the facility can demonstrate that the partial pressure of the regulated substance in the mixture (solution) under handling or storage conditions in any portion of the process is less than 10 millimeters of mercury (mm Hg), the amount of the substance in the mixture in that portion of a vessel need not be considered when determining the STQ. The facility shall document this partial pressure measurement or estimate.

(2) *Release-flammable chemicals.* If a release-flammable chemical of interest is present in a mixture in a concentration equal to or greater than one percent (1%) by weight of the mixture, and the mixture has a National Fire Protection Association (NFPA) flammability hazard rating of 4, the facility shall count the entire amount of the mixture toward the STQ. Except as provided in §27.203(b)(1)(v) for fuels that are stored in aboveground tank farms (including farms that are part of pipeline systems), if a release-flammable chemical of interest is present in a mixture in a concentration equal to or greater than one percent (1%) by weight of the mixture, and the mixture has a National Fire Protection Association (NFPA) flammability hazard rating of 1, 2, or 3, the facility need not count the mixture toward the STQ. The flammability hazard ratings are defined in NFPA 704: Standard System for the Identification of the Hazards of Materials for Emergency Response [2007 ed.]. The Director of the Federal Register approves the incorporation by reference of this standard in accordance with 5 U.S.C. 552(a) and 1 CFR part 51. You may obtain a copy of the incorporated standard from the National Fire Protection Association at 1 Batterymarch Park, Quincy, MA 02169–

7471 or *http://www.nfpa.org.* You may inspect a copy of the incorporated standard at the Department of Homeland Security, 1621 Kent Street, 9th Floor, Rosslyn VA (please call 703–235–0709) to make an appointment or at the or at the National Archives and Records Administration (NARA). For information on the availability of material at NARA, call 202–741–6030, or go to *http://www.archives.gov/federal_register/code_of_federal_regulations/ibr_locations.html.* If a release-flammable chemical of interest is present in a mixture, and the concentration of the chemical is less than one percent (1%) by weight, the facility need not count the mixture in determining whether the facility possesses the STQ.

(3) *Release-explosive chemicals.* For each release-explosive chemical of interest, a facility shall count the total quantity of all commercial grades of the chemical of interest toward the STQ, unless a specific minimum concentration is assigned in the Minimum Concentration column of appendix A to part 27, in which case the facility should count the total quantity of all commercial grades of the chemical at the specified minimum concentration.

(b) *Theft and diversion chemicals.* (1) Theft/Diversion-Chemical Weapons (CW) and Chemical Weapons Precursors (CWP Chemicals: Where a theft/diversion-CWC/CWP chemical of interest is not designated by "CUM 100g" in appendix A, and the chemical is present in a mixture at or above the minimum concentration amount listed in the Minimum Concentration column of appendix A to part 27, the facility shall count the entire amount of the mixture toward the STQ.

(2) Theft/Diversion-Weapon of Mass Effect (WME) Chemicals: If a theft/diversion-WME chemical of interest is present in a mixture at or above the minimum concentration amount listed in the Minimum Concentration column of appendix A to part 27, the facility shall count the entire amount of the mixture toward the STQ.

(3) *Theft/diversion-Explosives/Improvised Explosive Device Precursor (EXP/IEDP) chemicals.* For each theft/diversion-EXP/IEDP chemical of interest, a facility shall count the total quantity of all commercial grades of the chem-

ical toward the STQ, unless a specific minimum concentration is assigned in the Minimum Concentration column of appendix A to part 27, in which case the facility should count the total quantity of all commercial grades of the chemical at the specified minimum concentration.

(c) *Sabotage and contamination chemicals.* For each sabotage/contamination chemical of interest, a facility shall count the total quantity of all commercial grades of the chemical toward the STQ.

[72 FR 65419, Nov. 20, 2007]

§ 27.205 Determination that a chemical facility "presents a high level of security risk."

(a) *Initial determination.* The Assistant Secretary may determine at any time that a chemical facility presents a high level of security risk based on any information available (including any information submitted to the Department under § 27.200) that, in the Secretary's discretion, indicates the potential that a terrorist attack involving the facility could result in significant adverse consequences for human life or health, national security or critical economic assets. Upon determining that a facility presents a high level of security risk, the Department shall notify the facility in writing of such initial determination and may also notify the facility of the Department's preliminary determination of the facility's placement in a risk-based tier pursuant to § 27.220(a).

(b) *Redetermination.* If a covered facility previously determined to present a high level of security risk has materially altered its operations, it may seek a redetermination by filing a Request for Redetermination with the Assistant Secretary, and may request a meeting regarding the Request. Within 45 calendar days of receipt of such a Request, or within 45 calendar days of a meeting under this paragraph, the Assistant Secretary shall notify the covered facility in writing of the Department's decision on the Request for Redetermination.

§ 27.210 Submissions schedule.

(a) *Initial submission.* The timeframes in paragraphs (a)(2) and (a)(3) of this section also apply to covered facilities that submit an Alternative Security Program pursuant to §27.235.

(1) *Top-Screen.* Facilities shall complete and submit a Top-Screen within the following time frames:

(i) Unless otherwise notified, within 60 calendar days of November 20, 2007 for facilities that possess any of the chemicals listed in appendix A at or above the STQ for any applicable Security Issue, or within 60 calendar days for facilities that come into possession of any of the chemicals listed in appendix A at or above the STQ for any applicable Security Issue; or

(ii) Within the time frame provided in any written notification from the Department or specified in any subsequent FEDERAL REGISTER notice.

(2) *Security Vulnerability Assessment.* Unless otherwise notified, a covered facility must complete and submit a Security Vulnerability Assessment within 90 calendar days of written notification from the Department or within the time frame specified in any subsequent FEDERAL REGISTER notice.

(3) *Site Security Plan.* Unless otherwise notified, a covered facility must complete and submit a Site Security Plan within 120 calendar days of written notification from the Department or within the time frame specified in any subsequent FEDERAL REGISTER notice.

(b) *Resubmission schedule for covered facilities.* The timeframes in this subsection also apply to covered facilities who submit an Alternative Security Program pursuant to §27.235.

(1) *Top-Screen.* Unless otherwise notified, Tier 1 and Tier 2 covered facilities must complete and submit a new Top-Screen no less than two years, and no more than two years and 60 calendar days, from the date of the Department's approval of the facility's Site Security Plan; and Tier 3 and Tier 4 covered facilities must complete and submit a Top-Screen no less than 3 years, and no more than 3 years and 60 calendar days, from the date of the Department's approval of the facility's Site Security Plan.

(2) *Security Vulnerability Assessment.* Unless otherwise notified and following a Top-Screen resubmission pursuant to paragraph (b)(1) of this section, a cov-

ered facility must complete and submit a new Security Vulnerability Assessment within 90 calendar days of written notification from the Department or within the time frame specified in any subsequent FEDERAL REGISTER notice.

(3) *Site Security Plan.* Unless otherwise notified and following a Security Vulnerability Assessment resubmission pursuant to paragraph (b)(2) of this section , a covered facility must complete and submit a new Site Security Plan within 120 calendar days of written notification from the Department or within the time frame specified in any subsequent FEDERAL REGISTER notice.

(c) The Assistant Secretary retains the authority to modify the schedule in this part as needed. The Assistant Secretary may shorten or extend these time periods based on the operations at the facility, the nature of the covered facility's vulnerabilities, the level and immediacy of security risk, or for other reasons. If the Department alters the time periods for a specific facility, the Department will do so in written notice to the facility.

(d) If a covered facility makes material modifications to its operations or site, the covered facility must complete and submit a revised Top-Screen to the Department within 60 days of the material modification. In accordance with the resubmission requirements in §27.210(b)(2) and (3), the Department will notify the covered facility as to whether the covered facility must submit a revised Security Vulnerability Assessment, Site Security Plan, or both.

[72 FR 17729, Apr. 9, 2007, as amended at 72 FR 65420, Nov. 20, 2007]

§ **27.215 Security vulnerability assessments.**

(a) *Initial assessment.* If the Assistant Secretary determines that a chemical facility is high-risk, the facility must complete a Security Vulnerability Assessment. A Security Vulnerability Assessment shall include:

(1) Asset Characterization, which includes the identification and characterization of potential critical assets; identification of hazards and consequences of concern for the facility, its surroundings, its identified critical

asset(s), and its supporting infrastructure; and identification of existing layers of protection;

(2) Threat Assessment, which includes a description of possible internal threats, external threats, and internally-assisted threats;

(3) Security Vulnerability Analysis, which includes the identification of potential security vulnerabilities and the identification of existing countermeasures and their level of effectiveness in both reducing identified vulnerabilities and in meeting the applicable Risk-Based Performance Standards;

(4) Risk Assessment, including a determination of the relative degree of risk to the facility in terms of the expected effect on each critical asset and the likelihood of a success of an attack; and

(5) Countermeasures Analysis, including strategies that reduce the probability of a successful attack or reduce the probable degree of success, strategies that enhance the degree of risk reduction, the reliability and maintainability of the options, the capabilities and effectiveness of mitigation options, and the feasibility of the options.

(b) Except as provided in § 27.235, a covered facility must complete the Security Vulnerability Assessment through the CSAT process, or through any other methodology or process identified or issued by the Assistant Secretary.

(c) Covered facilities must submit a Security Vulnerability Assessment to the Department in accordance with the schedule provided in § 27.210.

(d) *Updates and revisions.* (1) A covered facility must update and revise its Security Vulnerability Assessment in accordance with the schedule provided in § 27.210.

(2) Notwithstanding paragraph (d)(1) of this section, a covered facility must update, revise or otherwise alter its Security Vulnerability Assessment to account for new or differing modes of potential terrorist attack or for other security-related reasons, if requested by the Assistant Secretary.

§ 27.220   Tiering.

(a) *Preliminary determination of risk-based tiering.* Based on the information the Department receives in accordance with §§ 27.200 and 27.205 (including information submitted through the Top-Screen process) and following its initial determination in § 27.205(a) that a facility presents a high level of security risk, the Department shall notify a facility of the Department's preliminary determination of the facility's placement in a risk-based tier.

(b) *Confirmation or alteration of risk-based tiering.* Following review of a covered facility's Security Vulnerability Assessment, the Assistant Secretary shall notify the covered facility of its final placement within a risk-based tier, or for covered facilities previously notified of a preliminary tiering, confirm or alter such tiering.

(c) The Department shall place covered facilities in one of four risk-based tiers, ranging from highest risk facilities in Tier 1 to lowest risk facilities in Tier 4.

(d) The Assistant Secretary may provide the facility with guidance regarding the risk-based performance standards and any other necessary guidance materials applicable to its assigned tier.

§ 27.225   Site security plans.

(a) The Site Security Plan must meet the following standards:

(1) Address each vulnerability identified in the facility's Security Vulnerability Assessment, and identify and describe the security measures to address each such vulnerability;

(2) Identify and describe how security measures selected by the facility will address the applicable risk-based performance standards and potential modes of terrorist attack including, as applicable, vehicle-borne explosive devices, water-borne explosive devices, ground assault, or other modes or potential modes identified by the Department;

(3) Identify and describe how security measures selected and utilized by the facility will meet or exceed each applicable performance standard for the appropriate risk-based tier for the facility; and

(4) Specify other information the Assistant Secretary deems necessary regarding chemical facility security.

(b) Except as provided in §27.235, a covered facility must complete the Site Security Plan through the CSAT process, or through any other methodology or process identified or issued by the Assistant Secretary.

(c) Covered facilities must submit a Site Security Plan to the Department in accordance with the schedule provided in §27.210.

(d) *Updates and revisions.* (1) When a covered facility updates, revises or otherwise alters its Security Vulnerability Assessment pursuant to §27.215(d), the covered facility shall make corresponding changes to its Site Security Plan.

(2) A covered facility must also update and revise its Site Security Plan in accordance with the schedule in §27.210.

(e) A covered facility must conduct an annual audit of its compliance with its Site Security Plan.

§27.230 Risk-based performance standards.

(a) Covered facilities must satisfy the performance standards identified in this section. The Assistant Secretary will issue guidance on the application of these standards to risk-based tiers of covered facilities, and the acceptable layering of measures used to meet these standards will vary by risk-based tier. Each covered facility must select, develop in their Site Security Plan, and implement appropriately risk-based measures designed to satisfy the following performance standards:

(1) *Restrict area perimeter.* Secure and monitor the perimeter of the facility;

(2) *Secure site assets.* Secure and monitor restricted areas or potentially critical targets within the facility;

(3) *Screen and control access.* Control access to the facility and to restricted areas within the facility by screening and/or inspecting individuals and vehicles as they enter, including,

(i) Measures to deter the unauthorized introduction of dangerous substances and devices that may facilitate an attack or actions having serious negative consequences for the population surrounding the facility; and

(ii) Measures implementing a regularly updated identification system that checks the identification of facility personnel and other persons seeking access to the facility and that discourages abuse through established disciplinary measures;

(4) *Deter, detect, and delay.* Deter, detect, and delay an attack, creating sufficient time between detection of an attack and the point at which the attack becomes successful, including measures to:

(i) Deter vehicles from penetrating the facility perimeter, gaining unauthorized access to restricted areas or otherwise presenting a hazard to potentially critical targets;

(ii) Deter attacks through visible, professional, well maintained security measures and systems, including security personnel, detection systems, barriers and barricades, and hardened or reduced value targets;

(iii) Detect attacks at early stages, through countersurveillance, frustration of opportunity to observe potential targets, surveillance and sensing systems, and barriers and barricades; and

(iv) Delay an attack for a sufficient period of time so to allow appropriate response through on-site security response, barriers and barricades, hardened targets, and well-coordinated response planning;

(5) *Shipping, receipt, and storage.* Secure and monitor the shipping, receipt, and storage of hazardous materials for the facility;

(6) *Theft and diversion.* Deter theft or diversion of potentially dangerous chemicals;

(7) *Sabotage.* Deter insider sabotage;

(8) *Cyber.* Deter cyber sabotage, including by preventing unauthorized on-site or remote access to critical process controls, such as Supervisory Control and Data Acquisition (SCADA) systems, Distributed Control Systems (DCS), Process Control Systems (PCS), Industrial Control Systems (ICS), critical business system, and other sensitive computerized systems;

(9) *Response.* Develop and exercise an emergency plan to respond to security incidents internally and with assistance of local law enforcement and first responders;

223

(10) *Monitoring.* Maintain effective monitoring, communications and warning systems, including,

(i) Measures designed to ensure that security systems and equipment are in good working order and inspected, tested, calibrated, and otherwise maintained;

(ii) Measures designed to regularly test security systems, note deficiencies, correct for detected deficiencies, and record results so that they are available for inspection by the Department; and

(iii) Measures to allow the facility to promptly identify and respond to security system and equipment failures or malfunctions;

(11) *Training.* Ensure proper security training, exercises, and drills of facility personnel;

(12) *Personnel surety.* Perform appropriate background checks on and ensure appropriate credentials for facility personnel, and as appropriate, for unescorted visitors with access to restricted areas or critical assets, including,

(i) Measures designed to verify and validate identity;

(ii) Measures designed to check criminal history;

(iii) Measures designed to verify and validate legal authorization to work; and

(iv) Measures designed to identify people with terrorist ties;

(13) *Elevated threats.* Escalate the level of protective measures for periods of elevated threat;

(14) *Specific threats, vulnerabilities, or risks.* Address specific threats, vulnerabilities or risks identified by the Assistant Secretary for the particular facility at issue;

(15) *Reporting of significant security incidents.* Report significant security incidents to the Department and to local law enforcement officials;

(16) *Significant security incidents and suspicious activities.* Identify, investigate, report, and maintain records of significant security incidents and suspicious activities in or near the site;

(17) *Officials and organization.* Establish official(s) and an organization responsible for security and for compliance with these standards;

(18) *Records.* Maintain appropriate records; and

(19) Address any additional performance standards the Assistant Secretary may specify.

(b) [Reserved]

§ 27.235 Alternative security program.

(a) Covered facilities may submit an Alternate Security Program (ASP) pursuant to the requirements of this section. The Assistant Secretary may approve an Alternate Security Program, in whole, in part, or subject to revisions or supplements, upon a determination that the Alternate Security Program meets the requirements of this part and provides for an equivalent level of security to that established by this part.

(1) A Tier 4 facility may submit an ASP in lieu of a Security Vulnerability Assessment, Site Security Plan, or both.

(2) Tier 1, Tier 2, or Tier 3 facilities may submit an ASP in lieu of a Site Security Plan. Tier 1, Tier 2, and Tier 3 facilities may not submit an ASP in lieu of a Security Vulnerability Assessment.

(b) The Department will provide notice to a covered facility about the approval or disapproval, in whole or in part, of an ASP, using the procedure specified in § 27.240 if the ASP is intended to take the place of a Security Vulnerability Assessment or using the procedure specified in § 27.245 if the ASP is intended to take the place of a Site Security Plan.

§ 27.240 Review and approval of security vulnerability assessments.

(a) *Review and approval.* The Department will review and approve in writing all Security Vulnerability Assessments that satisfy the requirements of § 27.215, including Alternative Security Programs submitted pursuant to § 27.235.

(b) If a Security Vulnerability Assessment does not satisfy the requirements of § 27.215, the Department will provide the facility with a written notification that includes a clear explanation of deficiencies in the Security Vulnerability Assessment. The facility shall then enter further consultations with the Department and resubmit a sufficient Security Vulnerability Assessment by the time specified in the written notification provided by the Department under this section. If the resubmitted Security Vulnerability Assessment does not satisfy the requirements of §27.215, the Department will provide the facility with written notification (including a clear explanation of deficiencies in the SVA) of the Department's disapproval of the SVA.

§27.245 Review and approval of site security plans.

(a) *Review and approval.* (1) The Department will review and approve or disapprove all Site Security Plans that satisfy the requirements of §27.225, including Alternative Security Programs submitted pursuant to §27.235.

(i) The Department will review Site Security Plans through a two-step process. Upon receipt of Site Security Plan from the covered facility, the Department will review the documentation and make a preliminary determination as to whether it satisfies the requirements of §27.225. If the Department finds that the requirements are satisfied, the Department will issue a Letter of Authorization to the covered facility.

(ii) Following issuance of the Letter of Authorization, the Department will inspect the covered facility in accordance with §27.250 for purposes of determining compliance with the requirements of this part.

(iii) If the Department approves the Site Security Plan in accordance with §27.250, the Department will issue a Letter of Approval to the facility, and the facility shall implement the approved Site Security Plan.

(2) The Department will not disapprove a Site Security Plan submitted under this part based on the presence or absence of a particular security measure. The Department may disapprove a Site Security Plan that fails to satisfy the risk-based performance standards established in §27.230.

(b) When the Department disapproves a preliminary Site Security Plan issued prior to inspection or a Site Security Plan following inspection, the Department will provide the facility with a written notification that includes a clear explanation of defi-

ciencies in the Site Security Plan. The facility shall then enter further consultations with the Department and resubmit a sufficient Site Security Plan by the time specified in the written notification provided by the Department under this section. If the resubmitted Site Security Plan does not satisfy the requirements of §27.225, the Department will provide the facility with written notification (including a clear explanation of deficiencies in the SSP) of the Department's disapproval of the SSP.

§27.250 Inspections and audits.

(a) *Authority.* In order to assess compliance with the requirements of this part, authorized Department officials may enter, inspect, and audit the property, equipment, operations, and records of covered facilities.

(b) Following preliminary approval of a Site Security Plan in accordance with §27.245, the Department will inspect the covered facility for purposes of determining compliance with the requirements of this part.

(1) If after the inspection, the Department determines that the requirements of §27.225 have been met, the Department will issue a Letter of Approval to the covered facility.

(2) If after the inspection, the Department determines that the requirements of §27.225 have not been met, the Department will proceed as directed by §27.245(b) in "Review and Approval of Site Security Plans."

(c) *Time and manner.* Authorized Department officials will conduct audits and inspections at reasonable times and in a reasonable manner. The Department will provide covered facility owners and/or operators with 24-hour advance notice before inspections, except

(1) If the Under Secretary or Assistant Secretary determines that an inspection without such notice is warranted by exigent circumstances and approves such inspection; or

(2) If any delay in conducting an inspection might be seriously detrimental to security, and the Director of the Chemical Security Division determines that an inspection without notice is warranted, and approves an inspector to conduct such inspection.

(d) *Inspectors.* Inspections and audits are conducted by personnel duly authorized and designated for that purpose as "inspectors" by the Secretary or the Secretary's designee.

(1) An inspector will, on request, present his or her credentials for examination, but the credentials may not be reproduced by the facility.

(2) An inspector may administer oaths and receive affirmations, with the consent of any witness, in any matter.

(3) An inspector may gather information by reasonable means including, but not limited to, interviews, statements, photocopying, photography, and video- and audio-recording. All documents, objects and electronically stored information collected by each inspector during the performance of that inspector's duties shall be maintained for a reasonable period of time in the files of the Department of Homeland Security maintained for that facility or matter.

(4) An inspector may request forthwith access to all records required to be kept pursuant to § 27.255. An inspector shall be provided with the immediate use of any photocopier or other equipment necessary to copy any such record. If copies can not be provided immediately upon request, the inspector shall be permitted immediately to take the original records for duplication and prompt return.

(e) *Confidentiality.* In addition to the protections provided under CVI in § 27.400, information received in an audit or inspection under this section, including the identity of the persons involved in the inspection or who provide information during the inspection, shall remain confidential under the investigatory file exception, or other appropriate exception, to the public disclosure requirements of 5 U.S.C. 552.

(f) *Guidance.* The Assistant Secretary shall issue guidance identifying appropriate processes for such inspections, and specifying the type and nature of documentation that must be made available for review during inspections and audits.

§ 27.255   Recordkeeping requirements.

(a) Except as provided in § 27.255(b), the covered facility must keep records of the activities as set out below for at least three years and make them available to the Department upon request. A covered facility must keep the following records:

(1) *Training.* For training, the date and location of each session, time of day and duration of session, a description of the training, the name and qualifications of the instructor, a clear, legible list of attendees to include the attendee signature, at least one other unique identifier of each attendee receiving the training, and the results of any evaluation or testing.

(2) *Drills and exercises.* For each drill or exercise, the date held, a description of the drill or exercise, a list of participants, a list of equipment (other than personal equipment) tested or employed in the exercise, the name(s) and qualifications of the exercise director, and any best practices or lessons learned which may improve the Site Security Plan;

(3) *Incidents and breaches of security.* Date and time of occurrence, location within the facility, a description of the incident or breach, the identity of the individual to whom it was reported, and a description of the response;

(4) *Maintenance, calibration, and testing of security equipment.* The date and time, name and qualifications of the technician(s) doing the work, and the specific security equipment involved for each occurrence of maintenance, calibration, and testing;

(5) *Security threats.* Date and time of occurrence, how the threat was communicated, who received or identified the threat, a description of the threat, to whom it was reported, and a description of the response;

(6) *Audits.* For each audit of a covered facility's Site Security Plan (including each audit required under § 27.225(e)) or Security Vulnerability Assessment, a record of the audit, including the date of the audit, results of the audit, name(s) of the person(s) who conducted the audit, and a letter certified by the covered facility stating the date the audit was conducted.

(7) *Letters of Authorization and Approval.* All Letters of Authorization and Approval from the Department,

and documentation identifying the results of audits and inspections conducted pursuant to §27.250.

(b) A covered facility must retain records of submitted Top-Screens, Security Vulnerability Assessments, Site Security Plans, and all related correspondence with the Department for at least six years and make them available to the Department upon request.

(c) To the extent necessary for security purposes, the Department may request that a covered facility make available records kept pursuant to other Federal programs or regulations.

(d) Records required by this section may be kept in electronic format. If kept in an electronic format, they must be protected against unauthorized access, deletion, destruction, amendment, and disclosure.

Subpart C—Orders and Adjudications

§27.300 Orders.

(a) *Orders generally.* When the Assistant Secretary determines that a facility is in violation of any of the requirements of this part, the Assistant Secretary may take appropriate action including the issuance of an appropriate Order.

(b) *Orders Assessing Civil Penalty and Orders to Cease Operations.* (1) Where the Assistant Secretary determines that a facility is in violation of an Order issued pursuant to paragraph (a) of this section, the Assistant may enter an Order Assessing Civil Penalty, Order to Cease Operations, or both.

(2) Following the issuance of an Order by the Assistant Secretary pursuant to paragraph (b)(1) of this section, the facility may enter further consultations with Department.

(3) Where the Assistant Secretary determines that a facility is in violation of an Order issued pursuant to paragraph (a) of this section and issues an Order Assessing Civil Penalty pursuant to paragraph (b)(1) of this section, a chemical facility is liable to the United States for a civil penalty of not more than $25,000 for each day during which the violation continues, if the violation of the Order occurred on or before November 2, 2015, or $34,013 for each day during which the violation of the Order

continues, if the violation occurred after November 2, 2015.

(c) *Procedures for Orders.* (1) At a minimum, an Order shall be signed by the Assistant Secretary, shall be dated, and shall include:

(i) The name and address of the facility in question;

(ii) A listing of the provision(s) that the facility is alleged to have violated;

(iii) A statement of facts upon which the alleged instances of noncompliance are based;

(iv) A clear explanation of deficiencies in the facility's chemical security program, including, if applicable, any deficiencies in the facility's Security Vulnerability Assessment, Site Security Plan, or both; and

(v) A statement, indicating what action(s) the chemical must take to remedy the instance(s) of noncompliance; and

(vi) The date by which the facility must comply with the terms of the Order.

(2) The Assistant Secretary may establish procedures for the issuance of Orders.

(d) A facility must comply with the terms of the Order by the date specified in the Order unless the facility has filed a timely Notice for Application for Review under §27.310.

(e) Where a facility or other person contests the determination of the Assistant Secretary to issue an Order, a chemical facility may seek an adjudication pursuant to §27.310.

(f) An Order issued under this section becomes final agency action when the time to file a Notice of Application of Review under §27.310 has passed without such a filing or upon the conclusion of adjudication or appeal proceedings under this subpart.

[72 FR 17729, Apr. 9, 2007, as amended at 81 FR 43001, July 1, 2016; 82 FR 8579, Jan. 27, 2017; 83 FR 13834, Apr. 2, 2018]

§27.305 Neutral adjudications.

(a) Any facility or other person who has received a Finding pursuant to §27.230(a)(12)(iv), a Determination pursuant to §27.245(b), or an Order pursuant to §27.300 is entitled to an adjudication, by a neutral adjudications officer, of any issue of material fact relevant to any administrative action which deprives that person of a cognizable interest in liberty or property.

(b) A neutral adjudications officer appointed pursuant to § 27.315 shall issue an Initial Decision on any material factual issue related to a Finding pursuant to § 27.230(a)(12)(iv), a Determination pursuant to § 27.245, or an Order pursuant to § 27.300 before any such administrative action is reviewed on appeal pursuant to § 27.345.

§ 27.310 Commencement of adjudication proceedings.

(a) *Proceedings instituted by facilities or other persons.* A facility or other person may institute proceedings to review a determination by the Assistant Secretary:

(1) Finding, pursuant to the § 27.230(a)(12)(iv), that an individual is a potential security threat;

(2) Disapproving a Site Security Plan pursuant to § 27.245(b); or

(3) Issuing an Order pursuant to § 27.300(a) or (b).

(b) *Procedure for applications by facilities or other persons.* A facility or other person may institute Proceedings by filing a Notice of Application for Review specifying that the facility or other person requests a Proceeding to review a determination specified in paragraph (a) of this section.

(1) An Applicant institutes a Proceeding by filing a Notice of Application for Review with the office of the Department hereinafter designated by the Secretary.

(2) An Applicant must file a Notice of Application for Review within seven calendar days of notification to the facility or other person of the Assistant Secretary's Finding, Determination, or Order.

(3) The Applicant shall file and simultaneously serve each Notice of Application for Review and all subsequent filings on the Assistant Secretary and the General Counsel.

(4) An Order is stayed from the timely filing of a Notice of Application for Review until the Presiding Officer issues an Initial Decision, unless the Secretary has lifted the stay due to exigent circumstances pursuant to paragraph (d) of this section.

(5) The Applicant shall file and serve an Application for Review within four-teen calendar days of the notification to the facility or other person of the Assistant Secretary's Finding, Determination, or Order.

(6) Each Application for Review shall be accompanied by all legal memoranda, other documents, declarations, affidavits, and other evidence supporting the position asserted by the Applicant.

(c) *Response.* The Assistant Secretary, through the Office of General Counsel, shall file and serve a Response, accompanied by all legal memoranda, other documents, declarations, affidavits and other evidence supporting the position asserted by the Assistant Secretary within fourteen calendar days of the filing and service of the Application for Review and all supporting papers.

(d) *Procedural modifications.* The Secretary may, in exigent circumstances (as determined in his sole discretion):

(1) Lift any stay applicable to any Order under § 27.300;

(2) Modify the time for a response;

(3) Rule on the sufficiency of Applications for Review; or

(4) Otherwise modify these procedures with respect to particular matters.

§ 27.315 Presiding officers for proceedings.

(a) Immediately upon the filing of any Application for Review, the Secretary shall appoint an attorney, who is employed by the Department and who has not performed any investigative or prosecutorial function with respect to the matter, to act as a neutral adjudications officer or Presiding Officer for the compilation of a factual record and the recommendation of an Initial Decision for each Proceeding.

(b) Notwithstanding paragraph (a) of this section, the Secretary may appoint one or more attorneys who are employed by the Department and who do not perform any investigative or prosecutorial function with respect to this subpart, to serve generally in the capacity as Presiding Officer(s) for such matters pursuant to such procedures as the Secretary may hereafter establish.

§ 27.320 Prohibition on ex parte communications during proceedings.

(a) At no time after the designation of a Presiding Officer for a Proceeding and prior to the issuance of a Final Decision pursuant to § 27.345 with respect to a facility or other person, shall the appointed Presiding Officer, or any person who will advise that official in the decision on the matter, discuss *ex parte* the merits of the proceeding with any interested person outside the Department, with any Department official who performs a prosecutorial or investigative function in such proceeding or a factually related proceeding, or with any representative of such person.

(b) If, after appointment of a Presiding Officer and prior to the issuance of a Final Decision pursuant to § 27.345 with respect to a facility or other person, the appointed Presiding Officer, or any person who will advise that official in the decision on the matter, receives from or on behalf of any party, by means of an *ex parte* communication, information which is relevant to the decision of the matter and to which other parties have not had an opportunity to respond, a summary of such information shall be served on all other parties, who shall have an opportunity to reply to the *ex parte* communication within a time set by the Presiding Officer.

(c) The consideration of classified information or CVI pursuant to an in camera procedure does not constitute a prohibited ex parte communication for purposes of this subpart.

§ 27.325 Burden of proof.

The Assistant Secretary bears the initial burden of proving the facts necessary to support the challenged administrative action at every proceeding instituted under this subpart.

§ 27.330 Summary decision procedures.

(a) The Presiding Officer appointed for each Proceeding shall immediately consider whether the summary adjudication of the Application for Review is appropriate based on the Application for Review, the Response, and all the supporting filings of the parties pursuant to §§ 27.310(b)(5) and 27.310(c).

(1) The Presiding Officer shall promptly issue any necessary scheduling order for any additional briefing of the issue of summary adjudication on the Application for Review and Response.

(2) The Presiding Officer may conduct scheduling conferences and other proceedings that the Presiding Officer determines to be appropriate.

(b) If the Presiding Officer determines that there is no genuine issue of material fact and that one party or the other is entitled to decision as a matter of law, then the record shall be closed and the Presiding Officer shall issue an Initial Decision on the Application for Review pursuant to § 27.340.

(c) If a Presiding Officer determines that any factual issues require the cross-examination of one or more witnesses or other proceedings at a hearing, the Presiding Officer, in consultation with the parties, shall promptly schedule a hearing to be conducted pursuant to § 27.335.

§ 27.335 Hearing procedures.

(a) Any hearing shall be held as expeditiously as possible at the location most conducive to a prompt presentation of any necessary testimony or other proceedings.

(1) Videoconferencing and teleconferencing may be used where appropriate at the discretion of the Presiding Officer.

(2) Each party offering the affirmative testimony of a witness shall present that testimony by declaration, affidavit, or other sworn statement submitted in advance as ordered by the Presiding Officer.

(3) Any witness presented for further examination shall be asked to testify under an oath or affirmation.

(4) The hearing shall be recorded verbatim.

(b)(1) A facility or other person may appear and be heard on his own behalf or through any counsel of his choice who is qualified to possess CVI.

(2) A facility of other person individually, or through counsel, may offer relevant and material information including written direct testimony which he believes should be considered in opposition to the administrative action or which may bear on the sanction being sought.

(3) The facility or other person individually, or through counsel, may conduct such cross-examination as may be specifically allowed by the Presiding Officer for a full determination of the facts.

§ 27.340 Completion of adjudication proceedings.

(a) The Presiding Officer shall close and certify the record of the adjudication promptly upon the completion of:

(1) Summary judgment proceedings,

(2) A hearing, if necessary,

(3) The submission of post hearing briefs, if any are ordered by the Presiding Officer, and

(4) The conclusion of oral arguments, if any are permitted by the Presiding Officer.

(b) The Presiding Officer shall issue an Initial Decision based on the certified record, and the decision shall be subject to appeal pursuant to § 27.345.

(c) An Initial Decision shall become a final agency action on the expiration of the time for an Appeal pursuant to § 27.345.

§ 27.345 Appeals.

(a) *Right to appeal.* A facility or any person who has received an Initial Decision under § 27.340(b) has the right to appeal to the Under Secretary acting as a neutral appeals officer.

(b) *Procedure for appeals.* (1) The Assistant Secretary, a facility or other person, or a representative on behalf of a facility or person, may institute an Appeal by filing a Notice of Appeal with the office of the Department hereinafter designated by the Secretary.

(2) The Assistant Secretary, a facility, or other person must file a Notice of Appeal within seven calendar days of the service of the Presiding Officer's Initial Decision.

(3) The Appellant shall file with the designated office and simultaneously serve each Notice of Appeal and all subsequent filings on the General Counsel.

(4) An Initial Decision is stayed from the timely filing of a Notice of Appeal until the Under Secretary issues a Final Decision, unless the Secretary lifts the stay due to exigent circumstances pursuant to § 27.310(d).

(5) The Appellant shall file and serve a Brief within 28 calendar days of the notification of the service of the Presiding Officer's Initial Decision.

(6) The Appellee shall file and serve its Opposition Brief within 28 calendar days of the service of the Appellant's Brief.

(c) The Under Secretary may provide for an expedited appeal for appropriate matters.

(d) *Ex parte communications.* (1) At no time after the filing of a Notice of Appeal pursuant to paragraph (b)(1) of this section and prior to the issuance of a Final Decision on an Appeal pursuant to paragraph (f) of this section with respect to a facility or other person shall the Under Secretary, his designee, or any person who will advise that official in the decision on the matter, discuss *ex parte* the merits of the proceeding with any interested person outside the Department, with any Department official who performs a prosecutorial or investigative function in such proceeding or a factually related proceeding, or with any representative of such person.

(2) If, after the filing of a Notice of Appeal pursuant to paragraph (b)(1) of this section and prior to the issuance of a Final Decision on an Appeal pursuant to paragraph (f) of this section with respect to a facility or other person, the Under Secretary, his designee, or any person who will advise that official in the decision on the matter, receives from or on behalf of any party, by means of an *ex parte* communication, information which is relevant to the decision of the matter and to which other parties have not had an opportunity to respond, a summary of such information shall be served on all other parties, who shall have an opportunity to reply to the *ex parte* communication within a time set by the Under Secretary or his designee.

(3) The consideration of classified information or CVI pursuant to an in camera procedure does not constitute a prohibited *ex parte* communication for purposes of this subpart.

(e) A facility or other person may elect to have the Under Secretary participate in any mediation or other resolution process by expressly waiving, in writing, any argument that such participation has compromised the Appeal process.

(f) The Under Secretary shall issue a Final Decision and serve it upon the parties. A Final Decision made by the Under Secretary constitutes final agency action.

(g) The Secretary may establish procedures for the conduct of Appeals pursuant to this section.

Subpart D—Other

§27.400 Chemical-terrorism vulnerability information.

(a) *Applicability.* This section governs the maintenance, safeguarding, and disclosure of information and records that constitute Chemical-terrorism Vulnerability Information (CVI), as defined in §27.400(b). The Secretary shall administer this section consistent with section 550(c) of the Homeland Security Appropriations Act of 2007, including appropriate sharing with Federal, State and local officials.

(b) *Chemical-terrorism vulnerability information.* In accordance with section 550(c) of the Department of Homeland Security Appropriations Act of 2007, the following information, whether transmitted verbally, electronically, or in written form, shall constitute CVI:

(1) Security Vulnerability Assessments under §27.215;

(2) Site Security Plans under §27.225;

(3) Documents relating to the Department's review and approval of Security Vulnerability Assessments and Site Security Plans, including Letters of Authorization, Letters of Approval and responses thereto; written notices; and other documents developed pursuant to §27.240 or §27.245;

(4) Alternate Security Programs under §27.235;

(5) Documents relating to inspection or audits under §27.250;

(6) Any records required to be created or retained under §27.255;

(7) Sensitive portions of orders, notices or letters under §27.300;

(8) Information developed pursuant to §§27.200 and 27.205; and

(9) Other information developed for chemical facility security purposes that the Secretary, in his discretion, determines is similar to the information protected in §27.400(b)(1) through

(8) and thus warrants protection as CVI.

(c) *Covered persons.* Persons subject to the requirements of this section are:

(1) Each person who has a need to know CVI, as specified in §27.400(e);

(2) Each person who otherwise receives or gains access to what they know or should reasonably know constitutes CVI.

(d) *Duty to protect information.* A covered person must—

(1) Take reasonable steps to safeguard CVI in that person's possession or control, including electronic data, from unauthorized disclosure. When a person is not in physical possession of CVI, the person must store it in a secure container, such as a safe, that limits access only to covered persons with a need to know;

(2) Disclose, or otherwise provide access to, CVI only to persons who have a need to know;

(3) Refer requests for CVI by persons without a need to know to the Assistant Secretary;

(4) Mark CVI as specified in §27.400(f);

(5) Dispose of CVI as specified in §27.400(k);

(6) If a covered person receives a record or verbal transmission containing CVI that is not marked as specified in §27.400(f), the covered person must—

(i) Mark the record as specified in §27.400(f) of this section; and

(ii) Inform the sender of the record that the record must be marked as specified in §27.400(f); or

(iii) If received verbally, make reasonable efforts to memorialize such information and mark the memorialized record as specified in §27.400(f) of this section, and inform the speaker of any determination that such information warrants CVI protection.

(7) When a covered person becomes aware that CVI has been released to persons without a need to know (including a covered person under §27.400(c)(2)), the covered person must promptly inform the Assistant Secretary.

(8) In the case of information that is CVI and also has been designated as critical infrastructure information

231

under section 214 of the Homeland Security Act, any covered person in possession of such information must comply with the disclosure restrictions and other requirements applicable to such information under section 214 and any implementing regulations.

(e) *Need to know.* (1) A person, including a State or local official, has a need to know CVI in each of the following circumstances:

(i) When the person requires access to specific CVI to carry out chemical facility security activities approved, accepted, funded, recommended, or directed by the Department.

(ii) When the person needs the information to receive training to carry out chemical facility security activities approved, accepted, funded, recommended, or directed by the Department.

(iii) When the information is necessary for the person to supervise or otherwise manage individuals carrying out chemical facility security activities approved, accepted, funded, recommended, or directed by the Department.

(iv) When the person needs the information to provide technical or legal advice to a covered person, who has a need to know the information, regarding chemical facility security requirements of Federal law.

(v) When the Department determines that access is required under § 27.400(h) or § 27.400(i) in the course of a judicial or administrative proceeding.

(2) *Federal employees, contractors, and grantees.* (i) A Federal employee has a need to know CVI if access to the information is necessary for performance of the employee's official duties.

(ii) A person acting in the performance of a contract with or grant from the Department has a need to know CVI if access to the information is necessary to performance of the contract or grant. Contractors or grantees may not further disclose CVI without the consent of the Assistant Secretary.

(iii) The Department may require that non-Federal persons seeking access to CVI complete a non-disclosure agreement before such access is granted.

(3) *Background check.* The Department may make an individual's access to the CVI contingent upon satisfactory completion of a security background check or other procedures and requirements for safeguarding CVI that are satisfactory to the Department.

(4) *Need to know further limited by the Department.* For some specific CVI, the Department may make a finding that only specific persons or classes of persons have a need to know.

(5) Nothing in § 27.400(e) shall prevent the Department from determining, in its discretion, that a person not otherwise listed in § 27.400(e) has a need to know CVI in a particular circumstance.

(f) *Marking of paper records.* (1) In the case of paper records containing CVI, a covered person must mark the record by placing the protective marking conspicuously on the top, and the distribution limitation statement on the bottom, of—

(i) The outside of any front and back cover, including a binder cover or folder, if the document has a front and back cover;

(ii) Any title page; and

(iii) Each page of the document.

(2) Protective marking. The protective marking is: CHEMICAL-TERRORISM VULNERABILITY INFORMATION.

(3) *Distribution limitation statement.* The distribution limitation statement is: WARNING: This record contains Chemical-terrorism Vulnerability Information controlled by 6 CFR 27.400. Do not disclose to persons without a "need to know" in accordance with 6 CFR 27.400(e). Unauthorized release may result in civil penalties or other action. In any administrative or judicial proceeding, this information shall be treated as classified information in accordance with 6 CFR 27.400(h) and (i).

(4) *Other types of records.* In the case of non-paper records that contain CVI, including motion picture films, videotape recordings, audio recording, and electronic and magnetic records, a covered person must clearly and conspicuously mark the records with the protective marking and the distribution limitation statement such that the viewer or listener is reasonably likely to see or hear them when obtaining access to the contents of the record.

(g) *Disclosure by the Department—In general.* (1) Except as otherwise provided in this section, and notwithstanding the Freedom of Information Act (5 U.S.C. 552), the Privacy Act (5 U.S.C. 552a), and other laws, records containing CVI are not available for public inspection or copying, nor does the Department release such records to persons without a need to know.

(2) Disclosure of Segregatable Information under the Freedom of Information Act and the Privacy Act. If a record is marked to signify both CVI and information that is not CVI, the Department, on a proper Freedom of Information Act or Privacy Act request, may disclose the record with the CVI redacted, provided the record is not otherwise exempt from disclosure under the Freedom of Information Act or Privacy Act.

(h) *Disclosure in administrative enforcement proceedings.* (1) The Department may provide CVI to a person governed by section 550, and his counsel, in the context of an administrative enforcement proceeding of section 550 when, in the sole discretion of the Department, as appropriate, access to the CVI is necessary for the person to prepare a response to allegations contained in a legal enforcement action document issued by the Department.

(2) *Security background check.* Prior to providing CVI to a person under §27.400(h)(1), the Department may require the individual or, in the case of an entity, the individuals representing the entity, and their counsel, to undergo and satisfy, in the judgment of the Department, a security background check.

(i) *Disclosure in judicial proceedings.* (1) In any judicial enforcement proceeding of section 550, the Secretary, in his sole discretion, may, subject to §27.400(i)(1)(i), authorize access to CVI for persons necessary for the conduct of such proceedings, including such persons' counsel, provided that no other persons not so authorized shall have access to or be present for the disclosure of such information.

(i) *Security background check.* Prior to providing CVI to a person under §27.400(i)(1), the Department may require the individual to undergo and satisfy, in the judgment of the Department, a security background check.

(ii) [Reserved]

(2) In any judicial enforcement proceeding of section 550 where a person seeks to disclose CVI to a person not authorized to receive it under paragraph (i)(1) of this section, or where a person not authorized to receive CVI under paragraph (i)(1) of this section seeks to compel its disclosure through discovery, the United States may make an ex parte application in writing to the court seeking authorization to—

(i) Redact specified items of CVI from documents to be introduced into evidence or made available to the defendant through discovery under the Federal Rules of Civil Procedure;

(ii) Substitute a summary of the information for such CVI; or

(iii) Substitute a statement admitting relevant facts that the CVI would tend to prove.

(3) The court shall grant a request under paragraph (i)(2) of this section if, after in camera review, the court finds that the redacted item, stipulation, or summary is sufficient to allow the defendant to prepare a defense.

(4) If the court enters an order granting a request under paragraph (i)(2) of this section, the entire text of the documents to which the request relates shall be sealed and preserved in the records of the court to be made available to the appellate court in the event of an appeal.

(5) If the court enters an order denying a request of the United States under paragraph (i)(2) of this section, the United States may take an immediate, interlocutory appeal of the court's order in accordance with 18 U.S.C. 2339B(f)(4), (5). For purposes of such an appeal, the entire text of the documents to which the request relates, together with any transcripts of arguments made ex parte to the court in connection therewith, shall be maintained under seal and delivered to the appellate court.

(6) Except as provided otherwise at the sole discretion of the Secretary, access to CVI shall not be available in any civil or criminal litigation unrelated to the enforcement of section 550.

(7) Taking of trial testimony—

(i) Objection—During the examination of a witness in any judicial proceeding, the United States may object to any question or line of inquiry that may require the witness to disclose CVI not previously found to be admissible.

(ii) Action by court—In determining whether a response is admissible, the court shall take precautions to guard against the compromise of any CVI, including—

(A) Permitting the United States to provide the court, ex parte, with a proffer of the witness's response to the question or line of inquiry; and

(B) Requiring the defendant to provide the court with a proffer of the nature of the information that the defendant seeks to elicit.

(iii) Obligation of defendant—In any judicial enforcement proceeding, it shall be the defendant's obligation to establish the relevance and materiality of any CVI sought to be introduced.

(8) *Construction.* Nothing in this subsection shall prevent the United States from seeking protective orders or asserting privileges ordinarily available to the United States to protect against the disclosure of classified information, including the invocation of the military and State secrets privilege.

(j) *Consequences of violation.* Violation of this section is grounds for a civil penalty and other enforcement or corrective action by the Department, and appropriate personnel actions for Federal employees. Corrective action may include issuance of an order requiring retrieval of CVI to remedy unauthorized disclosure or an order to cease future unauthorized disclosure.

(k) *Destruction of CVI.* (1) The Department of Homeland Security. Subject to the requirements of the Federal Records Act (5 U.S.C. 105), including the duty to preserve records containing documentation of a Federal agency's policies, decisions, and essential transactions, the Department destroys CVI when no longer needed to carry out the agency's function.

(2) *Other covered persons*—(i) *In general.* A covered person must destroy CVI completely to preclude recognition or reconstruction of the information when the covered person no longer needs the CVI to carry out security measures under paragraph (e) of this section.

(ii) *Exception.* Section 27.400(k)(2) does not require a State or local government agency to destroy information that the agency is required to preserve under State or local law.

§ 27.405 **Review and preemption of State laws and regulations.**

(a) As per current law, no law, regulation, or administrative action of a State or political subdivision thereof, or any decision or order rendered by a court under state law, shall have any effect if such law, regulation, or decision conflicts with, hinders, poses an obstacle to or frustrates the purposes of this regulation or of any approval, disapproval or order issued there under.

(1) Nothing in this part is intended to displace other federal requirements administered by the Environmental Protection Agency, U.S. Department of Justice, U.S. Department of Labor, U.S. Department of Transportation, or other federal agencies.

(2) [Reserved]

(b) State law, regulation or administrative action defined. For purposes of this section, the phrase "State law, regulation or administrative action" means any enacted law, promulgated regulation, ordinance, administrative action, order or decision, or common law standard of a State or any of its political subdivisions.

(c) *Submission for review.* Any chemical facility covered by these regulations and any State may petition the Department by submitting a copy of a State law, regulation, or administrative action, or decision or order of a court for review under this section.

(d) *Review and opinion*—(1) *Review.* The Department may review State laws, administrative actions, or opinions or orders of a court under State law and regulations submitted under this section, and may offer an opinion whether the application or enforcement of the State law or regulation would conflict with, hinder, pose an obstacle to or frustrate the purposes of this part.

(2) *Opinion.* The Department may issue a written opinion on any question regarding preemption. If the question

was submitted under subsection (c) of this part, the Assistant Secretary will notify the affected chemical facility and the Attorney General of the subject State of any opinion under this section.

(3) *Consultation with States.* In conducting a review under this section, the Department will seek the views of the State or local jurisdiction whose laws may be affected by the Department's review.

§ 27.410 **Third party actions.**

(a) Nothing in this part shall confer upon any person except the Secretary a right of action, in law or equity, for any remedy including, but not limited to, injunctions or damages to enforce any provision of this part.

(b) An owner or operator of a chemical facility may petition the Assistant Secretary to provide the Department's view in any litigation involving any issues or matters regarding this part.

APPENDIX A TO PART 27—DHS CHEMICALS OF INTEREST

Appendix A to Part 27. -- DHS Chemicals of Interest [1]

Chemicals of Interest (COI)	Synonym	Chemical Abstract Service (CAS) #	Release Minimum Concentration (%)	Release Screening Threshold Quantities (in pounds)	Theft Minimum Concentration (%)	Theft Screening Threshold Quantities (in pounds unless otherwise noted)	Sabotage Minimum Concentration (%)	Sabotage Screening Threshold Quantities	Release – Toxic	Release – Flammables	Release – Explosives	Theft – CW/CWP	Theft – WME	Theft – EXP/IEDP	Sabotage/Contamination
Acetaldehyde		75-07-0	1.00	10,000						X					
Acetone cyanohydrin, stabilized		75-86-5					ACG	APA							X
Acetyl bromide		506-96-7					ACG	APA							X
Acetyl chloride		75-36-5					ACG	APA							X
Acetyl iodide		507-02-8					ACG	APA							X
Acetylene	[Ethyne]	74-86-2	1.00	10,000						X					
Acrolein	[2-Propenal] or Acrylaldehyde	107-02-8	1.00	5,000					X						
Acrylonitrile	[2-Propenenitrile]	107-13-1	1.00	10,000						X					
Acrylyl chloride	[2-Propenoyl chloride]	814-68-6	1.00	10,000						X					
Allyl alcohol	[2-Propen-1-ol]	107-18-6	1.00	15,000					X						
Allylamine	[2-Propen-1-amine]	107-11-9	1.00	10,000						X					
Allyltrichlorosilane, stabilized		107-37-9					ACG	APA							X
Aluminum (powder)		7429-90-5			ACG	100								X	
Aluminum bromide, anhydrous		7727-15-3					ACG	APA							X
Aluminum chloride, anhydrous		7446-70-0					ACG	APA							X
Aluminum phosphide		20859-73-8					ACG	APA	X						X
Ammonia (anhydrous)		7664-41-7	1.00	10,000					X						
Ammonia (conc. 20% or greater)		7664-41-7	20.00	20,000					X						
Ammonium nitrate, [with more than 0.2 percent combustible substances, including any organic substance calculated as carbon, to the exclusion of any other added substance]		6484-52-2	ACG	5,000	ACG	400					X			X	

236

Appendix A to Part 27. – DHS Chemicals of Interest [1]

Chemicals of Interest (COI)	Synonym	Chemical Abstract Service (CAS) #	Release Min. Conc. (%)	Release Screening Threshold Quantities (in pounds)	Theft Min. Conc. (%)	Theft Screening Threshold Quantities (in pounds unless otherwise noted)	Sabotage Min. Conc. (%)	Sabotage Screening Threshold Quantities	Release – Toxic	Release – Flammables	Release – Explosives	Theft – CW/CWP	Theft – WME	Theft – EXP/IEDP	Sabotage/Contamination
Ammonium nitrate, solid [nitrogen concentration of 23% nitrogen or greater]		6484-52-2			33.00	2000								X	
Ammonium perchlorate		7790-98-9	ACG	5,000	ACG	400					X			X	
Ammonium picrate		131-74-8	ACG	5,000	ACG	400					X			X	
Amyltrichlorosilane		107-72-2					ACG	APA							X
Antimony pentafluoride		7783-70-2					ACG	APA							X
Arsenic trichloride	[Arsenous trichloride]	7784-34-1	1.00	15,000	30.00	2.2			X			X			
Arsine		7784-42-1	1.00	1,000	0.67	15			X			X	X		
Barium azide		18810-58-7	ACG	5,000	ACG	400					X			X	
1,4-Bis(2-chloroethylthio)-n-butane		142868-93-7			CUM	100g						X			
Bis(2-chloroethylthio)methane		63869-13-6			CUM	100g						X			
Bis(2-chloroethylthiomethyl)ether		63918-90-1			CUM	100g						X			
1,5-Bis(2-chloroethylthio)-n-pentane		142868-94-8			CUM	100g						X			
1,3-Bis(2-chloroethylthio)-n-propane		63905-10-2			CUM	100g						X			
Boron tribromide		10294-33-4			12.67	45	ACG	APA	X				X		X
Boron trichloride	[Borane, trichloro]	10294-34-5	1.00	5,000	84.70	45			X				X		
Boron trifluoride	[Borane, trifluoro]	7637-07-2	1.00	5,000	26.87	45			X				X		
Boron trifluoride compound with methyl ether (1:1)	[Boron, trifluoro [oxybis (methane)]-T-4-]	353-42-4	1.00	15,000					X						
Bromine		7726-95-6	1.00	10,000					X						
Bromine chloride		13863-41-7			9.67	45							X		
Bromine pentafluoride		7789-30-2					ACG	APA							X
Bromine trifluoride		7787-71-5			6.00	45	ACG	APA					X		X
Bromotrifluorethylene	[Ethene, bromotrifluoro-]	598-73-2	1.00	10,000						X					

Appendix A to Part 27. -- DHS Chemicals of Interest [1]

Chemicals of Interest (COI)	Synonym	Chemical Abstract Service (CAS) #	Release — Min. Conc. (%)	Release — Screening Threshold Quantities (in pounds)	Theft — Min. Conc. (%)	Theft — Screening Threshold Quantities (in pounds unless otherwise noted)	Sabotage — Min. Conc. (%)	Sabotage — Screening Threshold Quantities	Release – Toxic	Release – Flammables	Release – Explosives	Theft – CW/CWP	Theft – WME	Theft – EXP/IEDP	Sabotage/Contamination
1,3-Butadiene		106-99-0	1.00	10,000						X					
Butane		106-97-8	1.00	10,000						X					
Butene		25167-67-3	1.00	10,000						X					
1-Butene		106-98-9	1.00	10,000						X					
2-Butene		107-01-7	1.00	10,000						X					
2-Butene-cis		590-18-1	1.00	10,000						X					
2-Butene-trans	[2-Butene, (E)]	624-64-6	1.00	10,000						X					
Butyltrichlorosilane		7521-80-4					ACG	APA							X
Calcium hydrosulfite	[Calcium dithionite]	15512-36-4					ACG	APA							X
Calcium phosphide		1305-99-3					ACG	APA							X
Carbon disulfide		75-15-0	1.00	20,000					X						
Carbon oxysulfide	[Carbon oxide sulfide (COS); carbonyl sulfide]	463-58-1	1.00	10,000						X					
Carbonyl fluoride		353-50-4			12.00	45							X		
Carbonyl sulfide		463-58-1			56.67	500							X		
Chlorine		7782-50-5	1.00	2,500	9.77	500	ACG	APA	X				X		X
Chlorine dioxide	[Chlorine oxide, (ClO2)]	10049-04-4	1.00	1,000			ACG	APA	X						
Chlorine monoxide	[Chlorine oxide]	7791-21-1	1.00	10,000						X					
Chlorine pentafluoride		13637-63-3			4.07	15			X				X		
Chlorine trifluoride		7790-91-2			9.97	45			X				X		
Chloroacetyl chloride		79-04-9					ACG	APA							X
2-Chloroethylchloro-methylsulfide		2625-76-5				CUM 100g						X			
Chloroform	[Methane, trichloro-]	67-66-3	1.00	20,000					X						
Chloromethyl ether	[Methane, oxybis(chloro-)]	542-88-1	1.00	1,000					X						
Chloromethyl methyl ether	[Methane, chloromethoxy-]	107-30-2	1.00	5,000					X						
1-Chloropropylene	[1-Propene, 1-chloro-]	590-21-6	1.00	10,000						X					
2-Chloropropylene	[1-Propene, 2-chloro-]	557-98-2	1.00	10,000						X					

238

Appendix A to Part 27. – DHS Chemicals of Interest [1]

Chemicals of Interest (COI)	Synonym	Chemical Abstract Service (CAS) #	Release — Min. Conc. (%)	Release — Screening Threshold Quantities (in pounds)	Theft — Min. Conc. (%)	Theft — Screening Threshold Quantities (in pounds unless otherwise noted)	Sabotage — Min. Conc. (%)	Sabotage — Screening Threshold Quantities	Release – Toxic	Release – Flammables	Release – Explosives	Theft – CW/CWP	Theft – WME	Theft – EXP/IEDP	Sabotage/Contamination
Chlorosarin	[o-Isopropyl methylphosphonochloridate]	1445-76-7				CUM 100g						X			
Chlorosoman	[o-Pinacolyl methylphosphonochloridate]	7040-57-5				CUM 100g						X			
Chlorosulfonic acid		7790-94-5					ACG	APA							X
Chromium oxychloride		14977-61-8					ACG	APA							X
Crotonaldehyde	[2-Butenal]	4170-30-3	1.00	10,000						X					
Crotonaldehyde, (E)-	[2-Butenal], (E)-	123-73-9	1.00	10,000						X			X		
Cyanogen	[Ethanedinitrile]	460-19-5	1.00	10,000	11.67	45				X			X		
Cyanogen chloride		506-77-4	1.00	10,000	2.67	15			X						
Cyclohexylamine	[Cyclohexanamine]	108-91-8	1.00	15,000											
Cyclohexyltrichlorosilane		98-12-4					ACG	APA	X	X					X
Cyclopropane		75-19-4	1.00	10,000						X					
DF	Methyl phosphonyl difluoride	676-99-3				CUM 100g						X			
Diazodinitrophenol		87-31-0	ACG	5,000	ACG	400					X			X	
Diborane		19287-45-7	1.00	2,500	2.67	15			X				X		
Dichlorosilane	[Silane, dichloro-]	4109-96-0	1.00	10,000	10.47	45				X			X		
N,N-(2-diethylamino)ethanethiol		100-38-9			30.00	2.2						X			
Diethyldichlorosilane		1719-53-5					ACG	APA							X
o,o-Diethyl S-[2-(diethylamino)ethyl] phosphorothiolate		78-53-5			30.00	2.2						X			
Diethyleneglycol dinitrate		693-21-0	ACG	5,000	ACG	400					X			X	
Diethyl methylphosphonite		15715-41-0			30.00	2.2						X			
N,N-Diethyl phosphoramidic dichloride		1498-54-0			30.00	2.2						X			
N,N-(2-diisopropylamino)ethanethiol	N,N-diisopropyl-(beta)-aminoethane thiol	5842-07-9			30.00	2.2						X			

Appendix A to Part 27. -- DHS Chemicals of Interest [1]

Chemicals of Interest (COI)	Synonym	Chemical Abstract Service (CAS) #	Release – Minimum Concentration (%)	Release – Screening Threshold Quantities (in pounds)	Theft – Minimum Concentration (%)	Theft – Screening Threshold Quantities (in pounds unless otherwise noted)	Sabotage – Minimum Concentration (%)	Sabotage – Screening Threshold Quantities	Release – Toxic	Release – Flammables	Release – Explosives	Theft – CW/CWP	Theft – WME	Theft – EXP/IEDP	Sabotage/Contamination
Difluoroethane	[Ethane, 1,1-difluoro-]	75-37-6	1.00	10,000	30.00	2.2						X			
N,N-Diisopropyl phosphoramidic dichloride		23306-80-1					ACG	APA							X
1,1-Dimethylhydrazine	[Hydrazine, 1,1-dimethyl-]	57-14-7	1.00	10,000						X					
Dimethylamine	[Methanamine, N-methyl-]	124-40-3	1.00	10,000						X					
N,N-(2-dimethylamino)ethanethiol		108-02-1	1.00	10,000	30.00	2.2				X		X			
Dimethyldichlorosilane	[Silane, dichlorodimethyl-]	75-78-5					ACG	APA							X
N,N-Dimethyl phosphoramidic dichloride	[Dimethylphosphoramido-dichloridate]	677-43-0			30.00	2.2				X		X			
2,2-Dimethylpropane	[Propane, 2,2-dimethyl-]	463-82-1	1.00	10,000						X					
Dingu	[Dinitroglycoluril]	55510-04-8	ACG	5,000	ACG	400					X			X	
Dinitrogen tetroxide		10544-72-6			3.80	15							X		
Dinitrophenol		25550-58-7	ACG	5,000	ACG	400					X			X	
Dinitroresorcinol		519-44-8	ACG	5,000	ACG	400					X			X	
Diphenyldichlorosilane		80-10-4					ACG	APA							X
Dipicryl sulfide		2217-06-3	ACG	5,000	ACG	400					X			X	
Dipicrylamine [or] Hexyl	[Hexanitrodiphenylamine]	131-73-7	ACG	5,000	ACG	400					X			X	
N,N-(2-dipropylamino)ethanethiol		5842-06-8			30.00	2.2						X			
N,N-Dipropyl phosphoramidic dichloride		40881-99-9			30.00	2.2						X			
Dodecyltrichlorosilane		4484-72-4					ACG	APA							X
Epichlorohydrin	[Oxirane, (chloromethyl)-]	106-89-8	1.00	20,000					X						
Ethane		74-84-0	1.00	10,000						X					
Ethyl acetylene	[1-Butyne]	107-00-6	1.00	10,000						X					
Ethyl chloride	[Ethane, chloro-]	75-00-3	1.00	10,000						X					
Ethyl ether	[Ethane, 1,1-oxybis-]	60-29-7	1.00	10,000						X					
Ethyl mercaptan	[Ethanethiol]	75-08-1	1.00	10,000						X					

Appendix A to Part 27. — DHS Chemicals of Interest [1]

Chemicals of Interest (COI)	Synonym	CAS #	Release – Min Conc (%)	Release – Screening Threshold Quantities (in pounds)	Theft – Min Conc (%)	Theft – Screening Threshold Quantities (in pounds unless otherwise noted)	Sabotage – Min Conc (%)	Sabotage – Screening Threshold Quantities	Release – Toxic	Release – Flammables	Release – Explosives	Theft – CW/CWP	Theft – WME	Theft – EXP/IEDP	Sabotage/Contamination
Ethyl nitrite	[Nitrous acid, ethyl ester]	109-95-5	1.00	10,000						X					
Ethyl phosphonyl difluoride		753-98-0	1.00	10,000	CUM	100g						X			
Ethylamine	[Ethanamine]	75-04-7	1.00	10,000						X					
Ethyldiethanolamine		139-87-7			80.00	220						X			
Ethylene	[Ethene]	74-85-1	1.00	10,000						X					
Ethylene oxide	[Oxirane]	75-21-8	1.00	10,000						X					
Ethylenediamine	[1,2-Ethanediamine]	107-15-3	1.00	20,000						X					
Ethyleneimine	[Aziridine]	151-56-4	1.00	10,000						X					
Ethylphosphonothioic dichloride		993-43-1			30.00	2.2			X			X			
Ethyltrichlorosilane		115-21-9					ACG	APA							X
Fluorine		7782-41-4	1.00	1,000	6.17	15			X				X		
Fluorosulfonic acid		7789-21-1					ACG	APA	X						X
Formaldehyde (solution)		50-00-0	1.00	15,000						X					
Furan		110-00-9	1.00	10,000						X					
Germane		7782-65-2			20.73	45							X		
Germanium tetrafluoride		7783-58-6			2.11	15							X		
Guanyl nitrosaminoguanylidene hydrazine			ACG	5,000	ACG	400					X			X	
Hexaethyl tetraphosphate and compressed gas mixtures		757-58-4			33.37	500							X		
Hexafluoroacetone		684-16-2			15.67	45							X		
Hexanitrostilbene		20062-22-0	ACG	5,000	ACG	400					X			X	
Hexolite	[Hexotol]	121-82-4	ACG	5,000	ACG	400					X			X	
Hexyltrichlorosilane		928-65-4					ACG	APA							X
HMX	[Cyclotetramethylene-tetranitramine]	2691-41-0	ACG	5,000	ACG	400					X			X	X

Appendix A to Part 27. -- DHS Chemicals of Interest [1]

Chemicals of Interest (COI)	Synonym	Chemical Abstract Service (CAS) #	Release: Min Conc (%)	Release: Screening Threshold Quantities (in pounds)	Theft: Min Conc (%)	Theft: Screening Threshold Quantities (in pounds unless otherwise noted)	Sabotage: Min Conc (%)	Sabotage: Screening Threshold Quantities	Release – Toxic	Release – Flammables	Release – Explosives	Theft – CW/CWP	Theft – WME	Theft – EXP/IEDP	Sabotage/Contamination
HN1 (nitrogen mustard-1)	[Bis(2-chloroethyl)ethylamine]	538-07-8				CUM 100g						X			
HN2 (nitrogen mustard-2)	[Bis(2-chloroethyl)methylamine]	51-75-2				CUM 100g						X			
HN3 (nitrogen mustard-3)	[Tris(2-chloroethyl)amine]	555-77-1				CUM 100g						X			
Hydrazine		302-01-2	1.00	10,000						X					
Hydrochloric acid (conc. 37% or greater)		7647-01-0	37.00	15,000					X						
Hydrocyanic acid		74-90-8	1.00	2,500					X						
Hydrofluoric acid (conc. 50% or greater)		7664-39-3	50.00	1,000					X						
Hydrogen		1333-74-0	1.00	10,000						X					
Hydrogen bromide (anhydrous)		10035-10-6	1.00	10,000	95.33	500			X				X		
Hydrogen chloride (anhydrous)		7647-01-0	1.00	5,000	ACG	500			X						
Hydrogen cyanide	[Hydrocyanic acid]	74-90-8			4.67	15			X				X		
Hydrogen fluoride (anhydrous)		7664-39-3	1.00	1,000	42.53	45			X				X		
Hydrogen iodide, anhydrous		10034-85-2			95.33	500							X		
Hydrogen peroxide (concentration of at least 35%)		7722-84-1			35.00	400								X	
Hydrogen selenide		7783-07-5	1.00	10,000	0.07	15			X	X			X		
Hydrogen sulfide		7783-06-4	1.00	10,000	23.73	45							X		
Iodine pentafluoride		7783-66-6					ACG	APA							X
Iron, pentacarbonyl-	[Iron carbonyl (Fe (CO)5), (TB5-11)-]	13463-40-6	1.00	10,000						X					
Isobutane	[Propane, 2-methyl]	75-28-5	1.00	10,000						X					
Isobutyronitrile	[Propanenitrile, 2-methyl-]	78-82-0	1.00	20,000					X						
Isopentane	[Butane, 2-methyl-]	78-78-4	1.00	10,000						X					
Isoprene	[1,3-Butadiene, 2-methyl-]	78-79-5	1.00	10,000						X					

Appendix A to Part 27. -- DHS Chemicals of Interest [1]

Chemicals of Interest (COI)	Synonym	Chemical Abstract Service (CAS) #	Release – Minimum Concentration (%)	Release – Screening Threshold Quantities (in pounds)	Theft – Minimum Concentration (%)	Theft – Screening Threshold Quantities (in pounds unless otherwise noted)	Sabotage – Minimum Concentration (%)	Sabotage – Screening Threshold Quantities	Release – Toxic	Release – Flammables	Release – Explosives	Theft – CW/CWP	Theft – WME	Theft – EXP/IEDP	Sabotage/Contamination
Isopropyl chloride	[Propane, 2-chloro-]	75-29-6	1.00	10,000						X					
Isopropyl chloroformate	[Carbonochloridic acid, 1-methylethyl ester]	108-23-6	1.00	15,000					X						
Isopropylamine	[2-Propanamine]	75-31-0	1.00	10,000						X					
Isopropylphosphonothioic dichloride		1498-60-8			30.00	2.2						X			
Isopropylphosphonyl difluoride		677-42-9				CUM 100g						X			
Lead azide		13424-46-9	ACG	5,000	ACG	400					X			X	
Lead styphnate	[Lead trinitroresorcinate]	15245-44-0	ACG	5,000	ACG	400					X			X	
Lewisite 1	[2-Chlorovinyldichloroarsine]	541-25-3				CUM 100g						X			
Lewisite 2	[Bis(2-chlorovinyl)chloroarsine]	40334-69-8				CUM 100g						X			
Lewisite 3	[Tris(2-chlorovinyl)arsine]	40334-70-1				CUM 100g						X			
Lithium amide		7782-89-0					ACG	APA		X					X
Lithium nitride		26134-62-3					ACG	APA		X					X
Magnesium (powder)		7439-95-4			ACG	100				X				X	
Magnesium diamide		7803-54-5					ACG	APA		X					X
Magnesium phosphide		12057-74-8					ACG	APA		X					X
MDEA	[Methyldiethanolamine]	105-59-9			80.00	220						X			
Mercury fulminate		628-86-4	ACG	5,000	ACG	400			X					X	
Methacrylonitrile	[2-Propenenitrile, 2-methyl-]	126-98-7	1.00	10,000					X						
Methane		74-82-8	1.00	10,000						X					
2-Methyl-1-butene		563-46-2	1.00	10,000						X					
3-Methyl-1-butene		563-45-1	1.00	10,000						X					
Methyl chloride	[Methane, chloro-]	74-87-3	1.00	10,000						X					
Methyl chloroformate	[Carbonochloridic acid, methyl ester]	79-22-1	1.00	10,000					X						
Methyl ether	[Methane, oxybis-]	115-10-6	1.00	10,000						X					
Methyl formate	[Formic acid Methyl ester]	107-31-3	1.00	10,000						X					

Appendix A to Part 27. -- DHS Chemicals of Interest [1]

Chemicals of Interest (COI)	Synonym	CAS #	Release Min. Conc. (%)	Release Screening Threshold Quantities (in pounds)	Theft Min. Conc. (%)	Theft Screening Threshold Quantities (in pounds unless otherwise noted)	Sabotage Min. Conc. (%)	Sabotage Screening Threshold Quantities	Release – Toxic	Release – Flammables	Release – Explosives	Theft – CW/CWP	Theft – WME	Theft – EXP/IEDP	Sabotage/Contamination
Methyl hydrazine	[Hydrazine, methyl-]	60-34-4	1.00	15,000					X						
Methyl isocyanate	[Methane, isocyanato-]	624-83-9	1.00	10,000					X						
Methyl mercaptan	[Methanethiol]	74-93-1	1.00	10,000						X			X		
Methyl thiocyanate	[Thiocyanic acid, methyl ester]	556-64-9	1.00	20,000	45.00	500			X	X					
Methylamine	[Methanamine]	74-89-5	1.00	10,000						X					
Methylchlorosilane		993-00-0			20.00	45							X		
Methyldichlorosilane		75-54-7					ACG	APA							X
Methylphenyldichlorosilane		149-74-6					ACG	APA							X
Methylphosphonothioic dichloride		676-98-2			30.00	2.2						X			
2-Methylpropene	[1-Propene, 2-methyl-]	115-11-7	1.00	10,000						X					
Methyltrichlorosilane	[Silane, trichloromethyl-]	75-79-6	1.00	10,000			ACG	APA		X					X
Sulfur mustard (Mustard gas (H))	[Bis(2-chloroethyl)sulfide]	505-60-2				CUM 100g						X			
O-Mustard (T)	[Bis(2-chloroethylthioethyl)ether]	63918-89-8				CUM 100g						X			
Nickel Carbonyl		13463-39-3	1.00	10,000	68.00	400			X				X		
Nitric acid		7697-37-2	80.00	15,000	3.83	15								X	
Nitric oxide	[Nitrogen oxide (NO)]	10102-43-9	1.00	10,000	ACG	15			X						
Nitrobenzene		98-95-3			ACG	100								X	
5-Nitrobenzotriazol		2338-12-7	ACG	5,000	ACG	400					X			X	
Nitrocellulose		9004-70-0	ACG	5,000	ACG	400					X			X	
Nitrogen mustard hydrochloride	[Bis(2-chloroethyl)methylamine hydrochloride]	55-86-7			30.00	2.2						X			
Nitrogen trioxide		10544-73-7			3.83	15							X		
Nitroglycerine		55-63-0	ACG	5,000	ACG	400					X			X	
Nitromannite	[Mannitol hexanitrate, wetted]	15825-70-4	ACG	5,000	ACG	400					X			X	
Nitromethane		75-52-5			ACG	400								X	
Nitrostarch		9056-38-6	ACG	5,000	ACG	400					X			X	
Nitrosyl chloride		2696-92-6			1.17	15							X		

Appendix A to Part 27. -- DHS Chemicals of Interest [1]

Chemicals of Interest (COI)	Synonym	Chemical Abstract Service (CAS) #	Release Minimum Concentration (%)	Release Screening Threshold Quantities (in pounds)	Theft Minimum Concentration (%)	Theft Screening Threshold Quantities (in pounds unless otherwise noted)	Sabotage Minimum Concentration (%)	Sabotage Screening Threshold Quantities	Release – Toxic	Release – Flammables	Release – Explosives	Theft – CW/CWP	Theft – WME	Theft – EXP/IEDP	Sabotage/Contamination
Nitrotriazolone		932-64-9	ACG	5,000	ACG	400					X			X	
Nonyltrichlorosilane		5283-67-0					ACG	APA							X
Octadecyltrichlorosilane		112-04-9					ACG	APA							X
Octolite		57607-37-1	ACG	5,000	ACG	400					X			X	
Octonal		78413-87-3	ACG	5,000	ACG	400					X			X	
Octyltrichlorosilane		5283-66-9					ACG	APA							X
Oleum (Fuming Sulfuric acid)	[Sulfuric acid, mixture with sulfur trioxide]	8014-95-7	1.00	10,000					X						
Oxygen difluoride		7783-41-7			0.09	15							X		
1,3-Pentadiene		504-60-9	1.00	10,000						X					
Pentane		109-66-0	1.00	10,000						X					
1-Pentene		109-67-1	1.00	10,000						X					
2-Pentene, (E)-		646-04-8	1.00	10,000						X					
2-Pentene, (Z)-		627-20-3	1.00	10,000						X					
Pentolite		8066-33-9	ACG	5,000	ACG	400					X			X	
Peracetic acid	[Ethaneperoxic acid]	79-21-0	1.00	10,000						X					
Perchloromethylmercaptan	[Methanesulfenyl chloride, trichloro-]	594-42-3	1.00	10,000					X						
Perchloryl fluoride		7616-94-6			25.67	45							X		
PETN	[Pentaerythritol tetranitrate]	78-11-5	ACG	5,000	ACG	400					X			X	
Phenyltrichlorosilane		98-13-5					ACG	APA							X
Phosgene	[Carbonic dichloride] or [carbonyl dichloride]	75-44-5	1.00	500	0.17	15			X				X		
Phosphine		7803-51-2	1.00	10,000	0.67	15				X			X		
Phosphorus		7723-14-0			ACG	400	ACG	APA						X	X
Phosphorus oxychloride	[Phosphoryl chloride]	10025-87-3	1.00	5,000	80.00	220	ACG	APA	X			X			X
Phosphorus pentabromide		7789-69-7					ACG	APA							X
Phosphorus pentachloride		10026-13-8					ACG	APA							X
Phosphorus pentasulfide		1314-80-3					ACG	APA							X

245

Appendix A to Part 27. -- DHS Chemicals of Interest [1]

Chemicals of Interest (COI)	Synonym	Chemical Abstract Service (CAS) #	Release — Min Concentration (%)	Release — Screening Threshold Quantities (in pounds)	Theft — Min Concentration (%)	Theft — Screening Threshold Quantities (in pounds unless otherwise noted)	Sabotage — Min Concentration (%)	Sabotage — Screening Threshold Quantities	Release – Toxic	Release – Flammables	Release – Explosives	Theft – CW/CWP	Theft – WME	Theft – EXP/IEDP	Sabotage/Contamination
Phosphorus trichloride		7719-12-2	1.00	15,000	3.48	45	ACG	APA	X				X		X
Picrite	[Nitroguanidine]	556-88-7	ACG	5,000	ACG	400					X			X	
Piperidine		110-89-4	1.00	10,000						X					
Potassium chlorate		3811-04-9			ACG	400	ACG	APA						X	X
Potassium cyanide		151-50-8										X			
Potassium nitrate		7757-79-1			ACG	400								X	
Potassium perchlorate		7778-74-7			ACG	400								X	
Potassium permanganate		7722-64-7			ACG	400								X	
Potassium phosphide		20770-41-6					ACG	APA							X
Propadiene	[1,2-Propadiene]	463-49-0	1.00	10,000						X					
Propane		74-98-6	1.00	60,000						X					
Propionitrile	[Propanenitrile]	107-12-0	1.00	10,000					X						
Propyl chloroformate	[Carbonochloridic acid, propylester]	109-61-5	1.00	10,000						X					
Propylene	[1-Propene]	115-07-1	1.00	10,000						X					
Propylene oxide	[Oxirane, methyl-]	75-56-9	1.00	10,000						X					
Propyleneimine	[Aziridine, 2-methyl-]	75-55-8	1.00	10,000					X						
Propylphosphonothioic dichloride		2524-01-8			30.00	2.2						X			
Propylphosphonyl difluoride		690-14-2			CUM 100g							X			
Propyltrichlorosilane		141-57-1					ACG	APA							X
Propyne	[1-Propyne]	74-99-7	1.00	10,000						X					
QL	[o-Ethyl-o-2-diisopropylaminoethyl methylphosphonite]	57856-11-8			CUM 100g							X			
RDX	[Cyclotrimethylenetrinitramine]	121-82-4	ACG	5,000	ACG	400					X			X	
RDX and HMX mixtures		121-82-4	ACG	5,000	ACG	400					X			X	
Sarin	[o-Isopropyl methylphosphonofluoridate]	107-44-8			CUM 100g							X			
Selenium hexafluoride		7783-79-1			1.67	15							X		

Appendix A to Part 27. -- DHS Chemicals of Interest [1]

Chemicals of Interest (COI)	Synonym	Chemical Abstract Service (CAS) #	Release Min. Conc. (%)	Release Screening Threshold Quantities (in pounds)	Theft Min. Conc. (%)	Theft Screening Threshold Quantities (in pounds unless otherwise noted)	Sabotage Min. Conc. (%)	Sabotage Screening Threshold Quantities	Release – Toxic	Release – Flammables	Release – Explosives	Theft – CW/CWP	Theft – WME	Theft – EXP/IEDP	Sabotage/Contamination
Sesquimustard	[1,2-Bis(2-chloroethylthio)ethane]	3563-36-8				CUM 100g						X			
Silane		7803-62-5	1.00	10,000						X					
Silicon tetrachloride		10026-04-7					ACG	APA							X
Silicon tetrafluoride		7783-61-1			15.00	45							X	X	
Sodium azide		26628-22-8			ACG	400								X	
Sodium chlorate		7775-09-9			ACG	400								X	
Sodium cyanide		143-33-9					ACG	APA							X
Sodium hydrosulfite	[Sodium dithionite]	7775-14-6					ACG	APA							X
Sodium nitrate		7631-99-4			ACG	400								X	X
Sodium phosphide		12058-85-4					ACG	APA							X
Soman	[o-Pinacolyl methylphosphonofluoridate]	96-64-0				CUM 100g						X			
Stibine		7803-52-3			0.67	15	ACG	APA	X				X		X
Strontium phosphide		12504-16-4						APA	X				X		
Sulfur dioxide (anhydrous)		7446-09-5	1.00	5,000	84.00	500			X						
Sulfur tetrafluoride	[Sulfur fluoride (SF4), (T-4)-]	7783-60-0	1.00	2,500	1.33	15			X						
Sulfur trioxide		7446-11-9	1.00	10,000											
Sulfuryl chloride		7791-25-5					ACG	APA							X
Tabun	[o-Ethyl-N,N-dimethylphosphoramido-cyanidate]	77-81-6				CUM 100g						X			
Tellurium hexafluoride		7783-80-4	1.00	10,000	0.83	15							X		
Tetrafluoroethylene	[Ethene, tetrafluoro-]	116-14-3	1.00	10,000						X					
Tetramethyllead	[Plumbane, tetramethyl-]	75-74-1	1.00	10,000						X					
Tetramethylsilane	[Silane, tetramethyl-]	75-76-3	1.00	10,000						X					
Tetranitroaniline		53014-37-2	ACG	5,000	ACG	400					X			X	
Tetranitromethane	[Methane, tetranitro-]	509-14-8	1.00	10,000							X			X	
Tetrazene	[Guanyl nitrosaminoguanyltetrazene]	109-27-3	ACG	5,000	ACG	400					X			X	

Appendix A to Part 27. -- DHS Chemicals of Interest [1]

Chemicals of Interest (COI)	Synonym	CAS #	Release: Min Conc (%)	Release: Screening Threshold Quantities (lbs)	Theft: Min Conc (%)	Theft: Screening Threshold Quantities (lbs unless otherwise noted)	Sabotage: Min Conc (%)	Sabotage: Screening Threshold Quantities	Release – Toxic	Release – Flammables	Release – Explosives	Theft – CW/CWP	Theft – WME	Theft – EXP/IEDP	Sabotage/Contamination
1H-Tetrazole		288-94-8	ACG	5,000	ACG	400					X			X	
Thiodiglycol	[Bis(2-hydroxyethyl)sulfide]	111-48-8			30.00	2.2						X			
Thionyl chloride		7719-09-7					ACG	APA							X
Titanium tetrachloride	[Titanium chloride (TiCl4) (T-4)-]	7550-45-0	1.00	2,500	13.33	45	ACG	APA	X				X		X
TNT	[Trinitrotoluene]	118-96-7	ACG	5,000	ACG	400					X			X	
Torpex	[Hexotonal]	67713-16-0	ACG	5,000	ACG	400					X			X	
Trichlorosilane	[Silane, trichloro-]	10025-78-2	1.00	10,000			ACG	APA		X					X
Triethanolamine		102-71-6			80.00	220						X			
Triethanolamine hydrochloride		637-39-8			80.00	220						X			
Triethyl phosphite		122-52-1			80.00	220						X			
Trifluoroacetyl chloride		354-32-5			6.93	45							X		
Trifluorochloroethylene	[Ethene, chlorotrifluoro]	79-38-9	1.00	10,000	66.67	500				X			X		
Trimethylamine	[Methanamine, N,N-dimethyl-]	75-50-3	1.00	10,000						X					
Trimethylchlorosilane	[Silane, chlorotrimethyl-]	75-77-4	1.00	10,000			ACG	APA		X					X
Trimethyl phosphite		121-45-9			80.00	220						X			
Trinitroaniline		26952-42-1	ACG	5,000	ACG	400					X			X	
Trinitroanisole		606-35-9	ACG	5,000	ACG	400					X			X	
Trinitrobenzene		99-35-4	ACG	5,000	ACG	400					X			X	
Trinitrobenzenesulfonic acid		2508-19-2	ACG	5,000	ACG	400					X			X	
Trinitrobenzoic acid		129-66-8	ACG	5,000	ACG	400					X			X	
Trinitrochlorobenzene		88-88-0	ACG	5,000	ACG	400					X			X	
Trinitrofluorenone		129-79-3	ACG	5,000	ACG	400					X			X	
Trinitro-meta-cresol		602-99-3	ACG	5,000	ACG	400					X			X	
Trinitronaphthalene		55810-17-8	ACG	5,000	ACG	400					X			X	
Trinitrophenetole		4732-14-3	ACG	5,000	ACG	400					X			X	
Trinitrophenol		88-89-1	ACG	5,000	ACG	400					X			X	
Trinitroresorcinol		82-71-3	ACG	5,000	ACG	400					X			X	
Tritonal		54413-15-9	ACG	5,000	ACG	400					X			X	
Tungsten hexafluoride		7783-82-6			7.10	45							X		

Appendix A to Part 27. — DHS Chemicals of Interest [1]

Chemicals of Interest (COI)	Synonym	Chemical Abstract Service (CAS) #	Release		Theft		Sabotage		Security Issue						
			Minimum Concentration (%)	Screening Threshold Quantities (in pounds)	Minimum Concentration (%)	Screening Threshold Quantities (in pounds unless otherwise noted)	Minimum Concentration (%)	Screening Threshold Quantities	Release – Toxic	Release – Flammables	Release – Explosives	Theft – CW/CWP	Theft – WME	Theft – EXP/IEDP	Sabotage/Contamination
Vinyl acetate monomer	[Acetic acid ethenyl ester]	108-05-4	1.00	10,000						X					
Vinyl acetylene	[1-Buten-3-yne]	689-97-4	1.00	10,000						X					
Vinyl chloride	[Ethene, chloro-]	75-01-4	1.00	10,000						X					
Vinyl ethyl ether	[Ethene, ethoxy-]	109-92-2	1.00	10,000						X					
Vinyl fluoride	[Ethene, fluoro-]	75-02-5	1.00	10,000						X					
Vinyl methyl ether	[Ethene, methoxy-]	107-25-5	1.00	10,000						X					
Vinylidene chloride	[Ethene, 1,1-dichloro-]	75-35-4	1.00	10,000						X					
Vinylidene fluoride	[Ethene, 1,1-difluoro-]	75-38-7	1.00	10,000						X					
Vinyltrichlorosilane		75-94-5					ACG	APA				X			X
VX	[o-Ethyl-S-2-diisopropylaminoethyl methyl phosphonothiolate]	50782-69-9				CUM 100g									
Zinc hydrosulfite	[Zinc dithionite]	7779-86-4					ACG	APA							X

[1] The acronyms used in this appendix have the following meaning: ACG = A Commercial Grade; APA = A Placarded Amount; CW/CWP = Chemical Weapons/Chemical Weapons Precursors; WME = Weapons of Mass Effect; EXP/IEDP = Explosives/Improvised Explosive Device Precursors

[72 FR 65420, Nov. 20, 2007]

PART 29—PROTECTED CRITICAL INFRASTRUCTURE INFORMATION

Sec.
29.1 Purpose and scope.
29.2 Definitions.
29.3 Effect of provisions.
29.4 Protected Critical Infrastructure Information Program administration.
29.5 Requirements for protection.
29.6 Acknowledgment of receipt, validation, and marking.
29.7 Safeguarding of Protected Critical Infrastructure Information.
29.8 Disclosure of Protected Critical Infrastructure Information.
29.9 Investigation and reporting of violation of PCII procedures.

AUTHORITY: Pub. L. 107–296, 116 Stat. 2135 (6 U.S.C. 1 *et seq.*); 5 U.S.C. 301.

SOURCE: 71 FR 52271, Sept. 1, 2006, unless otherwise noted.

§ 29.1 Purpose and scope.

(a) *Purpose of this part.* This part implements sections 211 through 215 of the Homeland Security Act of 2002 (HSA) through the establishment of uniform procedures for the receipt, care, and storage of Critical Infrastructure Information (CII) voluntarily submitted to the Department of Homeland Security (DHS). Title II, Subtitle B, of the Homeland Security Act is referred to herein as the Critical Infrastructure Information Act of 2002 (CII Act). Consistent with the statutory mission of DHS to prevent terrorist attacks within the United States and reduce the vulnerability of the United States to terrorism, DHS will encourage the voluntary submission of CII by safeguarding and protecting that information from unauthorized disclosure and by ensuring that such information is, as necessary, securely shared with State and local government pursuant to section 214(a) through (g) of the CII Act. As required by the CII Act, these rules establish procedures regarding:

(1) The acknowledgement of receipt by DHS of voluntarily submitted CII;

(2) The receipt, validation, handling, storage, proper marking and use of information as PCII;

(3) The safeguarding and maintenance of the confidentiality of such information, appropriate sharing of such information with State and local governments pursuant to section 214(a) through (g) of the HSA.

(4) The issuance of advisories, notices and warnings related to the protection of critical infrastructure or protected systems in such a manner as to protect from unauthorized disclosure the source of critical infrastructure information that forms the basis of the warning, and any information that is proprietary or business sensitive, might be used to identify the submitting person or entity, or is otherwise not appropriately in the public domain.

(b) *Scope.* The regulations in this part apply to all persons and entities that are authorized to handle, use, or store PCII or that otherwise accept receipt of PCII.

§ 29.2 Definitions.

For purposes of this part:

(a) *Critical Infrastructure* has the meaning stated in section 2 of the Homeland Security Act of 2002 (referencing the term used in section 1016(e) of Public Law 107–56 (42 U.S.C. 5195c(e)).

(b) *Critical Infrastructure Information,* or *CII,* has the same meaning as established in section 212 of the CII Act of 2002 and means information not customarily in the public domain and related to the security of critical infrastructure or protected systems, including documents, records or other information concerning:

(1) Actual, potential, or threatened interference with, attack on, compromise of, or incapacitation of critical infrastructure or protected systems by either physical or computer-based attack or other similar conduct (including the misuse of or unauthorized access to all types of communications and data transmission systems) that violates Federal, State, local, or tribal law, harms interstate commerce of the United States, or threatens public health or safety;

(2) The ability of any critical infrastructure or protected system to resist such interference, compromise, or incapacitation, including any planned or

past assessment, projection, or estimate of the vulnerability of critical infrastructure or a protected system, including security testing, risk evaluation thereto, risk-management planning, or risk audit; or

(3) Any planned or past operational problem or solution regarding critical infrastructure or protected systems, including repair, recovery, reconstruction, insurance, or continuity, to the extent it is related to such interference, compromise, or incapacitation.

(c) *Information Sharing and Analysis Organization*, or *ISAO*, has the same meaning as is established in section 212 of the CII Act of 2002 and means any formal or informal entity or collaboration created or employed by public or private sector organizations for purposes of:

(1) Gathering and analyzing CII in order to better understand security problems and interdependencies related to critical infrastructure and protected systems, so as to ensure the availability, integrity, and reliability thereof;

(2) Communicating or disclosing CII to help prevent, detect, mitigate, or recover from the effects of an interference, compromise, or an incapacitation problem related to critical infrastructure or protected systems; and

(3) Voluntarily disseminating CII to its members, Federal, State, and local governments, or any other entities that may be of assistance in carrying out the purposes specified in paragraphs (c)(1) and (2) of this section.

(d) *In the public domain* means information lawfully, properly and regularly disclosed generally or broadly to the public. Information regarding system, facility or operational security is not "in the public domain." Information submitted with CII that is proprietary or business sensitive, or which might be used to identify a submitting person or entity will not be considered "in the public domain." Information may be "business sensitive" for this purpose whether or not it is commercial in nature, and even if its release could not demonstrably cause substantial harm to the competitive position of the submitting person or entity.

(e) *Local government* has the same meaning as is established in section 2 of the Homeland Security Act of 2002 and means:

(1) A county, municipality, city, town, township, local public authority, school district, special district, intrastate district, council of governments (regardless of whether the council of governments is incorporated as a nonprofit corporation under State law), regional or interstate government entity, or agency or instrumentality of a local government;

(2) An Indian tribe or authorized tribal organization, or in Alaska a Native village or Alaska Regional Native Corporation; and

(3) A rural community, unincorporated town or village, or other public entity.

(f) *Program Manager's Designee* means a Federal employee outside of the PCII Program Office, whether employed by DHS or another Federal agency, to whom certain functions of the PCII Program Office are delegated by the Program Manager, as determined on a case-by-case basis.

(g) *Protected Critical Infrastructure Information*, or *PCII*, means validated CII, including information covered by 6 CFR 29.6(b) and (f), including the identity of the submitting person or entity and any person or entity on whose behalf the submitting person or entity submits the CII, that is voluntarily submitted, directly or indirectly, to DHS, for its use regarding the security of critical infrastructure and protected systems, analysis, warning, interdependency study, recovery, reconstitution, or other appropriate purpose, and any information, statements, compilations or other materials reasonably necessary to explain the CII, put the CII in context, describe the importance or use of the CII, when accompanied by an express statement as described in 6 CFR 29.5.

(h) *Protected Critical Infrastructure Information Program*, or *PCII Program*, means the program implementing the CII Act, including the maintenance, management, and review of the information provided in furtherance of the protections provided by the CII Act.

(i) *Protected system* has the meaning set forth in section 212(6) of the CII

251

Act, and means any service, physical or computer-based system, process, or procedure that directly or indirectly affects the viability of a facility of critical infrastructure and includes any physical or computer-based system, including a computer, computer system, computer or communications network, or any component hardware or element thereof, software program, processing instructions, or information or data in transmission or storage therein, irrespective of the medium of transmission or storage.

(j) *Purposes of the CII Act* has the meaning set forth in section 214(a)(1) of the CII Act and includes the security of critical infrastructure and protected systems, analysis, warning, interdependency study, recovery, reconstitution, or other informational purpose.

(k) *Regulatory proceeding*, as used in section 212(7) of the CII Act and these rules, means administrative proceedings in which DHS is the adjudicating entity, and does not include any form or type of regulatory proceeding or other matter outside of DHS.

(l) *State* has the same meaning set forth in section 2 of the Homeland Security Act of 2002 and means any State of the United States, the District of Columbia, the Commonwealth of Puerto Rico, the Virgin Islands, Guam, American Samoa, the Commonwealth of the Northern Mariana Islands, and any possession of the United States.

(m) *Submission* as referenced in these procedures means any transmittal, either directly or indirectly, of CII to the DHS PCII Program Manager or the PCII Program Manager's designee, as set forth herein.

(n) *Submitted in good faith* means any submission of information that could reasonably be defined as CII or PCII under this section. Upon validation of a submission as PCII, DHS has conclusively established the good faith of the submission. Any information qualifying as PCII by virtue of a categorical inclusion identified by the Program Manager pursuant to section 214 of the CII Act and this part is submitted in good faith.

(o) *Voluntary* or *voluntarily*, when used in reference to any submission of CII, means the submittal thereof in the absence of an exercise of legal authority by DHS to compel access to or submission of such information. Voluntary submission of CII may be accomplished by (*i.e.*, come from) a single state or local governmental entity; private entity or person; or by an ISAO acting on behalf of its members or otherwise. There are two exclusions from this definition. In the case of any action brought under the securities laws—as is defined in section 3(a)(47) of the Securities Exchange Act of 1934 (15 U.S.C. 78c(a)(47))—the term "voluntary" or "voluntarily" does not include information or statements contained in any documents or materials filed, pursuant to section 12(i) of the Securities Exchange Act of 1934 (15 U.S.C. 78l(i)), with the U.S. Securities and Exchange Commission or with Federal banking regulators or a writing that accompanied the solicitation of an offer or a sale of securities. Information or statements previously submitted to DHS in the course of a regulatory proceeding or a licensing or permitting determination are not "voluntarily submitted." In addition, the submission of information to DHS for purposes of seeking a Federal preference or benefit, including CII submitted to support an application for a DHS grant to secure critical infrastructure will be considered a voluntary submission of information. Applications for SAFETY Act Designation or Certification under 6 CFR part 25 will also be considered a voluntary submission.

(p) The term *used directly by such agency, any other Federal, State, or local authority, or any third party, in any civil action arising under Federal or State law* in section 214(a)(1)(C) of the CII Act means any use in any proceeding other than a criminal prosecution before any court of the United States or of a State or otherwise, of any PCII, or any drafts or copies of PCII retained by the submitter, including the opinions, evaluations, analyses and conclusions prepared and submitted as CII, as evidence at trial or in any pretrial or other discovery, notwithstanding whether the United States, its agencies, officers, or employees is or are a party to such proceeding.

§ 29.3 Effect of provisions.

(a) *Freedom of Information Act disclosure exemptions.* Information that is separately exempt from public disclosure under the Freedom of Information Act or applicable State, local, or tribal law does not lose its separate exemption from public disclosure due to the applicability of these procedures or any failure to follow them.

(b) *Restriction on use of PCII by regulatory and other Federal, State, and Local agencies.* A Federal, State or local agency that receives PCII may utilize the PCII only for purposes appropriate under the CII Act, including securing critical infrastructure or protected systems. Such PCII may not be utilized for any other collateral regulatory purposes without the written consent of the PCII Program Manager and of the submitting person or entity. The PCII Program Manager or the PCII Program Manager's designee shall not share PCII with Federal, State or local government agencies without instituting appropriate measures to ensure that PCII is used only for appropriate purposes.

§ 29.4 Protected Critical Infrastructure Information Program administration.

(a) *Preparedness Directorate Program Management.* The Secretary of Homeland Security hereby designates the Under Secretary for Preparedness as the senior DHS official responsible for the direction and administration of the PCII Program. He shall administer this program through the Assistant Secretary for Infrastructure Protection.

(b) *Appointment of a PCII Program Manager.* The Under Secretary for Preparedness shall:

(1) Appoint a PCII Program Manager serving under the Assistant Secretary for Infrastructure Protection who is responsible for the administration of the PCII Program;

(2) Commit resources necessary for the effective implementation of the PCII Program;

(3) Ensure that sufficient personnel, including such detailees or assignees from other Federal national security, homeland security, or law enforcement entities as the Under Secretary deems appropriate, are assigned to the PCII Program to facilitate secure information sharing with appropriate authorities.

(4) Promulgate implementing directives and prepare training materials as ppropriate for the proper treatment of PCII.

(c) *Appointment of PCII Officers.* The PCII Program Manager shall establish procedures to ensure that each DHS component and each Federal, State, or local entity that works with PCII appoint one or more employees to serve as a PCII Officer in order to carry out the responsibilities stated in paragraph (d) of this section. Persons appointed to serve as PCII Officers shall be fully familiar with these procedures.

(d) *Responsibilities of PCII Officers.* PCII Officers shall:

(1) Oversee the handling, use, and storage of PCII;

(2) Ensure the secure sharing of PCII with appropriate authorities and individuals, as set forth in 6 CFR 29.1(a), and paragraph (b)(3) of this section;

(3) Establish and maintain an ongoing self-inspection program, to include periodic review and assessment of the compliance with handling, use, and storage of PCII;

(4) Establish additional procedures, measures and penalties as necessary to prevent unauthorized access to PCII; and

(5) Ensure prompt and appropriate coordination with the PCII Program Manager regarding any request, challenge, or complaint arising out of the implementation of these regulations.

(e) *Protected Critical Infrastructure Information Management System (PCIIMS).* The PCII Program Manager shall develop, for use by the PCII Program Manager and the PCII Manager's designees, an electronic database, to be known as the "Protected Critical Infrastructure Information Management System" (PCIIMS), to record the receipt, acknowledgement, validation, storage, dissemination, and destruction of PCII. This compilation of PCII shall be safeguarded and protected in accordance with the provisions of the CII Act. The PCII Program Manager may require the completion of appropriate background investigations of an individual before granting that individual access to any PCII.

§ 29.5 Requirements for protection.

(a) CII shall receive the protections of section 214 of the CII Act when:

(1) Such information is voluntarily submitted, directly or indirectly, to the PCII Program Manager or the PCII Program Manager's designee;

(2) The information is submitted for protected use regarding the security of critical infrastructure or protected systems, analysis, warning, interdependency study, recovery, reconstitution, or other appropriate purposes including, without limitation, for the identification, analysis, prevention, preemption, disruption, defense against and/or mitigation of terrorist threats to the homeland;

(3) The information is labeled with an express statement as follows:

(i) In the case of documentary submissions, written marking on the information or records substantially similar to the following: "This information is voluntarily submitted to the Federal government in expectation of protection from disclosure as provided by the provisions of the Critical Infrastructure Information Act of 2002"; or

(ii) In the case of oral information:

(A) Through an oral statement, made at the time of the oral submission or within a reasonable period thereafter, indicating an expectation of protection from disclosure as provided by the provisions of the CII Act; and

(B) Through a written statement substantially similar to the one specified above accompanied by a document that memorializes the nature of oral information initially provided received by the PCII Program Manager or the PCII Program Manager's designee within a reasonable period after using oral submission; and

(iii) In the case of electronic information:

(A) Through an electronically submitted statement within a reasonable period of the electronic submission indicating an expectation of protection from disclosure as provided by the provisions of the CII Act; and

(B) Through a non-electronically submitted written statement substantially similar to the one specified above accompanied by a document that memorializes the nature of e-mailed information initially provided, to be received by the PCII Program Manager or the PCII Program Manager's designee within a reasonable period after using e-mail submission.

(4) The submitted information additionally is accompanied by a statement, signed by the submitting person or an authorized person on behalf of an entity identifying the submitting person or entity, containing such contact information as is considered necessary by the PCII Program Manager, and certifying that the information being submitted is not customarily in the public domain;

(b) Information that is not submitted to the PCII Program Manager or the PCII Program Manager's designees will not qualify for protection under the CII Act. Only the PCII Program Manager or the PCII Program Manager's designees are authorized to acknowledge receipt of information being submitted for consideration of protection under the Act.

(c) All Federal, State and local government entities shall protect and maintain information as required by these rules or by the provisions of the CII Act when that information is provided to the entity by the PCII Program Manager or the PCII Program Manager's designee and is marked as required in 6 CFR 29.6(c).

(d) All submissions seeking PCII status shall be presumed to have been submitted in good faith until validation or a determination not to validate pursuant to these rules.

§ 29.6 Acknowledgment of receipt, validation, and marking.

(a) *Authorized officials.* Only the DHS PCII Program Manager is authorized to validate, and mark information as PCII. The PCII Program Manager or the Program Manager's designees, may mark information qualifying under categorical inclusions pursuant to 6 CFR 29.6(f).

(b) *Presumption of protection.* All information submitted in accordance with the procedures set forth hereby will be presumed to be and will be treated as PCII, enjoying the protections of section 214 of the CII Act, from the time the information is received by the PCII Program Office or the PCII

Program Manager's designee. The information shall remain protected unless and until the PCII Program Office renders a final decision that the information is not PCII. The PCII Program Office will, with respect to information that is not properly submitted, inform the submitting person or entity within thirty days of receipt, by a means of communication to be prescribed by the PCII Program Manager, that the submittal was procedurally defective. The submitter will then have an additional 30 days to remedy the deficiency from receipt of such notice. If the submitting person or entity does not cure the deficiency within thirty calendar days of the date of receipt of the notification provided in this paragraph, the PCII Program Office may determine that the presumption of protection is terminated. Under such circumstances, the PCII Program Office may cure the deficiency by labeling the submission with the information required in 6 CFR 29.5 or may notify the applicant that the submission does not qualify as PCII. No CII submission will lose its presumptive status as PCII except as provided in 6 CFR 29.6(g).

(c) *Marking of information.* All PCII shall be clearly identified through markings made by the PCII Program Office. The PCII Program Office shall mark PCII materials as follows: "This document contains PCII. In accordance with the provisions of 6 CFR part 29, this document is exempt from release under the Freedom of Information Act (5 U.S.C. 552(b)(3)) and similar laws requiring public disclosure. Unauthorized release may result in criminal and administrative penalties. This document is to be safeguarded and disseminated in accordance with the CII Act and the PCII Program requirements." When distributing PCII, the distributing person shall ensure that the distributed information contains this marking.

(d) *Acknowledgement of receipt of information.* The PCII Program Office or the PCII Program Manager's designees shall acknowledge receipt of information submitted as CII and accompanied by an express statement, and in so doing shall:

(1) Contact the submitting person or entity, within thirty calendar days of receipt of the submission of CII, by the means of delivery prescribed in procedures developed by the PCII Program Manager. In the case of oral submissions, receipt will be acknowledged in writing within thirty calendar days after receipt by the PCII Program Office or the PCII Program Manager's designee of a written statement, certification, and documents that memorialize the oral submission, as referenced in 6 CFR 29.5(a)(3)(ii);

(2) Enter the appropriate data into the PCIIMS as required in 6 CFR 29.4(e); and

(3) Provide the submitting person or entity with a unique tracking number that will accompany the information from the time it is received by the PCII Program Office or the PCII Program Manager's designees.

(e) *Validation of information.* (1) The PCII Program Manager shall be responsible for reviewing all submissions that request protection under the CII Act. The PCII Program Manager shall review the submitted information as soon as practicable. If a final determination is made that the submitted information meets the requirements for protection, the PCII Program Manager shall ensure that the information has been marked as required in paragraph (c) of this section, notify the submitting person or entity of the determination, and disclose it only pursuant to 6 CFR 29.8.

(2) If the PCII Program Office makes an initial determination that the information submitted does not meet the requirements for protection under the CII Act, the PCII Program Office shall:

(i) Notify the submitting person or entity of the initial determination that the information is not considered to be PCII. This notification also shall, as necessary:

(A) Request that the submitting person or entity complete the requirements of 6 CFR 29.5(a)(4) or further explain the nature of the information and the submitting person or entity's basis for believing the information qualifies for protection under the CII Act;

(B) Advise the submitting person or entity that the PCII Program Office will review any further information provided before rendering a final determination;

(C) Advise the submitting person or entity that the submission can be withdrawn at any time before a final determination is made;

(D) Notify the submitting person or entity that until a final determination is made the submission will be treated as PCII;

(E) Notify the submitting person or entity that any response to the notification must be received by the PCII Program Office no later than thirty calendar days after the date of the notification; and

(F) Request the submitting person or entity to state whether, in the event the PCII Program Office makes a final determination that any such information is not PCII, the submitting person or entity prefers that the information be maintained without the protections of the CII Act or returned to the submitter or destroyed. If a request for withdrawal is made, all such information shall be returned to the submitting person or entity.

(ii) If the information submitted has not been withdrawn by the submitting person or entity, and the PCII Program Office, after following the procedures set forth in paragraph (e)(2)(i) of this section, makes a final determination that the information is not PCII, the PCII Program Office, in accordance with the submitting person or entity's written preference, shall, within thirty calendar days of making a final determination, return the information to the submitter. If return to the submitter is impractical, the PCII Program Office shall destroy the information within 30 days. This process is consistent with the appropriate National Archives and Records Administration-approved records disposition schedule. If the submitting person or entity cannot be notified or the submitting person or entity's response is not received within thirty calendar days of the date of the notification as provided in paragraph (e)(2)(i) of this section, the PCII Program Office shall make the initial determination final and return the information to the submitter.

(f) *Categorical Inclusions of Certain Types of Infrastructure as PCII.* The PCII Program Manager has discretion to declare certain subject matter or types of information categorically protected as PCII and to set procedures for receipt and processing of such information. Information within a categorical inclusion will be considered validated upon receipt by the Program Office or any of the Program Manager's designees without further review, provided that the submitter provides the express statement required by section 214(a)(1). Designees shall provide to the Program Manager information submitted under a categorical inclusion.

(g) *Changing the status of PCII to non-PCII.* Once information is validated, only the PCII Program Office may change the status of PCII to that of non-PCII and remove its PCII markings. Status changes may only take place when the submitting person or entity requests in writing that the information no longer be protected under the CII Act; or when the PCII Program Office determines that the information was, at the time of the submission, customarily in the public domain. Upon making an initial determination that a change in status may be warranted, but prior to a final determination, the PCII Program Office, using the procedures in paragraph (e)(2) of this section, shall inform the submitting person or entity of the initial determination of a change in status. Notice of the final change in status of PCII shall be provided to all recipients of that PCII under 6 CFR 29.8.

§ 29.7 Safeguarding of Protected Critical Infrastructure Information.

(a) *Safeguarding.* All persons granted access to PCII are responsible for safeguarding such information in their possession or control. PCII shall be protected at all times by appropriate storage and handling. Each person who works with PCII is personally responsible for taking proper precautions to ensure that unauthorized persons do not gain access to it.

(b) *Background Checks on Persons with Access to PCII.* For those who require access to PCII, DHS will, to the extent practicable and consistent with the purposes of the Act, undertake appropriate background checks to ensure that individuals with access to PCII do not pose a threat to national security.

These checks may also be waived in exigent circumstances.

(c) *Use and Storage.* When PCII is in the physical possession of a person, reasonable steps shall be taken, in accordance with procedures prescribed by the PCII Program Manager, to minimize the risk of access to PCII by unauthorized persons. When PCII is not in the physical possession of a person, it shall be stored in a secure environment.

(d) *Reproduction.* Pursuant to procedures prescribed by the PCII Program Manager, a document or other material containing PCII may be reproduced to the extent necessary consistent with the need to carry out official duties, provided that the reproduced documents or material are marked and protected in the same manner as the original documents or material.

(e) *Disposal of information.* Documents and material containing PCII may be disposed of by any method that prevents unauthorized retrieval, such as shredding or incineration.

(f) *Transmission of information.* PCII shall be transmitted only by secure means of delivery as determined by the PCII Program Manager, and in conformance with appropriate federal standards.

(g) *Automated Information Systems.* The PCII Program Manager shall establish security requirements designed to protect information to the maximum extent practicable, and consistent with the Act, for Automated Information Systems that contain PCII. Such security requirements will be in conformance with the information technology security requirements in the Federal Information Security Management Act and the Office of Management and Budget's implementing policies.

§29.8 **Disclosure of Protected Critical Infrastructure Information.**

(a) *Authorization of access.* The Under Secretary for Preparedness, the Assistant Secretary for Infrastructure Protection, or either's designee may choose to provide or authorize access to PCII under one or more of the subsections below when it is determined that this access supports a lawful and authorized government purpose as enumerated in the CII Act or other law, regulation, or legal authority.

(b) *Federal, State and Local government sharing.* The PCII Program Manager or the PCII Program Manager's designees may provide PCII to an employee of the Federal government, provided, subject to subsection (f) of this section, that such information is shared for purposes of securing the critical infrastructure or protected systems, analysis, warning, interdependency study, recovery, reconstitution, or for another appropriate purpose including, without limitation, the identification, analysis, prevention, preemption, and/or disruption of terrorist threats to the homeland. PCII may not be used, directly or indirectly, for any collateral regulatory purpose. PCII may be provided to a State or local government entity for the purpose of protecting critical infrastructure or protected systems, or in furtherance of an investigation or the prosecution of a criminal act. The provision of PCII to a State or local government entity will normally be made only pursuant to an arrangement with the PCII Program Manager providing for compliance with the requirements of paragraph (d) of this section and acknowledging the understanding and responsibilities of the recipient. State and local governments receiving such information will acknowledge in such arrangements the primacy of PCII protections under the CII Act; agree to assert all available legal defenses to disclosure of PCII under State, or local public disclosure laws, statutes or ordinances; and will agree to treat breaches of the agreements by their employees or contractors as matters subject to the criminal code or to the applicable employee code of conduct for the jurisdiction.

(c) *Disclosure of information to Federal, State and local government contractors.* Disclosure of PCII to Federal, State, and local contractors may be made when necessary for an appropriate purpose under the CII Act, and only after the PCII Program Manager or a PCII Officer certifies that the contractor is performing services in support of the purposes of the CII Act. The contractor's employees who will be handling PCII must sign individual nondisclosure agreements in a form prescribed by the PCII Program Manager, and the contractor must agree by contract, whenever and to whatever extent possible, to comply with all relevant requirements of the PCII Program. The contractor shall safeguard PCII in accordance with these procedures and shall not remove any "PCII" markings. An employee of the contractor may, in the performance of services in support of the purposes of the CII Act and when authorized to do so by the PCII Program Manager or the PCII Program Manager's designee, communicate with a submitting person or an authorized person of a submitting entity, about a submittal of information by that person or entity. Contractors shall not further disclose PCII to any other party not already authorized to receive such information by the PCII Program Manager or PCII Program Manager's Designee, without the prior written approval of the PCII Program Manager or the PCII Program Manager's designee.

(d) *Further use or disclosure of information by State, and local governments.* (1) State and local governments receiving information marked "Protected Critical Infrastructure Information" shall not share that information with any other party not already authorized to receive such information by the PCII Program Manager or PCII Program Manager's designee, with the exception of their contractors after complying with the requirements of paragraph (c) of this section, or remove any PCII markings, without first obtaining authorization from the PCII Program Manager or the PCII Program Manager's designees, who shall be responsible for requesting and obtaining written consent from the submitter of the information.

(2) State and local governments may use PCII only for the purpose of protecting critical infrastructure or protected systems, or as set forth elsewhere in these rules.

(e) *Disclosure of information to appropriate entities or to the general public.* PCII may be used to prepare advisories, alerts, and warnings to relevant companies, targeted sectors, governmental entities, ISAOs or the general public regarding potential threats and vulnerabilities to critical infrastructure as appropriate pursuant to the CII Act. Unless exigent circumstances require otherwise, any such warnings to the general public will be authorized by the Secretary, Under Secretary for Preparedness, Assistant Secretary for Cyber Security and Telecommunications, or Assistant Secretary for Infrastructure Protection. Such exigent circumstances exist only when approval of the Secretary, the Under Secretary for Preparedness, Assistant Secretary for Cyber Security and Telecommunications, or the Assistant Secretary for Infrastructure Protection cannot be obtained within a reasonable time necessary to issue an effective advisory, alert, or warning. In issuing advisories, alerts and warnings, DHS shall consider the exigency of the situation, the extent of possible harm to the public or to critical infrastructure, and the necessary scope of the advisory or warning; and take appropriate actions to protect from disclosure any information that is proprietary, business sensitive, relates specifically to, or might be used to identify, the submitting person or entity, or any persons or entities on whose behalf the CII was submitted, or is not otherwise appropriately in the public domain. Depending on the exigency of the circumstances, DHS may consult or cooperate with the submitter in making such advisories, alerts or warnings.

(f) *Disclosure for law enforcement purposes and communication with submitters; access by Congress, the Comptroller General, and the Inspector General; and whistleblower protection*—(1) *Exceptions for disclosure.* (i) PCII shall not, without the written consent of the person or entity submitting such information, be used or disclosed for purposes other than the purposes of the CII Act, except—

(A) In furtherance of an investigation or the prosecution of a criminal act by the Federal government, or by a State, local, or foreign government, when such disclosure is coordinated by a Federal law enforcement official;

(B) To communicate with a submitting person or an authorized person on behalf of a submitting entity, about a submittal of information by that person or entity when authorized to do so by the PCII Program Manager or the PCII Program Manager's designee; or

(C) When disclosure of the information is made by any officer or employee of the United States—

(1) To either House of Congress, or to the extent of matter within its jurisdiction, any committee or subcommittee thereof, any joint committee thereof or subcommittee of any such joint committee; or

(2) To the Comptroller General, or any authorized representative of the Comptroller General, in the course of the performance of the duties of the Government Accountability Office.

(ii) If any officer or employee of the United States makes any disclosure pursuant to these exceptions, contemporaneous written notification must be provided to DHS through the PCII Program Manager.

(2) Consistent with the authority to disclose information for any of the purposes of the CII Act, disclosure of PCII may be made, without the written consent of the person or entity submitting such information, to the DHS Inspector General.

(g) *Responding to requests made under the Freedom of Information Act or State, local, and tribal information access laws.* PCII shall be treated as exempt from disclosure under the Freedom of Information Act and any State or local law requiring disclosure of records or information. Any Federal, State, local, or tribal government agency with questions regarding the protection of PCII from public disclosure shall contact the PCII Program Manager, who shall in turn consult with the DHS Office of the General Counsel.

(h) *Ex parte communications with decisionmaking officials.* Pursuant to section 214(a)(1)(B) of the Homeland Security Act of 2002, PCII is not subject to any agency rules or judicial doctrine regarding ex parte communications with a decisionmaking official.

(i) *Restriction on use of PCII in civil actions.* Pursuant to section 214(a)(1)(C) of the Homeland Security Act of 2002, PCII shall not, without the written consent of the person or entity submitting such information, be used directly by any Federal, State or local authority, or by any third party, in any civil action arising under Federal, State, local, or tribal law.

§29.9 Investigation and reporting of violation of PCII procedures.

(a) *Reporting of possible violations.* Persons authorized to have access to PCII shall report any suspected violation of security procedures, the loss or misplacement of PCII, and any suspected unauthorized disclosure of PCII immediately to the PCII Program Manager or the PCII Program Manager's designees. Suspected violations may also be reported to the DHS Inspector General. The PCII Program Manager or the PCII Program Manager's designees shall in turn report the incident to the appropriate Security Officer and to the DHS Inspector General.

(b) *Review and investigation of written report.* The PCII Program Manager, or the appropriate Security Officer shall notify the DHS Inspector General of their intent to investigate any alleged violation of procedures, loss of information, and/or unauthorized disclosure, prior to initiating any such investigation. Evidence of wrongdoing resulting from any such investigations by agencies other than the DHS Inspector General shall be reported to the Department of Justice, Criminal Division, through the DHS Office of the General Counsel. The DHS Inspector General also has authority to conduct such investigations, and shall report any evidence of wrongdoing to the Department of Justice, Criminal Division, for consideration of prosecution.

(c) *Notification to originator of PCII.* If the PCII Program Manager or the appropriate Security Officer determines that a loss of information or an unauthorized disclosure has occurred, the PCII Program Manager or the PCII Program Manager's designees shall notify the person or entity that submitted the PCII, unless providing such notification could reasonably be expected to hamper the relevant investigation or adversely affect any other law enforcement, national security, or homeland security interest.

(d) *Criminal and administrative penalties.* (1) As established in section 214(f) of the CII Act, whoever, being an officer or employee of the United States or of any department or agency thereof, knowingly publishes, divulges, discloses, or makes known in any manner or to any extent not authorized by law, any information protected from disclosure by the CII Act coming to the officer or employee in the course of his or her employment or official duties or by reason of any examination or investigation made by, or return, report, or record made to or filed with, such department or agency or officer or employee thereof, shall be fined under title 18 of the United States Code, imprisoned not more than one year, or both, and shall be removed from office or employment.

(2) In addition to the penalties set forth in paragraph (d)(1) of this section, if the PCII Program Manager determines that an entity or person who has received PCII has violated the provisions of this part or used PCII for an inappropriate purpose, the PCII Program Manager may disqualify that entity or person from future receipt of any PCII or future receipt of any sensitive homeland security information under section 892 of the Homeland Security Act, provided, however, that any such decision by the PCII Program Manager may be appealed to the Office of the Under Secretary for Preparedness.

PART 37—REAL ID DRIVER'S LICENSES AND IDENTIFICATION CARDS

Subpart A—General

AUTHORITY: 49 U.S.C. 30301 note; 6 U.S.C. 111, 112.

SOURCE: 73 FR 5331, Jan. 29, 2008, unless otherwise noted.

Subpart A—General

§ 37.1 Applicability.

(a) Subparts A through E of this part apply to States and U.S. territories that choose to issue driver's licenses and identification cards that can be accepted by Federal agencies for official purposes.

(b) Subpart F establishes certain standards for State-issued driver's licenses and identification cards issued by States that participate in REAL ID, but that are not intended to be accepted by Federal agencies for official purpose under section 202(d)(11) of the REAL ID Act.

§37.3 Definitions.

For purposes of this part:

Birth certificate means the record related to a birth that is permanently stored either electronically or physically at the State Office of Vital Statistics or equivalent agency in a registrant's State of birth.

Card means either a driver's license or identification card issued by the State Department of Motor Vehicles (DMV) or equivalent State office.

Certification means an assertion by the State to the Department of Homeland Security that the State has met the requirements of this part.

Certified copy of a birth certificate means a copy of the whole or part of a birth certificate registered with the State that the State considers to be the same as the original birth certificate on file with the State Office of Vital Statistics or equivalent agency in a registrant's State of birth.

Covered employees means Department of Motor Vehicles employees or contractors who are involved in the manufacture or production of REAL ID driver's licenses and identification cards, or who have the ability to affect the identity information that appears on the driver's license or identification card.

Data verification means checking the validity of data contained in source documents presented under this regulation.

DHS means the U.S. Department of Homeland Security.

DMV means the Department of Motor Vehicles or any State Government entity that issues driver's licenses and identification cards, or an office with equivalent function for issuing driver's licenses and identification cards.

Determination means a decision by the Department of Homeland Security that a State has or has not met the requirements of this part and that Federal agencies may or may not accept the driver's licenses and identification cards issued by the State for official purposes.

Digital photograph means a digital image of the face of the holder of the driver's license or identification card.

Document authentication means determining that the source document presented under these regulations is genuine and has not been altered.

Domestic violence and dating violence have the meanings given the terms in section 3, Universal definitions and grant provisions, of the Violence Against Women and Department of Justice Reauthorization Act of 2005 (Pub. L. 109–162, 119 Stat. 2960, 2964, Jan. 5, 2006); codified at section 40002, Definitions and grant provisions, 42 U.S.C. 13925, or State laws addressing domestic and dating violence.

Driver's license means a motor vehicle operator's license, as defined in 49 U.S.C. 30301.

Duplicate means a driver's license or identification card issued subsequent to the original document that bears the same information and expiration date as the original document and that is reissued at the request of the holder when the original is lost, stolen, or damaged and there has been no material change in information since prior issuance.

Federal agency means all executive agencies including Executive departments, a Government corporation, and an independent establishment as defined in 5 U.S.C. 105.

Federally-regulated commercial aircraft means a commercial aircraft regulated by the Transportation Security Administration (TSA).

Full compliance means that the Secretary or his designate(s) has determined that a State has met all the requirements of Subparts A through E.

Full legal name means an individual's first name, middle name(s), and last name or surname, without use of initials or nicknames.

IAFIS means the Integrated Automated Fingerprint Identification System, a national fingerprint and criminal history system maintained by the Federal Bureau of Investigation (FBI) that provides automated fingerprint search capabilities.

Identification card means a document made or issued by or under the authority of a State Department of Motor Vehicles or State office with equivalent function which, when completed with information concerning a particular individual, is of a type intended or commonly accepted for the purpose of identification of individuals.

INS means the former-Immigration and Naturalization Service of the U.S. Department of Justice.

Lawful status: A person in lawful status is a citizen or national of the United States; or an alien: lawfully admitted for permanent or temporary residence in the United States; with conditional permanent resident status in the United States; who has an approved application for asylum in the United States or has entered into the United States in refugee status; who has a valid nonimmigrant status in the United States; who has a pending application for asylum in the United States; who has a pending or approved application for temporary protected status (TPS) in the United States; who has approved deferred action status; or who has a pending application for lawful permanent residence (LPR) or conditional permanent resident status. This definition does not affect other definitions or requirements that may be contained in the Immigration and Nationality Act or other laws.

Material change means any change to the personally identifiable information of an individual as defined under this part. Notwithstanding the definition of personally identifiable information below, a change of address of principal residence does not constitute a material change.

Material compliance means a determination by DHS that a State has met the benchmarks contained in the Material Compliance Checklist.

NCIC means the National Crime Information Center, a computerized index of criminal justice information maintained by the Federal Bureau of Investigation (FBI) that is available to Federal, State, and local law enforcement and other criminal justice agencies.

Official purpose means accessing Federal facilities, boarding Federally-regulated commercial aircraft, and entering nuclear power plants.

Passport means a passport booklet or card issued by the U.S. Department of State that can be used as a travel document to gain entry into the United States and that denotes identity and citizenship as determined by the U.S. Department of State.

Personally identifiable information means any information which can be used to distinguish or trace an individual's identity, such as their name; driver's license or identification card number; social security number; biometric record, including a digital photograph or signature; alone, or when combined with other personal or identifying information, which is linked or linkable to a specific individual, such as a date and place of birth or address, whether it is stored in a database, on a driver's license or identification card, or in the machine readable technology on a license or identification card.

Principal residence means the location where a person currently resides (*i.e.,* presently resides even if at a temporary address) in conformance with the residency requirements of the State issuing the driver's license or identification card, if such requirements exist.

REAL ID Driver's License or Identification Card means a driver's license or identification card that has been issued by a State that has been certified by DHS to be in compliance with the requirements of the REAL ID Act and which meets the standards of subparts A through D of this part, including temporary or limited-term driver's licenses or identification cards issued under § 37.21.

Reissued card means a card that a State DMV issues to replace a card that has been lost, stolen or damaged, or to replace a card that includes outdated information. A card may not be reissued remotely when there is a material change to the personally identifiable information as defined by the Rule.

Renewed card means a driver's license or identification card that a State DMV issues to replace a renewable driver's license or identification card.

SAVE means the DHS Systematic Alien Verification for Entitlements system, or such successor or alternate verification system at the Secretary's discretion.

Secretary means the Secretary of Homeland Security.

Sexual assault and stalking have the meanings given the terms in section 3, universal definitions and grant provisions, of the Violence Against Women and Department of Justice Reauthorization Act of 2005 (Pub. L. 109–162, 119 Stat. 2960, 2964, Jan. 5, 2006); codified at section 40002, Definitions and grant provisions, 42 U.S.C. 13925, or State laws addressing sexual assault and stalking.

Source document(s) means original or certified copies (where applicable) of documents presented by an applicant as required under these regulations to the Department of Motor Vehicles to apply for a driver's license or identification card.

State means a State of the United States, the District of Columbia, Puerto Rico, the Virgin Islands, Guam, American Samoa, and the Commonwealth of the Northern Mariana Islands.

State address confidentiality program means any State-authorized or State-administered program that—

(1) Allows victims of domestic violence, dating violence, sexual assault, stalking, or a severe form of trafficking to keep, obtain, and use alternative addresses; or

(2) Provides confidential record-keeping regarding the addresses of such victims or other categories of persons.

Temporary lawful status: A person in temporary lawful status is a person who: has a valid nonimmigrant status in the United States; has a pending application for asylum in the United States; has a pending or approved application for temporary protected status (TPS) in the United States; has approved deferred action status; or has a pending application for LPR or conditional permanent resident status.

Verify means procedures to ensure that:

(1) The source document is genuine and has not been altered (*i.e.*, "document authentication"); and

(2) The identity data contained on the document is valid ("data verification").

§37.5 Validity periods and deadlines for REAL ID driver's licenses and identification cards.

(a) Driver's licenses and identification cards issued under this part, that are not temporary or limited-term driver's licenses and identification cards, are valid for a period not to exceed eight years. A card may be valid for a shorter period based on other State or Federal requirements.

(b) On or after October 1, 2020, Federal agencies shall not accept a driver's license or identification card for official purposes from any individual unless such license or card is a REAL ID-compliant driver's license or identification card issued by a State that has been determined by DHS to be in full compliance as defined under this subpart.

(c) Federal agencies cannot accept for official purpose driver's licenses and identification cards issued under §37.71 of this rule.

[73 FR 5331, Jan. 29, 2008, as amended at 79 FR 77838, Dec. 29, 2014]

Subpart B—Minimum Documentation, Verification, and Card Issuance Requirements

§37.11 Application and documents the applicant must provide.

(a) The State must subject each person applying for a REAL ID driver's license or identification card to a mandatory facial image capture, and shall maintain photographs of individuals even if no card is issued. The photographs must be stored in a format in accordance with §37.31 as follows:

(1) If no card is issued, for a minimum period of five years.

(2) If a card is issued, for a period of at least two years beyond the expiration date of the card.

(b) *Declaration.* Each applicant must sign a declaration under penalty of perjury that the information presented on the application is true and correct, and the State must retain this declaration. An applicant must sign a new declaration when presenting new source documents to the DMV on subsequent visits.

(c) *Identity.* (1) To establish identity, the applicant must present at least one of the following source documents:

(i) Valid, unexpired U.S. passport.

(ii) Certified copy of a birth certificate filed with a State Office of Vital Statistics or equivalent agency in the individual's State of birth.

(iii) Consular Report of Birth Abroad (CRBA) issued by the U.S. Department of State, Form FS–240, DS–1350 or FS–545.

(iv) Valid, unexpired Permanent Resident Card (Form I–551) issued by DHS or INS.

(v) Unexpired employment authorization document (EAD) issued by DHS, Form I–766 or Form I–688B.

(vi) Unexpired foreign passport with a valid, unexpired U.S. visa affixed accompanied by the approved I–94 form documenting the applicant's most recent admittance into the United States.

(vii) Certificate of Naturalization issued by DHS, Form N–550 or Form N–570.

(viii) Certificate of Citizenship, Form N–560 or Form N–561, issued by DHS.

(ix) REAL ID driver's license or identification card issued in compliance with the standards established by this part.

(x) Such other documents as DHS may designate by notice published in the FEDERAL REGISTER.

(2) Where a State permits an applicant to establish a name other than the name that appears on a source document (for example, through marriage, adoption, court order, or other mechanism permitted by State law or regulation), the State shall require evidence of the name change through the presentation of documents issued by a court, governmental body or other entity as determined by the State. The State shall maintain copies of the documentation presented pursuant to § 37.31, and maintain a record of both the recorded name and the name on the source documents in a manner to be determined by the State and in conformity with § 37.31.

(d) *Date of birth.* To establish date of birth, an individual must present at least one document included in paragraph (c) of this section.

(e) *Social security number (SSN).* (1) Except as provided in paragraph (e)(3) of this section, individuals presenting the identity documents listed in § 37.11(c)(1) and (2) must present his or her Social Security Administration account number card; or, if a Social Security Administration account card is not available, the person may present any of the following documents bearing the applicant's SSN:

(i) A W–2 form,

(ii) A SSA–1099 form,

(iii) A non-SSA–1099 form, or

(iv) A pay stub with the applicant's name and SSN on it.

(2) The State DMV must verify the SSN pursuant to § 37.13(b)(2) of this subpart.

(3) Individuals presenting the identity document listed in § 37.11(c)(1)(vi) must present an SSN or demonstrate non-work authorized status.

(f) *Documents demonstrating address of principal residence.* To document the address of principal residence, a person must present at least two documents of the State's choice that include the individual's name and principal residence. A street address is required except as provided in § 37.17(f) of this part.

(g) *Evidence of lawful status in the United States.* A DMV may issue a REAL ID driver's license or identification card only to a person who has presented satisfactory evidence of lawful status.

(1) If the applicant presents one of the documents listed under paragraphs (c)(1)(i), (c)(1)(ii), (c)(1)(iii), (c)(1)(iv), (c)(1)(vii) or (c)(1)(viii) of this section, the issuing State's verification of the applicant's identity in the manner prescribed in § 37.13 will also provide satisfactory evidence of lawful status.

(2) If the applicant presents one of the identity documents listed under paragraphs (c)(1)(v) or (c)(1)(vi), or (c)(1)(ix) of this section, the issuing State's verification of the identity document(s) does not provide satisfactory evidence of lawful status. The applicant must also present a second document from § 37.11(g)(1) or documentation issued by DHS or other Federal agencies demonstrating lawful status as determined by USCIS. All documents shall be verified in the manner prescribed in § 37.13.

(h) *Exceptions Process.* A State DMV may choose to establish a written, defined exceptions process for persons who, for reasons beyond their control, are unable to present all necessary documents and must rely on alternate documents to establish identity or date of birth. Alternative documents to demonstrate lawful status will only be allowed to demonstrate U.S. citizenship.

(1) Each State establishing an exceptions process must make reasonable efforts to establish the authenticity of alternate documents each time they are presented and indicate that an exceptions process was used in the applicant's record.

(2) The State shall retain copies or images of the alternate documents accepted pursuant to §37.31 of this part.

(3) The State shall conduct a review of the use of the exceptions process, and pursuant to subpart E of this part, prepare and submit a report with a copy of the exceptions process as part of the certification documentation detailed in §37.55.

(i) States are not required to comply with these requirements when issuing REAL ID driver's licenses or identification cards in support of Federal, State, or local criminal justice agencies or other programs that require special licensing or identification to safeguard persons or in support of their other official duties. As directed by appropriate officials of these Federal, State, or local agencies, States should take sufficient steps to safeguard the identities of such persons. Driver's licenses and identification cards issued in support of Federal, State, or local criminal justice agencies or programs that require special licensing or identification to safeguard persons or in support of their other official duties shall not be distinguishable from other REAL ID licenses or identification cards issued by the State.

§37.13 Document verification requirements.

(a) States shall make reasonable efforts to ensure that the applicant does not have more than one driver's license or identification card already issued by that State under a different identity. In States where an individual is permitted to hold both a driver's license and identification card, the State shall ensure that the individual has not been issued identification documents in multiple or different names. States shall also comply with the provisions of §37.29 before issuing a driver's license or identification card.

(b) States must verify the documents and information required under §37.11 with the issuer of the document. States shall use systems for electronic validation of document and identity data as they become available or use alternative methods approved by DHS.

(1) States shall verify any document described in §37.11(c) or (g) and issued by DHS (including, but not limited to, the I-94 form described in §37.11(c)(vi)) through the Systematic Alien Verification for Entitlements (SAVE) system or alternate methods approved by DHS, except that if two DHS-issued documents are presented, a SAVE verification of one document that confirms lawful status does not need to be repeated for the second document. In the event of a non-match, the DMV must not issue a REAL ID driver's license or identification card to an applicant, and must refer the individual to U.S. Citizenship and Immigration Services for resolution.

(2) States must verify SSNs with the Social Security Administration (SSA) or through another method approved by DHS. In the event of a non-match with SSA, a State may use existing procedures to resolve non-matches. If the State is unable to resolve the non-match, and the use of an exceptions process is not warranted in the situation, the DMV must not issue a REAL ID driver's license or identification card to an applicant until the information verifies with SSA.

(3) States must verify birth certificates presented by applicants. States should use the Electronic Verification of Vital Events (EVVE) system or other electronic systems whenever the records are available. If the document does not appear authentic upon inspection or the data does not match and the use of an exceptions process is not warranted in the situation, the State must not issue a REAL ID driver's license or identification card to the applicant until the information verifies, and should refer the individual to the issuing office for resolution.

(4) States shall verify documents issued by the Department of State with the Department of State or through methods approved by DHS.

(5) States must verify REAL ID driver's licenses and identification cards with the State of issuance.

(6) Nothing in this section precludes a State from issuing an interim license

or a license issued under § 37.71 that will not be accepted for official purposes to allow the individual to resolve any non-match.

§ 37.15 Physical security features for the driver's license or identification card.

(a) *General.* States must include document security features on REAL ID driver's licenses and identification cards designed to deter forgery and counterfeiting, promote an adequate level of confidence in the authenticity of cards, and facilitate detection of fraudulent cards in accordance with this section.

(1) These features must not be capable of being reproduced using technologies that are commonly used and made available to the general public.

(2) The proposed card solution must contain a well-designed, balanced set of features that are effectively combined and provide multiple layers of security. States must describe these document security features in their security plans pursuant to § 37.41.

(b) *Integrated security features.* REAL ID driver's licenses and identification cards must contain at least three levels of integrated security features that provide the maximum resistance to persons' efforts to—

(1) Counterfeit, alter, simulate, or reproduce a genuine document;

(2) Alter, delete, modify, mask, or tamper with data concerning the original or lawful card holder;

(3) Substitute or alter the original or lawful card holder's photograph and/or signature by any means; and

(4) Create a fraudulent document using components from legitimate driver's licenses or identification cards.

(c) *Security features to detect false cards.* States must employ security features to detect false cards for each of the following three levels:

(1) *Level 1.* Cursory examination, without tools or aids involving easily identifiable visual or tactile features, for rapid inspection at point of usage.

(2) *Level 2.* Examination by trained inspectors with simple equipment.

(3) *Level 3.* Inspection by forensic specialists.

(d) *Document security and integrity.* States must conduct a review of their card design and submit a report to DHS with their certification that indicates the ability of the design to resist compromise and document fraud attempts. The report required by this paragraph is SSI and must be handled and protected in accordance with 49 CFR part 1520. Reports must be updated and submitted to DHS whenever a security feature is modified, added, or deleted. After reviewing the report, DHS may require a State to provide DHS with examination results from a recognized independent laboratory experienced with adversarial analysis of identification documents concerning one or more areas relating to the card's security.

§ 37.17 Requirements for the surface of the driver's license or identification card.

To be accepted by a Federal agency for official purposes, REAL ID driver's licenses and identification cards must include on the front of the card (unless otherwise specified below) the following information:

(a) *Full legal name.* Except as permitted in § 37.11(c)(2), the name on the face of the license or card must be the same as the name on the source document presented by the applicant to establish identity. Where the individual has only one name, that name should be entered in the last name or family name field, and the first and middle name fields should be left blank. Place holders such as NFN, NMN, and NA should not be used.

(b) *Date of birth.*

(c) *Gender,* as determined by the State.

(d) *Unique Driver's license or identification card number.* This cannot be the individual's SSN, and must be unique across driver's license or identification cards within the State.

(e) *Full facial digital photograph.* A full facial photograph must be taken pursuant to the standards set forth below:

(1) States shall follow specifically ISO/IEC 19794–5:2005(E) Information technology—Biometric Data Interchange Formats—Part 5: Face Image Data. The Director of the Federal Register approves this incorporation by

reference in accordance with 5 U.S.C. 552(a) and 1 CFR part 51. You may obtain a copy of these incorporated standards from *http://www.ansi.org*, or by contacting ANSI at ANSI, 25 West 43rd Street, 4th Floor, New York, New York 10036. You may inspect a copy of the incorporated standard at the Department of Homeland Security, 1621 Kent Street, 9th Floor, Rosslyn, VA (please call 703–235–0709 to make an appointment) or at the National Archives and Records Administration (NARA). For information on the availability of material at NARA, call 202–741–6030, or go to *www.archives.gov/federal_register/code_of_federal_regulations/ibr_locations.html.*

These standards include:

(i) Lighting shall be equally distributed on the face.

(ii) The face from crown to the base of the chin, and from ear-to-ear, shall be clearly visible and free of shadows.

(iii) Veils, scarves or headdresses must not obscure any facial features and not generate shadow. The person may not wear eyewear that obstructs the iris or pupil of the eyes and must not take any action to obstruct a photograph of their facial features.

(iv) Where possible, there must be no dark shadows in the eye-sockets due to the brow. The iris and pupil of the eyes shall be clearly visible.

(v) Care shall be taken to avoid "hot spots" (bright areas of light shining on the face).

(2) Photographs may be in black and white or color.

(f) *Address of principal residence*, except an alternative address may be displayed for:

(1) Individuals for whom a State law, regulation, or DMV procedure permits display of an alternative address, or

(2) Individuals who satisfy any of the following:

(i) If the individual is enrolled in a State address confidentiality program which allows victims of domestic violence, dating violence, sexual assault, stalking, or a severe form of trafficking, to keep, obtain, and use alternative addresses; and provides that the addresses of such persons must be kept confidential, or other similar program;

(ii) If the individual's address is entitled to be suppressed under State or Federal law or suppressed by a court order including an administrative order issued by a State or Federal court; or

(iii) If the individual is protected from disclosure of information pursuant to section 384 of the Illegal Immigration Reform and Immigrant Responsibility Act of 1996.

(3) In areas where a number and street name has not been assigned for U.S. mail delivery, an address convention used by the U.S. Postal Service is acceptable.

(g) *Signature.* (1) The card must include the signature of the card holder. The signature must meet the requirements of the March 2005 American Association of Motor Vehicle Administrators (AAMVA) standards for the 2005 AAMVA Driver's License/Identification Card Design Specifications, Annex A, section A.7.7.2. This standard includes requirements for size, scaling, cropping, color, borders, and resolution. The Director of the Federal Register approves this incorporation by reference in accordance with 5 U.S.C. 552(a) and 1 CFR part 51. You may obtain a copy of these standards from AAMVA on-line at *http://www.aamva.org*, or by contacting AAMVA at 4301 Wilson Boulevard, Suite 400, Arlington, VA 22203. You may inspect a copy of these incorporated standards at the Department of Homeland Security, 1621 Kent Street, 9th Floor, Rosslyn, VA (please call 703–235–0709 to make an appointment) or at the National Archives and Records Administration (NARA). For information on the availability of material at NARA, call 202–741–6030, or go to *http://www.archives.gov/federal_register/code_of_federal_regulations/ibr_locations.html.*

(2) The State shall establish alternative procedures for individuals unable to sign their name.

(h) *Physical security features*, pursuant to §37.15 of this subpart.

(i) *Machine-readable technology on the back of the card*, pursuant to §37.19 of this subpart.

(j) *Date of transaction.*

(k) *Expiration date.*

(l) *State or territory of issuance.*

(m) *Printed information.* The name, date of birth, gender, card number, issue date, expiration date, and address on the face of the card must be in Latin alpha-numeric characters. The name must contain a field of no less than a total of 39 characters, and longer names shall be truncated following the standard established by International Civil Aviation Organization (ICAO) 9303, "Machine Readable Travel Documents," Volume 1, part 1, Sixth Edition, 2006. The Director of the Federal Register approves this incorporation by reference in accordance with 5 U.S.C. 552(a) and 1 CFR part 51. You may obtain a copy of ICAO 9303 from the ICAO, Document Sales Unit, 999 University Street, Montreal, Quebec, Canada H3C 5H7, e-mail: *sales@icao.int.* You may inspect a copy of the incorporated standard at the Department of Homeland Security, 1621 Kent Street, 9th Floor, Rosslyn, VA (please call 703-235-0709 to make an appointment) or at the National Archives and Records Administration (NARA). For information on the availability of material at NARA, call 202-741-6030, or go to *http:// www.archives.gov/federal_register/ code_of_federal_regulations/ ibr_locations.html.*

(n) The card shall bear a DHS-approved security marking on each driver's license or identification card that is issued reflecting the card's level of compliance as set forth in § 37.51 of this Rule.

§ 37.19 Machine readable technology on the driver's license or identification card.

For the machine readable portion of the REAL ID driver's license or identification card, States must use the ISO/IEC 15438:2006(E) Information Technology—Automatic identification and data capture techniques—PDF417 symbology specification. The Director of the Federal Register approves this incorporation by reference in accordance with 5 U.S.C. 552(a) and 1 CFR part 51. You may obtain a copy of these incorporated standards at *http:// www.ansi.org,* or by contacting ANSI at ANSI, 25 West 43rd Street, 4th Floor, New York, New York 10036. You may inspect a copy of the incorporated standard at the Department of Home-

land Security, 1621 Kent Street, 9th Floor, Rosslyn, VA (please call 703-235-0709 to make an appointment) or at the National Archives and Records Administration (NARA). For information on the availability of material at NARA, call 202-741-6030, or go to *http:// www.archives.gov/federal_register/ code_of_federal_regulations/ ibr_locations.html.* The PDF417 bar code standard must have the following defined minimum data elements:

(a) Expiration date.

(b) Full legal name, unless the State permits an applicant to establish a name other than the name that appears on a source document, pursuant to § 37.11(c)(2).

(c) Date of transaction.

(d) Date of birth.

(e) Gender.

(f) Address as listed on the card pursuant to § 37.17(f).

(g) Unique driver's license or identification card number.

(h) Card design revision date, indicating the most recent change or modification to the visible format of the driver's license or identification card.

(i) Inventory control number of the physical document.

(j) State or territory of issuance.

§ 37.21 Temporary or limited-term driver's licenses and identification cards.

States may only issue a temporary or limited-term REAL ID driver's license or identification card to an individual who has temporary lawful status in the United States.

(a) States must require, before issuing a temporary or limited-term driver's license or identification card to a person, valid documentary evidence, verifiable through SAVE or other DHS-approved means, that the person has lawful status in the United States.

(b) States shall not issue a temporary or limited-term driver's license or identification card pursuant to this section:

(1) For a time period longer than the expiration of the applicant's authorized stay in the United States, or, if there is no expiration date, for a period longer than one year; and

(2) For longer than the State's maximum driver's license or identification card term.

(c) States shall renew a temporary or limited-term driver's license or identification card pursuant to this section and §37.25(b)(2), only if:

(1) the individual presents valid documentary evidence that the status by which the applicant qualified for the temporary or limited-term driver's license or identification card is still in effect, or

(2) the individual presents valid documentary evidence that he or she continues to qualify for lawful status under paragraph (a) of this section.

(d) States must verify the information presented to establish lawful status through SAVE, or another method approved by DHS.

(e) Temporary or limited-term driver's licenses and identification cards must clearly indicate on the face of the license and in the machine readable zone that the license or card is a temporary or limited-term driver's license or identification card.

§37.23 Reissued REAL ID driver's licenses and identification cards.

(a) *State procedure.* States must establish an effective procedure to confirm or verify an applicant's identity each time a REAL ID driver's license or identification card is reissued, to ensure that the individual receiving the reissued REAL ID driver's license or identification card is the same individual to whom the driver's license or identification card was originally issued.

(b) *Remote/Non-in-person reissuance.* Except as provided in paragraph (c) of this section a State may conduct a non-in-person (remote) reissuance if State procedures permit the reissuance to be conducted remotely. Except for the reissuance of duplicate driver's licenses and identification cards as defined in this rule, the State must reverify pursuant to §37.13, the applicant's SSN and lawful status prior to reissuing the driver's license or identification card.

(c) *In-person reissuance.* The State may not remotely reissue a driver's license or identification card where there has been a material change in

any personally identifiable information since prior issuance. All material changes must be established through an applicant's presentation of an original source document as provided in this subpart, and must be verified as specified in §37.13.

§37.25 Renewal of REAL ID driver's licenses and identification cards.

(a) *In-person renewals.* States must require holders of REAL ID driver's licenses and identification cards to renew their driver's licenses and identification cards with the State DMV in person, no less frequently than every sixteen years.

(1) The State DMV shall take an updated photograph of the applicant, no less frequently than every sixteen years.

(2) The State must reverify the renewal applicant's SSN and lawful status through SSOLV and SAVE, respectively (or other DHS-approved means) as applicable prior to renewing the driver's license or identification card. The State must also verify electronically information that it was not able to verify at a previous issuance or renewal if the systems or processes exist to do so.

(3) Holders of temporary or limited-term REAL ID driver's licenses and identification cards must present evidence of continued lawful status via SAVE or other method approved by DHS when renewing their driver's license or identification card.

(b) *Remote/Non-in-person renewal.* Except as provided in (b)(2) a State may conduct a non-in-person (remote) renewal if State procedures permit the renewal to be conducted remotely.

(1) The State must reverify the applicant's SSN and lawful status pursuant to §37.13 prior to renewing the driver's license or identification card.

(2) The State may not remotely renew a REAL ID driver's license or identification card where there has been a material change in any personally identifiable information since prior issuance. All material changes must be established through the applicant's presentation of an original source document as provided in Subpart B, and must be verified as specified in §37.13.

§ 37.27 Driver's licenses and identification cards issued during the age-based enrollment period.

Driver's licenses and identification cards issued to individuals prior to a DHS determination that the State is materially compliant may be renewed or reissued pursuant to current State practices, and will be accepted for official purposes until the validity dates described in § 37.5.

[73 FR 5331, Jan. 29, 2008, as amended at 79 FR 77838, Dec. 29, 2014]

§ 37.29 Prohibition against holding more than one REAL ID card or more than one driver's license.

(a) An individual may hold only one REAL ID card. An individual cannot hold a REAL ID driver's license and a REAL ID identification card simultaneously. Nothing shall preclude an individual from holding a REAL ID card and a non-REAL ID card unless prohibited by his or her State.

(b) Prior to issuing a REAL ID driver's license,

(1) A State must check with all other States to determine if the applicant currently holds a driver's license or REAL ID identification card in another State.

(2) If the State receives confirmation that the individual holds a driver's license in another State, or possesses a REAL ID identification card in another State, the receiving State must take measures to confirm that the person has terminated or is terminating the driver's license or REAL ID identification card issued by the prior State pursuant to State law, regulation or procedure.

(c) Prior to issuing a REAL ID identification card,

(1) A State must check with all other States to determine if the applicant currently holds a REAL ID driver's license or identification card in another State.

(2) If the State receives confirmation that the individual holds a REAL ID card in another State the receiving State must take measures to confirm that the person has terminated or is terminating the REAL ID driver's license or identification card issued by the prior State pursuant to State law, regulation or procedure.

Subpart C—Other Requirements

§ 37.31 Source document retention.

(a) States must retain copies of the application, declaration and source documents presented under § 37.11 of this part, including documents used to establish all names recorded by the DMV under § 37.11(c)(2). States shall take measures to protect any personally identifiable information collected pursuant to the REAL ID Act as described in their security plan under § 37.41(b)(2).

(1) States that choose to keep paper copies of source documents must retain the copies for a minimum of seven years.

(2) States that choose to transfer information from paper copies to microfiche must retain the microfiche for a minimum of ten years.

(3) States that choose to keep digital images of source documents must retain the images for a minimum of ten years.

(4) States are not required to retain the declaration with application and source documents, but must retain the declaration consistent with applicable State document retention requirements and retention periods.

(b) States using digital imaging to retain source documents must store the images as follows:

(1) Photo images must be stored in the Joint Photographic Experts Group (JPEG) 2000 standard for image compression, or a standard that is interoperable with the JPEG standard. Images must be stored in an open (consensus) format, without proprietary wrappers, to ensure States can effectively use the image captures of other States as needed.

(2) Document and signature images must be stored in a compressed Tagged Image Format (TIF), or a standard that is interoperable with the TIF standard.

(3) All images must be retrievable by the DMV if properly requested by law enforcement.

(c) Upon request by an applicant, a State shall record and retain the applicant's name, date of birth, certificate numbers, date filed, and issuing agency in lieu of an image or copy of the applicant's birth certificate, where such procedures are required by State law.

§ 37.33 DMV databases.

(a) States must maintain a State motor vehicle database that contains, at a minimum—

(1) All data fields printed on driver's licenses and identification cards issued by the State, individual serial numbers of the card, and SSN;

(2) A record of the full legal name and recorded name established under § 37.11(c)(2) as applicable, without truncation;

(3) All additional data fields included in the MRZ but not printed on the driver's license or identification card; and

(4) Motor vehicle driver's histories, including motor vehicle violations, suspensions, and points on driver's licenses.

(b) States must protect the security of personally identifiable information, collected pursuant to the REAL ID Act, in accordance with § 37.41(b)(2) of this part.

Subpart D—Security at DMVs and Driver's License and Identification Card Production Facilities

§ 37.41 Security plan.

(a) *In General.* States must have a security plan that addresses the provisions in paragraph (b) of this section and must submit the security plan as part of its REAL ID certification under § 37.55.

(b) Security plan contents. At a minimum, the security plan must address—

(1) Physical security for the following:

(i) Facilities used to produce driver's licenses and identification cards.

(ii) Storage areas for card stock and other materials used in card production.

(2) Security of personally identifiable information maintained at DMV locations involved in the enrollment, issuance, manufacture and/or production of cards issued under the REAL ID Act, including, but not limited to, providing the following protections:

(i) Reasonable administrative, technical, and physical safeguards to protect the security, confidentiality, and integrity of the personally identifiable information collected, stored, and maintained in DMV records and information systems for purposes of complying with the REAL ID Act. These safeguards must include procedures to prevent unauthorized access, use, or dissemination of applicant information and images of source documents retained pursuant to the Act and standards and procedures for document retention and destruction.

(ii) A privacy policy regarding the personally identifiable information collected and maintained by the DMV pursuant to the REAL ID Act.

(iii) Any release or use of personal information collected and maintained by the DMV pursuant to the REAL ID Act must comply with the requirements of the Driver's Privacy Protection Act, 18 U.S.C. 2721 *et seq.* State plans may go beyond these minimum privacy requirements to provide greater protection, and such protections are not subject to review by DHS for purposes of determining compliance with this part.

(3) Document and physical security features for the card, consistent with the requirements of § 37.15, including a description of the State's use of biometrics, and the technical standard utilized, if any;

(4) Access control, including the following:

(i) Employee identification and credentialing, including access badges.

(ii) Employee background checks, in accordance with § 37.45 of this part.

(iii) Controlled access systems.

(5) Periodic training requirements in—

(i) Fraudulent document recognition training for all covered employees handling source documents or engaged in the issuance of driver's licenses and identification cards. The fraudulent document training program approved by AAMVA or other DHS approved method satisfies the requirement of this subsection.

(ii) Security awareness training, including threat identification and handling of SSI as necessary.

(6) Emergency/incident response plan;

(7) Internal audit controls;

(8) An affirmation that the State possesses both the authority and the means to produce, revise, expunge, and protect the confidentiality of REAL ID driver's licenses or identification cards issued in support of Federal, State, or local criminal justice agencies or similar programs that require special licensing or identification to safeguard persons or support their official duties. These procedures must be designed in coordination with the key requesting authorities to ensure that the procedures are effective and to prevent conflicting or inconsistent requests. In order to safeguard the identities of individuals, these procedures should not be discussed in the plan and States should make every effort to prevent disclosure to those without a need to know about either this confidential procedure or any substantive information that may compromise the confidentiality of these operations. The appropriate law enforcement official and United States Attorney should be notified of any action seeking information that could compromise Federal law enforcement interests.

(c) *Handling of Security Plan.* The Security Plan required by this section contains Sensitive Security Information (SSI) and must be handled and protected in accordance with 49 CFR part 1520.

§ 37.43 Physical security of DMV production facilities.

(a) States must ensure the physical security of facilities where driver's licenses and identification cards are produced, and the security of document materials and papers from which driver's licenses and identification cards are produced or manufactured.

(b) States must describe the security of DMV facilities as part of their security plan, in accordance with § 37.41.

§ 37.45 Background checks for covered employees.

(a) *Scope.* States are required to subject persons who are involved in the manufacture or production of REAL ID driver's licenses and identification cards, or who have the ability to affect the identity information that appears on the driver's license or identification card, or current employees who will be assigned to such positions ("covered employees" or "covered positions"), to a background check. The background check must include, at a minimum, the validation of references from prior employment, a name-based and fingerprint-based criminal history records check, and employment eligibility verification otherwise required by law. States shall describe their background check process as part of their security plan, in accordance with § 37.41(b)(4)(ii). This section also applies to contractors utilized in covered positions.

(b) *Background checks.* States must ensure that any covered employee under paragraph (a) of this section is provided notice that he or she must undergo a background check and the contents of that check.

(1) *Criminal history records check.* States must conduct a name-based and fingerprint-based criminal history records check (CHRC) using, at a minimum, the FBI's National Crime Information Center (NCIC) and the Integrated Automated Fingerprint Identification (IAFIS) database and State repository records on each covered employee identified in paragraph (a) of this section, and determine if the covered employee has been convicted of any of the following disqualifying crimes:

(i) *Permanent disqualifying criminal offenses.* A covered employee has a permanent disqualifying offense if convicted, or found not guilty by reason of insanity, in a civilian or military jurisdiction, of any of the felonies set forth in 49 CFR 1572.103(a).

(ii) *Interim disqualifying criminal offenses.* The criminal offenses referenced in 49 CFR 1572.103(b) are disqualifying if the covered employee was either convicted of those offenses in a civilian or military jurisdiction, or admits having committed acts which constitute the essential elements of any of those criminal offenses within the seven years preceding the date of employment in the covered position; or the covered employee was released from incarceration for the crime within the five years preceding the date of employment in the covered position.

(iii) *Under want or warrant.* A covered employee who is wanted or under indictment in any civilian or military jurisdiction for a felony referenced in this section is disqualified until the want or warrant is released.

(iv) *Determination of arrest status.* When a fingerprint-based check discloses an arrest for a disqualifying crime referenced in this section without indicating a disposition, the State must determine the disposition of the arrest.

(v) *Waiver.* The State may establish procedures to allow for a waiver of the requirements of paragraphs (b)(1)(ii) or (b)(1)(iv) of this section under circumstances determined by the State. These procedures can cover circumstances where the covered employee has been arrested, but no final disposition of the matter has been reached.

(2) *Employment eligibility status verification.* The State shall ensure it is fully in compliance with the requirements of section 274A of the Immigration and Nationality Act (8 U.S.C. 1324a) and its implementing regulations (8 CFR part 274A) with respect to each covered employee. The State is encouraged to participate in the USCIS E-Verify program (or any successor program) for employment eligibility verification.

(3) *Reference check.* Reference checks from prior employers are not required if the individual has been employed by the DMV for at least two consecutive years since May 11, 2006.

(4) *Disqualification.* If results of the State's CHRC reveal a permanent disqualifying criminal offense under paragraph (b)(1)(i) or an interim disqualifying criminal offense under paragraph (b)(1)(ii), the covered employee may not be employed in a position described in paragraph (a) of this section. An employee whose employment eligibility has not been verified as required by section 274A of the Immigration and Nationality Act (8 U.S.C. 1324a) and its implementing regulations (8 CFR part 274A) may not be employed in any position.

(c) *Appeal.* If a State determines that the results from the CHRC do not meet the standards of such check the State must so inform the employee of the determination to allow the individual an opportunity to appeal to the State or Federal government, as applicable.

(d) Background checks substantially similar to the requirements of this section that were conducted on existing employees on or after May 11, 2006 need not be re-conducted.

Subpart E—Procedures for Determining State Compliance

§37.51 Compliance—general requirements.

(a) *Full compliance.* To be in full compliance with the REAL ID Act of 2005, 49 U.S.C. 30301 note, States must meet the standards of subparts A through D or have a REAL ID program that DHS has determined to be comparable to the standards of subparts A through D. States certifying compliance with the REAL ID Act must follow the certification requirements described in §37.55. States must be fully compliant with Subparts A through D on or before January 15, 2013. States must file the documentation required under §37.55 at least 90 days prior to the effective date of full compliance.

(b) *Material compliance.* States must be in material compliance by January 1, 2010 to receive an additional extension until no later than May 10, 2011 as described in §37.63. Benchmarks for material compliance are detailed in the Material Compliance Checklist found in DHS' Web site at *http://www.dhs.gov.*

[73 FR 5331, Jan. 29, 2008, as amended at 76 FR 12271, Mar. 7, 2011]

EFFECTIVE DATE NOTE: At 74 FR 68478, Dec. 28, 2009, in §37.51, paragraph (b) was stayed from Jan. 1, 2010, until further notice.

§37.55 State certification documentation.

(a) States seeking DHS's determination that its program for issuing REAL ID driver's licenses and identification cards is meeting the requirements of this part (full compliance), must provide DHS with the following documents:

(1) A certification by the highest level Executive official in the State overseeing the DMV reading as follows:

"I, [name and title (name of certifying official), (position title) of the State (Commonwealth))] of _____, do hereby certify that the State (Commonwealth) has implemented a program for issuing driver's licenses and identification cards in compliance with the requirements of the REAL ID Act of 2005, as further defined in 6 CFR part 37, and intends to remain in compliance with these regulations."

(2) A letter from the Attorney General of the State confirming that the State has the legal authority to impose requirements necessary to meet the standards established by this part.

(3) A description of the State's exceptions process under § 37.11(h), and the State's waiver processes under § 37.45(b)(1)(v).

(4) The State's Security Plan under § 37.41.

(b) After DHS's final compliance determination, States shall recertify compliance with this part every three years on a rolling basis as determined by DHS.

§ 37.59 DHS reviews of State compliance.

State REAL ID programs will be subject to DHS review to determine whether the State meets the requirements for compliance with this part.

(a) *General inspection authority.* States must cooperate with DHS's review of the State's compliance at any time. In addition, the State must:

(1) Provide any reasonable information pertinent to determining compliance with this part as requested by DHS;

(2) Permit DHS to conduct inspections of any and all sites associated with the enrollment of applicants and the production, manufacture, personalization and issuance of driver's licenses or identification cards; and

(3) Allow DHS to conduct interviews of the State's employees and contractors who are involved in the application and verification process, or the manufacture and production of driver's licenses or identification cards. DHS shall provide written notice to the State in advance of an inspection visit.

(b) *Preliminary DHS determination.* DHS shall review forms, conduct audits of States as necessary, and make a preliminary determination on whether the State has satisfied the requirements of

this part within 45 days of receipt of the Material Compliance Checklist or State certification documentation of full compliance pursuant to § 37.55.

(1) If DHS determines that the State meets the benchmarks of the Material Compliance Checklist, DHS may grant the State an additional extension until no later than May 10, 2011.

(2) If DHS determines that the State meets the full requirements of subparts A through E, the Secretary shall make a final determination that the State is in compliance with the REAL ID Act.

(c) *State reply.* The State will have up to 30 calendar days to respond to the preliminary determination. The State's reply must explain what corrective action it either has implemented, or intends to implement, to correct any deficiencies cited in the preliminary determination or, alternatively, detail why the DHS preliminary determination is incorrect. Upon request by the State, an informal conference will be scheduled during this time.

(d) *Final DHS determination.* DHS will notify States of its final determination of State compliance with this part, within 45 days of receipt of a State reply.

(e) *State's right to judicial review.* Any State aggrieved by an adverse decision under this section may seek judicial review under 5 U.S.C. Chapter 7.

§ 37.61 Results of compliance determination.

(a) A State shall be deemed in compliance with this part when DHS issues a determination that the State meets the requirements of this part.

(b) The Secretary will determine that a State is not in compliance with this part when it—

(1) Fails to submit a timely certification or request an extension as prescribed in this subpart; or

(2) Does not meet one or more of the standards of this part, as established in a determination by DHS under § 37.59.

§ 37.63 Extension of deadline.

(a) A State may request an initial extension by filing a request with the Secretary no later than March 31, 2008. In the absence of extraordinary circumstances, such an extension request will be deemed justified for a period lasting until, but not beyond, December 31, 2009. DHS shall notify a State of its acceptance of the State's request for initial extension within 45 days of receipt.

(b) States granted an initial extension may file a request for an additional extension until no later than May 10, 2011, by submitting a Material Compliance Checklist demonstrating material compliance, per § 37.51(b) with certain elements of subparts A through E as defined by DHS. Such additional extension request must be filed by December 1, 2009. DHS shall notify a State whether an additional extension has been granted within 45 days of receipt of the request and documents described above.

(c) Subsequent extensions, if any, will be at the discretion of the Secretary.

[73 FR 5331, Jan. 29, 2008, as amended at 74 FR 49309, Sept. 28, 2009]

§ 37.65 Effect of failure to comply with this part.

(a) Any driver's license or identification card issued by a State that DHS determines is not in compliance with this part is not acceptable as identification by Federal agencies for official purposes.

(b) Driver's licenses and identification cards issued by a State that has obtained an extension of the compliance date from DHS per § 37.51 are acceptable for official purposes until the end of the applicable enrollment period under § 37.5; or the State subsequently is found by DHS under this Subpart to not be in compliance.

(c) Driver's licenses and identification cards issued by a State that has been determined by DHS to be in material compliance and that are marked to identify that the licenses and cards are materially compliant will continue to be accepted by Federal agencies after the expiration of the enrollment period under § 37.5, until the expiration date on the face of the document.

Subpart F—Driver's Licenses and Identification Cards Issued Under section 202(d)(11) of the REAL ID Act

§ 37.71 Driver's licenses and identification cards issued under section 202(d)(11) of the REAL ID Act.

(a) Except as authorized in § 37.27, States that DHS determines are compliant with the REAL ID Act that choose to also issue driver's licenses and identification cards that are not acceptable by Federal agencies for official purposes must ensure that such driver's licenses and identification cards—

(1) Clearly state on their face and in the machine readable zone that the card is not acceptable for official purposes; and

(2) Have a unique design or color indicator that clearly distinguishes them from driver's licenses and identification cards that meet the standards of this part.

(b) DHS reserves the right to approve such designations, as necessary, during certification of compliance.

PART 46—PROTECTION OF HUMAN SUBJECTS

46.119 Research undertaken without the intention of involving human subjects.
46.120 Evaluation and disposition of applications and proposals for research to be conducted or supported by a Federal department or agency.
46.121 [Reserved]
46.122 Use of Federal funds.
46.123 Early termination of research support: Evaluation of applications and proposals.
46.124 Conditions.

AUTHORITY: 5 U.S.C. 301; Pub. L. 107–296, sec. 102, 306(c); Pub. L. 108–458, sec. 8306.

SOURCE: 82 FR 7269, Jan. 19, 2017, unless otherwise noted.

§ 46.101 To what does this policy apply?

(a) Except as detailed in § 46.104, this policy applies to all research involving human subjects conducted, supported, or otherwise subject to regulation by any Federal department or agency that takes appropriate administrative action to make the policy applicable to such research. This includes research conducted by Federal civilian employees or military personnel, except that each department or agency head may adopt such procedural modifications as may be appropriate from an administrative standpoint. It also includes research conducted, supported, or otherwise subject to regulation by the Federal Government outside the United States. Institutions that are engaged in research described in this paragraph and institutional review boards (IRBs) reviewing research that is subject to this policy must comply with this policy.

(b) [Reserved]

(c) Department or agency heads retain final judgment as to whether a particular activity is covered by this policy and this judgment shall be exercised consistent with the ethical principles of the Belmont Report.[62]

(d) Department or agency heads may require that specific research activities or classes of research activities conducted, supported, or otherwise subject to regulation by the Federal department or agency but not otherwise covered by this policy comply with some or all of the requirements of this policy.

(e) Compliance with this policy requires compliance with pertinent federal laws or regulations that provide additional protections for human subjects.

(f) This policy does not affect any state or local laws or regulations (including tribal law passed by the official governing body of an American Indian or Alaska Native tribe) that may otherwise be applicable and that provide additional protections for human subjects.

(g) This policy does not affect any foreign laws or regulations that may otherwise be applicable and that provide additional protections to human subjects of research.

(h) When research covered by this policy takes place in foreign countries, procedures normally followed in the foreign countries to protect human subjects may differ from those set forth in this policy. In these circumstances, if a department or agency head determines that the procedures prescribed by the institution afford protections that are at least equivalent to those provided in this policy, the department or agency head may approve the substitution of the foreign procedures in lieu of the procedural requirements provided in this policy. Except when otherwise required by statute, Executive Order, or the department or agency head, notices of these actions as they occur will be published in the FEDERAL REGISTER or will be otherwise published as provided in department or agency procedures.

(i) Unless otherwise required by law, department or agency heads may waive the applicability of some or all of the provisions of this policy to specific research activities or classes of research activities otherwise covered by this policy, provided the alternative procedures to be followed are consistent with the principles of the Belmont Report.[63] Except when otherwise required by statute or Executive Order, the department or agency head shall forward advance notices of these actions to the

---

[62] The National Commission for the Protection of Human Subjects of Biomedical and Behavioral Research.– Belmont Report. Washington, DC: U.S. Department of Health and Human Services. 1979.

[63] Id.

Office for Human Research Protections, Department of Health and Human Services (HHS), or any successor office, or to the equivalent office within the appropriate Federal department or agency, and shall also publish them in the FEDERAL REGISTER or in such other manner as provided in department or agency procedures. The waiver notice must include a statement that identifies the conditions under which the waiver will be applied and a justification as to why the waiver is appropriate for the research, including how the decision is consistent with the principles of the Belmont Report.

(j) Federal guidance on the requirements of this policy shall be issued only after consultation, for the purpose of harmonization (to the extent appropriate), with other Federal departments and agencies that have adopted this policy, unless such consultation is not feasible.

(k) [Reserved]

(l) Compliance dates and transition provisions:

(1) *Pre-2018 Requirements.* For purposes of this section, the *pre-2018 Requirements* means this subpart as published in the 2016 edition of the Code of Federal Regulations.

(2) *2018 Requirements.* For purposes of this section, the *2018 Requirements* means the Federal Policy for the Protection of Human Subjects requirements contained in this part. The general compliance date for the 2018 Requirements is January 21, 2019. The compliance date for §46.114(b) (cooperative research) of the 2018 Requirements is January 21, 2020.

(3) *Research subject to pre-2018 requirements.* The pre-2018 Requirements shall apply to the following research, unless the research is transitioning to comply with the 2018 Requirements in accordance with paragraph (l)(4) of this section:

(i) Research initially approved by an IRB under the pre-2018 Requirements before January 21, 2019;

(ii) Research for which IRB review was waived pursuant to §46.101(i) of the pre-2018 Requirements) before January 21, 2019; and

(iii) Research for which a determination was made that the research was

exempt under §46.101(b) of the pre-2018 Requirements before January 21, 2019.

(4) *Transitioning research.* If, on or after July 19, 2018, an institution planning or engaged in research otherwise covered by paragraph (l)(3) of this section determines that such research instead will transition to comply with the 2018 Requirements, the institution or an IRB must document and date such determination.

(i) If the determination to transition is documented between July 19, 2018, and January 20, 2019, the research shall:

(A) Beginning on the date of such documentation through January 20, 2019, comply with the pre-2018 Requirements, except that the research shall comply with the following:

(*1*) Section 46.102(l) of the 2018 Requirements (definition of research) (instead of §46.102(d) of the pre-2018 Requirements);

(*2*) Section 46.103(d) of the 2018 Requirements (revised certification requirement that eliminates IRB review of application or proposal) (instead of §46.103(f) of the pre-2018 Requirements); and

(*3*) Section 46.109(f)(1)(i) and (iii) of the 2018 Requirements (exceptions to mandated continuing review) (instead of §46.103(b), as related to the requirement for continuing review, and in addition to §46.109, of the pre-2018 Requirements); and

(B) Beginning on January 21, 2019, comply with the 2018 Requirements.

(ii) If the determination to transition is documented on or after January 21, 2019, the research shall, beginning on the date of such documentation, comply with the 2018 Requirements.

(5) *Research subject to 2018 Requirements.* The 2018 Requirements shall apply to the following research:

(i) Research initially approved by an IRB on or after January 21, 2019;

(ii) Research for which IRB review is waived pursuant to paragraph (i) of this section on or after January 21, 2019; and

(iii) Research for which a determination is made that the research is exempt on or after January 21, 2019.

(m) Severability: Any provision of this part held to be invalid or unenforceable by its terms, or as applied to any person or circumstance, shall be construed so as to continue to give maximum effect to the provision permitted by law, unless such holding shall be one of utter invalidity or unenforceability, in which event the provision shall be severable from this part and shall not affect the remainder thereof or the application of the provision to other persons not similarly situated or to other dissimilar circumstances.

[82 FR 7269, Jan. 19, 2017, as amended at 83 FR 2890, Jan. 22, 2018; 83 FR 28510, June 19, 2018]

§ 46.102 Definitions for purposes of this policy.

(a) *Certification* means the official notification by the institution to the supporting Federal department or agency component, in accordance with the requirements of this policy, that a research project or activity involving human subjects has been reviewed and approved by an IRB in accordance with an approved assurance.

(b) *Clinical trial* means a research study in which one or more human subjects are prospectively assigned to one or more interventions (which may include placebo or other control) to evaluate the effects of the interventions on biomedical or behavioral health-related outcomes.

(c) *Department or agency head* means the head of any Federal department or agency, for example, the Secretary of HHS, and any other officer or employee of any Federal department or agency to whom the authority provided by these regulations to the department or agency head has been delegated.

(d) *Federal department or agency* refers to a federal department or agency (the department or agency itself rather than its bureaus, offices or divisions) that takes appropriate administrative action to make this policy applicable to the research involving human subjects it conducts, supports, or otherwise regulates (*e.g.*, the U.S. Department of Health and Human Services, the U.S. Department of Defense, or the Central Intelligence Agency).

(e)(1) *Human subject* means a living individual about whom an investigator (whether professional or student) conducting research:

(i) Obtains information or biospecimens through intervention or interaction with the individual, and uses, studies, or analyzes the information or biospecimens; or (ii) Obtains, uses, studies, analyzes, or generates identifiable private information or identifiable biospecimens.

(2) *Intervention* includes both physical procedures by which information or biospecimens are gathered (*e.g.*, venipuncture) and manipulations of the subject or the subject's environment that are performed for research purposes.

(3) *Interaction* includes communication or interpersonal contact between investigator and subject.

(4) *Private information* includes information about behavior that occurs in a context in which an individual can reasonably expect that no observation or recording is taking place, and information that has been provided for specific purposes by an individual and that the individual can reasonably expect will not be made public (*e.g.*, a medical record).

(5) *Identifiable private information* is private information for which the identity of the subject is or may readily be ascertained by the investigator or associated with the information.

(6) *An identifiable biospecimen* is a biospecimen for which the identity of the subject is or may readily be ascertained by the investigator or associated with the biospecimen.

(7) Federal departments or agencies implementing this policy shall:

(i) Upon consultation with appropriate experts (including experts in data matching and re-identification), reexamine the meaning of "identifiable private information," as defined in paragraph (e)(5) of this section, and "identifiable biospecimen," as defined in paragraph (e)(6) of this section. This reexamination shall take place within 1 year and regularly thereafter (at least every 4 years). This process will be conducted by collaboration among the Federal departments and agencies implementing this policy. If appropriate and permitted by law, such Federal departments and agencies may alter the interpretation of these terms, including through the use of guidance.

(ii) Upon consultation with appropriate experts, assess whether there are analytic technologies or techniques that should be considered by investigators to generate "identifiable private information," as defined in paragraph (e)(5) of this section, or an "identifiable biospecimen," as defined in paragraph (e)(6) of this section. This assessment shall take place within 1 year and regularly thereafter (at least every 4 years). This process will be conducted by collaboration among the Federal departments and agencies implementing this policy. Any such technologies or techniques will be included on a list of technologies or techniques that produce identifiable private information or identifiable biospecimens. This list will be published in the FEDERAL REGISTER after notice and an opportunity for public comment. The Secretary, HHS, shall maintain the list on a publicly accessible Web site.

(f) *Institution* means any public or private entity, or department or agency (including federal, state, and other agencies).

(g) *IRB* means an institutional review board established in accord with and for the purposes expressed in this policy.

(h) *IRB approval* means the determination of the IRB that the research has been reviewed and may be conducted at an institution within the constraints set forth by the IRB and by other institutional and federal requirements.

(i) *Legally authorized representative* means an individual or judicial or other body authorized under applicable law to consent on behalf of a prospective subject to the subject's participation in the procedure(s) involved in the research. If there is no applicable law addressing this issue, *legally authorized representative* means an individual recognized by institutional policy as acceptable for providing consent in the nonresearch context on behalf of the prospective subject to the subject's participation in the procedure(s) involved in the research.

(j) *Minimal risk* means that the probability and magnitude of harm or discomfort anticipated in the research are not greater in and of themselves than those ordinarily encountered in daily life or during the performance of routine physical or psychological examinations or tests.

(k) *Public health authority* means an agency or authority of the United States, a state, a territory, a political subdivision of a state or territory, an Indian tribe, or a foreign government, or a person or entity acting under a grant of authority from or contract with such public agency, including the employees or agents of such public agency or its contractors or persons or entities to whom it has granted authority, that is responsible for public health matters as part of its official mandate.

(l) *Research* means a systematic investigation, including research development, testing, and evaluation, designed to develop or contribute to generalizable knowledge. Activities that meet this definition constitute research for purposes of this policy, whether or not they are conducted or supported under a program that is considered research for other purposes. For example, some demonstration and service programs may include research activities. For purposes of this part, the following activities are deemed not to be research:

(1) Scholarly and journalistic activities (*e.g.*, oral history, journalism, biography, literary criticism, legal research, and historical scholarship), including the collection and use of information, that focus directly on the specific individuals about whom the information is collected.

(2) Public health surveillance activities, including the collection and testing of information or biospecimens, conducted, supported, requested, ordered, required, or authorized by a public health authority. Such activities are limited to those necessary to allow a public health authority to identify, monitor, assess, or investigate potential public health signals, onsets of disease outbreaks, or conditions of public health importance (including trends, signals, risk factors, patterns in diseases, or increases in injuries from using consumer products). Such activities include those associated with providing timely situational awareness and priority setting during the course of an event or crisis that threatens

public health (including natural or man-made disasters).

(3) Collection and analysis of information, biospecimens, or records by or for a criminal justice agency for activities authorized by law or court order solely for criminal justice or criminal investigative purposes.

(4) Authorized operational activities (as determined by each agency) in support of intelligence, homeland security, defense, or other national security missions.

(m) *Written,* or *in writing,* for purposes of this part, refers to writing on a tangible medium (*e.g.,* paper) or in an electronic format.

§ 46.103 Assuring compliance with this policy—research conducted or supported by any Federal department or agency.

(a) Each institution engaged in research that is covered by this policy, with the exception of research eligible for exemption under § 46.104, and that is conducted or supported by a Federal department or agency, shall provide written assurance satisfactory to the department or agency head that it will comply with the requirements of this policy. In lieu of requiring submission of an assurance, individual department or agency heads shall accept the existence of a current assurance, appropriate for the research in question, on file with the Office for Human Research Protections, HHS, or any successor office, and approved for Federalwide use by that office. When the existence of an HHS-approved assurance is accepted in lieu of requiring submission of an assurance, reports (except certification) required by this policy to be made to department and agency heads shall also be made to the Office for Human Research Protections, HHS, or any successor office. Federal departments and agencies will conduct or support research covered by this policy only if the institution has provided an assurance that it will comply with the requirements of this policy, as provided in this section, and only if the institution has certified to the department or agency head that the research has been reviewed and approved by an IRB (if such certification is required by § 46.103(d)).

(b) The assurance shall be executed by an individual authorized to act for the institution and to assume on behalf of the institution the obligations imposed by this policy and shall be filed in such form and manner as the department or agency head prescribes.

(c) The department or agency head may limit the period during which any assurance shall remain effective or otherwise condition or restrict the assurance.

(d) Certification is required when the research is supported by a Federal department or agency and not otherwise waived under § 46.101(i) or exempted under § 46.104. For such research, institutions shall certify that each proposed research study covered by the assurance and this section has been reviewed and approved by the IRB. Such certification must be submitted as prescribed by the Federal department or agency component supporting the research. Under no condition shall research covered by this section be initiated prior to receipt of the certification that the research has been reviewed and approved by the IRB.

(e) For nonexempt research involving human subjects covered by this policy (or exempt research for which limited IRB review takes place pursuant to § 46.104(d)(2)(iii), (d)(3)(i)(C), or (d)(7) or (8)) that takes place at an institution in which IRB oversight is conducted by an IRB that is not operated by the institution, the institution and the organization operating the IRB shall document the institution's reliance on the IRB for oversight of the research and the responsibilities that each entity will undertake to ensure compliance with the requirements of this policy (*e.g.,* in a written agreement between the institution and the IRB, by implementation of an institution-wide policy directive providing the allocation of responsibilities between the institution and an IRB that is not affiliated with the institution, or as set forth in a research protocol).

(Approved by the Office of Management and Budget under Control Number 0990–0260)

§ 46.104 Exempt research.

(a) Unless otherwise required by law or by department or agency heads, research activities in which the only involvement of human subjects will be in one or more of the categories in paragraph (d) of this section are exempt from the requirements of this policy, except that such activities must comply with the requirements of this section and as specified in each category.

(b) Use of the exemption categories for research subject to the requirements of subparts B, C, and D: Application of the exemption categories to research subject to the requirements of 45 CFR part 46, subparts B, C, and D, is as follows:

(1) *Subpart B.* Each of the exemptions at this section may be applied to research subject to subpart B if the conditions of the exemption are met.

(2) *Subpart C.* The exemptions at this section do not apply to research subject to subpart C, except for research aimed at involving a broader subject population that only incidentally includes prisoners.

(3) *Subpart D.* The exemptions at paragraphs (d)(1), (4), (5), (6), (7), and (8) of this section may be applied to research subject to subpart D if the conditions of the exemption are met. Paragraphs (d)(2)(i) and (ii) of this section only may apply to research subject to subpart D involving educational tests or the observation of public behavior when the investigator(s) do not participate in the activities being observed. Paragraph (d)(2)(iii) of this section may not be applied to research subject to subpart D.

(c) [Reserved]

(d) Except as described in paragraph (a) of this section, the following categories of human subjects research are exempt from this policy:

(1) Research, conducted in established or commonly accepted educational settings, that specifically involves normal educational practices that are not likely to adversely impact students' opportunity to learn required educational content or the assessment of educators who provide instruction. This includes most research on regular and special education instructional strategies, and research on the effectiveness of or the comparison among instructional techniques, curricula, or classroom management methods.

(2) Research that only includes interactions involving educational tests (cognitive, diagnostic, aptitude, achievement), survey procedures, interview procedures, or observation of public behavior (including visual or auditory recording) if at least one of the following criteria is met:

(i) The information obtained is recorded by the investigator in such a manner that the identity of the human subjects cannot readily be ascertained, directly or through identifiers linked to the subjects;

(ii) Any disclosure of the human subjects' responses outside the research would not reasonably place the subjects at risk of criminal or civil liability or be damaging to the subjects' financial standing, employability, educational advancement, or reputation; or

(iii) The information obtained is recorded by the investigator in such a manner that the identity of the human subjects can readily be ascertained, directly or through identifiers linked to the subjects, and an IRB conducts a limited IRB review to make the determination required by § 46.111(a)(7).

(3)(i) Research involving benign behavioral interventions in conjunction with the collection of information from an adult subject through verbal or written responses (including data entry) or audiovisual recording if the subject prospectively agrees to the intervention and information collection and at least one of the following criteria is met:

(A) The information obtained is recorded by the investigator in such a manner that the identity of the human subjects cannot readily be ascertained, directly or through identifiers linked to the subjects;

(B) Any disclosure of the human subjects' responses outside the research would not reasonably place the subjects at risk of criminal or civil liability or be damaging to the subjects' financial standing, employability, educational advancement, or reputation; or

(C) The information obtained is recorded by the investigator in such a manner that the identity of the human subjects can readily be ascertained, directly or through identifiers linked to the subjects, and an IRB conducts a limited IRB review to make the determination required by §46.111(a)(7).

(ii) For the purpose of this provision, benign behavioral interventions are brief in duration, harmless, painless, not physically invasive, not likely to have a significant adverse lasting impact on the subjects, and the investigator has no reason to think the subjects will find the interventions offensive or embarrassing. Provided all such criteria are met, examples of such benign behavioral interventions would include having the subjects play an online game, having them solve puzzles under various noise conditions, or having them decide how to allocate a nominal amount of received cash between themselves and someone else.

(iii) If the research involves deceiving the subjects regarding the nature or purposes of the research, this exemption is not applicable unless the subject authorizes the deception through a prospective agreement to participate in research in circumstances in which the subject is informed that he or she will be unaware of or misled regarding the nature or purposes of the research.

(4) Secondary research for which consent is not required: Secondary research uses of identifiable private information or identifiable biospecimens, if at least one of the following criteria is met:

(i) The identifiable private information or identifiable biospecimens are publicly available;

(ii) Information, which may include information about biospecimens, is recorded by the investigator in such a manner that the identity of the human subjects cannot readily be ascertained directly or through identifiers linked to the subjects, the investigator does not contact the subjects, and the investigator will not re-identify subjects;

(iii) The research involves only information collection and analysis involving the investigator's use of identifiable health information when that use is regulated under 45 CFR parts 160 and 164, subparts A and E, for the purposes of "health care operations" or "research" as those terms are defined at

45 CFR 164.501 or for "public health activities and purposes" as described under 45 CFR 164.512(b); or

(iv) The research is conducted by, or on behalf of, a Federal department or agency using government-generated or government-collected information obtained for nonresearch activities, if the research generates identifiable private information that is or will be maintained on information technology that is subject to and in compliance with section 208(b) of the E-Government Act of 2002, 44 U.S.C. 3501 note, if all of the identifiable private information collected, used, or generated as part of the activity will be maintained in systems of records subject to the Privacy Act of 1974, 5 U.S.C. 552a, and, if applicable, the information used in the research was collected subject to the Paperwork Reduction Act of 1995, 44 U.S.C. 3501 *et seq.*

(5) Research and demonstration projects that are conducted or supported by a Federal department or agency, or otherwise subject to the approval of department or agency heads (or the approval of the heads of bureaus or other subordinate agencies that have been delegated authority to conduct the research and demonstration projects), and that are designed to study, evaluate, improve, or otherwise examine public benefit or service programs, including procedures for obtaining benefits or services under those programs, possible changes in or alternatives to those programs or procedures, or possible changes in methods or levels of payment for benefits or services under those programs. Such projects include, but are not limited to, internal studies by Federal employees, and studies under contracts or consulting arrangements, cooperative agreements, or grants. Exempt projects also include waivers of otherwise mandatory requirements using authorities such as sections 1115 and 1115A of the Social Security Act, as amended.

(i) Each Federal department or agency conducting or supporting the research and demonstration projects must establish, on a publicly accessible Federal Web site or in such other manner as the department or agency head may determine, a list of the research and demonstration projects that the

Federal department or agency conducts or supports under this provision. The research or demonstration project must be published on this list prior to commencing the research involving human subjects.

(ii) [Reserved]

(6) Taste and food quality evaluation and consumer acceptance studies:

(i) If wholesome foods without additives are consumed, or

(ii) If a food is consumed that contains a food ingredient at or below the level and for a use found to be safe, or agricultural chemical or environmental contaminant at or below the level found to be safe, by the Food and Drug Administration or approved by the Environmental Protection Agency or the Food Safety and Inspection Service of the U.S. Department of Agriculture.

(7) Storage or maintenance for secondary research for which broad consent is required: Storage or maintenance of identifiable private information or identifiable biospecimens for potential secondary research use if an IRB conducts a limited IRB review and makes the determinations required by §46.111(a)(8).

(8) Secondary research for which broad consent is required: Research involving the use of identifiable private information or identifiable biospecimens for secondary research use, if the following criteria are met:

(i) Broad consent for the storage, maintenance, and secondary research use of the identifiable private information or identifiable biospecimens was obtained in accordance with §46.116(a)(1) through (4), (a)(6), and (d);

(ii) Documentation of informed consent or waiver of documentation of consent was obtained in accordance with §46.117;

(iii) An IRB conducts a limited IRB review and makes the determination required by §46.111(a)(7) and makes the determination that the research to be conducted is within the scope of the broad consent referenced in paragraph (d)(8)(i) of this section; and (iv) The investigator does not include returning individual research results to subjects as part of the study plan. This provision does not prevent an investigator from abiding by any legal requirements to return individual research results.

(Approved by the Office of Management and Budget under Control Number 0990–0260)

§§46.105–46.106 [Reserved]

§46.107 IRB membership.

(a) Each IRB shall have at least five members, with varying backgrounds to promote complete and adequate review of research activities commonly conducted by the institution. The IRB shall be sufficiently qualified through the experience and expertise of its members (professional competence), and the diversity of its members, including race, gender, and cultural backgrounds and sensitivity to such issues as community attitudes, to promote respect for its advice and counsel in safeguarding the rights and welfare of human subjects. The IRB shall be able to ascertain the acceptability of proposed research in terms of institutional commitments (including policies and resources) and regulations, applicable law, and standards of professional conduct and practice. The IRB shall therefore include persons knowledgeable in these areas. If an IRB regularly reviews research that involves a category of subjects that is vulnerable to coercion or undue influence, such as children, prisoners, individuals with impaired decision-making capacity, or economically or educationally disadvantaged persons, consideration shall be given to the inclusion of one or more individuals who are knowledgeable about and experienced in working with these categories of subjects.

(b) Each IRB shall include at least one member whose primary concerns are in scientific areas and at least one member whose primary concerns are in nonscientific areas.

(c) Each IRB shall include at least one member who is not otherwise affiliated with the institution and who is not part of the immediate family of a person who is affiliated with the institution.

(d) No IRB may have a member participate in the IRB's initial or continuing review of any project in which the member has a conflicting interest, except to provide information requested by the IRB.

(e) An IRB may, in its discretion, invite individuals with competence in special areas to assist in the review of issues that require expertise beyond or in addition to that available on the IRB. These individuals may not vote with the IRB.

§ 46.108   IRB functions and operations.

(a) In order to fulfill the requirements of this policy each IRB shall:

(1) Have access to meeting space and sufficient staff to support the IRB's review and recordkeeping duties;

(2) Prepare and maintain a current list of the IRB members identified by name; earned degrees; representative capacity; indications of experience such as board certifications or licenses sufficient to describe each member's chief anticipated contributions to IRB deliberations; and any employment or other relationship between each member and the institution, for example, full-time employee, part-time employee, member of governing panel or board, stockholder, paid or unpaid consultant;

(3) Establish and follow written procedures for:

(i) Conducting its initial and continuing review of research and for reporting its findings and actions to the investigator and the institution;

(ii) Determining which projects require review more often than annually and which projects need verification from sources other than the investigators that no material changes have occurred since previous IRB review; and

(iii) Ensuring prompt reporting to the IRB of proposed changes in a research activity, and for ensuring that investigators will conduct the research activity in accordance with the terms of the IRB approval until any proposed changes have been reviewed and approved by the IRB, except when necessary to eliminate apparent immediate hazards to the subject.

(4) Establish and follow written procedures for ensuring prompt reporting to the IRB; appropriate institutional officials; the department or agency head; and the Office for Human Research Protections, HHS, or any successor office, or the equivalent office within the appropriate Federal department or agency of

(i) Any unanticipated problems involving risks to subjects or others or any serious or continuing noncompliance with this policy or the requirements or determinations of the IRB; and

(ii) Any suspension or termination of IRB approval.

(b) Except when an expedited review procedure is used (as described in § 46.110), an IRB must review proposed research at convened meetings at which a majority of the members of the IRB are present, including at least one member whose primary concerns are in nonscientific areas. In order for the research to be approved, it shall receive the approval of a majority of those members present at the meeting.

(Approved by the Office of Management and Budget under Control Number 0990–0260)

§ 46.109   IRB review of research.

(a) An IRB shall review and have authority to approve, require modifications in (to secure approval), or disapprove all research activities covered by this policy, including exempt research activities under § 46.104 for which limited IRB review is a condition of exemption (under § 46.104(d)(2)(iii), (d)(3)(i)(C), and (d)(7), and (8)).

(b) An IRB shall require that information given to subjects (or legally authorized representatives, when appropriate) as part of informed consent is in accordance with § 46.116. The IRB may require that information, in addition to that specifically mentioned in § 46.116, be given to the subjects when in the IRB's judgment the information would meaningfully add to the protection of the rights and welfare of subjects.

(c) An IRB shall require documentation of informed consent or may waive documentation in accordance with § 46.117.

(d) An IRB shall notify investigators and the institution in writing of its decision to approve or disapprove the proposed research activity, or of modifications required to secure IRB approval of the research activity. If the IRB decides to disapprove a research activity, it shall include in its written notification a statement of the reasons for its decision and give the investigator an opportunity to respond in person or in writing.

(e) An IRB shall conduct continuing review of research requiring review by the convened IRB at intervals appropriate to the degree of risk, not less than once per year, except as described in § 46.109(f).

(f)(1) Unless an IRB determines otherwise, continuing review of research is not required in the following circumstances:

(i) Research eligible for expedited review in accordance with § 46.110;

(ii) Research reviewed by the IRB in accordance with the limited IRB review described in § 46.104(d)(2)(iii), (d)(3)(i)(C), or (d)(7) or (8);

(iii) Research that has progressed to the point that it involves only one or both of the following, which are part of the IRB-approved study:

(A) Data analysis, including analysis of identifiable private information or identifiable biospecimens, or

(B) Accessing follow-up clinical data from procedures that subjects would undergo as part of clinical care.

(2) [Reserved.]

(g) An IRB shall have authority to observe or have a third party observe the consent process and the research.

(Approved by the Office of Management and Budget under Control Number 0990–0260)

§ 46.110 **Expedited review procedures for certain kinds of research involving no more than minimal risk, and for minor changes in approved research.**

(a) The Secretary of HHS has established, and published as a Notice in the FEDERAL REGISTER, a list of categories of research that may be reviewed by the IRB through an expedited review procedure. The Secretary will evaluate the list at least every 8 years and amend it, as appropriate, after consultation with other federal departments and agencies and after publication in the FEDERAL REGISTER for public comment. A copy of the list is available from the Office for Human Research Protections, HHS, or any successor office.

(b)(1) An IRB may use the expedited review procedure to review the following:

(i) Some or all of the research appearing on the list described in paragraph (a) of this section, unless the reviewer determines that the study involves more than minimal risk;

(ii) Minor changes in previously approved research during the period for which approval is authorized; or

(iii) Research for which limited IRB review is a condition of exemption under § 46.104(d)(2)(iii), (d)(3)(i)(C), and (d)(7) and (8).

(2) Under an expedited review procedure, the review may be carried out by the IRB chairperson or by one or more experienced reviewers designated by the chairperson from among members of the IRB. In reviewing the research, the reviewers may exercise all of the authorities of the IRB except that the reviewers may not disapprove the research. A research activity may be disapproved only after review in accordance with the nonexpedited procedure set forth in § 46.108(b).

(c) Each IRB that uses an expedited review procedure shall adopt a method for keeping all members advised of research proposals that have been approved under the procedure.

(d) The department or agency head may restrict, suspend, terminate, or choose not to authorize an institution's or IRB's use of the expedited review procedure.

§ 46.111 **Criteria for IRB approval of research.**

(a) In order to approve research covered by this policy the IRB shall determine that all of the following requirements are satisfied:

(1) Risks to subjects are minimized:

(i) By using procedures that are consistent with sound research design and that do not unnecessarily expose subjects to risk, and

(ii) Whenever appropriate, by using procedures already being performed on the subjects for diagnostic or treatment purposes.

(2) Risks to subjects are reasonable in relation to anticipated benefits, if any, to subjects, and the importance of the knowledge that may reasonably be expected to result. In evaluating risks and benefits, the IRB should consider only those risks and benefits that may

result from the research (as distinguished from risks and benefits of therapies subjects would receive even if not participating in the research). The IRB should not consider possible long-range effects of applying knowledge gained in the research (*e.g.*, the possible effects of the research on public policy) as among those research risks that fall within the purview of its responsibility.

(3) Selection of subjects is equitable. In making this assessment the IRB should take into account the purposes of the research and the setting in which the research will be conducted. The IRB should be particularly cognizant of the special problems of research that involves a category of subjects who are vulnerable to coercion or undue influence, such as children, prisoners, individuals with impaired decision-making capacity, or economically or educationally disadvantaged persons.

(4) Informed consent will be sought from each prospective subject or the subject's legally authorized representative, in accordance with, and to the extent required by, § 46.116.

(5) Informed consent will be appropriately documented or appropriately waived in accordance with § 46.117.

(6) When appropriate, the research plan makes adequate provision for monitoring the data collected to ensure the safety of subjects.

(7) When appropriate, there are adequate provisions to protect the privacy of subjects and to maintain the confidentiality of data.

(i) The Secretary of HHS will, after consultation with the Office of Management and Budget's privacy office and other Federal departments and agencies that have adopted this policy, issue guidance to assist IRBs in assessing what provisions are adequate to protect the privacy of subjects and to maintain the confidentiality of data.

(ii) [Reserved]

(8) For purposes of conducting the limited IRB review required by § 46.104(d)(7)), the IRB need not make the determinations at paragraphs (a)(1) through (7) of this section, and shall make the following determinations:

(i) Broad consent for storage, maintenance, and secondary research use of identifiable private information or identifiable biospecimens is obtained in accordance with the requirements of § 46.116(a)(1)–(4), (a)(6), and (d);

(ii) Broad consent is appropriately documented or waiver of documentation is appropriate, in accordance with § 46.117; and

(iii) If there is a change made for research purposes in the way the identifiable private information or identifiable biospecimens are stored or maintained, there are adequate provisions to protect the privacy of subjects and to maintain the confidentiality of data.

(b) When some or all of the subjects are likely to be vulnerable to coercion or undue influence, such as children, prisoners, individuals with impaired decision-making capacity, or economically or educationally disadvantaged persons, additional safeguards have been included in the study to protect the rights and welfare of these subjects.

§ 46.112   Review by institution

Research covered by this policy that has been approved by an IRB may be subject to further appropriate review and approval or disapproval by officials of the institution. However, those officials may not approve the research if it has not been approved by an IRB.

§ 46.113   Suspension or termination of IRB approval of research.

An IRB shall have authority to suspend or terminate approval of research that is not being conducted in accordance with the IRB's requirements or that has been associated with unexpected serious harm to subjects. Any suspension or termination of approval shall include a statement of the reasons for the IRB's action and shall be reported promptly to the investigator, appropriate institutional officials, and the department or agency head.

(Approved by the Office of Management and Budget under Control Number 0990–0260)

§ 46.114   Cooperative research.

(a) Cooperative research projects are those projects covered by this policy that involve more than one institution. In the conduct of cooperative research projects, each institution is responsible for safeguarding the rights and welfare of human subjects and for complying with this policy.

(b)(1) Any institution located in the United States that is engaged in cooperative research must rely upon approval by a single IRB for that portion of the research that is conducted in the United States. The reviewing IRB will be identified by the Federal department or agency supporting or conducting the research or proposed by the lead institution subject to the acceptance of the Federal department or agency supporting the research.

(2) The following research is not subject to this provision:

(i) Cooperative research for which more than single IRB review is required by law (including tribal law passed by the official governing body of an American Indian or Alaska Native tribe); or

(ii) Research for which any Federal department or agency supporting or conducting the research determines and documents that the use of a single IRB is not appropriate for the particular context.

(c) For research not subject to paragraph (b) of this section, an institution participating in a cooperative project may enter into a joint review arrangement, rely on the review of another IRB, or make similar arrangements for avoiding duplication of effort.

§46.115 IRB records.

(a) An institution, or when appropriate an IRB, shall prepare and maintain adequate documentation of IRB activities, including the following:

(1) Copies of all research proposals reviewed, scientific evaluations, if any, that accompany the proposals, approved sample consent forms, progress reports submitted by investigators, and reports of injuries to subjects.

(2) Minutes of IRB meetings, which shall be in sufficient detail to show attendance at the meetings; actions taken by the IRB; the vote on these actions including the number of members voting for, against, and abstaining; the basis for requiring changes in or disapproving research; and a written summary of the discussion of controverted issues and their resolution.

(3) Records of continuing review activities, including the rationale for conducting continuing review of research that otherwise would not require continuing review as described in §46.109(f)(1).

(4) Copies of all correspondence between the IRB and the investigators.

(5) A list of IRB members in the same detail as described in §46.108(a)(2).

(6) Written procedures for the IRB in the same detail as described in §46.108(a)(3) and (4).

(7) Statements of significant new findings provided to subjects, as required by §46.116(c)(5).

(8) The rationale for an expedited reviewer's determination under §46.110(b)(1)(i) that research appearing on the expedited review list described in §46.110(a) is more than minimal risk.

(9) Documentation specifying the responsibilities that an institution and an organization operating an IRB each will undertake to ensure compliance with the requirements of this policy, as described in §46.103(e).

(b) The records required by this policy shall be retained for at least 3 years, and records relating to research that is conducted shall be retained for at least 3 years after completion of the research. The institution or IRB may maintain the records in printed form, or electronically. All records shall be accessible for inspection and copying by authorized representatives of the Federal department or agency at reasonable times and in a reasonable manner.

(Approved by the Office of Management and Budget under Control Number 0990–0260)

§46.116 General requirements for informed consent.

(a) *General.* General requirements for informed consent, whether written or oral, are set forth in this paragraph and apply to consent obtained in accordance with the requirements set forth in paragraphs (b) through (d) of this section. Broad consent may be obtained in lieu of informed consent obtained in accordance with paragraphs (b) and (c) of this section only with respect to the storage, maintenance, and secondary research uses of identifiable private information and identifiable biospecimens. Waiver or alteration of consent in research involving public benefit and service programs conducted

287

by or subject to the approval of state or local officials is described in paragraph (e) of this section. General waiver or alteration of informed consent is described in paragraph (f) of this section. Except as provided elsewhere in this policy:

(1) Before involving a human subject in research covered by this policy, an investigator shall obtain the legally effective informed consent of the subject or the subject's legally authorized representative.

(2) An investigator shall seek informed consent only under circumstances that provide the prospective subject or the legally authorized representative sufficient opportunity to discuss and consider whether or not to participate and that minimize the possibility of coercion or undue influence.

(3) The information that is given to the subject or the legally authorized representative shall be in language understandable to the subject or the legally authorized representative.

(4) The prospective subject or the legally authorized representative must be provided with the information that a reasonable person would want to have in order to make an informed decision about whether to participate, and an opportunity to discuss that information.

(5) Except for broad consent obtained in accordance with paragraph (d) of this section:

(i) Informed consent must begin with a concise and focused presentation of the key information that is most likely to assist a prospective subject or legally authorized representative in understanding the reasons why one might or might not want to participate in the research. This part of the informed consent must be organized and presented in a way that facilitates comprehension.

(ii) Informed consent as a whole must present information in sufficient detail relating to the research, and must be organized and presented in a way that does not merely provide lists of isolated facts, but rather facilitates the prospective subject's or legally authorized representative's understanding of the reasons why one might or might not want to participate.

(6) No informed consent may include any exculpatory language through which the subject or the legally authorized representative is made to waive or appear to waive any of the subject's legal rights, or releases or appears to release the investigator, the sponsor, the institution, or its agents from liability for negligence.

(b) *Basic elements of informed consent.* Except as provided in paragraph (d), (e), or (f) of this section, in seeking informed consent the following information shall be provided to each subject or the legally authorized representative:

(1) A statement that the study involves research, an explanation of the purposes of the research and the expected duration of the subject's participation, a description of the procedures to be followed, and identification of any procedures that are experimental;

(2) A description of any reasonably foreseeable risks or discomforts to the subject;

(3) A description of any benefits to the subject or to others that may reasonably be expected from the research;

(4) A disclosure of appropriate alternative procedures or courses of treatment, if any, that might be advantageous to the subject;

(5) A statement describing the extent, if any, to which confidentiality of records identifying the subject will be maintained;

(6) For research involving more than minimal risk, an explanation as to whether any compensation and an explanation as to whether any medical treatments are available if injury occurs and, if so, what they consist of, or where further information may be obtained;

(7) An explanation of whom to contact for answers to pertinent questions about the research and research subjects' rights, and whom to contact in the event of a research-related injury to the subject;

(8) A statement that participation is voluntary, refusal to participate will involve no penalty or loss of benefits to which the subject is otherwise entitled, and the subject may discontinue participation at any time without penalty or loss of benefits to which the subject is otherwise entitled; and

(9) One of the following statements about any research that involves the collection of identifiable private information or identifiable biospecimens:

(i) A statement that identifiers might be removed from the identifiable private information or identifiable biospecimens and that, after such removal, the information or biospecimens could be used for future research studies or distributed to another investigator for future research studies without additional informed consent from the subject or the legally authorized representative, if this might be a possibility; or

(ii) A statement that the subject's information or biospecimens collected as part of the research, even if identifiers are removed, will not be used or distributed for future research studies.

(c) *Additional elements of informed consent.* Except as provided in paragraph (d), (e), or (f) of this section, one or more of the following elements of information, when appropriate, shall also be provided to each subject or the legally authorized representative:

(1) A statement that the particular treatment or procedure may involve risks to the subject (or to the embryo or fetus, if the subject is or may become pregnant) that are currently unforeseeable;

(2) Anticipated circumstances under which the subject's participation may be terminated by the investigator without regard to the subject's or the legally authorized representative's consent;

(3) Any additional costs to the subject that may result from participation in the research;

(4) The consequences of a subject's decision to withdraw from the research and procedures for orderly termination of participation by the subject;

(5) A statement that significant new findings developed during the course of the research that may relate to the subject's willingness to continue participation will be provided to the subject;

(6) The approximate number of subjects involved in the study;

(7) A statement that the subject's biospecimens (even if identifiers are removed) may be used for commercial profit and whether the subject will or will not share in this commercial profit;

(8) A statement regarding whether clinically relevant research results, including individual research results, will be disclosed to subjects, and if so, under what conditions; and

(9) For research involving biospecimens, whether the research will (if known) or might include whole genome sequencing (*i.e.*, sequencing of a human germline or somatic specimen with the intent to generate the genome or exome sequence of that specimen).

(d) *Elements of broad consent for the storage, maintenance, and secondary research use of identifiable private information or identifiable biospecimens.* Broad consent for the storage, maintenance, and secondary research use of identifiable private information or identifiable biospecimens (collected for either research studies other than the proposed research or nonresearch purposes) is permitted as an alternative to the informed consent requirements in paragraphs (b) and (c) of this section. If the subject or the legally authorized representative is asked to provide broad consent, the following shall be provided to each subject or the subject's legally authorized representative:

(1) The information required in paragraphs (b)(2), (b)(3), (b)(5), and (b)(8) and, when appropriate, (c)(7) and (9) of this section;

(2) A general description of the types of research that may be conducted with the identifiable private information or identifiable biospecimens. This description must include sufficient information such that a reasonable person would expect that the broad consent would permit the types of research conducted;

(3) A description of the identifiable private information or identifiable biospecimens that might be used in research, whether sharing of identifiable private information or identifiable biospecimens might occur, and the types of institutions or researchers that might conduct research with the identifiable private information or identifiable biospecimens;

(4) A description of the period of time that the identifiable private information or identifiable biospecimens may be stored and maintained (which period

of time could be indefinite), and a description of the period of time that the identifiable private information or identifiable biospecimens may be used for research purposes (which period of time could be indefinite);

(5) Unless the subject or legally authorized representative will be provided details about specific research studies, a statement that they will not be informed of the details of any specific research studies that might be conducted using the subject's identifiable private information or identifiable biospecimens, including the purposes of the research, and that they might have chosen not to consent to some of those specific research studies;

(6) Unless it is known that clinically relevant research results, including individual research results, will be disclosed to the subject in all circumstances, a statement that such results may not be disclosed to the subject; and

(7) An explanation of whom to contact for answers to questions about the subject's rights and about storage and use of the subject's identifiable private information or identifiable biospecimens, and whom to contact in the event of a research-related harm.

(e) *Waiver or alteration of consent in research involving public benefit and service programs conducted by or subject to the approval of state or local officials*—(1) *Waiver.* An IRB may waive the requirement to obtain informed consent for research under paragraphs (a) through (c) of this section, provided the IRB satisfies the requirements of paragraph (e)(3) of this section. If an individual was asked to provide broad consent for the storage, maintenance, and secondary research use of identifiable private information or identifiable biospecimens in accordance with the requirements at paragraph (d) of this section, and refused to consent, an IRB cannot waive consent for the storage, maintenance, or secondary research use of the identifiable private information or identifiable biospecimens.

(2) *Alteration.* An IRB may approve a consent procedure that omits some, or alters some or all, of the elements of informed consent set forth in paragraphs (b) and (c) of this section provided the IRB satisfies the require-

ments of paragraph (e)(3) of this section. An IRB may not omit or alter any of the requirements described in paragraph (a) of this section. If a broad consent procedure is used, an IRB may not omit or alter any of the elements required under paragraph (d) of this section.

(3) *Requirements for waiver and alteration.* In order for an IRB to waive or alter consent as described in this subsection, the IRB must find and document that:

(i) The research or demonstration project is to be conducted by or subject to the approval of state or local government officials and is designed to study, evaluate, or otherwise examine:

(A) Public benefit or service programs;

(B) Procedures for obtaining benefits or services under those programs;

(C) Possible changes in or alternatives to those programs or procedures; or

(D) Possible changes in methods or levels of payment for benefits or services under those programs; and

(ii) The research could not practicably be carried out without the waiver or alteration.

(f) *General waiver or alteration of consent*—(1) *Waiver.* An IRB may waive the requirement to obtain informed consent for research under paragraphs (a) through (c) of this section, provided the IRB satisfies the requirements of paragraph (f)(3) of this section. If an individual was asked to provide broad consent for the storage, maintenance, and secondary research use of identifiable private information or identifiable biospecimens in accordance with the requirements at paragraph (d) of this section, and refused to consent, an IRB cannot waive consent for the storage, maintenance, or secondary research use of the identifiable private information or identifiable biospecimens.

(2) *Alteration.* An IRB may approve a consent procedure that omits some, or alters some or all, of the elements of informed consent set forth in paragraphs (b) and (c) of this section provided the IRB satisfies the requirements of paragraph (f)(3) of this section. An IRB may not omit or alter any

of the requirements described in paragraph (a) of this section. If a broad consent procedure is used, an IRB may not omit or alter any of the elements required under paragraph (d) of this section.

(3) *Requirements for waiver and alteration.* In order for an IRB to waive or alter consent as described in this subsection, the IRB must find and document that:

(i) The research involves no more than minimal risk to the subjects;

(ii) The research could not practicably be carried out without the requested waiver or alteration;

(iii) If the research involves using identifiable private information or identifiable biospecimens, the research could not practicably be carried out without using such information or biospecimens in an identifiable format;

(iv) The waiver or alteration will not adversely affect the rights and welfare of the subjects; and

(v) Whenever appropriate, the subjects or legally authorized representatives will be provided with additional pertinent information after participation.

(g) *Screening, recruiting, or determining eligibility.* An IRB may approve a research proposal in which an investigator will obtain information or biospecimens for the purpose of screening, recruiting, or determining the eligibility of prospective subjects without the informed consent of the prospective subject or the subject's legally authorized representative, if either of the following conditions are met:

(1) The investigator will obtain information through oral or written communication with the prospective subject or legally authorized representative, or

(2) The investigator will obtain identifiable private information or identifiable biospecimens by accessing records or stored identifiable biospecimens.

(h) *Posting of clinical trial consent form.* (1) For each clinical trial conducted or supported by a Federal department or agency, one IRB-approved informed consent form used to enroll subjects must be posted by the awardee or the Federal department or agency component conducting the trial on a publicly available Federal Web site

that will be established as a repository for such informed consent forms.

(2) If the Federal department or agency supporting or conducting the clinical trial determines that certain information should not be made publicly available on a Federal Web site (*e.g.* confidential commercial information), such Federal department or agency may permit or require redactions to the information posted.

(3) The informed consent form must be posted on the Federal Web site after the clinical trial is closed to recruitment, and no later than 60 days after the last study visit by any subject, as required by the protocol.

(i) *Preemption.* The informed consent requirements in this policy are not intended to preempt any applicable Federal, state, or local laws (including tribal laws passed by the official governing body of an American Indian or Alaska Native tribe) that require additional information to be disclosed in order for informed consent to be legally effective.

(j) *Emergency medical care.* Nothing in this policy is intended to limit the authority of a physician to provide emergency medical care, to the extent the physician is permitted to do so under applicable Federal, state, or local law (including tribal law passed by the official governing body of an American Indian or Alaska Native tribe).

(Approved by the Office of Management and Budget under Control Number 0990–0260)

§ **46.117 Documentation of informed consent.**

(a) Except as provided in paragraph (c) of this section, informed consent shall be documented by the use of a written informed consent form approved by the IRB and signed (including in an electronic format) by the subject or the subject's legally authorized representative. A written copy shall be given to the person signing the informed consent form.

(b) Except as provided in paragraph (c) of this section, the informed consent form may be either of the following:

(1) A written informed consent form that meets the requirements of § 46.116. The investigator shall give either the

subject or the subject's legally authorized representative adequate opportunity to read the informed consent form before it is signed; alternatively, this form may be read to the subject or the subject's legally authorized representative.

(2) A short form written informed consent form stating that the elements of informed consent required by § 46.116 have been presented orally to the subject or the subject's legally authorized representative, and that the key information required by § 46.116(a)(5)(i) was presented first to the subject, before other information, if any, was provided. The IRB shall approve a written summary of what is to be said to the subject or the legally authorized representative. When this method is used, there shall be a witness to the oral presentation. Only the short form itself is to be signed by the subject or the subject's legally authorized representative. However, the witness shall sign both the short form and a copy of the summary, and the person actually obtaining consent shall sign a copy of the summary. A copy of the summary shall be given to the subject or the subject's legally authorized representative, in addition to a copy of the short form.

(c)(1) An IRB may waive the requirement for the investigator to obtain a signed informed consent form for some or all subjects if it finds any of the following:

(i) That the only record linking the subject and the research would be the informed consent form and the principal risk would be potential harm resulting from a breach of confidentiality. Each subject (or legally authorized representative) will be asked whether the subject wants documentation linking the subject with the research, and the subject's wishes will govern;

(ii) That the research presents no more than minimal risk of harm to subjects and involves no procedures for which written consent is normally required outside of the research context; or

(iii) If the subjects or legally authorized representatives are members of a distinct cultural group or community in which signing forms is not the norm, that the research presents no more than minimal risk of harm to subjects and provided there is an appropriate alternative mechanism for documenting that informed consent was obtained.

(2) In cases in which the documentation requirement is waived, the IRB may require the investigator to provide subjects or legally authorized representatives with a written statement regarding the research.

(Approved by the Office of Management and Budget under Control Number 0990–0260)

§ 46.118 Applications and proposals lacking definite plans for involvement of human subjects.

Certain types of applications for grants, cooperative agreements, or contracts are submitted to Federal departments or agencies with the knowledge that subjects may be involved within the period of support, but definite plans would not normally be set forth in the application or proposal. These include activities such as institutional type grants when selection of specific projects is the institution's responsibility; research training grants in which the activities involving subjects remain to be selected; and projects in which human subjects' involvement will depend upon completion of instruments, prior animal studies, or purification of compounds. Except for research waived under § 46.101(i) or exempted under § 46.104, no human subjects may be involved in any project supported by these awards until the project has been reviewed and approved by the IRB, as provided in this policy, and certification submitted, by the institution, to the Federal department or agency component supporting the research.

§ 46.119 Research undertaken without the intention of involving human subjects.

Except for research waived under § 46.101(i) or exempted under § 46.104, in the event research is undertaken without the intention of involving human subjects, but it is later proposed to involve human subjects in the research, the research shall first be reviewed and approved by an IRB, as provided in this policy, a certification submitted by the institution to the Federal department or agency component supporting the research, and final approval given to the proposed change by the Federal department or agency component.

§ 46.120 Evaluation and disposition of applications and proposals for research to be conducted or supported by a Federal department or agency.

(a) The department or agency head will evaluate all applications and proposals involving human subjects submitted to the Federal department or agency through such officers and employees of the Federal department or agency and such experts and consultants as the department or agency head determines to be appropriate. This evaluation will take into consideration the risks to the subjects, the adequacy of protection against these risks, the potential benefits of the research to the subjects and others, and the importance of the knowledge gained or to be gained.

(b) On the basis of this evaluation, the department or agency head may approve or disapprove the application or proposal, or enter into negotiations to develop an approvable one.

§ 46.121 [Reserved]

§ 46.122 Use of Federal funds.

Federal funds administered by a Federal department or agency may not be expended for research involving human subjects unless the requirements of this policy have been satisfied.

§ 46.123 Early termination of research support: Evaluation of applications and proposals.

(a) The department or agency head may require that Federal department or agency support for any project be terminated or suspended in the manner prescribed in applicable program requirements, when the department or agency head finds an institution has materially failed to comply with the terms of this policy.

(b) In making decisions about supporting or approving applications or proposals covered by this policy the department or agency head may take into account, in addition to all other eligibility requirements and program criteria, factors such as whether the applicant has been subject to a termi-

nation or suspension under paragraph (a) of this section and whether the applicant or the person or persons who would direct or has/have directed the scientific and technical aspects of an activity has/have, in the judgment of the department or agency head, materially failed to discharge responsibility for the protection of the rights and welfare of human subjects (whether or not the research was subject to federal regulation).

§ 46.124 Conditions.

With respect to any research project or any class of research projects the department or agency head of either the conducting or the supporting Federal department or agency may impose additional conditions prior to or at the time of approval when in the judgment of the department or agency head additional conditions are necessary for the protection of human subjects.

PART 115—SEXUAL ABUSE AND ASSAULT PREVENTION STANDARDS

Sec.
115.5 General definitions.
115.6 Definitions related to sexual abuse and assault.

Subpart A—Standards for Immigration Detention Facilities

COVERAGE

115.10 Coverage of DHS immigration detention facilities.

PREVENTION PLANNING

115.11 Zero tolerance of sexual abuse; Prevention of Sexual Assault Coordinator.
115.12 Contracting with non-DHS entities for the confinement of detainees.
115.13 Detainee supervision and monitoring.
115.14 Juvenile and family detainees.
115.15 Limits to cross-gender viewing and searches.
115.16 Accommodating detainees with disabilities and detainees who are limited English proficient.
115.17 Hiring and promotion decisions.
115.18 Upgrades to facilities and technologies.

RESPONSIVE PLANNING

115.21 Evidence protocols and forensic medical examinations.
115.22 Policies to ensure investigation of allegations and appropriate agency oversight.

AUTHORITY: 5 U.S.C. 301, 552, 552a; 8 U.S.C. 1103, 1182, 1223, 1224, 1225, 1226, 1227, 1228, 1231, 1251, 1253, 1255, 1330, 1362; 18 U.S.C. 4002, 4013(c)(4); Pub. L. 107–296, 116 Stat. 2135 (6 U.S.C. 101, et seq.); 8 CFR part 2.

SOURCE: 79 FR 13165, Mar. 7, 2014, unless otherwise noted.

§115.5 General definitions.

For purposes of this part, the term—

Agency means the unit or component of DHS responsible for operating or supervising any facility, or part of a facility, that confines detainees.

Agency head means the principal official of an agency.

Contractor means a person who or entity that provides services on a recurring basis pursuant to a contractual agreement with the agency or facility.

Detainee means any person detained in an immigration detention facility or holding facility.

Employee means a person who works directly for the agency.

Exigent circumstances means any set of temporary and unforeseen circumstances that require immediate action in order to combat a threat to the security or institutional order of a facility or a threat to the safety or security of any person.

Facility means a place, building (or part thereof), set of buildings, structure, or area (whether or not enclosing a building or set of buildings) that was built or retrofitted for the purpose of detaining individuals and is routinely used by the agency to detain individuals in its custody. References to requirements placed on facilities extend to the entity responsible for the direct operation of the facility.

Facility head means the principal official responsible for a facility.

Family unit means a group of detainees that includes one or more non-United States citizen juvenile(s) accompanied by his/her/their parent(s) or legal guardian(s), whom the agency will evaluate for safety purposes to protect juveniles from sexual abuse and violence.

Gender nonconforming means having an appearance or manner that does not conform to traditional societal gender expectations.

Holding facility means a facility that contains holding cells, cell blocks, or other secure enclosures that are:

(1) Under the control of the agency; and

(2) Primarily used for the short-term confinement of individuals who have recently been detained, or are being transferred to or from a court, jail, prison, other agency, or other unit of the facility or agency.

Immigration detention facility means a confinement facility operated by or pursuant to contract with U.S. Immigration and Customs Enforcement (ICE) that routinely holds persons for over 24 hours pending resolution or completion of immigration removal operations or processes, including facilities that are operated by ICE, facilities that provide detention services under a contract awarded by ICE, and facilities used by ICE pursuant to an Intergovernmental Service Agreement.

Intersex means having sexual or reproductive anatomy or chromosomal pattern that does not seem to fit typical definitions of male or female. Intersex medical conditions are sometimes referred to as disorders of sex development.

Juvenile means any person under the age of 18.

Law enforcement staff means officers or agents of the agency or facility that are responsible for the supervision and control of detainees in a holding facility.

Medical practitioner means a health professional who, by virtue of education, credentials, and experience, is permitted by law to evaluate and care for patients within the scope of his or her professional practice. A "qualified medical practitioner" refers to such a professional who has also successfully completed specialized training for treating sexual abuse victims.

Mental health practitioner means a mental health professional who, by virtue of education, credentials, and experience, is permitted by law to evaluate and care for patients within the scope of his or her professional practice. A "qualified mental health practitioner" refers to such a professional who has also successfully completed specialized training for treating sexual abuse victims.

Pat-down search means a sliding or patting of the hands over the clothed body of a detainee by staff to determine whether the individual possesses contraband.

Security staff means employees primarily responsible for the supervision and control of detainees in housing units, recreational areas, dining areas, and other program areas of an immigration detention facility.

Staff means employees or contractors of the agency or facility, including any entity that operates within the facility.

Strip search means a search that requires a person to remove or arrange some or all clothing so as to permit a visual inspection of the person's breasts, buttocks, or genitalia.

Substantiated allegation means an allegation that was investigated and determined to have occurred.

Transgender means a person whose gender identity (*i.e.*, internal sense of feeling male or female) is different from the person's assigned sex at birth.

Unfounded allegation means an allegation that was investigated and determined not to have occurred.

Unsubstantiated allegation means an allegation that was investigated and the investigation produced insufficient evidence to make a final determination as to whether or not the event occurred.

Volunteer means an individual who donates time and effort on a recurring basis to enhance the activities and programs of the agency or facility.

§ 115.6 Definitions related to sexual abuse and assault.

For purposes of this part, the term—

Sexual abuse includes—

(1) Sexual abuse and assault of a detainee by another detainee; and

(2) Sexual abuse and assault of a detainee by a staff member, contractor, or volunteer.

Sexual abuse of a detainee by another detainee includes any of the following acts by one or more detainees, prisoners, inmates, or residents of the facility in which the detainee is housed who, by force, coercion, or intimidation, or if the victim did not consent or was unable to consent or refuse, engages in or attempts to engage in:

(1) Contact between the penis and the vulva or anus and, for purposes of this paragraph (1), contact involving the penis upon penetration, however slight;

(2) Contact between the mouth and the penis, vulva, or anus;

(3) Penetration, however slight, of the anal or genital opening of another person by a hand or finger or by any object;

(4) Touching of the genitalia, anus, groin, breast, inner thighs or buttocks, either directly or through the clothing, with an intent to abuse, humiliate, harass, degrade or arouse or gratify the sexual desire of any person; or

(5) Threats, intimidation, or other actions or communications by one or more detainees aimed at coercing or

pressuring another detainee to engage in a sexual act.

Sexual abuse of a detainee by a staff member, contractor, or volunteer includes any of the following acts, if engaged in by one or more staff members, volunteers, or contract personnel who, with or without the consent of the detainee, engages in or attempts to engage in:

(1) Contact between the penis and the vulva or anus and, for purposes of this paragraph (1), contact involving the penis upon penetration, however slight;

(2) Contact between the mouth and the penis, vulva, or anus;

(3) Penetration, however slight, of the anal or genital opening of another person by a hand or finger or by any object that is unrelated to official duties or where the staff member, contractor, or volunteer has the intent to abuse, arouse, or gratify sexual desire;

(4) Intentional touching of the genitalia, anus, groin, breast, inner thighs or buttocks, either directly or through the clothing, that is unrelated to official duties or where the staff member, contractor, or volunteer has the intent to abuse, arouse, or gratify sexual desire;

(5) Threats, intimidation, harassment, indecent, profane or abusive language, or other actions or communications, aimed at coercing or pressuring a detainee to engage in a sexual act;

(6) Repeated verbal statements or comments of a sexual nature to a detainee;

(7) Any display of his or her uncovered genitalia, buttocks, or breast in the presence of an inmate, detainee, or resident, or

(8) Voyeurism, which is defined as the inappropriate visual surveillance of a detainee for reasons unrelated to official duties. Where not conducted for reasons relating to official duties, the following are examples of voyeurism: staring at a detainee who is using a toilet in his or her cell to perform bodily functions; requiring an inmate detainee to expose his or her buttocks, genitals, or breasts; or taking images of all or part of a detainee's naked body or of a detainee performing bodily functions.

Subpart A—Standards for Immigration Detention Facilities

COVERAGE

§115.10 Coverage of DHS immigration detention facilities.

This subpart covers ICE immigration detention facilities. Standards set forth in this subpart A are not applicable to Department of Homeland Security (DHS) holding facilities.

PREVENTION PLANNING

§115.11 Zero tolerance of sexual abuse; Prevention of Sexual Assault Coordinator.

(a) The agency shall have a written policy mandating zero tolerance toward all forms of sexual abuse and outlining the agency's approach to preventing, detecting, and responding to such conduct.

(b) The agency shall employ or designate an upper-level, agency-wide Prevention of Sexual Assault Coordinator (PSA Coordinator) with sufficient time and authority to develop, implement, and oversee agency efforts to comply with these standards in all of its immigration detention facilities.

(c) Each facility shall have a written policy mandating zero tolerance toward all forms of sexual abuse and outlining the facility's approach to preventing, detecting, and responding to such conduct. The agency shall review and approve each facility's written policy.

(d) Each facility shall employ or designate a Prevention of Sexual Assault Compliance Manager (PSA Compliance Manager) who shall serve as the facility point of contact for the agency PSA Coordinator and who has sufficient time and authority to oversee facility efforts to comply with facility sexual abuse prevention and intervention policies and procedures.

§115.12 Contracting with non-DHS entities for the confinement of detainees.

(a) When contracting for the confinement of detainees in immigration detention facilities operated by non-DHS private or public agencies or other entities, including other government agencies, the agency shall include in any new contracts, contract renewals, or substantive contract modifications the entity's obligation to adopt and comply with these standards.

(b) Any new contracts, contract renewals, or substantive contract modifications shall provide for agency contract monitoring to ensure that the contractor is complying with these standards.

§ 115.13 Detainee supervision and monitoring.

(a) Each facility shall ensure that it maintains sufficient supervision of detainees, including through appropriate staffing levels and, where applicable, video monitoring, to protect detainees against sexual abuse.

(b) Each facility shall develop and document comprehensive detainee supervision guidelines to determine and meet the facility's detainee supervision needs, and shall review those guidelines at least annually.

(c) In determining adequate levels of detainee supervision and determining the need for video monitoring, the facility shall take into consideration generally accepted detention and correctional practices, any judicial findings of inadequacy, the physical layout of each facility, the composition of the detainee population, the prevalence of substantiated and unsubstantiated incidents of sexual abuse, the findings and recommendations of sexual abuse incident review reports, and any other relevant factors, including but not limited to the length of time detainees spend in agency custody.

(d) Each facility shall conduct frequent unannounced security inspections to identify and deter sexual abuse of detainees. Such inspections shall be implemented for night as well as day shifts. Each facility shall prohibit staff from alerting others that these security inspections are occurring, unless such announcement is related to the legitimate operational functions of the facility.

§ 115.14 Juvenile and family detainees.

(a) Juveniles shall be detained in the least restrictive setting appropriate to the juvenile's age and special needs, provided that such setting is consistent with the need to protect the juvenile's well-being and that of others, as well as with any other laws, regulations, or legal requirements.

(b) The facility shall hold juveniles apart from adult detainees, minimizing sight, sound, and physical contact, unless the juvenile is in the presence of an adult member of the family unit, and provided there are no safety or security concerns with the arrangement.

(c) In determining the existence of a family unit for detention purposes, the agency shall seek to obtain reliable evidence of a family relationship.

(d) The agency and facility shall provide priority attention to unaccompanied alien children as defined by 6 U.S.C. 279(g)(2), including transfer to a Department of Health and Human Services Office of Refugee Resettlement facility within 72 hours, except in exceptional circumstances, in accordance with 8 U.S.C. 1232(b)(3).

(e) If a juvenile who is an unaccompanied alien child has been convicted as an adult of a crime related to sexual abuse, the agency shall provide the facility and the Department of Health and Human Services Office of Refugee Resettlement with the releasable information regarding the conviction(s) to ensure the appropriate placement of the alien in a Department of Health and Human Services Office of Refugee Resettlement facility.

§ 115.15 Limits to cross-gender viewing and searches.

(a) Searches may be necessary to ensure the safety of officers, civilians and detainees; to detect and secure evidence of criminal activity; and to promote security, safety, and related interests at immigration detention facilities.

(b) Cross-gender pat-down searches of male detainees shall not be conducted unless, after reasonable diligence, staff of the same gender is not available at the time the pat-down search is required or in exigent circumstances.

(c) Cross-gender pat-down searches of female detainees shall not be conducted unless in exigent circumstances.

(d) All cross-gender pat-down searches shall be documented.

(e) Cross-gender strip searches or cross-gender visual body cavity searches shall not be conducted except in exigent circumstances, including consideration of officer safety, or when performed by medical practitioners. Facility staff shall not conduct visual body cavity searches of juveniles and, instead, shall refer all such body cavity searches of juveniles to a medical practitioner.

(f) All strip searches and visual body cavity searches shall be documented.

(g) Each facility shall implement policies and procedures that enable detainees to shower, perform bodily functions, and change clothing without being viewed by staff of the opposite gender, except in exigent circumstances or when such viewing is incidental to routine cell checks or is otherwise appropriate in connection with a medical examination or monitored bowel movement. Such policies and procedures shall require staff of the opposite gender to announce their presence when entering an area where detainees are likely to be showering, performing bodily functions, or changing clothing.

(h) The facility shall permit detainees in Family Residential Facilities to shower, perform bodily functions, and change clothing without being viewed by staff, except in exigent circumstances or when such viewing is incidental to routine cell checks or is otherwise appropriate in connection with a medical examination or monitored bowel movement.

(i) The facility shall not search or physically examine a detainee for the sole purpose of determining the detainee's genital characteristics. If the detainee's gender is unknown, it may be determined during conversations with the detainee, by reviewing medical records, or, if necessary, learning that information as part of a standard medical examination that all detainees must undergo as part of intake or other processing procedure conducted in private, by a medical practitioner.

(j) The agency shall train security staff in proper procedures for conducting pat-down searches, including cross-gender pat-down searches and searches of transgender and intersex detainees. All pat-down searches shall be conducted in a professional and respectful manner, and in the least intrusive manner possible, consistent with security needs and agency policy, including consideration of officer safety.

§115.16 Accommodating detainees with disabilities and detainees who are limited English proficient.

(a) The agency and each facility shall take appropriate steps to ensure that detainees with disabilities (including, for example, detainees who are deaf or hard of hearing, those who are blind or have low vision, or those who have intellectual, psychiatric, or speech disabilities) have an equal opportunity to participate in or benefit from all aspects of the agency's and facility's efforts to prevent, detect, and respond to sexual abuse. Such steps shall include, when necessary to ensure effective communication with detainees who are deaf or hard of hearing, providing access to in-person, telephonic, or video interpretive services that enable effective, accurate, and impartial interpretation, both receptively and expressively, using any necessary specialized vocabulary. In addition, the agency and facility shall ensure that any written materials related to sexual abuse are provided in formats or through methods that ensure effective communication with detainees with disabilities, including detainees who have intellectual disabilities, limited reading skills, or who are blind or have low vision. An agency or facility is not required to take actions that it can demonstrate would result in a fundamental alteration in the nature of a service, program, or activity, or in undue financial and administrative burdens, as those terms are used in regulations promulgated under title II of the Americans with Disabilities Act, 28 CFR 35.164.

(b) The agency and each facility shall take steps to ensure meaningful access to all aspects of the agency's and facility's efforts to prevent, detect, and respond to sexual abuse to detainees who are limited English proficient, including steps to provide in-person or telephonic interpretive services that enable effective, accurate, and impartial interpretation, both receptively and expressively, using any necessary specialized vocabulary.

(c) In matters relating to allegations of sexual abuse, the agency and each facility shall provide in-person or telephonic interpretation services that enable effective, accurate, and impartial interpretation, by someone other than another detainee, unless the detainee expresses a preference for another detainee to provide interpretation and the agency determines that such interpretation is appropriate and consistent with DHS policy. The provision of interpreter services by minors, alleged abusers, detainees who witnessed the alleged abuse, and detainees who have a significant relationship with the alleged abuser is not appropriate in matters relating to allegations of sexual abuse.

§ 115.17 Hiring and promotion decisions.

(a) An agency or facility shall not hire or promote anyone who may have contact with detainees, and shall not enlist the services of any contractor or volunteer who may have contact with detainees, who has engaged in sexual abuse in a prison, jail, holding facility, community confinement facility, juvenile facility, or other institution (as defined in 42 U.S.C. 1997); who has been convicted of engaging or attempting to engage in sexual activity facilitated by force, overt or implied threats of force, or coercion, or if the victim did not consent or was unable to consent or refuse; or who has been civilly or administratively adjudicated to have engaged in such activity.

(b) An agency or facility considering hiring or promoting staff shall ask all applicants who may have contact with detainees directly about previous misconduct described in paragraph (a) of this section, in written applications or interviews for hiring or promotions and in any interviews or written self-evaluations conducted as part of reviews of current employees. Agencies and facilities shall also impose upon employees a continuing affirmative duty to disclose any such misconduct. The agency, consistent with law, shall make its best efforts to contact all prior institutional employers of an applicant for employment, to obtain information on substantiated allegations of sexual abuse

or any resignation during a pending investigation of alleged sexual abuse.

(c) Before hiring new staff who may have contact with detainees, the agency or facility shall conduct a background investigation to determine whether the candidate for hire is suitable for employment with the facility or agency, including a criminal background records check. Upon request by the agency, the facility shall submit for the agency's approval written documentation showing the detailed elements of the facility's background check for each staff member and the facility's conclusions. The agency shall conduct an updated background investigation every five years for agency employees who may have contact with detainees. The facility shall require an updated background investigation every five years for those facility staff who may have contact with detainees and who work in immigration-only detention facilities.

(d) The agency or facility shall also perform a background investigation before enlisting the services of any contractor who may have contact with detainees. Upon request by the agency, the facility shall submit for the agency's approval written documentation showing the detailed elements of the facility's background check for each contractor and the facility's conclusions.

(e) Material omissions regarding such misconduct, or the provision of materially false information, shall be grounds for termination or withdrawal of an offer of employment, as appropriate.

(f) Unless prohibited by law, the agency shall provide information on substantiated allegations of sexual abuse involving a former employee upon receiving a request from an institutional employer for whom such employee has applied to work.

(g) In the event the agency contracts with a facility for the confinement of detainees, the requirements of this section otherwise applicable to the agency also apply to the facility and its staff.

§ 115.18 Upgrades to facilities and technologies.

(a) When designing or acquiring any new facility and in planning any substantial expansion or modification of existing facilities, the facility or agency, as appropriate, shall consider the effect of the design, acquisition, expansion, or modification upon their ability to protect detainees from sexual abuse.

(b) When installing or updating a video monitoring system, electronic surveillance system, or other monitoring technology in an immigration detention facility, the facility or agency, as appropriate, shall consider how such technology may enhance their ability to protect detainees from sexual abuse.

RESPONSIVE PLANNING

§115.21 Evidence protocols and forensic medical examinations.

(a) To the extent that the agency or facility is responsible for investigating allegations of sexual abuse involving detainees, it shall follow a uniform evidence protocol that maximizes the potential for obtaining usable physical evidence for administrative proceedings and criminal prosecutions. The protocol shall be developed in coordination with DHS and shall be developmentally appropriate for juveniles, where applicable.

(b) The agency and each facility developing an evidence protocol referred to in paragraph (a) of this section, shall consider how best to utilize available community resources and services to provide valuable expertise and support in the areas of crisis intervention and counseling to most appropriately address victims' needs. Each facility shall establish procedures to make available, to the full extent possible, outside victim services following incidents of sexual abuse; the facility shall attempt to make available to the victim a victim advocate from a rape crisis center. If a rape crisis center is not available to provide victim advocate services, the agency shall provide these services by making available a qualified staff member from a community-based organization, or a qualified agency staff member. A qualified agency staff member or a qualified community-based staff member means an individual who has received education concerning sexual assault and forensic examination issues in general. The outside or internal victim advocate shall provide emotional support, crisis intervention, information, and referrals.

(c) Where evidentiarily or medically appropriate, at no cost to the detainee, and only with the detainee's consent, the facility shall arrange for an alleged victim detainee to undergo a forensic medical examination by qualified health care personnel, including a Sexual Assault Forensic Examiner (SAFE) or Sexual Assault Nurse Examiner (SANE) where practicable. If SAFEs or SANEs cannot be made available, the examination can be performed by other qualified health care personnel.

(d) As requested by a victim, the presence of his or her outside or internal victim advocate, including any available victim advocacy services offered by a hospital conducting a forensic exam, shall be allowed for support during a forensic exam and investigatory interviews.

(e) To the extent that the agency is not responsible for investigating allegations of sexual abuse, the agency or the facility shall request that the investigating agency follow the requirements of paragraphs (a) through (d) of this section.

§115.22 Policies to ensure investigation of allegations and appropriate agency oversight.

(a) The agency shall establish an agency protocol, and shall require each facility to establish a facility protocol, to ensure that each allegation of sexual abuse is investigated by the agency or facility, or referred to an appropriate investigative authority. The agency shall ensure that an administrative or criminal investigation is completed for all allegations of sexual abuse.

(b) The agency shall ensure that the agency and facility protocols required by paragraph (a) of this section, include a description of responsibilities of the agency, the facility, and any other investigating entities; and require the documentation and maintenance, for at least five years, of all reports and referrals of allegations of sexual abuse.

(c) The agency shall post its protocols on its Web site; each facility shall also post its protocols on its Web site, if it has one, or otherwise make the protocol available to the public.

(d) Each facility protocol shall ensure that all allegations are promptly reported to the agency as described in paragraphs (e) and (f) of this section, and, unless the allegation does not involve potentially criminal behavior, are promptly referred for investigation to an appropriate law enforcement agency with the legal authority to conduct criminal investigations. A facility may separately, and in addition to the above reports and referrals, conduct its own investigation.

(e) When a detainee, prisoner, inmate, or resident of the facility in which an alleged detainee victim is housed is alleged to be the perpetrator of detainee sexual abuse, the facility shall ensure that the incident is promptly reported to the Joint Intake Center, the ICE Office of Professional Responsibility or the DHS Office of Inspector General, as well as the appropriate ICE Field Office Director, and, if it is potentially criminal, referred to an appropriate law enforcement agency having jurisdiction for investigation.

(f) When a staff member, contractor, or volunteer is alleged to be the perpetrator of detainee sexual abuse, the facility shall ensure that the incident is promptly reported to the Joint Intake Center, the ICE Office of Professional Responsibility or the DHS Office of Inspector General, as well as to the appropriate ICE Field Office Director, and to the local government entity or contractor that owns or operates the facility. If the incident is potentially criminal, the facility shall ensure that it is promptly referred to an appropriate law enforcement agency having jurisdiction for investigation.

(g) The agency shall ensure that all allegations of detainee sexual abuse are promptly reported to the PSA Coordinator and to the appropriate offices within the agency and within DHS to ensure appropriate oversight of the investigation.

(h) The agency shall ensure that any alleged detainee victim of sexual abuse that is criminal in nature is provided timely access to U nonimmigrant status information.

TRAINING AND EDUCATION

§ 115.31 Staff training.

(a) The agency shall train, or require the training of, all employees who may have contact with immigration detainees, and all facility staff, to be able to fulfill their responsibilities under this part, including training on:

(1) The agency's and the facility's zero-tolerance policies for all forms of sexual abuse;

(2) The right of detainees and staff to be free from sexual abuse, and from retaliation for reporting sexual abuse;

(3) Definitions and examples of prohibited and illegal sexual behavior;

(4) Recognition of situations where sexual abuse may occur;

(5) Recognition of physical, behavioral, and emotional signs of sexual abuse, and methods of preventing and responding to such occurrences;

(6) How to avoid inappropriate relationships with detainees;

(7) How to communicate effectively and professionally with detainees, including lesbian, gay, bisexual, transgender, intersex, or gender nonconforming detainees;

(8) Procedures for reporting knowledge or suspicion of sexual abuse; and

(9) The requirement to limit reporting of sexual abuse to personnel with a need-to-know in order to make decisions concerning the victim's welfare and for law enforcement or investigative purposes.

(b) All current facility staff, and all agency employees who may have contact with immigration detention facility detainees, shall be trained within one year of May 6, 2014, and the agency or facility shall provide refresher information every two years.

(c) The agency and each facility shall document that staff that may have contact with immigration facility detainees have completed the training.

§ 115.32 Other training.

(a) The facility shall ensure that all volunteers and other contractors (as defined in paragraph (d) of this section) who have contact with detainees have been trained on their responsibilities under the agency's and the facility's sexual abuse prevention, detection, intervention and response policies and procedures.

(b) The level and type of training provided to volunteers and other contractors shall be based on the services they provide and level of contact they have with detainees, but all volunteers and other contractors who have contact with detainees shall be notified of the agency's and the facility's zero-tolerance policies regarding sexual abuse and informed how to report such incidents.

(c) Each facility shall receive and maintain written confirmation that volunteers and other contractors who have contact with immigration facility detainees have completed the training.

(d) In this section, the term *other contractor* means a person who provides services on a non-recurring basis to the facility pursuant to a contractual agreement with the agency or facility.

§115.33 Detainee education.

(a) During the intake process, each facility shall ensure that the detainee orientation program notifies and informs detainees about the agency's and the facility's zero-tolerance policies for all forms of sexual abuse and includes (at a minimum) instruction on:

(1) Prevention and intervention strategies;

(2) Definitions and examples of detainee-on-detainee sexual abuse, staff-on-detainee sexual abuse and coercive sexual activity;

(3) Explanation of methods for reporting sexual abuse, including to any staff member, including a staff member other than an immediate point-of-contact line officer (e.g., the compliance manager or a mental health specialist), the DHS Office of Inspector General, and the Joint Intake Center;

(4) Information about self-protection and indicators of sexual abuse;

(5) Prohibition against retaliation, including an explanation that reporting sexual abuse shall not negatively impact the detainee's immigration proceedings; and

(6) The right of a detainee who has been subjected to sexual abuse to receive treatment and counseling.

(b) Each facility shall provide the detainee notification, orientation, and instruction in formats accessible to all detainees, including those who are limited English proficient, deaf, visually impaired or otherwise disabled, as well as to detainees who have limited reading skills.

(c) The facility shall maintain documentation of detainee participation in the intake process orientation.

(d) Each facility shall post on all housing unit bulletin boards the following notices:

(1) The DHS-prescribed sexual assault awareness notice;

(2) The name of the Prevention of Sexual Abuse Compliance Manager; and

(3) The name of local organizations that can assist detainees who have been victims of sexual abuse.

(e) The facility shall make available and distribute the DHS-prescribed "Sexual Assault Awareness Information" pamphlet.

(f) Information about reporting sexual abuse shall be included in the agency Detainee Handbook made available to all immigration detention facility detainees.

§115.34 Specialized training: Investigations.

(a) In addition to the general training provided to all facility staff and employees pursuant to §115.31, the agency or facility shall provide specialized training on sexual abuse and effective cross-agency coordination to agency or facility investigators, respectively, who conduct investigations into allegations of sexual abuse at immigration detention facilities. All investigations into alleged sexual abuse must be conducted by qualified investigators.

(b) The agency and facility must maintain written documentation verifying specialized training provided to investigators pursuant to this section.

§115.35 Specialized training: Medical and mental health care.

(a) The agency shall provide specialized training to DHS or agency employees who serve as full- and part-time medical practitioners or full- and part-time mental health practitioners in immigration detention facilities where medical and mental health care is provided.

(b) The training required by this section shall cover, at a minimum, the following topics:

(1) How to detect and assess signs of sexual abuse;

(2) How to respond effectively and professionally to victims of sexual abuse,

(3) How and to whom to report allegations or suspicions of sexual abuse, and

(4) How to preserve physical evidence of sexual abuse. If medical staff employed by the agency conduct forensic examinations, such medical staff shall receive the appropriate training to conduct such examinations.

(c) The agency shall review and approve the facility's policy and procedures to ensure that facility medical staff is trained in procedures for examining and treating victims of sexual abuse, in facilities where medical staff may be assigned these activities.

ASSESSMENT FOR RISK OF SEXUAL VICTIMIZATION AND ABUSIVENESS

§ 115.41 Assessment for risk of victimization and abusiveness.

(a) The facility shall assess all detainees on intake to identify those likely to be sexual aggressors or sexual abuse victims and shall house detainees to prevent sexual abuse, taking necessary steps to mitigate any such danger. Each new arrival shall be kept separate from the general population until he/she is classified and may be housed accordingly.

(b) The initial classification process and initial housing assignment should be completed within twelve hours of admission to the facility.

(c) The facility shall also consider, to the extent that the information is available, the following criteria to assess detainees for risk of sexual victimization:

(1) Whether the detainee has a mental, physical, or developmental disability;

(2) The age of the detainee;

(3) The physical build and appearance of the detainee;

(4) Whether the detainee has previously been incarcerated or detained;

(5) The nature of the detainee's criminal history;

(6) Whether the detainee has any convictions for sex offenses against an adult or child;

(7) Whether the detainee has self-identified as gay, lesbian, bisexual, transgender, intersex, or gender nonconforming;

(8) Whether the detainee has self-identified as having previously experienced sexual victimization; and

(9) The detainee's own concerns about his or her physical safety.

(d) The initial screening shall consider prior acts of sexual abuse, prior convictions for violent offenses, and history of prior institutional violence or sexual abuse, as known to the facility, in assessing detainees for risk of being sexually abusive.

(e) The facility shall reassess each detainee's risk of victimization or abusiveness between 60 and 90 days from the date of initial assessment, and at any other time when warranted based upon the receipt of additional, relevant information or following an incident of abuse or victimization.

(f) Detainees shall not be disciplined for refusing to answer, or for not disclosing complete information in response to, questions asked pursuant to paragraphs (c)(1), (c)(7), (c)(8), or (c)(9) of this section.

(g) The facility shall implement appropriate controls on the dissemination within the facility of responses to questions asked pursuant to this standard in order to ensure that sensitive information is not exploited to the detainee's detriment by staff or other detainees or inmates.

§ 115.42 Use of assessment information.

(a) The facility shall use the information from the risk assessment under § 115.41 of this part to inform assignment of detainees to housing, recreation and other activities, and voluntary work. The agency shall make individualized determinations about how to ensure the safety of each detainee.

(b) When making assessment and housing decisions for a transgender or intersex detainee, the facility shall consider the detainee's gender self-identification and an assessment of the effects of placement on the detainee's health and safety. The facility shall consult a medical or mental health professional as soon as practicable on this assessment. The facility should not base placement decisions of transgender or intersex detainees solely on the identity documents or physical anatomy of the detainee; a detainee's self-identification of his/her gender and self-assessment of safety needs shall always be taken into consideration as well. The facility's placement of a transgender or intersex detainee shall be consistent with the safety and security considerations of the facility, and placement and programming assignments for each transgender or intersex detainee shall be reassessed at least twice each year to review any threats to safety experienced by the detainee.

(c) When operationally feasible, transgender and intersex detainees shall be given the opportunity to shower separately from other detainees.

§ 115.43 Protective custody.

(a) The facility shall develop and follow written procedures consistent with the standards in this subpart for each facility governing the management of its administrative segregation unit. These procedures, which should be developed in consultation with the ICE Enforcement and Removal Operations Field Office Director having jurisdiction for the facility, must document detailed reasons for placement of an individual in administrative segregation on the basis of a vulnerability to sexual abuse or assault.

(b) Use of administrative segregation by facilities to protect detainees vulnerable to sexual abuse or assault shall be restricted to those instances where reasonable efforts have been made to provide appropriate housing and shall be made for the least amount of time practicable, and when no other viable housing options exist, as a last resort. The facility should assign detainees vulnerable to sexual abuse or assault to administrative segregation for their protection until an alternative means of separation from likely abusers can be arranged, and such an assignment shall not ordinarily exceed a period of 30 days.

(c) Facilities that place vulnerable detainees in administrative segregation for protective custody shall provide those detainees access to programs, visitation, counsel and other services available to the general population to the maximum extent practicable.

(d) Facilities shall implement written procedures for the regular review of all vulnerable detainees placed in administrative segregation for their protection, as follows:

(1) A supervisory staff member shall conduct a review within 72 hours of the detainee's placement in administrative segregation to determine whether segregation is still warranted; and

(2) A supervisory staff member shall conduct, at a minimum, an identical review after the detainee has spent seven days in administrative segregation, and every week thereafter for the first 30 days, and every 10 days thereafter.

(e) Facilities shall notify the appropriate ICE Field Office Director no later than 72 hours after the initial placement into segregation, whenever a detainee has been placed in administrative segregation on the basis of a vulnerability to sexual abuse or assault.

(f) Upon receiving notification pursuant to paragraph (e) of this section, the ICE Field Office Director shall review the placement and consider:

(1) Whether continued placement in administrative segregation is warranted;

(2) Whether any alternatives are available and appropriate, such as placing the detainee in a less restrictive housing option at another facility or other appropriate custodial options; and

(3) Whether the placement is only as a last resort and when no other viable housing options exist.

REPORTING

§ 115.51 Detainee reporting.

(a) The agency and each facility shall develop policies and procedures to ensure that detainees have multiple ways to privately report sexual abuse, retaliation for reporting sexual abuse, or staff neglect or violations of responsibilities that may have contributed to such incidents. The agency and each facility shall also provide instructions on how detainees may contact their consular official, the DHS Office of the Inspector General or, as appropriate, another designated office, to confidentially and, if desired, anonymously, report these incidents.

(b) The agency shall also provide, and the facility shall inform the detainees of, at least one way for detainees to report sexual abuse to a public or private entity or office that is not part of the agency, and that is able to receive and immediately forward detainee reports of sexual abuse to agency officials, allowing the detainee to remain anonymous upon request.

(c) Facility policies and procedures shall include provisions for staff to accept reports made verbally, in writing, anonymously, and from third parties and to promptly document any verbal reports.

§ 115.52 Grievances.

(a) The facility shall permit a detainee to file a formal grievance related to sexual abuse at any time during, after, or in lieu of lodging an informal grievance or complaint.

(b) The facility shall not impose a time limit on when a detainee may submit a grievance regarding an allegation of sexual abuse.

(c) The facility shall implement written procedures for identifying and handling time-sensitive grievances that involve an immediate threat to detainee health, safety, or welfare related to sexual abuse.

(d) Facility staff shall bring medical emergencies to the immediate attention of proper medical personnel for further assessment.

(e) The facility shall issue a decision on the grievance within five days of receipt and shall respond to an appeal of the grievance decision within 30 days. Facilities shall send all grievances related to sexual abuse and the facility's decisions with respect to such grievances to the appropriate ICE Field Office Director at the end of the grievance process.

(f) To prepare a grievance, a detainee may obtain assistance from another detainee, the housing officer or other facility staff, family members, or legal representatives. Staff shall take reasonable steps to expedite requests for assistance from these other parties.

§ 115.53 Detainee access to outside confidential support services.

(a) Each facility shall utilize available community resources and services to provide valuable expertise and support in the areas of crisis intervention, counseling, investigation and the prosecution of sexual abuse perpetrators to most appropriately address victims' needs. The facility shall maintain or attempt to enter into memoranda of understanding or other agreements with community service providers or, if local providers are not available, with national organizations that provide legal advocacy and confidential emotional support services for immigrant victims of crime.

(b) Each facility's written policies shall establish procedures to include outside agencies in the facility's sexual abuse prevention and intervention protocols, if such resources are available.

(c) Each facility shall make available to detainees information about local organizations that can assist detainees who have been victims of sexual abuse, including mailing addresses and telephone numbers (including toll-free hotline numbers where available). If no such local organizations exist, the facility shall make available the same information about national organizations. The facility shall enable reasonable communication between detainees and these organizations and agencies, in as confidential a manner as possible.

(d) Each facility shall inform detainees, prior to giving them access to outside resources, of the extent to which such communications will be monitored and the extent to which reports of abuse will be forwarded to authorities in accordance with mandatory reporting laws.

§ 115.54 Third-party reporting.

Each facility shall establish a method to receive third-party reports of sexual abuse in its immigration detention facilities and shall make available to the public information on how to report sexual abuse on behalf of a detainee.

OFFICIAL RESPONSE FOLLOWING A
DETAINEE REPORT

§115.61 Staff reporting duties.

(a) The agency and each facility shall require all staff to report immediately and according to agency policy any knowledge, suspicion, or information regarding an incident of sexual abuse that occurred in a facility; retaliation against detainees or staff who reported or participated in an investigation about such an incident; and any staff neglect or violation of responsibilities that may have contributed to an incident or retaliation. The agency shall review and approve facility policies and procedures and shall ensure that the facility specifies appropriate reporting procedures, including a method by which staff can report outside of the chain of command.

(b) Staff members who become aware of alleged sexual abuse shall immediately follow the reporting requirements set forth in the agency's and facility's written policies and procedures.

(c) Apart from such reporting, staff shall not reveal any information related to a sexual abuse report to anyone other than to the extent necessary to help protect the safety of the victim or prevent further victimization of other detainees or staff in the facility, or to make medical treatment, investigation, law enforcement, or other security and management decisions.

(d) If the alleged victim is under the age of 18 or considered a vulnerable adult under a State or local vulnerable persons statute, the agency shall report the allegation to the designated State or local services agency under applicable mandatory reporting laws.

§115.62 Protection duties.

If an agency employee or facility staff member has a reasonable belief that a detainee is subject to a substantial risk of imminent sexual abuse, he or she shall take immediate action to protect the detainee.

§115.63 Reporting to other confinement facilities.

(a) Upon receiving an allegation that a detainee was sexually abused while confined at another facility, the agency or facility whose staff received the allegation shall notify the appropriate office of the agency or the administrator of the facility where the alleged abuse occurred.

(b) The notification provided in paragraph (a) of this section shall be provided as soon as possible, but no later than 72 hours after receiving the allegation.

(c) The agency or facility shall document that it has provided such notification.

(d) The agency or facility office that receives such notification, to the extent the facility is covered by this subpart, shall ensure that the allegation is referred for investigation in accordance with these standards and reported to the appropriate ICE Field Office Director.

§115.64 Responder duties.

(a) Upon learning of an allegation that a detainee was sexually abused, the first security staff member to respond to the report, or his or her supervisor, shall be required to:

(1) Separate the alleged victim and abuser;

(2) Preserve and protect, to the greatest extent possible, any crime scene until appropriate steps can be taken to collect any evidence;

(3) If the abuse occurred within a time period that still allows for the collection of physical evidence, request the alleged victim not to take any actions that could destroy physical evidence, including, as appropriate, washing, brushing teeth, changing clothes, urinating, defecating, smoking, drinking, or eating; and

(4) If the sexual abuse occurred within a time period that still allows for the collection of physical evidence, ensure that the alleged abuser does not take any actions that could destroy physical evidence, including, as appropriate, washing, brushing teeth, changing clothes, urinating, defecating, smoking, drinking, or eating.

(b) If the first staff responder is not a security staff member, the responder shall be required to request that the alleged victim not take any actions that could destroy physical evidence and then notify security staff.

§ 115.65 Coordinated response.

(a) Each facility shall develop a written institutional plan to coordinate actions taken by staff first responders, medical and mental health practitioners, investigators, and facility leadership in response to an incident of sexual abuse.

(b) Each facility shall use a coordinated, multidisciplinary team approach to responding to sexual abuse.

(c) If a victim of sexual abuse is transferred between facilities covered by subpart A or B of this part, the sending facility shall, as permitted by law, inform the receiving facility of the incident and the victim's potential need for medical or social services.

(d) If a victim is transferred from a DHS immigration detention facility to a facility not covered by paragraph (c) of this section, the sending facility shall, as permitted by law, inform the receiving facility of the incident and the victim's potential need for medical or social services, unless the victim requests otherwise.

§ 115.66 Protection of detainees from contact with alleged abusers.

Staff, contractors, and volunteers suspected of perpetrating sexual abuse shall be removed from all duties requiring detainee contact pending the outcome of an investigation.

§ 115.67 Agency protection against retaliation.

(a) Staff, contractors, and volunteers, and immigration detention facility detainees, shall not retaliate against any person, including a detainee, who reports, complains about, or participates in an investigation into an allegation of sexual abuse, or for participating in sexual activity as a result of force, coercion, threats, or fear of force.

(b) The agency shall employ multiple protection measures, such as housing changes, removal of alleged staff or detainee abusers from contact with victims, and emotional support services for detainees or staff who fear retaliation for reporting sexual abuse or for cooperating with investigations.

(c) For at least 90 days following a report of sexual abuse, the agency and facility shall monitor to see if there are facts that may suggest possible retaliation by detainees or staff, and shall act promptly to remedy any such retaliation. Items the agency should monitor include any detainee disciplinary reports, housing or program changes, or negative performance reviews or reassignments of staff. DHS shall continue such monitoring beyond 90 days if the initial monitoring indicates a continuing need.

§ 115.68 Post-allegation protective custody.

(a) The facility shall take care to place detainee victims of sexual abuse in a supportive environment that represents the least restrictive housing option possible (e.g., protective custody), subject to the requirements of § 115.43.

(b) Detainee victims shall not be held for longer than five days in any type of administrative segregation, except in highly unusual circumstances or at the request of the detainee.

(c) A detainee victim who is in protective custody after having been subjected to sexual abuse shall not be returned to the general population until completion of a proper re-assessment, taking into consideration any increased vulnerability of the detainee as a result of the sexual abuse.

(d) Facilities shall notify the appropriate ICE Field Office Director whenever a detainee victim has been held in administrative segregation for 72 hours.

(e) Upon receiving notification that a detainee victim has been held in administrative segregation, the ICE Field Office Director shall review the placement and consider:

(1) Whether the placement is only as a last resort and when no other viable housing options exist; and

(2) In cases where the detainee has been held in administrative segregation for longer than 5 days, whether the placement is justified by highly unusual circumstances or at the detainee's request.

INVESTIGATIONS

§ 115.71 Criminal and administrative investigations.

(a) If the facility has responsibility for investigating allegations of sexual abuse, all investigations into alleged sexual abuse must be prompt, thorough, objective, and conducted by specially trained, qualified investigators.

(b) Upon conclusion of a criminal investigation where the allegation was substantiated, an administrative investigation shall be conducted. Upon conclusion of a criminal investigation where the allegation was unsubstantiated, the facility shall review any available completed criminal investigation reports to determine whether an administrative investigation is necessary or appropriate. Administrative investigations shall be conducted after consultation with the appropriate investigative office within DHS, and the assigned criminal investigative entity.

(c)(1) The facility shall develop written procedures for administrative investigations, including provisions requiring:

(i) Preservation of direct and circumstantial evidence, including any available physical and DNA evidence and any available electronic monitoring data;

(ii) Interviewing alleged victims, suspected perpetrators, and witnesses;

(iii) Reviewing prior complaints and reports of sexual abuse involving the suspected perpetrator;

(iv) Assessment of the credibility of an alleged victim, suspect, or witness, without regard to the individual's status as detainee, staff, or employee, and without requiring any detainee who alleges sexual abuse to submit to a polygraph;

(v) An effort to determine whether actions or failures to act at the facility contributed to the abuse; and

(vi) Documentation of each investigation by written report, which shall include a description of the physical and testimonial evidence, the reasoning behind credibility assessments, and investigative facts and findings; and

(vii) Retention of such reports for as long as the alleged abuser is detained

or employed by the agency or facility, plus five years.

(2) Such procedures shall govern the coordination and sequencing of the two types of investigations, in accordance with paragraph (b) of this section, to ensure that the criminal investigation is not compromised by an internal administrative investigation.

(d) The agency shall review and approve the facility policy and procedures for coordination and conduct of internal administrative investigations with the assigned criminal investigative entity to ensure non-interference with criminal investigations.

(e) The departure of the alleged abuser or victim from the employment or control of the facility or agency shall not provide a basis for terminating an investigation.

(f) When outside agencies investigate sexual abuse, the facility shall cooperate with outside investigators and shall endeavor to remain informed about the progress of the investigation.

§ 115.72 Evidentiary standard for administrative investigations.

When an administrative investigation is undertaken, the agency shall impose no standard higher than a preponderance of the evidence in determining whether allegations of sexual abuse are substantiated.

§ 115.73 Reporting to detainees.

The agency shall, when the detainee is still in immigration detention, or where otherwise feasible, following an investigation into a detainee's allegation of sexual abuse, notify the detainee as to the result of the investigation and any responsive action taken.

DISCIPLINE

§ 115.76 Disciplinary sanctions for staff.

(a) Staff shall be subject to disciplinary or adverse action up to and including removal from their position and the Federal service for substantiated allegations of sexual abuse or for violating agency or facility sexual abuse policies.

(b) The agency shall review and approve facility policies and procedures regarding disciplinary or adverse actions for staff and shall ensure that the facility policy and procedures specify disciplinary or adverse actions for staff, up to and including removal from their position and from the Federal service, when there is a substantiated allegation of sexual abuse, or when there has been a violation of agency sexual abuse rules, policies, or standards. Removal from their position and from the Federal service is the presumptive disciplinary sanction for staff who have engaged in or attempted or threatened to engage in sexual abuse, as defined under the definition of sexual abuse of a detainee by a staff member, contractor, or volunteer, paragraphs (1)–(4) and (7)–(8) of the definition of "sexual abuse of a detainee by a staff member, contractor, or volunteer" in § 115.6.

(c) Each facility shall report all removals or resignations in lieu of removal for violations of agency or facility sexual abuse policies to appropriate law enforcement agencies, unless the activity was clearly not criminal.

(d) Each facility shall make reasonable efforts to report removals or resignations in lieu of removal for violations of agency or facility sexual abuse policies to any relevant licensing bodies, to the extent known.

§ 115.77 Corrective action for contractors and volunteers.

(a) Any contractor or volunteer who has engaged in sexual abuse shall be prohibited from contact with detainees. Each facility shall make reasonable efforts to report to any relevant licensing body, to the extent known, incidents of substantiated sexual abuse by a contractor or volunteer. Such incidents shall also be reported to law enforcement agencies, unless the activity was clearly not criminal.

(b) Contractors and volunteers suspected of perpetrating sexual abuse shall be removed from all duties requiring detainee contact pending the outcome of an investigation.

(c) The facility shall take appropriate remedial measures, and shall consider whether to prohibit further contact with detainees by contractors or volunteers who have not engaged in sexual abuse, but have violated other provisions within these standards.

§ 115.78 Disciplinary sanctions for detainees.

(a) Each facility shall subject a detainee to disciplinary sanctions pursuant to a formal disciplinary process following an administrative or criminal finding that the detainee engaged in sexual abuse.

(b) At all steps in the disciplinary process provided in paragraph (a), any sanctions imposed shall be commensurate with the severity of the committed prohibited act and intended to encourage the detainee to conform with rules and regulations in the future.

(c) Each facility holding detainees in custody shall have a detainee disciplinary system with progressive levels of reviews, appeals, procedures, and documentation procedure.

(d) The disciplinary process shall consider whether a detainee's mental disabilities or mental illness contributed to his or her behavior when determining what type of sanction, if any, should be imposed.

(e) The facility shall not discipline a detainee for sexual contact with staff unless there is a finding that the staff member did not consent to such contact.

(f) For the purpose of disciplinary action, a report of sexual abuse made in good faith based upon a reasonable belief that the alleged conduct occurred shall not constitute falsely reporting an incident or lying, even if an investigation does not establish evidence sufficient to substantiate the allegation.

MEDICAL AND MENTAL CARE

§ 115.81 Medical and mental health assessments; history of sexual abuse.

(a) If the assessment pursuant to § 115.41 indicates that a detainee has experienced prior sexual victimization or perpetrated sexual abuse, staff shall, as appropriate, ensure that the detainee is immediately referred to a qualified medical or mental health practitioner for medical and/or mental health follow-up as appropriate.

(b) When a referral for medical follow-up is initiated, the detainee shall receive a health evaluation no later than two working days from the date of assessment.

(c) When a referral for mental health follow-up is initiated, the detainee shall receive a mental health evaluation no later than 72 hours after the referral.

§115.82 Access to emergency medical and mental health services.

(a) Detainee victims of sexual abuse shall have timely, unimpeded access to emergency medical treatment and crisis intervention services, including emergency contraception and sexually transmitted infections prophylaxis, in accordance with professionally accepted standards of care.

(b) Emergency medical treatment services provided to the victim shall be without financial cost and regardless of whether the victim names the abuser or cooperates with any investigation arising out of the incident.

§115.83 Ongoing medical and mental health care for sexual abuse victims and abusers.

(a) Each facility shall offer medical and mental health evaluation and, as appropriate, treatment to all detainees who have been victimized by sexual abuse while in immigration detention.

(b) The evaluation and treatment of such victims shall include, as appropriate, follow-up services, treatment plans, and, when necessary, referrals for continued care following their transfer to, or placement in, other facilities, or their release from custody.

(c) The facility shall provide such victims with medical and mental health services consistent with the community level of care.

(d) Detainee victims of sexually abusive vaginal penetration by a male abuser while incarcerated shall be offered pregnancy tests. If pregnancy results from an instance of sexual abuse, the victim shall receive timely and comprehensive information about lawful pregnancy-related medical services and timely access to all lawful pregnancy-related medical services.

(e) Detainee victims of sexual abuse while detained shall be offered tests for sexually transmitted infections as medically appropriate.

(f) Treatment services shall be provided to the victim without financial cost and regardless of whether the victim names the abuser or cooperates with any investigation arising out of the incident.

(g) The facility shall attempt to conduct a mental health evaluation of all known detainee-on-detainee abusers within 60 days of learning of such abuse history and offer treatment when deemed appropriate by mental health practitioners.

DATA COLLECTION AND REVIEW

§115.86 Sexual abuse incident reviews.

(a) Each facility shall conduct a sexual abuse incident review at the conclusion of every investigation of sexual abuse and, where the allegation was not determined to be unfounded, prepare a written report within 30 days of the conclusion of the investigation recommending whether the allegation or investigation indicates that a change in policy or practice could better prevent, detect, or respond to sexual abuse. The facility shall implement the recommendations for improvement, or shall document its reasons for not doing so in a written response. Both the report and response shall be forwarded to the agency PSA Coordinator.

(b) The review team shall consider whether the incident or allegation was motivated by race; ethnicity; gender identity; lesbian, gay, bisexual, transgender, or intersex identification, status, or perceived status; or gang affiliation; or was motivated or otherwise caused by other group dynamics at the facility.

(c) Each facility shall conduct an annual review of all sexual abuse investigations and resulting incident reviews to assess and improve sexual abuse intervention, prevention and response efforts. If the facility has not had any reports of sexual abuse during the annual reporting period, then the facility shall prepare a negative report. The results and findings of the annual review shall be provided to the facility administrator, Field Office Director or his or her designee, and the agency PSA Coordinator.

§ 115.87　Data collection.

(a) Each facility shall maintain in a secure area all case records associated with claims of sexual abuse, including incident reports, investigative reports, offender information, case disposition, medical and counseling evaluation findings, and recommendations for post-release treatment, if necessary, and/or counseling in accordance with these standards and applicable agency policies, and in accordance with established schedules. The DHS Office of Inspector General shall maintain the official investigative file related to claims of sexual abuse investigated by the DHS Office of Inspector General.

(b) On an ongoing basis, the PSA Coordinator shall work with relevant facility PSA Compliance Managers and DHS entities to share data regarding effective agency response methods to sexual abuse.

(c) On a regular basis, the PSA Coordinator shall prepare a report for ICE leadership compiling information received about all incidents or allegations of sexual abuse of detainees in immigration detention during the period covered by the report, as well as ongoing investigations and other pending cases.

(d) On an annual basis, the PSA Coordinator shall aggregate, in a manner that will facilitate the agency's ability to detect possible patterns and help prevent future incidents, the incident-based sexual abuse data, including the number of reported sexual abuse allegations determined to be substantiated, unsubstantiated, or unfounded, or for which investigation is ongoing, and for each incident found to be substantiated, information concerning:

(1) The date, time, location, and nature of the incident;

(2) The demographic background of the victim and perpetrator (including citizenship, age, gender, and whether either has self-identified as gay, lesbian, bisexual, transgender, intersex, or gender nonconforming);

(3) The reporting timeline for the incident (including the name of individual who reported the incident, and the date and time the report was received);

(4) Any injuries sustained by the victim;

(5) Post-report follow up responses and action taken by the facility (e.g., housing placement/custody classification, medical examination, mental health counseling, etc.); and

(6) Any sanctions imposed on the perpetrator.

(e) Upon request, the agency shall provide all data described in this section from the previous calendar year to the Office for Civil Rights and Civil Liberties no later than June 30.

§ 115.88　Data review for corrective action.

(a) The agency shall review data collected and aggregated pursuant to § 115.87 of this part in order to assess and improve the effectiveness of its sexual abuse prevention, detection, and response policies, practices, and training, including by:

(1) Identifying problem areas;

(2) Taking corrective action on an ongoing basis; and

(3) Preparing an annual report of its findings and corrective actions for each immigration detention facility, as well as the agency as a whole.

(b) Such report shall include a comparison of the current year's data and corrective actions with those from prior years and shall provide an assessment of the agency's progress in preventing, detecting, and responding to sexual abuse.

(c) The agency's report shall be approved by the agency head and made readily available to the public through its Web site.

(d) The agency may redact specific material from the reports, when appropriate for safety or security, but must indicate the nature of the material redacted.

§ 115.89　Data storage, publication, and destruction.

(a) The agency shall ensure that data collected pursuant to § 115.87 are securely retained in accordance with agency record retention policies and the agency protocol regarding investigation of allegations.

(b) The agency shall make all aggregated sexual abuse data from immigration detention facilities under its direct control and from any private agencies with which it contracts available to the public at least annually on its Web site consistent with existing agency information disclosure policies and processes.

(c) Before making aggregated sexual abuse data publicly available, the agency shall remove all personal identifiers.

(d) The agency shall maintain sexual abuse data collected pursuant to §115.87 for at least 10 years after the date of the initial collection unless Federal, State, or local law requires otherwise.

<small>AUDITS AND COMPLIANCE</small>

§115.93 Audits of standards.

(a) During the three-year period starting on July 6. 2015, and during each three-year period thereafter, the agency shall ensure that each immigration detention facility that has adopted these standards is audited at least once.

(b) The agency may require an expedited audit if the agency has reason to believe that a particular facility may be experiencing problems relating to sexual abuse. The agency may also include referrals to resources that may assist the facility with PREA-related issues.

(c) Audits under this section shall be conducted pursuant to §§115.201 through 115.205.

(d) Audits under this section shall be coordinated by the agency with the DHS Office for Civil Rights and Civil Liberties, which may request an expedited audit if it has reason to believe that an expedited audit is appropriate.

<small>ADDITIONAL PROVISIONS IN AGENCY POLICIES</small>

§115.95 Additional provisions in agency policies.

The regulations in this subpart A establish minimum requirements for agencies and facilities. Agency and facility policies may include additional requirements.

Subpart B—Standards for DHS Holding Facilities

<small>COVERAGE</small>

§115.110 Coverage of DHS holding facilities.

This subpart B covers all DHS holding facilities. Standards found in subpart A of this part are not applicable to DHS facilities except ICE immigration detention facilities.

<small>PREVENTION PLANNING</small>

§115.111 Zero tolerance of sexual abuse; Prevention of Sexual Assault Coordinator.

(a) The agency shall have a written policy mandating zero tolerance toward all forms of sexual abuse and outlining the agency's approach to preventing, detecting, and responding to such conduct.

(b) The agency shall employ or designate an upper-level, agency-wide PSA Coordinator with sufficient time and authority to develop, implement, and oversee agency efforts to comply with these standards in all of its holding facilities.

§115.112 Contracting with non-DHS entities for the confinement of detainees.

(a) An agency that contracts for the confinement of detainees in holding facilities operated by non-DHS private or public agencies or other entities, including other government agencies, shall include in any new contracts, contract renewals, or substantive contract modifications the entity's obligation to adopt and comply with these standards.

(b) Any new contracts, contract renewals, or substantive contract modifications shall provide for agency contract monitoring to ensure that the contractor is complying with these standards.

(c) To the extent an agency contracts for confinement of holding facility detainees, all rules in this subpart that apply to the agency shall apply to the contractor, and all rules that apply to staff or employees shall apply to contractor staff.

§ 115.113 Detainee supervision and monitoring.

(a) The agency shall ensure that each facility maintains sufficient supervision of detainees, including through appropriate staffing levels and, where applicable, video monitoring, to protect detainees against sexual abuse.

(b) The agency shall develop and document comprehensive detainee supervision guidelines to determine and meet each facility's detainee supervision needs, and shall review those supervision guidelines and their application at each facility at least annually.

(c) In determining adequate levels of detainee supervision and determining the need for video monitoring, agencies shall take into consideration the physical layout of each holding facility, the composition of the detainee population, the prevalence of substantiated and unsubstantiated incidents of sexual abuse, the findings and recommendations of sexual abuse incident review reports, and any other relevant factors, including but not limited to the length of time detainees spend in agency custody.

§ 115.114 Juvenile and family detainees.

(a) Juveniles shall be detained in the least restrictive setting appropriate to the juvenile's age and special needs, provided that such setting is consistent with the need to protect the juvenile's well-being and that of others, as well as with any other laws, regulations, or legal requirements.

(b) Unaccompanied juveniles shall generally be held separately from adult detainees. The juvenile may temporarily remain with a non-parental adult family member where:

(1) The family relationship has been vetted to the extent feasible, and

(2) The agency determines that remaining with the non-parental adult family member is appropriate, under the totality of the circumstances.

§ 115.115 Limits to cross-gender viewing and searches.

(a) Searches may be necessary to ensure the safety of officers, civilians and detainees; to detect and secure evidence of criminal activity; and to promote security, safety, and related interests at DHS holding facilities.

(b) Cross-gender strip searches or cross-gender visual body cavity searches shall not be conducted except in exigent circumstances, including consideration of officer safety, or when performed by medical practitioners. An agency shall not conduct visual body cavity searches of juveniles and, instead, shall refer all such body cavity searches of juveniles to a medical practitioner.

(c) All strip searches and visual body cavity searches shall be documented.

(d) The agency shall implement policies and procedures that enable detainees to shower (where showers are available), perform bodily functions, and change clothing without being viewed by staff of the opposite gender, except in exigent circumstances or when such viewing is incidental to routine cell checks or is otherwise appropriate in connection with a medical examination or monitored bowel movement under medical supervision. Such policies and procedures shall require staff of the opposite gender to announce their presence when entering an area where detainees are likely to be showering, performing bodily functions, or changing clothing.

(e) The agency and facility shall not search or physically examine a detainee for the sole purpose of determining the detainee's gender. If the detainee's gender is unknown, it may be determined during conversations with the detainee, by reviewing medical records (if available), or, if necessary, learning that information as part of a broader medical examination conducted in private, by a medical practitioner.

(f) The agency shall train law enforcement staff in proper procedures for conducting pat-down searches, including cross-gender pat-down searches and searches of transgender and intersex detainees. All pat-down searches shall be conducted in a professional and respectful manner, and in the least intrusive manner possible, consistent with security needs and agency policy, including consideration of officer safety.

§ 115.116 Accommodating detainees with disabilities and detainees who are limited English proficient.

(a) The agency shall take appropriate steps to ensure that detainees with disabilities (including, for example, detainees who are deaf or hard of hearing, those who are blind or have low vision, or those who have intellectual, psychiatric, or speech disabilities), have an equal opportunity to participate in or benefit from all aspects of the agency's efforts to prevent, detect, and respond to sexual abuse. Such steps shall include, when necessary to ensure effective communication with detainees who are deaf or hard of hearing, providing access to in-person, telephonic, or video interpretive services that enable effective, accurate, and impartial interpretation, both receptively and expressively, using any necessary specialized vocabulary. In addition, the agency shall ensure that any written materials related to sexual abuse are provided in formats or through methods that ensure effective communication with detainees with disabilities, including detainees who have intellectual disabilities, limited reading skills, or who are blind or have low vision. An agency is not required to take actions that it can demonstrate would result in a fundamental alteration in the nature of a service, program, or activity, or in undue financial and administrative burdens, as those terms are used in regulations promulgated under title II of the Americans with Disabilities Act, 28 CFR 35.164.

(b) The agency shall take reasonable steps to ensure meaningful access to all aspects of the agency's efforts to prevent, detect, and respond to sexual abuse to detainees who are limited English proficient, including steps to provide in-person or telephonic interpretive services that enable effective, accurate, and impartial interpretation, both receptively and expressively, using any necessary specialized vocabulary.

(c) In matters relating to allegations of sexual abuse, the agency shall provide in-person or telephonic interpretation services that enable effective, accurate, and impartial interpretation, by someone other than another detainee, unless the detainee expresses a preference for another detainee to provide interpretation, and the agency determines that such interpretation is appropriate and consistent with DHS policy. The provision of interpreter services by minors, alleged abusers, detainees who witnessed the alleged abuse, and detainees who have a significant relationship with the alleged abuser is not appropriate in matters relating to allegations of sexual abuse is not appropriate in matters relating to allegations of sexual abuse.

§ 115.117 Hiring and promotion decisions.

(a) The agency shall not hire or promote anyone who may have contact with detainees, and shall not enlist the services of any contractor or volunteer who may have contact with detainees, who has engaged in sexual abuse in a prison, jail, holding facility, community confinement facility, juvenile facility, or other institution (as defined in 42 U.S.C. 1997); who has been convicted of engaging or attempting to engage in sexual activity facilitated by force, overt or implied threats of force, or coercion, or if the victim did not consent or was unable to consent or refuse; or who has been civilly or administratively adjudicated to have engaged in such activity.

(b) When the agency is considering hiring or promoting staff, it shall ask all applicants who may have contact with detainees directly about previous misconduct described in paragraph (a) of this section, in written applications or interviews for hiring or promotions and in any interviews or written self-evaluations conducted as part of reviews of current employees. The agency shall also impose upon employees a continuing affirmative duty to disclose any such misconduct.

(c) Before hiring new employees who may have contact with detainees, the agency shall require a background investigation to determine whether the candidate for hire is suitable for employment with the agency. The agency shall conduct an updated background investigation for agency employees every five years.

(d) The agency shall also perform a background investigation before enlisting the services of any contractor who may have contact with detainees.

(e) Material omissions regarding such misconduct, or the provision of materially false information, shall be grounds for termination or withdrawal of an offer of employment, as appropriate.

(f) Unless prohibited by law, the agency shall provide information on substantiated allegations of sexual abuse involving a former employee upon receiving a request from an institutional employer for whom such employee has applied to work.

(g) In the event the agency contracts with a facility for the confinement of detainees, the requirements of this section otherwise applicable to the agency also apply to the facility.

§ 115.118 Upgrades to facilities and technologies.

(a) When designing or acquiring any new holding facility and in planning any substantial expansion or modification of existing holding facilities, the agency shall consider the effect of the design, acquisition, expansion, or modification upon the agency's ability to protect detainees from sexual abuse.

(b) When installing or updating a video monitoring system, electronic surveillance system, or other monitoring technology in a holding facility, the agency shall consider how such technology may enhance the agency's ability to protect detainees from sexual abuse.

RESPONSIVE PLANNING

§ 115.121 Evidence protocols and forensic medical examinations.

(a) To the extent that the agency is responsible for investigating allegations of sexual abuse in its holding facilities, the agency shall follow a uniform evidence protocol that maximizes the potential for obtaining usable physical evidence for administrative proceedings and criminal prosecutions. The protocol shall be developed in coordination with DHS and shall be developmentally appropriate for juveniles, where applicable.

(b) In developing the protocol referred to in paragraph (a) of this sec-tion, the agency shall consider how best to utilize available community resources and services to provide valuable expertise and support in the areas of crisis intervention and counseling to most appropriately address victims' needs.

(c) Where evidentiarily or medically appropriate, at no cost to the detainee, and only with the detainee's consent, the agency shall arrange for or refer the alleged victim detainee to a medical facility to undergo a forensic medical examination, including a Sexual Assault Forensic Examiner (SAFE) or Sexual Assault Nurse Examiner (SANE) where practicable. If SAFEs or SANEs cannot be made available, the examination can be performed by other qualified health care personnel.

(d) If, in connection with an allegation of sexual abuse, the detainee is transported for a forensic examination to an outside hospital that offers victim advocacy services, the detainee shall be permitted to use such services to the extent available, consistent with security needs.

(e) To the extent that the agency is not responsible for investigating allegations of sexual abuse, the agency shall request that the investigating agency follow the requirements of paragraphs (a) through (d) of this section.

§ 115.122 Policies to ensure investigation of allegations and appropriate agency oversight.

(a) The agency shall establish a protocol to ensure that each allegation of sexual abuse is investigated by the agency, or referred to an appropriate investigative authority.

(b) The agency protocol shall be developed in coordination with DHS investigative entities; shall include a description of the responsibilities of both the agency and the investigative entities; and shall require the documentation and maintenance, for at least five years, of all reports and referrals of allegations of sexual abuse. The agency shall post its protocol on its Web site, redacted if appropriate.

(c) The agency protocol shall ensure that each allegation is promptly reported to the Joint Intake Center and, unless the allegation does not involve potentially criminal behavior, promptly referred for investigation to an appropriate law enforcement agency with the legal authority to conduct criminal investigations. The agency may separately, and in addition to the above reports and referrals, conduct its own investigation.

(d) The agency shall ensure that all allegations of detainee sexual abuse are promptly reported to the PSA Coordinator and to the appropriate offices within the agency and within DHS to ensure appropriate oversight of the investigation.

(e) The agency shall ensure that any alleged detainee victim of sexual abuse that is criminal in nature is provided timely access to U nonimmigrant status information.

TRAINING AND EDUCATION

§ **115.131 Employee, contractor, and volunteer training.**

(a) The agency shall train, or require the training of all employees, contractors, and volunteers who may have contact with holding facility detainees, to be able to fulfill their responsibilities under these standards, including training on:

(1) The agency's zero-tolerance policies for all forms of sexual abuse;

(2) The right of detainees and employees to be free from sexual abuse, and from retaliation for reporting sexual abuse;

(3) Definitions and examples of prohibited and illegal sexual behavior;

(4) Recognition of situations where sexual abuse may occur;

(5) Recognition of physical, behavioral, and emotional signs of sexual abuse, and methods of preventing such occurrences;

(6) Procedures for reporting knowledge or suspicion of sexual abuse;

(7) How to communicate effectively and professionally with detainees, including lesbian, gay, bisexual, transgender, intersex, or gender nonconforming detainees; and

(8) The requirement to limit reporting of sexual abuse to personnel with a need-to-know in order to make decisions concerning the victim's welfare and for law enforcement or investigative purposes.

(b) All current employees, contractors and volunteers who may have contact with holding facility detainees shall be trained within two years of the effective date of these standards, and the agency shall provide refresher information, as appropriate.

(c) The agency shall document those employees who may have contact with detainees have completed the training and receive and maintain for at least five years confirmation that contractors and volunteers have completed the training.

§ **115.132 Notification to detainees of the agency's zero-tolerance policy.**

The agency shall make public its zero-tolerance policy regarding sexual abuse and ensure that key information regarding the agency's zero-tolerance policy is visible or continuously and readily available to detainees, for example, through posters, detainee handbooks, or other written formats.

§ **115.133 [Reserved]**

§ **115.134 Specialized training: Investigations.**

(a) In addition to the training provided to employees, DHS agencies with responsibility for holding facilities shall provide specialized training on sexual abuse and effective cross-agency coordination to agency investigators who conduct investigations into allegations of sexual abuse at holding facilities. All investigations into alleged sexual abuse must be conducted by qualified investigators.

(b) The agency must maintain written documentation verifying specialized training provided to agency investigators pursuant to this section.

ASSESSMENT FOR RISK OF SEXUAL VICTIMIZATION AND ABUSIVENESS

§ **115.141 Assessment for risk of victimization and abusiveness.**

(a) Before placing any detainees together in a holding facility, agency staff shall consider whether, based on the information before them, a detainee may be at a high risk of being sexually abused and, when appropriate, shall take necessary steps to mitigate any such danger to the detainee.

(b) All detainees who may be held overnight with other detainees shall be assessed to determine their risk of being sexually abused by other detainees or sexually abusive toward other detainees; staff shall ask each such detainee about his or her own concerns about his or her physical safety.

(c) The agency shall also consider, to the extent that the information is available, the following criteria to assess detainees for risk of sexual victimization:

(1) Whether the detainee has a mental, physical, or developmental disability;

(2) The age of the detainee;

(3) The physical build and appearance of the detainee;

(4) Whether the detainee has previously been incarcerated or detained;

(5) The nature of the detainee's criminal history; and

(6) Whether the detainee has any convictions for sex offenses against an adult or child;

(7) Whether the detainee has self-identified as gay, lesbian, bisexual, transgender, intersex, or gender nonconforming;

(8) Whether the detainee has self-identified as having previously experienced sexual victimization; and

(9) The detainee's own concerns about his or her physical safety.

(d) If detainees are identified pursuant to the assessment under this section to be at high risk of victimization, staff shall provide such detainees with heightened protection, to include continuous direct sight and sound supervision, single-cell housing, or placement in a cell actively monitored on video by a staff member sufficiently proximate to intervene, unless no such option is determined to be feasible.

(e) The facility shall implement appropriate controls on the dissemination of sensitive information provided by detainees under this section.

REPORTING

§ 115.151 Detainee reporting.

(a) The agency shall develop policies and procedures to ensure that the detainees have multiple ways to privately report sexual abuse, retaliation for reporting sexual abuse, or staff ne-

glect or violations of responsibilities that may have contributed to such incidents, and shall provide instructions on how detainees may contact the DHS Office of the Inspector General or, as appropriate, another designated office, to confidentially and, if desired, anonymously, report these incidents.

(b) The agency shall also provide, and shall inform the detainees of, at least one way for detainees to report sexual abuse to a public or private entity or office that is not part of the agency, and that is able to receive and immediately forward detainee reports of sexual abuse to agency officials, allowing the detainee to remain anonymous upon request.

(c) Agency policies and procedures shall include provisions for staff to accept reports made verbally, in writing, anonymously, and from third parties and to promptly document any verbal reports.

§§ 115.152–115.153 [Reserved]

§ 115.154 Third-party reporting.

The agency shall establish a method to receive third-party reports of sexual abuse in its holding facilities. The agency shall make available to the public information on how to report sexual abuse on behalf of a detainee.

OFFICIAL RESPONSE FOLLOWING A
DETAINEE REPORT

§ 115.161 Staff reporting duties.

(a) The agency shall require all staff to report immediately and according to agency policy any knowledge, suspicion, or information regarding an incident of sexual abuse that occurred to any detainee; retaliation against detainees or staff who reported or participated in an investigation about such an incident; and any staff neglect or violation of responsibilities that may have contributed to an incident or retaliation. Agency policy shall include methods by which staff can report misconduct outside of their chain of command.

(b) Staff members who become aware of alleged sexual abuse shall immediately follow the reporting requirements set forth in the agency's written policies and procedures.

(c) Apart from such reporting, the agency and staff shall not reveal any information related to a sexual abuse report to anyone other than to the extent necessary to help protect the safety of the victim or prevent further victimization of other detainees or staff in the facility, or to make medical treatment, investigation, law enforcement, or other security and management decisions.

(d) If the alleged victim is under the age of 18 or considered a vulnerable adult under a State or local vulnerable persons statute, the agency shall report the allegation to the designated State or local services agency under applicable mandatory reporting laws.

§115.162 Agency protection duties.

When an agency employee has a reasonable belief that a detainee is subject to a substantial risk of imminent sexual abuse, he or she shall take immediate action to protect the detainee.

§115.163 Reporting to other confinement facilities.

(a) Upon receiving an allegation that a detainee was sexually abused while confined at another facility, the agency that received the allegation shall notify the appropriate office of the agency or the administrator of the facility where the alleged abuse occurred.

(b) The notification provided in paragraph (a) of this section shall be provided as soon as possible, but no later than 72 hours after receiving the allegation.

(c) The agency shall document that it has provided such notification.

(d) The agency office that receives such notification, to the extent the facility is covered by this subpart, shall ensure that the allegation is referred for investigation in accordance with these standards.

§115.164 Responder duties.

(a) Upon learning of an allegation that a detainee was sexually abused, the first law enforcement staff member to respond to the report, or his or her supervisor, shall be required to:

(1) Separate the alleged victim and abuser;

(2) Preserve and protect, to the greatest extent possible, any crime scene until appropriate steps can be taken to collect any evidence;

(3) If the sexual abuse occurred within a time period that still allows for the collection of physical evidence, request the alleged victim not to take any actions that could destroy physical evidence, including, as appropriate, washing, brushing teeth, changing clothes, urinating, defecating, smoking, drinking, or eating; and

(4) If the abuse occurred within a time period that still allows for the collection of physical evidence, ensure that the alleged abuser does not take any actions that could destroy physical evidence, including, as appropriate, washing, brushing teeth, changing clothes, urinating, defecating, smoking, drinking, or eating.

(b) If the first staff responder is not a law enforcement staff member, the responder shall be required to request that the alleged victim not take any actions that could destroy physical evidence and then notify law enforcement staff.

§115.165 Coordinated response.

(a) The agency shall develop a written institutional plan and use a coordinated, multidisciplinary team approach to responding to sexual abuse.

(b) If a victim of sexual abuse is transferred between facilities covered by subpart A or B of this part, the agency shall, as permitted by law, inform the receiving facility of the incident and the victim's potential need for medical or social services.

(c) If a victim is transferred from a DHS holding facility to a facility not covered by paragraph (b) of this section, the agency shall, as permitted by law, inform the receiving facility of the incident and the victim's potential need for medical or social services, unless the victim requests otherwise.

§115.166 Protection of detainees from contact with alleged abusers.

Agency management shall consider whether any staff, contractor, or volunteer alleged to have perpetrated sexual abuse should be removed from duties requiring detainee contact pending the outcome of an investigation, and shall do so if the seriousness and plausibility of the allegation make removal appropriate.

§ 115.167 Agency protection against retaliation.

Agency employees shall not retaliate against any person, including a detainee, who reports, complains about, or participates in an investigation into an allegation of sexual abuse, or for participating in sexual activity as a result of force, coercion, threats, or fear of force.

INVESTIGATIONS

§ 115.171 Criminal and administrative investigations.

(a) If the agency has responsibility for investigating allegations of sexual abuse, all investigations into alleged sexual abuse must be prompt, thorough, objective, and conducted by specially trained, qualified investigators.

(b) Upon conclusion of a criminal investigation where the allegation was substantiated, an administrative investigation shall be conducted. Upon conclusion of a criminal investigation where the allegation was unsubstantiated, the agency shall review any available completed criminal investigation reports to determine whether an administrative investigation is necessary or appropriate. Administrative investigations shall be conducted after consultation with the appropriate investigative office within DHS and the assigned criminal investigative entity.

(c) The agency shall develop written procedures for administrative investigations, including provisions requiring:

(1) Preservation of direct and circumstantial evidence, including any available physical and DNA evidence and any available electronic monitoring data;

(2) Interviewing alleged victims, suspected perpetrators, and witnesses;

(3) Reviewing prior complaints and reports of sexual abuse involving the suspected perpetrator;

(4) Assessment of the credibility of an alleged victim, suspect, or witness, without regard to the individual's status as detainee, staff, or employee, and without requiring any detainee who alleges sexual abuse to submit to a polygraph;

(5) Documentation of each investigation by written report, which shall include a description of the physical and testimonial evidence, the reasoning behind credibility assessments, and investigative facts and findings; and

(6) Retention of such reports for as long as the alleged abuser is detained or employed by the agency, plus five years. Such procedures shall establish the coordination and sequencing of the two types of investigations, in accordance with paragraph (b) of this section, to ensure that the criminal investigation is not compromised by an internal administrative investigation.

(d) The departure of the alleged abuser or victim from the employment or control of the agency shall not provide a basis for terminating an investigation.

(e) When outside agencies investigate sexual abuse, the agency shall cooperate with outside investigators and shall endeavor to remain informed about the progress of the investigation.

§ 115.172 Evidentiary standard for administrative investigations.

When an administrative investigation is undertaken, the agency shall impose no standard higher than a preponderance of the evidence in determining whether allegations of sexual abuse are substantiated.

DISCIPLINE

§ 115.176 Disciplinary sanctions for staff.

(a) Staff shall be subject to disciplinary or adverse action up to and including removal from their position and the Federal service for substantiated allegations of sexual abuse or violating agency sexual abuse policies.

(b) The agency shall review and approve policy and procedures regarding disciplinary or adverse action for staff and shall ensure that the policy and procedures specify disciplinary or adverse actions for staff, up to and including removal from their position and from the Federal service, when there is a substantiated allegation of sexual abuse, or when there has been a violation of agency sexual abuse rules, policies, or standards. Removal from their position and from the Federal service is the presumptive disciplinary sanction for staff who have engaged in or attempted or threatened to engage in sexual abuse, as defined under the definition of sexual abuse of a detainee by a staff member, contractor, or volunteer, paragraphs (1)–(4) and (7)–(8) of the definition of "sexual abuse of a detainee by a staff member, contractor, or volunteer" in §115.6.

(c) Each facility shall report all removals or resignations in lieu of removal for violations of agency or facility sexual abuse policies to appropriate law enforcement agencies, unless the activity was clearly not criminal.

(d) Each agency shall make reasonable efforts to report removals or resignations in lieu of removal for violations of agency or facility sexual abuse policies to any relevant licensing bodies, to the extent known.

§115.177 Corrective action for contractors and volunteers.

(a) Any contractor or volunteer suspected of perpetrating sexual abuse shall be prohibited from contact with detainees. The agency shall also consider whether to prohibit further contact with detainees by contractors or volunteers who have not engaged in sexual abuse, but have violated other provisions within these standards. The agency shall be responsible for promptly reporting sexual abuse allegations and incidents involving alleged contractor or volunteer perpetrators to an appropriate law enforcement agency as well as to the Joint Intake Center or another appropriate DHS investigative office in accordance with DHS policies and procedures. The agency shall make reasonable efforts to report to any relevant licensing body, to the extent known, incidents of substantiated sexual abuse by a contractor or volunteer.

(b) Contractors and volunteers suspected of perpetrating sexual abuse may be removed from all duties requiring detainee contact pending the outcome of an investigation, as appropriate.

MEDICAL AND MENTAL CARE

§115.181 [Reserved]

§115.182 Access to emergency medical services.

(a) Detainee victims of sexual abuse shall have timely, unimpeded access to emergency medical treatment and crisis intervention services, including emergency contraception and sexually transmitted infections prophylaxis, in accordance with professionally accepted standards of care.

(b) Emergency medical treatment services provided to the victim shall be without financial cost and regardless of whether the victim names the abuser or cooperates with any investigation arising out of the incident.

DATA COLLECTION AND REVIEW

§115.186 Sexual abuse incident reviews.

(a) The agency shall conduct a sexual abuse incident review at the conclusion of every investigation of sexual abuse and, where the allegation was not determined to be unfounded, prepare a written report recommending whether the allegation or investigation indicates that a change in policy or practice could better prevent, detect, or respond to sexual abuse. Such review shall ordinarily occur within 30 days of the agency receiving the investigation results from the investigative authority. The agency shall implement the recommendations for improvement, or shall document its reasons for not doing so in a written response. Both the report and response shall be forwarded to the agency PSA Coordinator.

(b) The agency shall conduct an annual review of all sexual abuse investigations and resulting incident reviews to assess and improve sexual abuse intervention, prevention and response efforts.

§115.187 Data collection.

(a) The agency shall maintain in a secure area all agency case records associated with claims of sexual abuse, in accordance with these standards and applicable agency policies, and in accordance with established schedules. The DHS Office of Inspector General shall maintain the official investigative file related to claims of sexual abuse investigated by the DHS Office of Inspector General.

(b) On an annual basis, the PSA Coordinator shall aggregate, in a manner that will facilitate the agency's ability to detect possible patterns and help prevent future incidents, the incident-based sexual abuse data available, including the number of reported sexual abuse allegations determined to be substantiated, unsubstantiated, or unfounded, or for which investigation is ongoing, and for each incident found to be substantiated, such information as is available to the PSA Coordinator concerning:

(1) The date, time, location, and nature of the incident;

(2) The demographic background of the victim and perpetrator (including citizenship, age, gender, and whether either has self-identified as gay, lesbian, bisexual, transgender, intersex, or gender nonconforming);

(3) The reporting timeline for the incident (including the name of individual who reported the incident, and the date and time the report was received);

(4) Any injuries sustained by the victim;

(5) Post-report follow up responses and action taken by the agency (e.g., supervision, referral for medical or mental health services, etc.); and

(6) Any sanctions imposed on the perpetrator.

(c) The agency shall maintain, review, and collect data as needed from all available agency records.

(d) Upon request, the agency shall provide all such data from the previous calendar year to the Office for Civil Rights and Civil Liberties no later than June 30.

§ 115.188 Data review for corrective action.

(a) The agency shall review data collected and aggregated pursuant to § 115.187 in order to assess and improve the effectiveness of its sexual abuse prevention, detection, and response policies, practices, and training, including by:

(1) Identifying problem areas;

(2) Taking corrective action on an ongoing basis; and

(3) Preparing an annual report of its findings and corrective actions for the agency as a whole.

(b) Such report shall include a comparison of the current year's data and corrective actions with those from prior years and shall provide an assessment of the agency's progress in preventing, detecting, and responding to sexual abuse.

(c) The agency's report shall be approved by the agency head and made readily available to the public through its Web site.

(d) The agency may redact specific material from the reports, when appropriate for safety or security, but must indicate the nature of the material redacted.

§ 115.189 Data storage, publication, and destruction.

(a) The agency shall ensure that data collected pursuant to § 115.187 are securely retained in accordance with agency record retention policies and the agency protocol regarding investigation of allegations.

(b) The agency shall make all aggregated sexual abuse data from holding facilities under its direct control and from any private agencies with which it contracts available to the public at least annually on its Web site consistent with agency information disclosure policies and processes.

(c) Before making aggregated sexual abuse data publicly available, the agency shall remove all personal identifiers.

(d) The agency shall maintain sexual abuse data collected pursuant to § 115.187 for at least 10 years after the date of the initial collection unless Federal, State, or local law requires otherwise.

AUDITS AND COMPLIANCE

§ 115.193 Audits of standards.

(a) Within three years of July 6, 2015, the agency shall ensure that each of its immigration holding facilities that houses detainees overnight and has adopted these standards is audited. For any such holding facility established after July 6, 2015, the agency shall ensure that the facility is audited within three years. Audits of new holding facilities as well as holding facilities that have previously failed to meet the standards shall occur as soon as practicable within the three-year cycle; however, where it is necessary to prioritize, priority shall be given to facilities that have previously failed to meet the standards.

(1) Audits required under this paragraph (a) shall:

(i) Include a determination whether the holding facility is low-risk based on its physical characteristics and whether it passes the audit conducted pursuant to paragraph (a)(1)(ii) of this section,

(ii) Be conducted pursuant to §§ 115.201 through 115.205, and

(iii) Be coordinated by the agency with the DHS Office for Civil Rights and Civil Liberties, which may request an expedited audit if it has reason to believe that an expedited audit is appropriate.

(2) [Reserved]

(b) Following an audit, the agency shall ensure that any immigration holding facility that houses detainees overnight and is determined to be low-risk, based on its physical characteristics and passing its most recent audit, is audited at least once every five years.

(1) Audits required under this paragraph (b) shall:

(i) Include a determination whether the holding facility is low-risk based on its physical characteristics and whether it passes the audit conducted pursuant to paragraph (b)(1)(ii) of this section,

(ii) Be conducted pursuant to §§ 115.201 through 115.205, and

(iii) Be coordinated by the agency with the DHS Office for Civil Rights and Civil Liberties, which may request an expedited audit if it has reason to believe that an expedited audit is appropriate.

(2) [Reserved]

(c) Following an audit, the agency shall ensure that any immigration holding facility that houses detainees overnight and is determined to not be low-risk, based on its physical characteristics or not passing its most recent audit, is audited at least once every three years.

(1) Audits required under this paragraph (c) shall:

(i) Include a determination whether the holding facility is low-risk based on its physical characteristics and whether it passes the audit conducted by paragraph (c)(1)(ii) of this section,

(ii) Be conducted pursuant to §§ 115.201 through 115.205, and

(iii) Be coordinated by the agency with the DHS Office for Civil Rights and Civil Liberties, which may request an expedited audit if it has reason to believe that an expedited audit is appropriate.

(2) [Reserved]

ADDITIONAL PROVISIONS IN AGENCY POLICIES

§ 115.195 Additional provisions in agency policies.

The regulations in this subpart B establish minimum requirements for agencies. Agency policies may include additional requirements.

Subpart C—External Auditing and Corrective Action

§ 115.201 Scope of audits.

(a) The agency shall develop and issue an instrument that is coordinated with the DHS Office for Civil Rights and Civil Liberties, which will provide guidance on the conduct of and contents of the audit;

(b) The auditor shall review all relevant agency policies, procedures, reports, internal and external audits, and accreditations for each facility type.

(c) The audits shall review, at a minimum, a sampling of relevant documents and other records and information for the most recent one-year period.

(d) The auditor shall have access to, and shall observe, all areas of the audited facilities.

(e) The agency shall provide the auditor with relevant documentation to complete a thorough audit of the facility.

(f) The auditor shall retain and preserve all documentation (including, e.g., videotapes and interview notes) relied upon in making audit determinations. Such documentation shall be provided to the agency upon request.

(g) The auditor shall interview a representative sample of detainees and of staff, and the facility shall make space available suitable for such interviews.

(h) The auditor shall review a sampling of any available videotapes and other electronically available data that may be relevant to the provisions being audited.

(i) The auditor shall be permitted to conduct private interviews with detainees.

(j) Detainees shall be permitted to send confidential information or correspondence to the auditor.

(k) Auditors shall attempt to solicit input from community-based or victim advocates who may have insight into relevant conditions in the facility.

(l) All sensitive but unclassified information provided to auditors will include appropriate designations and limitations on further dissemination. Auditors will be required to follow all appropriate procedures for handling and safeguarding such information.

§ 115.202   Auditor qualifications.

(a) An audit shall be conducted by entities or individuals outside of the agency and outside of DHS that have relevant audit experience.

(b) All auditors shall be certified by the agency, in coordination with DHS. The agency, in coordination with DHS, shall develop and issue procedures regarding the certification process, which shall include training requirements.

(c) No audit may be conducted by an auditor who has received financial compensation from the agency being audited (except for compensation received for conducting other audits, or other consulting related to detention reform) within the three years prior to the agency's retention of the auditor.

(d) The agency shall not employ, contract with, or otherwise financially compensate the auditor for three years subsequent to the agency's retention of the auditor, with the exception of contracting for subsequent audits or other consulting related to detention reform.

§ 115.203   Audit contents and findings.

(a) Each audit shall include a certification by the auditor that no conflict of interest exists with respect to his or her ability to conduct an audit of the facility under review.

(b) Audit reports shall state whether facility policies and procedures comply with relevant standards.

(c) For each of these standards, the auditor shall determine whether the audited facility reaches one of the following findings: Exceeds Standard (substantially exceeds requirement of standard); Meets Standard (substantial compliance; complies in all material ways with the standard for the relevant review period); Does Not Meet Standard (requires corrective action). The audit summary shall indicate, among other things, the number of provisions the facility has achieved at each grade level.

(d) Audit reports shall describe the methodology, sampling sizes, and basis for the auditor's conclusions with regard to each standard provision for each audited facility, and shall include recommendations for any required corrective action.

(e) Auditors shall redact any personally identifiable detainee or staff information from their reports, but shall provide such information to the agency upon request.

(f) The agency shall ensure that the auditor's final report is published on the agency's Web site if it has one, or is otherwise made readily available to the public. The agency shall redact any sensitive but unclassified information (including law enforcement sensitive information) prior to providing such reports publicly.

§ 115.204   Audit corrective action plan.

(a) A finding of "Does Not Meet Standard" with one or more standards shall trigger a 180-day corrective action period.

(b) The agency and the facility shall develop a corrective action plan to achieve compliance.

(c) The auditor shall take necessary and appropriate steps to verify implementation of the corrective action plan, such as reviewing updated policies and procedures or re-inspecting portions of a facility.

(d) After the 180-day corrective action period ends, the auditor shall issue a final determination as to whether the facility has achieved compliance with those standards requiring corrective action.

(e) If the facility does not achieve compliance with each standard, it may (at its discretion and cost) request a subsequent audit once it believes that is has achieved compliance.

§115.205 Audit appeals.

(a) A facility may lodge an appeal with the agency regarding any specific audit finding that it believes to be incorrect. Such appeal must be lodged within 90 days of the auditor's final determination.

(b) If the agency determines that the facility has stated good cause for a re-evaluation, the facility may commission a re-audit by an auditor mutually agreed upon by the agency and the facility. The facility shall bear the costs of this re-audit.

(c) The findings of the re-audit shall be considered final.

PARTS 116–199 [RESERVED]

CHAPTER X—PRIVACY AND CIVIL LIBERTIES OVERSIGHT BOARD

PART 1000—ORGANIZATION AND DELEGATION OF POWERS AND DUTIES OF THE PRIVACY AND CIVIL LIBERTIES OVERSIGHT BOARD

Sec.
1000.1 Purpose.
1000.2 Definitions.
1000.3 Organization.
1000.4 Functions.
1000.5 Delegations of authority.

AUTHORITY: 5 U.S.C. 552.

SOURCE: 78 FR 33689, June 5, 2013, unless otherwise noted.

§ 1000.1 Purpose.

This part describes the organization of the Board, and the assignment of authorities and the responsibilities of the Board, individual Board members, and employees.

§ 1000.2 Definitions.

As used in this part:

Board means the Privacy and Civil Liberties Oversight Board, established by the Implementing Recommendations of the 9/11 Commission Act of 2007, Public Law 110–53.

Chairman means the Chairman of the Board, as appointed by the President and confirmed by the Senate under section 801(a) of the Implementing Recommendations of the 9/11 Commission Act of 2007, Public Law 110–53.

General Counsel means the Board's principal legal advisor.

Member means an individual appointed by the President, with the advice and consent of the Senate, to be a member of the Board.

§ 1000.3 Organization.

(a) The Board is comprised of four part-time Board members and a full-time Chairman, each appointed by the President with the advice and consent of the Senate.

(b) The Board's staff is comprised of the following administrative units:

(1) Office of Management and Operations;

(2) Office of the General Counsel; and

(3) Office of Liaison and Oversight.

§ 1000.4 Functions.

(a) The Board provides advice and counsel to the President and executive departments and agencies to ensure that privacy and civil liberties are appropriately considered in proposed legislation, regulations, and policies, and in the implementation of new and existing legislation, regulations, and policies, related to efforts to protect the Nation from terrorism;

(b) The Board oversees actions by the executive branch relating to efforts to protect the Nation from terrorism to determine whether such actions appropriately protect privacy and civil liberties and are consistent with governing laws, regulations, and policies regarding privacy and civil liberties; and

(c) The Board receives and reviews reports and other information from privacy and civil liberties officers under 42 U.S.C. 2000ee-1 and, when appropriate, makes recommendations to and coordinates the activities of privacy and civil liberties officers on relevant interagency matters.

§ 1000.5 Delegations of authority.

(a) *The Board.* The Board is the head of the agency. The Board is responsible for the overall planning, direction, and control of the agency's agenda. The delegations of authority in this part do not extend to the following actions which are reserved to the Board:

(1) Disposition of all rulemaking and similar proceedings involving the promulgation of rules or the issuance of statements of general policy.

(2) Determination of advice or recommendations to the President or executive departments and agencies regarding the matters described in 42 U.S.C. 2000ee(d).

(3) Determination of the Board's annual agenda or other statement of operational priorities; and

(4) Redelegation to one or more Board members or staff of those responsibilities delegated to the Chairman in § 1000.3(b), in the event of a vacancy.

(5) Any authority that is not delegated by the Board in this part, or otherwise vested in officials other than the Board, is reserved to the Board. Except as otherwise provided, the Board

may exercise powers and duties delegated or assigned to individuals other than the Board.

(b) *The Chairman.* The Chairman is the executive and administrative head of the Board. The Chairman has the authority, duties, and responsibilities assigned to the Chairman under 42 U.S.C. 2000ee(h)(5) and (j)(1) and is responsible for the agency's day-to-day operations. The Chairman is delegated the authority to:

(1) Exercise control over the Board's management and functioning;

(2) Implement and execute the Board's budget;

(3) Develop and effectively use staff support to carry out the functions of the Board, including, but not limited to, the supervision and removal of Board employees and the assignment and distribution of work among staff;

(4) Convene and preside at all meetings of the Board and ensure that every vote and official act of the Board required by law to be recorded is accurately and promptly recorded by the General Counsel;

(5) Act as the Board's spokesman on all matters where an official expression of the Board is required, or as otherwise directed by the Board;

(6) Approve for publication all publicly issued documents, except:

(i) Those authorized by an individual Board Member;

(ii) Decisions or informal opinions of the Board; and

(iii) The semi-annual report required to be published by the Board under 42 U.S.C. 2000ee(e).

(7) Serve as the Board's Chief FOIA Officer under 5 U.S.C. 552(j).

(8) Serves as the Board's Equal Employment Opportunity Director, as described in 29 CFR part 1614.

(9) Redelegate to one or more Board staff persons those responsibilities delegated to the Executive Director or General Counsel under this part, in the event that either position is unfilled.

(10) Authorize any officer, employee, or administrative unit of the Board to perform a function vested in, delegated, or otherwise designated to the Chairman.

(c) *Executive Director.* The Executive Director manages the staff and assists the Chairman with the day-to-day operation of the Board. The Executive Director is delegated authority to:

(1) Formulate and implement plans and policies designed to assure the effective administration of the Board's operations and the efficient operations of the staff;

(2) Serve as the Board's Senior Agency Official for Privacy;

(3) Administer the Board's programs under the Freedom of Information Act, 5 U.S.C. 552, and the Privacy Act of 1974, 5 U.S.C. 552a.; and

(4) Authorize any officer or employee of the Board to perform a function vested in, delegated, or otherwise designated to the Executive Director.

(d) *General Counsel.* The General Counsel is the Board's chief legal officer, and serves as legal advisor to the Board. The General Counsel is delegated authority to:

(1) Serve as the Board's Designated Ethics Official in accordance with 5 CFR 2638.202;

(2) Certify Board votes consistent with Board policies and procedures; and

(3) Authorize any officer or employee of the Board to perform a function vested in, delegated, or otherwise designated to the General Counsel.

(e) *Individual Board Members.* Any member delegated authority vested in the Chairman under paragraph (a) of this section may redelegate that authority to one or more Board employees.

(f) *Exercise of authority.* In carrying out any functions delegated under this part, members and staff are governed in the exercise of those functions by all applicable Federal statutes and regulations, and by the regulations, orders, and rules of the Board.

[78 FR 33689, June 5, 2013, as amended at 78 FR 38811, June 28, 2013]

PART 1001—PROCEDURES FOR DISCLOSURE OF RECORDS UNDER THE FREEDOM OF INFORMATION ACT

1001.6 Responsibility for responding to requests.
1001.7 Administrative appeals.
1001.8 Time frame for Board response.
1001.9 Business information.
1001.10 Fees.
1001.11 Other rights and services.

AUTHORITY: 5 U.S.C. 552, as amended; Executive Order 12600.

SOURCE: 78 FR 66997, Nov. 8, 2013, unless otherwise noted.

§ 1001.1 Purpose and scope.

The regulations in this part implement the provisions of the FOIA.

§ 1001.2 Definitions.

The following definitions apply to this part:

Board means the Privacy and Civil Liberties Oversight Board, established by the Implementing Recommendations of the 9/11 Commission Act of 2007, Public Law 110–53.

Chairman means the Chairman of the Board, as appointed by the President and confirmed by the Senate under section 801(a) of the Implementing Recommendations of the 9/11 Commission Act of 2007, Public Law 110–53, or any person to whom the Board has delegated authority for the matter concerned.

Chief FOIA Officer means the senior official to whom the Board delegated responsibility for efficient and appropriate compliance with the FOIA.

Commercial use request means a FOIA request from or on behalf of a person who seeks information for a use or purpose that furthers his or her commercial, trade, or profit interests, including pursuit of those interests through litigation.

Confidential business information means trade secrets and confidential, privileged, or proprietary business or financial information submitted to the Board by a person.

Direct costs mean in the case of commercial use requesters those expenses the Board has actually incurred to search for, duplicate, and review documents in response to a FOIA request. Direct costs include, but are not limited to, the salary of the employee performing the work and costs associated with duplication.

Educational institution means a preschool, a public or private elementary or secondary school, an institution of undergraduate or graduate higher education, an institution of professional education, or an institution of vocational education, which operates a program or programs of scholarly research.

Fee waiver means the waiver or reduction of processing fees if a requester can demonstrate that OMB's Fee Guidelines' standards are satisfied, including that the information is in the public interest and is not a commercial interest.

FOIA means the Freedom of Information Act, 5 U.S.C. 552, as amended. The FOIA applies to third-party requests for documents concerning the general activities of the government and the Board in particular. A request by a U.S. citizen or an individual lawfully admitted for permanent residence for access to his or her own records is considered a Privacy Act request, under the Privacy Act of 1974, 5 U.S.C. 552a, as amended. *See* 6 CFR 1002.3.

FOIA Officer means the individual to whom the Board has delegated authority to carry out the Board's day-to-day FOIA administration.

FOIA Public Liaison means the individual designated by the Chairman to assist FOIA requesters with concerns about the Board's processing of their FOIA request, including assistance in resolving disputes.

Non-commercial scientific institution means an organization operated solely for the purpose of conducting scientific research, the results of which are not intended to promote any product or research, and not operated on a commercial basis.

Person includes an individual, partnership, corporation, association, or public or private organization other than an agency.

Record means any writing, drawing, map, recording, diskette, DVD, CD–ROM, tape, film, photograph, or other documentary material, regardless of medium, by which information is preserved, including documentary material stored electronically.

Redact means delete or mark over.

Representative of the news media means any person or entity that gathers information of potential public interest to a segment of the public, uses its editorial skills to turn the raw materials into a distinct work, and distributes that work to an audience.

Requester category means one of the three categories in which requesters will be placed for the purpose of determining whether a requester will be charged fees for search, review, or duplication. They are:

(1) Commercial requestors,

(2) Non-commercial scientific or educational institutions or news media requestors, and

(3) All other requestors.

Submitter means any person or entity from whom the Board obtains confidential business information, directly or indirectly.

Unusual circumstances means, to the extent reasonably necessary for the proper processing of a FOIA request:

(1) The need to search for and collect the requested records from physically separate facilities;

(2) The need to search for, collect and appropriately examine a voluminous amount of separate and distinct records which are demanded in a single request; or

(3) The need for consultation, which shall be conducted with all practicable speed, with another agency having a substantial interest in the determination of the request.

[78 FR 66997, Nov. 8, 2013, as amended at 82 FR 34835, July 27, 2017]

§ 1001.3 Availability of records.

(a) In accordance with 5 U.S.C. 552(a)(1), the Board publishes the following records in the FEDERAL REGISTER and makes an index of the records publicly available:

(1) Descriptions of the Board's organization and the established places at which, the employees from whom, and the methods by which, the public may obtain information, submit documents, or obtain decisions;

(2) Statements of the general course and method by which the Board's functions are channeled and determined, including the nature and requirements of all formal and informal procedures available;

(3) Rules of procedure, descriptions of forms available or the places at which forms may be obtained, and instructions as to the scope and contents of all papers, reports, or examinations;

(4) Substantive rules of general applicability adopted as authorized by law and statements of general policy or interpretations of general applicability formulated and adopted by the Board; and

(5) Each amendment, revision, or repeal of any material listed in paragraphs (a)(1) through (4) of this section.

(b) In accordance with 5 U.S.C. 552(a)(2), the Board shall make the following materials available for public inspection and copying:

(1) Statements of policy and interpretation that have been adopted by the Board and not published in the FEDERAL REGISTER;

(2) Administrative staff manuals and instructions to staff that affect a member of the public;

(3) Copies of all records, regardless of the form or format, which have been released to any person under paragraph (c) of this section and that, because of their nature or subject matter, the Board determines have become or are likely to become the subject of subsequent requests for substantially the same records; and

(4) A general index of the records referred to in paragraph (b)(3) of this section.

(c) In accordance with 5 U.S.C. 552(a)(3), the Board shall make available, upon proper request, as described in section 5 of this part, all non-exempt Board records, or portions of records, not previously made public under paragraphs (a) and (b) of this section.

(d) The FOIA applies only to Board records in existence at the time of the request; the FOIA does not require that the Board create new records in order to respond to FOIA requests. When responsive records are located, the Board adopts a presumption of disclosure and openness.

§ 1001.4 Categories of exemptions.

(a) The FOIA does not require disclosure of matters that are:

(1) Specifically authorized under criteria established by an executive order

to be kept secret in the interest of national defense or foreign policy and are, in fact, properly classified under executive order;

(2) Related solely to the internal personnel rules and practices of the Board;

(3) Specifically exempted from disclosure by statute (other than the Government in the Sunshine Act, 5 U.S.C. 552b, as amended), provided that such statute:

(i) Requires that the matters be withheld from the public in such a manner as to leave no discretion on the issue, establishes particular criteria for withholding, or refers to particular types of matters to be withheld; and

(ii) If enacted after October 28, 2009, specifically cites to Exemption 3 of the FOIA, 5 U.S.C. 552(b)(3);

(4) Trade secrets and commercial or financial information obtained from a person and privileged or confidential;

(5) Inter-agency or intra-agency memoranda or letters, which would not be available at law to a party other than an agency in litigation with the Board;

(6) Personnel and medical files and similar files the disclosure of which would constitute a clearly unwarranted invasion of personal privacy;

(7) Records or information compiled for law enforcement purposes, but only to the extent that the production of such law enforcement records or information:

(i) Could reasonably be expected to interfere with enforcement proceedings;

(ii) Would deprive a person of a right to a fair trial or impartial adjudication;

(iii) Could reasonably be expected to constitute an unwarranted invasion of personal privacy;

(iv) Could reasonably be expected to disclose the identity of a confidential source, including a state, local, or foreign agency or authority or any private institution that furnished information on a confidential basis, and, in the case of a record or information compiled by a criminal investigation, or by an agency conducting a lawful national security intelligence investigation, information furnished by a confidential source;

(v) Would disclose techniques and procedures for law enforcement investigations or prosecutions or would disclose guidelines for law enforcement investigations or prosecutions if such disclosure could reasonably be expected to risk circumvention of the law; or

(vi) Could reasonably be expected to endanger the life or physical safety of any individual.

(8) Contained in or related to examination, operating, or condition reports prepared by, on behalf of, or for the use of an agency responsible for the regulation or supervision of financial institutions; or

(9) Geological and geophysical information and data, including maps, concerning wells.

(b) [Reserved]

§ 1001.5 Requests for records.

(a) You may request copies of records under this part by email to *FOIA@pclob.gov* or in writing addressed to FOIA Officer, Privacy and Civil Liberties Oversight Board. Requestors should check the Board's Web site at *https://www.pclob.gov* for the Board's current mailing address. Please provide contact information, such as your phone number, email address, and/or mailing address, to assist the Board in communicating with you and providing released records.

(b) Your request shall reasonably describe the records sought with sufficient specificity, and when possible, include names, dates, and subject matter, in order to permit the FOIA Officer to locate the records with a reasonable amount of effort. If the FOIA Officer cannot locate responsive records based on your written description, you will be notified and advised that further identifying information is necessary before the request can be fulfilled. Requesters who are attempting to reformulate or modify such a request may discuss their request with the Board's FOIA Officer or FOIA Public Liaison. If a request does not reasonably describe the records sought, the Board's response to the request is likely to be delayed.

(c) Although requests are considered either FOIA or Privacy Act requests, the Board processes requests for records in accordance with both laws so as to provide the greatest degree of lawful access while safeguarding an individual's personal privacy.

(d) Your request should specify your preferred form or format (including electronic formats) for the records you seek. We will accommodate your request if the record is readily available in that form or format. When you do not specify the form or format of the response, we will provide responsive records in the form or format most convenient to us.

[82 FR 34835, July 27, 2017]

§ 1001.6 Responsibility for responding to requests.

(a) *In general.* The Board delegates authority to grant or deny FOIA requests in whole or in part to the FOIA Officer. When conducting a search for responsive records, the FOIA Officer generally will search for records in existence on the date of the search. If another date is used, the FOIA Officer shall inform the requester of the date used.

(b) *Responses.* The FOIA Officer will notify you of his or her determination to grant or deny your FOIA request in the time frame stated in § 1001.8. The Board will release reasonably segregable non-exempt information. For any adverse determination, including those regarding any disputed fee matter; a denial of a request for a fee waiver; or a determination to withhold a record, in whole or in part, that a record does not exist or cannot be located; or to deny a request for expedited processing; the notice shall include the following information:

(1) The name(s) of any person responsible for the determination to deny the request in whole or in part;

(2) A brief statement of the reason(s) for the denial, including any FOIA exemption applied in denying the request. The FOIA Officer will indicate, if technically feasible, the amount of information deleted and the exemption under which a deletion is made on the released portion of the record, unless including that indication would harm an interest protected by the exemption;

(3) An estimate of the volume of information withheld, if applicable. This estimate does not need to be provided if it is ascertainable based on redactions in partially disclosed records or if the disclosure of the estimate would harm an interest protected by an applicable FOIA exemption;

(4) A statement that the adverse determination may be appealed and a description of the requirements for an appeal under § 1001.7; and

(5) A statement notifying you of the assistance available from the Board's FOIA Public Liaison and the dispute resolution services offered by OGIS.

(c) *Consultations and referrals.* (1) Upon receipt of a FOIA request for a record within the Board's possession, the FOIA Officer should determine if the Board or another federal agency is best able to determine eligibility for disclosure under the FOIA. If the FOIA Officer determines that another agency is better able to evaluate the releasibility of the record, the FOIA Officer shall:

(1) Upon receipt of a FOIA request for a record within the Board's possession, the FOIA Officer should determine if the Board or another federal agency is best able to determine eligibility for disclosure under the FOIA. As to any such record, the FOIA Officer must proceed in one of the following ways:

(i) *Consultation.* When records originated with the Board, but contain within them information of interest to or originated by another agency or Federal Government office, the FOIA Officer must consult with that other entity prior to making a release determination.

(ii) *Referral.* When the FOIA Officer believes that a different agency is best able to determine whether to disclose the record the FOIA Officer will refer the responsibility for responding to the request regarding that record to that agency (but only if that other department or agency is subject to FOIA). Ordinarily, the department or agency that originated the record will be presumed best able to determine whether to disclose it. However, if the FOIA Officer and the originating agency jointly agree that the Board is in the best position to respond regarding the record, then the record may be handled as a consultation.

(2) Whenever a request is made for information that is classified, the FOIA Officer shall refer the responsibility for responding to that portion of the request to the agency that originated the information, or has the primary interest in it, as appropriate. Whenever a record contains information that the Board has derivatively classified because it contains information classified by another agency, the FOIA Officer shall refer the responsibility for responding to the request regarding that information to the agency that classified the underlying information or originated the record.

(3) If responsibility for responding to a request is referred to another department or agency, the FOIA Officer shall notify you of the referral. This notice shall identify the part of the request that has been referred and the name of each department or agency to which the request, or part of the request, has been referred, when appropriate and available, the notice will include a point of contact for the referral agency or department.

(d) *Coordination.* The standard referral procedure is not appropriate where disclosure of the identity of the agency to which the referral would be made is classified for national security reasons or otherwise could harm an interest protected by an applicable exemption, such as the exemptions that protect personal privacy or national security interests. For instance, if the Board locates within its files materials originating with an Intelligence Community agency, and the involvement of that agency in the matter is classified and not publicly acknowledged, then to disclose or give attribution to the involvement of that Intelligence Community agency could cause national security harms. In such an instance, in order to avoid harm to an interest protected by an applicable exemption, the Board will coordinate with the originating agency to seek its views on the disclosability of the record. The release determination for the record that is the subject of the coordination will then be conveyed to the requester by the Board.

[78 FR 66997, Nov. 8, 2013, as amended at 82 FR 34836, July 27, 2017]

§1001.7 Administrative appeals.

(a) You may appeal an adverse determination related to your FOIA request, or the Board's failure to respond to your FOIA request within the prescribed time limits, to the Chief FOIA Officer, Privacy and Civil Liberties Oversight Board. Requestors should check the Board's Web site at *https://www.pclob.gov* for the Board's current mailing address.

(b) Your appeal must be in writing, sent to the address posted on the Board's Web site in accordance with paragraph (a) of this section, and it must be postmarked, or in the case of electronic submissions, transmitted, within 90 calendar days after the date of the letter denying your request, in whole or in part. The appeal should clearly identify the agency determination that is being appealed and the assigned case request number. In case of the Board's failure to respond within the statutory time frame, you may submit an administrative appeal at any time until an agency response has been provided. For the most expeditious handling, your appeal letter and envelope, or subject line of the electronic transmission, should be marked "Freedom of Information Act appeal."

(c) Your appeal letter should state facts and may cite legal or other authorities in support of your request.

(d) On receipt of any appeal involving classified information, the Chief FOIA Officer must take appropriate action to ensure compliance with applicable classification rules.

(e) The Chief FOIA Officer shall respond to all administrative appeals in writing and within the time frame stated in §1001.8(d). If the decision affirms, in whole or in part, the FOIA Officer's determination, the letter shall contain a statement of the reasons for the affirmance, including any FOIA exemption(s) applied, and will inform you of the FOIA's provisions for court review. If the Chief FOIA Officer reverses or modifies the FOIA Officer's determination, in whole or in part, you will be notified in writing and your request will be reprocessed in accordance with that decision. The Board may work with Office of Government Information Services (OGIS) to resolve disputes between FOIA requestors and the Board.

A requester may also contact OGIS in the following ways: Via mail to OGIS, National Archives and Records Administration, 8601 Adelphi Road—OGIS, College Park, MD 20740 (*ogis.archives.gov*), via email at *ogis@nara.gov*, or via the telephone at 202–741–5770 or 877–684–6448. Facsimile is also available at 202–741–5769.

[82 FR 34836, July 27, 2017]

§ 1001.8 **Time frame for Board response.**

(a) *In general.* The Board ordinarily shall respond to requests according to their order of receipt.

(b) *Multi-track processing.* The Board may use two or more processing tracks by distinguishing between simple and more complex requests based on the amount of work or time needed to process the request.

(c) *Initial decisions.* The Board shall determine whether to comply with a FOIA request within 20 working days after our receipt of the request, unless the time frame for response is extended due to unusual circumstances as further described in paragraph (f) of this section. A request is received by the Board, for purposes of commencing the 20-day timeframe for its response, on the day it is received by the FOIA Officer or, in any event, not later than ten days after the request is first received by any Board office.

(d) *Administrative appeals.* The Chief FOIA Officer shall determine whether to affirm or overturn a decision subject to administrative appeal within 20 working days after receipt of the appeal, unless the time frame for response is extended in accordance with subsection (e) of this section.

(e) *Tolling timelines.* We may toll the 20-day timeframe set forth in paragraphs (c) or (d) of this section:

(1) One time to await information that we reasonably requested from you, as permitted by 5 U.S.C. 552(a)(6)(A)(iii)(I);

(2) As necessary to clarify with you issues regarding the fee assessment.

(3) If we toll the time frame for response under paragraphs (e)(1) or (2) of this section, the tolling period ends upon our receipt of your response.

(f) *Unusual circumstances.* In the event of unusual circumstances, we may extend the time frame for response provided in paragraphs (c) or (d) of this section by providing you with written notice of the unusual circumstances and the date on which a determination is expected to be made. Where the extension is for more than ten working days, we will provide you with an opportunity either to modify your request so that it may be processed within the statutorily-prescribed time limits or to arrange an alternative time period for processing your request or modified request.

(g) *Aggregating requests.* When we reasonably believe that multiple requests submitted by a requester, or by a group of requesters acting in concert, involving clearly related matters, can be viewed as a single request that involves unusual circumstances, we may aggregate the requests for the purposes of fees and processing activities, which may result in an extension of the processing time.

(h) *Expedited processing.* You may request that the Board expedite processing of your FOIA request. To receive expedited processing, you must demonstrate a compelling need for such processing.

(1) For requests for expedited processing, a "compelling need" involves:

(i) Circumstances in which the lack of expedited treatment could reasonably be expected to pose an imminent threat to the life or physical safety of an individual; or

(ii) A request made by a person primarily engaged in disseminating information, with a time urgency to inform the public of actual or alleged federal government activity.

(2) Your request for expedited processing must be in writing and may be made at the time of the initial FOIA request or at any later time.

(3) Your request for expedited processing must include a statement, certified to be true and correct to the best of your knowledge and belief, explaining in detail the basis for requesting expedited processing. If you are a person primarily engaged in disseminating information, you must establish a particular urgency to inform the public about the federal government activity involved in the request.

(4) The FOIA Officer will decide whether to grant or deny your request for expedited processing within ten calendar days of receipt. You will be notified in writing of the determination. Appeals of adverse decisions regarding expedited processing shall be processed expeditiously.

§ 1001.9 Business information.

(a) *Designation of confidential business information.* In the event a FOIA request is made for confidential business information previously submitted to the Government by a commercial entity or on behalf of it (hereinafter 'submitter'), the regulations in this section apply. When submitting confidential business information, you must use a good-faith effort to designate, by use of appropriate markings, at the time of submission or at a reasonable time thereafter, any portions of your submission that you consider to be exempt from disclosure under FOIA Exemption 4, 5 U.S.C. 552(b)(4). Your designation will expire ten years after the date of submission unless you request, and provide justification for, a longer designation period.

(b) *Notice to submitters.* Whenever you designate confidential business information as provided in paragraph (a) of this section, or the Board has reason to believe that your submission may contain confidential business information, we will provide you with prompt written notice of a FOIA request that seeks your business information. The notice shall:

(1) Give you an opportunity to object to disclosure of your information, in whole or in part;

(2) Describe the business information requested or include copies of the requested records or record portions containing the information; and

(3) Inform you of the time frame in which you must respond to the notice.

(c) *Opportunity to object to disclosure.* The Board shall allow you a reasonable time to respond to the notice described in paragraph (b) of this section. If you object to the disclosure of your information, in whole or in part, you must provide us with a detailed written statement of your objection. The statement must specify all grounds for withholding any portion of the information

under any FOIA exemption and, when relying on FOIA Exemption 4, it must explain why the information is a trade secret or commercial or financial information that is privileged and confidential. If you fail to respond within the time frame specified in the notice, the Board will conclude that you have no objection to disclosure of your information. The Board will only consider information that we receive within the time frame specified in the notice. Any information provided by a submitter under this subpart may itself be subject to disclosure under the FOIA.

(d) *Notice of intent to disclose.* The Board will consider your objection and specific grounds for non-disclosure in deciding whether to disclose business information. Whenever the Board decides to disclose business information over your objection, we will provide you with written notice that includes:

(1) A statement of the reasons why each of your bases for withholding were not sustained;

(2) A description of the business information to be disclosed; and

(3) A specified disclosure date, which shall be a reasonable time after the notice.

(e) *Exceptions to the notice requirement.* The notice requirements of paragraphs (c) and (d) of this section shall not apply if:

(1) The Board determines that the information shall not be disclosed;

(2) The information lawfully has been published or has been officially made available to the public;

(3) Disclosure of the information is required by statute (other than the FOIA) or by a regulation issued in accordance with the requirements of Executive Order 12600;

(4) The designation made by the submitter under paragraph (a) of this section appears obviously frivolous, except that, in such a case, the Board shall, within a reasonable time prior to the date the disclosure will be made, give the submitter written notice of the final decision to disclose the information.

(f) *Notice to requesters.* Whenever we provide a submitter with the notice described in paragraph (b) of this section, we also will provide notice to the requester that notice and opportunity to object to the disclosure are being provided to the submitter. The Board also must notify the requester when it notifies the submitter of its intent to disclose the requested information, and whenever a submitter files a lawsuit to prevent the disclosure of the information.

[78 FR 66997, Nov. 8, 2013, as amended at 82 FR 34836, July 27, 2017]

§ 1001.10 Fees.

(a) We will charge fees that recoup the full allowable direct costs we incur in processing your FOIA request. Fees may be charged for search, review or duplication. As a matter of administrative discretion, the Board may release records without charge or at a reduced rate whenever the Board determines that the interest of the United States government would be served. We will use the most efficient and least costly methods to comply with your request. The Board may charge for search time even if no records are located or the records located are exempt from disclosure. If the Board fails to comply with the FOIA's time limits in which to respond to a request, it may not charge search fees, unless the circumstances outlined in paragraph (o) of this section are met.

(b) With regard to manual searches for records, we will charge the salary rate(s) (calculated as the basic rate of pay plus 16 percent of that basic rate to cover benefits) of the employee(s) performing the search.

(c) In calculating charges for computer searches for records, we will charge at the actual direct cost of providing the service, including the cost of operating computers and other electronic equipment, such as photocopiers and scanners, directly attributable to searching for records potentially responsive to your FOIA request and the portion of the salary of the operators/programmers performing the search.

(d) We may only charge requesters seeking documents for commercial use for time spent reviewing records to determine whether they are exempt from mandatory disclosure. Charges may be assessed only for the initial review— that is, the review undertaken the first time we analyze the applicability of a specific exemption to a particular record or portion of a record. Records or portions of records withheld in full under an exemption that is subsequently determined not to apply may be reviewed again to determine the applicability of other exemptions not previously considered. We may assess the costs for such subsequent review. No charge will be made for review at the administrative appeal stage of exemptions applied at the initial review stage.

(e) Records will be duplicated at a rate of $.10 per page, except that the Board may adjust this rate from time to time by rule published in the FEDERAL REGISTER. For copies prepared by computer, such as tapes, CDs, DVDs, or printouts, we will charge the actual cost, including operator time, of production. For other methods of reproduction or duplication, we will charge the actual direct costs of producing the document(s). If we estimate that duplication charges are likely to exceed $25, we will notify you of the estimated amount of fees, unless you indicated in advance your willingness to pay fees as high as those anticipated. Our notice will offer you an opportunity to confer with Board personnel to reformulate the request to meet your needs at a lower cost. If the Board notifies you that the actual or estimated fees are in excess of $25.00, your request will not be considered received and further work will not be completed until you commit in writing to pay the actual or estimated total fee, or designate some amount of fees you are willing to pay, or in the case of a noncommercial use requester who has not yet been provided with your statutory entitlements, you designate that you seek only that which can be provided by the statutory entitlements. The Board's FOIA Officer or Public Liaison are available to assist you in reformulating your request to meet your needs at a lower cost.

(f) We will charge you the full costs of providing you with the following services:

(1) Certifying that records are true copies; or

(2) Sending records by special methods such as express mail.

(g) We may assess interest charges on an unpaid bill starting on the 31st calendar day following the day on which the billing was sent. Interest shall be at the rate prescribed in 31 U.S.C. 3717 and will accrue from the date of the billing until payment is received by the Board.

(h) We will not charge a search fee for requests by educational institutions, non-commercial scientific institutions, or representatives of the news media. A search fee will be charged for a commercial use request.

(i) The Board will not charge duplication fees for requests by educational institutions, non-commercial scientific institutions, or representatives of the news media for a non-commercial use request if the agency fails to comply with the FOIA's time limits in which to respond to a request.

(j) Except for a commercial use request, we will not charge you for the first 100 pages of duplication and the first two hours of search.

(k) You may not file multiple requests, each seeking portions of a document or documents, solely for the purpose of avoiding payment of fees. When the Board reasonably believes that a requester, or a group of requesters acting in concert, has submitted requests that constitute a single request involving clearly related matters, we may aggregate those requests and charge accordingly.

(l) We may not require you to make payment before we begin work to satisfy the request or to continue work on a request, unless:

(1) We estimate or determine that the allowable charges that you may be required to pay are likely to exceed $250; or

(2) You have previously failed to pay a fee charged within 30 calendar days of the date of billing.

(m) In cases in which the Board requires advance payment, the request will not be considered received and further work will not be completed until the required payment is received. If you do not pay the advance payment within 30 calendar days after the date of the Board's fee determination, the request will be closed.

(n) Upon written request, we may waive or reduce fees that are otherwise chargeable under this part. If you request a waiver or reduction in fees, you must demonstrate that a waiver or reduction in fees is in the public interest because disclosure of the requested records is likely to contribute significantly to the public understanding of the operations or activities of the government and is not primarily in your commercial interest. After processing, actual fees must exceed $25, for the Board to require payment of fees.

(o) If the Board has determined that unusual circumstances, as defined by the FOIA, apply and more than 5,000 pages are necessary to respond to the request, the Board may charge search fees, or, in the case of requesters described in paragraph (h) of this section, may charge duplication fees, if the following steps are taken. The Board must have provided timely written notice of unusual circumstances to the requester in accordance with the FOIA and the agency must have discussed with the requester via written mail, email, or telephone (or made not less than three good-faith attempts to do so) how the requester could effectively limit the scope of the request in accordance with 5 U.S.C. 552(a)(6)(B)(ii). If this exception is satisfied, the Board may charge all applicable fees incurred in the processing of the request.

[82 FR 34847, July 27, 2017]

§ 1001.11 Other rights and services.

Nothing in this subpart shall be construed to entitle any person, as of right, to any service or to the disclosure of any record to which such person is not entitled under the FOIA.

[82 FR 34837, July 27, 2017]

PART 1002—IMPLEMENTATION OF THE PRIVACY ACT OF 1974

AUTHORITY: 5 U.S.C. 552a.

SOURCE: 78 FR 66997, Nov. 8, 2013, unless otherwise noted.

339

§ 1002.1 Purpose and scope.

The regulations in this part implement the provisions of the Privacy Act.

§ 1002.2 Definitions.

The following terms used in this part are defined in the Privacy Act: *Individual, maintain, record, system of records, statistical record,* and *routine use.* The following definitions also apply in this part:

Board means the Privacy and Civil Liberties Oversight Board, established by the Implementing Recommendations of the 9/11 Commission Act of 2007, Pub. L. 110–53.

Chairman means the Chairman of the Board, as appointed by the President and confirmed by the Senate under section 801(a) of the Implementing Recommendations of the 9/11 Commission Act of 2007, Pub. L. 110–53, or any person to whom the Board has delegated authority in the matter concerned.

General Counsel means the Board's principal legal advisor, or his or her designee.

Privacy Act means the Privacy Act of 1974, 5 U.S.C. 552a, as amended.

Privacy Act Officer means the person designated by the Board to be responsible for the day-to-day administration of the Privacy Act.

§ 1002.3 Privacy Act requests.

(a) *Requests to determine if you are the subject of a record.* You may request that the Board inform you if we maintain a system of records that contains records about you. Your request must follow the procedures described in paragraph (b) of this section.

(b) *Requests for access.* You may request access to a Board record about you in writing or by appearing in person. You should direct your request to the Privacy Act Officer. Written requests may be sent to: Privacy Act Officer, Privacy and Civil Liberties Oversight Board, 2100 K Street NW., Suite 500, Washington, DC 20427. Your request should include the following information:

(1) Your name, address, and telephone number;

(2) The system(s) of records in which the requested information is contained; and

(3) At your option, authorization for copying expenses.

(4) *Written requests.* In addition to the information described in paragraphs (b)(1) through (3) of this section, written requests must include a statement affirming your identity, signed by you and witnessed by two persons (including witnesses' addresses) or notarized.

(i) *Witnessed.* If your statement is witnessed, it must include a sentence above the witnesses' signatures attesting that they personally know you or that you have provided satisfactory proof of your identity.

(ii) *Notarized.* If your statement is notarized, you must provide the notary with adequate proof of your identity in the form of a drivers' license, passport, or other identification acceptable to the notary.

(iii) The Board, in its discretion, may require additional proof of identification depending on the nature and sensitivity of the records in the system of records.

(iv) For the quickest possible handling, your letter and envelope should be marked "Privacy Act Request".

(5) *In person requests.* In addition to the information described in paragraphs (b)(1) through (3) of this section, if you make your request in person, you must provide adequate proof of identification at the time of your request. Adequate proof of identification includes a valid drivers' license, valid passport, or other current identification that includes your address and photograph.

(c) *Requests for amendment or correction of records.* You may request an amendment to or correction of a record about you in person or by writing to the Privacy Act Officer following the procedures described in paragraph (b) of this section. Your request for amendment or correction should identify each particular record at issue, state the amendment or correction sought, and describe why the record is not accurate, relevant, timely, or complete.

(d) *Requests for an accounting of disclosures.* Except for those disclosures for which the Privacy Act does not require an accounting, you may request an accounting of any disclosure by the

Board of a record about you. Your request for an accounting of disclosures must be made in writing following the procedures described in subsection (b) of this section.

(e) *Requests for access on behalf of someone else.* (1) If you are making a request on behalf of someone else, your request must include a statement from that individual verifying his or her identity, as provided in paragraph (b)(4) of this section. Your request also must include a statement certifying that individual's agreement that records about him or her may be released to you.

(2) If you are the parent or guardian of the individual to whom the requested record pertains, or the individual to whom the record pertains has been deemed incompetent by a court, your request for access to records about that individual must include:

(i) The identity of the individual who is the subject of the record, including his or her name, current address, and date and place of birth;

(ii) Verification of your identity in accordance with paragraph (b)(4) of this section;

(iii) Verification that you are the subject's parent or guardian, which may be established by a copy of the subject's birth certificate identifying you as his or her parent, or a court order establishing you as guardian; and

(iv) A statement certifying that you are making the request on the subject's behalf.

§ 1002.4 Responses to Privacy Act requests.

(a) *Acknowledgement.* The Privacy Act Officer shall provide you with a written acknowledgment of your written request under section 3 within ten business days of our receipt of your request.

(b) *Grants of requests.* If you make your request in person, the Privacy Act Officer shall respond to your request directly, either by granting you access to the requested records, upon payment of any applicable fee and with a written record of the grant of your request and receipt of the records, or by informing you when a response may be expected. If you are accompanied by another person, you must authorize in writing any discussion of the records in the presence of the third person. If your request is in writing, the Privacy Act Officer shall provide you with written notice of the Board's decision to grant your request and the amount of any applicable fee. The Privacy Act Officer shall disclose the records to you promptly, upon payment of any applicable fee.

(c) *Denials of requests in whole or in part.* The Privacy Act Officer shall notify you in writing of his or her determination to deny, in whole or in part, your request. This writing shall include the following information:

(1) The name and title or position of the person responsible for the denial;

(2) A brief statement of the reason for the denial(s), including any applicable Privacy Act exemption;

(3) A statement that you may appeal the denial and a brief description of the requirements for appeal under § 1002.5.

(d) *Request for records not covered by the Privacy Act or subject to Privacy Act exemption.* If the Privacy Act Officer determines that a requested record is not subject to the Privacy Act or the records are subject to Privacy Act exemption, your request will be processed in accordance with the Board's Freedom of Information Act procedures at 6 CFR part 1001.

§ 1002.5 Administrative appeals.

Appeal procedures.

(1) You may appeal any decision by the Board to deny, in whole or in part, your request under § 1002.3 no later than 60 days after the decision is rendered.

(2) Your appeal must be in writing, sent to the General Counsel at the address specified in § 1002.3(b) and contain the following information:

(i) Your name;

(ii) Description of the record(s) at issue;

(iii) The system of records in which the record(s) is contained;

(iv) A statement of why your request should be granted.

(3) The General Counsel shall determine whether to uphold or reverse the initial determination within 30 working days of our receipt of your appeal. The General Counsel shall notify you of his or her decision, including a brief

statement of the reasons for the decision, in writing. The General Counsel's decision will be the final action of the Board.

(b) *Statement of disagreement.* If your appeal of our determination related to your request for amendment or correction is denied in whole or in part, you may file a Statement of Disagreement that states the basis for your disagreement with the denial. Statements of Disagreement must be concise and must clearly identify each part of any record that is disputed. The Privacy Act Officer will place your Statement of Disagreement in the system of records in which the disputed record is maintained and shall mark the disputed record to indicate that a Statement of Disagreement has been filed and where it may be found.

(c) *Notification of amendment, correction, or disagreement.* Within 30 working days of the amendment or correction of a record, the Privacy Act Officer shall notify all persons, organizations, or agencies to which the Board previously disclosed the record, if an accounting of that disclosure was made, that the record has been corrected or amended. If you filed a Statement of Disagreement, the Privacy Act Officer shall append a copy of it to the disputed record whenever it is disclosed and also may append a concise statement of its reason(s) for denying the request to amend or correct the record.

§ 1002.6 Fees.

We will not charge a fee for search or review of records requested under this part, or for the correction of records. If you request copies of records, we may charge a fee of $.10 per page.

§ 1002.7 Penalties.

Any person who makes a false statement in connection with any request for a record or an amendment or correction thereto under this part is subject to the penalties prescribed in 18 U.S.C. 494 and 495 and 5 U.S.C. 552a(i)(3).

PART 1003—IMPLEMENTATION OF THE GOVERNMENT IN THE SUNSHINE ACT

Sec.

AUTHORITY: 5 U.S.C. 552b.

SOURCE: 78 FR 67002, Nov. 8, 2013, unless otherwise noted.

§ 1003.1 Purpose and scope.

(a) The regulations in this part implement the provisions of the Sunshine Act.

(b) Requests for all records other than those described in § 1003.9, shall be governed by the Board's Freedom of Information Act procedures at 6 CFR part 1001.

§ 1003.2 Definitions.

The following definitions apply in this part:

Board means the Privacy and Civil Liberties Oversight Board, established by the Implementing Recommendations of the 9/11 Commission Act of 2007, Public Law 110–53.

Chairman means the Chairman of the Board, as appointed by the President and confirmed by the Senate under section 801(a) of the Implementing Recommendations of the 9/11 Commission Act of 2007, Public Law 110–53, or any person to whom the Board delegated authority in the matter concerned.

General Counsel means the Board's principal legal advisor, or his or her designee.

Meeting means the deliberations of three or more Board members that determine or result in the joint conduct or disposition of official Board business. A meeting does not include:

(1) Notational voting or similar consideration of business for the purpose of recording votes, whether by circulation of material to members' individually in writing or by a polling of the members individually by phone.

(2) Action by three or more members to:

(i) Open or close a meeting or to release or withhold information pursuant to section 1003.6 of this part;

(ii) Set an agenda for a proposed meeting;

(iii) Call a meeting on less than seven days' notice, as permitted by §1003.4; or

(iv) Change the subject matter or the determination to open or to close a publicly announced meeting under §1003.7.

(3) A session attended by three or more members for the purpose of having the Board's staff or expert consultants, another federal agency, or other persons or organizations brief or otherwise provide information to the Board concerning any matters within the purview of the Board, provided that the members do not engage in deliberations that determine or result in the joint conduct or disposition of official business on such matters.

(4) A gathering of members for the purpose of holding informal, preliminary discussions or exchanges of views which do not effectively predetermine official action.

Member means an individual duly appointed and confirmed to the Board.

Public observation means attendance by the public at a meeting of the Board, but does not include public participation.

Public participation means the presentation or discussion of information, raising of questions, or other manner of involvement in a meeting of the Board by the public in a manner that contributes to the disposition of official Board business.

Sunshine Act means the Government in the Sunshine Act, 5 U.S.C. 552b.

§1003.3 Open meetings.

(a) Except as otherwise provided in this part, every portion of a Board meeting shall be open to public observation.

(b) Board meetings, or portions thereof, shall be open to public partici-

pation when an announcement to that effect is published under §1003.4. Public participation shall be conducted in an orderly, non-disruptive manner and in accordance with any procedures the Chairman may establish. Public participation may be terminated for good cause as determined by the Board upon the advice of the General Counsel based on unanticipated developments.

§1003.4 Procedures for public announcement of meetings.

(a) Except as otherwise provided in this section, the Board shall make a public announcement at least seven days prior to a meeting. The public announcement shall include:

(1) The time and place of the meeting;

(2) The subject matter of the meeting;

(3) Whether the meeting is to be open, closed, or portions of a meeting will be closed;

(4) Whether public participation will be allowed;

(5) The name and telephone number of the person who will respond to requests for information about the meeting;

(b) The seven day prior notice required by paragraph (a) of this section may be reduced only if:

(1) A majority of all members determine by recorded vote that Board business requires that such meeting be scheduled in less than seven days; and

(2) The public announcement required by this section is made at the earliest practicable time.

(c) When a meeting has been called by the Chairman, the notice shall contain such agenda items as the Chairman designates. The notice shall be circulated to Members in advance of publication and Members, by majority vote, may add additional agenda items.

(d) When a meeting is called by a majority of Members, the notice shall contain such agenda items as have been approved by a majority of the Board.

(e) The Executive Director will ensure that the final agenda for the meeting conforms to the notice published in the FEDERAL REGISTER.

(f) If public notice is provided by means other than publication in the FEDERAL REGISTER, notice will be promptly submitted to the FEDERAL REGISTER for publication.

[78 FR 67002, Nov. 8, 2013, as amended at 82 FR 34838, July 27, 2017]

§ 1003.5 Grounds on which meetings may be closed or information withheld.

A meeting, or portion thereof, may be closed and information pertinent to such meeting withheld if the Board determines that the meeting or release of information is likely to disclose matters that are:

(a) Specifically authorized under criteria established by an executive order to be kept secret in the interests of national defense or foreign policy; and, in fact, are properly classified pursuant to such executive order. In making the determination that this exemption applies, the Board shall rely on the classification assigned to the document or assigned to the information from the federal agency from which the document was received.

(b) Related solely to the internal personnel rules and practices of the Board;

(c) Specifically exempt from disclosure by statute (other than 5 U.S.C. 552), provided that such statute:

(1) Requires that the matters be withheld from the public in such a manner as to leave no discretion on the issue; or

(2) Establishes particular criteria for withholding or refers to particular types of matters to be withheld;

(d) Trade secrets and commercial or financial information obtained from a person and privileged or confidential;

(e) Involved with accusing any person of a crime or formally censuring any person;

(f) Of a personal nature, if disclosure would constitute a clearly unwarranted invasion of personal privacy;

(g) Either investigatory records compiled for law enforcement purposes or information which, if written, would be contained in such records, but only to the extent that the production of records or information would:

(1) Interfere with enforcement proceedings;

(2) Deprive a person of a right to either a fair trial or an impartial adjudication;

(3) Constitute an unwarranted invasion of personal privacy;

(4) Disclose the identity of a confidential source or sources and, in the case of a record compiled either by a criminal law enforcement authority or by an agency conducting a lawful national security intelligence investigation, confidential information furnished only by the confidential source(s);

(5) Disclose investigative techniques and procedures; or

(6) Endanger the life or physical safety of law enforcement personnel;

(h) Contained in or relating to examination, operating, or condition reports prepared by, on behalf of, or for the use of an agency responsible for the regulation or supervision of financial institutions;

(i) If prematurely disclosed, likely to significantly frustrate implementation of a proposed action of the Board, except that this subsection shall not apply in any instance where the Board has already disclosed to the public the content or nature of its proposed action or is required by law to make such disclosure on its own initiative prior to taking final action on such proposal; and

(j) Specifically concerned with the Board's issuance of a subpoena, or its participation in a civil action or proceeding, an action in a foreign court or international tribunal, or an arbitration, or the initiation, conduct, or disposition by the Board of a particular case or formal agency adjudication pursuant to the procedures in 5 U.S.C. 554 or otherwise involving a determination on the record after opportunity for a hearing.

§ 1003.6 Procedures for closing meetings or withholding information, and requests by affected persons to close a meeting.

(a) A meeting or portion of a meeting may be closed and information pertaining to a meeting withheld under § 1003.5 only by vote of a majority of members.

(b) A separate vote of the members shall be taken with respect to each meeting or portion of a meeting proposed to be closed and with respect to information which is proposed to be withheld. A single vote may be taken with respect to a series of meetings or portions of a meeting that are proposed to be closed, so long as each meeting or portion thereof in the series involves the same particular matter and is scheduled to be held no more than 30 days after the initial meeting in the series. The vote of each member shall be recorded and no proxies shall be allowed.

(c) A person whose interests may be directly affected by a portion of a meeting may request in writing that the Board close that portion for any of the reasons referred to in § 1003.5(e), (f) and (g). Upon the request of a member, a recorded vote shall be taken whether to close such meeting or portion thereof.

(d) For every meeting closed, the General Counsel shall publicly certify that, in his or her opinion, the meeting may be closed to the public and shall state each relevant basis for closing the meeting. If the General Counsel invokes the bases set forth in § 1003.5(a) or (c), he/she shall rely upon the classification or designation assigned to the information by the originating agency. A copy of such certification, together with a statement by the presiding officer setting forth the time and place of the meeting and the persons present, shall be retained by the Board as part of the transcript, recording, or minutes required by § 1003.8.

§ 1003.7 Changes following public announcement.

(a) The time, place, and agenda items of a meeting following the public announcement described in § 1003.4, or the determination of the Board to open or close a meeting, or a portion thereof, to the public may be changed following public announcement only if:

(1) A majority of all members determine by recorded vote that Board business so requires and that no earlier announcement of the change was possible; and

(2) The Board publicly announces such change and the vote of each member thereon at the earliest practicable time.

(b) Changes to the time, place and agenda items of a meeting called by the Chairman pursuant to § 1003.4(c) must be made with the concurrence of the Chairman, except that when Members have, by majority vote, added additional agenda items, the addition of those agenda items does not require the Chairman's concurrence.

[82 FR 34838, July 27, 2017]

§ 1003.8 Transcripts, recordings, or minutes of closed meetings.

Along with the General Counsel's certification and presiding officer's statement referred to in § 1003.6(d), the Board shall maintain a complete transcript or electronic recording adequate to record fully the proceedings of each meeting, or a portion thereof, closed to the public. Alternatively, for any meeting closed pursuant to § 1003.5(h) or (j), the Board may maintain a set of minutes adequate to record fully the proceedings, including a description of each of the views expressed on any item and the record of any roll call vote.

§ 1003.9 Public availability and retention of transcripts, recordings, and minutes, and applicable fees.

(a) The Board shall make available, in a place easily accessible, such as *www.pclob.gov*, to the public the transcript, electronic recording, or minutes of a meeting, except for items of discussion or testimony related to matters the Board determines may be withheld under § 1003.6.

(b) Copies of the nonexempt portions of the transcripts or minutes shall be provided upon receipt of the actual costs of the transcription or duplication.

(c) The Board shall maintain meeting transcripts, recordings, or minutes of each meeting closed to the public for a period ending at the later of two years following the date of the meeting, or one year after the conclusion of any Board proceeding with respect to the closed meeting.

PARTS 1004–1099 [RESERVED]

FINDING AIDS

A list of CFR titles, subtitles, chapters, subchapters and parts, and an alphabetical list of agencies publishing in the CFR are included in the CFR Index and Finding Aids volume to the Code of Federal Regulations which is published separately and revised annually.

Table of CFR Titles and Chapters

(Revised as of January 1, 2019)

Title 1—General Provisions

Title 2—Grants and Agreements

Title 2—Grants and Agreements—Continued

Title 3—The President

Title 4—Accounts

Title 5—Administrative Personnel

Title 5—Administrative Personnel—Continued

Title 6—Domestic Security

Title 7—Agriculture

Title 7—Agriculture—Continued

Title 15—Commerce and Foreign Trade—Continued

Title 16—Commercial Practices

Title 17—Commodity and Securities Exchanges

Title 18—Conservation of Power and Water Resources

Title 19—Customs Duties

Title 20—Employees' Benefits

357

Title 25—Indians

Title 26—Internal Revenue

Title 27—Alcohol, Tobacco Products and Firearms

Title 28—Judicial Administration

Title 29—Labor

Title 29—Labor—Continued

Title 30—Mineral Resources

Title 31—Money and Finance: Treasury

Title 34—Education—Continued

Title 35 [Reserved]

Title 36—Parks, Forests, and Public Property

Title 37—Patents, Trademarks, and Copyrights

Title 38—Pensions, Bonuses, and Veterans' Relief

Title 48—Federal Acquisition Regulations System

Alphabetical List of Agencies Appearing in the CFR

(Revised as of January 1, 2019)

Agency	CFR Title, Subtitle or Chapter
Administrative Conference of the United States	1, III
Advisory Council on Historic Preservation	36, VIII
Advocacy and Outreach, Office of	7, XXV
Afghanistan Reconstruction, Special Inspector General for	5, LXXXIII
African Development Foundation	22, XV
Federal Acquisition Regulation	48, 57
Agency for International Development	2, VII; 22, II
Federal Acquisition Regulation	48, 7
Agricultural Marketing Service	7, I, IX, X, XI
Agricultural Research Service	7, V
Agriculture, Department of	2, IV; 5, LXXIII
Advocacy and Outreach, Office of	7, XXV
Agricultural Marketing Service	7, I, IX, X, XI
Agricultural Research Service	7, V
Animal and Plant Health Inspection Service	7, III; 9, I
Chief Financial Officer, Office of	7, XXX
Commodity Credit Corporation	7, XIV
Economic Research Service	7, XXXVII
Energy Policy and New Uses, Office of	2, IX; 7, XXIX
Environmental Quality, Office of	7, XXXI
Farm Service Agency	7, VII, XVIII
Federal Acquisition Regulation	48, 4
Federal Crop Insurance Corporation	7, IV
Food and Nutrition Service	7, II
Food Safety and Inspection Service	9, III
Foreign Agricultural Service	7, XV
Forest Service	36, II
Grain Inspection, Packers and Stockyards Administration	7, VIII; 9, II
Information Resources Management, Office of	7, XXVII
Inspector General, Office of	7, XXVI
National Agricultural Library	7, XLI
National Agricultural Statistics Service	7, XXXVI
National Institute of Food and Agriculture	7, XXXIV
Natural Resources Conservation Service	7, VI
Operations, Office of	7, XXVIII
Procurement and Property Management, Office of	7, XXXII
Rural Business-Cooperative Service	7, XVIII, XLII
Rural Development Administration	7, XLII
Rural Housing Service	7, XVIII, XXXV
Rural Telephone Bank	7, XVI
Rural Utilities Service	7, XVII, XVIII, XLII
Secretary of Agriculture, Office of	7, Subtitle A
Transportation, Office of	7, XXXIII
World Agricultural Outlook Board	7, XXXVIII
Air Force, Department of	32, VII
Federal Acquisition Regulation Supplement	48, 53
Air Transportation Stabilization Board	14, VI
Alcohol and Tobacco Tax and Trade Bureau	27, I
Alcohol, Tobacco, Firearms, and Explosives, Bureau of	27, II
AMTRAK	49, VII
American Battle Monuments Commission	36, IV
American Indians, Office of the Special Trustee	25, VII
Animal and Plant Health Inspection Service	7, III; 9, I

|

	CFR Title, Subtitle or Chapter

List of CFR Sections Affected

All changes in this volume of the Code of Federal Regulations (CFR) that were made by documents published in the FEDERAL REGISTER since January 1, 2014 are enumerated in the following list. Entries indicate the nature of the changes effected. Page numbers refer to FEDERAL REGISTER pages. The user should consult the entries for chapters, parts and subparts as well as sections for revisions.

For changes to this volume of the CFR prior to this listing, consult the annual edition of the monthly List of CFR Sections Affected (LSA). The LSA is available at *www.govinfo.gov*. For changes to this volume of the CFR prior to 2001, see the "List of CFR Sections Affected, 1949–1963, 1964–1972, 1973–1985, and 1986–2000" published in 11 separate volumes. The "List of CFR Sections Affected 1986–2000" is available at *www.govinfo.gov*.

www.ingramcontent.com/pod-product-compliance
Lightning Source LLC
Chambersburg PA
CBHW060540200326
41521CB00007B/431